KU-620-422

Collecting
and Interpreting
Qualitative
Materials

WITHDRAWN
FROM STOCK

EDITION **4**

Norman K. Denzin
University of Illinois

Yvonna S. Lincoln
Texas A&M University

Editors

SAGE

Los Angeles | London | New Delhi
Singapore | Washington DC

SAGE

Los Angeles | London | New Delhi
Singapore | Washington DC

FOR INFORMATION:

SAGE Publications, Inc.
2455 Teller Road
Thousand Oaks, California 91320
E-mail: order@sagepub.com

SAGE Publications Ltd.
1 Oliver's Yard
55 City Road
London EC1Y 1SP
United Kingdom

SAGE Publications India Pvt. Ltd.
B 1/I 1 Mohan Cooperative Industrial Area
Mathura Road, New Delhi 110 044
India

SAGE Publications Asia-Pacific Pte. Ltd.
3 Church Street
#10-04 Samsung Hub
Singapore 049483

Acquisitions Editor: Helen Salmon
Editorial Assistant: Kaitlin Perry
Production Editor: Laura Stewart
Typesetter: C&M Digitals (P) Ltd.
Proofreader: Stefanie Storholt
Indexer: Jeanne Busemeyer
Cover Designer: Candice Harman
Marketing Manager: Nicole Elliott
Permissions Editor: Jason Kelley

Copyright © 2013 by SAGE Publications, Inc.

All rights reserved. No part of this book may be reproduced or utilized in any form or by any means, electronic or mechanical, including photocopying, recording, or by any information storage and retrieval system, without permission in writing from the publisher.

Printed in the United States of America

Library of Congress Cataloging-in-Publication Data

Collecting and interpreting qualitative materials / editors, Normal K. Denzin, University of Illinois, Urbana-Champaign, Yvonna S. Lincoln, Texas A&M University.—Fourth Edition.

pages cm
Includes bibliographical references and index.

ISBN 978-1-4522-5804-1 (pbk.)

1. Social sciences—Research—Methodology.
2. Qualitative reasoning.
I. Denzin, Normal K. II. Lincoln, Yvonna S.

H62.C566 2013
001.4′2—dc23   2012035579

This book is printed on acid-free paper.

SUSTAINABLE FORESTRY INITIATIVE

Certified Chain of Custody
Promoting Sustainable Forestry
www.sfiprogram.org
SFI-01268

SFI label applies to text stock

12 13 14 15 16 10 9 8 7 6 5 4 3 2 1

014545478 Liverpool Univ

Collecting
and Interpreting
Qualitative
Materials

EDITION

UNIVERSITY OF
LIVERPOOL

**University
Library**

Contents

Preface

For nearly five decades, a quiet methodological revolution has been taking place in the social sciences. A blurring of disciplinary boundaries has occurred. The social sciences and humanities have drawn closer together in a mutual focus on an interpretive, qualitative approach to research and theory. Although these trends are not new, the extent to which the "qualitative revolution" has overtaken the social sciences and related professional fields has been nothing short of amazing.

Reflecting this revolution, a host of textbooks, journals, research monographs, and readers have been published in recent years. In 1994 we published the first edition of the *Handbook of Qualitative Research* in an attempt to represent the field in its entirety, to take stock of how far it had come and how far it might yet go. The immediate success of the first edition suggested the need to offer the *Handbook* in terms of three separate volumes. So in 1998 we published a three-volume set, *The Landscape of Qualitative Research: Theories and Issues; Strategies of Inquiry; Collecting and Interpreting Qualitative Materials.* In 2013 we offer a new three-volume set, based on the fourth edition of the handbook.[1]

By 2005 we had published the third edition of the *Handbook*. Although it became abundantly clear that the "field" of qualitative research is still defined primarily by tensions, contradictions, and hesitations—and that they exist in a less-than-unified arena—we believed that the handbook could and would be valuable for solidifying, interpreting, and organizing the field in spite of the essential differences that characterize it.

The first edition attempted to define the field of qualitative research. The second and third editions went one step further. Building on themes in the first edition we asked how the practices of qualitative inquiry could be used to address issues equity and of social justice. The fourth edition continues where the third edition ended. The transformations that were taking place in the first decade of this new century continue to gain momentum in the second decade.

---

[1]To review: the first three-volume set was offered in 1998, the second in 2003, and the third in 2008.

Not surprisingly, this quiet revolution has been met by resistance. In many quarters, a resurgent, scientifically based research paradigm has gained the upper hand. Borrowing form the field of biomedical research, the National Research Council (NRC) has appropriated neo-positivist, evidence-based epistemologies. Calls for Randomized Control Trials and mixed-methods designs are now common. Interpretive methods are read as being unsuitable for those who legislate social policy.

The days of value-free inquiry based on a God's-eye of reality are over. Today many agree that inquiry is moral, and political. Experimental, reflexive ways of writing and performing first-person autoethnographic texts are now commonplace. There continues to be a pressing need to show how the practices of qualitative research can help change the world in positive ways. It is necessary to reengage the promise of qualitative research as a form of radical democratic practice. At the same time there is an urgent need to train students in the new qualitative methodologies.

We have been enormously gratified and heartened by the response to the *Handbook* since its publication. Especially gratifying has been that it has been used and adapted by such a wide variety of scholars and graduate students in precisely the way we had hoped: as a starting point, a springboard for new thought and new work.

The Paperback Project

The fourth edition of the *Handbook of Qualitative Research* is virtually all new. Over half of the authors from the first edition have been replaced by new contributors. Indeed there are 33 new chapter authors or co-authors. There are fifteen totally new chapter topics, including contributions on: mixed methods, the sacred and the spiritual, critical humanism and queer theory, Asian epistemologies, disability communities and transformative research, performance ethnography, participatory action inquiry, oral history focus groups in feminist research, applied ethnography, and anthropological poetics. All returning authors have substantially revised their original contributions, in many cases producing a totally new and different chapter.

A handbook, we were told by our publisher, should ideally represent the distillation of knowledge of a field, a benchmark volume that synthesizes an existing literature, helping to define and shape the present and future of that discipline. In metaphoric terms, if you were to take one book on qualitative research with you to a desert island (or for a comprehensive graduate examination), a handbook would be the book.

It was decided that the part structure of the *Handbook* could serve as useful point of departure for the organization of the paperbacks. Thus Volume 1, titled *The Landscape of Qualitative Research: Theories and Issues*, takes a look at the field from a broadly theoretical perspective, and is composed of the *Handbook*'s Parts I ("Locating the Field"), II ("Major Paradigms and Perspectives"), and VI ("The Future of Qualitative Research"). Volume 2, titled *Strategies of Qualitative Inquiry*, focuses on just that, and consists of Part III of the *Handbook*. Volume 3, titled *Collecting and Interpreting Qualitative Materials*, considers the tasks of collecting, analyzing, and interpreting empirical materials, and comprises the *Handbook*'s Parts IV ("Methods of Collecting and Analyzing Empirical Materials") and V ("The Art of Interpretation, Evaluation, and Presentation").

As with the first edition of the Landscape series, we decided that nothing should be cut from the original *Handbook*. Nearly everyone we spoke to who used the *Handbook* had his or her own way of using it, leaning heavily on certain chapters and skipping others altogether. But there was consensus that this reorganization made a great deal of sense both pedagogically and economically. We and Sage are committed to making this iteration of the *Handbook* accessible for classroom use. This commitment is reflected in the size, organization, and price of the paperbacks, as well as in the addition of end-of-book bibliographies.

It also became clear in our conversations with colleagues who used the *Handbook* that the single-volume, hard-cover version has a distinct place and value, and Sage will keep the original version available until a revised edition is published.

ORGANIZATION OF THIS VOLUME

Collecting and Interpreting Qualitative Materials introduces the researcher to basic methods of gathering, analyzing and interpreting qualitative empirical materials. Part 1 moves from narrative inquiry, to critical arts-based inquiry, to oral history, observations, observing, visual methodologies, autoethnographic methods. It then takes up analysis methods, including computer assisted methodologies, focus groups, as well as strategies for analyzing talk, and text. The chapters in Part II discuss evidence, interpretive adequacy, forms of representation, post qualitative inquiry, the new information technologies and research, the politics of evidence, writing, and evaluation practices.

Acknowledgments

This *Handbook* would not be without its authors, and the editorial board members who gave freely, often on very short notice, of their time, advice and ever courteous suggestions. We acknowledge *en masse* the support of the authors, and the editorial board members, whose names are listed facing the title page. These individuals were able to offer both long-term, sustained commitments to the project and short-term emergency assistance.

There are other debts, intensely personal and closer to home. The *Handbook* would never have been possible without the ever present help, support, wisdom, and encouragement of our editors and publishers at Sage: Michele Sordi, Vicki Knight, Sean Connelly, and Lauren Habib Their grasp of this field, its history, and diversity is extraordinary. Their conceptions of what this project should look like were extremely valuable. Their energy kept us moving forward. Furthermore, whenever we confronted a problem Michele, Vicki and Lauren were there with their assistance and good natured humor.

We would also like to thank the following individuals, and institutions for their assistance, support, insights and patience: our respective universities, administrations and departments. In Urbana James Salvo, Melba Velez, Koeli Goel, and Katia Curbelo were the *sine qua non.* Their good-humor and grace kept our ever -growing files in order, and everyone on the same timetable. Without them, this project would never have been completed!

Laura Stewart at SAGE Publications helped move this project through production. We are extremely grateful to her, as well as to Stefanie Storholt and Jeanne Busemeyer for their excellent work during the proofreading and indexing phases of production. Our spouses, Katherine Ryan and Egon Guba, helped keep us on track, listened to our complaints, and generally displayed extraordinary patience, forbearance and support.

Finally, there is another group of individuals who gave unstintingly of their time and energy to provide us with their expertise and thoughtful reviews when we needed additional guidance. Without the help of these individuals we would often have found ourselves with less than complete understandings of the various traditions, perspectives and methods represented in this volume. We would also like to acknowledge the important contributions of the following special readers to this project: Bryant Alexander, Susan Chase, Michele Fine, Susan Finley, Andrea Fontana, Jaber Gubrium, James Holstein, Alison Jones, Stacy Holman Jones, Tony Kuzel, Luis Miron, Ron Pelias, John Prosser, Johnny Saldana, Harry Torrance.

Norman K. Denzin
University of Illinois at Urbana-Champaign

Yvonna S. Lincoln
Texas A & M University
24 April 2012

About the Editors

Norman K. Denzin is Distinguished Professor of Communications, College of Communications Scholar, and Research Professor of Communications, Sociology and Humanities, at the University of Illinois, Urbana-Champaign. He is the author, editor, or coeditor of numerous books, including *The Qualitative Manifesto; Qualitative Inquiry Under Fire; Flags in the Window: Dispatches From the American War Zone; Searching for Yellowstone: Identity, Politics and Democracy in the New West; Performance Ethnography: Critical Pedagogy and the Politics of Culture; Screening Race: Hollywood and a Cinema of Racial Violence; Performing Ethnography; and 9/11 in American Culture*. He is past editor of *The Sociological Quarterly*; coeditor of *The SAGE Handbook of Qualitative Research*, Fourth Edition; coeditor of *Qualitative Inquiry*; editor of *Cultural Studies <=> Critical Methodologies*; editor of *International Review of Qualitative Research*, editor of *Studies in Symbolic Interaction*, and founding President of the International Association of Qualitative Inquiry.

Yvonna S. Lincoln is Ruth Harrington Chair of Educational Leadership and Distinguished Professor of Higher Education at Texas A&M University, where she also serves as Program Chair for the higher education program area. She is the coeditor, with Norman K. Denzin, of the journal *Qualitative Inquiry*, and of the first and second, third and now fourth editions of *the SAGE Handbook of Qualitative Research* and the *Handbook of Critical and Indigenous Methodologies*. As well, she is the coauthor, editor, or coeditor of more than a half dozen other books and volumes. She has served as the President of the Association for the Study of Higher Education and the American Evaluation Association, and as the Vice President for Division J (Postsecondary Education) for the American Educational Research Association. She is the author or coauthor of more than 100 chapters and journal articles on aspects of higher education or qualitative research methods and methodologies. Her research interests include development of qualitative methods and methodologies, the status and future of research libraries, and other issues in higher education. And, she's fun.

About the Contributors

Tineke A. Abma is Professor in Client Participation in Elderly Care at the department of Medical Humanities, VU University Medical Center and senior researcher at the EMGO+ Institute for Health and Care Research at the same university in Amsterdam. Her scholarly work concentrates on the methodology of interactive approaches to qualitative research and program evaluation, including the participation and empowerment of patients and vulnerable groups. More recently she works in the field of bioethics with a special interest in ethics of care and hermeneutic ethics. Practice fields include chronic care and disabilities, elderly care, and psychiatry.

David L. Altheide is Regents' Professor in the School of Justice and Social Inquiry at Arizona State University, where he has taught for 36 years. A sociologist who uses qualitative methods, his work has focused on the role of mass media and information technology in social control. Dr. Altheide received the 2005 George Herbert Mead Award for lifetime contributions from the Society for the Study of Symbolic Interaction (SSSI). He is also a three-time recipient of the SSSI's Cooley Award, for the best book of the year in 2007 for *Terrorism and the Politics of Fear* (2006); in 2004 for *Creating Fear: News and the Construction of Crisis* (2002); and in 1986 for *Media Power* (2005). His most recent book is *Terror Post 9/11 and the Media* (2009). His teaching efforts were recognized with the SSSI's Mentor Excellence Award in 2007.

Michael Angrosino is Professor Emeritus of Anthropology at the University of South Florida. He is an applied medical anthropologist who specializes in mental health policy and service delivery issues and in studies of religion in secular society. His most recent books are *Exploring Oral History: A Window on the Past* (2008) and *How Do They Know That? The Process of Social Research* (2010).

Susan E. Chase is Professor of Sociology at the University of Tulsa. Her most recent book is *Learning to Speak, Learning to Listen: How Diversity Works on Campus.* Using the methods of narrative ethnography and narrative analysis, she presents a case study of how undergraduates engage diversity issues at City University (a pseudonym). The book portrays how some students at this predominantly white university learn to speak and listen to each other across social differences, especially race. She is also the author of *Ambiguous Empowerment: The Work Narratives of Women School Superintendents,* and *Mothers and Children: Feminist Analyses and Personal Narratives* (with Mary Rogers).

Judith Davidson is an Associate Professor in the Graduate School of Education at the University of Massachusetts-Lowell (UML). Her major interest is in the area of qualitative research methodology, with an emphasis on technologies for qualitative research. She has served as a qualitative researcher on projects investigating a diverse range of areas, from early childhood education for at-risk students and elementary arts education to K–12 technology planning, math/science instruction for in-service teachers, and preservice teacher recruitment. She is a founder of the cross-campus Qualitative Research Network and has worked with faculty, staff, and graduate students to implement qualitative research technologies in diverse disciplinary areas on the UML campus. She is the author of *Living Reading: Exploring the Lives of Reading Teachers* (2005), and coauthor of *Qualitative Research Design for Software Users* (2008) and *Adolescent Literacy: What Works and Why* (1998). She was a leader in the organization of the "A Day in Technology in Qualitative Research" preconference day at the International Congress on Qualitative Inquiry 2008 conference. She has presented and published widely on topics related to qualitative research and its technologies. Currently she is working on a project that blends a cluster of qualitative research techniques—document analysis, self-study, arts-based research, and use of qualitative data analysis software—to create a new approach to artful computing in qualitative research. She received a PhD from the University of Illinois College of Education, an MS from Bank Street College of Education, and her BA from Antioch University.

Greg Dimitriadis is Professor of Sociology of Education in Graduate School of Education at the State University of New York at Buffalo. He is interested in urban education and the policies that serve urban youth. More specifically, he is interested in the potential value and importance of nontraditional educational curricula (e.g., popular culture), programs (e.g., arts-based initiatives), and institutions (e.g., community centers) in the lives of disenfranchised young people. His most recent work has dealt with the contemporary complexities of qualitative inquiry, including its history and philosophical and theoretical underpinnings, as well as the ways "theory" generated outside the field of education can be brought to bear on the questions and concerns facing educational researchers and practitioners today. He is author or editor (alone and with others) of more than 10 books and 50 articles and book chapters. His books include *Performing Identity/Performing Culture: Hip Hop as Text, Pedagogy, and Lived Practice; Friendship, Cliques, and Gangs: Young Black Men Coming of Age in Urban America;* and *Studying Urban Youth Culture.* His work has appeared in journals, including *Teachers College Record, Anthropology and Education Quarterly,* and *British Journal of Sociology of Education.* He edits the book series Critical Youth Studies and coedits Key Ideas and Education, both published by Routledge.

Laura L. Ellingson, PhD, University of South Florida, is Associate Professor of Communication and Women's & Gender Studies at Santa Clara University. Her research focuses on gender, qualitative methodology, extended and chosen family, and interdisciplinary communication in health care organizations. She is author of *Communicating in the Clinic: Negotiating Frontstage and Backstage Teamwork* (2005) and *Engaging Crystallization in Qualitative Research* (2009), and coauthor (with Patricia J. Sotirin) of *Aunting: Cultural Practices That Sustain Family and Community Life* (2010). She is the Senior Editor for Qualitative, Interpretive, and Rhetorical Methods at the journal *Health Communication.*

Susan Finley—researcher, teacher, artist, and author—is an activist who has implemented community-based educational efforts with people living in tent communities, with street youths, and among economically poor children and their families, housed and unhoused. Her artworks have been exhibited in galleries and in professional research venues, and have been published as covers and illustrations of research texts. Her original poetry and drama, as well as coauthored theater scripts, have been performed in arts venues, on campuses, and at professional research meetings. Curricular innovations for K–8 students and preservice teachers have been developed through the At Home At School Community Education effort that Susan designed and directs (2002–).

Sarah N. Gatson is Associate Professor of Sociology at Texas A&M University. Her research interests include race/ethnicity, gender, culture, legal studies, identity, community, citizenship, media and technology, and qualitative methods. Her work has appeared in *Law & Social Inquiry, Research in Community Sociology, Qualitative Research, Qualitative Inquiry, Contemporary Sociology, Feminist Media Studies,* and *Advances in Physiology Education,* and as book chapters in *Fighting the Forces: What's at Stake in Buffy the Vampire Slayer* (edited by David Lavery and Rhonda Wilcox, 2002), *Faculty of Color Teaching in Predominantly White Institutions* (edited by Christine Stanley, 2006), and *Real Drugs in a Virtual World: Drug Discourse and Community Online* (edited by Edward Murguia,

Melissa Tackett-Gibson, and Anne Lessem, 2007). Gatson is the coauthor of the book *Interpersonal Culture on the Internet—Television, the Internet, and the Making of a Community* (2004).

Silvana di Gregorio received her PhD in social policy and administration from the London School of Economics and Political Science. She has worked in several applied research settings including the Nuffield Centre for Health Services Studies, University of Leeds, and the Department of Social Policy, Cranfield University, where she was involved in numerous practitioner-research studies. During the 1990s, she was Director of Graduate Research Training at Cranfield School of Management, where she developed her interest in methodological issues, particularly looking at the affordances of software to support the analysis of qualitative data. In 1996, she resigned her position at Cranfield to focus on consulting and teaching on a range of packages that support qualitative analysis. SdG Associates is her consulting business. She is coauthor with Judith Davidson of *Qualitative Research Design for Software Users* (2008), which addresses both methodological and practical issues related to working with qualitative data analysis software packages—regardless of which brand of package is used. She is currently updating her skills by doing an MSc in E-Learning at the University of Edinburgh. She is also exploring the use of Web 2.0 tools to support the analysis of qualitative data. She is on the Advisory Board of the European Chapter of the Merlien Institute, which promotes innovations in qualitative research.

John M. Johnson is Professor of Justice Studies at Arizona State University, where he has taught for almost 40 years with his close friend David Altheide. They have changed in many ways during their lives, including many of their views about qualitative methods.

George Kamberelis is a Wyoming Excellence Chair of Literacy Education at the University of Wyoming. He received a PhD in Education and Psychology and an MS in Psychology from the University of Michigan, an MA in Literature and Religion from the University of Chicago, and a BA in Philosophy and Religion from Bates College. Most of his research and writing has focused on the philosophical foundations of qualitative inquiry, methods of qualitative inquiry, and sociocultural dimensions of literacy practice. He has coauthored two books with Greg Dimitriadis (*On Qualitative Inquiry* and *Theory for Education*) and contributed chapters to many edited volumes. His work has also been published in various journals including *Qualitative Inquiry, Annals of the American Academy of Political and Social Science, Journal of Russian & East European Psychology, Journal of Contemporary Legal Issues, Reading Research Quarterly,*

Research in the Teaching of English, and *Linguistics and Education*. Over the years, Kamberelis has taught courses on social theory, the logics of inquiry, qualitative research methods, literacy and society, classroom discourse, and media literacy.

Ronald J. Pelias, Professor, teaches performance studies in the Department of Speech Communication at Southern Illinois University, Carbondale. His most recent books are *Writing Performance: Poeticizing the Researcher's Body* (1999), *A Methodology of the Heart: Evoking Academic & Daily Life* (2004) and *Leaning: A Poetics of Personal Relations* (2011).

Anssi Peräkylä is Professor of Sociology at the University of Helsinki. His research interests include medical communication, psychotherapy, emotional communication, and conversation analysis. His books include *AIDS Counselling* (1995) and *Conversation Analysis and Psychotherapy* (coedited, 2008), both published by Cambridge University Press. His work has appeared in journals such as *Sociology, Sociology of Health and Illness, Social Psychology Quarterly, Research on Language and Social Interaction,* and *Psychotherapy Research*. In his current research project, he is exploring the linkages between interactional management of emotion, and psychophysiological processes in the body.

Jon Prosser is Director of the International Education Management program and a member of the Leeds Social Science Institute at Leeds University, United Kingdom. He was project leader for the Economic and Social Research Council's Building Capacity in Visual Methods program, which was part of the UK Researcher Development Initiative. He was involved as a visual methodologist in the Real Life Methods project based at Leeds and Manchester universities. Currently he is contributing to the groundbreaking Realities program based at the Morgan Centre, University of Manchester, and a study of Visual Ethics, both funded by the National Centre for Research Methods, University of Southampton. He is also involved in the Campaigning for Social Change: Understanding the Motive and Experiences of People With Dementia project with Bradford University. He is perhaps best known for editing *Image-based Research: A Sourcebook for Qualitative Researchers* (1998), which was the first book in the field to present visual research not as a stand-alone strategy taking one particular form or perspective, but as a theoretically and methodologically varied approach that drew on other approaches to conducting research. He sees his current work, which involves taking photographs for the local Riding for the Disabled Association calendar, as challenging and important.

Judith Rosenberg works as a nurse practitioner and ethnographic researcher in the Department of Pediatrics at the University of South Florida's College of

Medicine. Her research has focused on adolescents, particularly those with disabilities and those at risk for domestic violence. She earned her doctorate in applied anthropology at the University of South Florida.

Johanna Ruusuvuori is Senior Researcher at the Finnish Institute of Occupational Health. Her research interests include professional–client interaction in health care encounters (general practice, homeopathy, maternity health care, psychotherapy), interaction in multiprofessional meetings, emotion in social interaction, intertwine of facial expression and spoken interaction, qualitative methodology and conversation analysis. She has published in journals such as *Social Psychology Quarterly, Social Science & Medicine,* and *Journal of Pragmatics.* In her current research, she develops evaluation methods for occupational health promotion.

Linda Shopes is a freelance developmental editor and consultant in oral and public history. She has written widely on oral and public history with a focus on interpretive issues, community history, and ethics, including institutional review board (IRB) review of oral history. She coedited *Oral History and Public Memories* (2008) and *The Baltimore Book: New Views of Local History* (1991), served as contributing editor for oral history to the *Journal of American History,* and is co-general editor of Palgrave's *Studies in Oral History* series. She is a past president of the U.S. Oral History Association.

Tami Spry is a Professor of Performance Studies in the Communication Studies Department at St. Cloud State University in Minnesota. Using autoethnographic writing and performance as a critical method of inquiry into culture and communication, Spry's national and international performance work, publications, directing, and pedagogy focuses on the development of cultural critique that engenders dialogue about difficult sociocultural issues in our everyday communal and global lives. Her publications appear in *Text and Performance Quarterly, Critical Studies <=> Critical Methodologies, Qualitative Inquiry, International Review of Qualitative Research, Women and Language, The SAGE Handbook of Qualitative Research,* and various anthologies. Her book, *Body, Paper, Stage: Writing and Performing Autoethnography* is available in Spring 2011.

Elizabeth Adams St. Pierre is Professor of Language and Literacy Education and Affiliated Professor of both the Qualitative Research Program and the Women's Studies Institute at the University of Georgia. Her interests focus on the work of language in the construction of subjectivity, a poststructural critique of conventional qualitative inquiry, and a critique of "scientifically based research."

Harry Torrance is Professor of Education and Director of the Education and Social Research Institute, Manchester Metropolitan University, UK. His research interests include the interrelation of assessment, teaching, and learning; testing and educational standards; the role of assessment in educational reform and policy development; qualitative research methodology; the development of applied research; and the relationship between research and policy, research governance, and research management. He has undertaken many research projects investigating these topics, funded by a wide range of sponsors. He is editor of the four-volume *SAGE Handbook of Qualitative Research Methods in Education* (2010), a former editor of the *British Educational Research Journal,* and an elected member of the UK Academy of Social Sciences.

Guy A. M. Widdershoven is Professor in Medical Philosophy and Ethics and head of the department of Medical Humanities, VU University Medical Center, and senior researcher at the EMGO+ Institute for Health and Care Research at the same university in Amsterdam. He has published on hermeneutic ethics and its application in empirical ethics, moral deliberation, and the ethics of chronic care (psychiatry and elderly care). He is Scientific Director of the Netherlands School of Primary Care Research (CaRe) and former president of the European Association of Centers of Medical Ethics (EACME).

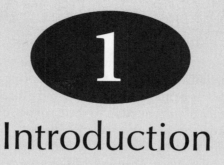

Introduction

The Discipline and Practice of Qualitative Research

Norman K. Denzin and Yvonna S. Lincoln

The global community of qualitative researchers is midway between two extremes, searching for a new middle, moving in several different directions at the same time.[1] Mixed methodologies and calls for scientifically based research, on the one side, renewed calls for social justice inquiry from the critical social science tradition on the other. In the methodological struggles of the 1970s and 1980s, the very existence of qualitative research was at issue. In the new paradigm war, "every overtly social justice-oriented approach to research . . . is threatened with de-legitimization by the government-sanctioned, exclusivist assertion of positivism . . . as the 'gold standard' of educational research" (Wright, 2006, pp. 799–800).

The evidence-based research movement, with its fixed standards and guidelines for conducting and evaluating qualitative inquiry, sought total domination: one shoe fits all (Cannella & Lincoln, Chapter 5, volume 1; Lincoln, 2010). The heart of the matter turns on issues surrounding the politics and ethics of evidence and the value of qualitative work in addressing matters of equity and social justice (Torrance, Chapter 11, this volume).

In this introductory chapter, we define the field of qualitative research, then navigate, chart, and review the history of qualitative research in the human disciplines. This will allow us to locate this handbook and its contents within their historical moments. (These historical moments are somewhat artificial; they are socially constructed, quasi-historical, and overlapping conventions. Nevertheless, they permit a "performance" of developing ideas. They also facilitate an increasing sensitivity to and sophistication about the pitfalls and promises of ethnography and qualitative research.) A conceptual framework for reading the qualitative research act as a multicultural, gendered process is presented.

We then provide a brief introduction to the chapters, concluding with a brief discussion of qualitative research. We will also discuss the threats to qualitative human-subject research from the methodological conservatism movement, which was noted in our Preface. As indicated there, we use the metaphor of the bridge to structure what follows. This volume provides a bridge between historical moments, politics, the decolonization project, research methods, paradigms, and communities of interpretive scholars.

History, Politics, and Paradigms

To better understand where we are today and to better grasp current criticisms, it is useful to return to the so-called paradigm wars of the 1980s, which resulted in the serious crippling of quantitative research in education. Critical pedagogy, critical theorists, and feminist analyses fostered struggles to acquire power and cultural capital for the poor, non-whites, women, and gays (Gage, 1989).

Charles Teddlie and Abbas Tashakkori's history is helpful here. They expand the time frame of the 1980s war to embrace at least three paradigm wars, or periods of conflict: the postpositivist-constructivist war against positivism (1970–1990); the conflict between competing postpositivist, constructivist, and critical theory paradigms (1990–2005); and the current conflict between evidence-based methodologists and the mixed methods, interpretive, and critical theory schools (2005–present).[2]

Egon Guba's (1990a) *The Paradigm Dialog* signaled an end to the 1980s wars. Postpositivists, constructivists, and critical theorists talked to one another, working through issues connected to ethics, field studies, praxis, criteria, knowledge accumulation, truth, significance, graduate training, values, and politics. By the early 1990s, there was an explosion of published work on qualitative research; handbooks and new journals appeared. Special interest groups committed to particular paradigms appeared, some with their own journals.[3]

The second paradigm conflict occurred within the mixed methods community and involved disputes "between individuals convinced of the 'paradigm purity' of their own position" (Teddlie & Tashakkori, 2003b, p. 7). Purists extended and repeated the argument that quantitative and qualitative methods and postpositivism and the other "isms" cannot be combined because of the differences between their underlying paradigm assumptions. On the methodological front, the incompatibility thesis was challenged by those who invoked triangulation as a way of combining multiple methods to study the same phenomenon (Teddlie & Tashakkori, 2003a, p. 7). This ushered in a new round of arguments and debates over paradigm superiority.

A soft, apolitical pragmatic paradigm emerged in the post-1990 period. Suddenly, quantitative and qualitative methods became compatible, and researchers could use both in their empirical inquiries (Teddlie & Tashakkori, 2003a, p. 7). Proponents made appeals to a "what works" pragmatic argument, contending that "no incompatibility between quantitative and qualitative methods exists at either the level of practice or that of epistemology . . . there are thus no good reasons for educational researchers to fear forging ahead with 'what works'" (Howe, 1988, p. 16). Of course, what works is more than an empirical question. It involves the politics of evidence.

This is the space that evidence-based research entered. It became the battleground of the third war, "the current upheaval and argument about 'scientific' research in the scholarly world of education" (Clark & Scheurich, 2008; Scheurich & Clark, 2006, p. 401). Enter Teddlie and Tashakkori's third moment: Mixed methods and evidence-based inquiry meet one another in a soft center. C. Wright Mills (1959) would say this is a space for abstracted empiricism. Inquiry is cut off from politics. Biography and history recede into the background. Technological rationality prevails.

RESISTANCES TO QUALITATIVE STUDIES

The academic and disciplinary resistances to qualitative research illustrate the politics embedded in this field of discourse. The challenges to qualitative research are many. To better understand these criticisms, it is necessary to "distinguish analytically the political (or external) role of [qualitative] methodology from the procedural (or internal) one" (Seale, Gobo, Gubrium, & Silverman, 2004, p. 7). Politics situate methodology within and outside the academy. Procedural issues define how qualitative methodology is used to produce knowledge about the world (Seale et al., 2004, p. 7).

Often, the political and the procedural intersect. Politicians and hard scientists call qualitative researchers *journalists* or "soft" scientists. Their work is termed unscientific, only exploratory, or subjective. It is called criticism and not theory, or it is interpreted politically, as a disguised version of Marxism or secular humanism (see Huber, 1995; also Denzin, 1997, pp. 258–261).

These political and procedural resistances reflect an uneasy awareness that the interpretive traditions of qualitative research commit one to a critique of the positivist or postpositivist project. But the positivist resistance to qualitative research goes beyond the "ever-present desire to maintain a distinction between hard science and soft scholarship" (Carey, 1989, p. 99). The experimental (positivist) sciences (physics, chemistry, economics, and psychology, for example) are often seen as the crowning achievements of Western civilization, and in their practices, it is assumed that "truth" can transcend opinion and personal bias (Carey, 1989, p. 99; Schwandt, 1997b, p. 309). Qualitative research is seen as an assault on this tradition, whose adherents often retreat into a "value-free objectivist science" (Carey, 1989, p. 104) model to defend their position. The positivists seldom attempt to make explicit, and critique the "moral and political commitments in their own contingent work" (Carey, 1989, p. 104; Lincoln, Lynham, & Guba, Chapter 6, volume 1).

Positivists further allege that the so-called new experimental qualitative researchers write fiction, not science, and have no way of verifying their truth statements. Ethnographic poetry and fiction signal the death of empirical science, and there is little to be gained by attempting to engage in moral criticism. These critics presume a stable, unchanging reality that can be studied with the empirical methods of objective social science (see Huber, 1995). The province of qualitative research, accordingly, is the world of lived experience, for this is where individual belief and action intersect with culture. Under this model, there is no preoccupation with discourse and method as material interpretive practices that constitute representation and description. This is the textual, narrative turn rejected by the positivists.

The opposition to positive science by the poststructuralists is seen, then, as an attack on reason and truth. At the same time, the positivist science attack on qualitative research is regarded as an attempt to legislate one version of truth over another.

THE LEGACIES OF SCIENTIFIC RESEARCH

Writing about scientific research, including qualitative research, from the vantage point of the colonized, a position that she chooses to privilege, Linda Tuhiwai Smith states that "the term 'research' is inextricably linked to European imperialism and colonialism." She continues, "the word itself is probably one of the dirtiest words in the indigenous world's vocabulary . . . It is "implicated in the worst excesses of colonialism" (p. 1), with the ways in which "knowledge about indigenous peoples was collected, classified, and then represented back to the West" (Smith, 1999, p. 1). This dirty word stirs up anger, silence, distrust. "It is so powerful that indigenous people even write poetry about research " (Smith, 1999, p. 1). It is one of colonialism's most sordid legacies, she says.

Frederick Erickson's Chapter 3 of volume 1 charts many key features of this painful history. He notes with some irony that qualitative research in sociology and anthropology was born out of concern to understand the exotic, often dark-skinned "other." Of course, there were colonialists long before there were anthropologists and ethnographers. Nonetheless, there would be no colonial—and now no neo-colonial—history, were it not for this investigative mentality that turned the dark-skinned other into the object of the ethnographer's gaze. From the very beginning, qualitative research was implicated in a racist project.[4]

Definitional Issues

Qualitative research is a field of inquiry in its own right. It crosscuts disciplines, fields, and subject matter.[5] A complex, interconnected family of terms, concepts, and assumptions surrounds the term. These include the traditions associated with foundationalism, positivism, postfoundationalism, postpositivism, post-structuralism, postmodernism, post-humanism, and the many qualitative research perspectives and methods connected to cultural and interpretive studies (the chapters in Part II of this volume take up these paradigms).[6] There are separate and detailed literatures on the many methods and approaches that fall under the category of qualitative research, such as case study, politics and ethics, participatory inquiry, interviewing, participant observation, visual methods, and interpretive analysis.

In North America, qualitative research operates in a complex historical field that crosscuts at least eight historical moments. These moments overlap and simultaneously operate in the present.[7] We define them as the traditional (1900–1950), the modernist or golden age (1950–1970), blurred genres (1970–1986), the crisis of representation (1986–1990), the postmodern, a period of experimental and new ethnographies (1990–1995), postexperimental inquiry (1995–2000), the methodologically contested present (2000–2010), and the future (2010–), which is now. The future, the eighth moment, confronts the methodological backlash associated with the evidence-based social movement. It is concerned with moral discourse, with the development of sacred textualities. The eighth moment asks that the social sciences and the humanities become sites for critical conversations about democracy, race, gender, class, nation-states, globalization, freedom, and community.[8]

The postmodern and postexperimental moments were defined in part by a concern for literary and rhetorical tropes and the narrative turn, a concern for storytelling, for composing ethnographies in new ways (Ellis, 2009; and in this volume, Hamera, Chapter 6, volume 2; Tedlock, Chapter 7 volume 2; Spry, Chapter 7; Ellingson, Chapter 13; St.Pierre, Chapter 14; and Pelias, Chapter 17).

Successive waves of epistemological theorizing move across these eight moments. The traditional period is associated with the positivist, foundational paradigm. The modernist or golden age and blurred genres moments are connected to the appearance of postpositivist arguments. At the same time, a variety of new interpretive, qualitative perspectives were taken up, including hermeneutics, structuralism, semiotics, phenomenology, cultural studies, and feminism.[9] In the blurred genre phase, the humanities became central resources for critical, interpretive theory and the qualitative research project broadly conceived. The researcher became a *bricoleur* (as discussed later), learning how to borrow from many different disciplines.

The blurred genres phase produced the next stage, the crisis of representation. Here researchers struggled with how to locate themselves and their subjects in reflexive texts. A kind of methodological diaspora took place, a two-way exodus. Humanists migrated to the social sciences, searching for new social theory and new ways to study popular culture and its local ethnographic contexts. Social scientists turned to the humanities, hoping to learn how to do complex structural and poststructural readings of social texts. From the humanities, social scientists also learned how to produce texts that refused to be read in simplistic, linear, incontrovertible terms. The line between a text and a context blurred. In the postmodern experimental moment, researchers continued to move away from foundational and quasifoundational criteria (in this volume, see Altheide & Johnson, Chapter 12; St.Pierre, Chapter 14). Alternative evaluative criteria were sought, ones that might prove evocative, moral, critical, and rooted in local understandings.

Any definition of qualitative research must work within this complex historical field. Qualitative research means different things in each of these moments. Nonetheless, an initial, generic definition can be offered. *Qualitative research* is a situated activity that locates the observer in the world. Qualitative research consists of a set of interpretive, material practices that make the world visible. These practices transform the world. They turn the world into a series of representations, including fieldnotes, interviews, conversations, photographs, recordings, and memos to the self. At this level, qualitative research involves an interpretive, naturalistic approach to the world. This means that qualitative researchers study things in their natural settings, attempting to make sense of or interpret phenomena in terms of the meanings people bring to them.[10]

Qualitative research involves the studied use and collection of a variety of empirical materials—case study, personal experience, introspection, life story, interview, artifacts, and cultural texts and productions, along with observational, historical, interactional, and visual texts—that describe routine and problematic moments and meanings in individuals' lives. Accordingly, qualitative researchers deploy a wide-range of interconnected interpretive practices, hoping always to get a better understanding of the subject matter at hand. It is understood, however, that each practice makes the world visible in a different way. Hence, there is frequently a commitment to using more than one interpretive practice in any study.

The Qualitative Researcher-as-Bricoleur and Quilt Maker

Multiple gendered images may be brought to the qualitative researcher: scientist, naturalist, fieldworker, journalist, social critic, artist, performer, jazz musician, filmmaker, quilt maker, essayist. The many methodological practices of qualitative research may be viewed as soft science, journalism, ethnography, *bricolage,* quilt making, or montage. The researcher, in turn, may be seen as a *bricoleur,* as a maker of quilts, or in filmmaking, a person who assembles images into montages (on montage, see Cook, 1981, pp. 171–177; Monaco, 1981, pp. 322–328; and discussion below; on quilting, see hooks, 1990, pp. 115–122; Wolcott, 1995, pp. 31–33).

Douglas Harper (1987, pp. 9, 74–75, 92); Michel de Certeau (1984, p. xv); Cary Nelson, Paula A. Treichler, and Lawrence Grossberg (1992, p. 2); Claude Lévi-Strauss (1962/1966, p. 17); Deena and Michael Weinstein (1991, p. 161); and Joe L. Kincheloe (2001) clarify the meaning of bricolage and bricoleur.[11] A bricoleur makes do by "adapting the bricoles of the world. Bricolage is 'the poetic making do'" (de Certeau, 1984, p. xv), with "such bricoles—the odds and ends, the bits left over" (Harper, 1987, p. 74). The bricoleur is a "Jack of all trades, a kind of professional do-it-yourself[er]" (Lévi-Strauss, 1962/1966, p. 17). In Harper's (1987) work, the bricoleur defines herself and extends herself (p. 75). Indeed, her life story, her biography, "may be thought of as bricolage" (Harper, 1987, p. 92).

There are many kinds of bricoleurs—interpretive, narrative, theoretical, political. The interpretive bricoleur produces a bricolage; that is, a pieced-together set of representations that are fitted to the specifics of a complex situation. "The solution (bricolage) which is the result of the bricoleur's method is an [emergent] construction" (Weinstein & Weinstein, 1991, p. 161), which changes and takes new forms as different tools, methods, and techniques of representation and interpretation are added to the puzzle. Nelson et al. (1992) describe the methodology of cultural studies "as a bricolage. Its choice of practice, that is, is pragmatic, strategic, and self-reflexive" (p. 2). This understanding can be applied, with qualifications, to qualitative research.

The qualitative-researcher-as-bricoleur or a maker of quilts uses the aesthetic and material tools of his or her craft, deploying whatever strategies, methods, or empirical materials are at hand (Becker, 1998, p. 2). If new tools or techniques have to be invented or pieced together, then the researcher will do this. The choice of which interpretive practices to employ is not necessarily set in advance. The "choice of research practices depends upon the questions that are asked, and the questions depend on their context" (Nelson et al., 1992, p. 2), what is available in the context, and what the researcher can do in that setting.

These interpretive practices involve aesthetic issues, an aesthetics of representation that goes beyond the pragmatic or the practical. Here the concept of *montage* is useful (see Cook, 1981, p. 323; Monaco, 1981, pp. 171–172). Montage is a method of editing cinematic images. In the history of cinematography, montage is associated with the work of Sergei Eisenstein, especially his film, *The Battleship Potemkin* (1925). In montage, a picture is made by superimposing several different images on one another. In a sense, montage is like *pentimento*, where something painted out of a picture (an image the painter "repented," or denied) now becomes visible again, creating something new. What is new is what had been obscured by a previous image.

Montage and pentimento, like jazz, which is improvisation, create the sense that images, sounds, and understandings are blending together, overlapping, and forming a composite, a new creation. The images seem to shape and define one another; an emotional gestalt effect is produced. Often, these images are combined in a swiftly run sequence. When done, this produces a dizzily revolving collection of several images around a central or focused picture or sequence; such effects signify the passage of time.

Perhaps the most famous instance of montage is given in the Odessa Steps sequence in *The Battleship Potemkin*.[12] In the climax of the film, the citizens of Odessa are being massacred by tsarist troops on the stone steps leading down to the city's harbor. Eisenstein cuts to a young mother as she pushes her baby's carriage across the landing in front of the firing troops. Citizens rush past her, jolting the carriage, which she is afraid to push down to the next flight of stairs. The troops are above her firing at the citizens. She is trapped between the troops and the steps. She screams. A line of rifles pointing to the sky erupts in smoke. The mother's head sways back. The wheels of the carriage teeter on the edge of the steps. The mother's hand clutches the silver buckle of her belt. Below her, people are being beaten by soldiers. Blood drips over the mother's white gloves. The baby's hand reaches out of the carriage. The mother sways back and forth. The troops advance. The mother falls back against the carriage. A woman watches in horror as the rear wheels of the carriage roll off the edge of the landing. With accelerating speed, the carriage bounces down the steps, past the dead citizens. The baby is jostled from side to side inside the carriage. The soldiers fire their rifles into a group of wounded citizens. A student screams, as the carriage leaps across the steps, tilts, and overturns (Cook, 1981, p. 167).[13]

Montage uses sparse images to create a clearly defined sense of urgency and complexity. Montage invites viewers to construct interpretations that build on one another as a scene unfolds. These interpretations are built on associations based on the contrasting images that blend into one another. The underlying assumption of montage is that viewers perceive and interpret the shots in a "montage sequence not *sequentially*, or one at a time, but rather *simultaneously*" (Cook, 1981, p. 172, italics in original). The viewer puts the sequences together into a meaningful emotional whole, as if at a glance, all at once.

The qualitative researcher who uses montage is like a quilt maker or a jazz improviser. The quilter stitches, edits, and puts slices of reality together. This process creates and brings psychological and emotional unity to an interpretive experience. There are many examples of montage in current qualitative research. Using multiple voices and different textual formations, voices, and narrative styles, Marcelo Diversi and Claudio Moreira (2009) weave a complex text about race, identity, nation, class, sexuality, intimacy, and family. As in quilt making and jazz improvisation, many different things are going on at the same time: different voices, different perspectives, points of views, angles of vision. Autoethnographic performance texts use montage simultaneously to create and enact moral meaning. They move from the personal to the political, the local to the historical and the cultural. These are dialogical texts. They presume an active audience. They create spaces for give and take between reader and writer. They do more than turn the other into the object of the social science gaze (in this volume, see Spry, Chapter 7; Pelias, Chapter 17).

Of course, qualitative research is inherently multimethod in focus (Flick, 2002, pp. 226–227; 2007). However, the use of multiple methods, or triangulation, reflects an attempt to secure an in-depth understanding of the phenomenon in question. Objective reality can never be captured. We know a thing only through its representations. Triangulation is not a tool or a strategy of validation but an alternative to validation (Flick, 2002, p. 227; 2007). The combination of multiple methodological practices, empirical materials, perspectives, and observers in a single study is best understood, then, as a strategy that adds rigor, breadth complexity, richness, and depth to any inquiry (see Flick, 2002, p. 229; 2007, pp. 102–104).

Laura L. Ellingson (Chapter 13, this volume; also 2009) disputes a narrow conception of triangulation, endorsing instead a postmodern form (2009, p. 190). It asserts that the central image for qualitative inquiry is the crystal—multiple lenses—not the triangle. She sees crystallization as embodying an energizing, unruly discourse, drawing raw energy from artful science and scientific artwork (p. 190). Mixed-genre texts in the postexperimental moment have more than three sides. Like crystals, Eisenstein's montage, the jazz solo, or the pieces in a quilt, the mixed-genre text combines "symmetry and substance with an infinite variety of shapes, substances, transmutations . . . crystals grow, change, alter . . . crystals are prisms that reflect externalities and refract within themselves, creating different colors, patterns, arrays, casting off in different directions" (Richardson, 2000, p. 934).

In the crystallization process, the writer tells the same tale from different points of view. Crystallized projects mix genres and writing formats, offering partial, situated, open-ended conclusions. In *Fires in the Mirror* (1993) Anna Deavere Smith presents a series of performance pieces based on interviews with people involved in a racial conflict in Crown Heights, Brooklyn, on August 19, 1991. Her play has multiple speaking parts, including conversations with gang members, the police, and anonymous young girls and boys. There is no correct telling of this event. Each telling, like light hitting a crystal, gives a different reflection of the racial incident.

Viewed as a crystalline form, as a montage, or as a creative performance around a central theme, triangulation as a form of, or alternative to, validity thus can be extended. Triangulation is the display of multiple, refracted realities simultaneously. Each of the metaphors "works" to create simultaneity rather than the sequential or linear. Readers and audiences are then invited to explore competing visions of the context, to become immersed in and merge with new realities to comprehend.

The methodological bricoleur is adept at performing a large number of diverse tasks, ranging from interviewing to intensive self-reflection and introspection. The theoretical bricoleur reads widely and is knowledgeable about the many interpretive paradigms (feminism, Marxism, cultural studies, constructivism, queer theory) that can be brought to any particular problem. He or she may not, however, feel that paradigms can be mingled or synthesized. If paradigms are overarching philosophical systems denoting particular ontologies, epistemologies, and methodologies, one cannot move easily from one to the other. Paradigms represent belief systems that attach the user to a particular worldview. Perspectives, in contrast, are less well developed systems, and it can be easier to move between them. The researcher-as-bricoleur-theorist works between and within competing and overlapping perspectives and paradigms.

The interpretive bricoleur understands that research is an interactive process shaped by one's personal history, biography, gender, social class, race, and ethnicity and those of the people in the setting. Critical bricoleurs stress the dialectical and hermeneutic nature of interdisciplinary inquiry, knowing that the boundaries between traditional disciplines no longer hold (Kincheloe, 2001, p. 683). The political bricoleur knows that science is power, for all research findings have political implications. There is no value-free science. A civic social science based on a politics of hope is sought (Lincoln, 1999). The gendered, narrative bricoleur also knows that researchers all tell stories about the worlds they have studied. Thus, the narratives or stories scientists tell are accounts couched and framed within specific storytelling traditions, often defined as paradigms (e.g., positivism, postpositivism, constructivism).

The product of the interpretive bricoleur's labor is a complex, quilt-like bricolage, a reflexive collage or montage; a set of fluid, interconnected images and representations. This interpretive structure is like a quilt, a performance text, or a sequence of representations connecting the parts to the whole.

Qualitative Research as a Site of Multiple Interpretive Practices

Qualitative research, as a set of interpretive activities, privileges no single methodological practice over another. As a site of discussion or discourse, qualitative research is difficult to define clearly. It has no theory or paradigm that is distinctly its own. As Part II of this volume reveals, multiple theoretical paradigms claim use of qualitative research methods and strategies, from constructivism to cultural studies, feminism, Marxism, and ethnic models of study. Qualitative research is used in many separate disciplines, as we will discuss below. It does not belong to a single discipline.

Nor does qualitative research have a distinct set of methods or practices that are entirely its own. Qualitative researchers use semiotics, narrative, content, discourse, archival, and phonemic analysis—even statistics, tables, graphs, and numbers. They also draw on and use the approaches, methods, and techniques of ethnomethodology, phenomenology, hermeneutics, feminism, rhizomatics, deconstructionism, ethnographies, interviews, psychoanalysis, cultural studies, survey research, and participant observation, among others.[14] All of these research practices "can provide important insights and knowledge" (Nelson et al., 1992, p. 2). No specific method or practice can be privileged over another.

Many of these methods or research practices are used in other contexts in the human disciplines. Each bears the traces of its own disciplinary history. Thus, there is an extensive history of the uses and meanings of ethnography and ethnology in education (Erickson, Chapter 3, volume 1); of participant observation and ethnography in anthropology (Tedlock, Chapter 7, volume 2); sociology (Holstein & Gubrium, Chapter 8, volume 2); communications (in volume 2, Hamera, Chapter 6; Spry, Chapter 7); cultural studies (Giardina & Newman, Chapter 10, this volume); textual, hermeneutic, feminist, psychoanalytic, arts-based, semiotic, and narrative analysis in cinema and literary studies (in volume 1, Olesen, Chapter 7; Chase, Chapter 2; Finley, Chapter 3); and narrative, discourse, and conversational analysis in sociology, medicine, communications, and education (in this volume, Chase, Chapter 2; Peräkylä & Ruusuvuori, Chapter 9).

The many histories that surround each method or research strategy reveal how multiple uses and meanings are brought to each practice. Textual analyses in literary studies, for example, often treat texts as self-contained systems. On the other hand, a cultural studies or feminist perspective reads a text in terms of its location within a historical moment marked by a particular gender, race, or class ideology. A cultural studies use of ethnography would bring a set of understandings from feminism, postmodernism, and poststructuralism to the project. These understandings would not be shared by mainstream postpositivist sociologists. Similarly, postpositivist and poststructural historians bring different understandings and uses to the methods and findings of historical research. These tensions and contradictions are evident in many of the chapters in this handbook.

These separate and multiple uses and meanings of the methods of qualitative research make it difficult to agree on any essential definition of the field, for it is never just one thing.[15] Still, a definition must be made. We borrow from and paraphrase Nelson et al.'s (1992, p. 4) attempt to define cultural studies:

> Qualitative research is an interdisciplinary, transdiciplinary, and sometimes counterdisciplinary field. It crosscuts the humanities, as well as the social and the physical sciences. Qualitative research is many things at the same time. It is multiparadigmatic in focus. Its practitioners are sensitive to the

value of the multimethod approach. They are committed to the naturalistic perspective and to the interpretive understanding of human experience. At the same time, the field is inherently political and shaped by multiple ethical and political positions.

Qualitative research embraces two tensions at the same time. On the one hand, it is drawn to a broad, interpretive, postexperimental, postmodern, feminist, and critical sensibility. On the other hand, it is drawn to more narrowly defined positivist, postpositivist, humanistic, and naturalistic conceptions of human experience and its analysis. Furthermore, these tensions can be combined in the same project, bringing both postmodern and naturalistic, or both critical and humanistic, perspectives to bear.

This rather awkward statement means that qualitative research is a set of complex interpretive practices. As a constantly shifting historical formation, it embraces tensions and contradictions, including disputes over its methods and the forms its findings and interpretations take. The field sprawls between and crosscuts all of the human disciplines, even including, in some cases, the physical sciences. Its practitioners are variously committed to modern, postmodern, and postexperimental sensibilities and the approaches to social research that these sensibilities imply.

POLITICS AND REEMERGENT SCIENTISM

In the first decade of this new century, the scientifically based research movement (SBR) initiated by the National Research Council (NRC) created a new and hostile political environment for qualitative research (Howe, 2009). Connected to the No Child Left Behind Act of 2001 (NCLB), SBR embodied a reemergent scientism (Maxwell, 2004), a positivist evidence-based epistemology. Researchers are encouraged to employ "rigorous, systematic, and objective methodology to obtain reliable and valid knowledge" (Ryan & Hood, 2004, p. 80). The preferred methodology has well-defined causal models using independent and dependent variables. Causal models are examined in the context of randomized controlled experiments, which allow replication and generalization (Ryan & Hood, 2004, p. 81).

Under this framework, qualitative research becomes suspect. There are no well-defined variables or causal models. Observations and measurements are not based on random assignment to experimental groups. Hard evidence is not generated by these methods. At best, case study, interview, and ethnographic methods offer descriptive materials that can be tested with experimental methods. The epistemologies of critical race, queer, postcolonial, feminist, and postmodern theories are rendered useless, relegated at best to the category of scholarship, not science (Ryan & Hood, 2004, p. 81; St.Pierre & Roulston, 2006, p. 132).

Critics of the evidence movement are united on the following points. The movement endorses a narrow view of science (Lather, 2004; Maxwell, 2004), celebrating a "neoclassical experimentalism that is a throwback to the Campbell-Stanley era and its dogmatic adherence to an exclusive reliance on quantitative methods" (Howe, 2004, p. 42). There is "nostalgia for a simple and ordered universe of science that never was" (Popkewitz, 2004, p. 62). With its emphasis on only one form of scientific rigor, the NRC ignores the need for and value of complex historical, contextual, and political criteria for evaluating inquiry (Bloch, 2004).

Neoclassical experimentalists extol evidence-based "medical research as the model for educational research, particularly the random clinical trial" (Howe, 2004, p. 48). But the random clinical trial—dispensing a pill—is quite unlike "dispensing a curriculum" (Howe, 2004, p. 48), nor can the "effects" of the educational experiment be easily measured, unlike a "10-point reduction in diastolic blood pressure" (Howe, 2004, p. 48).

Qualitative researchers must learn to think outside the box as they critique the NRC and its methodological guidelines (Atkinson, 2004). We must apply our critical imaginations to the meaning of such terms as *randomized design, causal model, policy studies,* and *public science* (Cannella & Lincoln, 2004; Weinstein, 2004). At a deeper level, we must resist conservative attempts to discredit qualitative inquiry by placing it back inside the box of positivism.

CONTESTING MIXED METHODS EXPERIMENTALISM

Kenneth R. Howe (2004) observes that the NRC finds a place for qualitative methods in mixed methods experimental designs. In such designs, qualitative methods may be "employed either singly or in combination with quantitative methods, including the use of randomized experimental designs" (Howe, 2004, p. 49; also Clark & Creswell, 2008; Hesse-Biber & Leavy, 2008). Clark, Creswell, Green, and Shope (2008) define mixed methods research "as a design for collecting, analyzing, and mixing both quantitative and qualitative data in a study in order to understand a research problem" (p. 364).[16] Mixed methods are direct descendants of classical experimentalism and the triangulation movement of the 1970s (Denzin, 1989b). They presume a methodological hierarchy, with quantitative methods at the top, relegating qualitative methods to "a largely auxiliary role in pursuit of the *technocratic* aim of accumulating knowledge of 'what works'" (Howe, 2004, pp. 53–54).

The *incompatibility thesis* disputes the key claim of the mixed methods move-ment, namely that methods and perspectives can be combined. Recalling the para-digm wars of the 1980s, this thesis argues that "compatibility between quantitative and qualitative methods is impossible due to incompatibility of the paradigms that underlie the methods" (Teddlie & Tashakkori 2003a, pp. 14–15; 2003b). Others disagree with this conclusion, and some contend that the incompatibility thesis has been largely discredited because researchers have demonstrated that it is possible to successfully use a mixed methods approach.

There are several schools of thought on this thesis, including the four identified by Teddlie and Tashakkori (2003a); that is, the complementary, single paradigm, dialectical, and multiple paradigm models. There is by no means con-sensus on these issues. Morse and Niehaus (2009) warn that ad hoc mixing of methods can be a serious threat to validity. Pragmatists and transformative emancipatory action researchers posit a dialectical model, working back and forth between a variety of tension points, such as etic–emic, value neutrality–value committed. Others (Guba & Lincoln, 2005; Lather, 1993) deconstruct validity as an operative term. Sharlene Nagy Hesse-Biber and Patricia Leavy's (2008) emphasis on emergent methods pushes and blurs the methodological boundaries between quantitative and qualitative methods.[17] Their model seeks to recover subjugated knowledges hidden from everyday view.

The traditional mixed methods movement takes qualitative methods out of their natural home, which is within the critical interpretive framework (Howe, 2004, p. 54; but see Teddlie and Tashakkori, 2003a, p. 15; also Chapter 16 in this volume). It divides inquiry into dichotomous categories, exploration versus con-firmation. Qualitative work is assigned to the first category, quantitative research to the second (Teddlie & Tashakkori, 2003a, p. 15). Like the classic experimental model, this movement excludes stakeholders from dialogue and active participa-tion in the research process. Doing so weakens its democratic and dialogical dimensions and decreases the likelihood that previously silenced voices will be heard (Howe, 2004, pp. 56–57).

Howe (2004) cautions that it is not just

> [the] "methodological fundamentalists" who have bought into [this] approach. A sizeable number of rather influential . . . educational research-ers . . . have also signed on. This might be a compromise to the current political climate; it might be a backlash against the perceived excesses of postmodernism; it might be both. It is an ominous development, whatever the explanation. (p. 57; also 2009, p. 438; Lincoln, 2010, p. 7)

The hybrid dialogical model, in contrast, directly confronts these criticisms.

THE PRAGMATIC CRITICISMS OF ANTI-FOUNDATIONALISM

Clive Seale et al. (2004) contest what they regard as the excesses of an anti-methodological, "anything goes," romantic postmodernism that is associated with our project. They assert that too often the approach we value produces "low quality qualitative research and research results that are quite stereotypical and close to common sense" (p. 2). In contrast they propose a practice-based, pragmatic approach that places research practice at the center. Research involves an engagement "with a variety of things and people: research materials . . . social theories, philosophical debates, values, methods, tests . . . research participants" (p. 2). (Actually this approach is quite close to our own, especially our view of the bricoleur and bricolage).

Their situated methodology rejects the antifoundational claim that there are only partial truths, that the dividing line between fact and fiction has broken down (Seale et al., 2004, p. 3). They believe that this dividing line has not collapsed and that we should not accept stories if they do not accord with the best available facts (p. 6). Oddly, these pragmatic procedural arguments reproduce a variant of the evidence-based model and its criticisms of poststructural performative sensibilities. They can be used to provide political support for the methodological marginalization of many of the positions advanced in this handbook.

This complex political terrain defines the many traditions and strands of qualitative research: the British and its presence in other national contexts; the American pragmatic, naturalistic, and interpretive traditions in sociology, anthropology, communications, and education; the German and French phenomenological, hermeneutic, semiotic, Marxist, structural, and poststructural perspectives; feminist, African American, Latino, and queer studies; and studies of indigenous and aboriginal cultures. The politics of qualitative research create a tension that informs each of the above traditions. This tension itself is constantly being reexamined and interrogated, as qualitative research confronts a changing historical world, new intellectual positions, and its own institutional and academic conditions.

To summarize, qualitative research is many things to many people. Its essence is two-fold: (1) a commitment to some version of the naturalistic, interpretive approach to its subject matter and (2) an ongoing critique of the politics and methods of postpositivism. We turn now to a brief discussion of the major differences between qualitative and quantitative approaches to research. We will then discuss ongoing differences and tensions within qualitative inquiry.

QUALITATIVE VERSUS QUANTITATIVE RESEARCH

The word *qualitative* implies an emphasis on the qualities of entities and on processes and meanings that are not experimentally examined or measured (if measured at all) in terms of quantity, amount, intensity, or frequency. Qualitative researchers stress the socially constructed nature of reality, the intimate relationship between the researcher and what is studied, and the situational constraints that shape inquiry. Such researchers emphasize the value-laden nature of inquiry. They seek answers to questions that stress *how* social experience is created and given meaning. In contrast, quantitative studies emphasize the measurement and analysis of causal relationships between variables, not processes. Proponents claim that their work is done from within a value-free framework.

RESEARCH STYLES: DOING THE SAME THINGS DIFFERENTLY?

Of course, both qualitative and quantitative researchers "think they know something about society worth telling to others, and they use a variety of forms, media, and means to communicate their ideas and findings" (Becker, 1986, p. 122). Qualitative research differs from quantitative research in five significant ways (Becker, 1996). These points of difference turn on different ways of addressing the same set of issues. They return always to the politics of research and who has the power to legislate correct solutions to these problems.

Using Positivism and Postpositivism: First, both perspectives are shaped by the positivist and postpositivist traditions in the physical and social sciences (see discussion below). These two positivist science traditions hold to naïve and critical realist positions concerning reality and its perception. Proponents of the positivist version contend that there is a reality out there to be studied, captured, and understood, whereas the postpositivists argue that reality can never be fully apprehended, only approximated (Guba, 1990a, p. 22). Postpositivism relies on multiple methods as a way of capturing as much of reality as possible. At the same time, emphasis is placed on the discovery and verification of theories. Traditional evaluation criteria like internal and external validity are stressed, as are the use of qualitative procedures that lend themselves to structured (sometimes statistical) analysis. Computer-assisted methods of analysis, which permit frequency counts, tabulations, and low-level statistical analyses, may also be employed.

The positivist and postpositivist traditions linger like long shadows over the qualitative research project. Historically, qualitative research was defined within the positivist paradigm, where qualitative researchers attempted to do good positivist research with less rigorous methods and procedures. Some mid-century qualitative researchers (Becker, Geer, Hughes, & Strauss, 1961) reported findings from participant observations in terms of quasi-statistics. As recently as 1999 (Strauss & Corbin, 1999), two leaders of the grounded theory approach to qualitative research attempted to modify the usual canons of good (positivistic) science to fit their own postpositivist conception of rigorous research (but see Charmaz, Chapter 9, volume 2; also see Glaser, 1992). Some applied researchers, while claiming to be atheoretical, often fit within the positivist or postpositivist framework by default.

Uwe Flick (2002, pp. 2–3) usefully summarizes the differences between these two approaches to inquiry. He observes that the quantitative approach has been used for purposes of isolating "causes and effects . . . operationalizing theoretical relations . . . [and] measuring and . . . quantifying phenomena . . . allowing the generalization of findings" (p. 3). But today, doubt is cast on such projects.

> Rapid social change and the resulting diversification of life worlds are increasingly confronting social researchers with new social contexts and perspectives . . . traditional deductive methodologies . . . are failing . . . thus research is increasingly forced to make use of inductive strategies instead of starting from theories and testing them . . . knowledge and practice are studied as local knowledge and practice. (Flick, 2002, p. 2)

George and Louise Spindler (1992) summarize their qualitative approach to quantitative materials.

> Instrumentation and quantification are simply procedures employed to extend and reinforce certain kinds of data, interpretations and test hypotheses across samples. Both must be kept in their place. One must avoid their premature or overly extensive use as a security mechanism. (p. 69)

While many qualitative researchers in the postpositivist tradition will use statistical measures, methods, and documents as a way of locating a group of subjects within a larger population, they will seldom report their findings in terms of the kinds of complex statistical measures or methods that quantitative researchers are drawn to (i.e., path, regression, log-linear analyses).

Accepting Postmodern Sensibilities: The use of quantitative, positivist methods and assumptions has been rejected by a new generation of qualitative researchers who are attached to poststructural or postmodern sensibilities. These researchers argue that positivist methods are but one way of telling a story about society or the social world. They may be no better or no worse than any other method; they just tell a different kind of story.

This tolerant view is not shared by everyone. Many members of the critical theory, constructivist, poststructural, and postmodern schools of thought reject positivist and postpositivist criteria when evaluating their own work. They see these criteria as being irrelevant to their work and contend that positivist and postpositivist research reproduces only a certain kind of science, a science that silences too many voices. These researchers seek alternative methods for evaluating their work, including verisimilitude, emotionality, personal responsibility, an ethic of caring, political praxis, multivoiced texts, dialogues with subjects, and so on. In response, positivist and postpositivists argue that what they do is good science, free of individual bias and subjectivity. As noted above, they see postmodernism and poststructuralism as attacks on reason and truth.

Capturing the Individual's Point of View: Both qualitative and quantitative researchers are concerned with the individual's point of view. However, qualitative investigators think they can get closer to the actor's perspective by detailed interviewing and observation. They argue that quantitative researchers are seldom able to capture the subject's perspective because they have to rely on more remote, inferential empirical methods and materials. Many quantitative researchers regard empirical materials produced by interpretive methods as unreliable, impressionistic, and not objective.

Examining the Constraints of Everyday Life: Qualitative researchers are more likely to confront and come up against the constraints of the everyday social world. They see this world in action and embed their findings in it. Quantitative researchers abstract from this world and seldom study it directly. They seek a nomothetic or etic science based on probabilities derived from the study of large numbers of randomly selected cases. These kinds of statements stand above and outside the constraints of everyday life. Qualitative researchers, on the other hand, are committed to an emic, ideographic, case-based position, which directs their attention to the specifics of particular cases.

Securing Rich Descriptions: Qualitative researchers believe that rich descriptions of the social world are valuable, whereas quantitative researchers, with their etic, nomothetic commitments, are less concerned with such detail. They are deliberately unconcerned with such descriptions because such detail interrupts the process of developing generalizations.

These five points of difference described above (using positivism and post-positivism, accepting postmodern sensibilities, capturing the individual's point of view, examining the constraints of everyday life, securing thick descriptions) reflect commitments to different styles of research, different epistemologies, and different forms of representation. Each work tradition is governed by a different set of genres, and each has its own classics and its own preferred forms of representation, interpretation, trustworthiness, and textual evaluation (see Becker, 1986, pp. 134–135). Qualitative researchers use ethnographic prose, historical narratives, first-person accounts, still photographs, life history, fictionalized "facts," and biographical and autobiographical materials, among others. Quantitative researchers use mathematical models, statistical tables, and graphs and usually write in an impersonal, third-person prose.

Tensions Within Qualitative Research

It is erroneous to presume that qualitative researchers share the same assumptions about these five points of difference. As the discussion below will reveal, positivist, postpositivist, and poststructural differences define and shape the discourses of qualitative research. Realists and postpositivists within the interpretive, qualitative research tradition criticize poststructuralists for taking the textual, narrative turn. These critics contend that such work is navel-gazing. It produces the conditions "for a dialogue of the deaf between itself and the community" (Silverman, 1997, p. 240). Those who attempt to capture the point of view of the interacting subject in the world are accused of naïve humanism, of reproducing a Romantic impulse that elevates the experiential to the level of the authentic (Silverman, 1997, p. 248).

Still others argue that lived experience is ignored by those who take the textual, performance turn. David Snow and Calvin Morrill (1995) argue that

This performance turn, like the preoccupation with discourse and story-telling, will take us further from the field of social action and the real dramas of everyday life and thus signal the death knell of ethnography as an empirically grounded enterprise. (p. 361)

Of course, we disagree.

According to Martyn Hammersley (2008, p. 1), qualitative research is currently facing a crisis symbolized by an ill-conceived postmodernist image of qualitative research, which is dismissive of traditional forms of inquiry. He feels that "unless this dynamic can be interrupted the future of qualitative research is endangered" (p. 11).

Paul Atkinson and Sara Delamont (2006), two qualitative scholars in the traditional, classic Chicago School tradition,[18] offer a corrective. They remain committed to qualitative (and quantitative) research *provided that they are conducted rigorously and contribute to robustly useful knowledge*" (p. 749, italics in original). Of course, these scholars are committed to social policy initiatives at some level. But, for them, the postmodern image of qualitative inquiry threatens and undermines the value of traditional qualitative inquiry. Atkinson and Delamont exhort qualitative researchers to "think hard about whether their investigations are the best social science they could be" (p. 749). Patricia and Peter Adler (2008) implore the radical postmodernists to "give up the project for the good of the discipline and for the good of society" (p. 23).

Hammersley (2008, pp. 134–136, 144), extends the traditional critique, finding little value in the work of ethnographic postmodernists and literary ethnographers.[19] This new tradition, he asserts, legitimates speculative theorizing, celebrates obscurity, and abandons the primary task of inquiry, which is to produce truthful knowledge about the world (p. 144). Poststructural inquirers get it from all sides. The criticisms, Carolyn Ellis (2009, p. 231) observes, fall into three overlapping categories. Our work (1) is too aesthetic and not sufficiently realistic; it does not provide hard data; (2) is too realistic and not mindful of poststructural criticisms concerning the "real" self and its place in the text; and (3) is not sufficiently aesthetic, or literary; that is, we are second-rate writers and poets (p. 232).

THE POLITICS OF EVIDENCE

The critics' model of science is anchored in the belief that there is an empirical world that is obdurate and talks back to investigators. This is an empirical science based on evidence that corroborates interpretations. This is a science that returns to and is lodged in the real, a science that stands outside nearly all of the turns listed above; this is Chicago School neo-postpositivism.

Contrast this certain science to the position of those who are preoccupied with the politics of evidence. Jan Morse (2006), for example, says: "Evidence is not just something that is out there. Evidence has to be produced, constructed, represented. Furthermore, the politics of evidence cannot be separated from the ethics of evidence" (pp. 415–416). Under the Jan Morse model, representations of empirical reality become problematic. Objective representation of reality is impossible. Each representation calls into place a different set of ethical questions regarding evidence, including how it is obtained and what it means. But surely a middle ground can be found. If there is a return to the spirit of the paradigm dialogues of the 1980s, then multiple representations of a situation should be encouraged, perhaps placed alongside one another.

Indeed, the interpretive camp is not antiscience, per se. We do something different. We believe in multiple forms of science: soft, hard, strong, feminist, interpretive, critical, realist, postrealist, and post-humanist. In a sense, the traditional and postmodern projects are incommensurate. We interpret, we perform, we interrupt, we challenge, and we believe nothing is ever certain. We want performance texts that quote history back to itself, texts that focus on epiphanies; on the intersection of biography, history, culture, and politics; on turning point moments in people's lives. The critics are correct on this point. We have a political orientation that is radical, democratic, and interventionist. Many postpositivists share these politics.

CRITICAL REALISM

For some, there is a third stream between naïve positivism and poststructuralism. Critical realism is an antipositivist movement in the social sciences closely associated with the works of Roy Bhaskar and Rom Harré (Danermark, Ekstrom, Jakobsen, & Karlsson, 2002). Critical realists use the word *critical* in a particular way. This is not Frankfurt School critical theory, although there are traces of social criticism here and there (Danermark et al., 2002, p. 201). *Critical,* instead, refers to a transcendental realism that rejects methodological individualism and universal claims to truth. Critical realists oppose logical positivist, relativist, and antifoundational epistemologies. Critical realists agree with the positivists that there is a world of events out there that is observable and independent of human consciousness. Knowledge about this world is socially constructed. Society is made up of feeling, thinking human beings, and their interpretations of the world must be studied (Danermark et al., 2002, p. 200). A correspondence theory of truth is rejected. Critical realists believe that reality is arranged in levels. Scientific work must go beyond statements of regularity to the analysis of the mechanisms, processes, and structures that account for the patterns that are observed.

Still, as postempiricist, antifoundational, critical theorists, we reject much of what is advocated here. Throughout the last century, social science and philosophy were continually tangled up with one another. Various "isms" and philosophical movements criss-crossed sociological and educational discourse, from positivism to postpositivism to analytic and linguistic philosophy, to hermeneutics, structuralism, and poststructuralism; to Marxism, feminism, and current post-post-versions of all of the above. Some have said that the logical positivists steered the social sciences on a rigorous course of self-destruction.

We do not think critical realism will keep the social science ship afloat. The social sciences are normative disciplines, always already embedded in issues of value, ideology, power, desire, sexism, racism, domination, repression, and control. We want a social science committed up front to issues of social justice, equity, nonviolence, peace, and universal human rights. We do not want a social science that says it can address these issues if it wants to do so. For us, this is no longer an option.

Qualitative Research as Process

Three interconnected, generic activities define the qualitative research process. They go by a variety of different labels, including theory, method, and analysis; or ontology, epistemology, and methodology. Behind these terms stands the personal biography of the researcher, who speaks from a particular class, gendered, racial, cultural, and ethnic community perspective. The gendered, multiculturally situated researcher approaches the world with a set of ideas, a framework (theory, ontology) that specifies a set of questions (epistemology), which are then examined (methodology, analysis) in specific ways. That is, empirical materials bearing on the question are collected and then analyzed and written about. Every researcher speaks from within a distinct interpretive community, which configures, in its special way, the multicultural, gendered components of the research act.

In this volume, we treat these generic activities under five headings or phases: the researcher and the researched as multicultural subjects, major paradigms and interpretive perspectives, research strategies, methods of collecting and analyzing empirical materials, and the art of interpretation. Behind and within each of these phases stands the biographically situated researcher. This individual enters the research process from inside an interpretive community. This community has its own historical research traditions, which constitute a distinct point of view. This perspective leads the researcher to adopt particular views of the "other" who is studied. At the same time, the politics and the ethics of research must also be considered, for these concerns permeate every phase of the research process.

The Other as Research Subject

From its turn-of-the-century birth in modern, interpretive form, qualitative research has been haunted by a double-faced ghost. On the one hand, qualitative researchers have assumed that qualified, competent observers could, with objectivity, clarity, and precision, report on their own observations of the social world, including the experiences of others. Second, researchers have held to the belief in a real subject or real individual who is present in the world and able, in some form, to report on his or her experiences. So armed, researchers could blend their own observations with the self-reports provided by subjects through interviews, life story, personal experience, and case study documents.

These two beliefs have led qualitative researchers across disciplines to seek a method that would allow them to record accurately their own observations while also uncovering the meanings their subjects brought to their life experiences. This method would rely on the subjective verbal and written expressions of meaning given by the individuals, which are studied as windows into the inner life of the person. Since Wilhelm Dilthey (1900/1976), this search for a method has led to a perennial focus in the human disciplines on qualitative, interpretive methods.

Recently, as noted above, this position and its beliefs have come under assault. Poststructuralists and postmodernists have contributed to the understanding that there is no clear window into the inner life of an individual. Any gaze is always filtered through the lenses of language, gender, social class, race, and ethnicity. There are no objective observations, only observations socially situated in the worlds of—and between—the observer and the observed. Subjects, or individuals, are seldom able to give full explanations of their actions or intentions; all they can offer are accounts or stories about what they did and why. No single method can grasp the subtle variations in ongoing human experience. Consequently, qualitative researchers deploy a wide-range of interconnected interpretive methods, always seeking better ways to make more understandable the worlds of experience that have been studied.

Table 1.1 depicts the relationships we see among the five phases that define the research process (the researcher; major paradigms; research strategies; methods of collecting and analyzing empirical materials; and the art, practices, and politics of interpretation). Behind all but one of these phases stands the biographically situated researcher. These five levels of activity, or practice, work their way through the biography of the researcher. We take them up in brief order here, for each phase is more fully discussed in the transition sections between the various parts of this volume.

Table 1.1 The Research Process

Phase 1: The Researcher as a Multicultural Subject	Historical method
	Action and applied research
History and research traditions	Clinical research
Conceptions of self and the other	
The ethics and politics of research	*Phase 4: Methods of Collection and Analysis*
Phase 2: Theoretical Paradigms and Perspectives	Interviewing
	Observing
Positivism, postpositivism	Artifacts, documents, and records
Interpretivism, constructivism, hermeneutics	Visual methods
	Autoethnography
Feminism(s)	Data management methods
Racialized discourses	Computer-assisted analysis
Critical theory and Marxist models	Textual analysis
Cultural studies models	Focus groups
Queer theory	Applied ethnography
Post-colonialism	
	Phase 5: The Art, Practices, and Politics of Interpretation and Evaluation
Phase 3: Research Strategies	
Design	Criteria for judging adequacy
Case study	Practices and politics of interpretation
Ethnography, participant observation, performance ethnography	Writing as interpretation
Phenomenology, ethnomethodology	Policy analysis
Grounded theory	Evaluation traditions
Life history, **testimonio**	Applied research

PHASE 1: THE RESEARCHER

Our remarks above indicate the depth and complexity of the traditional and applied qualitative research perspectives into which a socially situated researcher enters. These traditions locate the researcher in history, simultaneously guiding and constraining work that will be done in any specific study. This field has been constantly characterized by diversity and conflict, and these are its most enduring traditions (see Levin & Greenwood, Chapter 2, volume 1). As a carrier of this complex and contradictory history, the researcher must also confront the ethics and politics of research (Christians, Chapter 4, volume 1). It is no longer possible for the human disciplines to research the native, the indigenous other, in a spirit of value-free inquiry. Today researchers struggle to develop situational and transsituational ethics that apply to all forms of the research act and its human-to-human relationships. We no longer have the option of deferring the decolonization project.

PHASE 2: INTERPRETIVE PARADIGMS

All qualitative researchers are philosophers in that "universal sense in which all human beings . . . are guided by highly abstract principles" (Bateson, 1972, p. 320). These principles combine beliefs about *ontology* (What kind of being is the human being? What is the nature of reality?), *epistemology* (What is the relationship between the inquirer and the known?), and *methodology* (How do we know the world or gain knowledge of it?) (see Guba, 1990a, p. 18; Lincoln & Guba, 1985, pp. 14–15; and Lincoln, Lynham, & Guba in Chapter 6 of volume 1). These beliefs shape how the qualitative researcher sees the world and acts in it. The researcher is "bound within a net of epistemological and ontological premises which—regardless of ultimate truth or falsity—become partially self-validating" (Bateson, 1972, p. 314).

The net that contains the researcher's epistemological, ontological, and methodological premises may be termed a *paradigm* (Guba, 1990a, p. 17) or interpretive framework, a "basic set of beliefs that guides action" (Guba, 1990a, p. 17). All research is interpretive: guided by a set of beliefs and feelings about the world and how it should be understood and studied. Some beliefs may be taken for granted, invisible, or only assumed, whereas others are highly problematic and controversial. Each interpretive paradigm makes particular demands on the researcher, including the questions that are asked and the interpretations that are brought to them.

At the most general level, four major interpretive paradigms structure qualitative research: positivist and postpositivist, constructivist-interpretive, critical (Marxist, emancipatory), and feminist-poststructural. These four abstract paradigms become more complicated at the level of concrete specific interpretive communities. At this level, it is possible to identify not only the constructivist but also multiple versions of feminism (Afrocentric and poststructural),[20] as well as specific ethnic, feminist, endarkened, social justice, Marxist, cultural studies, disability, and non-Western-Asian paradigms. These perspectives or paradigms are examined in Part II of this volume.

The paradigms examined in Part II work against or alongside (and some within) the positivist and postpositivist models. They all work within relativist ontologies (multiple constructed realities), interpretive epistemologies (the knower and known interact and shape one another), and interpretive, naturalistic methods.

Table 1.2 presents these paradigms and their assumptions, including their criteria for evaluating research, and the typical form that an interpretive or theoretical statement assumes in the paradigm.[21]

Each paradigm is explored in considerable detail in chapters 6 through 10. The positivist and postpositivist paradigms were discussed above. They work from within a realist and critical realist ontology and objective epistemologies, and they rely on experimental, quasi-experimental, survey, and rigorously defined qualitative methodologies.

The *constructivist paradigm* assumes a relativist ontology (there are multiple realities), a subjectivist epistemology (knower and respondent co-create understandings), and a naturalistic (in the natural world) set of methodological procedures. Findings are usually presented in terms of the criteria of grounded theory or pattern theories (in this volume, see Lincoln, Lynham, & Guba, Chapter 6; Creswell, Chapter 3, volume 2; Teddlie & Tashakkori, Chapter 4, volume 2; Charmaz, Chapter 9, volume 2; Morse, Chapter 12, volume 2; Altheide & Johnson, Chapter 12; and St.Pierre, Chapter 14). Terms like credibility, transferability, dependability, and confirmability replace the usual positivist criteria of internal and external validity, reliability, and objectivity.

Feminist, ethnic, Marxist, cultural studies, queer theory, Asian, and disability models privilege a materialist-realist ontology; that is, the real world makes a material difference in terms of race, class, and gender. Subjectivist epistemologies and naturalistic methodologies (usually ethnographies) are also employed. Empirical materials and theoretical arguments are evaluated in terms of their emancipatory implications. Criteria from gender and racial communities (e.g., African American) may be applied (emotionality and feeling, caring, personal accountability, dialogue).

Poststructural feminist theories emphasize problems with the social text, its logic, and its inability to ever represent the world of lived experience fully. Positivist and postpositivist criteria of evaluation are replaced by other terms, including the reflexive, multivoiced text, which is grounded in the experiences of oppressed people.

The cultural studies and queer theory paradigms are multifocused, with many different strands drawing from Marxism, feminism, and the postmodern sensibility (in volume 1, Giardina & Newman, Chapter 10; Plummer, Chapter 11 , volume 1; St.Pierre, Chapter 14). There is a tension between a humanistic cultural studies, which stresses lived experiences (meaning), and a more structural cultural studies project, which

Table 1.2 Interpretive Paradigms

Paradigm/ Theory	Criteria	Form of Theory	Type of Narration
Positivist/ postpositivist	Internal, external validity	Logical-deductive, grounded	Scientific report
Constructivist	Trustworthiness, credibility, transferability, confirmability	Substantive-formal, standpoint	Interpretive case studies, ethnographic fiction
Feminist	Afrocentric, lived experience, dialogue, caring, accountability, race, class, gender, reflexivity, praxis, emotion, concrete grounding, embodied	Critical, standpoint	Essays, stories, experimental writing
Ethnic	Afrocentric, lived experience, dialogue, caring, accountability, race, class, gender	Standpoint, critical, historical	Essays, fables, dramas
Marxist	Emancipatory theory, falsifiability, dialogical, race, class, gender	Critical, historical, economic	Historical, economic, sociocultural analyses
Cultural studies	Cultural practices, praxis, social texts, subjectivities	Social criticism	Cultural theory-as-criticism
Queer theory	Reflexivity, deconstruction	Social criticism, historical analysis	Theory-as-criticism, autobiography

stresses the structural and material determinants and effects (race, class, gender) of experience. Of course, there are two sides to every coin; both sides are needed and are indeed critical. The cultural studies and queer theory paradigms use methods strategically, that is, as resources for understanding and for producing resistances to local structures of domination. Such scholars may do close textual readings and discourse analysis of cultural texts (in this volume, Olesen, Chapter 7, volume 1; Chase, Chapter 2), as well as local, online, reflexive, and critical ethnographies; open-ended interviewing; and participant observation. The focus is on how race, class, and gender are produced and enacted in historically specific situations.

Paradigm and personal history in hand, focused on a concrete empirical problem to examine, the researcher now moves to the next stage of the research process, namely working with a specific strategy of inquiry.

PHASE 3: STRATEGIES OF INQUIRY AND INTERPRETIVE PARADIGMS

Table 1.1 presents some of the major strategies of inquiry a researcher may use. Phase 3 begins with research design, which broadly conceived involves a clear focus on the research question, the purposes of the study, "what information most appropriately will answer specific research questions, and which strategies are most effective for obtaining it" (LeCompte & Preissle with Tesch, 1993, p. 30; see also Cheek, Chapter 2, volume 2). A research design describes a flexible set of guidelines that connect theoretical paradigms, first, to strategies of inquiry and, second, to methods for collecting empirical material. A research design situates researchers in the empirical world and connects them to specific sites, people, groups, institutions, and bodies of relevant interpretive material, including documents and archives. A research design also specifies how the investigator will address the two critical issues of representation and legitimation.

A strategy of inquiry refers to a bundle of skills, assumptions, and practices that researchers employ as they move from their paradigm to the empirical world. Strategies of inquiry put paradigms of interpretation into motion. At the same time, strategies of inquiry also connect the researcher to specific methods of collecting and analyzing empirical materials. For example, the case study relies on interviewing, observing, and document analysis. Research strategies implement and anchor paradigms in specific empirical sites or in specific methodological practices, for example, making a case an object of study. These strategies include the case study, phenomenological and ethnomethodological techniques, the use of grounded theory, and biographical, autoethnographic, historical, action, and clinical methods. Each of these strategies is connected to a complex literature; each has a separate history, exemplary works, and preferred ways for putting the strategy into motion.

PHASE 4: METHODS OF COLLECTING AND ANALYZING EMPIRICAL MATERIALS

The researcher has several methods for collecting empirical materials.[22] These methods are taken up in Part IV. They range from the interview to direct observation, the use of visual materials or personal experience. The researcher may also use a variety of different methods of reading and analyzing interviews or cultural texts, including content, narrative, and semiotic strategies. Faced with large amounts of qualitative materials, the investigator seeks ways of managing and interpreting these documents, and here data management methods and computer-assisted models of analysis may be of use. In this volume, David L. Altheide and John M. Johnson (Chapter 12), Laura L. Ellingson (Chapter 13), and Judith Davidson and Silvana di Gregorio (Chapter 15) take up these techniques.

PHASE 5: THE ART AND POLITICS OF INTERPRETATION AND EVALUATION

Qualitative research is endlessly creative and interpretive. The researcher does not just leave the field with mountains of empirical materials and easily write up his or her findings. Qualitative interpretations are constructed. The researcher first creates a field text consisting of fieldnotes and documents from the field, what Roger Sanjek (1992, p. 386) calls "indexing" and David Plath (1990, p. 374) "filework." The writer-as-interpreter moves from this text to a research text; notes and interpretations based on the field text. This text is then re-created as a working interpretive document that contains the writer's initial attempts to make sense out of what has been learned. Finally, the writer produces the public text that comes to the reader. This final tale from the field may assume several forms: confessional, realist, impressionistic, critical, formal, literary, analytic, grounded theory, and so on (see Van Maanen, 1988).

The interpretive practice of making sense of one's findings is both artistic and political. Multiple criteria for evaluating qualitative research now exist, and those we emphasize stress the situated, relational, and textual structures of the ethnographic experience. There is no single interpretive truth. As argued earlier, there are multiple interpretive communities, each having its own criteria for evaluating an interpretation.

Program evaluation is a major site of qualitative research, and qualitative researchers can influence social policy in important ways. Applied, qualitative research in the social sciences has a rich history (discussed in this volume by

Levin & Greenwood, Chapter 2, volume 1; Cheek, Chapter 2, volume 2; Brydon-Miller, Kral, Maguire, Noffke, & Sabhlok, Chapter 11, volume 2; Morse, Chapter 12, volume 2; Torrance, Chapter 11; Abma & Widdershoven, Chapter 18). This is the critical site where theory, method, praxis, action, and policy all come together. Qualitative researchers can isolate target populations, show the immediate effects of certain programs on such groups, and isolate the constraints that operate against policy changes in such settings. Action and clinically oriented qualitative researchers can also create spaces for those who are studied (the other) to speak. The evaluator becomes the conduit for making such voices heard.

BRIDGING THE HISTORICAL MOMENTS: WHAT COMES NEXT?

St.Pierre (2004) argues that we are already in the post "post" period—post-poststructuralism, post-postmodernism, post-experimental. What this means for interpretive, ethnographic practices is still not clear. But it is certain that things will never again be the same. We are in a new age where messy, uncertain multivoiced texts, cultural criticism, and new experimental works will become more common, as will more reflexive forms of fieldwork, analysis, and intertextual representation. In a complex space like this, pedagogy becomes critical—that is, How do we teach qualitative methods? Judith Preissle (Chapter 14, volume 1) and Margaret Eisenhart and S. Jurow (Chapter 15, volume 1) offer insights on the future. It is true, as the poet said, the center no longer holds. We can reflect on what should be in this new center.

Thus, we come full circle. And returning to our bridge metaphor, the chapters that follow take the researcher back and forth through every phase of the research act. Like a good bridge, the chapters provide for two-way traffic, coming and going between moments, formations, and interpretive communities. Each chapter examines the relevant histories, controversies, and current practices that are associated with each paradigm, strategy, and method. Each chapter also offers projections for the future, where a specific paradigm, strategy, or method will be 10 years from now, deep into the formative years of the next century.

In reading this volume, it is important to remember that the field of qualitative research is defined by a series of tensions, contradictions, and hesitations. This tension works back and forth between and among (1) the broad, doubting, postmodern sensibility; (2) the more certain, more traditional positivist, post-positivist, and naturalistic conceptions of this project; and (3) an increasingly conservative, neoliberal global environment. All of the chapters that follow are caught in and articulate these tensions.

Notes

1. The following paragraphs draw from Denzin (2010, pp. 19–25).

2. They contend that our second moment, the Golden Age (1950–1970), was marked by the debunking of positivism, the emergence of postpositivism, and the development of designs that used mixed quantitative and qualitative methods. Full-scale conflict developed throughout the 1970–1990 period, the time of the first "paradigm war."

3. Conflict broke out between the many different empowerment pedagogies: feminist, anti-racist, radical, Freirean, liberation theology, postmodernists, poststructuralists, cultural studies, and so on (see Guba & Lincoln, 2005; also, Erickson, Chapter 3, volume 1).

4. Recall bell hooks's reading of the famous cover photo on *Writing Culture* (Clifford & Marcus, 1986), which consists of a picture of Stephen Tyler doing fieldwork in India. Tyler is seated some distance from three dark-skinned people. A child is poking its head out of a basket. A woman is hidden in the shadows of the hut. A male, a checkered white and black shawl across his shoulder, elbow propped on his knee, hand resting along the side of his face, is staring at Tyler. Tyler is writing in a field journal. A piece of white cloth is attached to his glasses, perhaps shielding him from the sun. This patch of whiteness marks Tyler as the white male writer studying these passive brown and black people. Indeed, the brown male's gaze signals some desire or some attachment to Tyler. In contrast, the female's gaze is completely hidden by the shadows and by the words in the book's title, which cross her face (hooks, 1990, p. 127).

5. Qualitative research has separate and distinguished histories in education, social work, communications, psychology, history, organizational studies, medical science, anthropology, and sociology.

6. Definitions: *positivism:* Objective accounts of the real world can be given; *postpositivism:* Only partially objective accounts of the world can be produced, for all methods are flawed; *foundationalism:* We can have an ultimate grounding for our knowledge claims about the world, and this involves the use of empiricist and positivist epistemologies (Schwandt, 1997a, p. 103); *nonfoundationalism:* We can make statements about the world without "recourse to ultimate proof or foundations for that knowing" (Schwandt, 1997a, p. 102); *quasifoundationalism:* Certain knowledge claims about the world based on neorealist criteria can be made, including the correspondence concept of truth. There is an independent reality that can be mapped.

7. Jameson (1991, pp. 3–4) reminds us that any periodization hypothesis is always suspect, even one that rejects linear, stage-like models. It is never clear to what reality a stage refers. What divides one stage from another is always debatable. Our seven moments are meant to mark discernible shifts in style, genre, epistemology, ethics, politics, and aesthetics.

8. See Denzin and Lincoln (2005, pp. 13–21) for an extended discussion of each of these phases. This model has been termed a progress narrative by Alasuutari (2004, pp. 599–600) and Seale, Gobo, Gubrium, and Silverman (2004, p. 2). The critics assert

that we believe that the most recent moment is the most up-to-date, the avant-garde, the cutting edge (Alasuutari, 2004, p. 601). Naturally, we dispute this reading. Teddlie and Tashakkori (2003a, pp. 5–8) have modified our historical periods to fit their historical analysis of the major moments in the emergence of mixed methods in the last century.

9. *Definitions: structuralism:* Any system is made up of a set of oppositional categories embedded in language; *semiotics:* the science of signs or sign systems—a structuralist project; *poststructuralism:* Language is an unstable system of referents, making it impossible to ever completely capture the meaning or an action, text, or intention; *postmodernism:* a contemporary sensibility, developing since World War II, which privileges no single authority, method, or paradigm; *hermeneutics:* An approach to the analysis of texts that stresses how prior understandings and prejudices shape the interpretive process; *phenomenology:* A complex system of ideas associated with the works of Edmund Husserl, Martin Heidegger, Jean-Paul Sartre, Maurice Merleau-Ponty, and Alfred Schutz; *cultural studies:* a complex, interdisciplinary field that merges with critical theory, feminism, and poststructuralism.

10. Of course, all settings are natural, that is, places where everyday experience takes place. Qualitative researchers study people doing things together in the places where these things are done (Becker, 1986). There is no field site or natural place where one goes to do this kind of work (see also Gupta & Ferguson, 1997, p. 8). The site is constituted through our interpretive practices. Historically, analysts have distinguished between experimental (laboratory) and field (natural) research settings; hence the argument that qualitative research is naturalistic. Activity theory erases this distinction (Keller & Keller, 1996, p. 20; Vygotsky, 1978).

11. "The meaning of *bricoleur* in French popular speech is 'someone who works with his (or her) hands and uses devious means compared to those of the craftsman . . . the bricoleur is practical and gets the job done" (Weinstein & Weinstein, 1991, p. 161). These authors provide a history of this term, connecting it to the works of the German sociologist and social theorist Georg Simmel, and by implication to Charles Baudelaire. Martyn Hammersley (2000) disputes our use of this term. Following Claude Lévi-Strauss, he reads the bricoleur as a myth maker. He suggests it be replaced with the notion of the boat builder. Hammersley also quarrels with our "moments" model of qualitative research, contending it implies some sense of progress.

12. Brian De Palma reproduces this baby carriage scene in his 1987 film, *The Untouchables.*

13. In the harbor, the muzzles of the Potemkin's two huge guns swing slowly into the camera. Words on screen inform us: "The brutal military power answered by guns of the battleship." A final famous three-shot montage sequence shows, first, a sculptured sleeping lion, then the lion rising from his sleep, and finally the lion roaring, symbolizing the rage of the Russian people (Cook, 1981, p. 167). In this sequence, Eisenstein uses montage to expand time, creating a psychological duration for this horrible event. By drawing out this sequence, by showing the baby in the carriage, the soldiers firing on the citizens, the blood on the mother's glove, the descending carriage on the steps, he suggests a level of destruction of great magnitude.

14. Here it is relevant to make a distinction between techniques that are used across disciplines and methods that are used within disciplines. Ethnomethodologists, for example, employ their approach as a method, whereas others selectively borrow that method-as-technique for their own applications. Harry Wolcott (in conversation) suggests this distinction. It is also relevant to make a distinction between topic, method, and resource. Methods can be studied as topics of inquiry; that is how a case study gets done. In this ironic, ethnomethodological sense, method is both a resource and a topic of inquiry.

15. Indeed any attempt to give an essential definition of qualitative research requires a qualitative analysis of the circumstances that produce such a definition.

16. They identify four major mixed methods designs: triangulation, embedded, explanatory, and exploratory (Clark et al., 2008, p. 371).

17. Their emergent model focuses on methods that break out of traditional frameworks and exploit new technologies and innovations; this is a process model that works between politics, epistemology, theory, and methodology.

18. There are several generations of the Chicago School, from Robert Park and Ernest Burgess, Herbert Blumer, and Everett Hughes (1920–1950) period, to second (Becker, Strauss, Goffman), to third (Hammersley, Atkinson, Delamont, Snow, Anderson, Fine, Adler and Adler, Prus, Maines, Flaherty, Sanders et al).

19. His blanket term for auto, performance, poststructural ethnography.

20. Olesen (Chapter 7, volume 1) identifies three strands of feminist research: mainstream empirical; standpoint and cultural studies; and poststructural, postmodern; placing Afrocentric and other models of color under the cultural studies and postmodern categories.

21. These, of course, are our interpretations of these paradigms and interpretive styles.

22. *Empirical materials* is the preferred term for what are traditionally described as data.

References

Adler, P. A., & Adler, P. (2008). Of rhetoric and representation: The four faces of ethnography. *Sociological Quarterly, 49*(4), 1–30.

Alasuutari, P. (2004). The globalization of qualitative research. In C. Seale, G. Gobo, J. F. Gubrium, & D. Silverman (Eds.), *Qualitative research practice* (pp. 595–608). London: Sage.

Atkinson, E. (2004). Thinking outside the box: An exercise in heresy. *Qualitative Inquiry, 10*(1), 111–129.

Atkinson, P., & Delamont, S. (2006). In the roiling smoke: Qualitative inquiry and contested fields. *International Journal of Qualitative Studies in Education, 19*(6), 747–755.

Bateson, G. (1972). *Steps to an ecology of mind.* New York: Ballantine.

Becker, H. S. (1986). *Doing things together.* Evanston, IL: Northwestern University Press.

Becker, H. S. (1996). The epistemology of qualitative research. In R. Jessor, A. Colby, & R. A. Schweder (Eds.), *Ethnography and human development* (pp. 53–71). Chicago: University of Chicago Press.

Becker, H. S. (1998). *Tricks of the trade.* Chicago: University of Chicago Press.

Becker, H S., Geer, B., Hughes, E. C., & Strauss, A. L. (1961). *Boys in white.* Chicago: University of Chicago Press.

Bloch, M. (2004). A discourse that disciplines, governs, and regulates: On scientific research in education. *Qualitative Inquiry, 10*(1), 96–110.

Cannella, G. S. (2004). Regulatory power: Can a feminist poststructuralist engage in research oversight? *Qualitative Inquiry, 10*(2), 235–245.

Cannella, G. S., & Lincoln, Y. S. (2004a). Dangerous discourses II: Comprehending and countering the redeployment of discourses (and resources) in the generation of liberatory inquiry. *Qualitative Inquiry, 10*(2), 165–174.

Cannella, G. S., & Lincoln, Y. S. (2004b). Epilogue: Claiming a critical public social science—reconceptualizing and redeploying research. *Qualitative Inquiry, 10*(2), 298–309.

Carey, J. W. (1989). *Culture as communication.* Boston: Unwin Hyman.

Cicourel, A. V. 1964. *Method and measurement in sociology.* New York: Free Press.

Clark, C., & Scheurich, J. (2008). Editorial: The state of qualitative research in the early twenty-first century. *International Journal of Qualitative Research in Education, 21*(4), 313.

Clark, V. L. P., & Creswell, J. W. (2008). Introduction. In V. L. Plano Clark & J. W. Creswell (Eds.), *The mixed methods reader* (pp. xv–xviii). Thousand Oaks: Sage.

Clark, V. L. P., Creswell, J. W., Green, D. O., & Shope, R. J. (2008). Mixing quantitative and qualitative approaches: An introduction to emergent mixed methods research. In S. N. Hesse-Biber & P. Leavy (Eds.), *Handbook of emergent methods* (pp. 363–388). New York: Guilford.

Clifford, J. (1988). *Predicament of culture.* Cambridge: Harvard University Press.

Clifford, J. (1997). *Routes: Travel and translation in the late twentieth century.* Cambridge: Harvard University Press.

Clifford, J., & Marcus, G. E. (Eds.). (1986). *Writing culture.* Berkeley: University of California Press.

Clough, P. T. (1992). *The end(s) of ethnography.* Newbury Park, CA: Sage.

Clough, P. T. (1998). *The end(s) of ethnography* (2nd ed.). New York: Peter Lang.

Clough, P. T. (2000). Comments on setting criteria for experimental writing. *Qualitative Inquiry, 6,* 278–291.

Cook, D. A. (1981). *A history of narrative film.* New York: W. W. Norton.

Creswell, J. W. (1998). *Qualitative inquiry and research design: Choosing among five traditions.* Thousand Oaks, CA: Sage.

Danermark, B., Ekstrom, M., Jakobsen, L., & Karlsson, J. C. (2002). *Explaining society: Critical realism in the social sciences.* London: Routledge.

de Certeau, M. (1984). *The practice of everyday life.* Berkeley: University of California Press.

Denzin, N. K. (1970). *The research act.* Chicago: Aldine.

Denzin, N. K. (1978). *The research act* (2nd ed.). New York: McGraw-Hill.

Denzin, N. K. (1989a). *Interpretive interactionism.* Newbury Park, CA: Sage.

Denzin, N. K. (1989b). *The research act* (3rd ed.). Englewood Cliffs, NJ: Prentice Hall.

Denzin, N. K. (1997). *Interpretive ethnography.* Thousand Oaks, CA: Sage.

Denzin, N. K. (2003). *Performance ethnography: Critical pedagogy and the politics of culture.* Thousand Oaks, CA: Sage.

Denzin, N. K. (2009). *Qualitative inquiry under fire: Toward a new paradigm dialogue.* Walnut Creek, CA: Left Coast Press.

Denzin, N. K. (2010). *The qualitative manifesto: A call to arms.* Walnut Creek, CA: Left Coast Press.

Denzin, N. K., & Lincoln, Y. S. (2005). Introduction: The discipline and practice of qualitative research. In N. K. Denzin & Y. S. Lincoln (Eds.), *The SAGE handbook of qualitative research* (3rd ed., pp. 1–32). Thousand Oaks, CA: Sage.

Dilthey, W. L. (1976). *Selected writings.* Cambridge, UK: Cambridge University Press. (Original work published 1900)

Diversi, M. (1998). Glimpses of street life: Representing lived experience through short stories. *Qualitative Inquiry, 4,* 131–137.

Diversi, M., & Moreira, C. (2009). *Betweener talk: Decolonizing knowledge production, pedagogy, and praxis.* Walnut Creek, CA: Left Coast Press.

Ellingson, L. L. (2009). *Engaging crystallization in qualitative research.* Thousand Oaks, CA: Sage.

Ellis, C. (2009). *Revision: Autoethnographic reflections on life and work.* Walnut Creek, CA: Left Coast Press.

Ellis, C., & Bochner, A. P. (Eds.). (2000). *Ethnographically speaking: Autoethnography, literature, and aesthetics.* Walnut Creek, CA: AltaMira Press.

Filstead, W. J. (Ed.). (1970). *Qualitative methodology.* Chicago: Markham.

Flick, U. (1998). *An introduction to qualitative research.* London: Sage.

Flick, U. (2002). *An introduction to qualitative research* (2nd ed.). London: Sage.

Flick, U. (2007). *Designing qualitative research.* London: Sage

Gage, N. L. (1989). The paradigm wars and their aftermath: A "historical" sketch of research and teaching since 1989. *Educational Researcher, 18*(7), 4–10.

Geertz, C. (1973). *Interpreting cultures.* New York: Basic Books.

Geertz, C. (1983). *Local knowledge.* New York: Basic Books.

Geertz, C. (1988). *Works and lives.* Stanford, CA: Stanford University Press.

Geertz, C. (1995). *After the fact: Two countries, four decades, one anthropologist.* Cambridge: Harvard University Press.

Glaser, B. G. (1992). *Emergence vs. forcing: Basics of grounded theory.* Mill Valley, CA: Sociology Press.

Glaser, B., & Strauss, A. (1967). *The discovery of grounded theory.* Chicago: Aldine.

Goodall, H. L., Jr. (2000). *Writing the new ethnography.* Walnut Creek, CA: AltaMira.

Gordon, D. A. (1988). Writing culture, writing feminism: The poetics and politics of experimental ethnography. *Inscriptions, 3/4* (8), 21–31.

Gordon, D. A. (1995). Conclusion: Culture writing women: Inscribing feminist anthropology. In R. Behar & D. A. Gordon (Eds.), *Women writing culture* (pp. 429–441). Berkeley: University of California Press.

Greenblatt, S. (1997). The touch of the real. In S. B. Ortner (Ed.), The fate of "culture": Geertz and beyond [Special issue]. *Representations, 59,* 14–29.

Grossberg, L., Nelson, C., & Treichler, P. (Eds.) (1992). *Cultural studies.* New York: Routledge.

Guba, E. G. (1990a). The alternative paradigm dialog. In E. G. Guba (Ed.), *The paradigm dialog* (pp. 17–30). Newbury Park, CA: Sage.

Guba, E. G. (1990b). Carrying on the dialog. In Egon G. Guba (Ed.), *The paradigm dialog* (pp. 368–378). Newbury Park, CA: Sage.

Guba, E., & Lincoln, Y. S. (1989). *Fourth generation evaluation.* Newbury Park, CA: Sage.

Guba, E., & Lincoln, Y. S. (2005). Paradigmatic controversies and emerging confluences. In N. K. Denzin & Y. S. Lincoln (Eds.), *The SAGE handbook of qualitative research* (3rd ed., pp. 191–216). Thousand Oaks, CA: Sage.

Gupta, A., & Ferguson, J. (Eds.). (1997). Discipline and practice: "The field" as site, method, and location in anthropology. In A. Gupta & J. Ferguson (Eds.), *Anthropological locations: Boundaries and grounds of a field science* (pp. 1–46). Berkeley: University of California Press.

Hammersley, M. (1992). *What's wrong with ethnography?* London: Routledge.

Hammersley, M. (2000). Not bricolage but boatbuilding. *Journal of Contemporary Ethnography, 28,* 5.

Hammersley, M. (2008). *Questioning qualitative inquiry: Critical essays.* London: Sage.

Harper, D. (1987). *Working knowledge: Skill and community in a small shop.* Chicago: University of Chicago Press.

Hesse-Biber, S. N., & Leavy, P. (2008). Introduction: Pushing on the methodological boundaries: The growing need for emergent methods within and across the disciplines. In S. N. Hesse-Biber & P. Leavy (Eds.), *Handbook of emergent methods* (pp. 1–15). New York: Guilford Press.

Holman-Jones, S. H. (1999). Torch. *Qualitative Inquiry, 5,* 235–250.

hooks, b.(1990). *Yearning: Race, gender, and cultural politics.* Boston: South End Press.

Howe, K. (1988). Against the quantitative-qualitative incompatibility thesis (Or dogmas die hard). *Educational Researcher, 17*(8), 10–16.

Howe, K. R. (2004). A critique of experimentalism. *Qualitative Inquiry, 10*(1), 42–61.

Howe, K. R. (2009). Positivist dogmas, rhetoric, and the education science question. *Education Researcher, 38* (August/September), 428–440.

Huber, J. (1995). Centennial essay: Institutional perspectives on sociology. *American Journal of Sociology, 101,* 194–216.

Jackson, M. (1998). *Minima ethnographica.* Chicago: University of Chicago Press.

Jameson, F. (1991). *Postmodernism, or the cultural logic of late capitalism.* Durham, NC: Duke University Press.

Keller, C. M., & Keller, J. D. (1996). *Cognition and tool use: The blacksmith at work.* New York: Cambridge University Press.

Kincheloe, J. L. (2001). Describing the bricolage: Conceptualizing a new rigor in qualitative research. *Qualitative Inquiry, 7*(6), 679–692.

Lather, P. (1993). Fertile obsession: Validity after poststructuralism. *Sociological Quarterly, 35,* 673–694.

Lather, P. (2004). This *is* your father's paradigm: Government intrusion and the case of qualitative research in education. *Qualitative Inquiry, 10*(1), 15–34.

Lather, P., & Smithies, C. (1997). *Troubling the angels: Women living with HIV/AIDS.* Boulder, CO: Westview Press.

LeCompte, M. D., & Preissle, J. with R. Tesch. (1993). *Ethnography and qualitative design in educational research* (2nd ed.). New York: Academic Press.

Lévi-Strauss, C. (1966). *The savage mind.* Chicago: University of Chicago Press. (Original work published 1962)

Lincoln, Y. S. (1997). Self, subject, audience, text: Living at the edge, writing in the margins. In W. G. Tierney & Y. S. Lincoln (Eds.*), Representation and the text: Re-framing the narrative voice* (pp. 37–56). Albany: SUNY Press.

Lincoln, Y. S. (1999, June 3–6). *Courage, vulnerability, and truth.* Paper presented to the Reclaiming Voice II Conference, University of California-Irvine, Irvine, CA.

Lincoln, Y. S. (2010). What a long, strange trip it's been . . . : Twenty-five years of qualitative and new paradigm research. *Qualitative Inquiry, 16*(1), 3–9.

Lincoln, Y. S., & Cannella, G. S. (2004a). Dangerous discourses: Methodological conservatism and governmental regimes of truth. *Qualitative Inquiry, 10*(1), 5–14.

Lincoln, Y. S., & Cannella, G. S. (2004b). Qualitative research, power, and the radical right. *Qualitative Inquiry, 10*(2), 175–201.

Lincoln, Y. S., & Guba, E. G. (1985). *Naturalistic inquiry.* Beverly Hills, CA: Sage.

Lincoln, Y. S., & Tierney, W. G. (2004). Qualitative research and institutional review boards. *Qualitative Inquiry, 10*(2), 219–234.

Lofland, J. (1971). *Analyzing social settings.* Belmont, CA: Wadsworth.

Lofland, J. (1995). Analytic ethnography: Features, failings, and futures. *Journal of Contemporary Ethnography, 24,* 30–67.

Lofland, J., & Lofland, L. H. (1984). *Analyzing social settings.* Belmont, CA: Wadsworth.

Lofland, J., & Lofland, L. H. (1995). *Analyzing social settings* (3rd ed.). Belmont, CA: Wadsworth.

Lofland, L. (1980). The 1969 Blumer-Hughes talk. *Urban Life and Culture, 8,* 248–260.

Malinowski, B. (1948). *Magic, science and religion, and other essays.* New York: Natural History Press. (Original work published 1916)

Malinowski, B. (1967). *A diary in the strict sense of the term.* New York: Harcourt.

Marcus, G., & Fischer, M. (1986). *Anthropology as cultural critique.* Chicago: University of Chicago Press.

Maxwell, J. A. (2004). Reemergent scientism, postmodernism, and dialogue across differences. *Qualitative Inquiry, 10*(1), 35–41.

Mills, C. W. (1959). *The sociological imagination*. New York: Oxford University Press.

Monaco, J. (1981). *How to read a film: The art, technology, language, history and theory of film* (Rev. ed.). New York: Oxford University Press.

Morse, J. M. (2006). The politics of evidence. In N. Denzin & M. Giardina (Eds.), *Qualitative inquiry and the conservative challenge* (pp. 79–92). Walnut Creek, CA: Left Coast Press.

Morse, J. M., & Niehaus, L. (2009). *Mixed method design: Principles and procedures*. Walnut Creek, CA: Left Coast Press.

Nelson. C., Treichler, P. A., & Grossberg, L. (1992). Cultural studies. In L. Grossberg, C. Nelson, & P. A. Treichler (Eds.), *Cultural studies* (pp. 1–16). New York: Routledge.

Ortner, S. B. (1997). Introduction. In S. B. Ortner (Ed.), The fate of "culture": Clifford Geertz and beyond [Special issue]. *representations, 59,* 1–13.

Pelias, R. J. (2004). *A methodology of the heart: Evoking academic & daily life*. Walnut Creek, CA: AltaMira.

Plath, David. (1990). Fieldnotes, filed notes, and the conferring of note. In R. Sanjek (Ed.), *Fieldnotes* (pp. 371–384). Albany: SUNY Press.

Popkewitz, T. S. (2004). Is the National Research Council committee's report on scientific research in education scientific? On trusting the manifesto. *Qualitative Inquiry, 10*(1), 62–78.

Richardson, L. (1991). Postmodern social theory. *Sociological Theory, 9,* 173–179.

Richardson, L. (1992). The consequences of poetic representation: Writing the other, rewriting the self. In C. Ellis & M. G. Flaherty (Eds.), *Investigating subjectivity: Research on lived experience*. Newbury Park, CA: Sage.

Richardson, L. (1997). *Fields of play*. New Brunswick, NJ: Rutgers University Press.

Richardson, L. (2000). Writing: A method of inquiry. In N. K. Denzin & Y. S. Lincoln (Eds.), *Handbook of qualitative research* (2nd ed., pp. 923–948). Thousand Oaks, CA: Sage.

Richardson, L., & Lockridge, E. (2004). *Travels with Ernest: Crossing the literary/ sociological divide*. Walnut Creek, CA: AltaMira.

Roffman, P., & Purdy, J. (1981). *The Hollywood social problem film*. Bloomington: Indiana University Press.

Ronai, C. R. (1998). Sketching with Derrida: An ethnography of a researcher/erotic dancer. *Qualitative Inquiry, 4,* 405–420.

Rosaldo, R. (1989). *Culture & truth*. Boston: Beacon.

Ryan, K. E., & Hood, L. K. (2004). Guarding the castle and opening the gates. *Qualitative Inquiry, 10*(1): 79–95.

Sanjek, R. (1992). *Fieldnotes*. Albany: SUNY Press.

Scheurich, J. & Clark, M. C. (2006). Qualitative studies in education at the beginning of the twenty-first century. *International Journal of Qualitative Studies in Education, 19*(4), 401.

Schwandt, T. A. (1997a). *Qualitative inquiry*. Thousand Oaks, CA: Sage.

Schwandt, T. A. (1997b). Textual gymnastics, ethics, angst. In W. G. Tierney & Y. S. Lincoln (Eds.*), Representation and the text: Re-framing the narrative voice* (pp. 305–313). Albany: SUNY Press.

Seale, C., Gobo, G., Gubrium, J. F., & Silverman, D. (2004). Introduction: Inside qualitative research. In C. Seale, G. Gobo, J. F. Gubrium, & D. Silverman (Eds.), *Qualitative research practice* (pp. 1–11). London: Sage.

Semaili, L. M., & Kincheloe, J. L. (1999). Introduction: What is indigenous knowledge and why should we study it? In L. M. Semaili & J. L. Kincheloe (Eds.), *What is indigenous knowledge? Voices from the academy* (pp. 3–57). New York: Falmer Press.

Silverman, D. (1997). Towards an aesthetics of research. In D. Silverman (Ed.), *Qualitative research: Theory, method, and practice* (pp. 239–253). London: Sage.

Smith, A. D. (1993). *Fires in the mirror.* New York: Anchor Books.

Smith, L. T. (1999). *Decolonizing methodologies: Research and indigenous peoples.* Dunedin, NZ: University of Otago Press.

Snow, D., & Morrill, C. (1995). Ironies, puzzles, and contradictions in Denzin and Lincoln's vision of qualitative research. *Journal of Contemporary Ethnography, 22,* 358–362.

Spindler, G., & Spindler, L. (1992). Cultural process and ethnography: An anthropological perspective. In M. D. LeCompte, W. L. Millroy, & J. Preissle (Eds.), *The handbook of qualitative research in education* (pp. 53–92). New York: Academic Press.

Stocking, G. W., Jr. (1986). Anthropology and the science of the irrational: Malinowski's encounter with Freudian psychoanalysis. In *History of anthropology: Vol. 4. Malinowski, Rivers, Benedict, and others: Essays on culture and personality* (pp. 13–49). Madison: University of Wisconsin Press.

Stocking, G. W., Jr. (1989). The ethnographic sensibility of the 1920s and the dualism of the anthropological tradition. In *History of anthropology: Vol. 6. Romantic Motives: Essays on anthropological sensibility* (pp. 208–276). Madison: University of Wisconsin Press.

Stoller, P., & Olkes, C. (1987). *In sorcery's shadow.* Chicago: University of Chicago Press.

St.Pierre, E. A. (2004). Refusing alternatives: A science of contestation. *Qualitative Inquiry, 10*(1), 130–139.

St.Pierre, E. A., & Roulston, K. (2006). The state of qualitative inquiry: A contested science. *International Jouranl of Qualitative Studies in Education, 19*(6), 673–684.

Strauss, A. (1987). *Qualitative analysis for social scientists.* New York: Cambridge.

Strauss, A., & Corbin, J. (1999). *Basics of qualitative research* (2nd ed.). Thousand Oaks, CA: Sage.

Taylor, S. J., & Bogdan, R. (1998). *Introduction to qualitative research methods: A phenomenological approach to the social sciences* (3rd ed.). New York: Wiley.

Teddlie, C., & Tashakkori, A. (2003a). Major issues and controversies in the use of mixed methods in the social and behavioral sciences. In A. Tashakkori & C. Teddlie (Eds.), *Handbook of mixed-methods in social and behavioral research* (pp. 3–50). Thousand Oaks, CA: Sage.

Teddlie, C., & Tashakkori, A. (2003b). Preface. In A. Tashakkori & C. Teddlie (Eds.), *Handbook of mixed-methods in social and behavioral research* (pp. ix-xv). Thousand Oaks, CA: Sage.

Turner, V., & Bruner, E. (Eds.). (1986). *The anthropology of experience.* Urbana: University of Illinois Press.

Van Maanen, J. (1988). *Tales of the field.* Chicago: University of Chicago Press.

Vygotsky, L. S. (1978). *Mind in society.* Cambridge, MA: Harvard University Press.

Weinstein, D., & Weinstein, M. A. (1991). Georg Simmel: Sociological *flaneur bricoleur. Theory, Culture & Society, 8,* 151–168.

Weinstein, M. (2004). Randomized design and the myth of certain knowledge: Guinea pig narratives and cultural critique. *Qualitative Inquiry, 10*(2), 246–260.

West, C. (1989). *The American evasion of philosophy.* Madison: University of Wisconsin Press.

Wolcott, H. F. (1990). *Writing up qualitative research.* Newbury Park, CA: Sage.

Wolcott, H. F. (1992). Posturing in qualitative research. In M. D. LeCompte, W. L. Millroy, & J. Preissle (Eds.), *The handbook of qualitative research in education* (pp. 3–52). New York: Academic Press, Inc.

Wolcott, H. F. (1995). *The art of fieldwork.* Walnut Creek, CA: AltaMira Press.

Wolfe, M. (1992). *A thrice-told tale.* Stanford, CA: Stanford University Press.

Wright, H. K. (2006). Are we there yet? Qualitative research in education's profuse and contested present. *International Journal of Qualitative Studies in Education, 19*(6), 793–802.

Part I

Methods of Collecting and Analyzing Empirical Materials

Nothing stands outside representation. Research involves a complex politics of representation. This world can never be captured directly; we only study representations of it. We study the way people represent their experiences to themselves and to others. Experience can be represented in multiple ways, including rituals, myth, stories, performances, films, songs, memoirs, and autobiography, writing stories, autoethnography. We are all storytellers, statisticians, and ethnographers alike.

The socially situated researcher creates through interaction and material practices those realities and representations that are the subject matter of inquiry. In such sites, the interpretive practices of qualitative research are implemented. These methodological practices represent different ways of generating and representing empirical materials grounded in the everyday world. Part IV examines the multiple practices and methods of analysis that qualitative researchers-as-methodological-bricoleurs now employ.

Narrative Inquiry

Today narrative inquiry is flourishing; it is everywhere. We know the world through the stories that are told about it. Even so, as Susan Chase reminds us, narrative inquiry as particular type of qualitative inquiry is a field in the making. Modifying her earlier formulation of narrative that focused on retrospective meaning making, Chase now defines narrative, after Jaber Gubrium and James Holstein, as "meaning making through the shaping or ordering of experience." She provides an excellent overview of this field, discussing the multiple approaches to narrative, storytelling as lived experience, narrative practices and narrative environments, the researcher and the story, autoethnography, performance narratives, methodological and ethical issues, big and small stories content analysis, going beyond written and oral texts, narrative and social change, Latin American *testimonios,* collective stories, public dialogue, the need for meta-analysis of the vast array of narrative studies.

Narratives are socially constrained forms of action, socially situated performances, ways of acting in and making sense of the world. Narrative researchers often write in the first person, thus "emphasizing their own narrative action. "Narrative inquiry can advance a social change agenda. Wounded storytellers can empower others to tell their stories. *Testimonios,* as emergency narratives, can mobilize a nation against social injustice, repression, and violence. Collective stories can form the basis of a social movement. Telling the stories of marginalized people can help create a public space requiring others to hear what they don't want to hear.

Critical Arts-Based Inquiry

Critical arts-based inquiry situates the artist-as-researcher in a research paradigm committed to democratic, ethical agendas. Like participatory action research (PAR), critical arts-based inquiry demonstrates an activist approach to inquiry. Arts-based inquiry uses the aesthetics, methods, and practices of the literary, performance, and visual arts, as well as dance, theater, drama, film, collage, video, and photography. Arts-based inquiry is intertextual. It crosses the borders of art and research. Susan Finley writes a history of this methodology, locating it in the postcolonial, postmodern context. As the same time, she critiques neoliberal trends that are critical of social-justice based projects. She takes up the performative turn in qualitative inquiry, moving to a people's pedagogy that performs a radical ethical aesthetic. She shows how activist art can be used to address issues of political significance, including engaging community participants in acts of political, self-expression.

When grounded in a critical performance pedagogy, arts-based work can be used to advance a progressive political agenda that addresses issues of social inequity. Thus do researchers take up their "pens, cameras, paintbrushes, bodies" and voices in the name of social justice projects. Such work exposes oppression, targets sites of resistance, and outlines a transformative praxis that performs resistance texts. Finley ends with a rubric for evaluating critical-arts based research, asking whether the research demonstrates indigenous skills, openly resists structures of domination, performs useful public service, gives a voice to the oppressed, critiques neoconservative discourse, and brings passion to its performances, moving persons to positive social action.

Oral History

Linda Shopes discusses moral history as a way of collecting and interpreting human memories to foster knowledge and human dignity. Because they interview persons, oral historians implement the open-ended interview as a form of social inquiry.

As Chase observed, we live in a narrative, storytelling, interview society, in a society whose members seem to believe that interviews (and stories) generate useful information about lived experience and its meanings. The interview and the life-story narrative have become taken-for-granted features of our mediated, mass culture. But the life story, the oral history, and the personal narrative are negotiated texts, sites where power, gender, race, and class intersect.

Andrea Fontana and James H. Frey (2005) review the history of the interview in the social sciences, noting its three major forms—structured, unstructured, and open-ended—while showing how the tool is modified and changed during use. They also oral history interviews, creative interviewing, gendered, feminist and postmodern, or multi-voiced interviewing. Shopes takes up where Fontana and Frey ended, with oral history.

The oral history is a recorded interview, preserved for the record and made accessible to others. The oral history interview is historical in intent—it seeks new knowledge about the past through an individual biography. Oral history is understood as both an act of memory and an inherently subjective account of the past. The oral history interview elicits information that requites interpretation. The oral history interview is an inquiry in depth.

Oral historians are closely aligned with the projects of interpretive sociologists and anthropologists such as Chase, Holstein, and Gubrium. Shopes reviews the history of oral history, discussing its different meanings, and interpretations, from the 19th century to the present, from slave narratives to elite interviews and the oral histories of underrepresented groups. Thus, the method has helped to democratize history, as have recent developments in digital media.

Oral histories, as noted in our Introduction to Part I, have taken the lead in confronting the legal and ethical issues involved in qualitative inquiry. The ethical initiatives by oral historians have created a space within current institutional review board (IRB) structures for truthful inquiry, for commitments to a "utopian striving to know how things really are, and of how things may be." Shopes has been the leader in this discourse.

Recontextualizing Observational Methods

Going into a social situation and looking is another important way of gathering materials about the social world. Drawing on previous arguments (Angrosino & Mays de Pérez, 2000), Michael Angrosino and Judith Rosenberg fundamentally rewrite the methods and practices of naturalistic observation. All observation involves participation in the world being studied. There is no pure, objective, detached observation; the effects of the observer's presence can never be erased. Further, the colonial concept of the subject (the object of the observer's gaze) is no longer appropriate. Observers now function as collaborative participants in action inquiry settings. Angrosino and Rosenberg argue that observational interaction is a tentative, situational process. It is shaped by shifts in gendered identity, as well as by existing structures of power. As relationships unfold, participants validate the cues generated by others in the sitting. Finally, during the observational process people assume situational identities, which may not be socially or culturally normative.

Like Clifford Christians (Chapter 4, volume 1) and Linda Shopes, Angrosino and Rosenberg offer compelling criticisms of institutional review boards (IRBs), noting that positivistic social scientists seldom recognize the needs of observational ethnographers. In many universities, the official IRB is tied to the experimental, hypothesis-testing, so-called scientific paradigm. This paradigm creates problems for the postmodern observer, for the scholar who becomes part of the world that is being studied. To get approval for their research, scholars may have to engage in deception (in this instance of the IRB). This leads some ethnographers to claim that their research will not be intrusive, and hence will not cause harm. Yet interactive observers are by definition intrusive. When collaborative inquiry is undertaken subjects become stakeholders, persons who shape the inquiry itself. What this means for consent forms—and forms of participatory inquiry more broadly—is not clear. Alternative forms of ethnographic writing, including the use of fictionalized stories, represent one avenue for addressing this ethical quandary.

An ethic of "proportionate reason" is offered. This utilitarian ethic attempts to balance the benefits, costs, and consequences of actions in the field, asking if the means to an end are justified by the importance and value of the goals attained. This ethic can then be translated into a progressive social agenda. This agenda stresses social, not commutative, distributive, or legal justice. A social justice ethic asks the researcher to become directly involved with the poor and the marginalized, to become an advocate, to facilitate empowerment in communities. Inquirers, seeking utopian visions, and progressive agendas, act as advocates, enacting pedagogies of service.

The worlds of observation are changing, new audio and visual technologies (see Prosser, Chapter 6, this volume) are now available, the stage has gone global, the Internet creates virtual worlds and virtual ethnographies (Gatson, Chapter 8, this volume) are commonplace. And the search for social justice continues. This chapter demystifies the observation method. Observation is no longer the key to some grand analysis of culture or society. Instead, observational research now becomes a method that focuses on differences, on the lives of particular people in concrete, but constantly changing, human relationships. The relevance and need for a radical ethics of care and commitment becomes even more apparent.

Visual Methodology: A More Seeing Research

Jon Prosser's chapter outlines the key facets of contemporary visual research, concluding with future challenges. Visual researchers use the word *visual* to refer to phenomena that can be seen, can be given meaning. Since the 1960s, researchers have used visual images for one of two purposes: empirically, to document reality, or symbolically, to study the meaning of images produced by visual culture. Today a visual fluency for qualitative researchers is presumed.

Today visual sociologists and anthropologists use digital photography, motion pictures, the World Wide Web, interactive CDs, CD-ROMs, and virtual reality as ways of forging connections between human existence and visual perception. These forms of visual representation represent different ways of recording and documenting what passes as social life. Often called the mirror with a memory, photography takes the researcher into the everyday world, where the issues of observer identity, the subject's point of view, and what to photograph become problematic.

Prosser discusses four current trends and issues in the evolving field of visual methodology: (1) the representations of visual research, (2) technology and visual methods, (3) participatory visual methods, and (4) training in visual methodology. We are moving into a space where data (empirical materials) can be better and more effectively represented visually. The digital camera, software for storing large volumes of imagery, and visual compliant software—ATLAS.ti, NVivo, Transana, Observer XT—enable researchers to store, analyze, map, measure, and represent complex human interactions and communication structures. New participatory visual methods use photo-elicitation methods, photovoice, video diaries, photo-narratives, and various other hypermedia techniques. Training in visual method is burgeoning. In the United Kingdom, the Economic and Social Research Council (ESRC) has sponsored a nationwide training program aimed at teaching visual methods to a cross-section of qualitative researchers.

Prosser predicts that in the next decade there will be a greater alignment between visual methodologies and arts-based research. This alignment will lead to innovations in visual sociology, visual ethnography, and disability studies. (Prosser offers moving visual examples from his current study, which explores the perceptions of disabled people with limited communication skills.) He concludes with observations on the threats to visual research from ethical review boards. He endorses an ethics of care model. A preoccupation with biomedical regulatory ethics will slow down the development of visual methods. IRBs insist that confidentiality be maintained, that subjects remain anonymous. But in many cases, subjects are pleased and willing to be identified, and further, their very identifiability is critical to the research project. In such situations, the researcher is urged to develop an ethical covenant with those being studied so that only mutually agreed upon materials will be published.

We need to learn how to experiment with visual (and nonvisual) ways of thinking. We need to develop a critical, visual sensibility, a sensibility that will allow us to bring the gendered material world into play in critically different ways. We need to interrogate critically the logics of cyberspace and its virtual realities. The rules and methods for establishing truth that hold these worlds together must also be better understood.

Authoethnography: Making the Personal Political

Personal experience reflects the flow of thoughts and meanings persons have in their immediate situations. These experiences can be routine or problematic. They occur within the life of a person. When they are talked about, they assume the shape of a story or a narrative. Lived experience cannot be studied directly, because language, speech, and systems of discourse mediate and define the very experience one attempts to describe. We study the representations of experience, not experience itself. We examine the stories people tell one another about the experiences they have had. These stories may be personal experience narratives, or self-stories, interpretations made up as the person goes along

Many now argue that we can only study our own experiences. The researcher becomes the research subject. This is the topic of autoethnography. Tami Spry's chapter (Chapter 7, this volume) reflexively presents the arguments for writing reflexive, personal narratives. Indeed her multivoiced text is an example of such writing; it performs its own narrative reflexivity. She masterfully reviews the arguments for studying personal experience narratives, anchoring her text in the discourses of critical performance studies.

She reviews the history of and arguments for this writing form, the challenge to create texts that unfold in the life of the writer, while embodying tactics that enact a progressive politics of resistance. Such texts, when performed (and writing is a form of performance), enact a politics of possibility. They shape a critical awareness, disturb the status quo, and probe questions of identity. Spry writes out of her own history with this method and in so doing takes the reader to Judith Hamera's (Chapter 6, volume 2) and Barbara Tedlock's (Chapter 7, volume 2) chapters on performance and narrative ethnography.

Spry shows how performative autoethnography, as a critical reflexive methodology, provides a framework for making the personal political in the spaces of a post–September 11, 2001, world. She writes and performs from the spaces of hurting, healing, and grieving bodies; her own grief at the loss of her son at childbirth, the death of her father, and the bombings of 9/11. She offers a pedagogy of hope, a critical and indigenous ethnography. Her essay is about autoethnography as a radical resistant democratic practice, a political practice intended to create a space for dialogue and debate about issues of injustice. Her chapter tells by showing performance fragments, absent histories, embodied possibilities, the storytelling, performative I. Personal biography collides with culture and structure, turning historical discourse back on itself. Her performative I is embodied, liminal, accountable, wild, free, moral.

Spry ends with writing exercises, performative practices, a call for collaborative performances grounded in the belief that together we can create a local and global respect, love, and care for one another.

Online Ethnography

Sarah Gatson (Chapter 8, this volume) discusses two main versions of online ethnography: as an extension of traditional collaborative and multisited/extended-case ethnography, on the one hand, and autoethnographic inquiry, on the other hand. Under this form, the inquirer grounds an online map upon herself. Gatson reviews the classic works in each of these genres, noting that the online site is already inscribed and performative. She suggests that computer-mediated construction of self, other, and social structure constitutes a unique phenomenon of study. Offline, the body is present, and can be responded to by others. Identity construction is a situated, face-to-face process. By contrast, online, the body is absent, and interaction is mediated by computer technology and the production of written discourse. Gatson examines many of the issues that can arise in the qualitative study of Internet-mediated situations. These are issues connected to definitions of what constitutes the field or boundaries of a text, as well as what counts as text or empirical material. How the other is interpreted and given a textual presence is also problematic, as are ethical issues that are complex.

Ethical guidelines for Internet research vary sharply across disciplines and nations. She acknowledges with Judith Davidson and Silvana di Gregorio (Chapter 15, this volume) the ethical complexities when virtual worlds are the inquiry site. Gatson troubles the issue of informed consent, asking who gives permission to who, and for what, when one's research site is a public venue "with not even an unlocked door whose opening announces a certain basic level of entry and at most slightly opaque windows that block certain kinds of participation." Of course, under a communitarian, feminist ethical model, researchers enter into a collaborative relationship with a moral community of online interactants. Attempts are made to establish agreed upon understandings concerning privacy, ownership of materials, the use of personal names, and the meaning of such broad principles as justice and beneficence.

Gatson draws material from several online multilocal ethnographies, arguing that we are in a new space—Ethnography 2.0—where online subjects talk back, interact with us, read our research, criticize our work, all while eroding the walls we build around ourselves as objective outsiders studying the virtual worlds of others. We have become the subject. In this space, it is essential to reflect carefully on the ethical issues framing our studies.

Analyzing Talk and Text

Qualitative researchers study spoken and written records of human experience, including transcribed talk, films, novels, and photographs. Interviews give the researcher accounts about the issues being studied. The topic of the research is not the interview itself. Research using naturally occurring empirical materials— tape recordings of mundane interaction—constitute topics of inquiry in their own right. This is the topic of Anssi Peräkylä and Johanna Ruusuvuori's chapter (Chapter 9).

With Chase, Shopes, and Gubrium and Holstein, Peräkylä and Ruusuvuori treat interview materials as narrative accounts, rather than pictures of reality. Texts are based on transcriptions of interviews, and other forms of talk. These texts are social facts; they are produced, shared, and used in socially organized ways. Peräkylä and Ruusuvuori discuss semiotics, discourse analysis (DA), critical discourse analysis (CDA), and historical critical discourse analysis (HAD), after Michel Foucault. They review instances of each of these types of discourse analysis.

Peräkylä and Ruusuvuori also discuss membership categorization analysis (MCA), which is a less familiar form of narrative analysis. Drawing on the work of Harvey Sacks (see Silverman, 1998), they illustrate the logic of MCA. With this method, the researcher asks how persons use everyday terms and categories in their interactions with others.

Peräkylä and Ruusuvuori then turn to the analysis of talk. Two main social science traditions inform the analysis of transcripts, conversation analysis (CA) and DA. Peräkylä and Ruusuvuori review and offer examples of both traditions, arguing that talk is socially organized action. It is structurally organized, and as such it creates and maintains its own version of intersubjective reality. They show how this work has direct relevance for political and social justice concerns. Many CA studies have shown, for example, how specific interactional practices contribute to the maintenance or change of the gender system.

To summarize: Text-based documents of experience are complex. But if talk constitutes much of what we have, then the forms of analysis outlined by Peräkylä and Ruusuvuori represent significant ways of making the world and its words more visible.

Focus Groups, Pedagogy, Politics, and Inquiry

George Kamberelis and Greg Dimitriadis (Chapter 10) continue to significantly advance the discourse on focus group methodology. Building on their previous treatments of this topic in earlier editions of the *Handbook*, they show how focus groups have been used in market and military research, in emancipatory pedagogy, and in first-, second-, and third-generation feminist inquiry. Kamberelis and Dimitriadis place these three genealogies in dialogue with one another while exploring new dangers faced by focus group research in the current political climate. They reimagine focus group work as performative, and as almost always involving multiple functions that are pedagogical, political, and empirical. The performative turn shapes a politics of evidence—that is how do we enact strong or weak evidence.

Kamberelis and Dimitriadis contrast the dialogical, critical theory approach to focus groups with their use in propaganda and market research. In the marketing context, focus groups are used to extract information from people on a given topic. This information is then used to manipulate people more effectively. Critical pedagogy theorists, such as Paulo Freire and Jonathan Kozol use focus groups for imagining and enacting the "emancipatory political possibilities of collective work."

They contrast these two approaches to the, history of focus groups in feminist inquiry, noting its use in first-, second-, and third-wave feminist formations for consciousness-raising purposes (CRP). They draw on Esther Madriz (2000), who offers a model of focus group interviewing that emphasizes a feminist ethic of empowerment, moral community, emotional engagement, and the development of long-term, trusting relationships. This method gives a voice to women of color, who have long been silenced. Focus groups facilitate women writing culture together. As a Latina feminist, Madriz places focus groups within the context of collective testimonies and group resistance narratives. Focus groups reduce the distance between the researcher and the researched. The multivocality of the participants limits the control of the researcher over the research process.

Within this history, focus groups have been used to elicit and validate collective testimonies, to give a voice to the previously silenced by creating a safe space for sharing one's life experiences. The critical insights and practices of consciousness-raising groups have helped us move more deeply into the praxis-oriented commitments of the seventh and eighth moments. In these spaces, as the work of Janice Radway, Patricia Lather, and Chris Smithies documents, focus groups can become the vehicle for allowing participants to take over and own the research. In these ways, focus groups become the sites where pedagogy, politics, and interpretive inquiry intersect and inform one another.

When this happens, inquiry becomes directly involved in the complexities of political activism and policy making. Often this clashes with local IRB offices. They offer examples from several sites showing how this can happen.

Virginia Olesen (Chapter 7, volume 1) reminds us that women of color experience a triple subjugation based on class, race, and gender oppression. Critical focus groups, as discussed by Kamberelis and Dimitriadis, create the conditions for the emergence of a critical race consciousness, a consciousness focused on social change. It seems that with critical focus groups, critical race theory and progressive politics have found their methodology.

Conclusion

The researcher-as-methodological bricoleur should have a working familiarity with each of the methods of collecting and analyzing empirical materials that are presented in this part of this handbook. This familiarity includes understanding the history of each method and technique, as well as hands-on experience with each. Only in this way can the limitations and strengths of each be fully appreciated. At the same time, the investigator will more clearly see how each, as a set of material, interpretive practices, creates its own subject matter.

In addition, it must be understood that each paradigm and perspective, as presented in Part II, has a distinct history with these methods of research. Although methods-as-tools are somewhat universal in application, they are not uniformly used by researchers from all paradigms, and when used, they are fitted and adapted to the particularities of the paradigm in question. However, researchers from all paradigms and perspectives can profitably make use of each of these methods of collecting and analyzing empirical materials.

References

Angrosino, M. V., & Mays de Pérez, K. A. (2000). Rethinking observation: From method to context. In N. K. Denzin & Y. S. Lincoln (Eds.), *Handbook of qualitative research* (2nd ed., pp. 673–702). Thousand Oaks: Sage.

Fontana, A., & Frey, J. H. (2005). The interview: From neutral stance to political involvement. In N. K. Denzin & Y. S. Lincoln (Eds.), *The SAGE handbook of qualitative research* (3rd ed., pp. 695–728). Thousand Oaks: Sage.

Madriz, E. (2000). Focus groups in feminist research. In N. K. Denzin & Y. S. Lincoln (Eds.), *Handbook of qualitative research* (2nd ed., pp. 835–850). Thousand Oaks: Sage.

Silverman, D. (1998). *Harvey Sacks: Social science & conversation analysis.* Oxford, UK: Polity Press.

2

Narrative Inquiry

Still a Field in the Making

Susan E. Chase

Much has happened in narrative inquiry since the third edition of this handbook. Many books have been published, including Michael Bamberg's *Narrative—State of the Art* (2007); D. Jean Clandinin's *Handbook of Narrative Inquiry* (2007); Jaber Gubrium and James Holstein's *Analyzing Narrative Reality* (2009); Mary Jo Maynes, Jennifer Pierce, and Barbara Laslett's *Telling Stories: The Use of Personal Narratives in the Social Sciences and History* (2008); Dan McAdams, Ruthellen Josselson, and Amia Lieblich's *Identity and Story: Creating Self in Narrative* (2006); and Catherine Kohler Riessman's *Narrative Methods for the Human Sciences* (2008). The journal *Narrative Inquiry* continues to thrive. So do research centers, such as the Life Story Center at the University of Southern Maine; the Center for Myth and Ritual in American Life at Emory University; the Narrative Therapy Centre of Toronto; the Centre for Narrative Practice in Sheffield, United Kingdom; and the Dulwich Centre in Adelaide, Australia. Digital collections of written, audio, and video narratives are expanding, including National Public Radio's StoryCorps project, the September 11 Digital Archive, and the Voices of the Holocaust Project.

Clearly, narrative inquiry is still flourishing. It is also still evolving. In this update of my chapter in the fourth edition of this book, I focus on recent contributions as I present multiple approaches to narrative research, address methodological issues, and explore how narratives and narrative research make personal and social change possible. I also sketch some ideas about the future of narrative inquiry.

Multiple Approaches

Narrative inquiry is a particular type—a subtype—of qualitative inquiry.[1] What distinguishes narrative inquiry is that it begins with the biographical aspect of C. Wright Mills' (1959) famous trilogy—biography, history, and society. Narrative inquiry revolves around an interest in life experiences as narrated by those who live them. Narrative theorists define narrative as a distinct form of discourse: as meaning making through the shaping or ordering of experience, a way of understanding one's own or others' actions, of organizing events and objects into a meaningful whole, of connecting and seeing the consequences of actions and events over time. Narrative researchers highlight what we can learn about anything—history and society as well as lived experience—by maintaining a focus on narrated lives.

Within this framework, however, researchers' interests differ substantially. Without claiming to be comprehensive or exhaustive in my categories, I outline several approaches within contemporary narrative inquiry.[2]

THE STORY AND THE LIFE

Some researchers focus on the relationship between people's life stories and the quality of their life experiences. These researchers usually emphasize *what* people's stories are about—their plots, characters, and sometimes the structure or sequencing of their content.[3] In explaining this approach, D. Jean Clandinin and Jerry Rosiek (2007) argue that everyday experience itself—that taken for granted, immediate, and engrossing daily reality in which we are all continuously immersed—is where narrative inquiry should begin and end. They implore researchers to listen to people's stories about everyday experience "with an eye to identifying new possibilities within that experience" (p. 55). Beginning and ending with experience means tempering the academic impulse to generalize from specific stories to broader concepts, or to impose theoretical concepts (such as false consciousness) on people's stories. Rather, the goal of this approach is to work collaboratively with research participants to improve the quality of their everyday experiences.[4] This approach can be thought of as pragmatic or applied.

Along similar lines, psychologists who conduct narrative research focus on the relationship between people's stories and their identity development or personal well-being.[5] In *Identity and Story: Creating Self in Narrative*, editors McAdams, Josselson, and Lieblich (2006) summarize Erik Erikson's classic theory of identity development and then demonstrate narrative inquiry's contribution to an understanding of identity. They define *narrative identity* as "internalized and evolving life stories" (p. 5), and they present research focused on three questions: whether people's identity constructions through storytelling reveal the self's unity, multiplicity, or both; how self and society contribute to people's constructions of narrative identity; and how people's stories display stability, growth, or both, in their identities.[6]

The question of how narrative makes personal growth possible grounds the field of narrative therapy (Adler & McAdams, 2007; Baddeley & Singer, 2007; Cohler, 2008; Josselson, 1996; McAdams, 2006; White & Epston, 1990). While acknowledging that biographical, social, cultural, and historical circumstances condition the stories people tell about themselves, narrative therapists propose that the stories people tell affect how they live their lives. The aim of narrative therapy is to "help people resolve problems by discovering new ways of storying their situation" (Lock, Epston, & Maisel, 2004, p. 278).[7]

STORYTELLING AS LIVED EXPERIENCE

Some researchers study narrative *as* lived experience, as itself social action. These researchers are as interested in *how* people narrate their experiences as in what their stories are about. These researchers treat an understanding of storytelling practices as essential to grasping what narrators are communicating. In this approach, narration is the practice of constructing meaningful selves, identities, and realities.

Many of these researchers use in-depth interviewing as their method of gathering narrative data. Some produce detailed transcripts of their interviews to pay close attention to the narrator's linguistic practices (such as word choice, repetition, hesitation, laughter, use of personal pronouns) and to how storytelling is embedded in the interaction between researcher and narrator (Bell, 2009; Chase, 1995, 2010; Riessman, 1990, 2002a, 2002b, 2008). Whether or not they produce detailed transcripts, however, these researchers are interested in how narrators make sense of personal experience in relation to cultural discourses.[8] In this approach, researchers treat narratives as a window to the contradictory and shifting nature of hegemonic discourses, which we tend to take for granted as stable monolithic forces. Unlike Clandinin and Rosiek, whose pragmatic approach resists theoretical abstraction, these researchers view identifying oppressive discourses—and the ways in which narrators disrupt them—as a worthy goal of narrative inquiry. These researchers show that people create a range of narrative strategies in relation to cultural discourses, and that individuals' stories are constrained but not determined by those discourses.

This approach to narrative inquiry has been used to explore a broad range of topics. Rachelle Hole (2007) examines how Deaf women construct their identities through incorporating and resisting cultural narratives about difference, normalcy, passing, and Deaf culture. Helena Austin and Lorelei Carpenter (2008) explore how mothers of children diagnosed with ADHD resist dominant cultural assumptions about mothering—which are expressed in friends' and professionals' judgments about them as troublesome and troubled mothers. Sunil Bhatia (2008) shows that first-generation Indian immigrants' stories about their lives after September 11, 2001, embody disruptions in their sense of race, place, and safety in the United States, thus challenging mainstream psychology's concept of acculturation as a linear process. Alexandra Adame and Roger Knudson (2007) argue that people in the psychiatric survivors' movement resist the dominant psychiatric discourse of chemical imbalance, "broken brains," and individual normalcy, and offer an alternative discourse. That alternative is about striving to live a good life through "a collective journey of peer-support and political activism" (p. 175).

NARRATIVE PRACTICES AND NARRATIVE ENVIRONMENTS

Some researchers focus specifically on the relationship between people's narrative practices and their local narrative environments. Gubrium and Holstein (2009) describe that relationship as a *reflexive interplay*, which means that people's narrative practices are shaped by and shape their narrative environments. These researchers are more interested in understanding *narrative reality* in any local context—what does and doesn't get said, about what, why, how, and to whom—than they are in understanding individuals' stories per se. They argue that understanding narrative reality in any context requires substantial attention both to narrative environments and narrative practices. Thus, this approach depends on "ethnographic sensibilities," that is, systematic consideration of "the communicative mechanisms, circumstances, purposes, strategies, and resources that shape narrative production" (pp. vii–viii). Gubrium and Holstein do not dismiss the use of in-depth interviews or a focus on broad cultural discourses, but they propose that understanding what gets said requires an ethnographic understanding of local contexts and interactional circumstances.

Gubrium and Holstein suggest that narrative environments include such diverse entities as intimate relationships, local cultures, occupations, and organizations. Each of these environments provides myriad circumstances and resources that condition but don't determine the stories people tell (and don't tell). Ethnographic sensibilities are needed for understanding narrative environments, but they are also needed for understanding narrative practices: the mechanics of how stories are activated, how storytellers create and develop meaning through interaction with each other, how speakers collaborate with each other or struggle for control over narrative meanings, and how narrators perform their identities for specific audiences and with specific (but not always intended) consequences. Gubrium and Holstein define a "good story" not in terms of linguistic criteria, but as *any* communication—even a word or a nod— that people treat as "narratively adequate in the circumstances, functioning to smoothly facilitate casual yet consequential interaction" (2009, p. 201).

Comparative ethnography lends itself to this approach. For example, in his study of addiction and mental illness, Darin Weinberg (2005) conducted fieldwork at two residential centers based in the same treatment model. Both centers aimed to "empower clients as agents of their own recoveries," but each center developed a distinct therapeutic orientation. One program addressed insanities and addictions as resources for understanding clients' past problems, but the other program addressed insanities and addictions in terms of clients' plans for their immediate futures (pp. 13–14). Comparative ethnography makes it possible to explore how narrative realities differ from place to place or shift over time.[9]

THE RESEARCHER AND THE STORY

Some researchers treat *their* stories about life experience (including research itself as a life experience) as a significant and necessary focus of narrative inquiry. Sometimes their aim is to create a more equitable relationship between the researcher and those she or he studies by subjecting the researched *and* the researcher to an analytic lens. And sometimes researchers' aim is to explore a topic or research question more fully by including the researcher's experience of it.

Barbara Myerhoff pioneered this approach in *Number Our Days* (1979/1994), an ethnographic study of a community of elderly immigrant Jews in California. Since Myerhoff's groundbreaking study, many researchers have become more explicit about their experiences as they work to understand the other's voice, life, and culture. In her study of Esperanza's (a Mexican woman's) life story, Ruth Behar (1993/2003) writes about her comadre relationship with Esperanza and dilemmas she encountered as she became an anthropologist. In her portrait of Jewish communities in Cuba, Behar (2007) discusses her roots in Jewish Cuban

culture and her search for home. As she explores women's struggles with anorexia and the discourses that govern treatment, Paula Saukko (2008) describes
her battle with the disease. C. J. Pascoe (2007) discusses her self-presentation—
her "least-gendered" identity—as a young woman doing ethnographic research
on teenagers' sexual and gender identities in high school. Kris Paap (2006) uses
the journal she kept while working as a carpenter's apprentice as the basis for her
cultural analyses of interactions at construction sites. Her experiences with
coworkers, bosses, and the work itself feature heavily in her argument that structural insecurity in construction work creates classed, racial, and gendered labor
practices that harm even the white male workers who engage in them.

Autoethnographers develop another version of this approach. They turn the
analytic lens fully and specifically on themselves as they write, interpret, or perform narratives about their own culturally significant experiences. In autoethnography, also called interpretive biography (Denzin, 2008), the researcher and
the researched are one and the same (Ellis, 2004, 2009; Jones, 2005). Recent
examples include stories of childhood (Denzin, 2008); stories about September
11, 2001 (Denzin, 2008; Schneider, 2006); and stories about learning about
autoethnography (Scott-Hoy and Ellis, 2008). Autoethnographers sometimes
present or perform their narratives as plays, as poems, or as novels (Denzin,
1997, 2000, 2003, 2008; Ellis, 2004, 2009; Madison, 2006; Richardson, 2002;
Saldaña, 2008). Scott-Hoy and Ellis (2008) experiment with painting as an
autoethnographic presentation. The goal of autoethnography, and of many performance narratives, is to *show* rather than to *tell* (Denzin, 2003, p. 203; Saldaña,
2008, p. 201) and thus to disrupt the politics of traditional research relationships,
traditional forms of representation, and traditional social science orientations to
audiences (Langellier & Peterson, 2006; Miller & Taylor, 2006).

Methodological Issues

No matter what approach they take, narrative researchers work closely with individuals and their stories. As a result, narrative inquiry involves a particular set of
issues concerning the research relationship, ethics, interpretation, and validity.
After discussing these briefly, I address two topics that have come to the fore in
recent years: the limits of interviews as a source of narrative data, and the use of
visual narratives as data and forms of presenting research.

When narrative researchers gather data through in-depth interviews, they
work at transforming the interviewee-interviewer relationship into one of

narrator and listener. This requires a shift from the conventional practice of asking research participants to generalize about their experiences (as qualitative researchers often do), to inviting narrators' specific stories (Chase, 2005). It also requires a shift from the conventional practice of treating the interview schedule as structuring or even semi-structuring the interview to treating it as a guide that may or may not be useful when one follows the narrator's story. Amia Lieblich (in Clandinin & Murphy, 2007) suggests that narrative interviewing requires emotional maturity, sensitivity, and life experience, all of which may take years to develop (p. 642). Similarly, Don Polkinghorne (in Clandinin & Murphy, 2007) suggests that narrative interviewing involves an intensive interaction with the narrator and the patience to encourage narrators to explore memories and deeper understandings of their experiences (p. 644). In my undergraduate course on qualitative research methods, as students prepare for interviewing, I ask them what they will do if the interviewee cries. Sometimes a student says that she or he will change the subject, a response that lets me know the student is not ready for narrative interviewing. The latter requires the researcher to be a witness to a wide range of emotions.

Specific ethical issues arise in narrative research. Unlike qualitative researchers in general, who usually present short excerpts from interviews or fieldwork in their published work, narrative researchers often publish or perform longer stories from individuals' narratives. This increases the risk that narrators will feel vulnerable or exposed by narrative work. Lieblich (in Clandinin & Murphy, 2007) suggests that because narrative researchers do not know in advance exactly how they will use the narratives they collect, they should return to narrators to inform them—and ask again for permission to use their stories—when they *do* know how they plan to present, publish, or perform the work.

Josselson's (2007b) article, "The Ethical Attitude in Narrative Research" may be most comprehensive discussion of ethical issues in narrative work. She writes about the need to explain narrative research to participants, the particular problems raised by informed consent forms (which usually assume a researcher can say in advance everything the narrator needs to know), how to work with institutional review boards (IRBs), and writing research reports. Rather than listing specific rules for ethical practice, she implores researchers to develop an "ethical attitude," which must be carefully developed in each research situation.

When narrative researchers interpret narratives heard during interviews, they begin with narrators' voices and stories, thereby extending the narrator–listener relationship and the active work of listening into the interpretive process (Chase, 2005). This is a move away from a traditional theme-oriented method of analyzing qualitative material. Rather than locating distinct themes *across* interviews, narrative researchers listen first to the voices *within* each narrative (Riessman 2008, p. 12). For Polkinghorne, this is what distinguishes narrative inquiry from qualitative inquiry generally (in Clandinin & Murphy, 2007, pp. 633–634).

Martyn Hammersley (2008) notes that all qualitative research needs to be assessed in terms of validity, which means evaluating whether researchers' claims are sufficiently supported by evidence (2008, pp. 162–163). But issues of validity also take particular forms in narrative research. Polkinghorne (2007) points out that narrative research "issues claims about the meaning life events hold for people. It makes claims about how people understand situations, others, and themselves" (p. 476). The researchers' primary aim is not to discover whether narrators' accounts are accurate reflections of actual events, but to understand the meanings people attach to those events (p. 479). Nonetheless, he reminds us that words are not always sufficient to communicate meaning, that narrators are selective in the meanings they narrate, and that context and audience (e.g., an interview situation) shape what meanings get expressed. Narrative researchers do not need to claim that their interpretation is the only possibility, but they do "need to cogently argue that theirs is a viable interpretation grounded in the assembled texts" (p. 484).

In discussing the validity of *narrators'* stories—or the trustworthiness of their stories, as she prefers to call it—Riessman (2008) argues that stories that "diverge from established 'truth' can sometimes be the most interesting, indicating silenced voices and subjugated knowledge" (p. 186). Similarly, Josselson (2007a) points out that narrative research allows for the study of "people's lives as lived, people whose life experience ha[s] been lost in the search for central tendencies" (p. 8). Because much narrative research reveals experiences and meanings that have not previously been exposed by other types of research, narrative researchers must present careful evidence for their claims from narrators' accounts (Riessman, 2008, p. 186). In addition, narrative researchers can strengthen their arguments by discussing cases that don't fit their claims and by considering alternative interpretations (p. 191). They should also document their procedures for collecting and interpreting data (p. 193).

BEYOND INTERVIEWS

Although narrative researchers have used many sources of data—diaries, letters, autobiographies, and field notes of naturally occurring conversations—in-depth interviews continue to be the most common source of narrative data (Bell, 2009, p. 171; Riessman 2008, p. 26; Hammersley, 2008, p. 89). In recent years, this privileging of interviews has been a topic of discussion and debate.

Big Stories and Small Stories

Mark Freeman (2006) calls the narrative material gathered from interviews *big stories*. He argues that their particular value as data is that they allow the narrator distance from and thus the opportunity to reflect on significant life events. Narrative researchers also value interviews for the window—a frequently used metaphor—they offer to the narrative environment external to the interview. Through close attention to both the content of narrators' stories and how they speak—for example, unselfconsciously, hesitantly, or defensively—a researcher can hear the influence of narrative environments on narrative practice. Analysis of patterns across interviews with similarly situated people contributes to a stronger understanding of those environments and their impact on individual narratives. But the metaphor of the window also indicates its limits. Looking out at narrative environments from inside the narrative, the narrative as a window limits how and how much of the narrative environment can be seen.

With this limit in mind, Riessman (2008) argues that ethnographic study of participants' settings facilitates stronger understanding of their stories (p. 26), including stories told during interviews. She describes this as the *dialogic/performance* approach, which highlights "'who' an utterance may be directed to, 'when,' and 'why,' that is, for what purposes?" (p. 105). Here, "Attention expands from detailed attention to a narrator's speech—what is said and/or how it is said—to the dialogic environment in all its complexity. Historical and cultural context, audiences for the narrative, and shifts in the interpreter's positioning over time are brought into interpretation" (pp. 136–137).

Some narrative theorists resist the privileged status of big stories produced during interviews by arguing for greater attention to *small stories*. Alexandra Georgakopoulou (2007) defines small stories as a constant and natural feature of everyday life; they include talk about very recent events, such as what happened this morning, as well talk about what might happen in the near future (2007, p. 150). Moreover, "with a small stories perspective in mind, it is not just tellings or retellings that form part of the analysis: refusals to tell or deferrals of telling are equally important in terms of how the participants orient to what is appropriate ... in a specific environment, what the norms for telling and tellability are" (p. 151). This resonates with Gubrium and Holstein's (2009) focus on the reflexive interplay between narrative environments and narrative practices. An interest in how stories are produced and received in society "requires that we step outside of narrative texts" to ask "who produces particular kinds of stories, where are they likely to be encountered, what are their purposes and consequences, who are the listeners, under what circumstances are particular narratives more or less accountable, how do they gain acceptance, and how are they challenged?" (p. 23)

Content Analyses

My own narrative work has relied heavily on in-depth interviews (for example, Chase, 1995). Recently though, I have been influenced by arguments about the limits of interviews and have sought ways to move beyond sole reliance on them. My book, *Learning to Speak, Learning to Listen: How Diversity Works on Campus* (Chase, 2010) offers an example of how it is possible to do this when long-term ethnographic study—and thus sustained attention to small stories— is not an option.

I conducted a case study of how students engage issues of race, class, gender, ability, and sexual orientation at City University (a pseudonym), a predominantly white private university. These days, most U.S. colleges and universities proclaim commitments to diversity (for example, in their mission statements), but this institutionalization of diversity does not always translate into serious engagement with diversity issues on campus. What interested me about City University (CU) is that a critical mass of students, faculty, and administrators has succeeded over the years in making organizational and cultural changes that strongly support students of color, women students, and gay, lesbian, bisexual, and transgender (GLBT) students. This critical mass of people has succeeded in making diversity issues an integral—if contentious—part of the narrative environment. One consequence is that CU students of color and GLBT students (among others) feel entitled to—and *do*—speak out when they perceive injustice on campus. Another consequence is that some CU students have learned to listen to those whose social identities and social locations differ from their own. I argue that students' speaking and listening across social differences are at once shaped by CU's narrative environment and contribute to it.

In my study I focused on events leading up to and culminating in a public protest by students of color who were frustrated by what they perceived as the university's lack of serious attention to racial issues. My major source of data was in-depth interviews with a wide range of individual students, groups of students in many different campus organizations, as well as with faculty, staff, and administrators. By interviewing people and groups that are differently situated on campus, I was able to get different views (or windows) on CU's narrative environment.

But I also wanted more direct access to that narrative environment. I did a limited amount of ethnographic observation, but long-term ethnography was not a practical option for me. Instead I conducted extensive quantitative and qualitative content analyses of key documents, most notably the student newspaper and the student government minutes, but also CU's curriculum, calendar of events, and website.

The broader understanding of CU's narrative environment that I gained from the content analyses allowed me to interpret puzzling aspects of the interviews. For example, I noticed a certain silence during my interview with Rachelle, one of the students who led the campus protest. As Rachelle told me about her personal development during college, she spoke about how she had become more open to GLBT people. As an African American raised in a Pentecostal tradition, this was a major change for her. She explained that while she was growing up, even *talking* about sexual orientation was taboo, never mind interacting with gays or lesbians. She said that at CU she had become more open-minded with the help of African American friends who showed her that it was possible to interact with—and even become friends with—GLBT people, without losing her faith.

Although Rachelle could tell me *this* story about becoming more open and tolerant, she said little about a related topic. When I asked about her current religious beliefs, she stated simply, "[homosexuality] is just something I don't feel is right but that's just for my own personal belief." If my study were *only* based on interviews, I would have noticed that Rachelle did not expand on this story of continuing to embrace her religious perspective that homosexuality is wrong, but I would not have understood *why* she had nothing more to say about this. The content analyses allowed me to see that Rachelle's relative silence about her belief that homosexuality is wrong was shaped by CU's narrative environment. The content analyses demonstrated that at CU an unquestioned acceptance of GLBT people and GLBT rights constitutes the *preferred story* (Gubrium and Holstein, 2009; Riessman, 2008) about sexual orientation. This preferred story is expressed routinely in articles, editorials, and letters in the student newspaper and in the student government's noncontroversial passage of resolutions in support of GLBT students and GLBT rights. Given that preferred story in CU's narrative environment, Rachelle's story about how she has become more open-minded about GLBT issues *and* her relative silence about how she still believes that homosexuality is wrong make sense. Both aspects of her personal narrative reflect the influence of that preferred story in CU's narrative environment.

The content analyses also showed that in CU's environment racial issues are much more contentious than are issues related to sexual orientation. The student newspaper, student government, and the administration were proactive and supportive in response to anonymous homophobic incidents on campus. By comparison, these same entities' responses to racial issues were interpreted by students of color as slow and unsupportive. The difference between the uncontentiousness of sexual orientation and the contentiousness of race in CU's narrative landscape helped me to understand students of color's frustration and thus their decision to stage a protest. The content analyses, in conjunction with the interviews, helped me to demonstrate the reflexive interplay between CU's narrative environment and students' narrative practices—such as Rachelle's relative silence about her religious belief and the student of color's public protest.

BEYOND WRITTEN AND ORAL TEXTS

Even when narrative researchers move beyond interviews, their data sources are usually oral or written texts—such as field notes about naturally occurring talk or the documents I used in my study. Some narrative researchers, however, challenge the assumption that narratives are found only or primarily in spoken or written formats. Riessman (2008) contends that visual images are so central to our everyday lives that social scientists must attend to them if they are to understand more fully how people communicate meaning (see also Bach, 2007; Harper, 2005; and Weber, 2008). Narrative researchers who study visual images treat them as socially situated narrative texts that demand interpretation.[10]

Some narrative researchers focus on visual images that others have already made—such as photographs, films, or paintings (Riessman, 2008, p. 141; Weber, 2008, p. 48). For instance, Susan Bell (2002) analyzes the photographs of Jo Spence, a British feminist photographer who was diagnosed with breast cancer before the emergence of the women's breast cancer movement. Bell chose three photographs out of hundreds Spence had taken to interpret what Spence was communicating about her illness experience. One photograph is of Spence getting a mammogram, another of her breast the day before surgery, and the third of herself in bed shortly before she died. Bell interprets the three photographs in detail, concentrating on Spence's face, posture, and body; the rooms in which she was located, the objects in the rooms (including technological devices and medical equipment); and the way Spence framed the images as photographs and described them in accompanying texts. Through her interpretations, Bell demonstrates how Spence resisted having her illness experience defined by the medical world (Bell, 2002, 2006; Riessman, 2008, pp. 153–159).

Other narrative researchers collaborate with research subjects in the construction of visual images (Riessman, 2008, p. 141; Weber, 2008, p. 47). For example, physician and filmmaker Gretchen Berland gave video equipment to three adults with physical disabilities who use wheelchairs for mobility. For 2 years, these adults recorded and commented on their everyday lives. Berland produced the film, *Rolling,* and appears in it from time to time, but the film foregrounds the three adults' stories (see http://www.thirteen.org/rolling/thefilm/ and Riessman, 2008, p. 143).

In her ethnographic study of a school program for pregnant teenagers, Wendy Luttrell (2003) discovered that the teens were uninterested in talking about their experiences in an in-depth interview format. So she suggested that they create self-portraits and collages, media that the teens found conducive to self-expression. As they worked on their projects, Luttrell listened to the girls converse with each other about the images they were constructing. When their work was complete, the girls presented the images to each other and engaged in further discussion about them. At the end of the year, Luttrell collected the images in a book format so that each girl could have a copy. Luttrell's data include the visual images, the words that each girl attached to the images she had made, the group's conversations about the images, as well as Luttrell's broader ethnographic observations about interactions in the classroom and the program's place in the school and community. She demonstrates that each girl, in her own way, struggles against demeaning portrayals of pregnant teens within narrative environments (the school and American culture broadly) that make that struggle painful and difficult (see also Riessman, 2008, pp. 164–172).

In her study of Muslim women's experiences in the United States after the terrorist attacks of September 11, 2001, Mei-Po Kwan (2008) uses visual narrative in yet another way. She asked 37 women in Columbus, Ohio, to carefully record their activities and trips outside the home on one particular day. Then she conducted interviews with the women about how their activities and sense of safety have changed since September 11th. She also asked them to indicate on a map where they go during their everyday lives, which areas they considered safe or unsafe before September 11th, and how their feelings about those areas have changed since then. Kwan uses these multiple sources of data to construct a visual narrative that shows changes in time and space in Muslim women's feelings of fear and safety pre– and post–September 11th. Kwan uses three-dimensional (3-D) geographical information systems (GIS) to "illuminate the impact of the fear of anti-Muslim hate violence on the daily lives of Muslim women and to help articulate their emotional geographies in the post–September 11 period" (p. 653). In Kwan's study, the visual narrative is not the data, but a powerful means of presenting Muslim women's narratives in the post–September 11th world.

Narrative Inquiry, Personal Change, and Social Change

Like other qualitative researchers, narrative researchers continue to be compelled by the relationship between their work and possibilities for change and social justice. Some study how narratives make change happen, and some collect and present narratives to make change happen. In either case, there is a sense of *urgency,* of the need for personal and social change. In the following, I characterize that urgency in several ways: the urgency of speaking, the urgency of being heard, the urgency of collective stories, and the urgency of public dialogue. When narrative inquiry focuses on personal or social change, the relation between narrator and audience becomes central.

THE URGENCY OF SPEAKING

Sometimes the act itself of narrating a significant life event facilitates positive change. In discussing a breast cancer survivor's narrative, Kristen Langellier (2001) writes, "The wounded storyteller reclaims the capacity to tell, and hold on to, her own story, resisting narrative surrender to the medical chart as the official story of the illness" (p. 146; see also Bell, 2002, 2009; Capps & Ochs, 1995; Frank, 1995; Lieblich, McAdams, & Josselson, 2004). Along similar lines, George Rosenwald and Richard Ochberg (1992) claim that self-narration can lead to personal emancipation—to "better" stories of life difficulties or traumas. In these cases, the narrator is his or her own audience, the one who needs to hear alternative versions of his or her identity or life events, and the one for whom changes in the narrative can "stir up changes" in the life (p. 8).

Researchers and practitioners in narrative therapy point out that creating alternative narratives of one's self or life can be extraordinarily difficult. For example, in their discussion of a woman who has been hospitalized multiple times for self-starvation, Andrew Lock, David Epston, and Richard Maisel (2004) show that it was only when the woman learned to treat "anorexia" as separate from herself that she began to develop a voice that confidently resisted the "voice of anorexia." In this case, the woman's externalization of anorexia was accomplished through therapeutic sessions in which one therapist literally spoke the punitive voice of "anorexia," the woman repudiated that voice in her own words, and a second therapist supported her in doing so.

The question of whether, how, and under what conditions the telling of traumatic experiences facilitates healing and emotional well-being is an important topic for narrative researchers (Naples, 2003). For instance, shortly after World War II, adult survivors of the Holocaust worked relentlessly to gather and publish child survivors' testimonies. At that time, some claimed that children's testimonies had therapeutic value for the children, but they did not always provide evidence for that claim (Cohen, 2007). Taking a life course perspective, Bertram Cohler (2008) suggests that *when* in the course of their lives survivors tell their stories shapes their meaning for survivors and the role the stories play in survivors' lives. He analyzes the memoirs of two Holocaust survivors, one of whom wrote her memoir right after the war. She described atrocities she had witnessed, but largely excluded her own experiences, as if she could not integrate them into her life story. The other woman wrote her memoir half a century after World War II as an émigré to the United States. She recounts her experiences before, during, and after the war, forming them into a "characteristic American redemptive account of successfully overcoming adversity" (Cohler, 2008, p. 1).

Some narrative therapists who work with Holocaust survivors find that successful therapy consists not in integrating the trauma into one's life story, but rather putting the traumatic narrative "into a capsule separated from other parts of the life story" (Shamai & Levin-Megged, 2006, p. 692). By defining successful therapy as separation of the traumatic story from the life story, these researchers counter traditional notions of therapeutic success. The difference lies, at least in part, in the severity of the trauma.

THE URGENCY OF BEING HEARD

For some individuals and groups, the urgency of storytelling arises from the need and desire to have *others* hear one's story. Citing René Jara, John Beverly (2005) describes Latin American *testimonios* as "emergency" narratives that involve "a problem of repression, poverty, marginality, exploitation, or simply survival. . . . The voice that speaks to the reader through the text . . . [takes] the form of an 'I' that demands to be recognized, that wants or needs to stake a claim on our attention" (p. 548).

Of course, more than Latin American *testimonios* are narrated with this urgent voice. The stories of many marginalized groups and oppressed people shape the contemporary narrative landscape. To name just a few: transgendered people (Girshick, 2008); parents of children with disabilities (Goodley & Tregaskis, 2006); Hmong immigrants to the United States after the Vietnam War (Faderman, 2005); Latino and Asian American college students on predominantly white campuses (Garrod & Kilkenny, 2007; Garrod, Kilkenny, & Gómez, 2007); and the victims and survivors of gendered, racial, ethnic, and sexual violence (Bales & Trodd, 2008; Deer, Clairmont, Martel, & While Eagle, 2008). Indeed, "naming silenced lives" and "giving voice" to marginalized people—or in Riessman's (2008) more collaborative term, "amplifying" others' voices

(p. 223)—have been primary goals of narrative research for several decades (McLaughlin & Tierney, 1993; Personal Narratives Group, 1989).

The urgency of speaking and being heard drives the ongoing collection and publication of narratives about many forms of social injustice. Examples include the personal narratives of refugees of the war in Bosnia and Croatia (Mertus, Tesanovic, Metikos, & Boric, 1997); the stories of September 11, 2001, survivors (www.911digitalarchive.org); testimonies about genocide in Rwanda (http://www .voicesofrwanda.org/); and the stories of survivors and witnesses of the Holocaust (the Voices of the Holocaust Project [www.iit.edu]; the Fortunoff Video Archive for Holocaust Testimonies at Yale University [http://www.library.yale.edu/testimo nies]; Voice/Vision: Holocaust Survivor Oral History Archive [http://holocaust .umd.umich.edu/interviews.php]; and the University of Southern California's Shoah Foundation Institute's archive [http://college.usc.edu/vhi/]).[11]

The same urgency to get survivors' voices heard drives the work of Father Patrick Desbois (2008), a French Catholic priest, who has traveled through the Ukraine to find the unmarked mass graves of a million and a half Jews killed by Nazi mobile death squads during World War II. In addition to honoring the victims with proper burials, he films the testimonies of eyewitnesses who were children at the time. These acts of genocide are not well known, and many of the eyewitnesses have never before spoken publicly about their experiences.[12]

The act of speaking to be heard references an "other" who needs to hear, to listen, to pay attention. Mary Gergen and Kenneth Gergen (2007) state, "Audiences who listen to a story from a witness become themselves second-order witnesses. They create for themselves the visual images, sounds, and visceral responses of the witness. One might say that they engage in empathetic listening, in which they come to feel with the storyteller" (p. 139). When the story is about pain, trauma, and injustice, listening itself can be painful. Listening requires the willingness to put the other's story at the center of one's attention, to resist defensive reactions, and to acknowledge the limits of one's ability to put oneself in another's shoes (Chase, 2010).

THE URGENCY OF COLLECTIVE STORIES

Stories about injustice are often more than individual stories. Laurel Richardson defines collective stories as those that connect an individual's story to the broader story of a marginalized social group (Richardson, 1990). In discussing the collective stories of sexual abuse survivors and gays and lesbians, Kenneth Plummer (1995) writes, "For narratives to flourish, there must be a community to hear. . . . For communities to hear, there must be stories which weave together their history, their identity, their politics. The one—community—feeds upon and into the other—story" (p. 87).

When survivors or marginalized or oppressed groups tell their collective stories, they demand social change. It may be a demand that people never forget the atrocities of the past. It may be a demand that educational curricula be transformed so that young people learn how to prevent what previous generations have suffered. It may be a demand that people who hold legal, cultural, or other forms of power take action to bring about justice. Thus, collective stories become integral to social movements (see also Davis, 2002).

Along these lines, Bell (2009) shows how women's personal narratives played a role in successfully challenging conventional medicine's treatment of women who were exposed prenatally to DES (a drug linked to a rare vaginal cancer and poor reproductive results). Bell gathered DES daughters' narratives through in-depth interviews as well as letters to the editor they had written in various media (which were collected and published in *DES Action Voice*). Through close attention to how DES daughters narrated their experiences, Bell shows how some of them became activists who created a feminist, embodied health movement. And through close examination of the proceedings of a National Institutes of Health–sponsored workshop, Bell demonstrates how DES daughters and biomedical scientists collaboratively "destabilized the discourse of science as usual" (p. 10).

In *To Plead Our Own Cause*, Kevin Bales and Zoe Trodd (2008) present verbatim the oral and written narratives of men, women, and children who have been enslaved in countries across the globe as soldiers, in prison camps, in workplaces, and as sexual objects. Some of these narrators have become activists, working with various organizations to get their stories heard. Many of the narratives in the book were originally elicited by or written for abolitionist and human rights organizations, public awareness campaigns, and congressional sessions on slavery-related bills. Indeed these testimonies were instrumental in getting the Victims of Trafficking and Violence Protection Act passed into U.S. law in 2000.

THE URGENCY OF PUBLIC DIALOGUE

William Gamson (2002) writes, "Deliberation and dialogue in a narrative mode . . . lends itself more easily [than abstract argument] to the expression of moral complexity." In this sense, "storytelling facilitates a healthy, democratic, public life" (p. 197).[13] Many narrative researchers hope their work will stimulate dialogue about complex moral matters and about the need for social change. And they look for creative ways to present their work to the public (Barone, 2007; Knowles & Cole, 2008; Madison & Hamera, 2006; Mattingly, 2007).

Some researchers use ethnotheater—turning narrative data into theater performances—as a means of accomplishing this goal. Anna Deavere Smith (1993, 1994, 2004) has been a leader in this regard. In her solo stage performances, based on the words of people she interviewed, Smith has explored events such as the riots in Los Angeles after the acquittal of the police officers who beat Rodney King, and the riots in Crown Heights, Brooklyn, after a car carrying a Hasidic spiritual leader killed a black 7-year-old child from Guyana. In her most recent one-woman show, *Let Me Down Easy*, Smith performs the narratives of many different people, all of whom address "the fragility and resilience of the human body" (Isherwood, 2008). In this show, she presents people's stories about "the steroid scandal in sports, cancer therapies, African folk healing, the genocide in Rwanda, the tragedy of Katrina and the ailing American health-care system" (Isherwood, 2008). In such performances, Smith presents a wide array of voices, and in so doing, attempts to create public dialogue about emotionally and politically charged issues and events.

During three years of ethnographic fieldwork in Ghana, Soyini Madison (2006) studied the debate surrounding a tradition of sending girls to a village shrine for years or even a lifetime to atone for a crime or violation committed by a (usually male) family member. Local human rights activists view that practice as tantamount to the girls' enslavement. Traditionalists view it as a matter of moral and cultural education and as protecting the girls from the shame of their family member's action. Traditionalists point out that the girls "are esteemed as 'queens' with special powers" (p. 398). On the basis of her fieldwork, Madison (2006) wrote, "*Is It a Human Being or a Girl?*," a play revolving around three major themes: the debate between the human rights activists and the traditionalists; critiques of corporate globalization, which produces the poverty underlying the traditional practice; and Madison's social location as an African American academic and how that shaped her ethnographic interests. In the play, five performers acted and spoke the various voices, based largely on narratives Madison collected during in-depth interviews. Madison's aim in presenting her fieldwork in the form of ethnotheater was to stimulate public dialogue in the local community about the moral issues involved.

Moisés Kaufman, a leading proponent and practitioner of ethnotheater, writes,

There are moments in history when a particular event brings the various ideologies and beliefs prevailing in a culture into sharp focus. At these junctures the event becomes a lightning rod of sorts, attracting and distilling the essence of these philosophies and convictions. By paying careful attention in moments like this to people's words, one is able to hear the way these prevailing ideas affect not only individual lives but also the culture at large. (2001, p. v)

Kaufman's play, *The Laramie Project,* is based on one such moment in history: the murder of Matthew Shepard in 1998. Four weeks after the murder, members of Kaufman's Tectonic Theater Project traveled to Laramie, Wyoming, to interview many of the people involved as well as other townspeople. A year and a half and 200 interviews later, the Tectonic Theater Project performed the first of many productions of the play, in which actors played the people they had interviewed, speaking their words verbatim.

Ten years later, Kaufman and his colleagues returned to Laramie and interviewed many of the same people again. One interviewed Aaron McKinney, who is currently serving two life sentences for the murder of Matthew Shepard. Kaufman and his colleagues turned these interviews into another play, which was staged in dozens of theaters across the United States and in other countries on October 12, 2009, the 11th anniversary of Shepard's death. The Tectonic Theater's goal in returning to Laramie was to find out what had and hadn't changed in the community during those 10 years. The new play shows that many Laramie residents have wanted to "move on," because "Laramie is not *that* kind of community."[14] Interestingly, Wyoming's hate crime legislation still excludes sexual orientation, but on October 28, 2009, President Barack Obama signed into law the Matthew Shepard and James Byrd, Jr. Hate Crimes Prevention Act. According to the Human Rights Campaign,

> [This law] gives the Department of Justice (DOJ) the power to investigate and prosecute bias-motivated violence by providing the DOJ with jurisdiction over crimes of violence where a perpetrator has selected a victim because of the person's actual or perceived race, color, religion, national origin, gender, sexual orientation, gender identity or disability.[15]

Whether or not *The Laramie Project* had a direct impact on the federal legislation, it certainly created public dialogue in theater venues across the country and the globe.

Still a Field in the Making

As I worked on this update to my original chapter in the fourth edition of this book, I found, as before, that it is easier to identify complexities and multiplicities in the field of narrative inquiry than it is to identify commonalities. As I think about the future of this field, I suspect that this will continue to be the case.

One small but poignant indicator of increasing complexity and multiplicity lies in how I changed the definition of narrative. In the original chapter, I wrote, "Narrative is *retrospective* meaning making—the shaping or ordering of *past* experience" [emphasis added]. In this update, I wrote that narrative is "meaning making through the shaping or ordering of experience." I deleted "retrospective" and "past" because of recent developments in this field. As noted earlier, in the last few years, some researchers have focused on "small stories" in everyday situated interaction (Bamberg, 2006; Georgakopoulou, 2007) and on the need for ethnographic sensibilities for understanding how small stories are produced in and organize social interaction (Gubrium & Holstein, 2009). These researchers demonstrate that the definition of narrative as *retrospective* meaning making is partial. They influenced me to broaden the definition.

I suspect that complexity and multiplicity will also persist in ideas about what narrative *inquiry* is. A number of researchers present overviews of and distinctions within narrative inquiry concerning its interests, goals, and methods (Bamberg, 2007; Clandinin & Rosiek, 2007; Gubrium & Holstein, 2009; Polkinghorne, in Clandinin & Murphy, 2007; Riessman, 2008). I have been influenced by their categories and yet I still came up with my own. Summarizing their conversation with Elliot Mishler about the future of narrative inquiry, D. Jean Clandinin and M. Shaun Murphy (2007) write, "Elliot notes that we cannot police the boundaries of narrative inquiry. For him, the field . . . will be defined from within the different communities of narrative inquirers with researchers picking up on each others' work that helps them address issues salient to their own research problems" (p. 636). This emphasis on different narrative research communities strikes me as an accurate description of what is happening and will continue to happen.

Yet the boundaries of narrative research communities are also fluid. Lieblich (in Clandinin & Murphy, 2007, pp. 640–641) notes that graduate students interested in narrative research still have trouble finding support for work they want to do. Mishler (in Clandinin & Murphy, 2007, p. 641) notes that even established narrative researchers often feel alone in their departments. As narrative researchers look outside their departments, disciplines, and across national boundaries to find colleagues with whom they share interests, narrative research communities will change and evolve.

Furthermore, it is not always clear which communities we should belong to, which colleagues we need to converse with, which conversations we need to cultivate. I still wonder sometimes who *my* colleagues are. Colleagues who use the same narrative methods but whose research covers different topics? Colleagues who work on the same topics, but who don't use narrative methods, or even qualitative methods? Practitioners in the fields for whom my research might provide useful insights? Ideally, of course, I would converse with all of these colleagues, but sometimes one has to choose. Because narrative inquiry is still a field in the making, I suspect that narrative researchers will continue to ask these questions about colleagues, conversations, and communities.

As discussed earlier, the last few years have seen an expansion in the kinds of data narrative researchers use in their studies. This will probably continue as well. Examples presented in this chapter speak to the value of combining interviews and ethnographic observation (Riessman, 2008); photographs and autobiographical writings (Bell, 2002, 2006; Behar, 2007); interviews, letters to the editor, autobiographical film, and workshop proceedings (Bell 2009); ethnography and participants' collages and self-portraits (Luttrell, 2003); activity diaries, in-depth interviews, maps, and geographical information systems (GIS) (Kwan, 2008); and interviews and content analyses of documents (Chase, 2010). Using multiple sources of data underscores that any view is partial and that narrative environments are multiple and layered. Given the explosion of new technologies, narrative researchers are likely to seek new data sources, adding to the complexity and multiplicity of narrative research. And with these new data sources, new ethical issues will arise. Mishler points out that the increased use of visual narratives raises questions about how to protect the rights of those whose images we use (in Clandinin & Murphy, 2007, p. 649). For example, presenting or publishing photos that include people's faces makes it impossible to conceal their identities.

Another issue that is close to my heart has to do with the generally critical character of narrative research. Like qualitative research generally, narrative research often critiques cultural discourses, institutions, organizations, and interactions that produce social inequalities. Narrative researchers frequently look for the collusive or resistant strategies that narrators develop in relation to the constraints of their narrative environments. As Plummer (1995) demonstrates, social movements research reveals resistant narratives that develop in activist communities. Narrative researchers note that those resistant narratives change others' beliefs, attitudes, and actions. But narrative researchers are less likely to study the *audience* side of this narrative process. The urgency to speak, to get heard, to develop collective narratives, and to create public dialogue—all of these are about the need to influence an audience. What does it look like when the audience *is* influenced. What does an audience's *listening* look like? A focus on these questions would encourage a hopeful aspect in narrative research.

Along similar lines, I suggest that we need to know more about narrative environments that make possible and even encourage creative explorations of self, identity, community, and reality. In this vein, some researchers study the intimate environment of therapy and some study the macro environment of social movements. I would also like to see studies of the mundane environments of everyday life. Even as they constrain, some families, friendships, classrooms, workplaces, and organizations *also* provide members with narrative resources for creating strong relationships and vibrant communities.

In other words, I suggest that we have as much to learn from narrative inquiry into environments where something is working as we do from inquiry into environments where injustice reigns. And I don't believe we have to give up intellectual skepticism to ask these questions. When something is working—when individuals, groups, or communities marshal ordinary resources in their everyday lives to strengthen their relationships and their communities—what is going on narratively in those environments? Karen Gallas (1994) offers an example. As a teacher, she did ethnographic research on sharing time in her own first-grade classroom. She discovered that certain sharing time (narrative) practices hindered and others supported a homeless student's social and language development. (See Riessman's [2008, pp. 125–136] analysis of Gallas's research.) Such research makes both a theoretical contribution to social science and a practical contribution to the field of education. Listening to and observing this child in interaction with her peers allowed Gallas to figure out what facilitated the child's effective speaking practices and the other students' listening. An interest in what works requires a focus on the urgency of speaking and the urgency of being heard, as well as on what it means to *listen*. Here, attention includes the recipients of stories, the audiences for performances.

The complexities and multiplicities in contemporary narrative inquiry offer novice and seasoned researchers a great deal of freedom in the topics and interests they pursue and the methods and approaches they use. At the same time, it is impossible for anyone to keep up with the field as a whole. Josselson (2007a) notes the proliferation of narrative studies, the "array of fascinating, richly-detailed expositions of life as lived, well-interpreted studies full of nuance and insight that befit the complexity of human lives" (p. 8). She also points out that it is impossible to read them all, an observation I share, having attempted to follow developments in this field over the years. Given this situation, Josselson (2007a) suggests that one important issue for contemporary narrative inquiry is "the challenge of accumulating knowledge." She argues that we need a meta-analysis of the vast array of narratives studies (pp. 7–8).

According to Josselson (2007a), a meta-analysis would include the comparison of narrators' language structures across studies, the search for patterns and differences across studies on the same topic, the creation of criteria for determining what constitutes a pattern or a difference, the assessment of whether similar findings across studies of the same phenomenon give us confidence in those findings, the search for patterns across studies of empirically different phenomena, and the articulation of "the frontiers of ignorance," what researchers do not yet understand. Finally, a meta-analysis would attend to the practical implications of narrative studies, what the findings of our studies tell us about how people act in the social world and about the kind of social world we all are creating (pp. 13–14).

I especially like Josselson's idea that this meta-analysis requires conversation among narrative researchers. It requires new colleagues and communities.

Notes

1. In my chapter in the third edition of this handbook, I covered important terms, historical background, and the analytic lenses that ground contemporary narrative inquiry.

2. Bamberg (2007), Mishler (1995), Polkinghorne (1995), and Riessman (2008) also make distinctions among types of narrative research in the social sciences, but because they exclude some kinds of work that I want to include (and include some kinds that I want to exclude), I construct my own categories here.

3. Riessman (2008) calls this focus on *what* questions a thematic approach to narrative analysis.

4. In outlining their approach to narrative inquiry, Clandinin and Rosiek (2007) draw heavily on the Deweyan definition of experience, which they explain in detail. They also describe the borders between their approach and several major theoretical paradigms (postpositivism, Marxism or critical theory, and poststructuralism).

5. Because quantitative modes of inquiry are so dominant in psychology, some psychologists treat narrative inquiry as synonymous with qualitative inquiry. But the psychologists I cite here carve out a distinctly narrative approach.

6. Josselson, Lieblich, and McAdams have edited four other books in the American Psychological Association's series, *The Narrative Study of Lives:* Josselson, Lieblich, and McAdams (2003; 2007); Lieblich, McAdams, and Josselson (2004); and McAdams, Josselson, and Lieblich (2001).

7. Several research centers focus specifically on narrative therapy: Narrative Therapy Centre of Toronto; Centre for Narrative Practice in Sheffield, United Kingdom; and the Dulwich Centre in Adelaide, Australia.

8. In Riessman's (2008) terms, this approach includes aspects of structural narrative analysis as well as aspects of dialogic/performative analysis.

9. For more examples of comparative ethnographies, see Gubrium and Holstein (2001) and Holstein and Gubrium (2000).

10. In the next three paragraphs, I rely heavily on Riessman's (2008) Chapter 6, "Visual Analysis."

11. These narrative collections are online, which means they are available to the general public as well as to researchers. In some cases, the websites make it possible for people to add their own stories.

12. See also a report about Father Patrick Desbois's work on the website of the U.S. Holocaust Memorial Museum (http://www.ushmm.org/museum/exhibit/focus/desbois/).

13. Gamson is writing specifically about media discourse about abortion, but his argument is useful for other topics and contexts.

14. Quotes in http://austinist.com/2009/10/14/the_laramie_project_ten_years_later.php. See also http://community.laramieproject.org/content/About/ and http://artsbeat.blogs.nytimes.com/2009/10/15/the-laramie-project-10-years-later-draws-50000-theatergoers/.

15. http://www.hrc.org/laws_and_elections/5660.htm

References

Adame, A. L., & Knudson, R. M. (2007). Beyond the counter-narrative: Exploring alternative narratives of recovery from the psychiatric survivor movement. *Narrative Inquiry, 17,* 157–178.

Adler, J. M., & McAdams, D. P. (2007). The narrative reconstruction of psychotherapy. *Narrative Inquiry, 17,* 179–202.

Austin, H., & Carpenter, L. (2008). Troubled, troublesome, troubling mothers: The dilemma of difference in women's personal motherhood narratives. *Narrative Inquiry, 18,* 378–392.

Bach, H. (2007). Composing a visual narrative inquiry. In D. J. Clandinin (Ed.), *Handbook of narrative inquiry: Mapping a methodology* (pp. 280–307). Thousand Oaks, CA: Sage.

Baddeley, J., & Singer, J. A. (2007). Charting the life story's path: Narrative identity across the life span. In D. J. Clandinin (Ed.), *Handbook of narrative inquiry: Mapping a methodology* (pp. 177–202). Thousand Oaks, CA: Sage.

Bales, K., & Trodd, Z. (Eds.). (2008). *To plead our own cause: Personal stories by today's slaves.* Ithaca, NY: Cornell University Press.

Bamberg, M. (2006). *Stories: Big or small: Why do we care? Narrative Inquiry, 16,* 139–147.

Bamberg, M. (Ed.). (2007). *Narrative—State of the art.* Philadelphia: John Benjamins.

Barone, T. (2007). A return to the gold standard? Questioning the future of narrative construction as educational research. *Qualitative Inquiry, 13,* 454–470.

Behar, R. (2003). *Translated woman: Crossing the border with Esperanza's story.* Boston: Beacon. (Original work published in 1993)

Behar, R. (2007). *An island called home: Returning to Jewish Cuba.* New Brunswick, NJ: Rutgers University Press.

Bell, S. E. (2002). Photo images: Jo Spence's narratives of living with illness. *Health: An Interdisciplinary Journal for the Social Study of Health, Illness and Medicine, 6,* 5–30.

Bell, S. E. (2006). Living with breast cancer in text and image: Making art to make sense. *Qualitative Research in Psychology, 3,* 31–44.

Bell, S. E. (2009). *DES daughters: Embodied knowledge and the transformation of women's health politics.* Philadelphia: Temple University Press.

Beverly, J. (2005). *Testimonio,* subalternity, and narrative authority. In N. K. Denzin & Y. S. Lincoln (Eds.), *The SAGE handbook of qualitative research* (3rd ed., pp. 547–557). Thousand Oaks, CA: Sage.

Bhatia, S. (2008). 9/11 and the Indian diaspora: Narratives of race, place, and immigrant identity. *Journal of Intercultural Studies, 29,* 21–39.

Capps, L., & Ochs, E. (1995). *Constructing panic: The discourse of agoraphobia.* Cambridge, MA: Harvard University Press.

Chase, S. E. (1995). *Ambiguous empowerment: The work narratives of women school super-intendents.* Amherst: University of Massachusetts Press.

Chase, S. (2005). Narrative inquiry: Multiple lenses, approaches, voices. In N. K. Denzin & Y. S. Lincoln (Eds.), *The SAGE handbook of qualitative research* (3rd ed., pp. 651–679). Thousand Oaks, CA: Sage.

Chase, S. E. (2010). *Learning to speak, learning to listen: How diversity works on campus.* Ithaca, NY: Cornell University Press.

Clandinin, D. J. (Ed.). (2007). *Handbook of narrative inquiry: Mapping a methodology.* Thousand Oaks, CA: Sage.

Clandinin, D. J., & Murphy, M. S. (2007). Looking ahead: Conversations with Elliot Mishler, Don Polkinghorne, and Amia Lieblich. In D. J. Clandinin (Ed.), *Handbook of narrative inquiry: Mapping a methodology* (pp. 632–650). Thousand Oaks, CA: Sage.

Clandinin, D. J., & Rosiek, J. (2007). Mapping a landscape of narrative inquiry: Borderland spaces and tensions. In D. J. Clandinin (Ed.), *Handbook of narrative inquiry: Mapping a methodology* (pp. 35–75). Thousand Oaks, CA: Sage.

Cohen, B. (2007). The children's voice: Postwar collection of testimonies from child survivors of the Holocaust. *Holocaust and Genocide Studies, 21,* 73–95.

Cohler, B. J. (2008). Two lives, two times: Life-writing after Shoah. *Narrative Inquiry, 18,* 1–28.

Davis, J. E. (Ed.). (2002). *Stories of change: Narrative and social movements.* Albany: SUNY Press.

Deer, S., Clairmont, B., Martel, C. A., & White Eagle, M. L. (Eds.). (2008). *Sharing our stories of survival: Native women surviving violence.* Lanham, MD: AltaMira Press.

Denzin, N. K. (1997). *Interpretive ethnography: Ethnographic practices for the 21st century.* Thousand Oaks, CA: Sage.

Denzin, N. K. (2000). The practices and politics of interpretation. In N. K. Denzin & Y. S. Lincoln (Eds.), *Handbook of qualitative research* (2nd ed., pp. 897–922). Thousand Oaks, CA: Sage.

Denzin, N. K. (2003). The call to performance. *Symbolic Interaction, 26,* 187–207.

Denzin, N. K. (2008). Interpretive biography. In J. G. Knowles & A. L. Cole (Eds.), *Handbook of the arts in qualitative research* (pp. 117–125). Thousand Oaks, CA: Sage.

Desbois, Father P. (2008). *The Holocaust by bullets: A priest's journey to uncover the truth behind the murder of 1.5 million Jews.* New York: Palgrave Macmillan.

Ellis, C. (2004). *The ethnographic I: A methodological novel about autoethnography.* Walnut Creek, CA: AltaMira Press.

Ellis, C. (2009). *Revision: Autoethnographic reflections on life and work.* Walnut Creek, CA: Left Coast Press.

Faderman, L., with Xiong, G. (2005). *I begin my life all over: The Hmong and the American immigrant experience.* Boston: Beacon.

Frank, A. W. (1995). *The wounded storyteller: Body, illness, and ethics.* Chicago: University of Chicago Press.

Freeman, M. (2006). Life "on holiday"? In defense of big stories. *Narrative Inquiry, 16,* 131–138.

Gallas, K. (1994). *The languages of learning: How children talk, write, dance, draw, and sing their understanding of the world.* New York: Teachers College Press.

Gamson, W. A. (2002). How storytelling can be empowering. In K. A. Cerulo (Ed.), *Culture in mind: Toward a sociology of culture and cognition* (pp. 187–198). New York: Routledge.

Garrod, A., & Kilkenny, R. (Eds.). (2007). *Balancing two worlds: Asian American college students tell their life stories.* Ithaca, NY: Cornell University Press.

Garrod, A., Kilkenny, R., & Gómez, C. (Eds.). (2007). *Mi voz, mi vida: Latino college students tell their life stories.* Ithaca, NY: Cornell University Press.

Georgakopoulou, A. (2007). Thinking big with small stories in narrative and identity analysis. In M. Bamberg (Ed.), *Narrative—State of the art* (pp. 145–154). Philadelphia: John Benjamins.

Gergen, M. M., & Gergen, K. J. (2007). Narratives in action. In M. Bamberg (Ed.), *Narrative—State of the art* (pp. 133–143). Philadelphia: John Benjamins.

Girshick, L. B. (2008). *Transgender voices: Beyond men and women.* Hanover, NH: University Press of New England.

Goodley, D., & Tregaskis, C. (2006). Storying disability and impairment: Retrospective accounts of disabled family life. *Qualitative Health Research, 16,* 630–646.

Gubrium, J. F., & Holstein, J. A. (Eds.). (2001). *Institutional selves: Troubled identities in a postmodern world.* New York: Oxford University Press.

Gubrium, J. F., & Holstein, J. A. (2009). *Analyzing narrative reality.* Thousand Oaks, CA: Sage.

Hammersley, M. (2008). *Questioning qualitative inquiry: Critical essays.* Thousand Oaks, CA: Sage.

Harper, D. (2005). What's new visually? In N. K. Denzin & Y. S. Lincoln (Eds.), *The SAGE handbook of qualitative research* (3rd ed., pp. 747–762). Thousand Oaks, CA: Sage.

Hole, R. (2007). Narratives of identity: A poststructural analysis of three Deaf women's life stories. *Narrative Inquiry, 17,* 259–278.

Holstein, J. A., & Gubrium, J. F. (2000). *The self we live by: Narrative identity in a postmodern world.* New York: Oxford University Press.

Isherwood, C. (2008). The body of her work: Hearing questions of life and death. *The New York Times,* January 22. Available at http://www.nytimes.com/2008/01/22/theater/reviews/22easy.html

Jones, S. H. (2005). Autoethnography: Making the personal political. In N. K. Denzin & Y. S. Lincoln (Eds.), *The SAGE handbook of qualitative research* (3rd ed., pp. 763–791). Thousand Oaks, CA: Sage.

Josselson, R. (1996). *Revising herself: The story of women's identity from college to midlife.* New York: Oxford University Press.

Josselson, R. (2007a). Narrative research and the challenge of accumulating knowledge. In M. Bamberg (Ed.), *Narrative—State of the art* (pp. 7–15). Philadelphia: John Benjamins.

Josselson, R. (2007b). The ethical attitude in narrative research: Principles and practicalities. In D. J. Clandinin (Ed.), *Handbook of narrative inquiry: Mapping a methodology* (pp. 537–566). Thousand Oaks, CA: Sage.

Josselson, R., Lieblich, A., & McAdams, D. P. (Eds.). (2003). *Up close and personal: The teaching and learning of narrative research.* Washington, DC: American Psychological Association.

Josselson, R., Lieblich, A., & McAdams, D. P. (Eds.). (2007). *The meaning of others: Narrative studies of relationships.* Washington, DC: American Psychological Association.

Kaufman, M., & the members of the Tectonic Theater Project. (2001). *The Laramie project.* New York: Vintage.

Knowles, J. G., & Cole, A. L. (Eds.). (2008). *Handbook of the arts in qualitative research: Perspectives, methodologies, examples, and issues.* Thousand Oaks, CA: Sage.

Kwan, M-P. (2008). From oral histories to visual narratives: Re-presenting the post–September 11 experiences of the Muslim women in the USA. *Social & Cultural Geography, 9,* 653–669.

Langellier, K. M. (2001). You're marked: Breast cancer, tattoo, and the narrative performance of identity. In J. Brockmeier & D. Carbaugh (Eds.), *Narrative and identity: Studies in autobiography, self, and culture* (pp. 145–184). Amsterdam: John Benjamins.

Langellier, K. M., & Peterson, E. E. (2006). Shifting contexts in personal narrative performance. In D. S. Madison & J. Hamera (Eds.), *The SAGE handbook of performance studies* (pp. 151–168). Thousand Oaks, CA: Sage.

Lieblich, A., McAdams, D. P., & Josselson, R. (Eds.). (2004). *Healing plots: The narrative basis of psychotherapy.* Washington, DC: American Psychological Association.

Lock, A., Epston, D., & Maisel, R. (2004). Countering that which is called anorexia. *Narrative Inquiry, 14,* 275–301.

Luttrell. W. (2003). *Pregnant bodies, fertile minds: Gender, race, and the schooling of pregnant teens*. New York: Routledge.

Madison, D. S. (2006). Staging fieldwork/performing human rights. In D. S. Madison & J. Hamera (Eds.), *The SAGE handbook of performance studies* (pp. 397–418). Thousand Oaks, CA: Sage.

Madison, D. S., & Hamera, J. (Eds.). (2006). *The SAGE handbook of performance studies*. Thousand Oaks, CA: Sage.

Mattingly, C. F. (2007). Acted narratives: From storytelling to emergent dramas. In D. J. Clandinin (Ed.), *Handbook of narrative inquiry: Mapping a methodology* (pp. 405–425). Thousand Oaks, CA: Sage.

Maynes, M. J., Pierce, J. L., & Laslett, B. (2008). *Telling stories: The use of personal narratives in the social sciences and history*. Ithaca, NY: Cornell University Press.

McAdams, D. P. (2006). *The redemptive self: Stories Americans live by*. New York: Oxford University Press.

McAdams, D. P., Josselson, R., & Lieblich, A. (Eds.). (2001). *Turns in the road: Narrative studies of lives in transition*. Washington, DC: American Psychological Association.

McAdams, D. P., Josselson, R., & Lieblich, A. (Eds.). (2006). *Identity and story: Creating self in narrative*. Washington, DC: American Psychological Association.

McLaughlin, D., & Tierney, W. G. (Eds.). (1993). *Naming silenced lives: Personal narratives and processes of educational change*. New York: Routledge.

Mertus, J., Tesanovic, J., Metikos, H., & Boric, R. (Eds.). (1997). *The suitcase: Refugee voices from Bosnia and Croatia*. Berkeley: University of California Press.

Miller, L. C., & Taylor, J. (2006). The constructed self: Strategic and aesthetic choices in autobiographical performance. In D. S. Madison & J. Hamera (Eds.), *The SAGE handbook of performance studies* (pp. 169–187). Thousand Oaks, CA: Sage.

Mills, C. W. (1959). *The sociological imagination*. London: Oxford University Press.

Mishler, E. G. (1995). Models of narrative analysis: A typology. *Journal of Narrative and Life History, 5,* 87–123.

Myerhoff, B. (1994). *Number our days: Culture and community among elderly Jews in an American ghetto*. New York: Meridian/Penguin. (Original work published in 1979)

Naples, N. (2003). Deconstructing and locating survivor discourse: Dynamics of narrative, empowerment, and resistance for survivors of childhood sexual abuse. *Signs: Journal of Women in Culture and Society, 28,* 1151–1185.

Paap, K. (2006). *Working construction: Why white working-class men put themselves—and the labor movement—in harm's way*. Ithaca, NY: ILR/Cornell University Press.

Pascoe, C. J. (2007). *Dude, you're a fag: Masculinity and sexuality in high school*. Berkeley: University of California Press.

Personal Narratives Group. (Eds.). (1989). *Interpreting women's lives: Feminist theory and personal narratives*. Bloomington: Indiana University Press.

Plummer, K. (1995). *Telling sexual stories: Power, change, and social worlds*. London: Routledge.

Polkinghorne, D. E. (1995). Narrative configuration in qualitative analysis. In J. A. Hatch & R. Wisniewski (Eds.), *Life history and narrative* (pp. 5–23). London: Falmer.

Polkinghorne, D. E. (2007). Validity issues in narrative research. *Qualitative Inquiry, 13,* 471–486.

Richardson, L. (1990). Narrative and sociology. *Journal of Contemporary Ethnography, 19,* 116–135.

Richardson, L. (2002). Poetic representation of interviews. In J. F. Gubrium & J. A. Holstein (Eds.), *Handbook of interview research: Context and method* (pp. 877–892). Thousand Oaks, CA: Sage.

Riessman, C. K. (1990). *Divorce talk: Women and men make sense of personal relationships.* New Brunswick, NJ: Rutgers University Press.

Riessman, C. K. (2002a). Analysis of personal narratives. In J. F. Gubrium & J. A. Holstein (Eds.), *Handbook of interview research: Context and method* (pp. 695–710). Thousand Oaks, CA: Sage.

Riessman, C. K. (2002b). Positioning gender identity in narratives of infertility: South Indian women's lives in context. In M. C. Inhorn & F. van Balen (Eds.), *Infertility around the globe: New thinking on childlessness, gender, and reproductive technologies* (pp. 152–170). Berkeley: University of California Press.

Riessman, C. K. (2008). *Narrative methods for the human sciences.* Thousand Oaks, CA: Sage.

Rosenwald, G. C., & Ochberg, R. L. (Eds.). (1992). *Storied lives: The cultural politics of self-understanding.* New Haven, CT: Yale University Press.

Saldaña, J. (2008). Ethnodrama and ethnotheatre. In J. G. Knowles & A. L. Cole (Eds.), *Handbook of the arts in qualitative research* (pp. 195–207). Thousand Oaks, CA: Sage.

Saukko, P. (2008). *The anorexic self: A personal, political analysis of a diagnostic discourse.* Albany: SUNY Press.

Schneider, R. (2006). Never, again. In D. S. Madison & J. Hamera (Eds.), *The SAGE handbook of performance studies* (pp. 21–32). Thousand Oaks, CA: Sage.

Scott-Hoy, K., & Ellis, C. (2008). Wording pictures: Discovering heartful autoethnography. In J. G. Knowles & A. L. Cole (Eds.), *Handbook of the arts in qualitative research* (pp. 127–140). Thousand Oaks, CA: Sage.

Shamai, M., & Levin-Megged, O. (2006). The myth of creating an integrative story: The therapeutic experience of Holocaust survivors. *Qualitative Health Research, 16,* 692–712.

Smith, A. D. (1993). *Fires in the mirror: Crown Heights, Brooklyn and other identities.* New York: Anchor.

Smith, A. D. (1994). *Twilight—Los Angeles, 1992 on the road: A search for American character.* New York: Anchor.

Smith, A. D. (2004). *House arrest: A search for American character in and around the White House, past and present.* New York: Anchor.

Weber, S. (2008). Visual images in research. In J. G. Knowles & A. L. Cole (Eds.), *Handbook of the arts in qualitative research* (pp. 41–53). Thousand Oaks, CA: Sage.

Weinberg, D. (2005). *Of others inside: Insanity, addiction and belonging in America.* Philadelphia: Temple University Press.

White, M., & Epston, D. (1990). *Narrative means to therapeutic ends.* New York: W. W. Norton.

3

Critical Arts-Based Inquiry

The Pedagogy and Performance of a Radical Ethical Aesthetic

Susan Finley

Critical arts-based inquiry situates the artist-as-researcher (or researcher-as-artist) in the new research paradigm of qualitative practitioners committed to democratic, ethical, and just research methodologies. It also demonstrates an activist approach to research in which the ultimate value of research derives from its usefulness to the community in which the research occurs.

Two recent events set the stage for my discussion of arts-based research. In the first example, I was invited to participate in an "Imagination Committee" to contemplate the future of education in a particular urban community. Participants were conscientiously drawn to honor cultural pluralism, with the intent of mobilizing culturally diverse communities within a single school district. We convened in one large group and then restructured into smaller learning pods that explored particular topics (e.g., student identity, technology, curriculum, etc.), with the instruction that each group would report back to the larger group in a closing exercise. The breakout groups were scheduled for about three hours work time.

In our smaller groups, we were encouraged to produce visual representations of our conversations, as well as written records. While we attended to our discussions in breakout groups, an artist traveled the room, talking with each work group, listening in on the various conversations, while sketching in a large pad. Our artist-researcher maintained his role as listener-observer throughout the morning and the lunch break, until we joined one another as one large group to recap our visionary insights about how to shape the future of education in the context of this community. As the large group meeting convened, the artist-as-researcher exhibited his portrayal of our day of reflection on the "big screen." He had produced a comic strip-like series of panels I associate with graphic novels. In the course of his drawings, he produced a sense of the complexities involved in developing a collaborative piece, which he conveyed through the nuance of his artistry—representations of movement, caricature portraits of individual speakers, and a Greek chorus that appeared in his cartoons. As he exhibited his work (sometimes collaged with drawings from the small group sessions), and with the assistance of a discussion moderator, the room buzzed with enthusiastic conversation, public responses to the art and its messages, and disagreements as to some of the representations (to which the artist-researcher responded by adding quick supplemental sketches).

The second example was a year later and with a different cast of characters—this time a group of individuals representing organizations that work with volunteers, refer volunteers, or who are committed to service learning as a pedagogical approach. In this setting, a visual artist was stationed in front of a large mural-like outline of buildings, parks, lakes, and the river that is central to the geography of the area. As large and small group discussions took place, the artist slowly completed the visual terrain using colored pencils until, at the end of the day, there existed a dynamic visual depiction of the future of service learning for the community.

These are examples of critical, qualitative arts-based research. It is a genre of research in which methodologies are emergent and egalitarian, local, and based in communal, reflective dialogue. These were performances of knowledge creation, taking shape in the context of complex conditions and in which art provided mechanisms and forms with which to see and hear each other's views on local socioeconomic systems, racial and cultural divides, and potential to develop common meeting spaces.

Each of these visual artists recorded images that emerged in dynamic conversations. Their visions were grounded in the particular place and the individual people who had committed themselves to the performance of a reflective dialogue with the other participants. Arts-based inquiry demystified the process of storytelling and facilitated participants' shared articulation of the experiences of living together, in harmony and in conflict. By engaging art as an emergent living practice, these research events brought audience and researcher to a place of possibility to experience the reciprocity of dialogue and representation, reflection and speaking, and speaking and listening. In each instance, art increased or rejuvenated participation and dialogue. The audience connected with the subject matter emotionally, simultaneously confirming the authenticity of their emotive, reflective dialogues that characterized their dialogues. These artists made no claims of truths, but clearly worked to represent reflective dialogue and explorations of futuristic possibility.

These examples drawn from my own experience represent a new approach to facilitating community discourse. They also speak to the ephemeral quality of many arts-based research methodologies. The art and the research are so localized as to be "in the moment." The intent in their creation is not to be replicated and distributed; in fact, in each of the given examples, the visual representations created in these localized discussions would be little appreciated outside the very local communities in which they were created. On a personal level, these instances of arts-based inquiry in community settings gave me a basis for optimism that arts-based research is one of the tools a community can use in the performance of community-based activism.

Critical Arts-Based Inquiry

In the third edition of the *SAGE Handbook of Qualitative Research,* my discussion of arts-based inquiry focused on "performing revolutionary pedagogy" and explicated the usefulness of critical arts-based research in "doing qualitative inquiry when political activism is the goal" (S. Finley, 2005, p. 681). Arts-based inquiry first developed in the historical moment of a "crisis of representation" among qualitative researchers in anthropology and sociology who struggled with ways to represent new wave research that was local in nature and based in an ethics of care (Denzin & Lincoln, 2000; Geertz, 1988; Guba, 1967; Hammersley, 1992). Research in the genres of arts and humanities has since proliferated to the point of "post-experimental" status (Denzin & Lincoln, 2000) and the proliferation of poetic forms of research in the social sciences has led Zali Gurevitch (2002) to declare a "poetic moment" (p. 403) in qualitative inquiry. More recently, a "performative turn" in arts-based research has shifted focus away from the written text to performance as a "form of research publication" (Denzin, 2003, p. 13; see also, Conquergood, 1988). Critical inquiry as performance art is particularly well suited to researchers who anticipate experiences of cultural resistance (Garoian, 1999) and positive social change through inclusive and emotional understandings created among communities of learner/participant/researchers.

In reworking my earlier handbook chapter for this newer edition, I have structured my discussion around three interrelated issues for critical arts-based researchers:

- First, I review neoliberal and neoconservative trends in research and curriculum that further institutionalize and reaffirm social divisions, deny access to creative participation and expression to particular groups of people, and stand in the way of post-colonizing research strategies (Cannella & Lincoln, 2004a, 2004b, Lincoln, 2005; Lincoln & Cannella, 2004a, 2004b).

- Second, I discuss the performative turn in qualitative inquiry and how it reinforces the potential of critical arts-based research as a revolutionary, activist, and aesthetic pedagogy (Alexander, 2005; Denzin, 2000; S. Finley, 2003a).

- Finally, the chapter moves into discussion (with examples) of arts-based inquiry at the heart of a people's pedagogy in which performances of critical arts-based research enact "a radical ethical aesthetic" (Denzin, 2000, p. 261) and attempt resistance to "the regressive structures of our every day lives" (Denzin, 1999, pp. 568, 572).

I believe that fulfillment of a resistance politics in research requires new urgency, requires renewed commitment, and calls for continuing development of research methodologies to support interpretive studies that extend democracy, freedom, and political voice into the everyday lives of politically oppressed people. What is called for in these times is political resistance that is intentional in its purpose of reversing efforts of neoliberal and neoconservative political forces that systematically counter progress that had been made to improve the human condition by "new wave" researchers whose work is based in an ethics of care (Lincoln, 1995).

In critical arts-based inquiry, arts are both a mode of inquiry and a methodology for performing social activism. Although many qualitative researchers draw on the arts and humanities as an epistemological construct that is useful as a communicative force, not all of these practitioners of arts-based research will join me in promoting a radical and revolutionary aesthetic. Instead, arts-based researchers have found "many and varied roles for the arts in social science research" (Knowles & Cole, 2008, p. xiii), not all of which consider social change the primary objective of their efforts.

In the wake of 9/11, neoconservative politics have taken hold in the United States. Coupled with economic collapse on a global scale, the face of new conservatism calls out qualitative researchers to political resistance. It is now more than ever the right for political activists in the academy to further develop and employ methodologies that inspire and facilitate progressive social action. Even those arts-based researchers who refuse the call to activate research for the purpose of cultural revolution (even in small, local efforts) cannot convincingly deny they have already entered the political fray. "It is an act of political defiance for arts-based researchers to say, 'I am doing art' and to mean, 'I am doing research.' . . . To hold that art and research can be synonymous is a charged political statement" (S. Finley, 2003a, p. 290; see also S. Finley, 2005, p. 685). The incidence of making political waves with research methodologies is not limited to qualitative or even arts-based researchers. All of research is political. Kenneth Howe (2009) declares the neoconservative regression in research methods to be "the new scientific ortho-doxy" and further argues, "Whatever the methods employed, decisions about what factors to fix in the design and conduct of social research are unavoidable—and are unavoidably political" (p. 428). Norman Denzin and Yvonna Lincoln (2005; see also Smith, 1999, cited in Denzin & Lincoln) write, "Sadly, qualitative research, in many if not all of its forms (observation, participation, interviewing, ethnogra-phy), serves as a metaphor for colonial knowledge, for power, and for truth" (p. 1). Thus, a key question for arts-based researchers is, "How do we break through the complex barriers of colonial social conformity to an inclusive, pluralist aesthetic situated in the lives of others?"

The Threat to Critical Arts-Based Inquiry Imposed by Reinvigorated Paleocon, Neocon, and Neoliberal Political Traditions in Research and Education

It stands to reason that social conditioning under what John Leaños and Anthony Villarreal (2007) have described as the "Judeo-Christian White Supremacist Heteronormative Capitalist Patriarchal Military Industrial Entertainment Prison University Complex" (p. 1) by definition limits possibility in an emerging tradi-tion of an ethical and socially engaged arts-based research. Roadblocks to arts-based inquiry are rooted in early education curricular issues that follow all the way through higher education and include public policy for the conduct and funding of human studies. Although arts inquiry holds promise for an emerging research tradition that is postcolonial, pluralistic, ethical, and transformative in positive ways, the forces of neoconservative political agendas jeopardize its implementation.

Liberal arts education that builds a particular skills-base encourages active imagination, and the ability to engage in critical critique and dialogue are central features of curriculum and pedagogy to prepare researchers for critical arts-based inquiry (Seidel, 2001). A profound shift toward capitalistic, business-strategies for educational organization and delivery, coupled with conservative schooling practices given emphasis in No Child Left Behind legislation, have depressed the value of arts and humanities education as they are pitted in competition for dollars against the profit-value assigned to sciences. The test-based, standardized accountability system in place in U.S. education holds little reward for arts-based teaching and learning. Richard Siegesmund observes "in an era of narrowly conceived outcomes for education, art is not taught" (1998, p. 199). As the character Shane Botin quips, kids go to school to "learn how to pass the weekly standardized tests to get the school more funding" (Benabib & Salsberg, 2009).

Also missing from the creative studies curriculum are opportunities and skills needed for critical analysis and social action. Leaños and Villarreal (2007) agree: "Critical pedagogy in general, and critical arts education in particular, have all but disappeared from school curriculum across the U.S." (p. 1).[1] Even more alarming is the long-term influence of conservative educational policy and its institutionalization as sustained social practice. "The educational force of the culture actually works pedagogically to reproduce neoliberal ideology, values, identifications and consent," write Henry Giroux and Susan Giroux (2008). Elliot Eisner (2001b) had it right: "Education in our schools should look more like the arts, rather than the arts looking more like our schools" (p. 9).

In an unseemly paradox, standardization of arts education has been offered as a solution to remand the trend toward severe cutbacks in public school-based arts education. Despite the potential truth to an argument that uniform art standards could ensure the continuation of arts education in public schools, arts-education standards threaten cultural pluralism and more likely promise cultural reproduction (Eisner, 2001a). Standardizing arts-education would reaffirm neoliberal educational policies and further force arts-education into a market model, whereas culturally responsive arts education is directly linked to academic achievement and its absence with educational disempowerment (Hanley & Noblit, 2009).

Standardized arts education draws its design from an aesthetic education tradition with the goal of teaching school children strategies for art appreciation and aesthetic engagement—the primary learning goal in this model is teaching children how to be a good audience for the arts, rather than a critic or producer of arts. Defending standardization in arts-education, Laura Zakaras and Julia Lowell (2008) claim the virtue of standardized arts curriculum in its universal applicability to students, "regardless of their artistic talent, to enable them to have more satisfying encounters with works of art, now and in the future" (p. 20). Consistent with neoliberal design, the experience of art could be standardized for all students—but not in furtherance of a democratic goal of inclusive pluralism. That which is identified as "quality" art suited for teaching all children would draw from a limited classification of arts created by "masters." Zakaras and Lowell write,

> It is generally agreed that these perceptual skills are best learned in encounters with masterpieces, exemplary works of art that reward close attention and bring the entire range of aesthetic skills into play. Ideally these works represent a variety of historical periods, regions of the world, and genres of the art form, including folk, popular, classical, and ethnic cultures. (2008, p. 21)

It cannot go unnoted that identification of the artist, regions, techniques, forms of arts, and so forth in such a curriculum can be reduced to multiple-choice testing. Furthermore, the selection of masterpieces will be politically grounded. Zakaras and Lowell actually move beyond student-as-audience to consider that immersion in the masters can be transferred to skills-based arts education as well as appreciation: "In music, for example, learning to perform a challenging work of art requires the kind of attention to the work's components that often develops aesthetic perception and appreciation" (Zakaras & Lowell, 2008, p. 22). I refer to artist and arts teacher Twila Tharp to counter the masters' argument, as Tharp begs room for students to engage in original, creative explorations of art making:

> Repetition is a problem if it forces us to cling to our past successes. Constant reminders of the things that worked inhibit us from trying something bold and new. We lose sight of the fact that we weren't searching for a formula when we first did something great; we were in unexplored territory, following our instincts and passions wherever they might lead us. (2003, p. 217)

Instincts and passions reach beyond the possibilities of standardization and formulaic art making. A standardized curriculum is unlikely to include the passionate artist whose work is culturally and historically situated but uses techniques inconsistent with those that have been designated masterpieces worthy of study and reproduction. Standardization in arts education as appreciation and duplication of strokes of master artists leaves begging the notion of cultural pluralism.

"Whose art?" becomes a pivotal question. It leaves to reason that indigenous, counterculture, and outsider art forms will be little represented by standardized arts-appreciation curricula. In place of pluralism, predefined value definitions reify social worlds revered by convention. Will the masters of graffiti arts, graphic artists who create computer games, and works of unschooled artists be included as masterpieces? Will pluralism give way to eroticism and exploitation in "pornomiseria" (Faguet, 2009)?[2] Will the arts canon be standardized to censor radical political expressions? "The censorship of arts is intimately linked to the censorship of political dissent," Leaños and Villarreal (2007, p. 1) agree. "Being *pissed* is one of the artist's most valuable conditions," wrote Tharp. "Creativity is an act of *defiance.* You're challenging the status quo. You're questioning accepted truths and principles" (Tharp, 2003, p. 133). Being pissed is what Denzin had in mind when he called qualitative researchers to engage "guerilla warfare" against the status quo in research. Leaños and Villarreal observe,

> In sum, the full range of art activity occurs within a "cultural arbitrary" (Bourdieu and Passeron, 1977) that establishes elite aesthetics as the norm, a norm further enacted and enforced by the everyday practices of arts education that privileges "beauty," "form," and "genius." As this high art aesthetic is central to the cultural arbitrary of traditional arts education in the U.S., artistic contributions that fall outside the narrow parameters of these norms, such as critical and politically engaged art practices, have been marginalized historically, and are practically absent from official school curriculum. (2007, p. 2)

Talent, genius, and *quality* are code words for cultural conservatism in arts. The narrow field of legitimacy introduced by these terms is the very definition of "high arts," the promotion of which further institutionalizes divisions along socioeconomic, racial, and gender lines. Expertism (and genius and natural talent) likewise can be traced to educational elitism. Tharp debunks the notion of natural genius through the example of Mozart: "Nobody worked harder than Mozart," Tharp observes, "By the time he was twenty-eight years old, his hands were deformed because of the hours he had spent practicing, performing, and gripping a quill pen to compose" (2003, p. 7). Yet, Mozart was born into the role of prodigy. "His first good fortune was to have a father who was a composer and a virtuoso on the violin, who could approach keyboard instruments with skill" (p. 7). Tharp concludes,

> Mozart was his father's son. Leopold Mozart had gone through an arduous education, not just in music, but also in philosophy and religion; he was a

sophisticated, broad-thinking man, famous throughout Europe as a composer and pedagogue.... Leopold taught the young Wolfgang everything
about music, including counterpoint and harmony. He saw to it that the
boy was exposed to everyone in Europe who was writing good music or
could be of use in Wolfgang's musical development. Destiny, quite often, is
a determined parent. Mozart was hardly some naïve prodigy who sat down
at the keyboard and, with God whispering in his ears, let the music flow
from his fingertips. (2003, pp. 7–8)

Mozart had the advantages of education in both musical theory and technique. Pierre Bourdieu, for one, emphasized that legitimacy among artists has
long depended on expertise with a particular set of craft skills ensconced within
a defined aesthetics. Mozart learned well the craft skills needed to master the
language of music. Tharp continues,

Skill gives you the wherewithal to execute whatever occurs to you. Without
it, you are just a font of unfulfilled ideas. Skill is how you close the gap
between what you can see in your mind's eye and what you can produce;
the more skill you have, the more sophisticated and accomplished your
ideas can be. With absolute skill comes absolute confidence, allowing you
to dare to be simple. Picasso once said, while examining an exhibition of
children's art, "When I was their age I could draw like Raphael, but it has
taken me a whole lifetime to learn to draw like them." (2003, p. 163)

Teach children the skills to play, to paint, to create with confidence—let their
hands form to the shape of pen, brush, or keyboard. If children don't have
opportunities to learn skills, there will be no new masters—and maybe that is the
point—cultural reproduction will not happen concurrently with social change.

In addition to financial restrictions that limit skills education in arts, also left
on the cutting room floor is the teaching of critical arts education. To know
about art or understand certain classical forms of art is not sufficient—as practitioners of a moral, ethical aesthetic, the goal is to move from knowledge and
understanding to action. When the value of art depends on standardization of
social conventions and traditions, the arts exist in a void of political and ethical
involvement by artists (performers) and audiences (performers in the experience). Moreover, isolating convention from critical question and interpretation
limits creative constructions of dynamic, evolutionary human activity. Simply,
public school students of the 21st century for the most part are not being educated to approach the world as active citizens. In the same way that neoconservative educational policies sorely limit students' learning of craft skills, they

displace critical discourse, performances of hope, and voices of public citizens sharing their creations of images of a better tomorrow. Giroux and Giroux (2006) write, "As the prevailing discourse of neoliberalism seizes the public imagination, there is no vocabulary for progressive social change, democratically inspired visions, critical notions of social agency, or the kinds of institutions that expand the meaning and purpose of democratic public life" (p. 25).

The conservative swell that threatens arts education repeats in form and content in the fields of human research. Forces of political conservatism reverberate in the call to claim human studies as "science" and to attach the notion of scientific rigor to understanding social phenomena. New life has returned to conservatism. Alternative ways of learning and knowing are cast aside as a traditionalist, capitalistic pedagogy (based in proof, truth, individualization, and competition) repeats its tired beat in the community of human researchers. This ideologically formed miseducation of arts and inquiry "prevents social art practices from becoming valued as a vital form of democratic engagement" (Leaños & Villarreal, 2007, p. 2).

Howe (2009) critiques positivist dogma "codified" in the National Research Council's (NRC) manifesto, *Scientific Research in Education* (2002) and "reinforced" in the American Educational Research Association's *Standards for Reporting on Empirical Social Science Research in AERA Publications* (2006). Howe is disturbed by the definition of research in technocratic parlance that is largely silent to the "relationship between education science and democratic politics." This is a poignant silence that sets up a dichotomous relationship as if science and politics exist as "separate domains" (p. x). Working his critique from within the conceptual framework of "deliberative democracy" (and with references to Gutmann & Thompson, 2004, and Young, 2004, on this point), Howe says, "The possibility—and desirability—of culling political values from education research depends on moribund positivist principles" (p. 432).

Following the lead of the *SRE* report, the AERA task force reflected similar positivistic dogma in their publication of "Standards for Reporting on Empirical Social Science Research in AERA Publications." Like the SRE guidelines, AERA narrowed the focus of its report to "empirical social science research" (AERA, 2006). AERA guidelines differentiate "research methods" from "other forms of scholarship." Approaches to be excluded from the category of research include reviews and critiques of research traditions and practices; theoretical, conceptual, and methodological studies; and historical types of work. Further, the AERA guidelines expand on the NRC specific exclusion of history and philosophy as outside the realm of research because they are not based in empirical experimentations. AERA specifies excluded methodologies should include "scholarship more grounded in the humanities (e.g., history, philosophy, literary analysis, *arts-based inquiry* [emphasis added])" and the authors reason that these approaches are "beyond the scope of this document."

Humanities-oriented research standards were the subject of a second AERA committee report, "Standards for Reporting on Humanities-Oriented Research in AERA Publications" (2009). Howe (2009) was a member of the humanities research committee and argues vociferously against the AERA's reinforcement of

> a reductionist conception of empirical social science research" that dichot-omizes educational science and the humanities. He defies the conclusion by the AERA task force authors who concluded that humanities-grounded research is not like scientific research because science is empirical and humanities is not. Howe argues that both methodologies are empirical but their differences are a matter of degree on a continuum of "blurred bound-aries . . . overlap and complementarity." (Howe, 2009, p. 432)

The AERA Humanities-Research Task Force and authors of the "Standards for Reporting on Humanities-Oriented Research in AERA Publications" (2009) ech-oed Howe's analysis of overlap and complementarity in their report. Howe fur-ther argues against the perception that scientific study is apolitical and objective "Characterizing science as rhetorical in the sense that, I suggest, applies to Kuhn, Harding, Code, and Hacking does not require denying that science is 'a pro-foundly powerful form of inquiry' (Lessl, 2005, p. 2)" (Howe, 2009, p. 437).

> It only requires denying that scientific claims are above and beyond persua-sive argumentation, that scientists are above and beyond weaknesses such as a blinkered perspective, ego involvement, resistance to novelty, an inter-est in the size of their paychecks, and the like, in the conduct of their research. (Howe, 2009, p. 437)

In much the same way that arts education has been compromised by neocon-servative, capitalistic, and corporate ideology, in the current climate of the first decade of the 21st century, so has the culture of university research. Giroux (2009) argues that this cultural shift (a reactionary shift that takes social science out of the realm of arts and humanities) removes faculty and students from democratic language, values, and work. Consequently, Giroux says, when educa-tional priorities labor to serve the "warfare state or the corporate state" (Giroux, p. 671), higher education falls short of its purpose of educating students in the performance of democratic governance. In such circumstances, higher education ceases to exist as "a crucial public sphere, responsible for both educating students for the workplace and providing them with the modes of critical discourse, interpretation, judgment, imagination, and experiences that deepen and expand a democracy" (Giroux, p. 671).

Roadblocks, Gatekeepers, and Other Issues for Critical Research Formed in Arts

Conditions that interfere with the acceptance of arts-based research as a forum for performance pedagogy and political emancipation come from both within the community of artist-researchers and from the dominating structures of positivism that privilege science over other forms of knowledge production. Cathy Coulter and Mary Lee Smith (2009) observe that purpose, methods, ethics, and validity form the contested terrain of narrative inquiry based in fiction. In my view, an even more divisive discussion revolves around the issues of standards for assessing quality in arts-based research. This discussion encompasses fictional narrative, poetry, dance, film, and all other art disciplines that have made their way into usage as forms of inquiry and expressions of inquiry through arts. Eisner (2008) notes,

> One of the most formidable obstacles to arts-informed research is the paucity of highly skilled, artistically grounded practitioners, people who know how to use image, language, movement, in artistically refined ways. Schools of education, for example, seldom provide courses or even workshops for doctoral students to develop such skills. As a result, it is not uncommon to find this type of research appearing amateurish to those who know what the potentialities of the medium are. (p. 9)

Donald Blumenfeld-Jones (2008) (a classically trained dancer and arts-based researcher) concurs. He holds that a "vigorous education in dance" (p. 183) is required preparation for arts-based researchers who choreograph or perform their research. "Dance is, first and foremost, an art form" (p. 183). Blumenfeld-Jones writes,

> The art needs to be practiced. . . . Insights discovered through the practice of dance as an art form are only available through that practice, and the practice focuses on making art, not on coming to understand. To consider using dance as a primary mode of research, persons must first develop

themselves as artists, understanding that the practice of art is, in many ways, no different than the practice of research (Blumenfeld-Jones, 2002, 2004a, 2004b). There are not many social scientists who are also well-educated dance artists, and without such grounding, the concern is that the emerging art will be poor and nothing significant can be gained from it. (2008, p. 184)

Johnny Saldaña (2008) takes a slightly different stance with regard to artistic expertism. He observes quality issues such as the over-inclusion of didactic content in ethnotheater scripts constructed by scholars who do not have theater training. He further notes that the director, designers, and performers need to be good at their craft if ethnotheater is to work as a research representation that is engaging and effective. Even so, he acquiesces that he would not want to discourage scholars who are inspired to playwriting. He asks only that those scholars, as with any playwright, would seek open critical feedback about the work.

Eisner (2008) suggests one solution to the dilemma of artistic expertism that I have tried. He encourages the formation of teams of social science researchers who work with practitioners of the arts. "It could be the case," Eisner wrote, "that such collaboration might provide a way to combine both theoretically sophisticated understandings and artistically inspired images" (2008, p. 9). For example, Macklin Finley and I worked with Saldaña (a theater professor and ethnodramatist) to condense a readers' theater script (S. Finley & M. Finley, 1998), a book of poetry (M. Finley, 2000) and other poems (e.g., S. Finley, 2000), as well as a short story (S. Finley & M. Finley, 1999) and several other artistic representations of our research with street youths into a single script. Elsewhere, Saldaña has opined that the goal of this type of shared work of adaptation has the goal of making the work "even better than its original source" (2008, p. 197). I disagree to some extent when this adage is applied to the *Street Rat* effort—in the instance of the readers' theater script, the adaptation was a vast improvement. In comparison with the short story and poetry formats, however, the forms of representation were different, but not improved. All of the dialogue of the play is excerpted from the previously published research poetry of S. Finley and M. Finley. Although I embrace the artfulness of the ethnodramatic staging of *Street Rat* and commend Saldaña for creating with us a work that maintained the integrity of the original representations, I question the accessibility of the new script for local audiences. Our (Finley and Finley) practice had been to interact with audiences during poetry readings as a way to provoke communication about the social issues of poverty, school leaving, the place of arts in street life, and so on that came about in audience responses to the work (M. Finley, 2003, p. 604). Likewise, the readers' theater was produced in several settings and was sufficiently provocative of conversation with diverse audiences that included academics, social workers, in-school youth, and street youths (including some who were present in the text). When rehearsals, directors, stage props, and even finding a stage are requisite to the performance, it is much more difficult to arrange.

It might also be that greater sophistication with regard to understanding the conventions of theater and performance are required of audiences of a fully developed script, constructed by an expert in theater. If a sound educational base in an art is requisite for social science research, and given the neoconservative backlash against arts education (as discussed in the early pages of this chapter), then the future of arts-based research is in serious doubt.

Fear that traditional members of the academy will demean our work (e.g., Mayer, 2000) stokes arts-based researchers' concerns for quality control. Instead, we should keep at the forefront that we serve the dual purpose of unveiling oppression and transforming praxis. Despite the movement to fuse arts and research that is taking place in many social science disciplines (e.g., education, nursing, social science), many researchers do not identify as "arts-based" their work that draws on arts for either inspiration or form. In response, I contest Melissa Cahnmann-Taylor's (Cahnmann-Taylor & Siegesmund, 2008) statement, "There are still more researchers writing *about* arts-based research criteria than those producing examples of what it looks like in each area of the literary, visual, and performing arts" (p. 12). First, I see examples of the arts in qualitative research in a wide variety of forums, but I puzzle over why so many researchers who clearly experience art as qualitative research do not choose to describe their work as "arts-based." A cynical possibility is that some arts-informed qualitative research is not identified as such because work of this type has a special place on what Tom Barone (2008) has referred to as the "blacklist of research methodologies (indeed, one that disparages all non-experimental forms)" (p. 34) of qualitative research.

An alternative explanation that intrigues me is that the many names for arts in qualitative research are confusing—is it arts-based research, arts-based inquiry, arts-informed research, or A/R/Tography (for history and definition, see Sinner et al., 2006)? Similarly, with the use of arts to reach a broader, community-centered audience for research, do the multiple terms and their fine-tuned differences counter the goal of accessibility? Are the terms obtuse in their verbiage, and, therefore, more accessible to an audience of scholars, researchers, and policy wonks than for local audiences situated in communities where the research took place? Instead, could it be that the clarity of the goal of audience-participant driven research results in work that is, indeed local, and does not make its way into publications and other professional forums accessed by scholars looking for examples of arts-based research? Much of the work is ephemeral and can only be captured as description and in analytic discussions of that which must go unseen and unexperienced by an academic audience. Although multimedia technology offers some possibilities for expanding audiences to performances of arts-based inquiry, Carl Bagley (2008) correctly observes such re-presentations "would still constitute a (re)reading and (re)presentation of what was performed" (p. 54).

New constructions of what is possible in the realm of human studies motivated Eisner, Barone, Denzin, and others to call arts-based researchers to action when the field was being formed. If, however, the roles of researchers and standards for assessing quality in research are hidebound by tradition and inalienable definitions of "research" and "art," this call to transformative inquiry through art will be a difficult act to perform. Breaking with tradition would feature transformations in pedagogy and praxis—art would of necessity be taught as a method for accessing multiple ways of understanding human conditions and experiences.

To prepare arts-based researchers, Eisner (e.g., 1991/1998) proposed a graduate school curriculum that enhances students' skills of imagination, perception, and interpretation of the qualities of things, as well as teaching mastery of skills of artistic representation. "Art, music, dance, prose, and poetry are some of the forms that have been invented to perform this function," Eisner wrote (p. 235). Clive Seale (1999) visualized a studio apprenticeship model to teach research skills "in much the same way as artists learn to paint, draw, or sculpt" (p. 476). "Working knowledge" (Harper, 1987) requires deep understanding of materials, the skills to manipulate them, and intuitive, imaginative, and reflective thinking (S. Finley, 2001). In working knowledge, there is "kinesthetic correctness . . . [an] interplay of the theoretical and the empirical, the marriage of hand and mind in solving practical problems" (Harper, 1987, pp. 117–118). The product crafted from working knowledge is secondary to the mental and cultural experiences of the work. "Work in this instance is both a noun and a verb—it performs the dual purpose [of being and acting]" (S. Finley, 2001, p. 20; see also Sullivan, 2005, p. 241). Creative work is the site for dialogue and the source of further action.

"Discourse is the power which is to be seized," wrote Michel Foucault (1984, p. 110). "The great challenge to neoliberalism can only come through the reclaiming of a language of power, social movements, politics, and ethics that is capable of examining the effects of the neoliberal order" (Giroux & Polychroniou, 2008, p. 1). "Higher education needs to be reclaimed as an ethical and political response to the demise of democratic public life," the authors conclude. In this contested terrain, art wields power to engender dialogue and can be a catalyst for reclaiming language and reviving the social imaginary to visions of hope. Leaños and Villarreal (2007) assert, "art's greatest potential to foster change is at the level of the micro-social, through tactical interruptions of bio-power, revealing the ways that we are complicit in the "normalizing" operations of power, opening up spaces for new forms of knowledge production, and spreading decolonial discourse" (p. 2).

Kathleen Casey (1995) explained that methodological shifts in research approaches are tied to political or theoretical interests charged by social and historical circumstances. She notes that, in the example of narrative research, the new paradigm researcher takes a stance that "deliberately defies the forces of alienation, anomie, annihilation, authoritarianism, fragmentation, commodification, deprecation, and dispossession" (p. 213). If it was important to defy such forces in the decades just past—during which academia saw the rise of arts-based inquiry in many (if not all) fields of human studies, it is even more important today, in the face of retrogressive conservatism, the loss of basic rights to free communication, and the commodification of the educational enterprise to capitalism.

The Performative Turn: Arts-Based Research as a Revolutionary, Critical, and Aesthetic Pedagogy

"Postmodern democracy cannot succeed," Denzin (2008a) argues, "unless critical qualitative scholars are able to adopt methodologies that transcend the limitations and constraints of a lingering, politically and racially conservative postpositivism" (p. x). He implores researchers (educational researchers in particular) to break the links that chain critical, qualitative inquiry to No Child Left Behind and similar politically and racially conservative postpositive frameworks for curriculum and pedagogy (Denzin, 2008a). For even longer, Denzin (1999) has urged a new movement in qualitative inquiry in which researchers "take up their pens" (and their cameras, paintbrushes, bodies, and voices) "so that we might conduct our own ground-level guerilla warfare against the oppressive structures of our everyday lives" (pp. 568, 572). This is the *performative turn* in qualitative research.

Resistance is a kind of performance that holds up for critique hegemonic texts that have become privileged stories told and retold. Performances "critique dominant cultural assumptions, to construct identity, and to attain political agency" (Garoian, 1999, p. 2). *Performativity* is the writing and rewriting of meanings to create a dynamic and open dialogue that continually disrupts the authority of meta-narratives. As Eisner (2001a) writes, artists "invent fresh ways to show us aspects of the world we had not noticed; they release us from the stupor of the familiar" (p. 136). With reference to performance artist Suzanne Lacy, Charles Garoian (1999) observed that performance art opens a liminal and ephemeral space in which a community can engage in critical discourse. The community aspects of Lacy's work are accomplished by the involvement of diverse communities of participants as experts and actors examining their own oppression, where expertise is defined by participants' lives in the community. The participants in her work are co-researchers, critiquing and challenging themselves to understand their community and to overcome cultural oppressions that occur there. Thus, art, politics, pedagogy, and inquiry are brought together in performance.

Denzin (2008a), Charles Garoian and Yvonne Gaudelius (2008), and others defend the potential for *performance pedagogy* in a post–9/11 world to transform "everyday lives" by exposing and critiquing neoconservative/neoliberal constraints on human dignity and social justice (Denzin, 2008a, p. x). In performance, the emphasis is on *doing* (see Dewey, 1934/1958; also Giroux, 2001; Grossberg, 1996). As Denzin says, within a performance studies paradigm "inquiry is a form of activism . . . that inspires and empowers persons to act on their utopian impulses" (2008a, p. x). Resistance performances are creative constructions that "can strengthen the capacity of research groups to implement qualitative research as a solution to public health, social welfare, and education problems" (Denzin, 2008a, p. x).

Contextualized by the September 11 attacks and war in Iraq, Garoian and Gaudelius (2008) claim mass-media visual images can be characterized as "spectacle pedagogy" (p. 24) and can open spaces for participatory democracy. Specifically, strategies of collage, montage, assemblage, installation, and performance art are based in reflection and critique and thereby present pedagogical means by which artists/researchers/teachers/students can involve themselves meaningfully in understanding and responding to the complex political, social, and ethical ideologies conveyed in mass media (p. 37). As involved learners, spectacle critics (Garoian and Gaudelius focus on "students") act as cultural citizens and participants in the political processes of democratic social justice. Garoian and Gaudelius write,

We characterize the spectacle pedagogy of visual culture in two opposing ways: First, as a ubiquitous form of representation, which constitutes the pedagogical objectives of mass mediated culture and corporate capitalism to manufacture our desires and determine our choices: the second, as a democratic form of practice that enables a critical examination of visual cultural codes and ideologies to resist social injustice. As the former spectacle pedagogy functions as an insidious, ever-present form of propaganda in the service of cultural imperialism, the latter represents critical citizenship, which aspires to cultural democracy. (2008, p. 24)

One of the creations of spectacle pedagogy of the first order—propaganda—is the myth that visual renditions in news, advertising, and other forms of mass media convey "truths." The historical context in which Garoian and Gaudelius situate their analysis of spectacle pedagogy accentuates the pervasiveness of visual cultural codes entrenched in capitalistic and colonial neocon political agendas. Thus, "critical performance pedagogy reflexively critiques those cultural practices that reproduce oppression" (Denzin, 2008a). Denzin writes, "Critical performance pedagogy moves from the global to the local, the political to the personal, the pedagogical to the performative" (2008b, p. 62).

Denzin writes, "In ethnodrama and radical pedagogy audience is transformed out of a consumer/consumption/entertainment space to a dialogical structure, a collaborative pedagogical assemblage, to use Garorian's term—a part of "spectacle pedagogy"" (Denzin, personal correspondence, October 29, 2009). The performance itself creates an open text in which "meanings emerge within the sociology of space and are connected within the reciprocal relationships that exist between people and the political, dynamic qualities of place" (S. Finley, 2003a, p. 288; 2005, p. 689). Thus, performance creates specialized (open and dialogic) space that is simultaneously asserted for inquiry and expression. In this liminal space, distinctions are made between private and public spheres, thereby rendering personal identity, culture, and social order unstable, indeterminate, inchoate, and amenable to change. Giroux (1995) notes, "It is within the tensions between what might be called the trauma of identity formation and the demands of public life that cultural work is both theorized and made performative" (p. 5, cited in Garoian, 1999, pp. 40–41).

From within the liminal openings that are created by the performance/ practice of arts-based inquiry, ordinary people, researchers as participants and as audiences can imagine new visions of dignity, care, democracy, and other decolonizing ways of being in the world. Once it has been imagined, it can be acted upon, or performed. In tracing the evolution of performance as a primary site for revolutionary research methodology, Denzin (2003) explained,

> Ethnography had to be taken out of a purely methodological framework and located first within a performative arena and then within the spaces

of pedagogy, where it was understood that the pedagogical is always political. We can now see that interpretive ethnography's subject matter is set by a dialectical pedagogy. This pedagogy connects oppressors and the oppressed in capital's liminal, epiphanic spaces. (p. 31; for a more comprehensive discussion of the "dramaturgical turn," see Denzin, 1997, 2003; Garoian, 1999)

Gregory Ulmer (1994) similarly argued for a revolutionary pedagogy that makes its task the transformation of institutions by using the formalizing structures of the institution itself to experimentally rearrange reality for critical effect. He cited Umberto Eco (1984, p. 409) to make his case for engaging in "revolutionary" interventionist works that entertain the possibility, as in an ideal "guerilla" semiotics of "changing the circumstances by virtue of which the receivers choose their own codes of reading. . . . This pragmatic energy of semiotic consciousness shows how a descriptive discipline can also be an active project" (Ulmer, 1994, p. 86; see also, Ulmer, 1989).

Arts-Based Inquiry at the Heart of a People's Pedagogy

In arts-based research within the paradigm of revolutionary pedagogy, the artfulness to be found in everyday living composes the aesthetic (Barone, 2001a; Barone & Eisner, 1997; Dewey, 1934/1958; Tolstoy, 1946/1996). For research to act locally, in its use of everyday, localized, and personal language, and in its reliance on texts that are ambiguous and open to interpretation, arts-based research draws audiences into dialogue and opens the possibility for critical critique of social structures (Barone, 2001a, 2001b). Denzin (2000) and others have encouraged artist-researchers to focus on the vernacular and to capture the visceral ephemeral moments in daily life in their representations of research. Communicating the "ordinary extraordinary" (Dissanayake, 1997) through vernacular expressions in the context of mass media popular culture—radio, television, film—does more than introduce dialogues that "automatically contain, constrain, or even liberate us," writes Joli Jensen (2002, p. 198). "Instead these cultural forms are part of an ongoing, humanly constructed conversation about the reality we are shaping as we participate in it" (p. 198). Thus, vernacular, expressive, and contextualized language forms open narratives that promote empathy and care (Barone, 2001b), and entreaties to the vernacular are encouraged as a means to more inclusive audience/participant voices in research representations.

Education in the arts is wrapped up in social privilege. I have previously noted my willingness to "hold open the possibility that the unschooled minds of untrained artists can construct and express ideas through the media of the arts. . . . I believe there is every possibility that the vernacular street performances of poetry, tagging, and fire dance are potentially meaningful" experiences of inquiry (S. Finley, 2003a, p. 292). If we define arts education through the informal venues of streets and communities, rather than through institutional delivery systems, arts-based researchers can perform a people's pedagogy.

Barone (2001a) observed that in arts-based inquiry representational media are "selected for their usefulness in recasting the contents of experience into a form with the potential for challenging (sometimes deeply held) beliefs and values" (p. 26). Connectivity among the forces of political resistance, pedagogy, interpretive performance, and arts-based methodological approaches crystallizes a way of understanding that is at once aesthetic and conducive to interpreting social structures and inspiring transformational action.

Arts-based research makes use of affective experiences, senses, and emotions. Its practitioners explore the bounds of space and place where the human body is a tool for gathering and exploring meaning in experience. Carl Bagley and Mary Beth Cancienne (2002) created a salon experience for artist-researchers to engage as a community of learners in the exploration of ways to use emotive, affective experiences, multiple senses, and bodies in coordination with intellect as ways of responding to the world. *Dancing the Data* (Bagley & Cancienne, 2002) is a compilation of performance research, accompanied by a CD-ROM where the researchers perform their interpretive work in a community setting. Denzin demonstrates the power of performance texts with his challenge to mythic, hegemonic texts and idealized views of Native American women and men (see *Searching for Yellowstone*, 2008a). Using family photographs, reminiscences from his own childhood, and descriptions of his family vacation retreat, he situates personal experiences within the complexities of political, social, and ethical ideologies conveyed in media and art. "Finding myself embedded in these representations" (p. 16), Denzin locates these stories in the current historical circumstances of race and gender "in a search for more realistic utopias, more just and more radically democratic social worlds for the twenty-first century" (p. 17). In constructing this text, Denzin uses strategies of assemblage that Garoian associates with spectacle pedagogy. Photo montage, personal journaling, script, poetry, and art criticism fold into each other and meld to create an experimental text that resists expectations for academic work. As a research text, it transforms the way that we perceive, read, write, and perform data and, in turn, challenges racial stereotypes with newly constructed representations of whiteness and of race. This movement from personal to global-political epito-mizes performance texts.

Further examples of the merger of arts-based inquiry with the field of perfor-mance pedagogy include, for example, reader's theater—Robert Donmoyer and June Yennie-Donmoyer (2008; see also 1995, 1998), ethno-drama—Jim Mienczakowski (2000; also see, Mienczakowski, Smith, & Sinclair, 1996) and Saldaña (2008; also see Saldaña, Finley, & Finley, 2005).

Examples that follow of arts-based research oriented toward educational praxis or "a people's pedagogy" come largely from my own work. As an arts-based researcher, I seek opportunities to locate work within local communities and subscribe to participants' everyday language and vernacular in discourse. Arts-based inquiry that is locally situated facilitates individual and communal reflection by diverse communities of participants. In general, its practitioners seek to understand and take action against the oppressive forces of politically conservative postpositivism that dominate and constrain the lives of ordinary citizens. In my work, I intend to create aesthetic spaces in which to experience transformational performances at a visceral level. I am, like Marcelo Diversi and Cláudio Moreira (2009), "reassured by the Rortyan notion that we are all stuck in a perpetual discussion about what the reality of oppression means to each and all of us" (p. 184). The potential exists for arts-based research to enact inquiry in the social world as one feature of a people's pedagogy (S. Finley, 2003b, 2005). Emancipation from colonizing human research that objectifies its participants (casting them as subjects) is not possible unless research is democratized and brought under the control of people in their daily lives.

Academic institutions—university classrooms, academic journals, and profes-sional conferences—are one contested site for a people's pedagogy to be enacted. Other work is more appropriately taken to the streets and gathering places that bring people together in everyday life. In this genre of arts-based research, the researcher attempts to involve people as experts of their own lives and to create forums for outreach to venues outside the academy (Woo, 2008).

Journals such as *Qualitative Inquiry*[3] and *Cultural Studies<=>Critical Methodologies* initiated unique spaces for arts-based inquiry that challenges the academic status quo (and several other journals have stretched to be inclusive of arts-based work, despite rather fierce opposition in academic circles). A recent special issue of *Cultural Studies<=>Critical Methodologies* (Diversi & S. Finley, 2010) devoted to "critical homelessness" incorporates prose and poetry variously written by street youth, homeless activists, and residents of Dignity Village—a tent city in Portland, Oregon. Two of the included manuscripts are e-mail mes-sages from homeless individuals reprinted in the pages of the journal.

Taken holistically, the special issue challenges the norms of academic research publication by including street authors—and crediting them for their own work as any journal would credit the work of an academic contributor. Poetry contributors were enlisted from my arts-based street research projects with homeless communities. To magnify the contrast between public citizens being included as authors of their own work in their own voices and being quoted as representative voices to illuminate points of view articulated by an academic voice, the journal also includes an article I have written about the experiences of a group of female street youth who participated in a poetry cooperative (S. Finley, 2010).

Through the structure of the co-op, female street youth shared their poetry and reflections on street life with each other and with me. Most of the exchanges of writing were accomplished through e-mail, which accommodated the transience of the youth participants. The group emerged from relationships I had developed with the participants while otherwise investigating the lives of street youth. The idea behind this emergent phase of the overall project was to shape a version of "street education" in which all participants were, simultaneously, teachers and students—I would teach literacy skills and the youth would teach me about street life. I also had a larger purpose in mind to use the experience of arts-based inquiry to challenge these female youths to exercise their leadership potential and restructure their street life to confront male domination among street youths. In this way, "experiences are being investigated narratively, including inquiry experiences. They become curricular experiences for the inquirer—and possibly also for the audience, if the experiential narratives are read or listened to by others" (Conle, 2003, p. 4).

Poetry is included here too, but it is inserted in the pages of *my* article, framed by me and in service to my subjective purposes. In this more traditional form of academic discourse, my voice dominates, even in an article that is inclusive of youth commentary. In each of these two examples from the special issue on critical homelessness, the purpose for doing the research and the purpose behind the assemblage of the contributions to form a holistic artful representation was to create aesthetic spaces for "resistance performances" to challenge beliefs and values and to encourage transformational action.

Performances of arts-based research for audiences outside the community (of participants in the research or others who share the community experience) often draw on empathetic understanding to "move" the audience to action—or at least to reflective contemplation of the roles of oppressors and the oppressed. At one level, the audience to critical research performances responds to sensory stimuli—sound, color, movement, and their composition. Empathy provides another inroad to understanding through artful performances. "We seek out the arts in order to take a ride on the wings that arts provide," Eisner wrote (2008, p. 3). Planning for the audience who will experience the aesthetic will further shape the researcher's approach to representation (Woo, 2008).

Street Rat (M. Finley, 2000; adapted to theater by Saldaña, Finley, & Finley, 2005) was constructed from research recordings and transcripts and then staged as performances on Bourbon Street in New Orleans for a varied audience of street youths, tourists, business people—anyone who would stop to listen (M. Finley, 2003, p. 603). "The performances generated continuing dialogues with the youths who were featured in the poems, and they opened up new dialogues about homelessness and street life with tourists, business people, and other observers," Finley wrote, "What developed was a cyclic process of dialogue, poetic responses to dialogic performance, and [continuing] dialogue" (M. Finley, 2003, p. 603). This was performance pedagogy for the audiences of participants and (casual) observers of the participants in their daily lives—with the potential for challenging some of the derogatory stereotypes the observers brought to their interactions with and understandings of the lives of street youths.

As part of the *At Home At School* (AHAS)[4] program, I designed a research project in which 20 youths (whose experiences were formed by poverty, homelessness, and living in foster care, and included several Deaf participants) were to engage in a new form of dialogic performance with *Street Rat*. As I proposed the project, the youth would read the poetry text (with the guidance of their theater teacher) and through their discussions of the text, participants would begin to substitute their own storied poems for those in the text to create a new and updated version of the poem/play that would include snippets of the original juxtaposed with new writings. Instead, the participants read the poetry together, discussed their responses to it, and put it aside to write their own script for a play entitled *All I Ask: A Look Into the Hardships Modern Teenagers Face* (AHAS, Not At-Risk Theatre Company, 2009). As Carola Conle (2003) observes, "Arts-based researchers use artistic means both to prompt inquiry and to represent their findings" (p. 10). Julia Colyar (2009) similarly discusses qualitative research writing as being "product, process, form of invention, and instrument of self-discovery" (p. 421). "Writing is product and process, noun and verb" (p. 423). Colyar (p. 424) quotes Denzin and Lincoln (2000): "'Fieldwork and writing blur into one another. There is, in the final analysis, no difference between writing and fieldwork'" (Denzin & Lincoln, 2000, p. 16). "Writing *is* inquiry. Writing is a kind of data collection" (Colyar, p. 424; also see Furman, 2006). For the AHAS Theatre Company, the duality of process and product, of inquiry and representation, manifested as self-reflective inquiry, reflection in community (and rewrite) and, finally, (re)presentation to a larger audience for the purpose of initiating discussion (the troupe performed their original work for a group of 150 youths enrolled in one of the AHAS summer programs).

Street Rat demonstrated to the theater group the potential of arts-based research as an approach to inquiry. Reading the poetry (often aloud to one another) served as a catalyst for the youths to initiate their own artistic processes. Their dialogue about their reading empowered them to action and encouraged them to take poetic "license" and to command their own arts-based research project. The theater troupe members then wrote and performed their own play—with themes that they chose to communicate their life experiences. They also changed their group name from the "AHAS Theatre Troupe" to the "Not at Risk Theatre Company." Their chosen purpose was to demonstrate to others that each individual in their group had faced tremendous systemic barriers, but that they individually and collectively regarded themselves as "not at risk." Their performance of their collective story ended with a group discussion with the actor/authors and the larger group of program participants (the audience comprised youths who were engaged in a variety of arts-inquiry projects that included mural painting and building a "green" and aesthetic outdoor classroom).

With their audience, the writer-performers explored the concepts of "at risk" and other labels that demean individual students and reinforce the systemic barriers experienced in educational settings. Through writing, they "named their reality" and created a product to communicate meaning about themselves (see Osterman & Kottkamp, 1993; see also Colyar, 2009). In the ensuing dialogue with the audience they further problematized the "at risk" label and engaged in a community dialogue about how they would live a future "not at risk." "It is the narrative repertoire of our imagination that helps us distinguish the world we live in from the world we want to live in" says Conle (2003, p. 4). Performance pedagogy enacted through the methods of writing and theater transformed the "everyday lives" of these youth through a process of exposing and critiquing insults to their personal dignity. In performance, they sought social justice. Inquiry took the form of activism and empowered the writers to act on their utopian impulses to change the way they were being defined by society. They created a resistance performance that implemented qualitative research as a solution to their real–world educational problems. For these youth, arts-based research was an active means by which to surpass oppressive social structures and rewrite their futures to include their personal dreams, desires, and goals as active citizens in a participatory democracy.

A good and productive discussion emanating from an artistic experience is only one step toward social change and break-through challenges to stereotyping. More powerful yet is that the youths have all continued with their educational pursuits (including reenrolling in school and seeking alternative educational options) and that they have continued to work as a group through the school year to improve their acting skills by engaging in workshops on body movement, expression, and so on, and one of their members created a new script performed by the Not at Risk Theatre Company.

A new kind of research pedagogy is needed in the context of diminishing democracy. Through arts-based research practices, citizen-scholars can employ the skills of the artist in creative roles such as shaping civic life so as to expand its democratic possibilities for all groups. The skills of the arts-based researcher include but are not limited to the manipulations of media or even the exercise of imagination, but also include preparedness to "directly confront the threat from fundamentalists of all varieties. . . . " To contest workplace inequalities, imagine democratically organized forms of work, and identify and challenge those injustices that contradict and undercut the most fundamental principles of freedom, equality, and respect for all people who make up the global public sphere (Giroux & Giroux, 2009, p. 29).

It is time to reaffirm the socially responsible political purpose of arts-based inquiry. Arts-based inquiry is a strategic means for political resistance to neo-cultural politics. It is a form of cultural resistance and a way to create a critical and dialogic space in which to engage in a struggle over the control of knowledge and the domination of discourse. The time is here to "perform revolutionary pedagogy" through an arts-based approach to inquiry that is socially responsible, locally useful, engaged in public criticism, and resistant to neoconservative discourses that threaten social justice and close down efforts toward a performative research ethics that facilitates critical race, indigenous, queer, feminist, and border studies.

Passion for a political cause or for individual people may be a better guide to creating quality arts-based inquiry than is preparatory education in the arts. For instance, Woo (2008) suggests important qualities of an artist-researcher include "an open mind, a tolerance for criticism, and willingness to learn [art-making techniques]" (p. 326). When the purpose of research is to provoke, to motivate, or to make meaning from experiences, it can be used to advance a progressive political agenda.

One objective the arts-based researcher can serve is to provide tools and opportunity for participants to perform inquiry, reflect on their performances, and preserve, create, and rewrite culture in dynamic indigenous spaces. Thus in critical arts-based inquiry, the location of research changes from the isolated sanctuaries of the laboratory and constructed and bounded environments to places where people meet, including schools, homeless shelters, and neighborhoods. Socially responsible research for and by "the people" cannot reside inside the lonely walls of academic institutions. (S. Finley, 2008, p. 73–74)

In practice of a people's pedagogy research can become a tool for advancing critical race theory and opening space for an aesthetic of artist-researchers and participant-observers belonging to oppressed groups and individuals traditionally excluded from research locations.

In other contexts, I have hashed through the expert-quality issue for arts-based researchers in some detail. I am not ready to embrace a requisite of expert training in art as a condition of producing quality arts-based inquiry (as defined by its potential for audience engagement and response, Knowles & Cole, 2008, p. 67). I wouldn't want it to be taken that I do not favor intensive education in the arts. (The AHAS program features a curriculum that includes arts as separate disciplines as well as arts integration, and my 13-year-old daughter is currently a student at the public Vancouver School for Arts and Academics.) Indeed, I would strongly prefer that all children engage in deep aesthetic experiences of education. With reference to the youth-authored *All I Ask* script, I believe the participants benefited greatly from the theater exercises, reading of scripts, and discussions led by their theater teacher, Anne Averre. Although their script was a dynamic force for portraying lives and generating discussion in a local audience of peers, I am quite sure it would not receive awards for writing or quality of performance. It is not a "masterpiece" but it is an imaginative and visceral performance of critical discourse that pushes against tradition, hegemony, and oppression.

Conclusion

The *Program for the Sixth International Congress of Qualitative Inquiry* (2010) continues the discussion about quality in arts-based research with a plenary session "On Rigor in Arts-Based Research." The question is not closed: How do we determine standards for both the processes and the products of arts-based inquiry? Are the expectations for critical arts-based inquiry different from other approaches to arts-and-research?

I have asked (S. Finley, 2003a): How do I assign grades to arts-based research? How do I determine which articles and proposals to recommend when I review my peers for publications and presentations of their arts-based research? Writing in *Qualitative Inquiry* (S. Finley, 2003a), I proposed a rubric to use in assessing arts-based inquiry; in the SAGE *Handbook of Qualitative Research,* third edition (S. Finley, 2005), I juxtaposed six traits of activist art with seven foundations that define arts-based research and seven bullets that form the framework of revolutionary pedagogy. Each of these movements is foundational to critical arts-based research, and each has its own expectations and standards. But I have to ask, Is "rigor" an appropriate term for contemplating arts-based research? Is the search for rigor in arts-based research another indication of neoconservative pedagogy working to reproduce the standards-laden language of education since 9/11?

Definitions and synonyms for *rigor* stand in stark contradiction with methodologies that are emergent, inclusive, and culturally responsive. Instead, rigor is likened to qualities of being unyielding or inflexible, austere and rigid, leading through fatality to the extremes of *rigor mortis* (S. Finley, 2007). For me, then, rigor is precluded by the key epistemological and ethical basis for using arts and research. Methodological rigor doesn't bring me any closer to understanding, How do we break through the complex barriers of colonial social conformity to an inclusive, pluralist aesthetic situated in the lives of others?

A people's pedagogy to replace neoconservative pedagogy and its constructs should define what is "good" in critical arts-based research. So I return to my initial rubric and refine it within the sociohistorical construct of neoconservatism.

What follows is a rubric for evaluating critical-arts based research in furtherance of a people's pedagogy and in opposition to post–9/11 neoconservative values.

- Does the research demonstrate indigenous or culturally relevant skills and practices?

- Does the research openly resist cultural dominance and demonstrations of meta-narratives of race, history, politics, and power?

- Are the researchers performing a useful, local, community service? Could the research be harmful in any way to the community of its participants?

- Who speaks? Are participants engaged in a process that uses the advantages of pluralism such as cacophony, bricolage, collage, and performance?

- Does the research defy limitations set by the hegemony of neoconservative research discourse?

- Is the research a performance of passionate and visceral communion?

- How likely are readers/viewers and participants to be moved to some kind of positive social action?

Notes

1. See Zakaras and Lowell (2008). This RAND report commissioned by the Wallace Foundation describes the fading optimism about public arts education of the 1960s and 1970s as the 1990s and beyond have ushered deep and continuing spending reductions in arts education (p. xiii). The focus of the report is determining conditions by which to "cultivate the capacity of individuals to have engaging experiences with works of art" (p. 14).

2. *Pornomiseria* describes voyeuristic, exploitive documentary-style films that depict poverty and human suffering in Latin American countries as a form of entertainment. See Michele Faguet, "Pornomiseria: or How Not to Make a Documentary Film," in *Afterall, 21,* Summer 2009, pp. 5–15.

3. For a review of the role *Qualitative Inquiry* has played in advancing arts-based inquiry, see S. Finley, 2003a).

4. For information about At Home At School programs, see http://AtHomeAtSchool.org

References

Alexander, B. K. (2005). Performance ethnography: The reenacting and inciting of culture. In N. K. Denzin & Y. S. Lincoln (Eds.), *The SAGE handbook of qualitative research* (3rd. ed., pp. 411–441). Thousand Oaks, CA: Sage.

American Educational Research Association. (2006). Standards for reporting on empirical social science research in AERA publications. *Educational Researcher, 35*(6), 33–40.

American Educational Research Association. (2009). Standards for reporting on humanities-oriented research in AERA publications. *Educational Researcher, 38*(6), 481–486.

At Home At School (AHAS) Not-At-Risk Theatre Company. (2009, August). *All I ask: A look into the hardships modern teenagers face.* [drama]. Unpublished script, At Home At School Program, Washington State University, Vancouver, WA.

Bagley, C. (2008). Educational ethnography as performance art: Towards a sensuous feeling and knowing. *Qualitative Research, 8,* 53–72.

Bagley, C., & Cancienne, M. B. (Eds.) (2002). *Dancing the data.* New York: Peter Lang.

Barone, T. (2001a). Science, art, and the predispositions of educational researchers. *Educational Researcher, 30*(7), 24–28.

Barone, T. (2001b). *Teaching eternity: The enduring outcomes of teaching.* New York: Columbia University, Teachers College Press.

Barone, T. (2008). How arts-based research can change minds. In M. Cahnmann-Taylor & R. Siegesmund (Eds.), *Arts-based research in education* (pp. 28–49). New York: Routledge.

Barone, T., & Eisner, E. (1997). Arts-based educational research. Section II of *Complementary Methods for Research in Education* (pp. 75–116, 2nd ed., R. M. Jaeger, Ed.). Washington, DC: American Educational Research Association.

Benabib, R., & Salsberg, M. (2009, July 20). *Weeds: Where the sidewalk ends.* [Television broadcast]. Showtime.

Blumenfeld-Jones, D. (2008). Dance, choreography, and social science research. In J. G. Knowles & A. L. Cole (Eds.), *Handbook of arts in qualitative research* (pp. 175–184). Thousand Oaks, CA: Sage.

Cahnmann-Taylor, M., & Siegesmund, R. (2008). *Arts-based research in education: Foundations for practice.* New York: Routledge.

Cannella, G. S., & Lincoln, Y. S. (2004a). Dangerous discourses II: Comprehending and countering the redeployment discourses (and resources) in the generation of liberatory inquiry. *Qualitative Inquiry, 10,* 165–174.

Cannella, G. S., & Lincoln, Y. S. (2004b). Epilogue: Claiming a critical public social science—Reconceptualizing and redeploying research. *Qualitative Inquiry, 10,* 298–309.

Casey, K. (1995). The new narrative research in education. *Review of Research in Education, 21,* 211–253.

Colyar, J. (2009). Becoming writing, becoming writers. *Qualitative Inquiry, 15*(2), 421–436.

Conle, C. (2003). An anatomy of narrative curricula. *Educational Researcher, 32*(3), 3–15.

Conquergood, D. (1988). Beyond the text: Toward a performance cultural politics. In S. J. Dailey (Ed.), *The future of performance studies: Visions and revisions* (pp. 25–36). Washington, DC: National Communication Association.

Coulter, C. A., & Smith, M. L. (2009). The construction zone: Literary elements in narrative research. *Educational Researcher, 38*(8), 577–590.

Denzin, N. K. (1997). Performance texts. In W. G. Tierney & Y. S. Lincoln (Eds.), *Representation and the text: Re-framing the narrative voice* (pp. 179–217). Albany: SUNY Press.

Denzin, N. K. (1999). Two-stepping in the 90s. *Qualitative Inquiry, 5,* 568–572.

Denzin, N. K. (2000). Aesthetics and the practices of qualitative inquiry. *Qualitative Inquiry, 6,* 256–265.

Denzin, N. K. (2003). *Performance ethnography: Critical pedagogy and the politics of culture.* Thousand Oaks, CA: Sage.

Denzin, N. K. (2004). *The First International Congress of Qualitative Inquiry.* Available at http://www.icqi.org/

Denzin, N. K. (2008a). *Searching for Yellowstone: Race, gender, family and memory in the postmodern west.* Walnut Creek, CA: Left Coast Press.

Denzin, N. K. (2008b). A critical performance pedagogy that matters. In J. A. Sandlin, B. D. Schultz, & J. Burdick. *Handbook of public pedagogy* (pp. 56–70). Thousand Oaks, CA: Sage.

Denzin, N. K., & Lincoln, Y. S. (2000). The discipline and practice of qualitative research. In N. K. Denzin & Y. S. Lincoln (Eds.), *Handbook of qualitative research* (2nd ed., pp. 1–28). Thousand Oaks, CA: Sage.

Denzin, N. K., & Lincoln, Y. S. (Eds.). (2005). *The SAGE handbook of qualitative research* (3rd ed.). Thousand Oaks, CA: Sage.

Dewey, J. (1958). *Art as experience.* New York: Capricorn. (Original work published in 1934)

Dissanayake, E. (1988). *What is art for?* Seattle: University of Washington Press.

Diversi, M., & Finley, S. (2010). Special issue on critical homelessness. *Cultural Studies<=>Critical Methodologies, 10*(1).

Diversi, M., & Moreira, C. (2009). *Betweener talk: Decolonizing knowledge production, pedagogy, and praxis.* Walnut Creek, CA: Left Coast Press.

Donmoyer, R., & Yennie-Donmoyer, J. (1995). Data as drama: Reflections on the use of readers' theater as a mode of qualitative data display. *Qualitative Inquiry, 20*(1), 74–83.

Donmoyer, R., & Yennie-Donmoyer, J. (1998). Reader's theater and educational research—Give me a for-instance: A commentary on Womentalkin'. *Qualitative Studies in Education, 11*(3), 397–402.

Donmoyer, R., & Yennie-Donmoyer, J. (2008). Readers' theater as a data display strategy. In J. G. Knowles & A. L. Cole (Eds.), *Handbook of arts in qualitative research* (pp. 209–224). Thousand Oaks, CA: Sage.

Eco, U. (1984). *La structure absente: Introduction a la reserche' semioteque* (U. Esposito-Torrigiani, Trans.). Paris: Mercured de France.

Eisner, E. (1998). *The enlightened eye: Qualitative inquiry and the enhancement of educational practice.* Upper Saddle River, NJ: Prentice Hall. (Original work published in 1991)

Eisner, E. (2001a). Concerns and aspirations for qualitative research in the new millennium. *Qualitative Research, 1,* 135–145.

Eisner, E. (2001b). Should we create new aims for art education? *National Art Education Association, 54*(5), 6–10.

Eisner, E. (2008). Arts and knowledge. In J. G. Knowles & A. L. Cole (Eds.), *Handbook of arts in qualitative research* (pp. 3–12). Thousand Oaks, CA: Sage.

Faguet, M. (2009). Pornomiseria: Or how not to make a documentary film. *Afterall, 21*(Summer), 5–15.

Finley, M. (2000). *Street rat.* Detroit: University of Detroit Press.

Finley, M. (2003). Fugue of the street rat: Writing research poetry. *Qualitative Studies in Education, 16*(4), 603–604.

Finley, S. (2000). "Dream child": The role of poetic dialogue in homeless research. *Qualitative Inquiry, 6,* 432–434.

Finley, S. (2001). Painting life histories. *Journal of Curriculum Theorizing, 17*(2), 13–26.

Finley S. (2003a). Arts-based inquiry in QI: Seven years from crisis to guerrilla warfare. *Qualitative Inquiry, 9,* 281–296.

Finley S. (2003b). The faces of dignity: Rethinking the politics of homelessness and poverty in America. *Qualitative Studies in Education, 16,* 509–531.

Finley, S. (2005). Arts-based inquiry: Performing revolutionary pedagogy. In N. K. Denzin & Y. S. Lincoln (Eds.), *The SAGE handbook of qualitative research* (3rd ed., pp. 681–694). Thousand Oaks, CA: Sage.

Finley, S. (2007). *Methodological rigor: Intellectual rigor mortis?* Paper presented at International Congress of Qualitative Inquiry, Urbana-Champaign, IL.

Finley, S. (2008). Arts-based research. In J. G. Knowles & A. L. Cole (Eds.), *Handbook of arts in qualitative research* (pp. 71–81). Thousand Oaks, CA: Sage.

Finley, S. (2010). "Freedom's just another word for nothin' left to lose": The power of poetry for young, nomadic women of the streets. *Cultural Studies<=>Critical Methodologies, 10,* 58–63.

Finley, S., & Finley, M. (1998). *Traveling through the cracks: Homeless youth speak out.* Paper presented at the American Educational Research Association, San Diego, CA.

Finley, S., & Finley, M. (1999). Sp'ange: A research story. *Qualitative Inquiry, 5,* 313–337.

Foucault, M. (1984). The order of discourse. In M. Shapiro (Ed.), *Language and politics* (pp. 108–138). London: Blackwell.

Furman, R. (2006). Poetic forms and structures in qualitative health research. *Qualitative Health Research, 16*(4), 560–566.

Garoian, C. R. (1999). *Performing pedagogy: Toward an art of politics.* Albany: SUNY Press.

Garoian, C. R., & Gaudelius, Y. M. (2008). *Spectacle pedagogy: Arts, politics, and visual culture.* Albany: SUNY Press.

Geertz, C. (1988). *Works and lives.* Cambridge, UK: Polity Press.

Giroux, H. A. (1995). Borderline artists, cultural workers, and the crisis of democracy. In C. Becker (Ed.), *The artist in society: Rights, rules, and responsibilities* (pp. 4–14). Chicago: New Art Examiner.

Giroux, H. A. (2001). Cultural studies as performative politics. *Cultural Studies<=>Critical Methodologies, 1,* 5–23.

Giroux, H. A. (2009). Democracy's nemesis: The rise of the corporate university. *Cultural Studies<=>Critical Methodologies, 9,* 669–695.

Giroux, H. A., & Giroux, S. S. (2006). Challenging neoliberalism's new world order: The promise of critical pedagogy. *Cultural Studies<=>Critical Methodologies, 6,* 21–32.

Giroux, H. A., & Giroux, S. S. (2008, December). Beyond bailouts: On the politics of education after neoliberalism. *Truthout.* Retrieved February 11, 2010, from http://www.truthout.org/123108A

Giroux, H. A., & Polychroniou, C. (2008, February). The scourge of global neoliberalism and the need to reclaim democracy. Retrieved January 19, 2011, from http://online-journal.com/artman/publish/article_2959.shtml

Grossberg, L. (1996). Toward a genealogy of the state of cultural studies. In C. Nelson & D. P. Gaonkar (Eds.), *Disciplinarity and dissent in cultural studies* (pp. 87–107). New York: Routledge.

Guba, E. (1967). The expanding concept of research. *Theory Into Practice, 6*(2), 57–65.

Gurevitch, Z. (2002). Writing through: The poetics of transfiguration. *Cultural Studies<=>Critical Methodologies, 2*(3), 403–413.

Gutmann, A., & Thompson, D. (2004). *Why deliberative democracy?* Princeton, NJ: Princeton University Press.

Hammersley, M. (1992). *What's wrong with ethnography?* London: Routledge.

Hanley, M. S., & Noblit, G. W. (2009). *Cultural responsiveness, racial identity and academic success: A review of the literature.* Pittsburgh, PA: Heinz Endowments.

Harper, D. (1987). *Working knowledge: Skill and community in a small shop.* Berkeley: University of California Press.

Howe, K. R. (2009). Positivist dogmas, rhetoric, and the education science question. *Educational Researcher, 38*(6), 428–440.

Jensen, J. (2002). *Is art good for us? Beliefs about high culture in American life.* Lanham, MD: Rowman & Littlefield.

Knowles, J. G., & Cole, A. L. (Eds.). (2008). *Handbook of the arts in qualitative research: Perspectives, methodologies, examples, and issues.* Thousand Oaks, CA: Sage.

Leaños, J. J., & Villarreal, A. J. (2007). Art education. In D. Gabbard (Ed.), *Knowledge and power in the global economy: The effects of school reform in a neoliberal/neoconservative age.* Available at http://www.leanos.net/Arts%20Education.html

Lincoln, Y. S. (1995). Emerging criteria for quality in qualitative and interpretative research. *Qualitative Inquiry, 1,* 275–289.

Lincoln, Y. S. (2005). Institutional review boards and methodological conservatism: The challenge to and from phenomenological paradigms. In N. K. Denzin & Y. S. Lincoln (Eds.), *The SAGE handbook of qualitative research* (3rd ed., pp. 165–181). Thousand Oaks, CA: Sage.

Lincoln, Y. S., & Cannella, G. S. (2004a). Dangerous discourses: Methodological conservatism and governmental regimes of truth. *Qualitative Inquiry, 10,* 5–14.

Lincoln, Y. S., & Cannella, G. S. (2004b). Qualitative research, power, and the radical right. *Qualitative Inquiry, 10,* 175–201.

Mayer, R. E. (2000). What is the place of science in education research? *Educational Researcher, 29*(6), 38–39.

Mienczakowski, J. (2000). Ethnodrama: Performed research—limitations and potential. In P. Atkinson, S. Delamont, & A. Coffey (Eds.), *Handbook of ethnography* (pp. 468–476). Thousand Oaks, CA: Sage.

Mienczakowski, J., Smith, R., & Sinclair, M. (1996). On the road to catharsis: A theoretical framework for change. *Qualitative Inquiry, 2*(4), 439–462.

National Research Council. (2002). *Scientific research in education.* Washington, DC: National Academy Press.

Osterman, K. F., & Kottkamp, R. B. (1993). *Reflective practice for educators: Improving schooling through professional development.* Newbury Park, CA: Corwin Press.

Program of the Sixth International Congress of Qualitative Inquiry (2010). University of Illinois at Urbana-Champaign. Retrieved January 20, 2011, from http://www.icqi.org/

Saldaña, J. (2008). Ethnodrama and ethnotheatre. In J. G. Knowles & A. L. Cole (Eds.), *Handbook of arts in qualitative research* (pp. 195–207). Thousand Oaks, CA: Sage.

Saldaña, J., Finley, S., & Finley, M. (2005). Street rat. In J. Saldaña (Ed.), *Ethnodrama: An anthology of reality theatre* (pp. 139–179). Walnut Creek, CA: AltaMira Press.

Seale, C. (1999). Quality in arts-based research. *Qualitative Inquiry, 5,* 465–478.

Seidel, K. (2001). Many issues, few answers—The role of research in K–12 arts education. *Arts Education Policy Review, 103*(2), 19–22.

Siegesmund, R. (1998). Why do we teach art today? Conceptions of art education and their justification. *Studies in Art Education, 39*(3), 197–214.

Sinner, A., Leggo, C., Irwin, R. L., Gouzouasis, P., & Grauer, K. (2006). Arts-based educational research dissertations: Reviewing the practices of new scholars. *Canadian Journal of Education, 29*(4), 1223–1270.

Smith, L. T. (1999). *Decolonizing methodologies: Research and indigenous peoples.* Dunedin, New Zealand: University of Otago Press.

Sullivan, G. (2005). *Art practice as research: Inquiry in the visual arts.* Thousand Oaks, CA: Sage.

Tharp, T. (2003). *The creative habit: Learn it and use it for life.* New York: Simon & Schuster.

Tolstoy, L. (1996). *What is art?* (A. Maude, Trans.). New York: Penguin. (Original work published in 1946)

Ulmer, G. (1989). *Teletheory.* New York: Routledge.

Ulmer, G. (1994). The heretics of deconstruction. In P. Brunette & D. Wills (Eds.), *Deconstruction and the visual arts: Art, media, architecture* (pp. 80–96). New York: Cambridge University Press.

Woo, Y. Y. J. (2008). Engaging new audiences: Translating research into popular media. *Educational Researcher, 37*(6), 321–329.

Young, I. M. (2004). *Inclusion and democracy.* New York: Oxford University Press.

Zakaras, L., & Lowell, J. F. (2008). *Cultivating demand for the arts: Arts learning, arts engagement, and state arts policy.* Santa Monica, CA: RAND Corporation.

Oral History

Linda Shopes

What Oral History Is, and Isn't

Oral history is a protean term: Within common parlance, it can refer to recorded speech of any kind or to talking about the past in ways ranging from casual reminiscing among family members, neighbors, or coworkers to ritualized accounts presented in formal settings by culturally sanctioned tradition-bearers. Most typically, the term refers to what folklorists call personal experience narratives—that is, orally transmitted, autobiographical stories crafted to communicate meaning or what is valued to others (Dolby, 1989). Oral history in this mode is exemplified most notably by the work of Studs Terkel (1967, 1970, 1974, 1984), whose multiple volumes have done much to popularize the term, and more recently, of David Isay (2007), whose StoryCorps project has been rekindling interest in the storied quality of everyday life. Typically, the term registers a certain democratic or populist meaning; *oral history* implies a recognition of the heroics of everyday life, a celebration of the quotidian, an appeal to the visceral.[1]

Among practitioners, however, oral history has a more precise meaning. The Oral History Association (2010) defines oral history as "a way of collecting and interpreting human memories to foster knowledge and human dignity." Donald Ritchie (2003), in his guide, *Doing Oral History,* describes it as "collect[ing] memories and personal commentaries of historical significance through recorded interviews." He continues, "An oral history interview generally consists of a well-prepared interviewer questioning an interviewee and recording their exchange in audio or video format. Recordings of the interview are transcribed, summarized, or indexed and then placed in a library or archives. These interviews may be used for research or excerpted in a publication, radio or video documentary, museum exhibition, dramatization, or other form of public presentation" (p. 19). Valerie

Yow (2005), in her *Recording Oral History,* states, "Oral history is the recording of personal testimony delivered in oral form." Distinguishing this practice from memoir, she notes that in oral history, "There is someone else involved who frames the topic and inspires the narrator to begin the act of remembering, jogs memory, and records and presents the narrator's words." Recognizing that various terms are used to describe this same activity, she concludes, "*Oral history* seems to be the [term] most frequently used to refer to the recorded in–depth interview" (pp. 3–4).

These definitions suggest six characteristics of oral history as a professional, disciplined practice. It is, *first,* an interview, an exchange between someone who asks questions, that is, the interviewer, and someone who answers them, referred to as the interviewee, narrator, or informant. It is not simply someone telling a story; it is someone telling a story in response to the queries of another; it is this dialogue that shapes the interview. Moreover, oral history generally involves only these two people. Although oral historians will occasionally conduct group interviews, these are generally done as preparation for or follow up to an individual interview. Oral historians value the intimacy of a one-on-one exchange. *Second,* oral history is recorded, preserved for the record, and made accessible to others for a variety of uses. Ritchie (2003) goes so far as to say, "An interview becomes an oral history only when it has been recorded, processed in some way, made available in an archive, library, or other repository, or reproduced in relatively verbatim form for publication. Availability for general research, reinterpretation, and verification defines oral history" (p. 24). These two primary characteristics of oral history suggest that it is properly understood as both process (that is the act of interviewing) and product (that is, the record that results from that interview).

Third, oral history interviewing is historical in intent; that is, it seeks new knowledge about and insights into the past through an individual biography. Although it always represents an interplay between past and present, the individual and the social, oral history is grounded in historical questions and hence requires that the interviewer has knowledge of both the subject at hand and the interviewee's relationship to that subject. *Fourth,* oral history is understood as both an act of memory and an inherently subjective account of the past. Interviews record what an interviewer draws out, what the interviewee remembers, what he or she chooses to tell, and how he or she understands what happened, not the unmediated "facts" of what happened in the past. An interview, therefore, renders an interpretation of the past that itself requires interpretation. *Fifth,* an oral history interview is an inquiry in depth. It is not a casual or serendipitous conversation but a planned and scheduled, serious and searching exchange, one that seeks a detailed, expansive, and reflective account of the past.

Although framed by a broad set of questions or areas of inquiry, an oral history interview admits a high degree of flexibility, allowing the narrator to speak about what he or she wishes, as he or she wishes. Finally, oral history is fundamentally oral, reflecting both the conventions and dynamics of the spoken word. This may seem self–evident, but decades of relying on transcripts, which can never fully represent what was said, have obscured this fact. Only with the widespread adoption of digital technology are oral historians beginning to engage seriously with the orality of oral history.

Oral history generally distinguishes between life history and topical interviews: Life history interviews, often undertaken within local or community settings, record a narrator's biography, addressing topics such as family life; educational and work experiences; social, political, and religious involvements; and, at their best, the relationship of personal history to broader historical events and social themes. Typically, life history interviews aim at recording everyday life within a particular setting. Topical interviews, often done as part of a larger research project, focus on specific elements of an individual's biography, for example, participation in the U.S. civil rights movement, a topic well documented by oral history. In practice, many interviews include both life history and topical elements; lives, after all, are not easily compartmentalized.

Whether a life history or topical interview or some combination of the two, the best interviews have a measured, thinking-out-loud quality, as perceptive questions work and rework a particular topic, encouraging the narrator to remember details, seeking to clarify what is muddled, making connections among seemingly disparate recollections, challenging contradictions, evoking assessments. The best interviewers listen carefully between the lines of what is being said to discern what the narrator is trying to get at and have the confidence to ask the hard questions. Yet all interviews are shaped by the context within which they are conducted, as well as the particular interpersonal dynamic between narrator and interviewer: An interview can be a history lecture, a confessional, a verbal sparring match, an exercise in nostalgia, a moral tale, or any other of the ways people talk about their experiences.

Although the act of interviewing lies at the heart of oral history, best practices define the oral history process as considerably more extensive (Larson, 2006; MacKay, 2007; Ritchie, 2003; Yow, 2005). The interview is preceded by careful preparation, including defining the focus of the inquiry, conducing background research in secondary and primary sources, developing skills in interview methods and in using recording technology, identifying and making contact with the narrator, cultivating rapport, conducting a preinterview, and developing an interview outline. An interview is then followed by a number of steps designed to facilitate preservation and access, including securing permission for others to use the interview by means of what is termed a *legal release;* making one or more copies of the original recording; placing these in a secure, publicly accessible repository; cataloguing or developing a finding aid for the interview; and developing a means of accessing what has been recorded without listening to the entire interview, by either transcribing or summarizing it, or, more recently, developing online search methods. If the interview is part of a larger project or program, additional considerations come into play, including project planning and design, management and staffing, office space, work flow, budget and funding, and the development of products or outcomes.

Oral history is thus distinguished from other kinds of interviewing. Its open-ended, subjective, historically inflected approach is quite unlike the highly structured opinion polls and surveys of current attitudes and behaviors conducted by sociologists, political scientists, and market researchers. Similarly, it is unlike interviews conducted by many journalists and documentary workers, who seek quotations to fit the story they are developing today rather than let the narrator define the plot of his or her own story for the historical record. (This is not to deny, however, that the line can be blurry; some journalists and documentarians are excellent oral historians, though they may not refer to themselves as such [Coles, 1997].) Oral history also differs from interviews done in a clinical or therapeutic setting. Although both are conducted in depth and recognize inter-subjectivity and personal biography—and notwithstanding that an oral history interview often has a salutary effect on both narrator and interviewer—clinical interviewing posits dysfunction and seeks to help a person resolve personal problems, sometimes, as in narrative psychology (Bruner, 1990; Polkinghorne, 1988; Spence, 1982), by reframing the person's story. Oral history, however, does not seek to change the narrator; it proceeds from the assumption that the narrator has been an active agent in fashioning his or her life and life story.

Oral historians are perhaps most closely allied with anthropologists and qualitative sociologists in their approach to interviewing; all, in Clifford Geertz's (1974) resonate phrase, seek "the native's point of view." Oral historians, especially those interviewing individuals who share a particular social setting, will often engage in the anthropologist's practice of participant observation; and anthropologists and sociologists, though generally focusing on the ethnographic present, do recognize at times a historical dimension to the topic at hand (Atkinson, Coffey, & Delamont, 2003; di Leonardo, 1987; Mintz, 1979; Silverman, 1997; Vansina, 1985). Oral historians also share certain approaches and practices with folklorists: Although folklorists focus on the formal and aesthetic qualities of traditional narratives, they and oral historians record firsthand accounts as part of the collective record of a culture; and within contemporary practice, both approach oral materials as subjective texts, constructions of language and mind, whose meaning demands a level of decoding (Abrahams, 1981; Davis, 1988; Jackson, 2007; Joyner, 1979).

Although oral history differs from the methods and purposes of other kinds of interviewing and allies most comfortably with the assumptions and intentions of history, it can be deeply interdisciplinary in the ways it seeks to understand interviews. Oral historians have looked to psychology for understanding the emotional undercurrents of an interview; to communications for the structure and dynamics of the interview exchange; to folklore and literary studies for the storied quality of interviews; to anthropology for the culture clash that often occurs as two different *mentalities* collide within the narrative; to cultural studies and critical race and gender studies for ways the social position of both narrator and interviewer underlies what is—and is not—said; to performance studies for the presentational quality of interviews; and to gerontology for understanding the way the imperatives of aging shape an interview. Indeed, much of the most creative thinking about oral history comes from practitioners trained and working in fields other than history.

This essay has thus far presented oral history in its own ethnographic present, for it has advanced a broad description of a practice that in fact has not been static but has evolved over several decades. Useful for laying out some generally—although not universally—agreed upon characteristics of oral history, for setting some boundaries, and for helping fix this indeed very protean term, this discussion has nonetheless stripped oral history of its own historical development. Thus, subsequent sections will discuss the development of oral history over time as both a method of research and mode of understanding the past (Gluck, 1999; Grele, 2007; Thomson, 2007). Collectively, they will address changes in practice, linking them to broader changes in the academy and within society, consider the politics of oral history as an intellectual and social practice, and outline oral history's institutional development. The chapter will conclude with a discussion of legal and ethical issues in oral history, including its problematic relationship with institutional review boards.

Early Developments: Oral History as an Archival Practice

Historians have long used oral sources for their work, either conducting interviews of their own or drawing on firsthand accounts recorded and preserved by others (Sharpless, 2006). No less than the ancient historian Thucydides interviewed participants for his history of the Peloponnesian War, observing that "different eye-witnesses give different accounts of the same events, speaking out of partiality for one side or the other or else from imperfect memories" (Ritchie, 2003, p. 20). Accounts of Aztec and Inca life recorded by Spanish chroniclers in the 16th century and of Mexican and American settlers in California recorded by Hubert Howe Bancroft and his assistants remain valuable sources for historians today. Similarly, Henry Mayhew's inquiry into the living and working conditions of London's working classes in the mid-19th century is only the first in a long line of investigations that have relied heavily on evidence obtained by talking with the subjects of the inquiry; these social studies have both goaded reform and informed scholarly history.

Nonetheless, reliance on oral sources fell into disfavor during the late 19th and much of the 20th centuries, as the practice of history became increasingly professionalized and as positivism became the reigning academic paradigm. The German historian Leopold von Ranke's dictum that the goal of history was to recount "how it really was" (*wie es eigentlich gewesen*) described a form of scholarship that increasingly relied on the (paper) documentary record, or as C.-V. Langlois and Charles Seignobos, two French historians, put it, "There is no substitute for documents: no documents, no history" (Thompson, 1988, p. 51). Reliance on what had often been an informal practice of talking with people thus became suspect. Indeed, early efforts to record firsthand accounts of the past were often idiosyncratic or extemporaneous affairs, conducted according to methods that were more or less rigorous in any given case and with no intention of developing a permanent archival collection. Furthermore, the absence of mechanical—or digital—recording devices necessitated reliance on human note-takers, raising questions about accuracy and reliability.

Dating oral history's beginnings in the United States is a quixotic exercise at best. Some reckon its origins in the Depression-era Federal Writers Project (FWP), which recorded thousands of life histories with individuals from various regional, occupational, and ethnic groups during the late 1930s and early 1940s (Hirsch, 2006, 2007). The best known of the FWP interviews are the slave narratives, accounts by elderly men and women who had experienced slavery firsthand. Rediscovered by scholars in the 1970s, these narratives have become important sources for a reorientation of the historiography of American slavery from one that views slaves primarily as victims to one that recognizes the active agency of enslaved persons within a system of bondage (Blassingame, 1972; Genovese, 1974; Rawick, 1972). But what about the interviews James McGregor conducted in 1940 with survivors of the 1890 Wounded Knee Massacre? Or the interviews done by Bancroft and his associates?

Nonetheless, the Oral History Research Office (OHRO) at Columbia University, established by Columbia historian Allan Nevins in the late 1940s, is generally acknowledged as the first oral history program in the United States, a distinction likely related to OHRO's prominence in institutionalizing and professionalizing oral history in its modern incarnation (Starr, 1984). Recognizing that the bureaucratization of public affairs was tending to standardize the paper trail and that the telephone was replacing personal correspondence, Nevins came up then with the idea of conducting interviews with participants in recent history to supplement the written record. He wrote of the need "for obtaining a little of the immense mass of information about the more recent American past—the past of the last half century—which might come fresh and direct from men once prominent in politics, in business, in the professions, and in other fields; information that every obituary column shows to be perishing" (Starr, 1984, p. 8). It took a decade for this idea to reach fruition: Nevins and his amanuensis—for these early interviews were recorded in longhand—conducted their first interview in 1948 with New York civic leader George McAneny.

Several universities soon followed Columbia's lead and established their own oral history programs: the University of Texas in 1952, the University of California at Berkeley in 1954, and the University of California at Los Angeles and the University of Michigan in 1959. The Harry S. Truman Library and Museum inaugurated its oral history project in 1961, interviewing Truman's family, friends, and associates, thus initiating the practice of oral history at presidential libraries. Columbia's 1965 annual report listed some 89 projects nationwide, fostered partly by the development of recording technologies.[2] By the mid-1960s, oral history was well enough established to form the Oral History Association (OHA), founded in 1967. After publishing its annual proceedings for five years, in 1973 OHA began publishing an annual journal, the *Oral History Review* ; in 1987 the *Review* became a biannual publication. Recognizing the need to codify standards for oral history, it developed the first iteration of the current *Principles and Best Practices for Oral History* (2009) in 1968. The document is generally regarded as defining the parameters of best practice.[3]

Unlike previous interviewing initiatives, these early oral history programs were distinguished by both their permanence and their systematic and disciplined approach to interviewing. Staff and affiliates developed projects that included a number of interviews on a single topic and were designed to fill in gaps in the extant record. These were explicitly archival: The point was to record on tape, preserve, and make available for future research recollections deemed of historical significance. Archival exigencies have thus defined what have been generally understood as fundamental features of oral history and have been codified in established best practices. Two merit particular attention. First is the matter of releases: Because an interview is understood as a creative work, it is subject to the laws of copyright; and these laws deem the interviewee, as "author" of the interview, to be the owner of the copyright. It is by means of the legal release form that the interviewee signs over or "releases" to the sponsoring institution—or individual researcher or the repository that accepts completed interviews—rights to the interview; and, if the interviewee chooses, sets certain limits to access. This is analogous to the deed of gift form by which archives typically acquire materials from donors, and indeed, some oral history interviews are transferred to an archive by a deed of gift (Neuenschwander, 2009). The legal status of the interviewer is unclear, but in practice he or she is often considered a cocreator of the interviewer and hence cosigner of the release.

Second is the matter of transcription: Transcribing interviews, that is rendering recorded speech in writing, has long been accepted as an essential part of the oral history process, on the assumption that a transcript will increase access considerably. Given that archives and the scholars who use them have historically been document driven, this assumption is understandable: Paper, unlike audio or visual media, is a familiar and comfortable form; it's easier and faster to scan a paper document than listen to or view an interview; words fixed on paper ensure accuracy of quotation in print; and they confer a certain intellectual authority on what could be construed as an ephemeral form. For years, oral historians accepted the transcript as the primary document of an oral history interview, despite its inevitable distortions, and early on, some programs destroyed or reused audiotapes (Allen, 1982; Baum, 1977; Mazé, 2006; Samuel, 1971). Only recently has the general consensus shifted away from the transcript and toward the recorded interview—the *oral* narrative—as the primary document; with the development of digital media has come a growing interest in supplementing—or supplanting—the transcript with digital access, topics that will be taken up later in this chapter.

Best practice also dictates that transcribed interviews be returned to the narrator for correction, amplification, and emendation, to obtain the fullest, most accurate account. This practice, coupled with the need for releases, can pit the rights and privileges of the narrator against the imperatives of scholarship. Law and custom give the narrator enormous control over the presentation of his or her story; and when, as is often the case, the narrator is someone who otherwise has little control over the circumstances of his or her life, this is certainly just. Still, a narrator can place restrictions on the interview by means of the release and can delete significant but unflattering, embarrassing, even incriminating information from the transcript, to the impoverishment of the historical record.

Because these early oral historians had been schooled in the Rankian document- and fact-based historiography of the times, they considered interviews to be a means of creating new facts that would lead to a more complete account of the past. The interviewee was viewed as a storehouse of information about "what actually happened"; the interviewer, a neutral presence who simply recorded these facts; and the interview, a document to be assessed like any other source for its reliability and verifiability. Michael Frisch (1990a, p. 160) has referred to this as the "more history" approach to oral history, "reducing [it] to simply another kind of evidence to be pushed through the historian's controlling mill." Because oral history was something of a maverick practice, dismissed by most historians as unreliable hearsay, a source of anecdote or color but little else, one finds a certain defensiveness among early practitioners and a strenuous effort to articulate systematic means of assuring and assessing the validity, reliability, and representativeness of interviews (Moss, 1977).

Social History and the Democratization of Oral History

The social movements and intellectual upheavals of the 1960s, 1970s, and beyond had enormous impact on oral history and, more modestly, vice versa. Who was interviewed, who interviewed them, what they were interviewed about, and the purpose of interviews all experienced significant shifts in these decades, not so much replacing the earlier, archival approach as building on it or occurring on a parallel track. Whereas early oral history programs, in line with the dominant historiography of the postwar era, had tended to interview the "elite"—that is, leaders in business, industry, and politics as well as distinguished individuals in the professions, the arts, and related fields—by the 1970s, oral history's scope widened considerably, in response to scholars' growing interest in the experiences of non-elites, ordinary people—anonymous Americans, as they were sometimes termed. As social history—that is, the history of social relationships among generally unequal and often competing groups—became the dominant historiographic paradigm, oral history became an essential tool for recovering the experiences of those to whom historians were now turning their attention. As Ronald Grele (2007, p. 12) has written, "The objective was to document the lives and past actions of classes of people heretofore ignored by historians; in particular the working class, but also racial and ethnic minorities, women, and sexual and political minorities. These are people whose lives were traditionally ignored or purposefully forgotten: people whose history [had been] ... understood by examining documents provided by those who were outsiders to the communities under study, upper class commentators for the most part, but also journalists, social and other service workers, or anyone who had left a written record." Interviewers thus began asking about everyday life in working-class communities, about the differing experiences of women and men within families, about ways minorities created purposeful lives within deeply constraining circumstances. Interviewers began to ask not only "What happened?" but also "What was it like?" "What did you do about ... ?" "How do you understand ... ?"

At the same time, oral history became a practice carried out less exclusively for archival purposes and increasingly by individual scholars conducting interviews for their own research projects. In some cases, scholarly interests catalyzed the development of ongoing, multifaceted oral history programs, such as the Southern Oral History Program at the University of North Carolina at Chapel Hill, where scholarly research and archival collection building have gone hand in hand since 1973. Yet some scholar-interviewers, operating outside of an institutional oral history archive, did not always adhere to established standards with the same rigor as the pioneering oral history projects. Some were unwilling to pursue topics that lay outside their immediate interests, thereby limiting interviews' usefulness to others; some, less concerned about the future use of interviews and often with fewer resources than ongoing projects, failed to secure release forms, or to transcribe interviews, or even to place them in public archives.[4] The last especially is of concern, for it violates historians' professional commitment to open access to sources.

These shortcomings notwithstanding, oral history has played an important role in democratizing our collective understanding of the past; interviews have added new knowledge about previously excluded or underdocumented groups and have restored voice and agency to those whom the extant record has often objectified. To cite only one example, John Bodnar's *The Transplanted* (1985), its title deliberately playing off Oscar Handlin's *The Uprooted* (1951) and its interpretation deeply informed by the biographical narratives of dozens of interviewees, represented Eastern and Southern European immigrants to the United States not as disoriented and "uprooted," anomic individuals, unable to gain a footing in the new world, but as men and women actively deploying creative strategies to fashion a new life as transplants to that world. Collectively, interviews conducted within the social history paradigm have challenged dominant, top-down narratives of the past and addressed the relationship between subordination and agency. More recently, this kind of oral history has occurred within the context of ethnic and queer studies, as scholars probe notions of identity, break long-held silences, and broaden our understanding of "who counts" in history.

Oral history has democratized not only the historical record but also the practice of history, involving people outside the academy and established archives as producers and interpreters of their own history in addition to serving as interviewees. Increasingly during the 1970s and on into the present, local organizations and groups—historical societies, museums, and libraries and also churches, unions, senior centers, and other grassroots groups—have carried out oral history projects to document their own history, often developing performances, exhibitions, media productions, and other creative work to extend the reach of the interviews. It is probably accurate to state that since the mid-1970s, at least as many oral history projects have been located outside the academy as within; as early as 1973, a directory listing oral history centers in the United States located half of them outside of a college or university setting (Starr, 1984, p. 12).

Still, scholars have often become involved in these projects as organizers, workshop leaders, consultants, collaborators, and interviewers in a self-conscious effort to engage with communities, often those they themselves are studying. In recent years, academic involvement in community oral history projects has taken place under the rubric of "civic engagement" or "public history," as students and faculty work with community collaborators to document and present aspects of the local past. Frisch (1990b) has written about oral and public history's capacity for sharing authority between interviewer and interviewee, creating opportunities for a "profound sharing of knowledges, an implicit and sometimes explicit dialogue from very different vantages about the shape, meaning, and implications of history" (p. xxii). Academically trained oral historians working "in public" and their local partners frequently struggle with the implications of such sharing, as they confront differences between scholarly understandings of history as an interpretive activity and vernacular notions of storytelling; between a scholar's interest in a critical approach to the past and a community's self-interest in promoting a positive image or in avoiding unsavory aspects of its past; between academic languages and styles of work and less formalized practices. These differences, difficult as they are to negotiate, point to larger social differences, in class and race, in generation, in education, in social and political views; and in that context are often resolved only uneasily, or partially (Diaz & Russell, 1999; Lewis, Waller, & Hinsdale, 1995; Shopes, 1986, 2002a).

In a practice that is less about community history and more about advocacy, some have connected oral history with broader humanitarian and civic concerns. Oral historians have, for example, been involved in reminiscence work with older adults, engaging in the integrative process of life review (Bornat, 1993;

Butler, 1963) and in "truth telling projects," designed to reconcile former antagonists (Lundy & McGovern, 2006; Minkley & Rassool, 1998). They have developed projects that both document and support redress for human rights abuses such as the internment of Japanese Americans during World War II (Densho, 2010; Dubrow, 2008) or more recently, the lengthy detention without trial of suspected Muslim terrorists in the United States (Shiekh, 2010). Oral historians have conducted interviews with displaced or homeless individuals as a means of stimulating and informing a broader activist agenda (Kerr, 2008), used the local knowledge gained in interviews to inform development projects around the globe (Cross & Barker, 2006; Slim & Thompson, 1993), and connected oral history with work for social change in numerous other ways.

Whether occurring inside or outside the academy or somewhere in between, oral history in this democratic mode has often been grounded not only in an interest in a more expansive sense of what counts as history and who counts as historians, but also in a progressive politics, an interest in using history to inform and at times to intervene in movements for equality and justice. As in other fields, the most forceful voice for a politically engaged oral history has often been feminist scholar/activists. Buoyed by the energy of the women's movement, they argued early on that "women's oral history was not merely *about* women. It was *by* and *for* women, as well" (Gluck, 2006, p. 360). Recognizing that the personal is political, interviewers were eager to discover the female experience. Given the nature of that experience, women, it was argued, brought an especial empathy to interviewing "their sisters." At times, the goal was as much about using oral history as a means of consciousness-raising, empowerment, and change as it was about generating new knowledge; indeed, flushed with the excitement of opening the new field of women's history, interviewers tended to take what narrators said at face value—not, it must be said, an entirely inappropriate response for people who had too often been historically silent, or silenced (Anderson & Jack, 1991; Bloom, 1977; Gluck, 1977; Oakley, 1981).

Practice and reflection challenged these rather naïve formulations (Armitage, 1983; Armitage & Gluck, 1998; Gluck & Patai, 1991): Documentation of "the female experience" often failed to account for social and ideological differences (Geiger, 1990). Empathy could be a manipulative ploy, resulting in unguarded revelations that were later regretted and unrealistic expectations for a continuing relationship with the interviewer (Stacey, 1991). Efforts to raise someone's consciousness could become a patronizing refusal to hear another's point of view. And failure to subject narrator accounts to critical analysis reflected what Frisch (1990a) has referred to as "anti-history"—a counterpoint to the "more history" approach noted earlier—by which he means viewing "oral historical evidence because of its immediacy and emotional resonance, as something almost beyond interpretation or accountability, as a direct window on the feelings and . . . [hence] on the meaning of past experience" (p. 160).

Recognizing that oral historians often share a broad sympathy with the people they interview and the intimacy that can develop in an interview, Yow (1997) has cautioned against "liking interviewees too much." Doing so can create an interview that is collusive, rather than searching: Hesitations, contradictions, and silences are not probed. Deeply painful memories are dismissed with ameliorative words. Cues to information that might shake the interviewer's positive view of a narrator are ignored. Challenging questions are not asked out of deference or to avoid an uncomfortable breach in mutual regard. To counter this tendency, Yow advocates a critical reflexivity, managing one's own emotional reactions to the narrator, challenging one's interests and ideological biases, thinking beyond the questions one intends to ask and developing alternative lines of inquiry.

Although not a concern of feminists exclusively, feminist oral historians were among the first to consider power relationships within the practice of oral history and, with colleagues addressing issues of race and ethnicity, have remained among the most sharply attentive to them (Coles, 1997; Gluck & Patai, 1991). How, they have asked, do knowledge production in oral history and the uses to which that knowledge is put reproduce unequal social relationship? Although doubts about "studying down" have somewhat attenuated over the years, it is still relevant to ask how the assumptions, questions, language, nonverbal cues, and modes of presentation of a relatively privileged interviewer can constrain a less privileged narrator. If scholars build careers based on recording and presenting life stories of others, however carefully and conscientiously they have pursued their work, it is still appropriate to ask how they might share some of the tangible rewards of that work with narrators and their communities. If oral history's much vaunted capacity to "give voice" assumes, naively, that narrators need the oral historian to find their voices, it is still useful to consider how, in the words of oral historian Alessandro Portelli (1997a, p. 69), we might responsibly "amplify their voices" within the public arena. If, as practice often demonstrates, a rough equality can exist within the bounded space of an interview, if indeed interviewees can retain the balance of power by deciding what to say and what to withhold, it is still useful to consider how one deploys power in presenting and interpreting the lives of those who have freely and in good faith shared them with us. Oral historians (James, 2000a; Kerr, 2003; Rouverol, 2003; Sitzia, 2003) continue to confront these questions, negotiating uneasy compromises with narrators, alternating their own interpretive voice with narrators' voices; sometimes letting narrators have their say with little comment sometimes deploying interviews within the context of their own narrative.

As a result of the range and depth of work in oral history since the 1960s, it has attained broad academic acceptance and the credibility it lacked in earlier years. Of course, the evidentiary value of oral history still had its critics. Historian Louise Tilly (1985, p. 41), with a bias toward quantitative evidence, referred to personal testimony, with its emphasis on the individual, as "ahistorical and unscientific."[5] Oral history has also shared in the critique of social history as overly concerned with the quotidian details of everyday life, celebratory of individual agency, and insufficiently attentive to ways the structures of power and relations of inequality constrain action. And local oral history work can be parochial and laced with nostalgia (Shopes, 1986, 2002a). Nonetheless, the dominance of social history during the 1970s and 1980s muted much of the earlier criticism, and we might summarize the two outstanding achievements of oral history in the democratic mode as restoring to our collective record of the past the voices of the historiographically—if not historically—silent and as providing a medium of exchange between the academy and communities.

Although the intent and topics of oral history interviews had shifted by the 1970s and the venues for practice broadened, as a source they were generally viewed much as they had always been, as transparent documents in the positivist tradition, purveyors of facts that were adjudged to be either true or false. Some oral historians, however, were gradually beginning to understand that something more was going on in an interview: that what a narrator said had something to do with the questions posed, the mental set of both narrator and interviewer, and the relationship between them; that narrators were telling stories, compressing years of living into a form that was shaped by language and culturally defined narrative conventions; that memory was not so much about the accuracy of an individual's recall and about how and why people remembered what they did; and that an interview was in many ways a performance, one that demanded our moral attention.

From Document to Text: Oral History's Move to Interpretive Complexity

Identifying a single turning point in the way oral history is understood is impossible; change has come from practitioners operating in a variety of intellectual contexts and has reflected broader theoretical currents. In the United States, Frisch (1990c) was perhaps the first to raise questions about the particular kind of historical evidence oral history provides in a review of Studs Terkel's *Hard Times appearing* in 1972. Unlike many reviewers, who lionized the book as the pure voice of the people, Frisch found the stories of individual failure and collective survival troubling, leading him to ask, "At what distance, in what ways, for what reasons, and in what patterns do people generalize, explain, and interpret experience? What cultural and historical categories do individuals use to help understand and present a view of experience?" (p. 11). By opening up these sorts of questions, Frisch suggested "oral history . . . encourages us to stand somewhat outside of cultural forms in order to observe their workings. Thus it permits us to track the elusive beats of consciousness and culture in way impossible to do within" (p. 13). Grele (1991a) brought a similar sort of reflexivity to oral history in a number of essays first published in the 1970s. Among his many insights is the especially fruitful one that an interview is a conversational narrative that incorporates three sets of structures—linguistic, performative, and cognitive— and that an analysis of these structures tells us a good deal about what, in addition to the obvious communication of information, is going on in an interview. In what is perhaps the most cited article in the oral history literature, Portelli (1991) analyzed why oral accounts of the death of Italian steel worker Luigi Trastulli, who had been shot during a workers' rally protesting NATO in 1949, routinely got the date, place, and reason for his death wrong, placing it instead in 1953, during street fights following announcement of the firing of more than two thousand steel workers. He argued that narrators manipulated the facts of Trastulli's death to render it less senseless, more comprehensible, and politically meaningful to them, concluding that "errors, inventions, and myths lead us through and beyond facts to their meaning" (p. 2).

These three seminal works and others (Passerini, 1980, 1987; Tonkin, 1992) initiated a gradual shift in the way oral historians think about their work. They did not change the methods of oral history—who is interviewed, what they are interviewed about, or how interviews are used; these elements of oral history have remained broadly democratic. Rather, these works have led practitioners into more theoretical territory, to focus less on the content of what a narrator has said and more on the meaning embedded in or lying underneath the words. This approach to interviews—as opposed to interviewing—arose from close attention to the dialogic exchange that lies at the heart of an interview, as well as sustained engagement with the narratives generated. This approach also reflected broader intellectual trends of the last decades of the 20th century, including what has been termed "the linguistic turn" in scholarship, in which attention to the semiotic and the symbolic have come to challenge the positivist paradigm. An interpretive approach to oral history has been further stimulated by the growing internationalization of oral history, bringing U.S. oral historians into closer contact with the work of their more theoretically inclined continental colleagues. Beginning in

1979, oral historians from around the world have been meeting biennially under the aegis of what became formalized in 1989 as the International Oral History Association. Beginning in 1980, work presented at these meetings has been published in a series of journals and annual publications, including the influential *International Journal of Oral History* published from 1980 through 1990.

It is difficult to summarize what is a diverse, complex, sometimes dense literature, but at bottom is the notion that interviews are hermeneutic acts, situated in time. Meaning is conveyed through language, which in turn is shaped by memory, myth, and ideology and through nonverbal expression and gesture, which give both immediacy and emotional depth to the exchange and further command the listener's attention. Interviews thus offer clues into narrators' subjectivities, or more accurately, the play of subjectivities—the intersubjectivity—between narrator and interviewer. Understood in this way, interviews are not documents in the traditional sense, to be mined for facts, but texts, to be interpreted for ways narrators understand—and want others to understand—their lives, their place in history, the way history works.

These more theoretical approaches to oral history can perhaps be approached by considering several examples from both published work and actual interviews. Consider the dialogic nature of an interview, the way it is the product—or expression—of two people talking. Historian Thomas Dublin (1998) came to understand this quite pointedly as he was reviewing family photographs with a husband and wife he had interviewed previously about the decline of the anthracite coal mining industry in Pennsylvania: "I expressed surprise at seeing so many pictures taken on [Tommy's] hunting trips with his buddies. When I commented that I had not realized how important hunting had been in Tommy's life, he responded good-naturedly, 'Well, you never asked'" (p. 21). Eva McMahan (1989, 2006) spins out the meaning of "asking"—and answering—by proposing a Conversational Analytic Framework for understanding the way meaning is actively negotiated within the interview exchange. By looking closely at the way the conversation moves and the rules that govern it, McMahon argues, we are able to see how "the oral history interview interaction is constitutive" (2006, p. 348) of meaning, not simply a recording of facts. Her work opens up rich possibilities for a rigorous analysis of interview dynamics. More practically, it has informed a more self-conscious, disciplined approach to interviewing.

Because an interview is a communicative event, communication sometimes becomes difficult or breaks down, pointing to issues of cognitive and social dissonance. Julie Cruikshank (1990) and David Neufeld (2008) describe how their interviews with Native Alaskan and First Nations Canadian elders resulted in life stories that did not conform to Western notions of autobiography as a chronological, ego-centered narrative, but rather mixed personal history with mythic, highly metaphorical stories. For Cruikshank, the challenge was to negotiate cultural differences about what properly constitutes a life history; for Neufeld, it was integrating these parallel narratives into historical programs for Parks Canada. Daniel James (2000b) describes the way incongruent expectations, an aggrieved narrator seeking to tell his version of Peronism, and James's own instance on penetrating the narrator's obfuscations while withholding his own views, resulted in a frustrating exchange and what he viewed as an act of symbolic violence.

Sometimes, meaning can be construed from what is not said, from silences in an interview. Luisa Passerini (1980, 1987) demonstrated the way the absence of talk can be not the result of "never asking," but of broad cultural significance. Recording life histories of members of the Turin, Italy, working class, she found that narrators frequently made no mention of Fascism, whose repressive regime nonetheless inevitably affected their lives. Even when questioned directly, narrators tended to jump directly from fascism's rise in the 1920s to its demise in World War II, avoiding any discussion of the years of fascism's reign. Passerini interprets this as evidence on the one hand "of a scar, a violent annihilation of many years in human lives, a profound wound in daily experience" among a broad swath of the population and, on the other, of people's preoccupation with the events of everyday life—"jobs, marriage, children"—even in deeply disruptive circumstances (1980, p. 9).

Addressing the narrative qualities of oral history, Mary Chamberlain (2006) has assessed ways that an oral history interviewee (or narrator) represents experience through language, drawing on a vast and diverse cultural repertoire to describe, structure, and make sense of his or her lived experience in ways that are, of necessity, highly selective. Chronology (first this, then this) and causality (this → this), for example, often are used to structure oral history interviews in Western societies. Similarly, narrators frequently make themselves the hero (or antihero) of their own stories, which can be partly attributed to the fundamentally ego-centered nature of oral history, but also represents the modern valorization of the individual, of living purposefully, overcoming odds (or not), progressing (or not) through life, achieving resolution (or not).

Interpreting oral history as narrative means looking for underlying patterns of meaning within the interview. Karen Fields (1994), reflecting on interviews she conducted with her grandmother, has argued that what "Gram" was trying to communicate to her, through anecdotes, stories, and commentaries, was not so much knowledge about her life as a black woman in the Jim Crow South, but wisdom and counsel for how Fields herself could live honorably in the present.

Similarly, Linda Shopes (2002b) has developed the notion of iconic stories—concrete, specific stories embedded within the interview that "stand for" or sum up something the narrator reckons of particular importance. Often these are presented as unique or totemic events in the person's history, even as they include tropes common in folklore or popular culture. Grele (1991b) has analyzed closely the contrasting "structures of consciousness" present in interviews with two Jewish immigrants to New York, identifying "the particular vision of history articulated in [each] interview" (p. 213). It's not the content of the interview that interests him, but the way what's said conveys the broader ideological bases of the narrators' understanding of their personal pasts.

Oral history narratives thus connect the individual and the social, drawing on culturally agreed upon (or disputed) mental sets and modes of expression to tell one's story. These sets and modes are themselves deeply embedded in the culture: Portelli (1997b) notes how men tell war stories, women hospital stories, in both cases connecting their lives with gendered social experiences. Writing about the 1921 race riot in Tulsa, Oklahoma, Scott Ellsworth (1982) coined the phrase "segregation of memory" to describe the opposing ways Blacks and Whites remembered this gruesome event, the result of their own racialized experience of it. Alistair Thomson (1990) uses the ambiguous term "composure" to suggest a more complicated relationship between self and society is articulated in an interview: "In one sense we 'compose' or construct memories using the public language and meaning of our culture. In another sense we 'compose' memories, . . . which gives us a feeling of composure. . . . an alignment of our past, present and future lives. . . . The link between the two senses of composure is that the apparently private process of composing safe memories is in fact very public. . . . We compose our memories so that they will fit with what is publicly acceptable or if we have been excluded from general public acceptance, we seek out particular publics which affirm our identities and the way we want to remember our lives" (p. 25).

Thomson's use of the term "memories" to refer to the construction of narrative in oral history suggests how deeply implicated memory is in oral history, in both an organic and social sense. Oral history records accounts about the past, but the recording takes place in the present; memory is the bridge between the two. In line with the interpretive turn, oral historians have become less defensive about the evidentiary value of these memories and, drawing on the work of psychologists, have come to recognize that narrators do misremember: They collapse events, skew chronology, forget, and get details wrong; they "remember" as firsthand experiences what others, in fact, have told them and recall as true that which is false because they wish it to be so. Moreover, concerns about the reliability and validity of individual memories have become less important in recent years as, following Frisch's and Portelli's work, oral historians have turned concerns about accuracy on their head, recognizing that memories, like narrative, are highly social, expressive of ways the present mediates a narrator's recollection of the past and are generated within ideological, often politically charged contexts. Kim Lacy Rogers's (2006) interviews with veterans of the U.S. civil rights movement decades after their years of peak activism reveal a pervasive sense of disappointment and grief, as the movement's promise of equality has been only partially realized and economic and social distress continues to plague their communities. Portelli's (2003) study of a Nazi massacre in Rome and Susana Kaiser's (2005) work on postmemories of the military dictatorship in Argentina demonstrate ways oral history serves as a counter-memory of events that official histories have erased, distorted, or manipulated in service of a false consensus.

Theories of performance, drawn from both folklore and communications studies, have also informed the interpretation of oral history narratives. An interview is, most obviously, a performance for the interviewer, in which the narrator presents himself or herself as much through embodied movements— gesture, facial expressions, and the like—as through actual words, a fact that supports the use of video in interviewing. As Samuel Schrager (1983) has argued, an interview is also a cultural performance that looks both backward as a narrator relates well-rehearsed accounts of the past, told and retold to create a certain version of events, and forward, as he or she self-consciously speaks through the interviewer to "history," to the audience of future users whom he or she wants to inform, persuade, inspire. Jeff Friedman (2003), Della Pollock (2005) and others (Bauman, 1986; Denzin, 2003) have further theorized oral history as a doubly charged performance: the narrative encounter itself operates in the charged or liminal space between two people focusing their careful attention on each other to create something of value. It also charges the listener, first the interviewer, but then all who receive the interview, to pay attention, to witness, and also to act in ways that respond to the teller's story, sometimes through actual acting, that is via a dramatic production scripted from interviews and acted before an audience, and sometimes through acting in the world, with a moral vision inspired by the stories one has heard.

Although the interpretive approach to interview texts has dominated the discussion of oral history in recent years, it must be acknowledged that it has not been fully embraced by all who conduct or use interviews. In fact, most continue to consider oral history in the traditional documentary sense as one source among many or to highlight voices that have previously been muted in our collective understanding of the past. Some are concerned that a focus on the subjective, textual nature of interviews will obviate the need to triangulate them with other sources and assess their veracity; others that oral history will become more self-referential rather than remain the intellectually and socially expansive practice it has become. Still others are uneasy that critical analyses of interview texts create scholarly products that objectify narrators, distancing them from their own words. These are among the many questions in the field that remain open.

The Digital Revolution

Like the invention of movable type in the 15th century, digital media are transforming the culture, changing the ways we record and receive information; our scholarly practices, patterns of social interaction, and leisure pursuits; and, as some argue, the very way our brains work. And, like those living in the 15th century, we don't know where the digital revolution will lead, how the changes it is setting in motion will affect everyday practices and modes of thought, as well as the global economic, social, and political landscape. Oral historians share in both the transformations and uncertainty of the digital revolution.

Undoubtedly, digital media are transforming the way interviews are recorded, preserved, and accessed. Digital is now the preferred format for recording audio interviews, and some consensus exists on recording and preservation standards. However, given the rapid development of relatively easy to use, inexpensive video recording devices, video interviews are rapidly becoming the norm, though standards are less well established. It has been said that widespread access to the tools of digital media is making everyone a documentarian, creating a certain elasticity in what properly constitutes oral history, raising legitimate questions about quality, and requiring archivists to think anew about what sorts of materials have the potential for lasting significance to warrant acceptance from donors. Migration of analog recordings to digital format and the lack of metadata standards for cataloguing digital interviews are also concerns for those overseeing archival collections.

Perhaps the most significant impact of new technology on oral history to date is the remarkable access the Internet provides to interview collections (Grele, 2007; Thomson, 2007). Interviews once languishing in archives, used only by the occasional researcher, now are widely accessed by students and the interested public as well as by the scholarly community. Though generally heralded as a positive development, opportunities for misuse, violation of copyright, and unwelcome exposure to a vast audience, always present to a degree in oral history, have increased exponentially with Internet access. Likewise, the ethics of placing online interviews recorded in the pre-digital era for which the narrator gave no explicit permission for such "future use" is a continuing concern.

However, new media's impact on oral history extends to matters that are far more than technical; it can be argued that digital technology is shifting the terrain on which oral history has been practiced for the past six decades. Fundamentally, by allowing direct access to the primary document—the recorded interview—new media offer opportunities to restore the oral and the kinesthetic to oral history, and hence the layers of meaning communicated by tone, volume, velocity, pauses, and other nonverbal elements of oral communication, as well as the performative elements of the speaking body. Although oral historians continue to look forward to the development of sophisticated voice recognition software that will automate transcribing, some are also suggesting that direct access to digital audio and video recordings and the continuing growth of online publication may obviate the need for transcribing at all. Furthermore, the sonic and visual qualities of oral history interviews are grounded in the senses of hearing and seeing, which in turn are linked to neurophysiological receptors that trigger emotion. In short, hearing and seeing oral history interviews create a more emotional response in the user than does reading transcripts—a fact that enhances oral history's cultural power, connects it more deeply to the imaginative realm of the humanities, and challenges traditional notions of history as rational, critical inquiry.

Currently, some of the more creative work in oral history lies in the development of digital tools by means of which "the audio-video materials themselves—not the transcribed text version—can be searched, browsed, accessed, studied, and selected for use at a high level of specificity" (Frisch, 2006, p. 103). The implication is not simply greater access within and across interviews, but a "postdocumentary sensibility," that is, the displacement of "the authority of the mediating intelligence or documentary authorship . . . by a sharable, dialogic capacity to explore, select, order, and interpret" interview materials in an "ongoing, contextually contingent, fluid construction of meaning," (p. 113); in other words, a radical democratization of the ways oral history can be used. This nonauthoritative approach to using interviews can be further enhanced by emerging modes of user-driven indexing via tagging. Steven High and David Sworn (2009, pp. 2–3), themselves advocates of digital oral history, nonetheless recognize "indexing can also conflict with the basic ethos of oral historical research: far from giving voice to interviewees, indexing risks sundering and de-contextualizing their life stories, . . . occluding the anomalous and specific in favour of the crossreferentiality afforded by topics and themes that are common to all interviews."

Again, this sort of misuse of oral history is not new to the digital era; digital tools simply magnify enormously possibilities for doing so.

In these ways, new media are transforming oral history from an archival and research practice to a presentational one. Increasingly interviews are being conducted not to create a formal archive or to inform a research project, but to form the basis of a website devoted to a specific topic. Often this involves collaboration among diverse partners across disciplines and institutions; equally often, allied practices such as digital storytelling include active citizen participation. Although these shifts can further democratize an already democratic practice, they also threaten the depth, range, and especially the critical cast of archival oral history, as interviewers interview with an ear to the sound bite and interviewees speak more guardedly, mindful that their words no longer enjoy the protection of archival gatekeepers. These concerns too are neither new nor unique to oral history; still, new media place them front and center of the craft, even as oral historians share in larger debates about democracy and authority in a digital environment.

Legal and Ethical Issues in Oral History

Whereas legal issues in oral history can be understood as state-sanctioned rules for specific elements of practice, ethics refers to a higher standard governing the right conduct of relationships within the broad context of an interview or project. In his definitive *A Guide to Oral History and the Law*, historian and attorney John A. Neuenschwander (2009) outlines key legal issues in oral history: release agreements, related to ownership of the interview and copyright; subpoenas and Freedom of Information Act requests compelling the release of interviews; defamation; and privacy. All have important implications for oral history, but the two issues most commonly encountered are copyright, discussed earlier as a *sine qua non* of archival oral history, and defamation, defined as "a false statement of fact printed or broadcast about a person which tends to injure that person's interest" (p. 32). Insofar as "one who repeats or otherwise republishes defamatory matter is subject to the liability as if he had originally published it" (p. 33), any oral history project or program that makes available an interview that includes defamatory material is equally liable as the party making the original statement. Defamation is thus a serious issue for oral history, but it is also subject to several constraints and difficult to prove. For one, the injured party must be living—one cannot defame the dead; for another, statements construed as opinion, "nothing more than conjecture and rumor," are not considered defamatory.

Confronted with a potentially defamatory statement, the oral historian has several courses of action: consult other sources in an attempt to determine if the statement, however extreme, is, in fact, true—if it's true, it's not defamatory; close the defamatory portion of the interview until the defamed person has died; carefully edit the statement to excise the defamatory material while not significantly distorting the record; and delete the defamatory material—a problematic action that violates norms of academic freedom.

Legal issues, though at times complicated, are relatively straightforward when compared with ethical issues, which often require the exercise of judgment and involve matters over which conscientious practitioners may reasonably disagree. While there is a lively ethical narrative within oral history (Blee, 1993; K'Meyer & Crothers, 2007; Shopes, 2006), perhaps the best place to start to understand both fundamental ethical principles and some of the nuances is the Oral History Association's *Principles and Best Practices for Oral History* (2009). To generalize, these *Principles* define standards governing the oral historian's relationship to the narrator, to standards of scholarship for history and related disciplines, and to both current and future users of the interview. The first two of these relationships concern us here. Fundamental to the interviewee-interviewer relationship is the notion of informed consent—that is, that the interviewee is fully informed about the purpose, scope, and value of the interview; how it will proceed; its final disposition and the uses to which it will or may be put; and issues of copyright—in other words, everything the interviewee needs to know to make an informed decision about whether to consent to the interview—or not. Recognizing the rights of scholarship, that is, the second set of relationships, the *Principles* also state, "Interviewers must take care to avoid making promises that cannot be met, such as guarantees of control over interpretation and presentation of the interviews" (n.p.).

The *Principles* also recognize the dialectic quality of these dual allegiances and at least imply the potential for conflict: "Oral historians respect the narrators as well as the integrity of the research. Interviewers are obliged to ask historically significant questions . . . [and] must also respect the narrators' equal authority in the interviews and honor their right to respond to questions in their own style and language. In the use of interviews, oral historians strive for intellectual honesty and the best application of the skills of their discipline, while avoiding stereotypes, misrepresentations, or manipulations of the narrators' words" (2009, n.p.).

The problem arises when responsibility to the narrator conflicts with the claims of scholarship and the broader public good. One might easily imagine lines of inquiry that discomfit a narrator or that lead to revelations, intended or not, that might be construed as damaging to the narrator or to others. One might just as easily imagine a narrator who deliberately misrepresents the facts of a situation, for whom intellectual honesty is not a value. Or consider the example of film-maker Claude Lanzmann, who exposed perpetrators of the Nazi Holocaust by filming them with a hidden camera—verboten in oral history and other field-based practices—and then included their testimony in his epic film *Shoah*. Does the public's right to hold war criminals accountable trump Lanzmann's failure to secure informed consent? Or not? Standard professional practice, privileging the rights of the individual narrator, would claim that Lanzmann acted unethically; broader civic or moral claims would suggest otherwise.

Although extreme, the example of Lanzmann points to what many oral historians believe to be a fundamental incongruity between their practice and federal regulations governing the ethics of research involving human subjects, codified as Title 45 Public Welfare, Part 46 Protection of Human Subjects (referred to as 45 CFR 46 or the Common Rule), with authority for implementation residing in the Office for Human Research Protections at the U.S. Department of Health and Human Services and delegated to local, often campus-based institutional review boards or IRBs (Schrag, 2010; Shopes, 2009) In brief, 45 CFR 46 includes "interaction" with human subjects as one of the research modes subject to ethical review by an IRB review and hence has been applied to oral history. Although the terms of 45 CFR 46 also "exempt" most interviewing from IRB review, only an IRB can confer an exemption, in effect requiring a researcher to submit his or her research for review.

Most problematic, however, is language in the Common Rule, which does not exempt—and hence raises concern about—interviews for which "disclosure of the human subjects' responses outside the research could reasonably place the subjects at risk of criminal or civil liability, or be damaging to the subjects' financial standing, employability, or reputation" (46.101 [b] [2]). IRBs have used this language to ask oral historians to submit detailed questionnaires in advance of any interview; to avoid sensitive, embarrassing, or potentially incriminating topics; to maintain narrator anonymity despite an interviewee's willingness to be identified; and to retain or destroy interviews and transcripts after the research project is completed—all of which violate fundamental practices and principles of oral history. At times information in an interview, if made public, can indeed place a person at risk of criminal or civil liability, or be damaging to one's financial standing, employability, or reputation. To constrain such inquiry *a priori*, many oral historians argue, undercuts the "integrity of the research" and impinges on academic freedom. The Oral History Association, in concert with the American Historical Association, has attempted to negotiate a broader exclusion from IRB review of oral history, but efforts to date have been largely unsuccessful. At best, they have alerted college- and university-based oral historians and their IRBs—which enjoy considerable autonomy—to potential conflicts and encouraged informed dialogue and mutual accommodation.

It is perhaps appropriate to conclude this section, and this essay, with Portelli's (1997a, p. 55) observation about law and ethics, which aptly summarizes the impulses, simultaneously humanistic, scholarly, and political, underlying much work in oral history: "Ultimately, in fact ethical and legal guidelines only make sense if they are the outward manifestation of a broader and deeper truth sense of personal and political commitment to honesty and to truth. . . . By commitment to honesty I mean personal respect for the people we work with and intellectual respect for the material we receive. By commitment to truth, I mean a utopian striving and urge to know 'how things really are' balanced by openness to the many variants of 'how things may be.'"

Notes

*In developing this article, the author has drawn in part on the background paper on oral history she wrote for the Mellon Project on Folklore, Ethnomusicology, and Oral History in the Academy; and gratefully acknowledges the American Folklore Society, copyright holder of the report, for permission to draw on it. The full text of the report is available at http://www.oralhistory.org/about/association-business/

1. First use of the term *oral history* to describe the practice of interviewing participants in past events is generally attributed to Allen Nevins, founder of Columbia University's Oral History Research Office. Oral historians find the term maddeningly imprecise and debated its utility during the early years of the Oral History Association's existence. Nevins's successor Louis Starr wrote in 1974, "Heaven knows, oral history is bad enough, but it has the sanction of a quarter century's usage, whereas presumably more beguiling substitutes like *living history* and *oral documentation* and sundry other variants have gone by the boards. Oral history is a misnomer to be sure. Let us cheerfully accept that fact that, like *social security* or the *Holy Roman Empire,* it is now hopelessly embedded in the language: one encounters it on every hand" (Morrissey, 1980, p. 40).

2. Wire recorders, based on German Magnetophones captured during World War II, first became available in 1948; Columbia began using them to record interviews in 1949. They were supplanted by reel-to-reel recorders, then in the mid-1960s by cassette tape recorders, which became standard for oral history until the digital revolution at the end of the 20th century.

3. The 1968 document, titled *Goals and Guidelines* (Oral History Association, 1969), was considerably amplified as a checklist of "evaluation guidelines" in 1979, and revised

in 1990 and again in 1998 to take into account new issues and concerns, including new technologies and increasingly diverse uses of oral history. A thorough revision was undertaken in 2008–2009 to abbreviate and consolidate what had become a rather cumbersome document developed by accretion.

4. Editors of two oral history book series have estimated that releases had not been secured for perhaps one half of the interviews used in manuscripts they have reviewed.

5. For the full debate, see Tilly, "People's History and Social Science History" (1983); Thompson et al., "Between Social Scientists: Reponses to Tilly" (1985); and Tilly, "Louise Tilly's Response to Thompson, Passerini, Bertaux-Wiame, and Portelli" (1985).

References

Abrahams, R. D. (1981). Story and history: A folklorist's view. *Oral History Review, 9,* 1–11.

Allen, S. E. (1982). Resisting the editorial ego: Editing oral history. *Oral History Review, 10,* 33–45.

Anderson, K., & Jack, D. C. (1991). Learning to listen: Interview techniques and analyses. In S. B. Gluck & D. Patai (Eds.), *Women's words: The feminist practice of oral history* (pp. 11–26). New York: Routledge.

Armitage, S. H. (1983). The next step. *Frontiers: Journal of Women's Studies, 7*(1), 3–8.

Armitage, S. H., & Gluck, S. B. (1998). Reflections on women's oral history: An exchange. *Frontiers: Journal of Women's Studies, 19*(3), 1–11.

Atkinson, P., Coffey, A., & Delamont, S. (2003). *Key themes in qualitative research: Continuities and change.* Walnut Creek, CA: AltaMira Press.

Baum, W. K. (1977). *Transcribing and editing oral history.* Nashville, TN: American Association for State and Local History.

Bauman, R. (1986). *Story, performance, and event: Contextual studies of oral narratives.* Cambridge, UK: Cambridge University Press.

Blassingame, J. (1972). *The slave community: Plantation life in the antebellum South.* New York: Oxford University Press.

Blee, K. M. (1993). Evidence, empathy, and ethics: Lessons from oral histories of the Klan. *Journal of American History, 80,* 596–606.

Bloom, L. Z. (1977). Listen! Women speaking. *Frontiers: Journal of Women's Studies, 2*(1), 1–3.

Bodnar, J. (1985). *The transplanted: A history of immigrants in urban America.* Bloomington: Indiana University Press.

Bornat, J. (Ed.). (1993). *Reminiscence reviewed: Perspectives, evaluations, achievements.* Buckingham, UK: Open University Press.

Bruner, J. (1990). *Acts of meaning.* Cambridge, MA: Harvard University Press.

Butler, R. N. (1963). The life review: An interpretation of reminiscence in the aged. *Psychiatry, 26,* 65–76.

Chamberlain, M. (2006). Narrative theory. In T. L. Charlton, L. E. Myers, & R. Sharpless (Eds.), *Handbook of oral history* (pp. 384–407). Lanham, MD: AltaMira Press.

Coles, R. (1997). *Doing documentary work.* New York: Oxford University Press.

Cross, N., & Barker, R. (2006). The Sahel Oral History Project. In R. Perks & A. Thomson (Eds.), *The oral history reader* (2nd ed., pp. 538–548). London: Routledge.

Cruikshank, J. (1990). *Life lived like a story: Life stories of three Yukon native elders.* Lincoln: University of Nebraska Press.

Davis, S. G. (1988). Review essay: Storytelling rights. *Oral History Review, 16,* 109–116.

Densho: The Japanese American Legacy Project. (2010). Available from http://densho .org

Denzin, N. K. (2003). The call to performance. *Symbolic Interaction, 26,* 187–208.

Diaz, R. T., & Russell, A. B. (1999). Oral historians: Community oral history and the cooperative ideal. In J. B. Gardner & P. S. LaPaglia (Eds.), *Public history: Essays from the field* (pp. 203–216). Malabar, FL: Kreiger Publishing.

di Leonardo, M. (1987). Oral history as ethnographic encounter. *Oral History Review, 15,* 1–20.

Dolby, S. S. (1989). *Literary folkloristics and the personal narrative.* Bloomington: Indiana University Press.

Dublin, T. With photographs by G. Harvan. (1998). *When the mines closed: Stories of struggles in hard times.* Ithaca, NY: Cornell University Press.

Dubrow, G. L. (2008). Contested places in public memory: Reflections on personal testimony and oral history in Japanese American heritage. In P. Hamilton & L. Shopes (Eds.), *Oral history and public memories* (pp. 125–143). Philadelphia: Temple University Press.

Ellsworth, S. (1982). *Death in a promised land: The Tulsa race riot of 1921.* Baton Rouge: Louisiana State University Press.

Fields, K. E. (1994). What one cannot remember mistakenly. In J. Jeffrey & G. Edwall (Eds.), *Memory and history: Essays on recalling and interpreting experience* (pp. 89–104). Lanham, MD: University Press of America.

Friedman, J. (2003). Muscle memory: Performing embodied knowledge. In R. C. Smith (Ed.), *The art and performance of memory: Sounds and gestures of recollection* (pp. 156–80). London: Routledge.

Frisch, M. (1990a). Oral history, documentary, and the mystification of power: A critique of *Vietnam: A Television History.* In M. Frisch, *A shared authority: Essays on the craft and meaning of oral and public history* (pp. 159–178). Albany: SUNY Press.

Frisch, M. (1990b). *A shared authority: Essays on the craft and meaning of oral and public history.* Albany: SUNY Press.

Frisch, M. (1990c). Oral history and *Hard Times:* A review essay. In M. Frisch, *A shared authority: Essays on the craft and meaning of oral and public history* (pp. 5–13). Albany: SUNY Press.

Frisch, M. (2006). Oral history and the digital revolution: Toward a post-documentary sensibility. In R. Perks & A. Thomson (Eds.), *The oral history reader* (2nd ed., pp. 102–114). London: Routledge.

Geertz, C. (1974). "From the native's point of view": On the nature of anthropological understanding. *Bulletin of the American Academy of Arts and Sciences, 28*(1), 26–45.

Geiger, S. (1990). What's so feminist about women's oral history? *Journal of Women's History, 2*(1), 169–182.

Genovese, E. (1974). *Roll, Jordon, roll: The world the slaves made.* New York: Pantheon.

Gluck, S. B. (1977). What's so special about women? Women's oral history. *Frontiers: Journal of Women's Studies, 2*(1), 3–13.

Gluck, S. B. (1999). From first generation oral historians to fourth and beyond. *Oral History Review, 26*(2), 1–9. Printed as part of Gluck, S. B., Ritchie, D. A., & Eynon, B. (1999). Reflections on oral history in the new millennium. *Oral History Review, 26*(2), 1–27.

Gluck, S. B. (2006). Women's oral history. Is it so special? In T. L. Charlton, L. E. Myers, & R. Sharpless (Eds.), *Handbook of oral history* (pp. 357–383). Lanham, MD: AltaMira Press.

Gluck, S. B., & Patai, D. (Eds.). (1991). Introduction. In S. B. Gluck & D. Patai (Eds.), *Women's words: The feminist practice of oral history* (pp. 1–5). New York: Routledge.

Grele, R. J. (1991a). *Envelopes of sound: The art of oral history* (2nd ed.). New York: Praeger.

Grele, R. J. (1991b). Listen to their voices: Two case studies in the interpretation of oral history interviews. In R. J. Grele, *Envelopes of sound: The art of oral history* (2nd ed., pp. 212–241). New York: Praeger.

Grele, R. J. (2007). Reflections on the practice of oral history: Retrieving what we can from an earlier critique. *Suomen Antropologi, 4,* 11–23.

Handlin, O. (1951). *The uprooted: The epic story of the great migrations that made the American people.* Boston: Little, Brown.

High, S. & Sworn, D. (2009). After the interview: The interpretive challenges of oral history video indexing. *Digital Studies Le champ numerique, 1*(2), 1–24.

Hirsch, J. (2006). *Portrait of America: A cultural history of the Federal Writers' Project.* Chapel Hill: University of North Carolina Press.

Hirsch, J. (2007). Before Columbia: The FWP and American oral history research. *Oral History Review, 34,* 1–16.

Isay, D. (2007). *Listening is an act of love.* New York: Penguin.

Jackson, B. (2007). *The story is true: The art and meaning of telling stories.* Philadelphia: Temple University Press.

James, D. (2000a). *Doña Maria's story: Life history, memory, and political identity.* Durham, NC: Duke University Press.

James, D. (2000b). Listening in the cold: The practice of oral history in an Argentine meatpacking community. In D. James, *Doña Maria's story: Life history, memory, and political identity* (pp. 119–156). Durham, NC: Duke University Press.

Joyner, C. W. (1979). Oral history as communicative event: A folkloristic perspective. *Oral History Review, 7,* 47–52.

Kaiser. S. (2005). *Postmemories of terror: A new generation copes with the legacy of the "dirty war."* New York: Palgrave Macmillan.

Kerr, D. (2003). "We know what the problem is": Using oral history to develop a collaborative analysis of homelessness from the bottom up. *Oral History Review, 30*(1), 27–46.

Kerr, D. (2008). Countering corporate narratives from the streets: The Cleveland Homeless Oral History Project. In P. Hamilton & L. Shopes (Eds.), *Oral history and public memories* (pp. 231–251). Philadelphia: Temple University Press.

K'Meyer, T. E., & Crothers, A. G. (2007). "If I see some of this in writing, I'm going to shoot you": Reluctant narrators, taboo topics, and the ethical dilemmas of the oral historian. *Oral History Review, 34,* 71–93.

Larson, M. A. (2006). Research design and strategies. In T. L. Charlton, L. E. Myers, & R. Sharpless (Eds.), *Handbook of oral history* (pp. 105–134). Lanham, MD: AltaMira Press.

Lewis, H. M., Waller, S. M., & Hinsdale, M. A. (1995). *It comes from the people: Community development and local theology.* Philadelphia: Temple University Press.

Lundy, P., & McGovern, M. (2006). "You understand again": Testimony and post-conflict transition in the North of Ireland. In R. Perks & A. Thomson (Eds.), *The oral history reader* (2nd ed., pp. 531–537). London: Routledge.

MacKay, N. (2007). *Curating oral histories: From interview to archive.* Walnut Creek, CA: Left Coast Press.

Mazé, E. A. (2006). The uneasy page: Transcribing and editing oral history. In T. L. Charlton, L. E. Myers, & R. Sharpless (Eds.), *Handbook of oral history* (pp. 237–271). Lanham, MD: AltaMira Press.

McMahan, E. M. (1989). *Elite oral history discourse: A study of cooperation and coherence.* Tuscaloosa: University of Alabama Press.

McMahan, E. M. (2006). A conversation analytic approach to oral history interviewing. In T. L. Charlton, L. E. Myers, & R. Sharpless (Eds.), *Handbook of oral history* (pp. 336–356). Lanham, MD: AltaMira Press.

Minkley, G., & Rassool, C. (1998). Orality, memory, and social history in South Africa. In S. Nuttall & C. Coetzee (Eds.), *Negotiating the past: The making of memory in South Africa* (pp. 89–99). Oxford, UK: Oxford University Press.

Mintz, S. W. (1979). The anthropological interview and the life history. *Oral History Review, 7,* 18–26.

Morrissey, C. T. (1980). Why call it "oral history"? Searching for early usage of a generic term. *Oral History Review, 8,* 20–48.

Moss, W. (1977). Oral history: An appreciation. *American Archivist, 40*(4), 429–439.

Neuenschwander, J. A. (2009). *A guide to oral history and the law.* New York: Oxford University Press.

Neufeld, D. (2008). Parks Canada, the commemoration of Canada, and northern Aboriginal oral history. In P. Hamilton & L. Shopes (Eds.), *Oral history and public memories* (pp. 3–29). Philadelphia: Temple University Press.

Oakley, A. (1981). Interviewing women: A contradiction in terms. In H. Roberts (Ed.), *Doing feminist research* (pp. 30–61). London: Routledge & Kegan Paul.

Oral History Association. (1969). Oral History Association adopts statement about goals and guidelines during Nebraska Colloquium. *Oral History Association Newsletter, 3*(1), 4.

Oral History Association. (2009). *Principles and best practices for oral history.* Available at http://www.oralhistory.org/do-oral-history/principles-and-practices

Oral History Association. (2010). Available at www.oralhistory.org

Passerini, L. (1980). Italian working-class culture between the wars: Consensus for fascism and work ideology. *International Journal of oral History, 1,* 1–27.

Passerini, L. (1987). *Fascism in popular memory: The cultural experience of the Turin working class.* (R. Lumley & J. Bloomfield, Trans.). Cambridge, UK: Cambridge University Press.

Polkinghorne, D. (1988). *Narrative knowing and the human sciences.* Albany: SUNY Press.

Pollock, D. (2005). Introduction: Remembering. In D. Pollock (Ed.), *Remembering: Oral history performance* (pp. 1–17). New York: Palgrave Macmillan.

Portelli, A. (1991). The death of Luigi Trastulli: Memory and the event. In A. Portelli, *The death of Luigi Trastulli and other stories: Form and meaning in oral history* (pp. 1–26). Albany: SUNY Press.

Portelli, A. (1997a). Tryin' to gather a little knowledge: Some thoughts on the ethics of oral history. In A. Portelli, *The battle of Valle Giulia: Oral history and the art of dialogue* (pp. 55–71). Madison: University of Wisconsin Press.

Portelli, A. (1997b). Oral history as genre. In A. Portelli, *The battle of Valle Giulia: Oral history and the art of dialogue* (pp. 3–23). Madison: University of Wisconsin Press.

Portelli, A. (2003). *The order has been carried out: History, memory, and meaning of a Nazi massacre in Rome.* New York: Palgrave Macmillan.

Rawick, G. P. (1972). *From sundown to sunup: The making of the Black community.* Westport, CT: Greenwood Press.

Ritchie, D. A. (2003). *Doing oral history: A practical guide* (2nd ed.). New York: Oxford University Press.

Rogers, K. L. (2006). *Life and death in the Delta: African American narratives of violence, resilience, and social change.* New York: Palgrave Macmillan.

Rouverol, A. J. (2003). Collaborative oral history in a correctional setting: Promise and pitfalls. *Oral History Review, 30*(1), 61–86.

Samuel, R. (1971). Perils of the transcript. *Oral History: Journal of the Oral History Society, 1*(2), 19–22.

Schrag, Z. (2010). *Ethical imperialism: Institutional review boards and the social sciences, 1965–2009.* Baltimore: Johns Hopkins University Press.

Schrager, S. (1983). What is social in oral history? *International Journal of Oral History, 4*(2), 76–98.

Sharpless, R. (2006). The history of oral history. In T. L. Charlton, L. E. Myers, & R. Sharpless (Eds.), *Handbook of oral history* (pp. 19–42). Lanham, MD: AltaMira Press.

Shiekh, I. (2010). *Being Muslim in America.* New York: Palgrave Macmillan.

Shopes, L. (1986). The Baltimore Neighborhood Heritage Project: Oral history and community involvement. In S. Benson, S. Brier, & R. Rosenzweig (Eds.), *Presenting the past: Critical perspectives on history and the public* (pp. 249–263). Philadelphia: Temple University Press.

Shopes, L. (2002a). Oral history and the study of communities: Problems, paradoxes, and possibilities. *Journal of American History, 69*(2), 588–598.

Shopes, L. (2002b). Making sense of oral history. *History matters: The U.S. survey course on the web.* Available from http://historymatters.gmu.edu/mse/oral/

Shopes, L. (2006). Legal and ethical issues in oral history. T. L. Charlton, L. E. Myers, & R. Sharpless (Eds.), *Handbook of oral history* (pp. 135–169). Lanham, MD: AltaMira Press.

Shopes, L. (2009). Human subjects and IRB review (2009). Available at http://www.oral history.org/do-oral-history/oral-history-and-irb-review

Silverman, D. (Ed.). (1997). *Qualitative research: Theory, method and practice.* London: Sage.

Sitzia, L. (2003). Shared authority: An impossible goal? *Oral History Review, 30*(1), 87–102.

Slim, H., & Thompson, P. (Eds.) (1993). *Listening for a change: Oral history and development.* London: Panos.

Spence, D. (1982). *Narrative truth and historical truth: Meaning and interpretation in psychoanalysis.* New York: W. W. Norton.

Stacey, J. (1991). Can there be a feminist ethnography? In S. B. Gluck & D. Patai (Eds.), *Women's words: The feminist practice of oral history* (pp. 111–119). New York: Routledge.

Starr, L. (1984). Oral history. In D. K. Dunn & W. K. Baum (Eds.), *Oral history: An interdisciplinary anthology* (pp. 3–26). Nashville, TN: American Association of State and Local History.

Terkel, S. (1967). *Division Street: America.* New York: Pantheon Books.

Terkel, S. (1970). *Hard times: An oral history of the Great Depression.* New York: New Press.

Terkel, S. (1974). *Working: People talk about what they do all day and how they feel about what they do.* New York: New Press.

Terkel, S. (1984). *The good war.* New York: Pantheon Books.

Thompson, P. (1988). *The voice of the past: Oral history.* New York: Oxford University Press.

Thompson, P., Passerini, L., Bertaux-Wiame, I., & Portelli, A. (1985). Between social scientists: Reponses to Tilly. *International Journal of Oral History, 6*(1), 19–40.

Thomson, A. (1990). Anzac memories: Putting popular memory theory into practice in Australia. *Oral History, 18*(2), 25–31.

Thomson, A. (2007). Four paradigm transformations in oral history. *Oral History Review, 34*(1), 49–70.

Tilly, L. (1983). People's history and social science history. *Social Science History, 7*(4), 457–474.

Tilly, L. (1985). Louise Tilly's response to Thompson, Passerini, Bertaux-Wiame, and Portelli with a concluding comment by Ronald J. Grele. *International Journal of Oral History, 6*(1), 40–47.

Tonkin, E. (1992). *Narrating our pasts: The social construction of oral history.* Cambridge, UK: Cambridge University Press.

Vansina, J. (1985). *Oral tradition as history.* Madison: University of Wisconsin Press.

Yow, V. R. (1997). "Do I like them too much?" Effects of the oral history interview on the interviewer and vice versa. *Oral History Review, 24,* 55–79.

Yow, V. R. (2005). *Recording oral history: A guide for the humanities and social sciences* (2nd ed.). Walnut Creek, CA: AltaMira Press.

5

Observations on Observation

Continuities and Challenges

Michael Angrosino and Judith Rosenberg

Observation has been characterized as "the fundamental base of all research methods" in the social and behavioral sciences (Adler & Adler, 1994, p. 389) and as "the mainstay of the ethnographic enterprise" (Werner & Schoepfle, 1987, p. 257). Qualitative social scientists are observers both of human activities and of the physical settings in which such activities take place. In qualitative research, observations typically take place in settings that are the natural loci of activity. Such naturalistic observation is therefore an integral part of ethnographic fieldwork.

Naturalistic observation is a technique for the collection of data that are, in the ideal at least, as unobtrusive as possible. Even fieldworkers who think of themselves as participant observers usually strive to make the process as objective as possible despite their quasi-insider status. The notion of unobtrusive, objective observation has not, however, gone uncontested. The prescient, discipline-spanning scholar Gregory Bateson (1972) developed a "cybernetic" theory in which the observer is inevitably tied to what is observed. More recently, postmodernists in various disciplines have emphasized the importance of understanding researchers' "situations" (e.g., their gender, social class, ethnicity) as part of interpreting the products of their research.

The potency and pervasiveness of the postmodernist critique of traditional assumptions about objectivity have led some qualitative researchers to rethink

151

and revise their approaches to observational methods. In a very important sense, we now function in a context of collaborative research in which the researcher no longer operates at a distance from those being observed. The latter are no longer referred to as "subjects" of research but as active partners who understand the goals of research and who help the researcher formulate and carry out the research plan. Judith Friedenberg (1998, p. 169), for example, has advocated the solicitation of feedback on ethnographic constructions from study populations "using techniques that minimize the researcher's control of the interview situation and enhance intellectual dialog." Valerie Matsumoto (1996) sent a prepared set of questions for the people she was interested in interviewing for an oral history project. She assured them that any questions to which they objected would be eliminated. The potential respondents reacted favorably to this invitation to participate in the formulation of the research plan. As such situations have become the norm, Michael Angrosino and Kimberly Mays de Pérez (2000) advocated a shift away from thinking of observation strictly as a data collection technique; rather, it should also be seen as a context in which those involved in the research collaboration can interact.

To clarify that shift, it may be helpful to briefly review both the classic tradition of naturalistic observation and the more contextualized analysis of the research collaboration as it has developed in response to current challenges both academic (e.g., the postmodernist critique) and in the society that we aim to study.

Observation-Based Research: The Classic Tradition

The creed of the classic tradition of observational research was explained by R. L. Gold (1997, p. 397), who noted that researchers believed it was both possible and desirable to develop standardized procedures that could "maximize observational efficacy, minimize investigator bias, and allow for replication and/or verification to check out the degree to which these procedures have enabled the investigator to produce valid, reliable data that, when incorporated into his or her published reports, will be regarded by peers as objective findings." Ethnographers were supposed to adhere to a "self-correcting investigative process" that included adequate and appropriate sampling procedures, systematic techniques for gathering and analyzing data, validation of data, avoidance of observer bias, and documentation of findings (Clifford, 1983, p. 129; Gold, 1997, p. 399).

According to Gold (1958), the sociological ethnographers of the first half of the 20th century often made implicit reference to a typology of roles that might characterize naturalistic research: the complete participant (a highly subjective stance whose scientific validity was automatically suspect), the participant-as-observer (only slightly less problematic), the observer-as-participant (more typically associated with anthropologists), and the complete (unobtrusive) observer. The purity of the latter type—difficult to attain even under controlled laboratory conditions, let alone in the field—was, as we can now see, compromised by the tendency of unobtrusive researchers to go about their business without informed consent, an ethical lapse that can no longer be tolerated. It is now very clear that the ethical imperative to provide informed consent paved the way toward the model of collaborative research that is now the norm because the process of obtaining such consent inevitably involves the people being studied in activity of research from the very beginning. In any case, the canons of observational research were modified long before the advent of the postmodernist critique as an awareness of relative degrees of researcher "membership" in a community under study entered the discussion (Adler & Adler, 1987). Nevertheless, even researchers who were active "members" were still enjoined to be careful "not to alter the flow of interaction unnaturally" (Adler & Adler, 1994, p. 380). The underlying assumption remained: A "natural" flow of social life could exist independent of the efforts of researchers to study it.

Anthropological ethnographers were less concerned than were their sociological cousins with obtrusiveness and its attendant delict, observer bias. Anthropological ethnographers were, however, still encouraged to seek objectivity in the midst of their acknowledged subjective immersion in a study community, and they did so by engaging in a three-step process of observation. First, there was "descriptive observation," which meant, to all intents and purposes, the observation of every conceivable aspect of the situation. Anthropologists at this point were supposed to be "childlike," assuming that they knew nothing and could take nothing for granted. There was, in effect, to be no sorting out of the important from the trivial based on assumptions carried into the field setting. As researchers became more familiar with the setting, however, they could move to the second step, "focused observation," at which point they could with some confidence discern the relevant from the irrelevant. Focused observation almost always involved interviewing because researchers could not rely on their own intuition to make such discernments. Focused observations usually concentrated on well-defined types of group activities (e.g., religious rituals, classroom instruction, political campaigns). The third and final step was the most systematic— "selective observation"—at which point ethnographers could concentrate on the elements of social action that are most salient, presumably from the "native" point of view (Werner & Schoepfle, 1987, pp. 262–264).

Observation-Based Research in Light of Current Concerns

Contemporary fieldwork has three major attributes: (1) the increasing willingness of ethnographers to affirm or develop a more than peripheral membership role in communities they study; (2) the recognition of the possibility that it may be neither feasible nor possible to harmonize observer and insider perspectives to achieve an objective consensus about "ethnographic truth"; (3) the transformation of the erstwhile subjects of research into collaborative partners in research (e.g., Angrosino, 2007a; Creswell, 2007). The goal of contemporary observational research is not to replace the classic ideal of pure objectivity with one of total, membership-driven empathy. Both of these approaches remain as constituent elements in the process of observation-based research; they represent, however, extreme points at opposite ends of a continuum of research practice. The problem with both extremes is that they assume that it is both feasible and desirable to describe or interpret cultures and societies as if those depictions could exist without ethnographers being part of the action. Observation-based research nowadays must certainly consider the attributes and activities of ethnographers themselves; it is therefore considerably more subjective than those of the classic tradition would have countenanced. But it cannot become so utterly subjective that it loses the rigor of carefully conducted, clearly recorded, and intelligently interpreted observations; ethnography is more than casually observed opinion.

Angrosino and Mays de Pérez (2000, pp. 678–690) discuss the ways in which these factors have come to be established in the current ethnographic literature and the implications of these changes for both the conduct and the interpretation of observation-based research. They note that whereas classic ethnographic fieldworkers insisted on their objectivity and adopted limited participatory roles only as the ethics of "pure observation" were questioned, latter-day researchers consciously seek out and adopt situational identities that give them defined membership roles in the communities they study. As their membership roles deepen, ethnographers must become attuned to life as it is actually lived, which means that they must pay increasing attention to the ways in which their potential collaborators in study communities want to be studied. The older notion of imposing a predetermined "scientific" agenda (itself now often seen as a product of a Western, elite bias), which was so integral to the objective aims of the classic period, has been set aside. Although rarely acknowledged at the time, the classic approach was based on a model of interaction in which power resided in the ethnographer (who set the research agenda and implicitly represented the more generalized power of elite institutions); power is now clearly shared. In the case of certain applied or advocate social scientists, power is actually ceded to the study community; researchers of this orientation may well see themselves as agents of those communities in the same way that they once thought of themselves as extensions of their academic institutions or granting organizations.

The imperative to acknowledge the shift in power to study communities takes on particular importance when, as is now so often the case, ethnography is conducted "without the ethnos" (Gupta & Ferguson, 1996b, p. 2). In other words, few ethnographers function within the circumscribed communities that lent coherence to the cultures or societies that figured so prominently in the conceptual frameworks of the classic period of observational research. It is no longer possible to assume that "the cultural object of study is fully accessible within a particular site" (Marcus, 1997, p. 96). Much of the current "field" in which "fieldwork" is conducted consists of people who inhabit the "borders between culture areas," of localities that demonstrate a diversity of behavioral and attitudinal patterns, of "postcolonial hybrid cultures," and of the social change and cultural transformations that are typically found "within interconnected spaces" (Gupta & Ferguson, 1996a, p. 35). In the classic period, it was assumed that because people lived in a common space they therefore came to share social institutions and cultural assumptions. Nowadays, "it is the communities that are accidental, not the happenings" (Malkki, 1996, p. 92), particularly in the case of "virtual" communities that spring up, flourish, and then vanish—seemingly overnight—on the Internet. Ethnographers therefore no longer enjoy the luxury of assuming that the local scenes they observe are somehow typical or representative of any single culture or society. Rather, any observed community is more likely to be understood as a "nexus of interactions defined by interstitiality and hybridity" (Gupta & Ferguson, 1996a, p. 48). Researchers who depend on observation must therefore be increasingly careful not to confuse the shifting interactions of people with multiple affiliations in both real and virtual space as if they were the bounded communities of old. To take a clearly articulated membership role in such diffuse settings, a researcher must be willing to be explicit about his or her own gender, sexual identity, age, class, and ethnicity because such factors form the basis of his or her affinity with potential study collaborators, rather than the simple fact of hanging around in a defined space. These situational factors are likely to shift from one research project to the next, so ethnographers are in a position of having to "reinvent themselves in diverse sites" (Giroux, 1995, p. 197). Norman Denzin (1997, p. 46) discusses the "mobile consciousness" of ethnographers who are aware of their "relationship to an ever-changing external world."

Much of the recent literature bearing on the creation, maintenance, and evolution of observers' identities has dealt with issues particular to women and lesbians and gay men. (This literature is vast, but a few representative studies that demonstrate the blending of observational sociocultural detail with analysis of personal "situations" include Behar, 1993; Blackwood, 1995; Lang, 1996; Walters, 1996; D. Wolf, 1996.) It is worth mentioning, however, that there are other identity issues that are of concern to researchers who study situations of political unrest and who come to be identified with politically proscribed groups (Hammond, 1996; Mahmood, 1996; Sluka, 1990), or who work with groups that are defined by their need for deceptive concealment, such as illegal immigrants (Chavez, Flores, & Lopez-Garza, 1990; Stepick & Stepick, 1990), or those involved in criminal activities (Agar & Feldman, 1980; Brewer, 1992; Dembo et al., 1993; Koester, 1994; van Gelder & Kaplan, 1992). In the post–9/11 era, it has been increasingly difficult to conduct ethnographic research in Muslim American communities, particularly if the research deals specifically with young men (Sirin & Fine, 2008).

The Question of Context: The Overlapping Roles of Observational Researchers

In the classic period, ethnographers had to be concerned with only one audience—the academic/scientific community. Although that community could hardly be said to have spoken with one voice, it certainly did share a set of assumptions about what a proper research report looked and sounded like. In our own time, however, there seem to be as many different formats in which a report can be disseminated as there are constituencies to which ethnographers are now responsible. Researchers must therefore be concerned with the ways in which their observations come to be translated into the different voices suitable for multiple audiences. Traditional research reports favored the supposedly objective third-person voice, emanating from the "omniscient narrator" (Tierney, 1997, p. 27). The shift to collaborative research allows ethnographers to acknowledge their own presence; the once-banned "I" is now much more common as subjective experience comes to the fore, a trend apparently encouraged by feminist scholars who often felt marginalized by the academic world and its objectifying tendencies (M. Wolf, 1992, p. 52). This shift is no mere matter of stylistic preference; it reflects evolving self-images of ethnographers, changing relations between observers and those they observe (with explicit permission), and new perceptions about the diverse, and possibly even contradictory, audiences to whom ethnographic research is now addressed.

Ethnographers can no longer claim to be the sole arbiters of knowledge about the societies and cultures they study because they are in a position to have their representations read and contested by those for whom they presume to speak (Bell & Jankowiak, 1992). In effect, objective truth about a society or culture cannot be established because there are inevitably going to be conflicting versions of what happened. Researchers can no longer claim the privilege of authoritative knowledge when there are all too many other collaborators ready and able to challenge them. Margery Wolf (1992, p. 5) notes that as a fledgling ethnographer she was "satisfied to describe what I thought I saw and heard as accurately as possible, to the point of trying to resolve differences of opinion among my informants." She eventually came to realize "the importance of retaining those 'contested meanings.'" She wryly concludes that any member of the study community is likely to "show up on your doorstep with an Oxford degree and your book in hand" (1992, p. 137). In sum, the results of observational research can never be "reducible to a form of knowledge that can be packaged in the monologic voice of the ethnographer alone" (Marcus, 1997, p. 92). To be sure, given the complexities of publication and other genres for the dissemination of ethnographic research, it is still almost always the case that the researcher is the visible "author" of a report. Attempts to get the actual voices of all collaborators onto the public record have been spotty at best.

Observation-based research is not simply a data-collection technique; it forms the context in which ethnographic fieldworkers assume membership roles in communities they want to study. They do so in a process of negotiation with those who are already members and who might act as collaborators in the research process. They bring to that negotiation their own "situations" (i.e., gender, sexual orientation, age, social class, ethnicity), all of which must necessarily figure in the kinds of roles they might assume and the ways in which they will be allowed to interact with those already involved in the setting. For these reasons, naturalistic observation can only be understood in light of the results of specific interactive negotiations in specific contexts representing (perhaps temporary) loci of interests. The old notion that cultures or social institutions have an independent existence has been set aside. By the same token, neither cultures nor social institutions are reducible to the experiences of those who observe them. Observation, if it is to be useful to the research process, must be as rigorously conducted as it was in the classic period; our social scientific powers of observation must, however, be turned on ourselves and the ways in which our experiences interface with those of others in the same context if we are to come to a full understanding of socio-cultural processes. Former generations of researchers were certainly not unaware of these experiential factors, but they were taught always to be aware of them so as to minimize them and hold them constant against the ethnographic truth.

The autonomous, enduring culture that embodies its own timeless truth may, however, no longer be an operative concept. After all, a researcher "never observes the behavioral event which 'would have taken place' in his or her absence, nor hears an account identical with that which the same narrator would have given to another person" (Behar, 1996, p. 6), so how could we ever be sure of that disembodied cultural reality? But the ways in which we as researchers negotiate the shifting sands of interaction, if we are careful to observe and ana-lyze them, are important clues to the ways in which societies and culture form, maintain themselves, and eventually dissolve. In other words, the contexts may be evanescent, but the ways in which those contexts come to be may well repre-sent enduring processes of human interaction.

Current Challenges for Observation-Based Researchers

The context of contemporary observation-based research is shaped by the situ-ational characteristics of the researchers themselves and their potential collabo-rators, and by several important changes in the general intellectual climate, in academic culture, and in the nature of an increasingly globalized, seemingly borderless society. These issues have been dealt with elsewhere by Angrosino (2007a, 2007b). Only a few of these trends, those with perhaps the most direct bearing on the conduct of observation-based research, will be summarized here.

ETHICAL/REGULATORY CONSTRAINTS

It has been noted that the old ideal of purely objective observation ultimately ran afoul of a new ethical climate that privileged informed consent and confi-dentiality to the extent that these principles were encoded in guidelines and institutional structures governing the conduct of research funded by public moneys—which, in the contemporary context, is just about everything. The early history of research ethics is covered by Murray Lionel Wax and Joan Cassell

(1979). The contemporary scene is covered by Carolyn Fluehr-Lobban (2003). A few of the highlights are discussed here.

Virtually all social research in our time is governed by the structure of institutional review boards (IRBs), which grew out of federal regulations beginning in the 1960s that mandated informed consent for all those participating in federally funded research. The perceived threat was from "intrusive" research (usually biomedical), participation in which was to be under the control of the "subjects," who had a right to know what was going to happen to them and to agree formally to all provisions of the research. They must be fully apprised of both direct benefits and potential risks (including risks to their privacy) entailed in the research. (See the National Commission for the Protection of Human Subjects of Biomedical and Behavioral Research, 1979.) The right of informed consent, and the review boards that were eventually created to enforce it at each institution receiving federal moneys, radically altered the power relationship between researcher and "subject," allowing both parties to have a say in the conduct and character of research.

Ethnographic researchers, however, were initially uncomfortable with this situation—not, of course, because they wanted to conduct covert, harmful research, but because they did not believe that their research was "intrusive." Such a claim was of a piece with the assumptions typical of the observer-as-participant role. As ethnographers became more comfortable with more engaged participatory roles, they came to agree that their very presence was an occasion of change, although they continued to resist the notion that their "intrusion" was by definition harmful. Ethnographers were also concerned that the proposals sent to IRBs had to be fairly complete, so that all possibilities for doing harm might be adequately assessed. Their research, they argued, often grew and changed as it went along and could not always be set out with the kind of predetermined specificity that the legal experts seemed to expect (and that has always been appropriate in biomedical and other forms of clinical/experimental research).

In the 1980s, social scientists won from the federal Department of Health and Human Services an exemption from review for all social research except that dealing with children, people with disabilities, and others defined as members of "vulnerable" populations. Nevertheless, legal advisers at many universities (including the University of South Florida [USF] where both the authors have been based) have opted for caution and have been very reluctant to allow this near-blanket exemption to be applied. As a result, at USF it is possible for a proposal to undergo "expedited" (or "partial") review if it seems to meet the federal criteria for exemption, but a formal proposal must still be filed. This practice is required under guidelines promulgated by the U.S. Department of Health and

Human Services in 2005 (Code of Federal Regulations, Title 45, Part 46) (see Office of the Federal Register, 2009).

USF now has two IRBs—one for biomedical research and one for "behavioral research." Because the latter is dominated by psychologists (by far the largest department in the social science division of the College of Arts and Sciences), this separate status rarely works to the satisfaction of qualitative researchers. Psychologists, used to dealing with hypothesis-testing, experimental, clinical/lab-based research, have been reluctant to recognize a subcategory of "observational" research design. As a result, the proposal format currently required by the behavioral research IRB is couched in terms of the individual subject rather than in terms of populations or communities, and it mandates the statement of a hypothesis to be tested and a "protocol for the experiment." Formats more congenial to the particular needs of qualitative researchers have not been fully explored or adopted at USF. It is perhaps plausible to maintain that qualitative research is really a species of humanistic scholarship and not "science" at all, social or otherwise. If qualitative inquiry is not "research" in the scientific sense, it must be automatically exempt from IRB oversight. This point of view, however, has not gained much traction. For one thing, qualitative researchers are, on the whole, unwilling to give up their scientific status. Moreover, they are unwilling to reinforce the suspicion that they are simply trying to evade their ethical responsibilities. The trick is to comply with currently accepted ethical standards without compromising the very premises of qualitative inquiry. But this form of inquiry as currently practiced really does confound traditional definitions of scientific research. For one thing, the kind of "collaborative" research currently in favor among qualitative researchers further militates against strict compliance with the guidelines for informed consent. In collaborative research, the ethnographer must discuss research plans with members of the prospective study community, so must these preliminary discussions also conform to norms of informed consent, or do the latter only apply to the formal research plans that ultimately emerge from the collaborative consultations?

Given the now widespread ethical suspicions about "pure" observational research, it is ironic that the only kind of social research that is explicitly mentioned and routinely placed in the "exempt" category at USF is that of observations of behavior in public spaces. But it was just this sort of "unobtrusive" observation that led to questions about the propriety of conducting research in the absence of informed consent in the first place. Having largely abandoned this genre of "public" research because of its ethical problems, will ethnographers return to it simply to avoid the philosophical and legal entanglements raised by the IRB structure for their kind of research?

A recent report from the Institute of Medicine (IOM, 2002), a body that one would think represents an old, established paradigm of research ethics, challenged researchers in all disciplines to rethink the fundamentals of research ethics. Its report pointed out that we have become used to asking basically negative questions (e.g., what is misconduct? how can it be prevented?). It might be preferable to consider the positive and ask, What is integrity? How do we find out whether we have it? How can we encourage it? The promotion of researcher integrity has both individual and institutional components, and those in charge of monitoring professional ethics should be in the business of "encouraging individuals to be intellectually honest in their work and to act responsibly, and encouraging research institutions to provide an environment in which that behavior can thrive" (Grinnell, 2002, p. B15). One possible way to accomplish this aim, constructed on a philosophy of "proportionate reason," was explored by Angrosino and Mays de Pérez (2000). The IOM went so far as to suggest that qualitative social researchers have a central role to play in the evolution of the structures of research ethics because they are particularly well equipped to conduct studies that could identify and assess the factors influencing integrity in research in both individuals and large social institutions.

THE CHANGING RESEARCH CONTEXT: TECHNOLOGY

Participant observation once implied a lone researcher working in a self-contained community, armed only with a notebook and pen, and perhaps a sketch pad and a simple camera. The mechanics of observation-based research were revitalized by the introduction of audiotape recorders, movie cameras, and later video recorders. Note-taking has been transformed by the advent of laptop computers and software programs for the analysis of narrative data. But as our technological sophistication has increased, ethnographers have begun to realize that the technology helps us capture and fix "reality" in ways that are somewhat at variance with our lived experience as fieldworkers. The great value of naturalistic observation has always been that we have immersed ourselves in the ebb and flow, in the ambiguities of life as it is lived by real people in real circumstances. To that traditional perception we have now become increasingly aware of our own part in that ever-changing interactive context. But the more we fix this or that snapshot of that life and the more we have the capacity to disseminate this or that image globally and instantaneously, the more we risk violating our sense of what makes real life so particular and therefore so endlessly fascinating. Video recording (still or moving) poses definite challenges to the ethical norms of the protection of privacy and the maintenance of confidentiality, issues explored in detail by Lauren Clark and Oswald Werner (1997) and Werner and Clark (1998).

It may, perhaps, become necessary to turn our observational powers on the very process of observation, to understand ourselves as users of technology. Technological change is never merely additive; it is never simply an aid to doing what has always been done. It is, rather, *ecological* in the sense that a change in one aspect of behavior has ramifications throughout the entire system of which that behavior is a part. So the more sophisticated our technology, the more we change the way we do business. We need to begin to understand not only what happens when "we" encounter "them," but when "we" do so with a particular kind of powerful technology. That we possess this technology (and the means to use it) while many of our likely research collaborators do not means that the power differential—which the shift to collaborative research was supposed to ameliorate—has only been exacerbated. (See Nardi & O'Day, 1999, for an elaboration of these points.)

THE CHANGING RESEARCH CONTEXT: GLOBALIZATION

Globalization is the process by which capital, goods, services, labor, ideas, and other cultural forms move freely across international borders. In our own time, communities that once existed in some degree of isolation have been drawn into interdependent relationships that extend around the globe. Globalization has been facilitated by the growth of information technology. News from all corners of the world is instantaneously available. Although once we could assume that the behaviors and ideas we observed or asked about in a particular community were somehow indigenous to that community, now we must ask literally where in the world they might have come from. Aihwa Ong and Stephen Collier (2005) provide an extended treatment of the implications of globalization on social research in general, and ethnographic research in particular. A few highlights are summarized here.

Communities are no longer necessarily place-bound, and the traditional influences of geography, topography, and climate are much less fixed than in days past. Increasing numbers of people are now explicitly "transnational" in their orientation, migrating from homeland to other places for work or study, but maintaining their ties to home. Such constant movement was difficult for earlier generations of migrants to achieve, as the high cost and relative inefficiency of earlier modes of transportation and communication were prohibitive for all but the most affluent. Doing observation-based research in a "transnational" community presents obvious challenges. We could, of course, contrive to follow people around the globe, but doing so hardly seems practical in most cases. More often than not, we will continue to be place-bound researchers, but we will have to keep reminding ourselves that the "place" we are participating in and observing may no longer be the total social or cultural reality for all the people who are in some way or another affiliated with the community.

We can discern several aspects of the modern world that may help us take observational research beyond the small, traditional communities in which it developed. For one thing, we can now speak in terms of a world in which nations are economically and politically interdependent. The relationships of units within this global system are shaped in large measure by the global capitalist economy, which is committed to the maximization of profits rather than to the satisfaction of domestic needs. Some settings and events that might be studied by observational methods to contribute to our understanding of the global system include the nature of labor migration (Zuniga and Hernandez-Léon, 2001); the emergence of "outsourcing" and its impact on the traditional societies that are thus brought into the world of the dominant powers (Saltzinger, 2003); the transformation of the old Soviet sphere of influence (Wedel, 2002); and the dynamics of cultural diversity, multiculturalism, and culture contact (Maybury-Lewis, 2002). In the modern world, people are less defined by traditions of "high culture" and more likely to be influenced (and to be drawn together as a global "community") by popular culture. The study of popular culture has been a staple of "cultural studies" for some time, and it is now well established in the mainstream disciplines as well (Bird, 2003; Fiske & Hartley, 2003).

THE CHANGING RESEARCH CONTEXT: VIRTUAL WORLDS

If they so choose, ethnographers can free themselves of "place" by means of the Internet—the "location" for so many of the most interesting communities on the contemporary scene. Virtual communities are characterized not by geographic proximity or long-established ties of heritage, but by computer-mediated communication and online interaction. They are "communities of interest" rather than communities of residence. Although some can last a while, they are mostly ephemeral in nature, and sometimes even by design.

Ethnography has demonstrably been carried out online (Jordan, 2009) although the nature of observation is necessarily somewhat altered. Living online is a 21st-century commonplace, and ethnography can certainly move into cyberspace along with the technology. Some cautions, however, are in order.

First, electronic communication is based almost exclusively on the written word, or on deliberately chosen images. The ethnographer who is used to "reading" behavior through the nuances of gesture, facial expression, and tone of voice is therefore at something of a disadvantage. Moreover, it is very easy for people online to disguise their identities; sometimes the whole purpose of participating in an online group is to assume a new identity. This is not to suggest that all individuals who may be found in virtual communities are engaging in deception. Indeed, members of such communities are all members of nonvirtual human organizations as well. Brigitte Jordan (2009) advances the paradigm of hybrid spaces, wherein the real and virtual personae of the members of online communities are considered.

A potential advantage to the use of the Internet as a vehicle for qualitative research is the potential for access to individuals who are reluctant to communicate directly. Russel Ayling and Avril Mewes (2009) describe Internet interviewing with gay men as one example of this process, although this advantage might also apply to other groups requiring or preferring concealment.

Using online interactions as a source of "observation" does, however, present certain challenges. For example, online conversations may well have deeply nuanced subtexts that depart markedly from the superficial meaning of the typed words. In the case of face-to-face conversations, a researcher can observe gestures, body language, use of space, and intonation patterns to go beneath the surface of the discourse. Other cues are almost certainly available to online in-groups, so it is imperative that researchers develop an understanding of the full range of communicative strategies available to members of a virtual community so that they do not rely on the words alone. Angela Garcia et al. (2009) cite an example of an online study of "skinheads" in which it was observed that the participants had established techniques for the conveyance of physicality, emotion, and feelings.

But are virtual communities really all that similar to traditional communities or social networks? How does electronic communication bring new communities into existence even as it enhances the ways in which older, established communities, now geographically dispersed, can keep in touch? Such questions lead us to the possibilities of research about specific people and their lives, as well as about the larger processes by which people define their lives.

Virtual ethnography also poses some ethical challenges that are similar to, but not exactly the same as, those that confront the fieldworker in traditional communities. The accepted norms of informed consent and protection of privacy and confidentiality continue to be important, even though we are dealing with people we do not see face-to-face. Although the Internet is a kind of public space (which means it might, in theory at least, be exempt from IRB rules), the people who "inhabit" it are still individuals entitled to the same rights as people in more conventional places. There are as yet no comprehensive ethical guidelines applicable to online research, but a few principles seem to be emerging by consensus. First, research based on content analysis of a public website need not pose an ethical problem, and it is *probably* acceptable to quote passages posted on public message boards, as long as they are not attributed to identifiable correspondents. Second, members of an online community should be informed if an ethnographer is also online "observing" their activities for research purposes. If at all possible, the researcher should obtain "signed" informed consent forms from the members before continuing to be an observing presence on the site. Doing so might be impossible if a site attracts transient users; it remains to be decided whether informing the webmaster alone is sufficient. Members of a virtual community under observation should be assured that the researcher will not use real names (or identifiable made-up names), e-mail addresses, or any other identifying markers in any publications based on the research. If the online group has posted its rules for entering and participating, those norms should be honored by the researcher, just as he or she would respect the values and expectations of any other community in which he or she intended to act as a participant observer. By conforming to those posted rules, the researcher is, in effect, drawing the members into a collaborative circle; the research is as much a result of the community's practices as it is of the researcher's agenda. Some online ethnographers have also decided to share drafts of research reports for comment by members of the virtual community. By allowing members to help decide how their comments are to be used, the researcher furthers the goals of collaborative research. Because researchers working in cyberspace are operating with social formations that are much potential as existing in current real time (that is, they are perpetually "under construction"), an ethical posture that is active and anticipatory is needed, in contrast to the essentially reactive ethics of prior forms of research (Hakken, 2003).[1]

The Search for Social Justice

The new contexts and challenges for observational research in our time as discussed earlier take on particular significance when researchers aim to move beyond academic discourse and use the fruits of their research to make an appreciable change in the world. As Norman Denzin and Michael Giardina

(2009, p. 11) insist, this is a "historical present that cries out for emancipator visions, for visions that inspire transformative inquiries, and for inquiries that can provide the moral authority to move people to struggle and resist oppression." Observation-based research can certainly play a role in the pursuit of an agenda of human rights-oriented social justice, if only by producing vivid, evocative descriptive analyses of situations (such as those reviewed in the previous section of this article) that can serve a consciousness-raising function. To the extent that observational research is conducted in a participatory/collaborative mode, it can empower formerly "voiceless" people and communities. To the extent that the fruits of such research are widely disseminated through multiple media (not just the traditional academic outlets) in ways that express the multivocalic nature of the research process, those formerly voiceless communities are able to participate in a variety of public forums in which their non-mainstream positions can be effectively aired.

Angrosino (2005, p. 739) has defined *social justice* as the obligation of all people to apply moral principles to the systems and institutions of society; individuals and groups who seek social justice should take an active interest in necessary social and economic reforms. To that end, I have suggested three ways in which researchers can make a contribution to the pursuit of social justice.

First, the researcher should be directly connected to those marginalized by mainstream society; that is, the researchers should feel some sort of kinship (be it political or emotional) with those being studied and not treat them solely as depersonalized objects of research. There may certainly be communities of people who are deservedly marginalized, and social justice is certainly not served by having ethnographers directly connected to, say, White supremacists or purveyors of child pornography. (It is certainly possible to argue that we cannot tell researchers which groups they can or cannot empathize with. But since the codes of professional ethics associated with the various social science disciplines all emphasize an adherence to standards of human rights, it seems fair to conclude that if researchers choose to affiliate with groups that exist explicitly to violate the rights of others, then they do so outside the limits of accepted ethical professional practice.) There is, however, no shortage of communities of people marginalized because of the structures of oppression built into the current economic and political world system. Helping them might well involve intensive study of power elites, but a progressive agenda goes by the boards if the researcher comes to identify with those elites and sees the marginalized simply as "target populations" for policies and programs formulated on high. Direct connection necessarily involves becoming part of the everyday life of a marginalized community. Research in service to a progressive agenda flows from a degree of empathy (not simply "rapport," as traditional ethnographers might have defined it) that is not available to those who strive to maintain an objective distance.[2]

Second, the researcher should ask questions and search for answers. This might seem like such an obvious piece of advice that it hardly seems worth discussing. But we are in the habit of asking questions based primarily of our scholarly (i.e., distanced) knowledge of the situation at hand. We move in a more productive direction if we begin to ask questions based on our experience of life as it is actually experienced in the community under study. By the same token, we must avoid the sentimental conclusion that "the people" have all the answers, as if poverty and oppression automatically conferred wisdom and foresight. Asking the relevant questions might lead us to look within the community for answers drawing on its own untapped (and perhaps unrecognized) resources, or it might lead us to explore options beyond the community. One very effective role for the committed collaborative researcher might be that of culture broker, putting people in the study community in touch with other circles of interest to which they might not otherwise have had access.

Third, the researcher should become an advocate, which might mean becoming a spokesperson for causes and issues already defined by the community. It might also mean helping the people discern and articulate issues that may have been unstated or unresolved to that point. Advocacy often means engaging in some sort of conflict (either among factions within the community or between the community and the powers-that-be), but it can also mean finding ways to achieve consensus in support of an issue that has the potential to unite. In either case, one ends up working *with* the community, rather than working *for* the community, which implies a more distanced stance.

The overall goal of this process is to empower the community to take charge of its own destiny—to use research for its own ends and to assert its own position relative to the power elite. A researcher may well retain a personal agenda (e.g., collecting data to complete a dissertation), but his or her main aim should be to work with the community to achieve shared goals that move it toward a more just situation. Such a philosophy can be difficult to convey to students or other apprentice researchers, and so it might be instructive to consider a form of pedagogy that, although not specifically designed for this purpose, certainly serves these ends.

"Service learning" is basically a way of integrating volunteer community service with active guided reflection. Although encouraging students to volunteer is certainly praiseworthy in and of itself, service learning programs give students the opportunity to study social issues from social scientific perspectives so they can understand what is going on in the agencies in which they are working. The combination of theory and action is sometimes referred to as *praxis*, and it is one way in which an engaged, committed, advocacy-oriented form of social science is carried out. Students do not simply carry out a set of tasks set by the agency—tasks that in and of themselves may not seem particularly meaningful but that take on very clear meaning when the students carefully observe the setting, the people, the interactions—in short, the total context in which those tasks are conducted. By combining academic learning with community service, students experience praxis—the linkage of theory and practice—firsthand (Roschelle, Turpin, & Elias, 2000, p. 840). Service learning was designed explicitly to reinvigorate the spirit of activism that energized campuses in the 1960s. Institutions that accepted this challenge formed a support network (Campus Compact) to develop and promote service learning as a pedagogical strategy. Service learning is now a national movement that has received recent additional public exposure in the form of the Clinton Global Initiative University. This nonpartisan project, founded by former President Bill Clinton, is designed to reach across college campuses and stimulate students to confront the challenges of pressing global issues (Clinton, 2008). It is the responsibility of concerned faculty to see that students have a service learning experience that expresses the three aspects of a social justice agenda as discussed earlier.

The philosophical antecedent and academic parent of service learning is experiential learning (e.g., cooperative education, internships, field placements), which was based on the direct engagement of the learner in the phenomenon being studied. The critical distinguishing characteristic of service learning is its emphasis on enriching student learning while revitalizing the community. To that end, service learning involves students in course-relevant activities that address real community needs. Community agencies are encouraged to take the initiative in defining their own needs and approaching the campus representatives to see if a group of students under faculty mentorship might be interested in helping them achieve their goals. Course materials (e.g., textbooks, lectures, discussions, reflections) inform students' service, and the service experience is brought back to the classroom to inform the academic dialogue and the quest for knowledge. This reciprocal process is based on the logical continuity between experience and knowledge. Anne Roschelle, Jennifer Turpin, and Robert Elias (2000) point out the critical importance of after-the-fact evaluation to ensure both a productive learning experience for the students and value to the community served. Elizabeth Paul (2006) argues for the inclusion of critical evaluation (or, perhaps more specifically, needs assessment) before the community-based effort to ensure that limited resources are most effectively applied.

The pedagogy of service learning reflects research indicating that we retain 60% of what we do, 80% of what we do with active guided reflection, and 90% of what we teach or give to others. The pedagogy is also based on the teaching of information processing skills rather than on the mere accumulation of information. In a complex society, it is nearly impossible to determine what information will be necessary to solve particular problems, especially those of intractable social inequalities. All too often, the content that students learn in class is obsolete by the time they obtain their degrees. Service learning advocates promote the importance of "lighting the fire" (i.e., teaching students how to think for themselves). Learning is not a predictable linear process. It may begin at any point during a cycle, and students might have to apply their limited knowledge in a service situation before consciously setting out to gain or comprehend a body of facts or the evolutionary development of a personal theory for future application. To ensure that this kind of learning takes place, however, skilled guidance in reflection on the experience must occur. By providing students with the opportunity to have a concrete experience and then assisting them in the intellectual processing of that experience, service learning takes advantage of a natural learning cycle and allows students to provide a meaningful contribution to the community (Marullo & Edwards, 2000).

It is important to emphasize that the projects that form the basis of the students' experience are generated by agencies or groups in the community, not by faculty researchers. These projects can be either specific one-time efforts (e.g., a Habitat for Humanity home-building effort) or longer-term initiatives (e.g., the development of an after-school recreation and tutoring program based at an inner-city community center). All such activities build on the fundamentals of observational research. Student volunteers gradually adopt membership identities in the community and must nurture their skills as observers of unfamiliar interactions to carry out the specific mandates of the chosen projects and to act as effective change agents. In this way, even service learning projects affiliated with courses outside the social sciences require students to become practitioners of observational research methods. At USF, service learning has been a key feature of a diverse set of courses, including an anthropology seminar on community development, a sociology course on the effects of globalization, an interdisciplinary social science course on farm-worker and other rural issues, a psychology course on responses to the HIV/AIDS epidemic, a social work course on racial and ethnic relations, and a business seminar on workplace communication and cultural diversity issues.

In sum, service learning affects the professional educator as well as the novice or student. Service learning is more than traditional "applied social science," which often had the character of "doing for" a community. Service learning begins with the careful observation of a community by a committed student adopting a membership identity; he or she goes on to an active engagement in and with the community in ways that foster the goals of a social justice-oriented progressive political and social agenda.

Prospects for Observation-Based Research: Are We in a Post-Postmodern Period?

Patricia Adler and Peter Adler (1994, p. 389) observed, "Forecasting the wax and wane of social science research methods is always uncertain." Nevertheless, it is probably safe to say that observation-based research is going to be increasingly committed to what Lila Abu-Lughod (1991, p. 154) called "the ethnography of the particular." Rather than attempting to describe the composite culture of a group or to analyze the full range of institutions that supposedly constitute the society, the observation-based researcher will be able to provide a rounded account of the lives of particular people, focusing on the lived experience of specific people and their ever-changing relationships. Angrosino (2005, p. 741) has expressed some doubt about the stability of the marriage between observation-based research and more positivistic forms of social science, but we are no longer so certain that a divorce is imminent, at least to the extent that there is an emerging consensus around a social justice agenda such that the disagreements are more about means rather than about the ends of research.

It also seems safe to predict that observation-based research, no less than any other genre of social research, will be influenced by changing technology and the inescapable presence of the online parallel world. Whether in the virtual world or the real world, observation-based researchers will continue to grapple with the ethical demands of their work. Those who seek "exemption" from the guidelines seem to be very much in the minority. On the other hand, the rise of a committed, social justice-oriented agenda means that ethical questions of an increasingly complex and vexing nature will continue to arise. A renewed framework for understanding research ethics, such as the one proposed by the IOM, may be one way to deal with this issue.

It seems clear that the once unquestioned hegemony of positivistic epistemology that encompassed even so apparently humanistic a research technique as observation has now been shaken to its roots by the postmodernist critique among other factors. But what lies beyond that critique? Postmodernists often seem to suggest that because absolute truth is an impossibility, any effort to take action is bound to be compromised by the situational biases of researchers and would-be reformers. But it is certainly possible to base sound reformist action on the foundation of the provisional truth that results in the negotiated contexts created by researchers and their collaborators in study communities, as the service learning experiment seems to demonstrate. The IOM-style reform of research ethics (see IOM, 2002, and the discussion thereof in an earlier section of this chapter) is also based on such provisional, negotiated, collaborative arrangements (rather than absolutist edicts from on high). It is clear in hindsight that we needed the postmodernist critique to help us rethink the assumptions of our traditions of research; it is equally clear that we now have the means to go forward with the fruits of our rethinking—if we but have the political will to do so.

Notes

1. The Association of Internet Researchers has produced a document on ethical practice (Ess & the AoIR Ethics Working Group, 2002), which may be a useful guide for those pursuing this type of research. See also Bruckman (2002).

2. As of this writing, the term *empathy* is at the center of a complex, but eye-opening political debate. We use the term here in a much more restricted sense, mainly to refer to the development of a researcher's primary commitment to the agenda of the community under study.

References

Abu-Lughod, L. (1991). Writing against culture. In R. G. Fox (Ed.), *Recapturing anthropology: Working in the present* (pp. 137–162). Santa Fe, NM: School of American Research.

Adler, P. A., & Adler, P. (1987). *Membership roles in field research.* Newbury Park, CA: Sage.

Adler, P. A., & Adler, P. (1994). Observational techniques. In N. K. Denzin & Y. S. Lincoln (Eds.), *Handbook of qualitative research* (pp. 377–392). Thousand Oaks, CA: Sage.

Agar, M., & Feldman, H. (1980). A four-city study of PCP users: Methodology and findings. In C. Akins & G. Beschner (Eds.), *Ethnography: A research tool for policymakers in the drug and alcohol fields* (pp. 80–146). Rockville, MD: National Institute on Drug Abuse.

Angrosino, M. V. (2005). Recontextualizing observation: Ethnography, pedagogy, and the prospects for a progressive political agenda. In N. K. Denzin & Y. S. Lincoln (Eds.), *The SAGE handbook of qualitative research* (3rd ed., pp. 729–745). Thousand Oaks, CA: Sage.

Angrosino, M. V. (2007a). *Doing ethnographic and observational research.* Thousand Oaks, CA: Sage.

Angrosino, M. V. (2007b). *Naturalistic observation.* Walnut Creek, CA: Left Coast Press.

Angrosino, M. V., & Mays de Pérez, K. A. (2000). Rethinking observation: From method to context. In N. K. Denzin & Y. S. Lincoln (Eds.), *Handbook of qualitative research* (2nd ed., pp. 673–702). Thousand Oaks, CA: Sage.

Ayling, R., & Mewes, A. J. (2009). Evaluating Internet interviews with gay men. *Qualitative Health Research, 19,* 566–576.

Bateson, G. (1972). *Steps to an ecology of mind: Collected essays in anthropology, psychiatry, evolution, and epistemology.* San Francisco: Chandler.

Behar, R. (1993). *Translated woman: Crossing the border with Esperanza's story.* Boston: Beacon Press.

Behar, R. (1996). *The vulnerable observer: Anthropology that breaks your heart.* Boston: Beacon Press.

Bell, J., & Jankowiak, W. R. (1992). The ethnographer vs. the folk expert: Pitfalls of contract ethnography. *Human Organization, 51,* 412–417.

Bird, S. E. (2003). *The audience in everyday life: Living in a media world.* New York: Routledge.

Blackwood. E. (1995). Falling in love with an-Other lesbian: Reflections on identity in fieldwork. In D. Kulick & M. Willson (Eds.), *Taboo: Sex, identity and erotic subjectivity in anthropological fieldwork* (pp. 51–75). London: Routledge.

Brewer, D. D. (1992). Hip hop graffiti writers' evaluations of strategies to control illegal graffiti. *Human Organization, 51,* 188–196.

Bruckman, A. (2002). *Ethical guidelines for research online.* Available at http://www.cc.gatech.edu/~asb/ethics

Chavez, L. R., Flores, E. T., & Lopez-Garza, M. (1990). Here today, gone tomorrow? Undocumented settlers and immigration reform. *Human Organization, 49,* 193–205.

Clark, L., & Werner, O. (1997). Protection of human subjects and ethnographic photography. *Cultural Anthropology Methods, 9,* 18–20.

Clifford, J. (1983). Power and dialogue in ethnography: Marcel Griaule's initiation. In G. W. Stocking, Jr. (Ed.), *Observers observed: Essays on ethnographic fieldwork* (pp. 121–156). Madison: University of Wisconsin Press.

Clinton, W. J. (2008). A new way for students and colleges to bring about global change. *Chronicle of Higher Education, 54*(25), A40.

Creswell, J. W. (2007). *Qualitative inquiry and research design: Choosing among five approaches* (2nd ed.). Thousand Oaks, CA: Sage.

Dembo, R., Hughes, P., Jackson, L., & Mieczkowski, T. (1993). Crack cocaine dealing by adolescents in two public housing projects: A pilot study. *Human Organization, 52,* 89–96.

Denzin, N. K. (1997). *Interpretive ethnography: Ethnographic practices for the 21st century.* Thousand Oaks, CA: Sage.

Denzin, N. K., & Giardina, M. D. (2009). Qualitative inquiry and social justice: Toward a politics of hope. In N. K. Denzin & M. D. Giardina (Eds.), *Qualitative inquiry and social justice* (pp. 11–52). Walnut Creek, CA: Left Coast Press.

Ess, C., & the Association of Internet Researchers (AoIR) Ethics Working Group. (2002). *Ethical decision-making and Internet research: Recommendations from the AoIR Ethics Working Group.* Available at http://www.aoir.org/reports/ethics.pdf

Fiske, J., & Hartley, J. (2003). *Reading television* (2nd ed.). New York: Routledge.

Fluehr-Lobban, C. (2003). Informed consent in anthropological research: We are not exempt. In C. Fluehr-Lobban (Ed.), *Ethics and the profession of anthropology* (2nd ed., pp. 159–178). Walnut Creek, CA: AltaMira Press.

Friedenberg, J. (1998). The social construction and reconstruction of the other: Fieldwork in El Barrio. *Anthropological Quarterly, 71,* 169–185.

Garcia, A. C., Standlee, A. J., Bechkoff, J., & Cui, Y. (2009). Ethnographic approaches to the Internet and computer-mediated communication. *Journal of Contemporary Ethnography, 38,* 52–84.

Giroux, H. A. (1995). Writing the space of the public intellectual. In G. A. Olson & E. Hirsh (Eds.), *Women writing culture* (pp. 195–198). Albany: SUNY Press.

Gold, R. L. (1958). Roles in sociological field observation. *Social Forces, 36,* 217–223.

Gold, R. L. (1997). The ethnographic method in sociology. *Qualitative Inquiry, 3,* 388–402.

Grinnell, F. (2002). *The impact of ethics on research.* Washington, DC: Institute of Medicine.

Gupta, A., & Ferguson, J. (1996a). Beyond "culture": Space, identity, and the politics of difference. In A. Gupta & J. Ferguson (Eds.), *Culture, power, place: Explorations in critical anthropology* (pp. 33–52). Durham, NC: Duke University Press.

Gupta, A., & Ferguson, J. (1996b). Culture, power, place: Ethnography at the end of an era. In A. Gupta & J. Ferguson (Eds.), *Culture, power, place: Explorations in critical anthropology* (pp. 1–32). Durham, NC: Duke University Press.

Hakken, D. (2003). An ethics for an anthropology in and of cyberspace. In C. Fluehr-Lobban (Ed.), *Ethics and the profession of anthropology* (2nd ed., pp. 179–195). Walnut Creek, CA: AltaMira Press.

Hammond, J. L. (1996). Popular education in the Salvadoran guerilla army. *Human Organization, 55,* 436–445.

Institute of Medicine. (2002). *Responsible research: A systems approach to protecting research participants.* Washington, DC: Institute of Medicine.

Jordan, B. (2009). Blurring boundaries: The "real" and the "virtual" in hybrid spaces. *Human Organization, 68,* 181–193.

Koester, S. K. (1994). Copping, running, and paraphernalia laws: Contextual variables and needle risk behavior among injection drug users in Denver. *Human Organization, 53,* 287–295.

Lang, S. (1996). Traveling woman: Conducting a fieldwork project on gender variance and homosexuality among North American Indians. In E. Lewin & W. L. Leap

(Eds.), *Out in the field: Reflections on lesbian and gay anthropologists* (pp. 86–110). Urbana: University of Illinois Press.

Mahmood, C. K. (1996). Why Sikhs fight. In A. Wolfe & H. Yang (Eds.), *Anthropological contributions to conflict resolution* (pp. 7–30). Athens: University of Georgia Press.

Malkki, L. H. (1996). News and culture: Transitory phenomena and the fieldwork tradition. In A. Gupta & J. Ferguson (Eds.), *Anthropological locations: Boundaries and grounds of a field science* (pp. 86–101). Berkeley: University of California Press.

Marcus, G. E. (1997). The uses of complicity in the changing mise-en-scene of anthropological fieldwork. *Reflections, 59,* 85–108.

Marullo, S., & Edwards, B. (2000). The potential of university-community collaborations for social change. *American Behavioral Scientist, 43,* 895–912.

Matsumoto, V. (1996). Reflections on oral history: Research in a Japanese-American community. In D. L. Wolf (Ed.), *Feminist dilemmas in fieldwork* (pp. 160–169). Boulder, CO: Westview Press.

Maybury-Lewis, D. (2002). *Indigenous people, ethnic groups, and the state* (2nd ed.). Boston: Allyn & Bacon.

Nardi, B., & O'Day, V. (1999). *Information ecologies: Using technology with heart.* Cambridge: MIT Press.

National Commission for the Protection of Human Subjects of Biomedical and Behavioral Research (1979). *The Belmont report: Ethical principles and guidelines for the protection of human subjects of research.* Washington, DC: U.S. Department of Health, Education, and Welfare.

Office of the Federal Register, National Archives and Records Administration, and U.S. Government Printing Office (2009). *Code of federal regulations.* Available from http:www.gpoaccess.gov/cfr

Ong, A., & Collier, S. J. (2005). *Global assemblages: Technology, politics and ethics as anthropological problems.* Malden, MA: Blackwell.

Paul, E. L. (2006). Community-based research as scientific and civic pedagogy. *Peer Review, 8,* 12–16.

Roschelle, A. R., Turpin, J., & Elias, R. (2000). Who learns from social learning? *American Behavioral Scientist, 43,* 839–847.

Saltzinger, L. (2003). *Genders in production: Making workers in Mexico's global factories.* Berkeley: University of California Press.

Sirin, S. R., & Fine, M. (2008). *Muslim American youth: Understanding hyphenated identities through multiple methods.* New York: New York University Press.

Sluka, J. A. (1990). Participant observation in violent social contexts. *Human Organization, 49,* 114–126.

Stepick, A., & Stepick, C. D. (1990). People in the shadows: Survey research among Haitians in Miami. *Human Organization, 49,* 64–77.

Tierney, W. G. (1997). Lost in translation: Time and voice in qualitative research. In W. G. Tierney & Y. S. Lincoln (Eds.), *Representation and the text: Re-framing the narrative voice* (pp. 23–36). Albany: SUNY Press.

van Gelder, P. J., & Kaplan, C. D. (1992). The finishing moment: Temporal and spatial features of sexual interactions between streetwalkers and car clients. *Human Organization, 51,* 253–263.

Walters, D. M. (1996). Cast among outcastes: Interpreting sexual orientation, racial, and gender identity in the Yemen Arab Republic. In E. Lewin & W. L. Leap (Eds.), *Out in the field: Reflections of lesbian and gay anthropologists* (pp. 58–69). Urbana: University of Illinois Press.

Wax, M. L., & Cassell, J. (1979). *Federal regulations: Ethical issues and social research.* Boulder, CO: Westview Press.

Wedel, J. (2002). *Blurring the boundaries of the state-private divide: Implications for corruption.* Available at http://www.anthrobase.com/Txt/W/Wedel_J_01.htm

Werner, O., & Clark, L. (1998). Ethnographic photographs converted to line drawings. *Cultural Anthropology Methods, 10,* 54–56.

Werner, O., & Schoepfle, G. M. (1987). *Systematic fieldwork: Vol. 1. Foundations of ethnography and interviewing.* Newbury Park, CA: Sage.

Wolf, D. L. (1996). Situating feminist dilemmas in fieldwork. In D. L. Wolf (Ed.), *Feminist dilemmas in fieldwork* (pp. 1–55). Boulder, CO: Westview Press.

Wolf, M. A. (1992). *A thrice-told tale: Feminism, postmodernism, and ethnographic responsibility.* Palo Alto, CA: Stanford University Press.

Zuniga, V., & Hernandez-Léon, R. (2001). A new destination for an old migration: Origins, trajectories, and labor market incorporation of Latinos in Dalton, Georgia. In A. D. Murphy, C. Blanchard, & J. A. Hill (Eds.), *Latino workers in the contemporary South* (pp. 126–146). Athens: University of Georgia Press.

6

Visual Methodology

Toward a More Seeing Research

Jon D. Prosser

A striking phenomenon of visual research a decade ago was its apparent invisibility. The malaise for things visual was replaced by positive engagement following a general awakening to the significance and ubiquity of imagery in contemporary lives. Visuals are pervasive in public, work, and private space, and we have no choice but to look. Qualitative researchers are taking up the challenge to understand a society increasingly dominated by visual rather than verbal and textual culture.

Visual research focuses on what can be seen. How humans "see" is part nature part nurture being governed by perception that, like other sensory modes, is mediated by physiology, culture, and history. Visual researchers use the term *visible* ontologically in referring to imagery and naturally occurring phenomena that can be seen, emphasizing the physiological dimension and disregarding their meaning or significance. *Visual*, however, is not about an image or object in of itself but more concerned with the perception and the meanings attributed to them. The terms *to visualize* and *visualization* refer to researchers' sense-making attributes that are epistemologically grounded and include concept formation, analytical processes, and modes of representation (Grady 1996; Wagner, 2006).

Current issues are best understood by reflecting on recent debates that shape contemporary visual research. Since the 1960s, there has been broad agreement that the type of media, mode of production, and context in which visual data are set are important in determining the meaning ascribed to imagery. In short, how researchers and others construct imagery and the kinds of technology used to produce them, are considered intrinsic to the interpretations of the phenomena they are intended to represent. Between 1970 and 2000, a dual paradigmatic disparity existed (what Harper in 1998, termed *the two-headed beast*) between researchers using images generated for empirical purposes and those who studied meanings of images produced by visual culture. The terms *empirical* and *symbolic* were used to denote the relative differences in perspectives during this period. Empirically orientated researchers stressed the importance of theory building and image creation and addressed the relationship between visual data, trustworthiness, and context, whereas symbolically inclined researchers focused on critical analysis of everyday popular visual culture. Hence, during this period an intellectual tension existed between those who read symbolic imagery and social scientists who created images for research purposes. By 2000, visual methods achieved normative status in sociology, anthropology, geography, health studies, history, the arts, and even traditionally quantitative disciplines such as psychology and medicine. Increasingly, we live in a visual world and currently, no topic, field of study, or discipline is immune to the influences of researchers adopting a visual perspective. The most important competency in societies around the world in the 21st century is visual fluency, and qualitative researchers are developing visual methodologies to study that phenomenon.

This chapter outlines key facets of contemporary visual research. Emphasis is placed on fieldwork undertaken in the qualitative tradition exemplifying insightful approaches, areas of concern, and future possibilities. I will begin by outlining *current trends* and conclude with a discussion of *future challenges*.

Current Trends

In this section, under four subheadings, I consider an eclectic mix of methods and studies to illustrate how the science and art of conducting visual research is currently evolving: *Representation of visual research*, a long-standing and contentious issue of considerable importance to visual researchers yet mostly ignored by nonvisual qualitative research; *technology and visual methods* are in the ascendancy because they provide powerful strategies for answering complex global research questions involving analysis of metadata; *participatory visual methods* are well established and included because they represent the most popular genre in visual methodology; and *training in visual methods* because it is not a luxury but an imperative following the burgeoning growth in visual research around the world.

REPRESENTATION OF VISUAL RESEARCH

Tim Berners-Lee created the World Wide Web in the early 1990s, and his graphical point-and-click browser, *WorldWideWeb,* was the precursor to providing access to multiple audiences worldwide. The subsequent standard graphics packages (Excel and Adobe) for creating tables, bar charts, graphs, and pie charts are adequate for most quantitative data but limit qualitative researchers' capacity to represent data effectively by their "one size fits all" approach and limited representational range. Scientists and social scientists are finding this new world of representation challenging, and Luc Pauwels (2006, p. x) points out why:

> While there seems to be an implicit but persistent belief that the rapid spread of visual technologies in almost every sector of society automatically will result in an increased visual literacy or competency, there is at least as much reason to believe that the already vulnerable link between the referent, its visual representation, and the functions it needs to serve will come under even greater pressure.

Currently there is a slow shift toward data visualization for summation of data, displaying information, and providing an opportunity for analysis. In their basic form, interactive graphics provide additional data as the cursor is moved around the screen. The *New York Times* has excellent examples including findings from the 2008 American Time Use Survey, which asked thousands of Americans to recall how they spent every minute of their day (do an Internet search for "How different groups spend their day interactive graphic"). Statistics, especially in the form of large numbers, are difficult to relate to a human scale. A project called *Running the Numbers*[1] (developed by Chris Jordan) adopts creative approach to making large numbers accessible and meaningful. The images, usually sets of photographs, portray specific quantities: 15 million sheets of office paper (5 minutes of paper use in the United States), 106,000 aluminum cans (30 seconds of can consumption in the United States), or the 32,000 breast augmentation surgeries that take place in the United States every month. But these are early days, and critical reflection is needed to determine what are advances in social science and visual representation and what are eye candy.

Representation of visual research is in a depressingly stagnant state because mainstream dissemination in academia remains hard copy text–based and conservative. The passion for the printed page, the "thingness" of books as a sensual experience, continues to dominate, and only slowly the screen is emerging as a site for presenting findings of visual research. Qualitative visual researchers currently struggle to present their work outside of the traditional word/print format despite the potential that digital delivery systems have to change the way visual research is represented (Banks, 2007, Pink, 2008; Ruby, 2005). Some multimedia presentations on the Web look little different from the usual sequential text on a printed page, whereas others work sympathetically with different media and connect to other online representation via digital video, clickable hypermedia links, and podcast or sound essays. Visual researchers' screen-based authoring and blogs are increasingly seen as places to publish and disseminate research and methods (see, for example, David Gauntlett's site: http://www.art lab.org.uk/). The combination of text, images, blogs, twitters, vlogging (video blogging), and digital hypermedia are now part of visual research vocabulary signposting a future direction of communicating visual research.

An unexpected twist in representational forms is the reemergence of photographs as visual presentations rather than representations of research—unexpected given long-standing arguments concerning "the myth of photographic truth." Barry Goldstein's "All Photos Lie" (2007) is yet another restatement of this argument. None of this is new to photographers or visual researchers. Photographers have always known that their photographs represent a highly selected sample of the "real" world about which their images convey some subjective and empirical truth (Becker, 1986; Fox Talbot,[2] 1844; Ruby, 2005) in the same way that wordsmiths know that structure, vocabulary, and tone of their texts contain misrepresentations.

Arguably, social scientists are too preoccupied by their own epistemology to reflect on how to take account of and apply other forms of inquiry. Jon Wagner (2007), in his essay *Observing Culture and Social Life: Documentary Photography, Fieldwork and Social Research,* provides a robust case for a more seeing research by revealing similarities in epistemology across the word-image interface. Central to visual studies and the representation of findings where imagery is involved is the relationship between words and images: Is the space taken up with mostly words or images; which is most influential; is it necessary to translate images into words; and is it necessary to provide captions for images? Marcus Banks (2007) opts for photographs as a quote within contextualizing text as though it were an interview quote. Elizabeth Chaplin (2006), in "The Convention of Captioning," being part artist and part visual sociologist, balances the arguments for and against captioning images before opting for the latter and prescribing that readers should work harder to interpret by relating text to image.

The next and most important step is for someone working within the epistemology of visual ethnography to represent a case for a photographic rather than word emphasis. Dona Schwartz's (2009a) domestic case study *In the Kitchen* is an exemplar of how this might look (see Figure 6.1). In her Keynote Photographer

Figure 6.1 "Inspector, 2005," *In the Kitchen* (2009a, p. 143, courtesy Dona Schwartz)

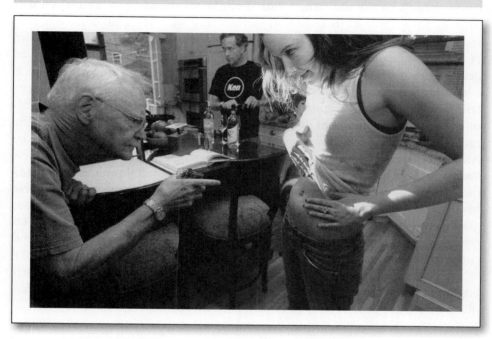

address at the 1st International Visual Methods Conference in 2009[3] and the challengingly titled "If a Picture Is Worth a Thousand Words, Why Are You Reading this Essay" paper (2007), she accepts that photographs are interpretations of the things to which they refer—they are not the thing itself. Schwartz acknowledges they are abstractions from ongoing time and space, a single arrested moment in time but, as Chaplin suggests, Schwartz challenges her audience to work harder at interpretation. More importantly, Schwartz makes strategic decisions and acts as a social scientist would but with important provisos:

> In making the case for making pictures I am suggesting that pictures can offer us ideas and an irreducible experience that cannot be restated or translated into linguistic terms. Articulations produced through photographs can offer us insights based on spatial and compositional arrangements, they can convey moods and emotions. They can generate novel ideas and inferences. . . . In the sciences, the idea of "productive ambiguity" with multiple readings giving rise to innovations that would have been unimagined had not a plurality of readings been possible. (2009b)

What Schwartz does is reverse the Banks and Chaplin call to place visual quotes in a contextualizing sea of words: "I am working to make pictures prime, to invest them with the thousand words I might otherwise write, and to present them in such a way as to insist that viewers read what the images have to say" (Schwartz, 2007, p. 320). A key element of this counterargument is the rejection of the widely held belief that visual literacy is somehow automatically improved because visual culture is so pervasive. Indeed, she argues that viewing images is a learned skill-based activity that differs from language, and being a fundamentally different communication system does not lend itself to context–free semiotic analysis. *In the Kitchen* has an erudite combination of word authors. The preface is a situating review of documentary photography of family settings by Alison Nordstrom (curator of photographs at George Eastman House in New York, the largest museum of photography in the world), followed by Schwartz's own rationale and methodological insights that are recognizable and acceptable to ethnographic and visual communication scholars. The following 170+ photographs are interspersed with poetry (by poet Marion Winik) that conjure up powerful mind imagery, inviting readers to search their own memory banks and examine their own values and beliefs about everyday family life. The history, ethnography, and humanities combination in this book illustrates how compelling interdisciplinary studies can be when research teams, working from a disciplinary base, are flexible enough to recognize the insights of others.

TECHNOLOGY AND VISUAL METHODS

Tools and techniques for seeing more and differently are key factors contributing to step changes in visual research. Advances such as the telescope, microscope, X-ray, ultrasound, MRI scanner, photography, and computers reflect our innate capacity to see, store, organize, and represent knowledge. Current documentary and participatory visual methods owe much to Steven Sasson's invention of the digital camera in 1975. Often, changes in research reflect changes in technology and vice versa, and qualitative visual researchers are well aware that technologies change what and how they study. With the advent of new technology for storing, organizing, analyzing, communicating, and presenting research, the qualitative-quantitative interface is being broadened, refined, and morphed. The cheapness and variety of image-making technology makes picture making and sharing a common activity. Still photography remains favored by participatory visual researchers, and video was widely used in the past by educationalists, anthropologists, ethnographers, and ethnomethodologists because it supports fine-grained analysis of complex social interaction (Goldman et al., 2007; Heath, Hindmarsh, & Luff, 2010).

Software for organizing and interpreting large volumes of imagery is becoming increasingly sophisticated. In the United Kingdom, the Economic and Social Research Council (ESRC) established the National Centre for e-Social Science (NCeSS), which increased interest in Computer Aided Qualitative Data Analysis Software (CAQDAS).[4] Consequently, there was an increased uptake of visual compliant software such as ATLAS.ti, NVivo, Transana (whose primary focus is audio/video analysis), and Observer XT, and the ESRC National Centre for Research Methods (NCRM) and Researcher Development Initiative (RDI) programs developed further software for analyzing digital data and provided nationwide training courses in their application. The combination of improved software and training capacity enabled researchers with metadata to store, analyze, map, measure, and represent, for example, complex human communication with other interconnected entities.

The use of innovative digital technology and software opens new methodological possibilities for visual researchers. With colleagues, I am currently interested in an education paradox—although visual culture has increasingly come to dominate many areas of the social and personal lives of students and teachers, relatively little is known about the significance of visual culture to learning and teaching. The objective of our study is to generate a theoretical model of the dynamic relationship between societal visual culture and the visual culture of classrooms, with a view to understanding pedagogic consequences. As a starting point, given the paucity of theoretical models and the partial and fragmented nature of current knowledge, we will identify elements central to understanding visual culture of classrooms and examine how those elements are dynamically interrelated using the tentative framework illustrated in Figure 6.2 as a starting point.

We (eight researchers, each knowledgeable in different aspects of the visual culture of schooling) will employ a qualitatively driven, visually orientated, mixed method, interdisciplinary, participatory approach to developing a model. Data will be collected using orthodox visual methods and different media, for example:

- Participatory visual methods, for example, graphical elicitation, photo elicitation, video diary, video elicitation, photovoice, timelines, and arts-based methods

- Data collected via dual camera video to document versions of talk, bodily communication (e.g., gesture and facial expression, proxemic and kinesthetic data) and material transitional resources such as computer screens, textbooks, interactive whiteboards, classroom walls, and the learning space

Figure 6.2   A Starting Point for Modeling the Visual Culture of Classrooms (from Prosser, 2007)

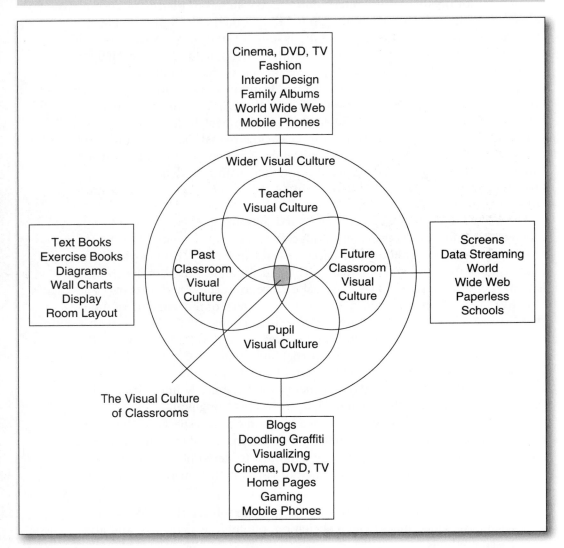

- Data collected by eye tracking software (Duchowski, 2003; Tai, Loehr, & Brigham, 2006) to aid understanding how screens and textbooks in classrooms are scanned, and employ new collaboration-friendly geographical information systems) software that enables coding, annotating, and analysis of the use of classroom physical space with CAQDAS functionality

We are faced with two major problems: The first is analyzing, contrasting, and combining a diverse range of data and media; the second is creating a positive climate where ideas can be exchanged among the eight researchers and participants. The digitized data from the case study schools will be archived on and displayed via the Digital Replay System (DRS) to help resolve both problems. The DRS (see Figure 6.3 for an example but not of school data) is a next generation CAQDAS tool developed through the ESRC e-Social Science program. Like other CAQDAS tools, DRS enables the synchronization, replay, and analysis of audio and video recordings. Distinctively, DRS also enables these conventional forms of recording to be combined with system logs, or data "born digital," which record interaction within computational environments, or are the product of using computational techniques, to analyze data. These novel forms of digital data may include global positioning system (GPS) or WiFi logs, systems management server (SMS) logs, logs of network traffic, or logs generated by vision recognition software. Systems logs may be visualized, synchronized, and replayed alongside video and transcripts, or other conventional data, through the construction of log viewers.

The capacity of DRS to store and compare multiple forms of digitized data that consist of interrelated elements of societal and classroom visual culture is clearly important. However, so is the capacity of DRS to draw down and display information on screens or a large white wall for simultaneous research team and participant viewing. The synergistic possibilities for evolving multilayered models are considerable. It is possible, for example, to compare different digitized media across time (see the horizontal overlapping circles in Figure 6.2) and to contrast pupil and teacher visual subcultures (see the vertical overlapping circles and boxes in Figure 6.2) and compare them. Exciting possibilities for theory generation occur when the researchers and participants collaborate. We intend drawing on psychodynamic theory and applying the concept of using the DRS screen as a transitional space to stimulate creative play throughout the study with the ultimate aim of improving the quality of learning and teaching in classrooms. In addition, establishing an internationally searchable DRS archive opens other future synergistic opportunities. We are able to share different forms of digital data between our team members who might be located in different geographical locations in the United Kingdom and allow other research teams in different countries to access our archive and load their own data, enabling international comparisons of models of visual culture of classrooms to be made. When funding for research is constrained through a global fiscal downturn and costs of collecting metadata for analysis and synthesis are high, archiving with DRS for secondary analysis by others makes economic sense.

Figure 6.3 Digital Replay System Example (courtesy Andrew Crabtree, Warwick University)

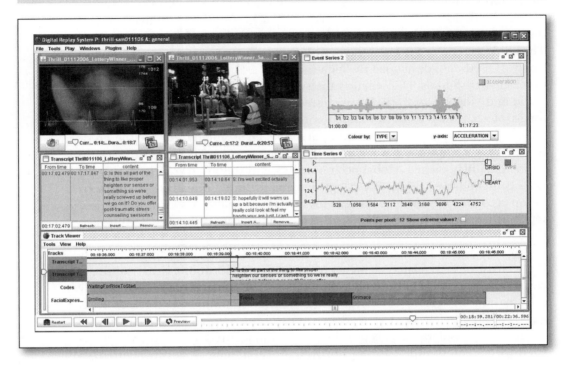

PARTICIPATORY VISUAL METHODS

Throughout the evolution of visual research, the researcher has been the instigator, designer, collector, interpreter, and producer in the research process. Post-1960 attention broadened to include the external narratives and combine researcher and participant insights. The earliest documented examples of this genre in visual research were by John Collier in mid-1950s (Collier & Collier, 1967/1986) who used photo elicitation as a way of stimulating interviewees' thinking during repeat interviews, and Sol Worth, John Adair, and Richard Chalfen's project (1972/1997) with Navajo in the mid-1960s. They were the forerunners of what is the most influential and abused methodological genre in contemporary visual research. Within the social sciences, broadly conceived participatory methodologies are evolving that are diverse and contested. Currently the role of technology, the potential gains and losses of participatory dissemination, and consequent ethical issues provide a major challenge. Participatory visual researchers are currently striving to meet that challenge.

Visual elicitation involves using photographs, drawings, or diagrams in a research interview to stimulate a response and remain the most popular and common method in participatory visual research. Photo elicitation is used as an "ice-breaker" or neutral third party when the power differential between researcher-researched is significant. Like most participatory visual methods, agreed upon protocols are rare. The method is not researcher-proof (Packard, 2008; Warren, 2005), and the biggest danger to democratization is when researchers come to the table with too many preconceptions in focus, process, or direction. After 50 years of application, even experienced practitioners think very carefully before exploring the meaning of images or objects with the interviewee (Harper, 2002).

Participants feel less pressured when discussing sensitive topics through intermediary artifacts. Because they do not speak directly about a topic on which they feel vulnerable but work through a material go-between (e.g., a doll, toy, line drawings, mobile phone, or memorabilia), they are more able to express difficult memories and powerful emotions. This approach is gaining in popularity because researchers believe that transitional objects have the capacity to be the locus of corporeal embodied memories. However, used injudiciously, without sensitivity, and under certain conditions, apparently innocuous visual stimuli and material culture can evoke inaccurate, distorted, unexpected, and even painful memories.

A long-standing strength of image/artifact elicitation is its capacity to evoke as well as create collective and personal memory. Chalfen's (1998) classic studies of how families in different cultures produce and use photographic albums and visual media to construct familial memory recognized that considering their temporal and contextual dimensions was of pivotal importance. The shift from looking in private through family snaps in plastic albums to semi-public browsing of web-based digitized multimedia family records illustrates changes in visual culture and the importance of considering lifestyle in any memory work. Making sense of web-based family photography is a relatively new but fast-growing area of study. Pauwels (2008) provides an insightful overview of this body of work by combining historical review, fieldwork, and identifying methodological problems. Current studies of the relationship between photography and memory draw on family collections, public archives, museums, newspapers, and art galleries for source material (see Kuhn & McAllister, 2006).

Marisol Clark-Ibanez (2007) uses participants' photographs in photo elicitation (she uses the term *auto-driving*) in her work with inner-city children to avoid overt voyeurism and to ensure topics relevant to the child remain central to the research agenda. Clark-Ibanez makes a strong case for using photo elicitation because she recognizes participants are expert in their own lives and able to define or refine the research, the agenda, and process. Obvious ground rules such as being sensitive to the participant's values, beliefs, lifestyle, and culture are emerging slowly, but some visual researchers use this method uncritically and without thinking through why or how it is to be used.

Photovoice and its variants (participative video, video diaries, photo-narratives, and photo-novella), which entail providing participants and collaborators with digital video or still cameras, remains the most commonly used visual method in social science research. An overtly political form entails giving participants cameras as an act of empowerment to generate changes in personal or community life or to influence policy directly. Here resultant photographs are circulated on the Internet; become local, regional, or national exhibitions; or are sent to government agencies as persuasive evidence. Such work tackles the power inequalities that create crises and sustain poverty and injustices through the suppression of marginalized voices. Researchers adopting this strategy are deeply committed to improving the lives of people with whom they work. Claudia Mitchell, for example, uses visual methods, particularly photovoice, to address problems arising from the rising tide of HIV and AIDS infection in sub-Saharan Africa. Mitchell has worked and lived in South Africa, Zambia, Malawi, Swaziland, Ethiopia, and Rwanda, serving community needs and acting as an adviser to various ministries. She draws together young people, researchers, and nongovernmental organizations and uses participatory visual and other arts-based methods to address issues of invisibility and marginalization. The work is important given that HIV/AIDS poses a major threat to development, poverty alleviation, and low life expectancy in sub-Saharan Africa. Five young people are being infected with HIV every minute, 7,000 every day, and 2.6 million every year. Worldwide, young people between the ages of 15 and 25 make up more than 40% of all new HIV and AIDS infections, with young women being disproportionately affected. Visual action research does not require publication to be life affirming and life saving.

Participatory video aims to create a narrative that conveys what respondents want to communicate in the manner they wish to communicate. Ruth Holliday (2007, p. 257) provides an insightful reflexive account of her use of video diaries to explore how "queer performances of identity are constructed as texts on the surface of bodies." She wanted to use a method in which participants were active in representing their own identities. The 15 diarists were given explicit instructions to explore their queer identities in three different spaces—work, rest (home), and play (the gay scene)—and to chart the similarities and differences in identity performances. They were also given specific instructions to film themselves in their typical choice of outfit for each setting and to comment on these settings, explaining to the camera what clothes, hairstyles, jewelry, and their other bodily arrangements were designed to portray. However, because of the constraints posed by the largely heterosexist culture in the United Kingdom, structured by "the closet," using a camera to film at a gay club (at play) proved impossible. Filming at work was equally difficult, and where it was done, it was carried out after hours so the spaces were strangely devoid of people. Hence much of the filming was carried out in the home.

Interestingly, Holliday considered and rejected feminist theory, the critique of objectivism, and masculine tendencies in research to arrive at distinctively queer methodology. She draws on the work of Judith Halberstam as partial justification of her choice of video diaries:

> A queer methodology, in a way, is a scavenger methodology that uses different methods to collect and produce information on subjects who have been deliberately or accidentally excluded from traditional studies of human behavior. (Holliday, 2007, p. 260)

In terms of generating theory, Holliday took the stance that given "self-filming" had an affinity with queer methodologies in their visual representations, encoding and decoding of queer (bodily) texts, a one-way (i.e., researcher) socio-semiotic reading of the videos was acceptable. The video diaries did, through the processes of watching, recording, and editing diaries before submission, afford participants the potential for a greater degree of reflection and control than other methods. However, clearly there were times when Holliday wanted to explore with the diarists, but did not, some of the points they had made, by follow-up video elicitation interviews.

It is interesting that beyond the initial specific instructions, the participants required no directions beyond working the video cameras. They knew how to behave in front of the camera and what was expected of them because they learned the technique from television. This is a clear demonstration of how visual methods and visual culture are inextricably linked. How so? In 1993, the British Broadcasting Corporation launched an audience interactivity project aimed at encouraging people to record their lives on video to be aired nationwide. The resultant television program, *Video Nation,*[5] ran until 2001, preceding vlogging (video blogging) by 8 years. The program comprised quirky 2-minute shorts featuring everything from the profound to the gloriously trivial (my favorite was Scottish clan chief filming a flower-filled toilet in Finland). The program was highly popular in the United Kingdom and helped make video diaries in visual research fashionable and a genre that many, as in Holliday's study, are keen to emulate.

Holliday's diarists operated at a sophisticated level thanks to *Big Brother,* another highly popular television program in the United Kingdom. At the heart of Holliday's discussion is the idea of the confessional that is now commonplace across postmodern media and reality TV. In *Big Brother,* the show's pervasive filming of housemates makes for a variety of more or less self-conscience performances, but the soundproof "diary room" is set aside as a private space to talk directly to a voice that is "Big Brother." The viewing audiences expect brazen "truths" to be revealed in such diary confessions, although they know these truths are performances for the camera and public at large. Participants in Holliday's study are not naive but, rather, media savvy and well able to draw on available cultural codes to know how to perform the kind of reflexive mediated video diary required. Holliday is very much aware of this:

> Self-storying in the video diaries suggest that mediated confession is a performance in which participants knowingly, reflexively, and willingly engage; in a media-saturated and confession-saturated culture, this confirms the value of this method and suggests that need to more fully understand the culture work of the confession as a site of local mediated meaning making. (Holliday, 2007, p. 278)

An unusual but important methodological twist in Holliday's study is that the participants, knowing how to behave in front of the camera and what was expected of them, are in control of the method.

Holliday ends with the familiar visual researchers' lament concerning representation of data and findings:

> In spite of the visual nature of the data that inform this chapter, I am left to present it using only text and a few still images. To capture the flavour of the diaries in the text is extremely difficult and takes up an enormous amount of writing space . . . The nuances available in an audiovisual text are such that many simultaneous interpretations are possible . . . The diarists and their views are foregrounded in presentations, and the audience is similarly skilled at reading video diaries due to their near-constant use in lifestyle and reality TV (and indeed beyond). (Holliday, 2007, p. 276)

She bemoans the lack of acceptance in the wider academic community for representation beyond paper-based renditions. Having seen the video diaries many times, I can understand this position because they are highly informative, data-rich representations of participants' understanding of their own queer performance. Holliday's comments echo Peter Biella's view back in 1993 in

"Beyond Ethnographic Film: Hypermedia and Scholarship" that mixed media studies are severely limited by text-based representations. Missing from major methodological texts are colors, movements, and sounds that are central representational forms in visual research.

TRAINING IN VISUAL METHODS

Visual research in North America, Australasia, Scandinavia, Italy, and the United Kingdom is long-standing, distinctive, and above all, burgeoning. The benefits accrued from the rapid uptake include increased vitality, diversity, and a firmament that invites intellectual exchange. However, with increased popularity comes the need to support those new to visual methodology.

Newcomers extemporize by drawing knowledge from journals such as *Visual Studies,* accessing online resources such as *Visualanthropology.net,* joining organizations such as the International Visual Sociology Association (IVSA), and attending conferences and workshops. Many turn to books for insight. The best of the current bunch is Gregory Stanczak's (2007) edited *Visual Research Methods: Image, Society, and Representation.* This critically reflexive text covers different visual methodologies and analytic approaches from photography to virtual research, and ranges from sociology to religion and political science. The *Handbook of the Arts in Qualitative Research* edited by J. Gary Knowles and Ardra Cole (2008) is a 54-chapter celebration of the concepts, processes, and representational forms from the arts and a must-buy book for aspiring visual researchers with a creative turn. Another concise and erudite text is Banks' *Using Visual Data in Qualitative Research* (2007), which draws on exemplars from an anthropological tradition. Gauntlett's (2007) playful *Creative Explorations: New Approaches to Identities and Audiences* draws usefully on an eclectic array of disciplines including neuroscience and philosophy to explore how creative methods can be employed to understand identity and individuals' connections with the wider world. Pauwel's (2006) edited book *Visual Cultures of Science* brings together some first-rate essays that plug a gap in the literature by rethinking representational and visualization practices in the communication of science. Finally, Paula Reavey's (2011) edited book *Visual Methods in Psychology: Using and Interpreting Images in Qualitative Research* will be welcomed by qualitatively orientated psychologists.

In the United Kingdom, as in many countries, the training provision before 2005 was mostly ad hoc. The ESRC began its involvement in visual methods training with the international seminar series Visual Evidence: the Use of Images in Social and Cultural Research (2000–2002), which brought together empirical and symbolic researchers from around the world. However, the Building

Capacity in Visual Methods program (2006–2009), part of the ESRC Researcher Development Initiative, was the first nationwide integrated program aimed at teaching visual methods to a cross-section of qualitative researchers. The program provided a strategic capacity building plan to meet the training needs of contemporary and future visual researchers in the social sciences in the United Kingdom. The objectives were threefold:

- To provide methodology trainers, users of research, and active researchers new to visual research with core skills and resources to enable them to build a deep understanding of visual research methods
- To provide an ongoing, visual methods resource for researchers with experience in visual methods at intermediate level that is stimulating, challenging and grounded in "best practice"
- To establish a national infrastructure that was self-sufficient and developmental that meets the ongoing needs of the research community

There were two progressive and interrelated levels: The first level targeted new visual researchers inside and outside academia and from a broad spectrum of social science disciplines. This training program spanned 3 years and comprised two 2-day Introduction to Visual Methods workshops held at six monthly intervals each year at different locations around the United Kingdom. The second level was aimed at more experienced visual researchers in need of an intermediate level of visual methods training and built on the level one workshops. Stress was placed on approaches that were generic and transferable across the social sciences rather than on unique or specialized methods or fields. The second level of the training program spanned 3 years and comprised two 1-day Visual Methods Symposiums held at six monthly intervals each year. The culminating event of the program was the staging of the *1st International Visual Methods Conference* at the University of Leeds, September 2009, attended by 300 delegates from around the world.

The pedagogic dimension of Building Capacity in Visual Methods is worth considering as a model of delivery for anyone envisaging a national scheme. The first level—An Introduction to Visual Methods—presented visual research in a workshop format not as a stand-alone strategy taking one particular form but as theoretically and methodologically varied and compliant with the needs of a broad cross-section of qualitative researchers. Special consideration was given to ensuring that specific methods were related to the research process as a whole rather than to a technique applied in isolation. Hence, visual methods were discussed relative to different visual paradigms, visual media, analytical perspectives, and applied the study of a wide range of topics.

The level one 2-day workshops included overviews of visual frameworks (for example, visual ethnography), researcher-generated data (for example, object/photo elicitation and record/documentary techniques), participant-created data (for example, video diaries and arts-based methods), technology-based capture and analysis (for example, CAQDAS software-based analysis and eye-tracker technology), modes of analysis (for example, visual socio-semiotics, the internal and external narrative of an image), forms of representation (for example, graphics, mixed media, photography, and film), and visual ethics (for example, legal requirements, institutional ethics committee requirements, and issues of anonymity and confidentiality). Generic skills and knowledge were viewed as transferable, and workshop participants, being an interdisciplinary mix, were encouraged to learn from each other. The workshops were designed to be intensive experiences, and total engagement and commitment were expected. The team of 14 tutors (who also designed the program) was drawn from the most able visual methodologists in the United Kingdom and included Marcus Banks, Sarah Pink, Steve Higgins, Rob Walker, Gillian Rose, David Gauntlet, and me. Each 2-day workshop was repeated around the United Kingdom and usually comprised 12 short talks, 8 discussion sessions, and 4 hands-on practical activities. In addition, each participant was given a pedagogically informed hard-copy material to take away and digest, and ongoing support provided through an e-learning resource.

Practical activities typically consisted of short exercises involving photo elicitation, visual analysis, documenting complex events, and research design, designed to reinforce theoretical understanding and application of first principles. This element was included to give students a hands-on experience so they could gain confidence of techniques in action and gain an understanding of their potential pitfalls (Wiles et al., 2005).

The *hard-copy material* and supplementary basic texts (for example, Prosser & Loxley, 2008) were designed to complement face-to-face activities. The material was designed to meet the educative rather than strictly academic needs of participants. Hence, the papers were shaped by the authors (the tutors) asking themselves the question, "If I were new to visual research what sort of 'take-away' document would I need to help me apply visual methods to my own the field?" Each paper contained background information—for example, brief history, visual framework, and origin of the method—a protocol of how the method is applied in practice, analytical approaches that are appropriate with the method, and exemplars of good practice. The hard-copy material avoided jargon, explained technical words, and provided a short bibliography of the best literature available.

Face-to-face activities and hard-copy materials were further supported by a purposely designed *e-learning resource*. The tutors created a dedicated, dynamic, and evolving online learning environment based on open-source software that complied with interoperability standards. The environment included resources such as interactive exercises, documents, banks of still and moving images, and social software to enable discussion and allowed students individually or collaboratively to share their research stories. In this way, students continued to construct and benefit from the e-learning resources thus becoming part of a community of practice that supports learning across the life course. Furthermore, the flexibility of e-learning media and resources allowed a high level of personalization and enabled the inclusion of students who, for reasons of location, disability, or life constraints, might not otherwise be able to access visual research methods training. The project used Ning (www.ning.com) to build a space in which to enable an online community to develop. The Ning site tools including image and video uploading, video playback, e-mail to all users, discussion boards, blogs, and individual member profiles. After each of the training workshops, participants were invited to join the Visual Methods community on Ning. In addition to providing an informal space for online communication, the site hosted several online events during the life of the project. At each of these events, one of the tutors hosted a themed expert seminar—for example, "visual ethics"—usually for 1 day. During that time, members of the community used the discussion boards to ask questions about the theme of the session and to discuss these questions with the expert visual researcher hosting the seminar.

The rapid growth of interest in visual methodology caught many institutions and training facilities by surprise. Although those new to visual research or with limited experience are able to draw from journals, access visual online resources, join organizations, attend conferences and workshops, or read visual methods books, there is no substitute for pedagogically led training. An effective and efficient way to educate new visual researchers is for countries to train the trainers via a nationwide program designed specifically for that purpose.

Future Challenges

In his summary for the visual chapter in the third edition of this book, Douglas Harper (2005, p. 760) looked to the future, partly in trepidation and partly in aspiration:

My hope is that visual methods will become ever more important in the various research traditions where it already has a foothold . . . I hope that during the next decade, visual studies will become a world movement . . .

Harper's hopes have been fulfilled, for visual methods have permeated all disciplines and topics. My hope for the next decade is that visual methodology will have a greater impact on social science globally through refining its strengths, developing creative elements, and resolving emergent problematic aspects. Hence, this final section will consider potential growth and a limitation:

- A strength of visual methods: the capacity to create and innovate
- An opportunity for visual methods: postcards from the edge
- A threat to the visual methods: ethics regulation

A STRENGTH OF VISUAL METHODS— THE CAPACITY TO CREATE AND INNOVATE

A limiting factor of interviews conducted verbally is the narrow parameters of responses and that they favor the articulate. One of the strengths of visual research is the wide range of response possibilities and their capacity to harness the creative abilities of researchers and participants. More thought and imagination is needed in academic debate and that is why art is so important in visual research. Art can comprise complexity and contradiction, and unlike the arguments in an academic paper, art need not be linear. Art can describe, reflect, and evoke emotion, which dry facts or figures and cool logic rarely do. Art is often about stories, of lives and characters with whom an audience can identify. Above all, art can help us (researchers, participants, and interested communities) imagine what it might be like to live that life. It may not be obvious what the art is saying and maybe the artists do not know themselves, or do not know in a way that is communicated by words. Art is a tool for thinking and a very powerful means of expression and promoting discussion. Arts-based approaches invoke beyond-text sensations employed to access sensory phenomena that are highly meaningful in ways that are ineffable and invisible using conventional text-based methods. Arts-based research is vibrant, evolving rapidly, and defined by Shaun McNiff (2008, p. 29) as

The systematic use of artistic process, the actual making of artistic expressions in all of the different forms of the arts, as a primary way of understanding and examining experience by both researchers and the people that they involve in their studies.

Elliot Eisner (2008, p. 7) claims a special provenance for including arts-based approaches to qualitative research:

> Langer (1957) claims that discursive language is the most useful scientific device humans have created but that the arts provide access to qualities of life that literal language has no great power to disclose.

Of the emergent visual paradigms, arts-based has the greatest potential to be innovative and insightful in terms of imagery, and Sandra Weber (2008, pp. 44–46) provides examples of why this might be the case:

> Images make us pay attention to things in new ways . . . images are likely to be memorable . . . images can be used to communicate more holistically, incorporating multiple layers, and evoking stories or questions; images can enhance empathic understanding and generalizability . . . through metaphor and symbol, artistic images can carry theory elegantly and eloquently . . . images encourage embodied knowledge . . . images can be more accessible than most forms of academic discourse . . . images provoke action for social justice.

Of course, there are different theoretical perspectives within arts-based research. Graeme Sullivan (2005) for example, critiques visual sociology and visual ethnography in particular as being too close to traditional sociological theory and methodological thinking that stress collaboration between "researchers and researched." Sullivan's hierarchical framework sees the artist occupying a position that is pivotal and supreme, where practice-based research within the artist's studio central, and hence the artist-as-researcher plays the sole role. It is somewhat ironic that Pink, a visual ethnographer who champions a variety of forms of arts-based participatory research, is criticized for limited reflexivity by Sullivan's version of art-based inquiry:

> Pink's text follows a strategy common to most research in critical and visual cultural inquiry in that it emphasizes the critique and analysis of phenomena, but has very little to say about the creation of new knowledge using visual means that might be taken within a research perspective. (Sullivan, 2005, p. xv)

Sullivan's provocative and narrow evocation of "artist as researcher" perspective underestimates Pink's capacity to work with diverse audiences and encourage agency in many. An indicator of the innovative possibilities, the energy and insights possible of an arts-based approach is revealed in Knowles and Cole's *Handbook of the Arts in Qualitative Research* (2008), mentioned earlier. It covers a gamut of arts-informed and arts-based research, each with a distinctive methodology and promoting the notion that art should be regarded as a form of knowledge and not merely an ornamental product of human experience. The 54 chapters cover mixed modes, media, methodologies, and representations, for example, "Collage as Inquiry" (Butler-Kisber, 2008), "From Research to Performance" (Cancienne, 2008), "Exhibiting as Inquiry" (Church, 2008), "Installation Art-as-Research" (Cole & McIntyre, 2008), "Psychology: Knowing the Self Through the Arts" (Higgs, 2008), and "Ethnodrama and Ethnotheatre" (Saldaña, 2008).

AN EXAMPLE OF THE CREATIVE POSSIBILITIES OF VISUAL METHODS

A distinctive capacity of visual methods is to improve the quality and trustworthiness of data and findings by drawing on participants' own resourcefulness and ingenuity. But what does an innovative visual enquiry look like? In *Creative Explorations* (2007), Gauntlett explains how, by adopting the methodological middle ground between method-sparse postmodern and cultural studies thinking and method-limiting word-dominated approaches, fresh insights about people's experiences are gained. He claims his "new creative methods" draw on people's needs to engage with the world. Participants are invited to spend time creatively making something metaphorical or symbolic about their lives and then reflect on their creation. Participants are introduced to the notion of "creative explorations" via simple experiments—for example, "build a creature" and then "in the next two minutes, turn the creature into how you feel on Monday morning or Friday afternoon." Participants play with this idea, and, for example, a walrus-type creature is turned into a Friday afternoon feeling by adding a wagging tail, a zingy hairstyle, or a set of wheels, to appear obviously excited and looking forward to the weekend (Figure 6.4).

Then the real work begins, and participants are asked to construct their identity and include key influences. In his current work, Gauntlett asks diverse groups of people, including architects, unemployed people, and social care workers, to construct models of their identity using LEGO blocks. He believes that a more hands-on, minds-on, approach by participants makes for more truthful results (see Figure 6.5 and www.artlab.org.uk).

Figure 6.4 Build a creature and turn it into a Friday afternoon feeling (courtesy David Gauntlett)

Gauntlett draws from an eclectic array of theories and disciplines ranging from neuroscience to philosophy to provide the theoretical underpinning and rationale for his method. His approach is far removed from the approaches of psychotherapists and art therapists of a past era who asked their subjects to construct or make something and then referred to a diagnostic manual to give them the expert insight into what a patient's artwork "actually" meant. Gauntlet draws on phenomenologist Maurice Merleau-Ponty to support his premise, that it is the process, particularly the embodied experience, of creating identity that is crucial to participants' capacity to provide a more realistic response than that obtained by word-only interviews. In addition, he cites Paul Ricoeur's *The Rule of the Metaphor* (2003) and his work on the concept of metaphor at the level of discourse and, more importantly, his work on narrative and identity. Gauntlett employs the human capacity to use metaphors to advantage by providing participants with full LEGO kits so a tiger could be used in a model to represent ambition, pride, a driving force, and so forth, and a bridge could represent variously challenges, connecting people, or the chance to reach higher places. He

Figure 6.5 LEGO serious play—each part represents something meaningful (courtesy David Gauntlett)

makes a strong claim for his creative explorations approach to building knowledge of society:

> Pictures or objects enable us to present information, ideas or feelings simultaneously, without the material being forced into an order or a hierarchy. Language may be needed to *explain* the visual, but the image remains primary and shows the relationships between parts most effectively. (Gauntlett, 2007, p. 15)

Gauntlett's critique of orthodox verbal interviews rests on the belief that interviewers have unreasonable expectations of interviewees. He feels that people's brains do not usually contain ready-made lists of "what I think" about topics such as identity. This gives rise, he believes, to participants generating "instant answers" that are imprecise and inaccurate. LEGO maps of identity help participants to form words and ideas at the speed and in the way they feel is their expression in the time that's best for them. The serious LEGO approach is one example of an innovative visual researcher using the creative capacities of participants.

AN OPPORTUNITY FOR VISUAL METHODS—POSTCARDS FROM THE EDGE

Because of the ubiquity of the semi-structured interview and the sample survey that favor the articulate (Mason,[6] 2002, 2008), participants with communication difficulties, learning difficulties, and other disabilities are inhibited from taking part in research. Despite the long-standing trend toward inclusive research and working "with" rather than "on" participants, the voice and agency of the least able in society is often missing. It is important to respect people with disability and to accept they can be powerful, beautiful, and sexy. Visual methodologists can make a major contribution here by adopting an egalitarian stance and by working alongside the most vulnerable, underrepresented, and least researched and understood members of society. Ontological and epistemological difficulties, coupled with the current global fiscal downturn and emergent enthusiasm for cost-effective research, will probably deflect the moral compass of research. It is relatively easy to obtain a research grant to fund social science curiosity but a lot tougher to make a difference to people's lives or advance social justice.

Currently in the United Kingdom, there are 850,000 people with dementia, 500,000 people with autistic spectrum disorders, and many others with intellectual disabilities who are habitually and systematically excluded from research data because of the underlying assumption that they are insufficiently articulate to contribute through interviews or sample surveys. Hence, little is known about the quality of life of autistic people after they leave school, research with dementia sufferers is limited, nothing is known about the quality of life of disabled people with a dual diagnosis (e.g., people with Down syndrome in their 50s who experience dementia 30 years ahead of the norm), and very little is known about the subjective well-being of disabled people with learning and communication difficulties.

Many in the disabled community communicate insights about themselves and their lives despite limited skills in speech and writing. Lester Magoogan,[7] for example, is a young man with Down syndrome who expresses his bubbly personality and unique perspectives on life through simple but evocative line drawings (see Figure 6.6). His images convey his cognitive understanding and emotional insight into "two-faced people," "coming out of nowhere," and "windy" in a way that language has no great power to reveal.

Figure 6.6 The Drawings of Lester Magoogan (copyright Lester Magoogan, www.lestermagoogan.co.uk)

Here I will provide three examples of using sensory methods with disabled people, each with an unadorned but important methodological message. The first is the simple strategy of asking two people with different disabilities to work together, the second illustrates the dangers of ocular centrism and participants "speaking" and the researcher hearing but not listening, and the third demonstrates the potential of technology as a collaborative tool of visual research to communicate with those previously considered noncommunicators. "Postcards from the edge" is an apt metaphor for this section because it comprises superficial messages on one side and concise, pithy visual statements from individuals on the other, and always the sender is a long way off—at the edge of research possibilities.

1. To be a child and disabled is to be doubly disadvantaged in terms of voice. A well-known "draw and write" method was used to help Jane, a young girl with a fire phobia who was experiencing recurrent nightmares with a fire theme. She is autistic, dyspraxic, aphasic with learning difficulties, experiences problems relating to others, and was unable to speak or write expressively. I asked Jane to draw her nightmare (Figure 6.7) and a disabled but slightly more able peer, her

Figure 6.7 "Dear Lord Happ me because cos I am ily sad" (published with permission)

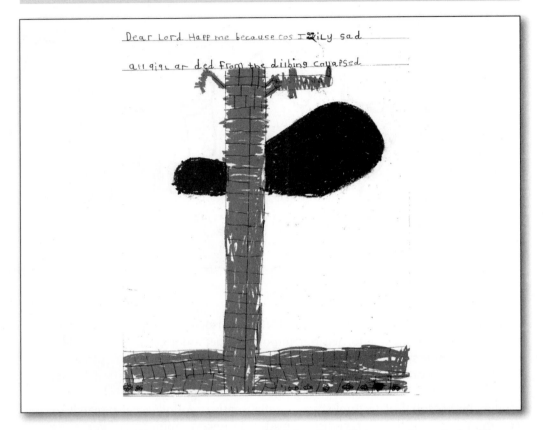

only friend, who through a language they had developed between them, helped her to write a prayer to accompany the image. It became apparent from the drawing and words and later gesticulations that Jane had seen TV footage of the New York 9/11 disaster. She was deeply disturbed by the experience particularly by the sight of people leaping from the building to avoid the fire (see bodies at the base). Later counseling based on the visual information enabled Jane to escape the nightly replay of the film loop in her mind that caused the nightmares to recur.

The draw and write technique and other visual methods (see Thomson, 2008) are often used with "normal" children. Jane and her friend were able to combine their strengths to communicate their views to me. This is not always the case, and the underlying assumption is that children with a mental disability or learning difficulty are neither well informed nor sufficiently able to contribute. This legitimizes not seeking or accepting their views and justifies researchers too quickly seeking professionals, parents, or guardians to speak for them. It is an undeniable right of all human beings to be heard and participate in studies in which they are expert.

I am currently undertaking a study to explore the perceptions of disabled people with limited communication skills of their subjective well-being through a "sensescape" approach.

2. Andrew is a participant in the project, and I have known him for 8 years. He is 42 years of age and suffered a brain hemorrhage when he was 12. He has significant physical and mental impairment. Despite very poor eyesight and motor skills, his paintings of his emotional state are skilful and insightful. However, for a long time I was unable to use them as part of an image-elicitation approach because of his limited interpersonal communication. When showing me his paintings, Andrew mostly sang apparently unrelated songs that were popular when he was 12 years old. I listened and tried to be patient, but it became very clear that he was becoming increasingly impatient with me. Then I realized that he was singing answers to my questions. When I asked him how he was feeling at the start of an interview, he would sing a Beatles song "It's been a hard day's night . . ." However, when asked about a drawing that to me denoted "sadness," he would come back with a Shakespearean quote "To be, or **NOT** to be: that is the question" (Andrew's emphasis), which I interpreted as a comment on his drawing and his state of mind (Is it better to live or to die?). In subsequent meetings, he continued to take songs memorized before his illness and by changing intonation or emphasis or by playing subtle word games with lyrics, he communicated his views. Now we conduct interviews by singing, and my job is to rotate his choice of song or turn of phrase until it catches the light of my reasoning.

When someone suffers a brain trauma as in Andrew's case, or has a congenital mental disability, elements of cognition are lost or depleted. The residual components reconfigure to make use of the remaining cerebral capacity, and this may entail increased capacity in one or more senses. Andrew communicates his views in two sensory forms—drawings and songs and verse—drawn from his memory stores. Like other visual researchers, I believed that photography (i.e., imagery) is *the* central mnemonic device (for example family photo albums), but Andrew accessed his memory banks not for images but for tunes, lyrics, and prose that he could manipulate to his own ends. Only when I understood the combined visual and auditory/oracy senses and their respective roles, did I and Andrew make sense of each other. Visual researchers should not assume that the visual has primacy over other senses but, rather, other senses are part, but not all, of our engagement with the world and therefore important to our understanding of society (Mason & Davies, 2009).

The capacity to communicate where communication was once thought impossible is changing. Improvements in intensive care have led to an increase in the number of patients who survive severe brain injury. Some of these patients go on to have a good recovery but others awaken from the acute comatose state and do not show any signs of awareness. Those who yield no evidence of purposeful sensory response are given a diagnosis of a vegetative state.

3.   Martin Monti et al. (2010) reported a study in *The New England Journal of Medicine* that gives credibility to the possibility that some patients classified as vegetative are actually conscious, and a few may be able to communicate. The researchers used functional magnetic resonance imaging (fMRI) to scan 54 patients' brains to record any activity generated following verbal prompts and questions from the doctors. They found signs of awareness in five patients who demonstrated the ability to generate willful, neuroanatomically specific responses during two established mental-imagery tasks, one of whom was able to answer basic "yes" or "no to questions by activating different parts of his brain after being instructed to do so. In conclusion, Monti et al. stated,

> These results show that a small proportion of patients in a vegetative or minimally conscious state have brain activation reflecting some awareness and cognition. Careful clinical examination will result in reclassification of the state of consciousness in some of these patients. This technique may be useful in establishing basic communication with patients who appear to be unresponsive. (Monti et al., 2010, p. 579)

The results indicate how much we still have to learn about visual methods and sensory consciousness. Researchers can potentially communicate with people diagnosed as in a vegetative state through auditory or other sensory stimuli, record responses visually (fMRI), and ask simple questions requiring a "yes" or "no" response. Ethical problems will arise if doctors ask bigger questions—for example, whether the patient wants to live or die, and the answer is "die." This development should stimulate sensory qualitative researchers to rethink communicating with participants who are sensorially challenged. The study also illustrates the power of applied technology to question our assumptions of what is possible in participatory research.

The sensorial experiences of people with disabilities are important because sensory relationships are pivotal domains of cultural expression and the medium through which well-being is enacted and depicted. Sensory relations are also social relations. Understanding how people with intellectual disabilities navigate changing social and cultural landscapes through their senses is fundamental to understanding how micro and macro contexts affect, for example, happiness and well-being. Disabled people make sense of their lives through the interplay of sensory relations not accessible through discourse; words are mere proxies for their direct experiences. Text- and verbal-based approaches are limited because they fail to move beyond inherent psychophysical characteristics to reveal taken-for-granted, embodied, sensorial lives.

A THREAT TO VISUAL RESEARCH—ETHICS REGULATION

In framing my argument for a more "seeing" research, I stressed the importance of normalizing visual methods within mainstream disciplines, paradigms, and practices. I conclude this chapter on a somber note by describing a significant threat to the collaborative and developmental possibilities of visual methods.

Increased regulation and bureaucratization of the ethical review process is particularly noticeable in Europe, the United States, Canada, Australia, New Zealand, and the developing world (van den Hoonaard, 2002). Researchers, institutions, and funding bodies are bound together by a web of ethical regulation that depends on limited value notions. Ethical regulations in the United States are viewed by Norman Denzin and Yvonna Lincoln (2005, p. 1123) as "out of date for the purposes of qualitative research and entirely useless for the development of culturally, racially, and ethically sensitive methods." Unfortunately, the U.S. regulatory/medical model of research ethics was widely adopted in the United Kingdom (Tinker & Coomber, 2004) and in mainland Europe. An empirical study of researchers' experience and understanding of visual ethics in the United Kingdom by Rose Wiles and colleagues (2010, p. 2) concluded,

> Critiques of the process of ethical approval for social scientific research include the following concerns: (1) the capacity of ethics committees to make ethical judgments across a wide range of research approaches and contexts, some of which might require particular and specialist knowledge; (2) the model of regulation which is perceived to be based on that of biomedical research where there are actual physical risks to participants and disproportionate for social science research relative to the level of potential

risk; (3) the consequences of ethical regulation on social research practice including making the use of some research approaches or topics difficult or impossible, impeding positive relations between researchers and participants, encouraging researchers to tell "half truths" (Atkinson, 2009) on forms for ethical approval and encouraging researchers to think of ethics as a one-off event rather than as a series of issues that need consideration through the lifetime of a research project. Thus paradoxically a case has been made that the new regimes of ethical approval might actually be discouraging ethical thinking among researchers.

Visual researchers working within the qualitative paradigm shoulder an additional burden because visual methods comprise a wide array of approaches and types of media and hence raise particular challenges for ethics committees adopting a conservative, regulatory/medical approach to ethics. Confidentiality, legal issues (such as copyright), and dissemination of visual data are problematic for visual researchers faced with ethics committees with limited knowledge of visual methods. Because, for example, anonymity is considered central to ethical research, ethics committees may adopt a restrictive "safety first" stance when faced with a visual study in which plans to use or publish images that make people identifiable. An important claim made by visual researchers is that visual methods can reveal important information that text or word-based methods cannot. Hence, any attempt to disguise people without careful reasoning and due cause can remove the very point of the data and the moral rights of participants who wish to have their voices heard.

The primary danger of the current system of bureaucratic regulation and review process is the preoccupation with gaining ethical approval. There is a real possibility that genuine discussions of sensitive visual ethical dilemmas will be put to one side in the effort to demonstrate that a study is ethically sound and acceptable to the legal, regulatory conscious members who constitute ethics committees. In encouraging making visual research appear to be respectable in the eyes of ethics committees, the potential for raising genuine ethical concerns will be discouraged and diminished to the detriment of visually located ethical debate and future good practice. Qualitative visual researchers should know enough about the culture, society, or community through their research to make sound sensitive moral decisions. The overarching aim of any ethical regulatory system should be to develop visual researchers' integrity and knowledge base:

Ethical reflexivity is a matter of awareness and sensitivity and is reflected in the degree of honesty and truthfulness in their dealings with others. These values are a measure of researchers' integrity and professionalism and are increasingly a requirement of research institutions and funding bodies aspiring to excellence. To act ethically is to value integrity, inclusiveness, personal security, privacy and dignity. For visual researchers, ethics guidelines and codes of practice cover important principles, but "visual" research brings additional, potentially distinct, ethical conundrums. (Clark, Prosser, & Wiles, 2010, p. 90)

For qualitative visual researchers, an "ethics of care" approach, which is an important but less common model that challenges the deontological framework underpinning biomedical ethics, is much preferred. Here, ethical decisions are made on the basis of care, compassion, and a desire to act in ways that benefit the individual or group that is the focus of research rather than following universalist principles or absolute norms and rules that may govern ethical decision making. Experienced qualitative visual researchers (e.g., Banks, 2007; Harper, 1998; Pink, 2008; Rose, 2007) seek to implement collaborative relationships in their research relationships that have some commonality with an ethics of care approach. The current trend toward a biomedical regulatory ethics may slow the development visual methods but nothing will stop visual methods' becoming one of the most important qualitative research methodologies in the 21st century.

Notes

1. Do an Internet search for "Running the Numbers" to find Chris Jordan's work. http://www.chrisjordan.com/current_set2.php

2. Stanczak (2007, p. 8) points out that William Fox Talbot, founder of paper-process photography, wrote, "It frequently happens, moreover—and this is one of the charms of photography—that the operator himself [sic] discovers on examination, perhaps long afterwards, that he has depicted many things he had no notion of at the time."

3. The 1st International Visual Methods Conference, convened by Jon Prosser, was held at Leeds University, United Kingdom, September 15–17, and was part of an Economic and Social Research Council (ESRC) Researcher Development Initiative program "Building Capacity in Visual Methods." The second conference will take place at the Open University, United Kingdom, in 2011.

4. CAQDAS Networking Project, University of Surrey: http://caqdas.soc.surrey .ac.uk/. The project is in receipt of its seventh consecutive term of funding by the UK ESRC. The research project Qualitative Innovations in CAQDAS (QUIC) is currently funded by the ESRC National Centre for Research Methods (NCRM).

5. See ongoing BBC *Video Nation* clips at http://www.bbc.co.uk/videonation/

6. Real Life Methods and Realities projects led by Jennifer Mason at the University of Manchester are both ESRC, National Centre for Research Methods projects that are at the cutting edge of creative, qualitatively driven research methods. The Morgan Centre is currently the main center in the United Kingdom for innovative qualitative research methods. See http://www.socialsciences.manchester.ac.uk/realities/ or search on the Internet for "Realities Manchester, UK."

7. Lester Magoogan has exhibited at Tate Modern and Lowry galleries in London and appeared on television in the United Kingdom and abroad. Lester Magoogan's art can be found at www.lestermagoogan.co.uk

References

Atkinson, P. (2009). Ethics and ethnography. *21st Century Society: Journal of the Academy of Social Sciences, 4*(1), 17–30.

Banks, M. (2007). *Using visual data in qualitative research*. London: Sage.

Becker, H. (1986). *Doing things together*. Evanston, IL: Northwestern University Press.

Biella, P. (1993). Beyond ethnographic film: Hypermedia and scholarship. In J. Rollwagen (Ed.), *Anthropological film and video in the 1990s*. New York: Institute Press.

Butler-Kisber, L. (2008). Collage as inquiry. In J. G. Knowles & A. L. Cole (Eds.), *Handbook of the arts in qualitative research* (pp. 265–276). Thousand Oaks, CA: Sage.

Cancienne, M. B. (2008). From research to performance. In J. G. Knowles & A. L. Cole (Eds.), *Handbook of the arts in qualitative research* (pp. 397–406). Thousand Oaks, CA: Sage.

Chalfen, R. (1998). Interpreting family photography as a pictorial communication. In J. Prosser (Ed.), *Image-based research: A sourcebook for qualitative researchers* (pp. 214–234). London: Falmer Press.

Chaplin, E. (2006). The convention of captioning: W. G. Sebald and the release of the captive image. *Visual Sociology, 21*(1), 42–54.

Church, K. (2008). Exhibiting as inquiry. In J. G. Knowles & A. L. Cole (Eds.), *Handbook of the arts in qualitative research* (pp. 421–434). Thousand Oaks, CA: Sage.

Clark, A., Prosser, J., & Wiles, R. (2010). Ethical issues in image-based research. *Arts & Health, 2*(1), 81–93. Available at http://dx.doi.org/10.1080/17533010903495298

Clark-Ibanez, M. (2007). Inner-city children in sharper focus: Sociology of childhood and photo-elicitation interviews. In G. Stanczak (Ed.), *Visual research methods: Image, society, and representation* (pp. 167–196). Thousand Oaks, CA: Sage.

Cole, A. L., & McIntyre, M. (2008). Installation art-as-research. In J. G. Knowles & A. L. Cole (Eds.), *Handbook of the arts in qualitative research* (pp. 287–298). Thousand Oaks, CA: Sage.

Collier, J., & Collier, M. (1986). *Visual anthropology: Photography as a research method.* Albuquerque: University of New Mexico Press. (Original work by J. Collier published in 1967)

Denzin, N. K., & Lincoln, Y. S. (Eds.). (2005). Epilogue. The eighth and ninth moments—Qualitative research in/and the fractured future. In *The SAGE handbook of qualitative research* (3rd ed., pp. 1115–1126). Thousand Oaks, CA: Sage.

Duchowski, A. T. (2003). *Eye tracking methodology: Theory and practice.* London: Springer.

Eisner, E. (2008). Art and knowledge. In J. G. Knowles & A. L. Cole (Eds.), *Handbook of the arts in qualitative research* (pp. 3–12). Thousand Oaks, CA: Sage.

Fox Talbot, W. H. (1844). *The pencil of nature.* Cambridge, MA: Capo Press. (Original published in a series 1844–1846)

Gauntlett, D. (2007). *Creative explorations: New approaches to identities and audiences.* New York: Routledge.

Goldman, R., Pea, R., Barron, B., & Derry, S. (Eds.). (2007). *Video research in the learning sciences.* Mahwah, NJ: Lawrence Erlbaum.

Goldstein, B. M. (2007). All photos lie: Images as data. In G. Stanczak (Ed.), *Visual research methods: Image, society, and representation.* Thousand Oaks, CA: Sage.

Grady, J. (1996). The scope of visual sociology. *Visual Sociology, 11*(1), 10–24.

Harper, D. (1998). An argument for visual sociology. In J. Prosser (Ed.), *Image-based research: A sourcebook for qualitative researchers* (pp. 20–35). London: Falmer Press.

Harper, D. (2002). Talking about pictures: A case for photo-elicitation. *Visual Studies, 17*(1), 13–26.

Harper, D. (2005). What's new visually? In N. K. Denzin & Y. S. Lincoln (Eds.), *The SAGE handbook of qualitative research* (3rd ed., pp. 747–762). Thousand Oaks, CA: Sage.

Heath, C., Hindmarsh, J., & Luff, P. (2010). *Video in qualitative research.* London: Sage.

Higgs, G. E. (2008). Psychology: Knowing the self through arts. In J. G. Knowles & A. L. Cole (Eds.), *Handbook of the arts in qualitative research* (pp. 545–556). Thousand Oaks, CA: Sage.

Holliday, R. (2007). Performances, confessions, and identities: Using video diaries to research sexualities. In G. Stanczak (Ed.), *Visual research methods: Image, society, and representation* (pp. 255–280). Thousand Oaks, CA: Sage.

Knowles, J. G., & Cole, A. L. (Eds.). (2008). *Handbook of the arts in qualitative research.* Thousand Oaks, CA: Sage.

Kuhn, A., & McAllister, K. E. (2006). *Locating memory: Photographic acts.* New York: Berghahn Books.

Langer, S. K. (1957). *Problems of art: Ten philosophical lectures.* New York: Scribner.

Mason, J. (2002). *Qualitative researching.* Thousand Oaks, CA: Sage.

Mason, J. (2008). Tangible affinities and the real life fascination of kinship. *Sociology, 42*(1), 29–45.

Mason, J., & Davies, K. (2009). Coming to our senses? A critical approach to sensory methodology. *Qualitative Research, 9*(5), 587–603.

McNiff, S. (2008). Art-based research. In J. G. Knowles & A. L. Cole (Eds.), *Handbook of the arts in qualitative research* (pp. 29–40). Thousand Oaks, CA: Sage.

Monti, M. M., Vanhaudenhuyse, A., Coleman, M. R., Boly, M., Pickard, J. D., Tshibanda, L., et al. (2010). Willful modulation of brain activity in disorders of consciousness. *New England Medical Journal, 362*(7), 579–589.

Packard, J. (2008). "I'm gonna show you what it's really like out here": The power and limitation of participatory visual methods. *Visual Studies, 23*(1, April), 63–77.

Pauwels, L. (Ed.). (2006). *Visual cultures of science.* Hanover, NH: Dartmouth College Press.

Pauwels, L. (2008). A private practice going public? Social functions and sociological research opportunities of web-based family photography. *Visual Studies, 23*(1, April), 34–49.

Pink, S. (2008). *Doing visual ethnography* (2nd ed.). Thousand Oaks, CA: Sage.

Prosser, J. (2007). Visual methods and the visual culture of schools. *Visual Studies, 22*(1), 13–30.

Prosser, J., & Loxley. A. (2008). *Introducing visual methods.* ESRC National Centre for Research Methods. NCRM/010 Review papers. Available at http://eprints.ncrm.ac.uk/420/

Reavey, P. (2011). *Visual methods in psychology: Using and interpreting images in qualitative research.* London: Routledge.

Rose, G. (2007). *Visual methodologies* (2nd ed.). London: Sage.

Ricoeur, P. (2003). *The rule of the metaphor: Multi-disciplinary studies of the creation of meaning in language.* Toronto, ON: University of Toronto. Toronto.

Ruby, J. (2005). The last 20 years of visual anthropology. *Visual Studies, 20*(2), 159–170.

Saldaña, J. (2008). Ethnodrama and ethnotheatre. In J. G. Knowles & A. L. Cole (Eds.), *Handbook of the arts in qualitative research* (pp. 195–208). Thousand Oaks, CA: Sage.

Schwartz, D. (2007). If a picture is worth a thousand words, why are you reading this essay? *Social Psychology Quarterly, 70*(4), 319–321.

Schwartz, D. (2009a). *In the kitchen.* Heidelberg, Germany: Kehrer Verlag.

Schwartz, D. (2009b). *Visual art meets visual methods: Making a case for making pictures.* Keynote photographer's address, 1st International Visual Methods Conference, Clothworkers' Hall, University of Leeds, Leeds, UK.

Stanczak, G. (Ed.). (2007). *Visual research methods: Image, society, and representation.* Thousand Oaks, CA: Sage.

Sullivan, G. (2005). *Art practice as research: Inquiry in the visual arts.* Thousand Oaks, CA: Sage.

Tai, R. H., Loehr, J. F., & Brigham, F. J. (2006). An exploration of the use of eye-gaze tracking to study problem-solving on standardized science assessments. *International Journal of Research and Method in Education, 29*(2), 185–208.

Thomson, P. (Ed.). (2008). *Doing visual research with children and young people.* New York: Routledge.

Tinker, A., & Coomber, V. (2004). *University research ethics committees: Their role, remit and conduct.* London: King's College.

Van den Hoonaard, W. C. (2002). *Walking the tightrope: Ethical issues for qualitative researchers.* Toronto, ON: University of Toronto Press.

Wagner, J. (2006). Visible materials, visualised theory and images of social research. *Visual Studies, 21*(1), 55–69.

Wagner. J. (2007). Observing culture and social life: Documentary photography, fieldwork and social research. In G. Stanczak (Ed.), *Visual research methods: Image, society, and representation.* Thousand Oaks, CA: Sage.

Warren, S. (2005). Photography and voice in critical qualitative management research. *Accounting, Auditing and Accountability Journal, 18,* 861–882.

Weber, S. (2008). Visual images in research. In J. G. Knowles & A. L. Cole (Eds.), *Handbook of the arts in qualitative research* (pp. 44–45). Thousand Oaks, CA: Sage.

Wiles, R., Coffey, A., Robison, J., & Prosser, J. (2010). Ethical regulation and visual methods: Making visual research impossible or developing good practice? *Sociological Research Online.* Retrieved February 2011 from http://www.socresonline.org.uk/

Wiles, R., Durrant, G., De Broe, S., & Powell. J., (2005). *Assessment of the needs for training in research methods in the UK social science community.* ESRC National Centre for Research Methods. Available at http://www.ncrm.ac.uk/research/outputs/publications/reports.php

Worth, S., Adair, J., & Chalfen, R. (1997). *Through Navajo eyes: An exploration in film communication and anthropology.* Albuquerque: University of New Mexico Press. (Original work published in 1972)

Performative Autoethnography

Critical Embodiments and Possibilities

Tami Spry

When the "I" seeks to give an account of itself, an account that must include the conditions of its own emergence, it must, as a matter of necessity, become a social theorist.

—Judith Butler (2005, p. 8)

S/he who writes, writes. In uncertainty, in necessity. And does not ask whether s/he is given the permission to do so or not.

—Trinh T. Minh-ha (1989, p. 8)

Performance sometimes resists, exceeds, and overwhelms the constraints and strictures of writing.

—Dwight Conquergood (1991, p. 193)

This chapter is an ensemble piece. . . . It asks for a performance, one in which we might discover that our autoethnographic texts are not alone.

—Stacy Holman Jones (2005, p. 764)

This chapter seeks engagement body to body, with hurting and healing bodies, with "articulate bodies" (Pineau, 2000), and with necessarily uncertain bodies; it seeks co-performance in the entanglements of accounting for "I" and in the rupture and rapture of performance that may well exceed the constraints of its (and this) writing. It seeks co-presence with others in the "chorus of discordant voices" (Denzin, 2008) in qualitative research. It is a bid for autoethnographic ensemble, for social theorizing with those laboring for disruptive dialogue and transformative pedagogies on the page and in the stages of our lives together post–9/11, postmodernity, postcolonially, post-political monologism.

Critical reflection on loss and the development of hope will comprise the autoethnographic bones of the chapter. Fragmentation, dismemberment, delivery of body/story will be implemented as metaphors to interrupt colonizing narratives of 9/11 and other personal/political and local/global issues of loss toward a performative pedagogy of hope and possibility. In performative autoethnographic fashion, the essay must *do* autoethnography as it articulates autoethnographic theory/methodology praxis, pushing and pulling between the "constraints and strictures of writing" (Conquergood, 1991) and the sometimes messy, resistant, and epistemologically overwhelming performing body.

Autoethnography Lost and Found

Autoethnography is body and verse.

It is self and other and one and many.

It is ensemble, a cappella, and accompaniment.

Autoethnography is place and space and time.

It is personal, political, and palpable.

It is art and craft. It is jazz and blues.

It is messy, bloody, and unruly.

It is agency, rendition, and dialogue.

It is danger, trouble, and pain.

It is critical, reflexive, performative, and often forgiving.

It is the string theories of pain and privilege

forever woven into fabrics of power/lessness.

It is skin/flints of melanin and bodies

in the gendered hues of sanctuary and violence.

It is a subaltern narrative revealing the understory of hegemonic systems.

It is skeptical and restorative.

It is an interpreted body

of evidence.

It is personally accountable.

It is wholly none of these, but fragments of each.

It is a performance of possibilities.

Performative autoethnography is a critically reflexive methodology resulting in a narrative of the researcher's engagement with others in particular sociocultural contexts. Performative autoethnography views the personal as inherently political, focuses on bodies-in-context as co-performative agents in interpreting knowledge, and holds aesthetic crafting of research as an ethical imperative of representation. At least, this is what I have come to know, because autoethnography, for me, has been about performing what I had thought impossible, about moving in and out of trauma with words and blood and bone. It has been about dropping down out of the personal and individual to find painful and comforting connection with others in sociocultural contexts of loss and hope.

Autoethnographically inhabiting the process of losing a son in childbirth felt like the identification of body parts, as if each described piece of the experience were a cumbersome limb that I could snap off my body and lay on the ground. There was a bizarre and profound comfort in admitting to and describing this feeling of dismemberment and fragmentation. I had been trying to glue myself together with dominant cultural narratives about grief, performed on its "five stages," and tried time and time again to stifle the waves of wails coming from an empty body and from Twin Towers of ashes. An 18-month period brought the loss of a child, the bombings of 9/11, the death of a close colleague from cancer, the loss of our beloved Minnesota Senator Paul Wellstone, and the death of my father.

I am thankful for the disciplinary wisdom to view lived experience through theories of embodiment because it was only in trusting the embodied knowledge that "I am an un/learning body in the process of feeling," that I began to heal (Madison, 2006, p. 245). Reinhabiting the only space I ever lived with my son motivated a deeply embodied theorizing about the narrative disposition of this grief (Spry, 2006). I felt a deep somatic connection to that fractured self and space, like I was moving back into my body, a body that I had abandoned with the birth and subsequent death of our son. Like bell hooks, "I came to theory desperate, wanting to comprehend—to grasp what was happening in and around me. Most importantly, I wanted the hurt to go away. I saw in theory then a location for healing" (hooks, 1994, p. 59). After years of moving through pain with pen and paper, asking the nurse for these tools the morning after losing our child was the only thing I could make my body do. Though it felt as if my arms had bounced stiff and clumsily about my ankles that day, the language of bodies came pouring out.

However, the resulting performative autoethnography, "Paper and Skin: Bodies of Loss and Life" (Spry, 2004), was certainly not written at the bedside of my grieving body. To believe so would be to romanticize the processes of grief and of performative autoethnography. Articulating my own personal pain is *not* autoethnography. Novelist David Foster Wallace suggests, "All the attention and engagement and work you need to get from the reader can't be for your benefit; it's got to be for hers" (quoted in Max, 2009, p. 48). It is the intentional and critically reflexive connection of this narrative to larger social issues, to the politics, pleasure, and pain of other people, that distinguishes performative autoethnography as a methodology grounded in forging knowledge with others to dismantle and transform the inequities of power structures.

In "Autoethnography: Making the Personal Political," Stacy Homan Jones describes autoethnography as "a performance that asks how our personal accounts count" (2005, p. 764). Like Jones, I, too, come to autoethnography and research from performance studies, particularly from the disciplinary turns of performance studies toward ethnography and ethnography toward performance studies; performative autoethnography emerges from this academic and artistic space. The "crisis of representation," which I have contended elsewhere, was not so much a crisis for performance studies artist/scholars as it was a recognition of a familiar (Spry, 2006). Our disciplinary roots are grounded in interpretation, a process wrought with the crisis and complexity of representation. The "performative turn" in ethnography (Turner, 1986) has expanded the scope and recognition of the cultural/political implications of performance studies (Spry, 2006). Similarly, performance studies theories of embodiment and textual interpretation inform ethnographic methods of ethics, researcher positionality, cultural performances, and fieldwork (Conquergood, 1985, 1991; Schechner, 1985). Mary Strine mapped the "cultural turn" in performance studies, asserting that the "cultural-performance matrix" refocused perspectives on how performative forms and practices have served to "produce, sustain, and transform" systems of power and dominance and directed us toward less traditional texts (personal narratives, oral histories, performance art) (1998, pp. 6–7). Strine, with

Conquergood, argued that this cultural-performance matrix signals a paradigmatic shift "from performance as a distinctive *act* of culture to performance as an integrated *agency* of culture" (Strine, 1998, p. 7).

Performance and ethnography continually turn back on themselves emerging as praxes of participatory civic social action (Alexander, 2006; Denzin, 2006, 2008; Jones, 2005; Madison & Hamera, 2006: Pelias, 2004). Nowhere is the complexity, utility, and ethical implications of these praxes more evident than in D. Soyini Madison's work, *Critical Ethnography: Method, Ethics, and Performance* (2005), which remains at this point in the development of critical/performative/pedagogical autoethnography the pivotal work informing auto/ethnographic performance scholarship. Performative autoethnography continues its epistemological development through insistence on the critique of our historical and sociocultural emergence. From this scholarly heritage, I find hope through loss with others in autoethnography.

Performative autoethnography then, as a personal, political, and social praxis, and as a critically reflexive methodology, can provide the framework to critically reflect on the ways in which our personal lives intersect, collide, and commune with others in the body politic in ways alternate to hegemonic cultural constructions. Autoethnography provides an apparatus to pose and engage the questions of our global lives.

This chapter is a textual "performance of possibilities" (Denzin, 2006b; Madison 2005) in a time when loss and hardship are found in our foreclosing homes, in our millions of No Children Left Behind, in our sisters and brothers recovering from and simultaneously shipping out to war(s). I hear Norman Denzin and Michael Giardina:

> Never before has there been a greater need for a militant utopianism that can help us imagine a world free of conflict, terror, and death; a world that is caring, loving, and truly compassionate: a world that honors healing. Postmodern democracy cannot succeed unless critical cultural scholars adopt methodologies that transcend the limitations and constraints of a lingering politically and racially conservative postpositivism. (2007, p. 12)

In a time of backlash with the rise in violent militia spurred on by media hate mongers (Keller, 2009) performative autoethnography is a methodology that can "transcend the limitations and constraints" of a lingering—and possibly growing—neoconservative postpositivism. It is a personal/political praxis, an aesthetic/epistemic performance, and a critical/indigenous/advocational ethnography that operates from a compassionate and lionhearted will to usurp and resist injustice.

What follows in this chapter then, is a response to Jones's 2005 call to "disrupt, produce, and imagine" co-performatively (p. 763). The essay will track representative histories ("Fragmented Histories Absent and Present"), offer interpretive criteria ("Performative Fragments and Embodied Possibilities"), discuss pedagogical developments ("Critical Fragments of Craft"), and posit future directions of autoethnography ("Concluding Fragments"). Throughout each section, the concept of the performative-I researcher disposition will be further developed as the nexus of performative autoethnography (Spry, 2006).

And so I have come to autoethnography yearning to know what is possible after absence, to embody the afterlife of loss, after 9/11, after an un/American politics of ignorance and bullying. In my/our body/politic are dark and empty and furtive places where things did not come to fruition, places from which there were no fruits of the labor. But writing performatively and autoethnographically with others in these darknesses reveals hope in the hollow, potential in the filling, and cleansing in the emptying.

Fragmented Histories Absent and Present

What we call *history* is strictly woven into each cultural environment. The making of historicizing therefore depends on "local knowledge."

—Antonis Liakos (2008, p. 139)

The past, home, is not a perfect memory—it will not save us.

—Elizabeth Adams St.Pierre (2008, p. 122)

In considering a history of autoethnography, it becomes clear that the contestation of history itself has been a catalyst of autoethnography as a methodology, revealing autoethnography's potential to break and remake canons of history through localized subaltern knowledges. Much autoethnographic work has been about the business of recognizing and articulating the multiplicity of histories that exist within any past event or historical epoch, and examining the ways in which dominant narratives of History with a capital "H" perpetuate and maintain the racism, classism, and sexism that in/forms dominant thought, memory, and imagination (Grande, 2008; Liakos, 2008; St.Pierre, 2008). In *Searching for Yellowstone: Race, Gender, Family, and Memory in the Postmodern West* (2008), Norman K. Denzin employs critical autoethnographic reflexivity concerning his childhood at Yellowstone, popular representations, and scholarly discourses to "create a new version of the past, a new history. I want to create a chorus of discordant voices (and images) concerning Native Americans and their place in Yellowstone Park as well as in our collective imagination" (p. 18). Here, critical reflection on how one's personal experiences collide with hegemonic History puts bodies in motion that break and remake historical memory and imagination, and foreground the power of performative autoethnography to empower critical collaborative meaning making to challenge and change, in this case, the romantic nostalgia reifying racist performances of Native Americans. Autoethnography can democratize historicizing by critically reflecting on the inherent collaboration and collisions between selves and others in the performativity of race, class, and other politicized identities. In critiquing the "minstrel shows that replay the Wild West," Denzin seeks to "replace old stereotypes with new understandings. I want to show how historical discourse can in fact turn back on itself, revise its stance toward the past, and perform new, progressive representations of cultural difference" (p. 23). Performative autoethnography makes present the absence of diverse, indigenous, and subaltern histories providing a multiplicity of representations that may challenge, argue, and disagree with one another, but, by their very presence, dispel the racial myths and minstrel shows of monologic history written by the politically powerful.

More specifically, the work of indigenous scholars critiques "history" as a hegemonic Westernized product of modernity in need of decolonization (Anzuldúa, 2007; Grande, 2008; Mutua-Kombo, 2009; Smith, 1999; Swadener & Mutua, 2008). In examining the process of canon and exclusion in historicizing, Liakos writes, "Since the eighteenth century, the tradition of history writing in Europe involves not only a description of the past, but also the imposition of a hierarchical view of the world, with Europe perched at the top" (2008, p. 143). And in the fashion of ethnography before the "crisis of representation," historians defined all that was non-Western and non-European as abject, abnormal, exotic, and "uncivilized." But here, for "historical discourse [to] in fact turn back upon itself" it must also view this "crisis" as a crisis only to colonizers; being represented as a subcategory to all that is moral and good was, and still is, merely a state of affairs to those colonized by History and the History of research. Research produced by privileged Whites sometimes reads as if they "discovered" the tragedy and inequity of racism, placing people of color as witnesses to their "findings" rather than as intellectual interlocutors, as evidence rather than as agents. In discussing decolonizing research schemata, Beth Blue Swadener and Kagendo Mutua argue,

> Non-Western knowledge forms are excluded from or marginalized in normative researched paradigms, and therefore non-Western/indigenous voices and epistemologies are silenced and subjects lack agency within such

representations. Furthermore, decolonizing research recognizes the role of colonizing in the scripting and encrypting of a silent, inarticulate, and inconsequential indigenous subject and how such encryptions legitimize oppression. (2008, pp. 33–34)

Though only one in a large and efficacious body of methods underpinned by indigenous methodologies, performative autoethnography breaks the colonized encrypted code of what counts as knowledge redefining silence as a form of agency and positioning local knowledge at the heart of epistemology and ontology (Spry, 2008; Visweswaran, 2006). Performative autoethnography interrupts and opens constructs of history, thereby reframing what a "crisis" is, and to whom, and who has the discursive power to define the crisis and its antecedents and antidotes in the first place.

HISTORY, TIME, AND THE OTHER

The process of performative autoethnography starts with a body, in a place, and in a time. In an earlier work, I considered autoethnography as an embodied praxis by employing Clifford Geertz's notion of "being here" and "being there" (Spry, 2001a). Though Geertz's construct recognizes time as an efficacious element in ethnography, its significance seems a taken–for–granted element, which, Johannes Fabian argues, can lead one to "disregard the many ways in which time is used to construct otherness" (2007, p. 49). How we represent the autoethnographic body "now" and "then" is of equal importance as "here" and "there." "What we know about the politics of time," writes Fabian, "should have epistemological consequences" (p. 49). Concepts of time and history go hand in hand in their ability to hegemonize and to proliferate representations of otherness as "inarticulate and inconsequential" (Swadener & Mutua, 2008). The Westernized terms *Third World, developing, underdeveloped,* and *primitive* exemplify attempts by dominant power systems to assign temporal constructs that situate the Other in the past, reifying Others as always and already "behind the times," as a quaint romanticized anecdote. Like the "Noble Savage," the Other is not represented as a contemporary, but as a hapless morally and intellectually inferior exotic. Fabian argues that the representation of time through language becomes a tool allowing the (auto)ethnographer to distance self from others, again positioning others as objects of study rather than as co-performers of knowledge, *co-present* in the time and process of knowledge production.

This is especially relevant to indigenous research where "natives" have been studied for the "richness of their past," rather than engaged as contemporary agents of epistemology (Denzin, 2008; Fabian, 1983; Grande, 2008; Liakos, 2008; Smith, 1999). Linda Tuhiwai Smith articulates the tradition of imperialism and colonialism in research, explaining in an understandably oft-quoted observation that the word *research* itself "is probably one of the dirtiest words in indigenous world's vocabulary" (1999, p. 1). Additionally, cultures view time in radically different ways, that is, circular, past and present as one, history as a space of still living experience, among other temporal constructs, which subsequently changes epistemological forms and content.

Living with others in time(s) and understanding the potentially colonizing apparatus of time is tantamount to autoethnographic research. In her discussion of a *Red* research construct of *Indianismo,* Sandy Grande explains that the "notion of *Indianismo* stands outside the polarizing debates of essentialism and postmodernism, recognizing that *both the timeless and temporal are essential for theorizing the complexity of indigenous realities*" (2008, p. 241, emphasis mine). In performative autoethnography, time is viewed as politically contested and contingent, as is cultural place, space, and identity—all of which effect and are effected by varying notions of temporality and history.

For a performative autoethnographer, the critical stance of the performing body constitutes a praxis of evidence and analysis through time and place. We offer our performing body as raw data of a critical cultural story. The performance work of Guillermo Gómez-Peña illustrates in stark clarity the exoticized and sexualized "Mexican" male body. Gómez-Peña embodies, and then flips these images by placing himself in a cage for audiences to observe "the noble savage." "The way in which society sees itself," writes Liakos, "determines both the historical view and vice versa: culture is historically determined not only because of its formation in time but also on account of the perceptions over time that constitute part of the warp and weft of culture" (2008, p. 139). Autoethnographic constructions and embodiments of history can trouble our perceptions of, "How far have we come, or not?" when considering cultural oppressions.

Performative autoethnography can interrupt master narratives that become "stuck in time" through its continual re/creation of knowledge by critically reflecting back on who we are, and where, and when. This kind of reflection constitutes a continual opening to the natures of temporality and its sociocultural representations, placing all of us in a coeval relationship with each other over time.

DÉJÀ VU BY ANY OTHER NAME

In a 2006 special issue of the *Journal of Contemporary Ethnography,* editors Scott Hunt and Natalia Junco presented essays that responded to Leon Anderson's work on "analytic autoethnography" where the ethnographic researcher is "a full member in the research group or setting" and is "committed to an analytic research agenda focused on improving theoretical understandings of broader social phenomenon" (Anderson, 2006, p. 375). I mention this special issue here because it presents significantly varying conceptions of the historical development of autoethnography. In his essay, Anderson decides that Carolyn Ellis and Arthur Bochner's (2006) work on "evocative or emotional ethnography" (Anderson, 2006, p. 374) constitutes a rejection of "realist and analytic ethnographic epistemological assumptions," and may "eclipse other versions of what autoethnography can be" (pp. 377, 374). Glaringly absent from Anderson's essay is a large body of autoethnographic work constituting many versions of what performative "autoethnography can be" and already is, including works by Bryant Alexander (2006), Ken Gale and Jonathan Wyatt (2008), Craig Gingrich-Philbrook (2001), H. Lloyd Goodall (2008), Stacy Holman Jones (2005), Ronald Pelias (2004), Elyse Lamm Pineau (2000), Chris Poulos (2009), Larry Russell (2004), Jonathan Wyatt (2008), and many others. In his response, "Analytic Autoethnography, or Déjà Vu All Over Again," Denzin writes, "Like others before him, Anderson does not want to review the debates that have gone on between the analytic and evocative schools of (auto)ethnography" (2006a, pp. 420–421). This want in literary review makes substantive comparative analysis difficult.

In their response, Ellis and Bochner, in concert with other essays in the series, argue that Anderson's defense of "realist" ethnography constitutes a call to stultify and bring under control the radicalizing, unruly, and creative elements of autoethnography that grew as a response to hegemonic reason/logic/analysis master narratives in anthropology and in academic discourse generally. In an essay outside of the special issue, "'Real Anthropology' and Other Nostalgias," Kath Weston argues that the term *real anthropology* encodes a certain historical consciousness when "the authority of the anthropologist remained intact, his or her identity secure . . . Its invocation implies that in recent times, when anthropology stumbled from grace, some policing of the boundaries of the discipline is necessary to separate acceptable from unacceptable topics or methods of study" (2008, pp. 128, 129). Surely, collaborative vigorous critique advances the development of theory and method; however, as Weston suggests, a policing of what is acceptable can draw us away from heuristic and pedagogical processes and possibilities.

Anderson is well advised by Denzin to engage the vast array of performance studies scholarship in autoethnography and critical ethnography. Performative autoethnography is forged within the ontological tension between its epistemological potential and its aesthetic imperative, the aesthetic/epistemic double-bind

(Gingrich-Philbrook, 2005). To Anderson's plea "that other scholars will join me in reclaiming and refining autoethnography as a part of the analytic ethnographic tradition" (2006, p. 392), authors in performative autoethnography are merely representative of the myriad scholars whose work is evidence that good autoethnography is, of course, theoretically grounded at its outset and methodologically heuristic in process and product, advancing itself as a praxis of inquiry as it performatively *does* analysis.

Ultimately, however discordant our voices may be in the articulation of autoethnography, as evidenced in the special issue of the *Journal of Contemporary Ethnography* (Hunt & Junco, 2006), our history, our historical present as researchers, is enriched by the constant conversation of what we are doing and why we are doing it. In their introduction to *Ethnographica Moralia: Experiments in Interpretive Anthropology*, Neni Panourgia and George Marcus caution us "not to rest comfortably in our assumptions, in our disciplinary boundaries . . . but to interrogate their certainty and interrupt their narratives" (2008, p. 3). I rely on the works of James Clifford, Dwight Conquergood, Craig Gingrich-Philbrook, D. Soyini Madison, George Marcus, Della Pollock, Mary Strine, Victor Turner, and others who view ethnography as performative, who see, as does Turner, performance as "the explanation and explication of life itself" (1986, p. 21). In the *co-performativity of meaning with others* I find myself, as autoethnographic researcher, in the constant negotiation of representation with others in always emergent, contingent, and power-laden historical contexts. I find scholarly desire and pedagogical purpose in Denzin's response in the special issue:

> Ethnography is not an innocent practice. Our research practices are performative, pedagogical, and political. Through our writing and our talk, we enact the worlds we study. These performances are messy and pedagogical. They instruct our readers about this world and how we see it. The pedagogical is always moral and political; by enacting a way of seeing and being, it challenges, contexts, or endorses the official, hegemonic ways of seeing and representing the other. (2006a, p. 422)

If autoethnography is knowledge forged collaboratively without a policing of disciplinary boundaries, then it may, in turn, become our history as well, always moving us forward, backward, in circle, or all at once. Rather than a historical modality of "civilizing" or "developing," performative autoethnography radicalizes scholarship through operating under the idea that, as Fabian argues, "In the real world *theory happens*" (2001, p. 5), in a present that includes the political inequities of privilege where researchers cannot displace otherness into a patronage of "native tradition," thus defining who and what is and is not "developed." "Theory," writes Fabian, "has no place unless it has time" (p. 5). In a post-9/11 America, autoethnography's local knowledge situates time and history as inherently critical tools.

Performative Fragments and Embodied Possibilities

I could tell a White band from a Black band. I could just tell, it wouldn't go into my body.

—Miles Davis (2001)

Experiencing language as a transformative force was not an awareness that I arrived at through writing. I discovered it through performance.

—bell hooks (1999, p. 35)

Davis' words illustrate the corporeal embeddedness of knowledge. They reveal the inherency, the seamlessness, the materiality of the personal and political, in a manner where we cannot tell where one ends and the other begins. His words speak a theory of embodiment, a theorizing of the embodied knowledge of, among other things, race. He could just "tell," his body telling, his telling body, that a particular composition wouldn't "go into my [his] body," not because he didn't *know* or understand the sound, but perhaps because he knew it too well, was *required* to know it, knew it as a racially compulsory verse in the soundscapes of power. In the agency of *telling,* of the telling body, in the critical assignment of language to experience, performative autoethnography is constructed. This is the basic foundation of autoethnography, the pulse of this methodology of the heart (Pelias, 2004), the peril of this anthropology that will break your heart (Behar, 1997). Embodied knowledge is the somatic (the body's interaction with culture) represented through the semantic (language), a linguistic articulation, a telling, of what does and does not go into the body, and why (Spry, 1998).

PERFORMATIVE-I EMBODIMENT: LOSS, CO-PRESENCE, AND (RE)LOCATION

But whose body? Whose words? Where or who does the telling come from? What is the sociocultural and temporal location and implication of the autoethnographer? What is the relationship between autoethnographer and others when considering and employing embodied theory and methodologies (embodied praxis)? The effect of theories of embodiment on autoethnography are deftly articulated by Jones; she addresses "how body and voice are inseparable from mind and thought as well as how bodies and voices move and are privileged (and are restricted and marked) in very particular and political ways" (2005, p. 767). The politics of/in the body are central in performance ethnography; Madison writes,

> In performance studies we do a lot of talking about the body. For performance ethnographers, this means we must embrace the body not only as the feeling/sensing home of our being—the harbor of our breath—but the vulnerability of how our body must move through the space and time of another—transporting our very being and breath—for the purpose of knowledge, for the purpose of realization and discovery. (2009, p. 191)

Embodied knowledge is the research home, the methodological toolbox, the "breath" of the performative autoethnographer. It allows the researcher to reflect on the myriad ways in which, for example, Miles' statement is packed with the politics of race, the politics of his body as the home of his being. It is, among other things, his social, cultural, and temporal embodied location as a distinguished musician, as an African American man, and as a person raised in financial privilege that embodies the ways in which he, and we as readers, make meaning of his words.

The consideration of *researcher location* in relation to others seems tantamount in the present development of autoethnography. As such, I am interested in continuing to develop a researcher location that I have termed a "performative-I" as a plural and performative researcher embodiment (Spry, 2006). The performative-I disposition is rooted in critical ethnography, critical cultural theory, politics of identity, and performance studies where the researcher seeks to develop a critique of her or his political standpoint and sociocultural situatedness to disarm the power structures restricting individual and group access and ability for social change and social justice. "Representation" writes Madison, "happens at different points along power's spectrum—we are all 'vehicles and targets' of power's contagion and omnipresence" (2009, p. 193). The performative-I disposition encourages the researcher to locate self in relation to others in the "both/and" of "power's contagion" seeking to understand how we—as both vehicles and targets—can effectively negotiate and transform power's contagion.

A performative-I location of autoethnography constitutes a focal shift away from identities as *constructed* socioculturally/politically/historically and more toward the *negotiation* of these subjectivities in meaning making. This process of negotiating—in this case, masculine subjectivities—is deeply salient in Gale and Wyatt's book, *Between the Two: A Nomadic Inquiry Into Collaborative Writing and Subjectivity*

(2009). Further, in *Performing Black Masculinity* (2006), Bryant Alexander writes, "identity politics are not situated on the body, but serve as a constellation of resources in the cultural negotiation of the ideal—in the form of nostalgia, remembrance, and remorse" (p. xiv); this "constellation of [sociocultural] resources" is central to the performative-I disposition, inviting us toward an examination of how we *co-performatively function* within a particular sociocultural, political, or historical context to (re)make meaning that illustrates the complex negotiations between selves and others in contexts, and reflects a multiplicity of cultural narratives. The performative-I research location embodies a plural sense of self collaboratively co-performing meaning in sociocultural contexts. The autoethnographer seeks to articulate with others the co-construction of culture, history, and power-provoking critical reflection on differences in power and privilege for the purpose of community efficacy.

Surely, the term "ethnographic-I" resonates here for many readers as it has been offered up and fruitfully developed in autoethnographic studies (Ellis, 2004). The conceptualization of "ethnographic-I" has served as a useful definitional guidepost for the conceptualization and composition of autoethnography (Ellis, 2009; Goodall, 2000; Richardson, 2007). In an intentional move away from realist ethnography, Ellis and Bochner (2006) advocate autoethnography that explicates emotional dimensions of self-reflection on lived experience. Goodall's work in "new ethnography" establishes a grounded rhetorical and literary stance while embracing the messy unpredictability of deep communicative engagements with others in cultural contexts (2000, 2008).

A performative-I location or disposition of embodiment, however, offers a different researcher positionality and perspective in autoethnography because of its foundational conflation of performativity, performance studies, and ethnography with established autoethnographic research. However, in the methodological fashion of autoethnography, the emergence of a performative-I was the result of a deep and all-consuming loss and the necessity to save my life after death.

All understandings of research and life broke apart for me into pieces large and small, sharp edged, inchoate, and seemingly irretrievable after the loss of our child. Writing was the only thing I could make myself do. My arms literally ached from the absence. I felt dismembered mentally and physically, phantom limbs holding a baby. My subject position went from a destabilized "me" to a chaotic but oddly comforting "we." And because, as hooks suggests, theory heals, Sidonie Smith's words acted as balm:

> And so the cultural injunction to be a deep, unified, coherent, autonomous "self" produces necessary failure, for the autobiographical subject is amnesiac, incoherent, heterogeneous, interactive. In that very failure lies the fascination of autobiographical storytelling as performativity. (1998, p. 108)

"Paper and Skin" is a "necessary failure" of a coherent unified self. In Smith's concept of autobiographical performativity, the autobiographical subject is not an intact coherent self waiting within the body to be recorded through language; rather, she is a conflation of effects, a "constellation of resources" created through a performative process of critical narration that resists notions of individual coherency; the performative-I disposition is a coupling of this sense of subjective incoherency with critical ethnographic reflexivity.

After much frustration with dominant cultural narratives of grief as well as my own writing process at the time, I finally gave in to the rupture. In their call for a "deconstructive autoethnography," Alecia Jackson and Lisa Mazzei deftly critique a hegemonic methodological trend of the "I" in autoethnography where "the goal is coherence, comfort, and continuity through mediated truth" (2008, p. 300). Rather, they argue for an "I" that confronts "experience as questionable, as problematic, and as incomplete—rather than as a foundation for truth" (p. 304). In the comfort of incoherency and incompleteness, I began to find relief. I began to experience rupture and fragmentation as a form and function of performative ethnographic representation. In her deeply moving book, *Telling Bodies Performing Birth*, Della Pollock speaks with women whose stories of birth suggest such rupture. She writes,

> The stories that emerge in each case rise up against the norms that deny their integrity, that prefer silence, conformity, and invisibility. In the corpo-realities of performance, they break through normative reiteration into the time-space of terrifying exhilarating possibility. They bend to the breaking point the comic-hero norm of birth storytelling, making story answer to performance, performance to difference, and difference to its origins in absence, in silence, in the blank expanse of not knowing and unknowing that remains impenetrably unknown. (1999, pp. 27–28)

As I let myself fall apart, I let myself see the pieces. I let myself fall into the presence of absence, into "the blank expanse of not knowing." My own experience of the multiplicity and partiality of knowledge became deeply embodied; I understood this as an autoethnographic stance, as a construction of self that seemed to navigate, to negotiate the interrelations between self/other/bodies/language/culture/history in ways that were markedly different from any previous "I" positionality in my research. Butler writes,

> I speak as an "I," but do not make the mistake of thinking that I know precisely all that I am doing when I speak in that way. I find that my very formation implicates the other in me, that my own foreignness to myself is, paradoxically, the source of my ethical connection with others. (2005, p. 84)

Butler (2005) suggests a decentering of epistemological authority in the "I" of autoethnographic writing. This decentering of authority made great sense walking in the fragments and rubble of loss personally in our family and nationally in 9/11. Pollock describes a performative self that "is not merely multiple," it moves itself "forward . . . and between selves/structures" (1998, p. 87). Any sense of knowledge located firmly within the boundaries of my own body fell away, and I began to feel within the concept of performativity and co-presence, an engagement with others in culture that was no longer centered in "I." As Conquergood believed, performance is about struggle to push through what seems fixed, static, or hopeless. My emptied body needed to speak of absence, of the incoherence of here/now/who, to embody "the indecidability of meaning, of self, of narrative—without requiring self-identification or mastery" (Jackson & Mazzei, 2008, p. 305). Performative writing can "make absence present and yet recover presence from structural, realist mimesis for poesies" (Pollock 1998, p. 81). Moving from mimetic imitation of "deep autonomous selfhood" into the deconstructive motile vision of empty arms falling, I began and structured the piecemeal form of "Paper and Skin: Bodies of Loss and Life."

Embodying this performative turn on grief activated an intervention on dominant cultural performances of grief, and I could feel a methodological shift in my positionality within this and other fields of study from participant-observer actor to co-performative agent within the research context; from within this experience, I understood more fully "the vulnerability of how our body must move through the space and time of another—transporting our very being and breath—for the purpose of knowledge, for the purpose of realization and discovery" (Madison, 2009, p. 191). From this embodied negotiation with others in loss emerged a performative-I disposition. The hearts and minds of words and lives of the works I had been reading began to make a more deeply embodied and more problematic "felt-sense."

The work of Dwight Conquergood, Norman Denzin, Kristen Langellier, Soyini Madison, Della Pollock, and others articulate performativity as having the capability of resisting and interrupting sedimented social meanings and normative performances that become oppressive, hegemonic, silencing. "Performativity," write Madison and Hamera, "is the interconnected triad of identity, experience, and social relations. . . . performativities are the many markings substantiating that all of us are subjects in a world of power relations" (2006, p. xix). Postcolonial critic Homi Bhabha (1993) enacts performativity to disrupt, dislodge, and dislocate hegemonic constructs of race and imperialism. Performative autoethnography presents alternate versions and options of reacting to and experiencing sociocultural expectations, thereby resisting and intervening on normative constructs of human being and reified structures of power. In this way performativity, a performative-I disposition, functions as agency of culture rather than as an act of culture (Strine, 1998).

Based in performativity, the performative-I location is a negotiation of critical agency and personal/political accountability.

Performative-I Critical Agency

With performativity and dialogue, the performative-I disposition requires collaborative co-performative meaning making and critical agency at once. Here, autoethnography is a collection of representational fragments of knowledge assembled with others from a plural sense of self, a dialectic of co-presence with others in the field of study concerning how bodies are read in various contexts of culture and power. In her work on Red pedagogy, Grande articulates a collaborative critical agency in research, "[Red pedagogy] is a space of engagement. It is the liminal and intellectual borderlands where indigenous and nonindigenous scholars encounter one another, working to remember, redefine, and reverse the devastation of the original colonialist 'encounter'" (2008, p. 234). The colonializing historicities of these encounters are critiqued and transformed, reassembled from a plural sense of self, a dialectic of co-presence where selves and others challenge and recognize their "overlapping cultural identifications" (p. 234) that may be in communion or in conflict with social and power relations. Vershawn Ashanti Young offers clarity of such overlaps in a dialectic of co-presence in *Your Average Nigga: Performing Race, Literacy, and Masculinity* where he seeks to "illustrate the intersection between what I call the burden of racial performance and the problems that I and other Blacks face in the ghetto and in school, particularly in college" (2007, p. 12). This kind of performative-I dialectic identification does not romanticize collaboration or assume that autoethnography is a manifestation of agreement or consensus or solution or emotional connection between selves and others. Within critical agency is the ethical awareness of representing one's own reflection on the complex interaction and negotiation between selves and others in complex sociocultural power-laden contexts.

For example, at a recent meeting of the Congress of Qualitative Inquiry, a groundbreaking conference that provides an international and interdisciplinary communal space for deep critical qualitative inquiry, I attended a panel on performance and metaphor. The presentations were provocative and heuristic, generating discussion that continued to open the epistemological efficacy of performance methodologies. The conversation turned to the uses of metaphor in autoethnographic research, and a participant asked how the autoethnographer gets others to understand his use of metaphor for the purposes of critical reflection. This was an iconic moment for me in relation to a performative-I research disposition. Though the young man seemed sincere and well-intentioned, his question illustrated, it seems to me, the imperialist impulse to "make others understand" rather than doing understanding with others. In "Rethinking Collaboration: Working the Indigene-Colonizer Hyphen," Alison Jones and Kuni Jenkins write, "I do not argue for a rejection of collaboration. Rather, I unpack its difficulties to suggest a less dialogical and more uneasy, unsettled relationship, based on learning (about difference) from the Other rather than learning about the Other" (2008, p. 471). Though I conceptualize dialogic engagement as inherently uneasy and unsettled, Jones and Jenkin's point is fundamental to the imperializing potential of research when the researcher's own power dynamics are left unconsidered and uncritiqued.

The performative-I autoethnographic positionality would encourage the researcher to seek understanding of others' uses of metaphor, and to critically reflect on the nuances and difficulties in the ontological situation of one's own in/ability to understand, or as Jackson and Mazzei write, "To interrogate the process of constituting a performative 'I' is to put experience under erasure, to expose the uncertainty of 'who' that 'I' could become, and to open up what can be known about the 'I'" (2008, p. 305). Through the performative-I re/positioning of the autoethnographer, a reader may learn about the complexity of cultural interaction, how the researcher's uses of dominant discourse effect these interactions, how we are all, as Madison suggests, "'vehicles and targets' of power's contagion and omnipresence" (2009, p. 193). The performative-I disposition calls forth dialogue between the personal and the politicized body.

Performative-I Accountability

Jazz great Wynton Marsalis writes of deep jazz swing, "It's a matter of understanding what a thing means to you, and being dedicated to playing that even if its meaning casts a cold eye on you yourself" (2005, p. 59). Marsalis captures the praxis of the performative-I in articulating the necessity for *agency* as well as *accountability.* The autoethnographer, who may certainly carry privilege into the research context, must be acutely aware of the power dynamics involved in representation; the autoethnographer must be able to engage in reflexive critique of her or his own social positioning, must be "dedicated to playing that," to recognize the necessity to be what Butler calls a "social theorist." She writes, "When the 'I' seeks to give an account of itself, it can start with itself, but will find that this self is already implicated in a social temporality that exceeds its own capacities for narration . . . an account that must include the conditions of its own emergence" (2005, pp. 8–9). The performative-I researcher disposition assumes the inherency of accountability in autoethnography. "There is no 'I,'" writes Butler, "that can stand apart from the social conditions of its emergence" (2005, p. 7). Performativity requires the perpetual critique of cultural performance, as well as intervening on sediment dominant patterns of oppression (Denzin 2003, 2005; Madison & Hamera, 2006).

In discussing the postcolonial notion of the *mestizaje,* an indigenous research positioning of critically reflexive multiple subjectivities, Grande writes, "Unlike liberal notions of subjectivity, it [mestizaje] also roots identity in the discourses of power" (2008, p. 239). Woven into a subversive performativity and Butler's accounting of "I" is the idea that one must critique the always and already power-laden structures of everyday life experience, that one cannot "stand apart from the social conditions" of one's emergence. The performative autoethnographer assumes that the complexity of her or his own sociocultural emergence or situatedness may exceed her or his capacity for narration—hence, if I am to claim agency, I also have the responsibility to account for my sociocultural whereabouts and its implications for myself and those with whom I work; I must be "dedicated to playing," dedicated to *doing* reflexivity even—and especially—while knowing it is never enough, never complete, never finished.

PERFORMATIVE EMBODIMENT

> *I love performance most when I enter into it, when it calls me forward shamelessly, across those hard-edged maps into spaces where I must go, terrains that are foreign, scary, uninhabitable, but necessary. I must go to them to know myself more, to know you more.*
>
> —Soyini Madison (2006, p. 244)

> *Knowledge becomes constantly embodied and bodying forth through past, present and future practices, sensorily and emotionally shared with persons, objects, and institutions—actual or imagined, seen or unseen or never to be seen.*
>
> —Eleni Papagaroufali (2008, p. 121)

Having discussed the conceptualization of a performative-I disposition, I would focus further on the development of embodiment in performative-I and in performative autoethnography because the centrality of the body is what characterizes performance studies research and, subsequently, performative autoethnography (Jones, 2005). Papagaroufali's and Madison's thoughts reflect why, since communing with loss, I have been uncomfortable with the conceptualization of "I" in autoethnographic research. Though dialogue and performativity have become tenants in autoethnographic description, there was, within my own embodied experience, the absence of a connective tissue in theoretical descriptions. But in writing this chapter through a conflation of performance studies, autoethnography, and critical ethnography, I find a multiplicity and accountability in the performative-I, and a felt-sense of liminality, of circularity, of inbetweeness as reflected in Papagaroufali's and Madison's words. In "bodying forth" with others "seen or unseen or never to be seen" in an embodied communion (pleasant and difficult) with others, I find embodied presence in performative autoethnography. Different from an "ethnographic-I," this is a troubled, sensual, contingent embodiment of communitas. Pollock guides me:

> Entanglement, ravishment, love, writing: what I want to call performance writing does not project a self, even a radically destabilized one, as much as *a relation of being and knowing* that cuts back and forth across multiple "divisions" among selves, contexts, affiliations. . . . the self that emerges from these shifting perspectives is, then, *a possibility rather than a fact,* a figure of relation emerging from between lines of difference. (1998, pp. 86–87, emphasis mine)

A disposition,

a relation of being and knowing that cuts back,

a possibility

a figure of relation emerging

from difference

from entanglement

from ravishment,

from . . .

and it is here that I must stop; for to speak of love in relation to research, in an academic

context, an academic handbook, even one edited by the roaming free radical Norman Denzin feels heresy,

not in the truth of my "un/learning body" (Madison, 2006),

because surely, truly, and ravishingly,

it is love and desire

for communitas, for Burke's consubstantiality, for articulation and interruption of the personally political pains that I inflict on others and that are inflicted upon me within the uneven, unjustified, and inequitable systems privileging some and disempowering others. Heresy or not, it is a disposition of love in autoethnographic research that has given me the courage to move into entanglements with others about race, gender, privilege, and more resulting in a different kind of knowing. Surely, it is only through a disposition of love, through love as an epistemological possibility, through a methodology of the heart that I have been able to fill the absence of loss with the linguistic presence of our child.

And so in speaking of an autoethnographic embodiment in research and in report, I am most comfortable in the liminal space of an embodied *disposition,* an embodied co-presence in conceptualizing the research and writing process of critical performative autoethnography, of the embodied performative-I. Engaging a liminal disposition then in performative autoethnography has *moved me out of* an autoethnographic, or "ethnographic–I." It has not moved me into the bodies of others; I do not "walk a mile in their shoes" or look at the world through their eyes. I do not *know* the Other through performing autoethnography, such would be hubris rather than pedagogy. Performance is not that innocent. Rather, through performance I come to know more fully what a painful and liberating process it is to try to represent the intimate nuances of a "hermeneutics of experience, relocation, co-presence, humility, and vulnerability" that Conquergood describes in conjunction with the texts of Frederick Douglass, where knowledge is located, engaged, and "forged from *solidarity with,* not separation from, the people" in research (Spry, 2006, p. 315). This is assuming, of course, that people would desire forging knowledge together, and, if not, that the autoethnographer has the humility to recognize resistance to collaboration and the courage to critically reflect upon why the resistance exists.

Seeking embodied knowledge through an embodied liminality with others has taken me out of my self, out of a singular self; it has taken me out of my body and pushed and pulled me into the liminal inbetweeness of meaning making with others, into the space where I am not me and not you, but where we are *us* in a place and time defined by the multiple and surely conflictual readings of our cultural situatedness and the meanings we make co-performatively/together. A performative-I embodied disposition has shifted me into the void between our materiality where we meet each other in dialogue, in argument, in communion, in anger, in the *mysterium tremendum* that performance studies scholar Leland Roloff (1973) describes where cultural presence is what our bodies in contexts are making together.

A liminally embodied disposition of performative-I autoethnography involves personal/political risk and vulnerability. A performative-I embodiment takes me out of my body and into the liminal space where I do not have the "safety" of "I," where I am vulnerable to contestation with others about what is what, about the critical readings and representations of bodies. Surely and without question, within a performative-I disposition, I am critically and unromantically aware that no matter how liminally out of my body I may move, it is a racially and financially privileged body that I live in. This material reality constitutes the reasons and need for the critical imagination (Denzin, 2005) needed to move out of body and into the rapture and entanglements of what Conquergood (1991) calls a "performance sensitive" way of knowing to articulate and transform dominant narratives that sediment systems of power.

We do not enter these spaces lightly or stumble into this process without strategy, without method, without a practice. The performative-I disposition wholly depends on performative embodiment where the body is the actor, agent, and text at once, where our views of the world are tested, refuted, and articulated through the negotiation of corporeal bodies in space and time. It is a "bodying forth" into critical social theorizing where the resulting text causes interruption, repudiation, and intervention on dominant narratives.

Critical Fragments of Craft: An Ethic of Aesthetics in Performative Autoethnography

Her vocabulary is so discriminating that each word wears the complex self-investigation that brought it into being.

—Carmine Starnino (2008, p. 149)

I only write or make art about myself when I am completely sure that the biographical paradigm intersects with larger social and cultural issues.

—Guillermo Gómez-Peña (2000, p. 7)

In the case of autoethnography, the two strands of barbed wire manifest as a demand to create knowledge (the epistemic) and a demand to create art (the aesthetic). While we need not see these demands as diametrically opposed, neither need we see them as synonymous. In any event, we leave the relationship between them unconsidered at our peril.

Craig Gingrich-Philbrook (2005, p. 303)

Performative autoethnography is a critical moral discourse (Conquergood, 1985, 1991; Denzin, 2003, 2008; Jones, 2005). It is grounded in "The performance paradigm [which] privileges particular, participatory, dynamic, intimate, precarious, embodied experience grounded in historical process, contingency, and ideology" (Conquergood 1991, p. 187). Consequently, in autoethnography's trajectory and development as a moral discourse it must be, at its foundation, epistemic. *All of the potentials and possibilities embodied in performative autoethnography depend upon the quality of its report, of its linguistic and aesthetic construction, of it its ability to make writing perform* (Alexander; 2006; Denzin, 2003, 2006b; Gingrich-Philbrook, 2001, 2005; Goodall, 2000, 2008; Hamera, 2006; Pelias, 2004; Pollock, 1998; Spry 2008, 2009; Trinh T. Minh-ha, 1989). The moral imperative, then, of autoethnography is as much situated in its aesthetic craft as in its epistemological potential. The depth of knowledge generated (epistemology) by performative autoethnography is directly related to its aesthetic acumen, and just as autoethnography is a critical moral discourse, the aesthetic crafting of autoethnography is a sociocultural and political action. "Performance exposes aesthetics' social work," writes Judith Hamera, "as embodied, processual, rhetorical, and political and especially, as daily, as routine, a practice of everyday life" (2006a, p. 47). Here performative autoethnography, the performative-I disposition, operates as a movement of epistemologically embodied art crafted within and between the representations of power and powerlessness and is motivated by the desire for local embodied knowledge of how unequal power systems can be called up, called out, disassembled, reimagined, and reconfigured.

Our need at this point in the development of autoethnographic writing is, it seems to me, to write more about writing, in particular, about the politics, power, and privilege of it, the various styles, forms, embodiment, and aesthetic functions of it—in other words, a focus on the aesthetic representation of how the body co-performs with others in sociopolitical contexts. In his 2008 essay "Contemporary Fieldwork Aesthetics in Art and Anthropology," George Marcus calls for "an explicit rearticulating of its [ethnography's] aesthetic of method" because of the varying "norms and forms of knowledge" (p. 32) since his groundbreaking work with James Clifford in *Writing Culture.*

We must continue to develop writing from/with/of the co-performative body as co-present with others, the body as epistemologically central, heuristically inspirational, politically catalytic. "In performative writing," writes Madison, "we recognize that the *body* writes. Critical ethnography adheres to radical empiricism: the intersection of bodies in motion and space" (2005, p. 195). We must write from within the entanglements of co-presence, from the rapture of communion, from the un/comfortable risk and intimacy of dialogue, from the vulnerable and liminal inbetweeness of self/other/context.

But it is, of course, *through language* that we "body forth" in interpreting and articulating what the body "knows." In postmodern research, we sometimes like to think of the body as inherently "knowing" things without remembering that *the body knows what language constructs* (Spry, 2009). In conceptualizing performative writing, Gingrich-Philbrook lives "in body-language-body-language. My body makes language. It makes language like hair" (2001, p. 3). Embodied knowledge is generated from a body-language rapture, elation, conflation, each affecting (and sometimes abjecting) the other.

I want to spin the aesthetic crafting of language in autoethnography as an ethical imperative, as *a movement of embodied art crafted within a performative-I disposition of liminality*. In a foundational article, "Autoethnography's Family Values: Easy Access to Compulsory Experiences" (2005), Gingrich-Philbrook deftly articulates the double bind of the aesthetic and the epistemic in autoethnography as a response, in part, to what he argues is a regulatory valuing and valorizing of a compulsory hegemonic emotionality in autoethnography at the expense of developing alternative theory, aesthetic practices and epistemological products of autoethnography. He states, "However much one applauds autoethnography's artistic and social intentions, those intentions do not in themselves secure artistic results" (p. 308). Performance studies practitioners have always worked with the embodiment of emotion in the production of knowledge and are aware of the potential dangers when expecting the expression of emotion in research to stand-in for aesthetic acumen. Emotion is not inherently epistemic. I have tomes of writing expressing the emotional turmoil of loss during childbirth; as significant as that writing is to my own personal grief process, it is not performative autoethnography. Hamera helps clarify:

> *Experience is not scholarship.* . . . Performance links experience, theory, and the work of close critique in ways that make precise analytical claims about cultural production and consumption, and expose how both culture and our claims are themselves constructed things, products of hearts and souls, minds and hands. (2006a, p. 241, emphasis mine)

Many aspects of my own personal grief are not yet critically reflective of how this experience is personally part of sociopolitics, of cultural production. "This does not mean," writes Butler, "that I cannot speak of such matters, but only when I do, I must be careful to understand the limits of what I can do, the limits that condition any and all such doing. In this sense, I must become critical" (2005, p. 82). In my own aesthetic production of critique, in the engagement of hearts and souls, minds, and hands, I understand the limits of my own condition in offering epistemologies concerning dominant hegemonic structures of grief.

I think at this point in our development of autoethnography, we look at the epistemic as more sociopolitically and academically relevant, while viewing the aesthetic or literary as an added scholarly bonus, or worse, as ideologically benign. Gingrich-Philbrook employs the work of Murray Krieger (1992), who argues that the aesthetic "alerts us to the illusionary, the merely arbitrary claims to reality that authoritarian discourse would impose upon us; because, unlike authoritarian discourse, the aesthetic takes back the 'reality' it offers us in the very act of offering it to us" (quoted in Gingrich-Philbrook 2005, p. 310). Performative autoethnography is forged in the ontological tension between its epistemological potential and its aesthetic imperative. It is through language, after all, that we "give an account of ourselves." Language's propensity toward imperializing, toward "merely arbitrary claims to reality," makes this accounting a moral commitment, an ethical imperative. Privileged peoples need not attend to imperializing aesthetics, as their words are framed by power. It is ethically imperative then, that the autoethnographer, who may certainly carry privilege into the research context, be acutely aware of the power dynamics involved in the aesthetics of performative autoethnography. Representation has risks (Denzin, 2003, 2006a, 2008; Denzin & Lincoln, 2007; Grande, 2008; Madison, 2005, 2009; Poulos, 2009; Smith, 1999; Spry, 2008). Aesthetics are not ideologically benign. Those risks can be negotiated by an ethic of care for aesthetic representation.

An ethic of aesthetic representation is illustrated through what Mindy Fenske calls an "ethic of answerability" where, in this case, the autoethnographer is responsible for and ethically liable for linguistic representations of the interpolations of self with others in contexts (2004, p. 8). Fenske argues that no hierarchy exists between craft and emotion, form and production, theory and practice, art and life. "Instead," she writes, "such relations are unified and dialogic. . . . Art and life are connected, one is not meant to transcend the other. Both content and experience, form and production . . . exist inside the unified act in constant interaction" (p. 9). In this dialogical ethic of care, emotion is not touted as the scholarly cure for realism, nor is aesthetic craft viewed as a mechanized technique handcuffing the raw essence of experience and emotion; rather, they are interdependent on one another, responsible to one another, liable to one another to represent the complex negotiations of meaning between selves and others in power-laden social structures. *Here art is not a reflection of life; they are, rather, answerable to one another.* "Form," writes Fenske "becomes a location inciting, rather than foreclosing, dialogue" (p. 11). The debilitating binary argument of craft over emotion, or practice over theory is deflated through Fenske's argument because these elements are mutually answerable to one another; knowledge is sought through their dialogic engagement suggesting a praxis, an ethical assembly, a resistance of hierarchy. Rather than a linear path from self to other, theory to practice, or emotion to craft, performative-I liminality is a dialogic space where experience and text effect and are effected by one another.

Clearly, embodiment is crucial in this ethics of aesthetics. Just as emotion and experience are not inherently epistemic, Fenske reminds us that "events are not ethical simply because they are embodied. . . . In order to achieve answerability, the embodied action must be responsible for its meaning, as well as liable to meaning" (2004, p. 12). The material body cannot be erased in composing autoethnography; rather the corporeal body is made fully present in performance and represented through critical reflections on the body's social constructions. In a recent student's performative autoethnography titled "Driving While Black," the truths of Anthony's life are not compromised by aesthetic craft, rather in the critical dialogic process of articulating, of crafting life, Anthony constructs and embodies knowledge that is subversive, pedagogical, and heuristic. Politically troubled aesthetics allow Anthony to read and re/write his social body as a transgressive text. To operate as if there is a hierarchy in art or life, in craft or emotion, in theory or practice is to engage, Fenske argues, "a type of aesthetic that lets the artist off the ethical hook" (2004, p. 13) by being tempted to offer simplistic notions of the "purity" (read "apolitical") of embodied experience in aesthetic composition. Any methodology, aesthetic or otherwise, that does not exercise as fundamental the critique of sociocultural systems and discourses of power sanitizes and imperializes critical reflexivity into a parlor game of identity construction where Self stands in front of a mirror trying on different cultural hats to see the "world" from the eyes of the Other. Epistemologically, these dialectics engaged in collaboration expand the depth and breadth of critical conversations and implementations. Autoethnography remains accountable by considering the political constructions of an "'I' that remains skeptical of authentic experience" (Jackson & Mazzei, 2008, p. 314) and, I would argue, of aesthetic purity.

Making writing perform. Making the story answerable to its own sociocultural emergence, to its own performance, to its own life as art and back again. Pelias writes, "Language is my most telling friend, my most fierce foe . . . power lurks, will grab me at every turn. I must stare it down, write it down" (2007, p. 193). Power lurks as much in aesthetic construction as in epistemological construction because surely, they are inseparable. And though they are answerable to one another, the answers do not foreclose one another. Performative autoethnographic writing is about the continual questioning, the naming and renaming and unnaming of experience through craft, through heart, through the fluent body.

Concluding Fragments: Entanglement, Rapture, and Writing

Did I actually reach out my arms
toward it, toward paradise falling, like
the fading of the dearest, wildest hope—
the dark heart of the story that is all
the reason for its telling?

—Mary Oliver (1986, p. 2)

There is a long time in me between knowing and telling.

—Grace Paley (1974, p. 127)

I write to show myself showing people who show me my own showing.
I-You: not one, not two. In this unwonted spectacle made of reality and fiction, where redoubled images form and reform, neither I nor you come first.

—Trinh T. Minh-ha (1989, p. 22)

Oliver, Paley, and Trinh T. Minh-ha write of the passionate liminality, the inchoate corporeality, the continual redoubling where you and I are collaboratively present and singularly absent on the page. The aesthetic and epistemic collapsing into one another

with such desire that we cannot tell where one ends and the other begins.

It is a strange and alternate plain where we can, at once, feel and speak and hear,

where we can bleed and bleed and not die,

or where we can die and be resurrected—or not,

thankful that through performance, words make flesh.

References

Alexander, B. (2006). *Performing Black masculinity: Race, culture, and queer identity.* Lanham, MD: AltaMira Press.

Anderson, L. (2006). Analytic autoethnography. *Journal of Contemporary Ethnography, 35*(4), 373–395.

Anzuldúa, G. (2007). *Borderlands/La Frontera: The new mestiza* (3rd ed.). San Francisco: Aunt Lute Books.

Behar, R. (1997). *The vulnerable observer: Anthropology that breaks your heart.* Boston: Beacon Press.

Bhabha, H. (1993). *The location of culture.* New York: Routledge.

Butler, J. (2005). *Giving an account of oneself.* New York: Fordham University Press.

Clifford, J., & Marcus, G. E. (1986). *Writing culture: The poetics and politics of ethnography.* Berkeley: University of California Press.

Conquergood, D. (1985). Performing as a moral act: Ethical dimensions of the ethnography of performance. *Literature in Performance, 5,* 1–13.

Conquergood, D. (1991). Rethinking ethnography: Towards a critical cultural politics. *Communication Monographs, 58,* 179–194.

Davis, M., & Dibbs, M. (Producer/Director). (2001). *The Miles Davis story* [TV documentary]. New York: Columbia Music Video.

Denzin, N. K. (2003). *Performance ethnography: Critical pedagogy and the politics of culture.* Thousand Oaks, CA: Sage.

Denzin, N. K. (2005). Politics and ethics of performance pedagogy: Toward a pedagogy of hope. In D. S. Madison & J. Hamera (Eds.), *The SAGE handbook of performance studies* (pp. 325–338). Thousand Oaks, CA: Sage.

Denzin, N. K. (2006). Analytic autoethnography, or déjà vu all over again. *Journal of Contemporary Ethnography, 35*(4), 419–428.

Denzin, N. K. (2008). *Searching for Yellowstone: Race, gender, family, and memory in the postmodern West.* Walnut Creek, CA: Left Coast Press.

Denzin, N. K., & Giardina, M. D. (2007). Introduction: Ethical futures in qualitative research. In N. K. Denzin & M. D. Giardina (Eds.), *Ethical futures in qualitative research* (pp. 9–39). Walnut Creek, CA: Left Coast Press.

Denzin, N. K., & Lincoln, Y. S. (2007). *The landscape of qualitative research* (3rd ed.). Thousand Oaks, CA: Sage.

Ellis, C. (2004). *The ethnographic-I: A methodological novel about autoethnography.* Walnut Creek, CA: AltaMira Press.

Ellis, C. (2009). *Revision: Autoethnographic reflections on life and work.* Walnut Creek, CA: Left Coast Press.

Ellis, C., & Bochner, A. P. (2006). Analyzing analytic autoethnography: An autopsy. *Journal of Contemporary Ethnography, 35,* 429–449.

Fabian, J. (1983). *Time and the Other: How anthropology makes its objects.* New York: Columbia University Press.

Fabian, J. (2001). *Anthropology with an attitude.* Palo Alto, CA: Stanford University Press.

Fabian, J. (2007). *Memory against culture: Arguments and reminders.* Durham, NC: Duke University Press.

Fenske, M. (2004). The aesthetic of the unfinished: Ethics and performance. *Text and Performance Quarterly, 24*(1), 1–19.

Gale, K., & Wyatt, J. (2008). Becoming men, becoming-men? A collective biography. *International Review of Qualitative Research, 1*(2), 235–253.

Gale, K., & Wyatt, J. (2009). *Between the two: A nomadic inquiry into collaborative writing and subjectivity.* Newcastle upon Tyne, UK: Cambridge Scholars.

Gingrich-Philbrook, C. (2001). Bite your tongue: Four songs of body and language. In R. J. Pelias & L. C. Miller (Eds.), *The green window: Proceedings of the Giant City Conference on Performative Writing* (pp. 1–7). Carbondale: Southern Illinois University Press.

Gingrich-Philbrook, C. (2005). Autoethnography's family values: Easy access to compulsory experiences. *Text and Performance Quarterly, 25*(4), 297–314.

Gómez-Peña, G. (2000). *Dangerous border crossers: The artist talks back.* New York: Routledge.

Goodall, H. L. (2000). *Writing the new ethnography.* Walnut Creek, CA: AltaMira Press.

Goodall, H. L. (2008). *Writing qualitative inquiry: Self, stories, and academic life.* Walnut Creek, CA: Left Coast Press.

Grande, S. (2008). Red pedagogy: The un-methodology. In N. K. Denzin, Y. S. Lincoln, & L. T. Smith (Eds.), *Handbook of critical and indigenous methodologies* (pp. 233–254). Thousand Oaks, CA: Sage.

Hamera, J. (2006). Performance, performativity, and cultural poesies in practices of everyday life. In D. S. Madison & J. Hamera (Eds.), *The SAGE handbook of performance studies* (pp. 49–64). Thousand Oaks, CA: Sage.

hooks, b. (1994). *Teaching to transgress: Education as the practice of freedom.* New York: Routledge.

hooks, b. (1999). *Remembered rapture: The writer at work.* New York: Henry Holt.

Hunt, S. A., & Junco, N. R. (Eds.). (2006). Introduction to two thematic issues: Defective memory and analytical autoethnography. *Journal of Contemporary Ethnography, 35*(4), 1–3.

Jackson, A. Y., & Mazzei, L. A. (2008). Experience and "I" in autoethnography: A deconstruction. *International Review of Qualitative Research, 1*(3), 299–317.

Jones, A., & Jenkins, K. (2008). Rethinking collaboration: Working the indigene-colonizer hyphen. In N. K. Denzin, Y. S. Lincoln, & L. T. Smith (Eds.), *The handbook of critical and indigenous methodologies.* Thousand Oaks, CA: Sage.

Jones, S. H. (2005). Autoethnography: Making the personal political. In N. K. Denzin & Y. S. Lincoln (Eds.), *The SAGE handbook of qualitative research* (pp. 763–792). Thousand Oaks, CA: Sage.

Keller, L. (2009). The second wave: Return of the militias. Montgomery, AL: Southern Poverty Law Center. Retrieved August 8, 2009, from http://www.splcenter.org

Krieger, M. (1992). *Words about words about words: Theory, criticism, and the literary text.* Baltimore: Johns Hopkins University Press.

Langellier, K. (1999). Personal narrative, performance, performativity: Two or three things I know for sure. *Text and Performance Quarterly, 19,* 125–144.

Liakos, A. (2008). Canonical and anticanonical histories. In N. Panourgia & G. Marcus (Eds.), *Ethnographic moralia: Experiments in interpretive anthropology* (pp. 138–156). New York: Fordham University Press.

Madison, D. S. (2005). *Critical ethnography: Method, ethics, and performance.* Thousand Oaks, CA: Sage.

Madison, D. S. (2006). Performing theory/embodied writing. In J. Hamera (Ed.), *Opening acts: Performance in/as communication and cultural studies* (pp. 243–266). Thousand Oaks, CA: Sage.

Madison, D. S. (2009). Dangerous ethnography. In N. K. Denzin & M. Giardina (Eds.), *Qualitative inquiry and social justice* (pp. 187–197). Walnut Creek, CA: Left Coast Press.

Madison, D. S., & Hamera, J. (Eds.). (2006). *The SAGE handbook of performance studies.* Thousand Oaks, CA: Sage.

Marcus, G. E. (2008). Contemporary fieldwork aesthetics in art and anthropology: Experiments in collaboration and intervention. In N. Panourgia & G. Marcus (Eds.), *Ethnographic moralia: Experiments in interpretive anthropology* (pp. 29–44). New York: Fordham University Press.

Marsalis, W., with Hinds, S. S. (2005). *To a young jazz musician: Letters from the road.* New York: Random House.

Max, D. T. (2009, March 9). The unfinished. *The New Yorker.*

Mutua-Kombo, E. (2009). Their words, actions, and meaning: A researcher's reflection on Rwandan women's experience of genocide. *Qualitative Inquiry, 15,* 308–323.

Oliver, M. (1986). The chance to love everything. In *Dream work* (pp. 8–9). Boston: Atlantic Monthly Press.

Paley, G. (1974). Debts. In *Enormous changes at the last minute* (pp. 15–23). New York: Farrar, Straus & Giroux.

Panourgia, N., & Marcus, G. (Eds.) (2008). *Ethnographic moralia: Experiments in interpretive anthropology.* New York: Fordham University Press.

Papagaroufali, E. (2008). Carnal hermeneutics: From "concepts" and "circles" to "dispositions" and "suspense." In N. Panourgia & G. Marcus (Eds.), *Ethnographic moralia: Experiments in interpretive anthropology* (pp. 113–125). New York: Fordham University Press.

Pelias, R. (2004). *A methodology of the heart: Evoking academic and daily life.* Walnut Creek, CA: AltaMira Press.

Pelias, R. (2007). Performative writing: The ethics of representation in form and body. In N. K. Denzin & M. Giardina (Eds.), *Ethical futures in qualitative research* (pp. 181–196). Walnut Creek, CA: Left Coast Press.

Pineau, E. L. (2000). Nursing mother and articulating absence. *Text and Performance Quarterly, 20*(1), 1–19.

Pollock, D. (1998). Performing writing. In P. Phelan & J. Lane (Eds.), *The ends of performance* (pp. 73–103). New York: New York University Press, 73–103.

Pollock, D. (1999). *Telling bodies performing birth.* New York: Columbia University Press.

Poulos, C. (2009). *Accidental ethnography: An inquiry into family secrecy.* Walnut Creek, CA: Left Coast Press.

Richardson, L. (2007). *Last writes: A daybook for a dying friend.* Walnut Creek, CA: Left Coast Press.

Roloff, L. (1973). *The perception and evocation of literature.* New York: Scott Foresman.

Russell, L. (2004). A long way toward compassion. *Text and Performance Quarterly, 24*(3 & 4), 233–254.

Schechner, R. (1985). *Between theater and anthropology.* Philadelphia: University of Pennsylvania Press.

Smith, L. T. (1999). *Decolonizing methodologies: Research and indigenous peoples.* New York: St. Martin's Press.

Smith, S. (1998). Performativity, autobiographical practice, resistance. In S. Smith & J. Watson (Eds.), *Women, autobiography, theory: A reader* (pp. 108–115). Madison: University of Wisconsin Press.

Spry, T. (1998). Performative autobiography: Presence and privacy. In S. J. Dailey (Ed.), *The future of performance studies: Visions and revisions* (pp. 254–259). Annandale, VA: National Communication Association.

Spry, T. (2001a). Performing autoethnography: An embodied methodological praxis. *Qualitative Inquiry, 7,* 706–732.

Spry, T. (2001b). From Goldilocks to dreadlocks: Racializing bodies. In R. J. Pelias & L. C. Miller (Eds.), *The green window: Proceedings of the Giant City Conference on Performative Writing* (pp. 52–65). Carbondale, IL: Southern Illinois University Press.

Spry, T. (2003). Illustrated woman: Autoperformance in "Skins: A daughter's (re)construction of cancer" and "Tattoo stories: A postscript to 'Skins.'" In L. C. Miller, J. Taylor, & M. H. Carver (Eds.), *Voices made flesh: Performing women's autobiography* (pp. 167–191). Madison: University of Wisconsin Press.

Spry, T. (2004). Paper and skin: Bodies of loss and life. An autoethnography performed in various venues across the country.

Spry, T. (2006). A performance-I copresence: Embodying the ethnographic turn in performance and the performative turn in ethnography. *Text and Performance Quarterly, 26*(4), 339–346.

Spry, T. (2008). Systems of silence: Word/less fragments of race in autoethnography. *International Review of Qualitative Research, 1*(1), 75–80.

Spry, T. (2009). *Bodies of/and evidence.* Paper performed at the 2008 Congress of Qualitative Inquiry, University of Illinois, Champaign-Urbana, IL.

St.Pierre, E. A. (2008). Home as a site of theory. *International Review of Qualitative Research, 1*(2), 119–124.

Starnino, C. (2008). Five from Ireland. *Poetry* (November), 149–161.

Strine, M. S. (1998). Mapping the "cultural turn" in performance studies. In S. J. Dailey (Ed.), *The future of performance studies: Visions and revisions* (pp. 3–9). Annandale, VA: National Communication Association.

Swadener, B. B., & Mutua, K. (2008). Decolonizing performances: Deconstructing the global postcolonial. In N. K. Denzin, Y. S. Lincoln, & L. T. Smith (Eds.), *Handbook of critical and indigenous methodologies* (pp. 31–43). Thousand Oaks, CA: Sage.

Trinh, T. Minh-Ha. (1989). *Woman, native, other.* Bloomington: Indiana University Press.

Turner, V. (1986). *The anthropology of performance.* New York: PAJ Publications.

Visweswaran, K. (2006). Betrayal: An analysis in three acts. In I. Grewal & C. Kaplan (Eds.), *Scattered hegemonies: Postmodernity and transnational feminist practices.* Minneapolis: University of Minnesota Press.

Weston, K. (2008). "Real anthropology" and other nostalgias. In N. Panourgia & G. Marcus (Eds.), *Ethnographic moralia: Experiments in interpretive anthropology* (pp. 126–137). New York: Fordham University Press.

Wyatt, J. (2008). No longer loss: Autoethnographic stammering. *Qualitative Inquiry, 14,* 955–967.

Young, V. A. (2007). *Your average Nigga: Performing race, literacy, and masculinity.* Detroit, MI: Wayne State University Press.

The Methods, Politics, and Ethics of Representation in Online Ethnography

Sarah N. Gatson

The Boundaries of Ethnography and the Internet

Any study of Internet interactions is challenging because of the simultaneous dense interconnectedness of the Internet and the normal boundaries between networks and communities. Moreover, online community development is inherently a multisited enterprise, and each locale in an identified network and its interactions must be thoroughly investigated to best discover its salient boundaries. In this chapter, I address the methods, politics, and ethics of representing these complex arenas through ethnography. I will provide a brief overview of the history and types of online ethnographies. Grounded in this discussion of online ethnographic works, and speculation about the future of such endeavors, I discuss the value of two ways to envision online ethnography: (1) The extension of traditional collaborative ethnography, in which a network of participant observers in offline laboratories or networks, as well as online, work together (sometimes unknowingly) to produce ethnography. This speculation is grounded in my experiences with online communities, one rooted in television fandom,[1] one rooted in research on drug use discourse,[2] and one that uses the Internet for research, training, and educational purposes.[3] (2) Emerging from these experiences, I discuss autoethnographic network mapping, in which a researcher grounds an online network map on herself or himself. I speculate that, in particular, this method would be useful in pedagogical and public sociological projects where media literacy/citizenship is the specific aim. The chapter concludes with the argument that these sorts of ethnographic practices both ground themselves in the traditions of the method, and address issues of the empiricist critique by explicitly exploring the meaning of "empirical" versus the meaning of "objective" in the practice of the social sciences.

In the way I understand methods, ethics, and politics, each of these concepts overlaps with the others, as each is concerned with distributions of power. Although ethics and politics are concepts that connote concomitant ideas of power, methods may not be. Decisions regarding exactly what tool in one's methodological kit to employ often hinge on power—that of the researcher, the researched, and the shifting power relations between the two over time, perhaps especially in the intensely interactive method of ethnography (e.g., Ferguson, 1991, pp. 130–132; Kurzman, 1991, p. 261). The power in method is the power of representation of others (Markham 2005a). It's a basic power—you get to choose the questions and the boundaries of the field, and you write the narrative. The ethnographic texts produced are models of social relations (Smith, 1990). The social relations involved in online ethnographies ultimately reveal that my position as arbiter of textual reality is a rather precarious power (see Marcus, 1998, p. 97).

Online Ethnographic Methods: Extending the Classics

Generally, ethnographic methods may be divided into three areas, and each of these and their well-known mechanics and methods are easily adaptable to the research site that begins, merges with, or ends up in an online setting,

- **Traditional field methods,** wherein a lone researcher enters a field site and becomes a covert or known participant observer. A subset of this classic type is collaborative ethnography, wherein pairs or teams of researchers, often a mentor plus field workers or students, engage the research site (e.g., Anderson, 1990; Burawoy, 1979; Drake & Cayton, 1945; Duneier, 1992; Geertz, 1973/2000; Hartigan, 1999; Kanter, 1977; Lynd & Lynd, 1927/1956; May & Patillo, 2000; Shostak, 1981; Tulloch & Jenkins, 1995).

- **Autoethnography,** wherein the researcher is the explicitly grounded native of a particular field site or social situation/status (e.g., Bochner & Ellis, 2002; Ellis, 2004; Gatson, 2003; Hancock, 2007; Markham, 2005a; May, 2003).

- **Multisited/extended-case ethnography,** wherein the goal is to situate contexts within a dialogue between theory and the field, and the micro mundane world to the macro systems that structure those worlds (Burawoy, 1991, 2000), where "Empirically following the thread of cultural process itself impels the move toward multisited ethnography" (Marcus, 1998, p. 80; see also the Center for Middletown Studies, which, like the Chicago School, has been an ethnographic factory).

Each of these types may be said to be mainly about presentation of the data, as it is possible to tease out the autoethnographic self of the researcher(s), and locate and highlight the place in the macro system(s) of the ethnographic site.

Whether using any of the ethnographic methods outlined, the Internet is ideally situated to be a part of extending the reach of ethnography. Although the boundaries of Internet sites are inherently more permeable and less physically bounded (if no less graphically or cognitively bounded) than offline sites, it is possible to note the predominant way in which authors have presented particular online ethnographies, although many of these publications may be placed in all three categories, and all can be placed in at least two, simultaneously. The bleed between the categories is not necessarily unique to the online settings of these ethnographies, but noting these categories and where we might place particular analyses within them tells us something about the ethical and political place of the contemporary ethnographer.

Although first emerging within the last two decades, with its classics only about 15 years old, and despite the ongoing question of whether online ethnography is either advisable or possible (e.g., Ashton & Thorns, 2007; Derteano, 2006; Ethnobase, n.d.; Holström, 2005; Howard, 2001; Nieckarz, 2005; Watson, 1997/2003), the online ethnography already has a vast tradition from which to draw.

TRADITIONAL FIELD METHODS ONLINE

The earliest online ethnography is arguably Howard Rheingold's *The Virtual Community* (1993/2000), wherein the "homesteading" metaphor of the "frontier" of cyberspace took root (see De Saille, 2006, for a critique of this metaphor). Although Rheingold's text is grounded in his personal experiences as one of the creators of online communities, as well as in an analysis that explores the multiple and connected online and offline places and spaces in which his community ultimately exists, his presentation is, without formally using the tools of ethnography (see Rheingold, 2000 edition, pp. 54–55), a rich and useful account of the state of online community in its nascent years. Others in this vein include Ali (2009a, 2009b), Baumle (2009), Baym (1995a; 1995b, 1998, 2000), Davis (2008), DiSalvo and Bruckman (2009), Gatson and Zweerink (2000, 2004a, 2004b), Harmon and Boeringer (2004), Kendall (2002), Lu (2009), Markham (1998), Millard (1997), Mizrach (1996), Nieckarz (2005), O'Brien (1997, 1999), Parpart (2003), Sharf (1997), Shaw (1997/2002), Stivale (1997), and Turkle (1995).

AUTOETHNOGRAPHY ONLINE

Unlike many works in the classical ethnographic tradition, online ethnographies are often written by consummate and acknowledged insiders in the communities of interest, often by individuals who start out as students, or indeed non-academics. Beginning again with Rheingold, these works explicitly ground the author(s) as a member (sometimes indeed as an architect) of the community of interest first and foremost, and they include Asim Ali (2009a, 2009b), Sarah Gatson and Amanda Zweerink (2004a, 2004b), Stacy Horn (1998), Jeffrey Ow (2000), Latoya Peterson (2009a, 2009b), Lisa Richards (2003), John Seabrook (1997), Sherry Turkle (1995), and Stephanie Tuszynski (2006).

MULTISITED ETHNOGRAPHY

One engages in this type of online ethnography by either exploring more than one online site, by including both online and offline sites, or building a multilayered narrative that develops the larger social context of a community under study (Marcus, 1998, pp. 84–88, 117–118, 241–242). Philip Howard's previous suggestion regarding the lack of appropriateness for straight ethnography in online settings did not hinge upon "real" versus "virtual" per se, but more specifically on a physical ideal of the field site, suggesting that most online sites are both non-physically bounded in any way, and "difficult to set . . . in a larger social context" (2001, p. 565; see also Derteano, 2006; Nieckarz, 2005). This position however has given way to one that is multisited (Celeste, Howard, & Hart, 2009), and includes Ashton and Thorns (2007), Bakardjieva (2005), Bandy (2007), Blasingame (2006), Christian (2009), Connery (1997), Gatson (2007a, 2007b),

Gatson and Zweerink (2004a, 2004b), Goodsell and Williamson (2008), Hampton and Wellman (2002, 2003), Heinecken (2004), Hine (2000), Islam (2008), Ito (1997), Kendall (2002), Knapp (1997), Komaki (2009), Leurs (2009), Mallapragada (2009), McPherson (2000), Mitchell (1999), Nakamura (2009), Ow (2000), Reid (2009), Richards (2003), Salaff (2002), Schmitz (1997/2002), Silver (2000), Stenger (2006), Stern and Dillman (2006), Tepper (1997), Tuszynski (2006), Watson (1997/2003), Williams (2004), and Zickmund (1997/2002).

It is worth noting again the difficulty of categorizing online ethnography. If we take a set of published texts by a research team (Busher & James, 2007a, 2007b; James, 2007; and James & Busher, 2006, 2007) together, these works present something other than only the online interviewing techniques that are their main stated methods. Instead, we could re-categorize this set as an autoethnographic multisited ethnography in that the authors set the research within academia where they are members, having prior knowledge of the bulk of their participants. A second set of examples occurs in *Race in Cyberspace*. Several of the chapters are never called *ethnography,* but arguably are, and are multisited: Nakamura analyzes advertising texts that are "popular media narratives of commercial cyberspace" (Kolko, Nakamura, & Rodman, 2000, p. 9). Jennifer González (2000) presents her sites as mainly text about graphics, discussing sites where users may purchase avatars. These sites, among some others in this edited volume (as well as in Porter's 1997 *Internet Culture*), are treated mainly as texts, and institutional review board (IRB) and methodological considerations are not explicitly discussed. Similarly, Henry Bial's keynote presentation at the 2009 Texas A&M University Race and Ethnic Studies Institute Symposium moves the author from film studies and analyses of actor performances, to the performances of Jewish identity in several online arenas. Finally, Jeffrey Ow's statement is most instructive:

> As an Asian male cyborg in my own right, I choose to play my own intellectual game with the *Shadow Warrior* controversy, acknowledging the perverse pleasures of weaving an oppositional read of the controversy, creating much more horrid creatures of the game designers and gaming public than the digital entities on the computer screen. In each level of my game, the Yellowfaced Cyborg Terminator morphs into different entities, from the individual gamer, to company representatives, ending with the corporate entities. (2000, p. 54)

Thus, Ow, though grounded in his own participation in both gaming and a racist culture, reflects George Marcus, "Cultural logics . . . are always multiple produced, and any ethnographic account of these logics finds that they are at least partly constituted within sites of the so-called system (i.e., modern interlocking institutions of media, markets, states, industries . . .)" (Marcus, 1998, p. 81).

Politicizing Methods and Ethics in the Online Field Site: Inherent Membership?

That none of the authors discussed in the previous paragraph called themselves ethnographers is generatively problematic. Max Travers (2009) argues that the newness and innovation claims of online ethnography are mainly political (see also Hine, 2008). In a basic sense of the mechanics of what it is that an ethnographer does (goes to a site, observes the location, the interactions, the boundaries, talks to or observes the inhabitants, records or transcribes all such observations and interactions, reads one's transcriptions, observes or talks more, transcribes more, and finally prepares a narrative wherein theory emerges or is tested), he is correct.[4] However, Travers's dismissal of the new *methods* of online ethnography misses the possibilities of the new *field*—in the sense of field site(s)—of online ethnography. The site of the online ethnography necessarily pushes the definitional boundaries of generally accepted concepts such as self, community, privacy, and text.

Gary Fine argues, "Ethnography is nothing until inscribed: sensory experiences become text" (1993, p. 288). The online site is already text, already inscribed (even more graphic sites, such as YouTube, have text); researcher elicitation from subjects is often unnecessary. This seems to be one reason for Travers to dismiss the online ethnography as one that "usually results in a 'thinner' level of description" (2009; p. 173). Despite the few examples Travers cites to prove this assertion, in which his sense seems to be that online ethnographers read "a" posting by a subject, the dozens of examples wherein the researcher(s) rather reads hundreds, perhaps thousands, of posts, often by the same set of participants, over years or as an archive, are ignored. Online research can provide either the same level of depth as a one-shot, one-hour interview, or the same level of depth as that produced by the daily participating, embedded offline ethnographer. It may also provide the same level of in-depth analysis as any historical or comparative historical text-based analysis, wherein the text is gleaned from archival sources (see also Marcus, 1998, p. 84).

Perhaps because the site of entry is so often (assumed to be) a private space (home, office; privately held online account), the idea that the online field has special ethical boundaries is often taken for granted. However, when reading the ethics sections of just about any work presenting itself as ethnographic, we find the same sorts of boundary-establishing behaviors outlined; indeed they are not inherently different than those found in offline ethnographies. I started my first online ethnographic project before the Association of Internet Researchers' (AoIR) "Ethical Decision-Making and Internet Research" guidelines were written (2002). From the outset, I followed the practices therein, paying particular attention to how various Internet venues across the terrain of a single community established their own ethical expectations (AoIR, 2002, pp. 4–5; Gatson & Zweerink, 2004a, pp. 17–19). I didn't get my sense of ethical boundaries from the AoIR, but rather from having been trained in sociological research methods.

ETHICAL GUIDELINES FOR ONLINE ETHNOGRAPHY: A SKETCH

Dorothy Smith has asserted, "There is no such thing as non-participant observation" (1990, pp. 87). As acknowledged by Judith Davidson and Silvana di Gregorio (Chapter 38, this volume), the higher scrutiny and surveillance of IRBs, coupled with the fact of "ordinary people . . . actively engaged as indigenous qualitative researchers in the virtual world," further complicates the already somewhat fraught professionally defined understandings of informed consent, participation, observation, authoritative narratives, discourse, and scholarship. The online arena then, is a field in which defining insiders and outsiders is more explicitly complicated than in traditionally understood conceptions of ethnographic field sites.

In contrast to Annette Markham's assertion, the first step in online environments is reading (see 2005a, p. 794). As well, in contrast to Hugh Busher and Nalita James (2007), it may be argued that academics are always already in the audience or group being studied when the research site is grounded in online interactions (see Turkle, 1995, pp. 29–30). The Internet itself is one of the only definable fields with which the overwhelming majority of its researchers are already intimately familiar, at least in the mechanical sense (we read, we post, we e-mail, etc.). The content of any particular subfield site within the Internet may be unfamiliar, but the method of becoming an entrant will not be. In other words, lurking or reading online content *is* participant observation in a way that unobtrusive observation isn't in an offline ethnographic situation; if we're a reader of online spaces, we are already "in," in a real way because most online content is read (interpreted), and not necessarily interacted with by adding the reader's own post. But is it always participant observation for which one needs

IRB permission to perform? When does reading become thinking become data gathering become data analysis? When is one a community member, a citizen, or a scholar? Does one need permission to read, or only to post or talk to others online? If, on the Internet, experience is already inscribed, already performed, and not in need of an ethnographer to validate it through scholarly revelation, we are again exposed as decision makers who arbitrate the definitions of the boundaries of appropriate interactions.

In a sense, all online ethnography is "disguised observation," but it is not also necessarily deceptive observation. The contemporary publicly accessible website carries with it an expectation of being under some level and type of observation, and it is questionable whether anyone participating in such sites has a reasonable or defensible expectation of being unobserved, or indeed of being able to control the observers' intentions or uses of such observation. The hegemonic bedrock of ethnographic ethics, however, involves both informed consent and an awareness of power differentials, both embedded in the historical excesses of human subjects research, as well as those of IRBs themselves. But, again, reading is its own form of interaction, and posting, submitting, and publishing one's text online invites readership and an audience, if not a community. Markham's concern with the researcher's "loss of authority [or power] in the presentation of research, and diminishment of one's academic role as observer/interpreter/archivist of social life" mirrors the loss of control the everyday online writer has once he or she presses post/submit/publish (2005a, p. 800; see also Marcus, 1998, p. 97).

In noting the "10 lies of ethnography," Fine discusses the positives of power and information control, assuming that the ethnographer has the greater share of salient power and control (1993, p. 276). In online settings though, the researcher is hardly the lone ranger (an ethnographic character Fine impugns) controlling the information flows and representations of an isolated or previously unknown/ ordinarily unknowable community; again this "lie" of offline ethnography is intensified online. One's colleagues may engage in open published critiques of one's work, but so may one's subjects, and *your* subjects are hardly yours alone.

The required online training manual for human subjects researchers states, "Researchers do not have the right to conduct research, especially research involving human subjects. Society grants researchers the privilege of conducting research. The granting of that privilege is based on the public's trust that research will be conducted responsibly. Erosion of that trust can result in the withdrawal of this privilege." I have discussed elsewhere (Gatson & Zweerink, 2004b) the complicated dynamics of who gives permission to who, and for what, when one's research site is a public venue with not even an unlocked door whose opening announces a certain basic level of entry, and at most slightly opaque windows that block certain kinds of participation. Those dynamics include the "privilege" of the researcher being just another subject in a way that classic offline ethnographers such as Clifford Geertz ([1973/2000] or even Joshua Gamson [1998]) did not have to confront. As well, Fine, citing Jack Douglas (1976), argues that the ethnographer has rights too. Given the very public nature of most online ethnography, those rights should be assessed under a model other than either a biomedical, or a 50-year-old social behavioral, one (see Stark, 2007). Rather, it should be one that takes the media literate citizen (including the online ethnographers themselves) into account (Fine, 1993, p. 271; see also Bassett & O'Riordan, 2002; Dingwall, 2007; Elm, Buchanan, & Stern, 2009; Feely, 2007a, pp. 766–770; 2007b; Johns, Hall, & Crowell, 2004; Katz, 2007; Kendall, 2004; Smith, 2004; Thomas, 2004). Online ethnographers have to engage in an exploration of our particular locations in connection to particular field sites, and it is fundamentally and qualitatively different exploring our place in the media-reading audience than it has been in exploring our place as outsiders to more or less bounded, easily identifiable, cultural or subcultural offline geographical locations. Thus, in a sense, we have to remake our guidelines for each online ethnography we decide to do, without at the same time abandoning our connections to professional and socio-legal ethics that we must simultaneously work under.

Finding the Edge of the Ethno: Representing Online Places and Experiences

How then does one go about using the political power one has as an online ethnographer? What is both useful and ethical in creating a representative narrative of an online site and its attendant identities and boundaries? I suggested earlier that one must understand one's place in the larger community and the ever-tightening circles that demarcate our memberships in groups and networks and thus understand one's multiple positions, identities, and power/resources, and how to ethically employ them.

THE INTERPENETRATION OF COMMUNITY BOUNDARIES ONLINE

'stina says:
(Mon Sep 14 10:27:21 1998)

QUESTION: This was in my local newspaper a couple of months ago, in the "letters" section:

As a high-school female student, it is troubling to me to think that my age group has been reduced to a simple stereotype of the child who has seen Titanic 18 times because Leonardo DiCaprio is "really really cute" and who religiously watches trashy, superficial programming like Buffy, the Vampire Slayer and Dawson's Creek.

I resent being told that I am so lucky to have role models like the short-skirted, thrift-store shopping, bubble-headed Buffy. . . . The empowerment of women is a long way off if the media think that portraying sexy, moronic, peroxided young girls will give us real teen-aged girls the power to take the world by storm. I have no problem with young—I am. I have no problem with sexy—that's cool. I have no problem with hair dye—that's between a girl and her hair-stylist. But what I do mind is moronic. To have "girl power," we must first learn to respect ourselves and others. And if the only images we see are those of heroines with no brains, how can we ever respect ourselves enough to believe we can be something more than Buffy, the vampire slayer?

Courtenay B. Symonds, Houston[5]

Why do you think that young women are consistently told it's "great" to have Buffy and Ally [McBeal] around as role models? Is it because t]here are so few role models out there for women, that the second [a] series that's not a sitcom comes out that's focused on women instead of men we're all supposed to follow that woman's lead?

Does this kid have a point?

'stina—who'd much rather be like Chris Carter's Dana Scully than Joss Whedon's Buffy Summers.

This textual excerpt from an online community—which generated an approximately hour-long analytical conversation about the gendered role-model appropriateness of Buffy Summers—in which I have spent more than a decade as a member, and more than 6 years as an autoethnographer presents an ideal framing device for a discussion of the methods, politics, and ethics of representation in online ethnography.[6] First, because **'stina** used a common strategy that in fact replicates an ethnographic technique—she made reference to a piece of conversation or text she'd overheard or read elsewhere to bring attention to a topic of concern to the community and herself as a member of it. Second, she quoted in full the words of someone else, whose original text appeared outside of the place of new inscription, for purposes of her own, again mimicking the technique of an ethnographer. Finally, by reproducing these texts in published form again (for the second time in Ms. Symonds' case, and for the first in 'stina's), I myself highlight methods, politics, and ethics—why these texts? Why these subjects? And, with whose permission?

Reuben May (2003) explored these issues in an article wherein he described himself as both a personal journal writer and a scholarly ethnographer. May's analysis is one of personal journals treated as archival textual evidence in and of themselves, not as field notes as his "statuses negate[d] the viability of formally studying college students' social behavior because his own behavior as a participant-observer would flirt with, rub against, or cross, social, administrative, or legal boundaries" (2003, p. 442). In exploring the difference between being an anonymous student participant-observer who "even wrote my first book about a neighborhood tavern because of my deep down urge to be around people and to share in their verbal games of sexual innuendo," and one who found it inappropriate to engage in the same techniques in exploring the nightlife in a college town wherein he was a non-anonymous and hypervisible Black professor, May tells us what he studied by telling us why he chose not to study it (2003, p. 443). In contrast to May's decisions, Markham (2005b), in a similarly contextualized article about sex/gender and class/race tensions and power dynamics, chose to present her narrative as a complex methodological piece that nevertheless presents findings from a formally defined ethnographic research project. Both of these authors were members of the contexts discussed but each made different choices about what could be defined as a legitimate research project, yet both published their accounts, and in the same journal.

Because of the very public nature of most World Wide Web sites (as opposed to online sites more generally, which includes more controlled access and private arenas from e-mail to newsgroups and bulletin boards, as well as intranet and Internet work- and education-based online arenas), the contentiousness over where the ethical boundaries are has been perhaps especially fraught because they raise issues perhaps thought settled already, as long as the formalities of the IRB process are followed. Is quoting from a blog the same thing as quoting from a newspaper, or a letter found in a historical archive? Is quoting from or reconstructing a face-to-face or overheard in-person conversation the same as quoting from or reconstructing a conversation or group discussion held through instant messaging or a bulletin/posting board? All self-identified online ethnographers, like their offline counterparts, discuss these sorts of issues, and must figure out what exactly their particular online arena(s) replicate about offline, perhaps settled, situations so that they can defend their ethical choices (e.g., Barnes, 2004; Bassett and O'Riordan, 2002; Elm, Buchanan, & Stern, 2009; Sharf, 1999).

Jan Fernback argues that online space is "socially constructed and reconstructed . . . [and] is a repository for collective cultural memory—it is popular culture, it is narratives created by its inhabitants that remind us who we are, it is life as lived and reproduced in pixels and virtual texts. . . . Cyberspace is essentially a reconceived public sphere for social, political, economic, and cultural interaction. . . . [its] users are . . . authors, public rhetoricians, statesmen, pundits" (1997/2002, p. 37). Thus, does a multivocal or dialogic set of texts produce a consensus picture of a community, a fragmented sense of what is or was important to it as a whole, or a reproduction—or indeed a continuation—of the community itself? Ethnographic narrative inscription presents a holistic and often linear story of a people, their place, and their identity. This linear structure may be a necessity of adhering to standards of coherent presentation (see Markham, 2005b, for another perspective). However, communities, identities, and places are contested entities. They also change over time. One (or even two) ethnographers can't cover every facet of a community, and the production of a coherent narrative requires choice-making. Although we as ethnographers can and do produce consecutive (or concurrent), multifocal narratives of one community, we are still the inscribers, interpreters, and authorities. What happens when there are other scholarly inscribers in one's research field, as well as "lay" inscribers whose inscription is at least as analytical as one's own (again, see Davidson and di Gregorio, Chapter 15, this volume)? One outcome could be a collaborative multivocal ethnography that combines the practices of each of the three main areas of ethnographic methodology. This becomes *macro-ethnography.*

Kate Millet's *Prostitution Papers* presents us with an example of multivocal ethnography (1973; see also Davis & Ellis, 2008). Although Millet is presented as the book's author, she is really its editor, soliciting and organizing a dialogue between four women, herself included. Millet presented the approaches of each writer in the form of essays authored by women who were identified only by their initials. She herself was K., the scholar activist. J. was the former sex worker–current psychologist, M. was the former sex worker–current PhD student, and L. was the lawyer and policy advocate for the rights of prostitutes. Although there was an overarching consensus offered by the authors—sex work is work, sex workers are positioned by patriarchy and re-victimized by the criminal justice system that seeks to punish prostitutes but not (or rarely) the men they service—as each woman comes from a different status position, their narratives are quite divergent.

Millet called the work a "candid dialogue," and the project actually produced both the book and a film. Millet was arguably a liminal ethnographer. She took on the ethnographer's timeline of observation, inscription, and interpretation. By offering space for their own developed narratives, she invited her ostensible subjects to become ethnographers as well, auto-ethnographers in particular. Millet's book is thus one that combines ethnography as the experience of the ethnographer and the text(s) that ethnographers and their subjects co-create. In the online ethnography, there is never just "'one beginning [or] one ending'" (Bochner & Ellis, 2002, p. 11), and no one position of unequivocal power. James and Busher worry that even with the shift in the balance of power that comes with using e-mail for interviews, "researchers cannot escape the power they exert from structuring the rules of the process" (2006, p. 416). Busher and James also worry about the insecure environments and lack of privacy inherent in the field (2007a, p. 3), [but they do not see that this is true for the researcher as well. As Stevienna De Saille notes, without making the Internet a utopia, power and access are quite different online, "As previously disenfranchised people increasingly put up their own boards, pages, and blogs, thus defining their heterogeneous subjectivity to the world, can it be ignored that the technologies of the web do indeed allow the subaltern to speak?" (2006, p. 7).

The "engagement medi[a]" that are both television and the Internet (Askwith, 2007) potentially take us far beyond team-based collaborative ethnographies and allow us to further parse the boundaries, ethical and otherwise, of television audiences, and the communities embedded within those audiences (Bandy, 2007; Islam, 2008; Lotz & Ross, 2004; Shirky, 2002; Whiteman, 2009). Around the same time that I was making the decision to formally study The Bronze, the book, *Bite Me! An Unofficial Guide to the World of Buffy the Vampire Slayer* was published (Stafford, 1998/2002). It contained a section on the first major offline gathering of the community, the soon-to-be annual Posting Board Party, and included photographs of Bronzers, captioned with both their Bronze posting names and their offline, everyday names. Its 2002 edition contains even more easily identifiable information about several individual Bronzers, as well as thoroughly identifying information about The Bronze as a website, and some interviews with members (Stafford, 2002, pp. 113–156). As well, the site was well advertised, and well trolled by journalists, and through linked websites such as The Who's Who and What's What of The Bronze (where Bronzers themselves created a pre-Friendster/MySpace/Facebook place for ease of social networking, long before the mainstream discourse of "Web 2.0" appeared) self-promoted as the communal place to be.

The audience-author feedback loop (Kociemba, 2006) of The Bronze has always been complex and multileveled—it wasn't just Joss Whedon who got to be an author, and he wasn't the only one to hear from his audience and community. Jane Espenson, eventually part of the production team, started out as a linguistics graduate student and provided the introduction to Michael Adams's *Slayer Slang* (2004). Meredyth Smith (~**mere**~) went the other direction, from Bronzer first to Whedonverse writer.[7] Others were lurking and posting, and ruminating on the implications of being Bronzers. **elusio** did a couple of papers for undergraduate courses at a university in the United Kingdom, **Kenickie** was an undergraduate sociology major in the United Kingdom throughout most of the research, and **Psyche** and **seraphim** were graduate students in psychology and anthropology, respectively, who—like several other acafans—while doing no formal studies on The Bronze, nonetheless brought their intellectual interests to their offline and online fandom activities, as **Tamerlane** did, when he delurked after several years and became a visible member of the community,

Tamerlane says:
(Tue Apr 11 17:10:39 2000)

> **'stina, Jaan Quidam, Closet Buffyholic, SarahNicole**, and others: This place really does interest me. More, I think, than the show. I think an awful lot of credit has to be given to **TV James** for instituting the format he did. One of my two long-time academic interests is Biology (the other of course being History). It always struck me as interesting the difference between your average college lecture class and a biology class with a field or even just a long, interactive lab component. Hanging around people for a three-hour open-ended lab, twice a week, where you spend the whole time wandering around looking at things and discussing them with others, led, I think, to a greatly increased connectivity (compared to even a three hour lecture). Not to mention the bonding that took place on long field excursions (one of my all time favorite camping trips remains a one-week Fire Ecology field-trip). Although I see communities develop at all the posting boards I visit (and I have been there at the beginning of a couple of others), I have never seen the cohesiveness of the Bronze duplicated elsewhere. This "message board" format, at least the way it has evolved, offers IMHO all of the best qualities of chatrooms . . . and threaded boards with few of the drawbacks. The ability to encompass a wide, free-flowing conversation that can be scrolled at leisure at any point within a one week period is pretty unique. The Usenet is similar of course, but the seemingly much higher level of anonymity and the much larger base of casual users seems to limit social interactions.

Here we see an example of how lurkers/readers have an acknowledged place as members of online communities and audiences—they may show up visibly at any time, and their observations/representations then become part of the communally produced text. Across the range of less formal photographic and inscribed observations, there were the Bronzers who wrote about their experiences on easily accessible websites (e.g., **Claris**'s site, www.NoDignity.com), wherein the ethnographer became the subject, where *sometimes* my informed consent was solicited before posting a quotation or a photo.

Other Bronzers (Ali, 2009a,[8] 2009b; Tuszynski, 2006) also wrote ethnographies, while Allyson Beatrice (2007) wrote a memoir that grounded her online communal experiences at The Bronze. Scholars who do not identify as Bronzers, but as aca-fans (*aca-fans* refers to academics who research the object of their fandom, or who identify as both fans and scholars) of *Buffy, the Vampire Slayer* (BtVS) to one degree or another, also wrote about Buffy fandom, and sometimes used The Bronze and Bronzers as data (Adams, 2004; Askwith, 2007; Bandy, 2007; Blasingame, 2006; Busse, 2002; Heinecken, 2004; Kem, 2005; Kociemba, 2006; Larbelestier, 2002; Parpart, 2003; Parrish, 2007; Richards, 2003; Stenger, 2006; Williams, 2004; see the Kirby-Diaz, 2009, collection for other broader BtVS fandom works). Dawn Heinecken and Michael Adams most explicitly use Bronzers as examples of audience members, with Adams acknowledging us/them as the hierarchical top of the fandom heap, whereas Heinecken does not draw a boundary around them as a community, but rather presents a division of fans that some Bronzers were a part of—Spike/Buffy 'shippers(short for "relationshippers"—fans of particular romantic pairings, either those actually appearing in a show/text, or those wished for)—without noting where these folks were on the Bronzer totem pole. Neither of these pieces nor most of the others include discussion of methods, or IRB issues. These authors generally do not position themselves as ethnographers (with the exceptions of Ali, Tuszynski, and Richards). In Adams's case, he is a linguist, accessing the publicly available development of slang stemming from a particular show and its fandom, without really drawing boundaries around the community(ies) that make up that fandom, and seeing his data as published text, part of the public flow of developing language.

THE NETWORKED SELF AND THE PEDAGOGY OF THE MEDIA LITERATE CITIZEN

As I have noted elsewhere (Gatson & Zweerink, 2004a), it is questionable how anonymous ethnographic sites have ever been. Thus, my comments in this section will mainly focus on field sites that are public arenas—not that there isn't a backstage, but they are backstages that one need not be a "professional" to gain access to. The (perhaps dirty) secret of online ethnography (all ethnography?)—like other mass media-based research, especially television studies—is that it exposes the lack of special knowledge needed to do it. It is intense, but its mechanics are fairly simple, and they're things we and our students are engaged in every day. All that is needed is the application of the sociological imagination to formalize the reading and posting I do at online communities where my membership ranges from the regular lurker, to the occasional poster, to the daily contributor, and where my online identity of **SarahNicole** remains a near-constant; I'm fairly certain that at the least one of my posts across these communities have already been incorporated into someone's thesis or dissertation at this point. Two examples demonstrate aspects of this experience of the Internet and create speculation of simultaneously teaching undergraduates responsible research methods and media literacy/citizenship.

In 2007, I did something common to academics; I read a review of my work. What was perhaps unusual but increasingly common was that I stumbled across the review online while "Googling myself" in a search for citations of my work (don't lie; you all do it too). What was truly unusual was that the review was written by some of the subjects of the research. This research was the outcome of a National Institute on Drug Abuse (NIDA)–funded study on raves and the use of "club drugs," which in our case focused on the online discourse surrounding these topics (Fire Erowid, 2007; Murguía, Tackett-Gibson, & Lessem, 2007). Early on, my co-principal investigator (PI) attended a conference at NIDA where he met Fire and Earth Erowid (Fire Erowid, 2002). Fire and Earth are the pseudonyms of the people who run Erowid, an online clearinghouse of information about drug use and alternative subcultures that was an important node in the network we were studying, so from nearly its inception, research subjects were involved in the research in ways that were previously unfamiliar to most of the research team. In their review, Fire characterized the work of Erowid thusly,

> Although our primary role is that of cultural documentarians rather than participants of the drug-using subculture, in the modern anthropological tradition we adhere to, the validity of one's understanding of a culture or community is based on whether one is a part of that culture or community. If there is too little connection between anthropologists, researchers, or documentarians and their subjects, the resulting research is likely to be inaccurate. Erowid was started out of our personal and academic interest in psychoactives, but we are only peripherally involved in many aspects of the field. We maintain connections and involvement with a variety of communities in order to better be able to serve their needs, represent their actions and viewpoints, and act as their trusted recorders and archivists. (2007).

These authors/subjects engage in a "contexting [of] the network" (Jones, 2004) of scholars and subjects that publicizes these connections in ways that go beyond publication in practically restricted-access journals read only by authoritatively legitimated experts.

The Internet exposes the fact that there's public, and then there's public; there's talking back (other scholars' letters to the editor, symposia/dialogue in journals; see Denzin, 2004), and then there's talking back (Borland, 2004; Chen, Hall, & Johns, 2004; Gatson & Zweerink, 2004b). The race and pop culture website Racialicious.com and some of the talk-back generated therein serve as examples of when subjects talk back. Racialicious is more moderated than many news outlets' comments section because it is partly meant to be a safe space to discuss issues related to race/ethnicity and racism (see http://www.racialicious.com/comment-moderation-policy/), but its capacity for generating talk-back with which many ethnographers may be unfamiliar is illustrative of the phenomenon wherein I think we can locate both scholars' place in the research network, as well as platform a teaching tool.

In 2009, as director of my university's Race and Ethnic Studies Institute, I hosted a symposium on race, ethnicity, and (new) media. Latoya Peterson, editrix of Racialicious, participated as both a keynote speaker (2009b) and research presenter (2009a). Peterson took copious notes on each presentation, and presented some of her synopses at Racialicious. The synopsis of Lisa Nakamura's keynote presentation and the article from which it was drawn (2009) drew sometimes angry commentary from fans of the game World of Warcraft, which, along with the gaming practice of creating machinima (animated music videos using images from the game), were the centerpiece of Nakamura's work. As well, danah boyd (2009) re-published at Racialicious some of her work looking at socioeconomic differences between MySpace and Facebook users, and some users of those social networking sites had much to critique about boyd's conclusions.[9]

These examples, along with my own experience with Erowid, demonstrate that both information and people, although theoretically having newly opened conduits, are also materially and ideologically embedded in truncated networks with less-than-permeable boundaries (Howard, 2004; Norris, 2004; Travers, 2000). The talk-back made possible by the Internet takes us beyond the professional deconstruction of our ethnographic pasts (Van Maanen, 2004; see also MacKinnon, 1997/2002), and pushes us as both scholars and teachers to explore our "distributed learning communities" (Haythornthwaite, 2002) and the "social context of user sophistication" (Hargittai, 2004). If it is important in the process of ethnographic research to locate the researcher as well as the subjects, and expose the connections between and among them, then the autoethnographic network mapping of particular research projects would be useful in pedagogical and public sociological projects where media literacy and online citizenship are the specific aims. In developing an undergraduate course on the sociology of the Internet, I use my own online network maps as an introduction to the major project of the class. The students will have to place themselves in their offline and online networks—where do they go and what do they read, watch, discuss, and publish? Do their experiences reflect the published works on their networked worlds? Why and why not?

Here, we have the inherent autoethnographic nature of Internet environments for the academic—being online is arguably (a large part of) our work environment, if not always our home or our third space. The Internet exposes us again in our quest for "unpolluted truth" (see Fine, 1993, p. 274)—if we ever were investigating isolated "primitives" outside of the macro system, we certainly aren't now. For every online interaction engaged in, every online observation logged, some other observer may be recording our actions, and observing us. Thus, we most especially "differ little from Erving Goffman's social actors" (Fine, 1993, p. 282), and increasingly our students are very likely to be more expert members of social worlds that they have the right to engage in and comment on, beyond their identities as nascent researchers. We should provide the tools for that commentary to be analytical and empirical, so that both they and we are aware of the political boundaries of our methods and ethics. Media-saturation is not the same thing as media-literacy, and navigating through representations across the field of mass media is an important skill, even if one chooses to opt out of much interaction with such media.

During the next decade and into the future as ethnography moves from face-to-face, to online textual and graphic communication, to the spaces of Second Life (Boellstorff, 2008) and such games as World of Warcraft, and back again to the offline context, the ethnographic experiences discussed herein both ground themselves in the traditions of the method and are generative of explicitly exploring the meaning of "empirical" versus the meaning of "objective" in the practice of the social sciences. We can tell empirically based trustworthy stories about human behavior online, perhaps especially because we as the ethnographers are eminently exposable as but one in a host of voices telling the stories, and we are un-removable subjects of those stories, perhaps waiting for someone else to tell our story for us. We could perhaps call this Ethnography 2.0, in an acknowledgement of the way in which this way of practicing ethnography "allows its [practitioners] to interact with other[s] or to change . . . content, in contrast to . . . [being] passive [subjects]" ("Web 2.0," 2/8/2010).[10] This visible and experiential reality does not remove our ethical responsibilities from us, but it does make the boundary surrounding the ostensibly objective outsider (the researcher, the lone scholar) especially permeable. It raises the question, can anyone be an ethnographer? If so, who watches the watchers?

Notes

1. Gatson and Zweerink, 2000, 2004a, 2004b; Zweerink and Gatson, 2002. These works, though driven by my sociological research agenda, were coauthored with Amanda Zweerink, a "lay" ethnographer I met online within the community I ended up researching. She was in advertising at the time we began working together and at present is director of community at CurrentTV.

2. Gatson, 2007a, 2007b. These are two of the three chapters I wrote for an edited volume that emerged from a National Institutes on Drug Abuse collaborative grant that looked at drug use discourse online.

3. Coughlin, Greenstein, Widmer, Meisner, Nordt, Young, Gatson, et al., 2007; Coughlin, Greenstein, Widmer, Meisner, Nordt, Young, Quick, and Bowden, 2007; Desai et al., 2008; Gatson et al., 2005; Gatson et al., 2009; Nordt et al., 2007. These represent some of the work emerging from a multiyear project exploring the ways in which a group of researchers, students, teachers, and others have worked together toward a paradigm shift in the production and use of science. This approach sought to integrate research, teaching, and service—the traditional triumvirate of evaluation for academics in college and university systems—by combining the reintroduction of an old animal model with new and emerging technologies and the development of a new online/offline community model that incorporated the development of formal and informal networks.

4. For specifically methodological discussions of the processes of online ethnography, see Chen, Hall, and Johns, 2004; Dicks and Mason, 2008; Dicks, Soyinka, and Coffey, 2006; Gatson and Zweerink, 2004b; Hine, 2000; 2008; Hine, Kendall, and boyd, 2009; Kendall, 1999, 2004; LeBesco, 2004; Mann and Stewart, 2004; Markham, 2004; Markham and Baym, 2009; Walstrom, 2004.

5. The italics used here indicate that the poster was quoting directly from another source, in this case, the letters to the editor section of the *Houston Chronicle*.

6. My field site was The Bronze, a linear posting board (which originally also hosted a threaded posting board and chat room) located at the official website for the television series *Buffy the Vampire Slayer* (BtVS). It was called The Bronze after the club where the main characters often hung out, and the denizens of the online community dubbed themselves Bronzers.

7. Both of these women now have writing and producing credits outside the Whedonverse.

8. The **Jaan Quidam** addressed by **Tamerlane** earlier; I am **SarahNicole** addressed earlier.

9. See http://www.racialicious.com/2009/05/11/dont-hate-the-player-hate-the-game-the-racialization-of-labor-in-world-of-warcraft-conference-notes/ and http://www.racialicious.com/2009/07/09/the-not-so-hidden-politics-of-class-online/. For another example of such researcher/ researched engagement, see also the discussion of Boellstorff's ethnography of Second Life, in which the ethnographer participates: http://savageminds.org/2008/06/12/ethnography-of-the-virtual/#comment-392629

10. I don't actually think it's appropriate to apply the concept of Web 3.0 to the concept of online ethnography I am explicating herein, because as a concept, there are too many varied definitions of what this even means (see "Web 2.0," retrieved February 8, 2010, from Wikipedia, http://en.wikipedia.org/wiki/Web_2.0; and "Semantic Web," retrieved from February 8, 2010, from Wikipedia, http://en.wikipedia.org/wiki/Semantic_Web). However, especially because some consider Web 3.0 "as the return of experts and authorities to the Web" ("Web 2.0") and I think the Internet (both the technology and the end users) have made the online ethnographic project one that is too inherently open to non-expert participation. Although we may continue to have easily separated reference groups relative to our particular ethnographic projects (e.g., our academic subjects versus our academic employers), and though to some degree we can still keep our finished products mainly to an academic audience if we choose, I think we have to deal with being no more necessarily experts in our online endeavors as our ostensible subjects, and I think this reality highlights and complicates the traditional ethnographic notion of participant observation in ways that "Web 3.0" doesn't.

References

Adams, M. (2004). *Slayer slang: A* Buffy the Vampire Slayer *lexicon.* Oxford, UK: Oxford University Press.

Ali, A. (2009a). "In the world, but not of it": An ethnographic analysis of an online *Buffy the Vampire Slayer* fan community. In M. K. Diaz (Ed.), *Buffy and Angel conquer the Internet: Essays on online fandom* (pp. 87–106). Jefferson, NC: McFarland.

Ali, A. (2009b). Community, language, and postmodernism at the mouth of hell. In M. Kirby-Diaz (Ed.), *Buffy and Angel conquer the Internet: Essays on online fandom* (pp. 107–126). Jefferson, NC: McFarland. (Original publication, 2000; available at http://terpconnect.umd.edu/~aali/buffnog.html)

Anderson, E. (1990). *Streetwise: Race, class, and change in an urban community.* Chicago: University of Chicago Press.

Ashton, H., & Thorns, D. C. (2007). The role of information communications technology in retrieving local community. *City & Community, 6*(3), 211–230.

Askwith, I. D. (2007). *Television 2.0: Reconceptualizing TV as an Engagement Medium.* Master's thesis, Massachusetts Institute of Technology, Boston, MA. Available at cms.mit.edu/research/theses/IvanAskwith2007.pdf

Association of Internet Researchers. (2002). Ethical decision-making and Internet research. Available at http://aoir.org/reports/ethics.pdf

Bakardjieva, M. (2005). *Internet society: The Internet in everyday life.* Thousand Oaks, CA: Sage.

Bandy, E. (2007, May 23). *From* Dawson's Creek *to "Dawson's Desktop": TV-web synergy in a multimedia world.* Paper presented at the annual meeting of the International Communication Association, San Francisco, CA. Available at http://www.allaca demic.com/meta/p172730_index.html

Barnes, S. B. (2004). Issues of attribution and identification in online social research. In M. D. Johns, S. S. Chen, & G. J. Hall (Eds.), *Online social research: Methods, issues, ethics* (pp. 203–222). New York: Peter Lang.

Bassett, E. H., & O'Riordan, K (2002). Ethics of Internet research: Contesting the human subjects research model. *Ethics and Information Technology, 4*(3), 233.

Baumle, A. K. (2009). *Sex discrimination and law firm culture on the Internet.* New York: Palgrave Macmillan.

Baym, N. K. (1995a). The emergence of community in CMC. In S. G. Jones (Ed.), *CyberSociety: Computer-mediated communication and community* (pp. 138–163). Thousand Oaks, CA: Sage.

Baym, N. K. (1995b). From practice to culture on Usenet. In S. L. Star (Ed.), *The cultures of computing* (pp. 29–52). Oxford, UK: Blackwell/Sociological Review.

Baym, N. K. (1998). The emergence of online community. In S. G. Jones (Ed.), *CyberSociety 2.0: Revisiting computer-mediated communication and community* (pp. 35–63). Thousand Oaks, CA: Sage.

Baym, N. K. (2000). *Tune in, log on: Soaps, fandom, and online community.* Thousand Oaks, CA: Sage.

Beatrice, A. (2007). *Will the vampire people please leave the lobby?: True adventures in cult fandom.* Naperville, IL: Sourcebooks.

Bial, H. (2009, April 30–May). *Jew media: Performance and technology in the 58th century.* Paper presented at the Texas A&M University Race & Ethnic Studies Institute Symposium: Race, Ethnicity, and (New) Media, Texas A&M University, College Station, TX.

Blasingame, K. S. (2006). "I can't believe I'm saying it twice in the same century. . . but 'Duh . . . '": The evolution of the *Buffy the Vampire Slayer* sub-culture language through the medium of fanfiction in *Buffy the Vampire Slayer. Slayage: The Online Journal of Buffy Studies, 20.* Available at http://slayageonline.com/essays/slayage20/Blasingame.htm

Bochner, A. P., & Ellis, C. (2002). *Ethnographically speaking: Autoethnography, literature, and aesthetics.* Walnut Creek, CA: AltaMira Press.

Boellstorff, T. (2008). *Coming of age in Second Life: An anthropologist explores the virtually human.* Princeton, NJ: Princeton University Press.

Borland, K. (2004). "That's not what I said": Interpretive conflict in oral narrative research. In S. N. Hesse-Biber & P. Leavy (Eds.), *Approaches to qualitative research: A reader on theory and practice* (pp. 522–534). New York: Oxford University Press.

boyd, d. (2009). The not-so-hidden politics of class online. Racialicious.com. Available at http://www.racialicious.com/2009/07/09/the-not-so-hidden-politics-of-class-online/

Burawoy, M. (1979). *Manufacturing consent: Changes in the labor process under monopoly capitalism.* Chicago: University of Chicago Press.

Burawoy, M. (1991). *Ethnography unbound: Power and resistance in the modern metropolis.* Berkeley: University of California Press.

Burawoy, M. (2000). *Global ethnography: Forces, connections, and imaginations in a postmodern world.* Berkeley: University of California Press.

Busher, H., & James, N. (2007a, April 12–14). *Email communication as a technology of oppression: Attenuating identity in online research.* Paper presented at the Annual Conference of the British Sociological Association, University of London Available at http://hdl.handle.net/2381/439

Busher, H., & James, N. (2007b, September 5–8). *Building castles in the air: Colonising the social space in online qualitative research.* Paper presented at the British Educational Research Association Annual Conference, Institute of Education, University of London. Available at http://www.leeds.ac.uk/educol/documents/165971.htm

Busse, K. (2002). Crossing the final taboo: Family, sexuality, and incest in Buffyverse fan fiction. In R. Wilcox & D. Lavery (Eds.), *Fighting the forces: What's at stake in* Buffy the Vampire Slayer (pp. 207–217). Lanham, MD: Rowman & Littlefield.

Celeste, M., Howard, P. N., & T. Hart (2009, April 30–May 2). *(Con)Testing identities: Haitian and Indian women's use of social networking platforms.* Paper presented at the Texas A&M University Race & Ethnic Studies Institute Symposium: Race, Ethnicity, and (New) Media, Texas A&M University, College Station, Texas.

Center for Middletown Studies. Available at http://cms.bsu.edu/Academics/Centersand Institutes/Middletown.aspx

Chen, S. S., Hall, G. J., & Johns, M. D. (2004). Research paparazzi in cyberspace: The voices of the researched. In M. D. Johns, S. S. Chen, & G. J. Hall (Eds.), *Online social research: Methods, issues, ethics* (pp. 157–173). New York: Peter Lang.

Christian, A. J. (2009, April 30–May 2). *YouTube: Black existentialism and network participation.* Paper presented at the Texas A&M University Race & Ethnic Studies Institute Symposium: Race, Ethnicity, and (New) Media, Texas A&M University, College Station, Texas.

Connery, B. (1997). IMHO: Authority and egalitarian rhetoric in the virtual coffeehouse. In D. Porter (Ed.), *Internet culture* (pp. 161–180). New York: Routledge.

Coughlin, D. J., Greenstein, E. E., Widmer, R. J. Meisner, J., Nordt, M. Young, M. F., Gatson, S. N., et al. (2007, April 29). *e-Research: A novel use of the Internet to perform live animal research from a laboratory distant from the site of animal care technicians and facilities.* Federation of American Societies for Experimental Biology meetings, Computers in Research and Teaching II poster session.

Coughlin, D. J., Greenstein, E. E., Widmer, R. J., Meisner, J., Nordt, M., Young, M. F., Quick, C. M., & Bowden, R. A. (2007). Characterization of an inflammatory response and hematology of the Pallid bat using "e-Research." *The FASEB Journal, 21,* 742.11.

Davis, J. L. (2008). *Presentation of self and the personal interactive homepage: An ethnography of MySpace.* Master's thesis, Texas A&M University, College Station, Texas.

Davis, C., & Ellis, C. (2008). Emergent methods in autoethnographic research: Autoethnographic narrative and the multiethnographic turn. In S. N. Hesse-Biber & P. Leavy (Eds.), *Handbook of emergent methods* (pp. 283–302). New York: Guilford Press.

Davis, J. L. (2008). *Presentation of self and the personal interactive homepage: An ethnography of MySpace.* Master's thesis, Texas A&M University, College Station, Texas.

Denzin, N. K. (2004). The art and politics of interpretation. In S. N. Hesse-Biber & P. Leavy (Eds.), *Approaches to qualitative research: A reader on theory and practice* (pp. 447–473). New York: Oxford University Press.

Derteano, P. F. M. (2006). Reflexiones para la reflexividad del investigador: Un acercamiento a través del estudio del fenómeno pornográfico (Reflections on the reflexivity of the investigator: An approach through the study of the pornographic phenomenon). Retrieved June 2006 from http://www.perio.unlp.edu.ar/question/nive12/articulos/ensayos/molinaderteano_1_ensayos_12primavera06.htm

Desai K. V., Gatson, S. N., Stiles, T., Laine, G. A., Stewart, R. H., & Quick, C. M. (2008). Integrating research and education at research-intensive universities with research-intensive communities. *Advances in Physiological Education, 32*(2), 136–141.

De Saille, S. (2006). A cyberian in the multiverse: Towards a feminist subject position for cyberspace. *Conference proceedings—Thinking gender—the NEXT generation.* UK Postgraduate Conference in Gender Studies, June 21–22, University of Leeds, UK, e-paper no. 19.

Dicks, B., & Mason, B. (2008). Hypermedia methods for qualitative research. In S. N. Hesse-Biber & P. Leavy (Eds.), *Handbook of emergent methods* (pp. 571–600). New York: Guilford Press.

Dicks, B., Soyinka, B., & Coffey, A. (2006). Multimodal ethnography. *Qualitative Research, 6*(1), 77–96.

Dingwall, R. (2007). "Turn off the oxygen . . . ' *Law & Society Review, 41*(4), 787–796.

DiSalvo, B. J., & Bruckman, A. (2009, April 30–May 2). *Gaming manhood in African American culture.* Paper presented at the Texas A&M University Race & Ethnic Studies Institute Symposium: Race, Ethnicity, and (New) Media, Texas A&M University, College Station, Texas.

Douglas, J. (1976). *Investigative social research.* Beverly Hills, CA: Sage.

Drake, S., & Cayton, H. R. (1945). *Black metropolis: A study of Negro life in a northern city.* New York: Harcourt, Brace.

Duneier, M. (1992). *Slim's table: Race, respectability, and masculinity.* Chicago: University of Chicago Press.

Ellis, C. (2004). *The ethnographic I: A methodological novel about autoethnography.* Walnut Creek, CA: AltaMira Press.

Elm, M. S., Buchanan, E. A., & Stern, S. A. (2009). How do various notions of privacy influence decisions in qualitative Internet research? In A. N. Markham & N. K. Baym (Eds.), *Internet inquiry: Conversations about method* (pp. 69–98). Thousand Oaks, CA: Sage.

Ethnobase. (n.d.). Available at http://webdb.lse.ac.uk/ethnobase/bibliography.asp

Feely, M. M. (2007a). Legality, social research, and the challenge of institutional review boards. *Law & Society Review, 41*(4) 757–776.

Feely, M. M. (2007b). Response to comments. *Law & Society Review, 41*(4), 811–818.

Ferguson, A. A. (1991). Managing without managers: Crisis and resolution in a collective bakery. In M. Burawoy (Ed.), *Ethnography unbound: Power and resistance in the modern metropolis* (pp. 108–132). Berkeley: University of California Press.

Fernback, J. (2002). The individual within the collective: Virtual ideology and the realization of collective principles. In S. G. Jones (Ed.), *Virtual culture: Identity and communication in cybersociety* (pp. 36–54). Thousand Oaks, CA: Sage. (Original work published 1997)

Fine, G. A. (1993). Ten lies of ethnography: Moral dilemmas of field research. *Journal of Contemporary Ethnography, 22*(3), 267–294.

Fire Erowid. (2002). Face to face with NIDA: A conference on drugs, youth and the Internet. *Erowid Extracts, 3*(2).

Fire Erowid. (2007). Review of *Real Drugs in a Virtual World. Erowid Newsletter, 13.* Available at http://www.erowid.org/library/review/review.php?p=265

Gamson, J. (1998). *Freaks talk back: Tabloid talk shows and sexual nonconformity.* Chicago: University of Chicago Press.

Gatson, S. N. (2003). On being amorphous: Autoethnography, genealogy, and a multiracial identity. *Qualitative Inquiry, 9*(1), 20–48.

Gatson, S. N. (2007a). Assessing the likelihood of Internet information-seeking leading to offline drug use by youth. In E. Murguía, M. Tackett-Gibson, & A. Lessem (Eds.), *Real drugs in a virtual world: Drug discourse and community online* (pp. 99–120). Lanham, MD: Lexington Books.

Gatson, S. N. (2007b). Illegal behavior and legal speech: Internet communities' discourse about drug use. In E. Murguía, M. Tackett-Gibson, & A. Lessem (Eds.), *Real drugs in a virtual world: Drug discourse and community online* (pp. 135–159). Lanham, MD: Lexington Books.

Gatson, S. N., Meisner, J. K., Young, M. F., Dongaonkar, R., & Quick, C. M. (2005). The eBat project: A novel model for live-animal distance learning labs. *FASEB Journal, 19*(5), A1352.

Gatson, S. N., Stewart, R. H., Laine, G. A., & Quick, C. M. (2009). A case for centralizing undergraduate summer research programs: The DeBakey research-intensive community. *FASEB Journal, 633*, 8.

Gatson, S. N., & Zweerink. A. (2000). Choosing community: Rejecting anonymity in cyberspace. In D. A. Chekki (Ed.), *Community structure and dynamics at the dawn of the new millennium* (pp. 105–137). Stamford, CT: JAI.

Gatson, S. N., & Zweerink. A. (2004a). *Interpersonal culture on the Internet: Television, the Internet, and the making of a community.* Studies in Sociology Series, no. 40. Lewiston, NY: Edwin Mellen Press.

Gatson, S. N., & Zweerink. A. (2004b). "Natives" practicing and inscribing community: Ethnography online. *Qualitative Research, 4*(2), 179–200.

Geertz, C. (2000). *The interpretation of cultures.* New York: Basic Books. (Original work published in 1973)

González, J. (2000). The appended subject: Race and identity as digital assemblage. In B. E. Kolko, L. Nakamura, & G. B Rodman (Eds.), *Race in cyberspace* (pp. 27–50). New York: Routledge.

Goodsell, T. L., & Williamson, O. (2008). The case of the brick huggers: The practice of an online community. *City & Community, 7*(3), 251–272.

Hampton, K., & Wellman, B. (2002). The not so global village of Netville. In B. Wellman & C. Haythornthwaite (Eds.), *The Internet in everyday life* (pp. 345–371). Malden, MA: Blackwell.

Hampton, K., & Wellman, B. (2003). Neighboring in Netville: How the Internet supports community and social capital in a wired suburb. *City & Community, 2*(4), 277–312.

Hancock, B. H. (2007). Learning how to make life swing. *Qualitative Sociology, 30*(2), 113–133.

Hargittai, E. (2004). Informed web surfing: The social context of user sophistication. In P. N. Howard & S. Jones (Eds.), *Society online: The Internet in context* (pp. 256–274). Thousand Oaks, CA: Sage.

Harmon, D., & Boeringer, S. B. (2004). A content analysis of Internet-accessible written pornographic depictions. In S.N. Hesse-Biber & P. Leavy (Eds.), *Approaches to qualitative research: A reader on theory and practice* (pp. 402–408). New York: Oxford University Press.

Hartigan, J. (1999). *Racial situations: Class predicaments of whiteness in Detroit.* Princeton, NJ: Princeton University Press.

Haythornthwaite, C. (2002). Building social networks via computer networks: Creating and sustaining distributed learning communities. In K. A. Renninger & W. Shumar, *Building virtual communities: Learning and change in cyberspace* (pp. 159–190). Cambridge, UK: Cambridge University Press.

Heinecken, D. (2004). Fan readings of sex and violence in *Buffy the Vampire Slayer. Slayage, 11–12.* Available at http://slayageonline.com/Numbers/slayage11_12.htm

Hine, C. (2000). *Virtual ethnography.* Thousand Oaks, CA: Sage.

Hine, C. (2008). Internet research as emergent practice. In S. N. Hesse-Biber & P. Leavy (Eds.), *Handbook of emergent methods* (pp. 525–542). New York: Guilford Press.

Hine, C., Kendall, L., & boyd, d. (2009). How can qualitative researchers define the boundaries of their projects? In A. N. Markham & N. K. Baym (Eds.), *Internet inquiry: Conversations about method* (pp. 1–32). Thousand Oaks, CA: Sage.

Holström, J. (2005, retrieved). Virtuell etnografi—vad är det? (Virtual ethnography—What is it?). Retrieved 2005 from http://www.hanken.fi/portals/studymaterial/2005–2006/

helsingfors/foretagsledningochorganisation/2235/material/handouts/virtuell_etno grafi.pdf

Horn, S. (1998). *Cyberville: Clicks, culture, and the creation of an online town.* New York: Warner Books.

Howard, P. N. (2001). Network ethnography and the hypermedia organization: New organizations, new media, new methods. *New Media & Society, 4*(4), 551–575.

Howard, P. N. (2004). Embedded media: Who we know, what we know, and society online. In P. N. Howard & S. Jones (Eds.), *Society online: The Internet in context* (pp. 1–28). Thousand Oaks, CA: Sage.

Islam, A. (2008). *Television and the Internet: Enabling global communities and its international implications on society and technology.* Master's thesis, Communication and Leadership Studies, School of Professional Studies, Gonzaga University, Spokane, WA.

Ito, M. (1997). Virtually embodied: The reality of fantasy in a multi-user dungeon. In D. Porter (Ed.), *Internet culture* (pp. 87–110). New York: Routledge.

James, N. (2007). The use of email interviewing as a qualitative method of inquiry in educational research. *British Educational Research Journal, 33*(6), 963–976.

James, N., & Busher, H. (2006). Credibility, authenticity and voice: Dilemmas in online interviewing. *Qualitative Research, 6*(3), 403–420.

James, N., & Busher, H. (2007). Ethical issues in online educational research: protecting privacy, establishing authenticity in email interviewing. *International Journal of Research & Method in Education, 30*(1), 101–113.

Johns, M. D., Hall, G. J., & Crowell, T. L. (2004). Surviving the IRB review: Institutional guidelines and research strategies. In M. D. Johns, S. S. Chen, & G. J. Hall (Eds.), *Online social research: Methods, issues, ethics* (pp. 105–124). New York: Peter Lang.

Jones, S. (2004). Contexting the network. In P. N. Howard & S. Jones (Eds.), *Society online: The Internet in context* (pp. 325–334). Thousand Oaks, CA: Sage.

Kanter, R .M. (1977). *Men and women of the corporation.* New York: Basic Books.

Katz, J. (2007). Toward a natural history of ethical censorship. *Law & Society Review, 41*(4), 797–810.

Kem, J. F. (2005). *Cataloging the Whedonverse: Potential roles for librarians in online fan fiction.* Master's thesis, School of Information and Library Science of the University of North Carolina at Chapel Hill.

Kendall, L. (1999). Recontextualizing "cyberspace": Methodological considerations for online research. In S. G. Jones (Ed.), *Doing Internet research: Critical issues and methods for examining the Net* (pp. 57–74). Thousand Oaks, CA: Sage.

Kendall, L. (2002). *Hanging out in the virtual pub: Masculinities and relationships online.* Berkeley: University of California Press.

Kendall, L. (2004). Participants and observers in online ethnography: Five stories about identity. In M. D. Johns, S. S. Chen, & G. J. Hall (Eds.), *Online social research: Methods, issues, ethics* (pp. 125–140). New York: Peter Lang.

Kirby-Diaz, M. (Ed.) (2009). *Buffy and Angel conquer the Internet: Essays on online fandom.* Jefferson, NC: McFarland.

Knapp, J. A. (1997). Essayistic messages: Internet newsgroups as electronic public sphere. In D. Porter (Ed.), *Internet culture* (pp. 181–200). New York: Routledge.

Kociemba, D. (2006). "Over-identify much?": Passion, "passion," and the author-audience feedback loop in *Buffy the Vampire Slayer. Slayage: The Online Journal of Buffy Studies, 19.* Available at http://slayageonline.com/essays/slayage19/Kociemba.htm

Kolko, B. E., Nakamura, L., & Rodman, G. G. (2000). *Race in cyberspace.* New York: Routledge.

Komaki, R. (2009, April 30–May 2). *A Japanese social network site mixi and the imagined boundary of "Japan."* Paper presented at the Texas A&M University Race & Ethnic Studies Institute Symposium: Race, Ethnicity, and (New) Media, Texas A&M University, College Station, TX.

Kurzman, C. (1991). Convincing sociologists: Values and interests in the sociology of knowledge. In M. Burawoy (Ed.), *Ethnography unbound: Power and resistance in the modern metropolis* (pp. 250–270). Berkeley: University of California Press.

Larbelestier, J. (2002). *Buffy's* Mary Sue is Jonathan: *Buffy* acknowledges the fans. In R. Wilcox & D. Lavery (Eds.), *Fighting the forces: What's at stake in* Buffy the Vampire Slayer (pp. 227–238). Lanham, MD: Rowman & Littlefield.

LeBosco, K. (2004). Managing visibility, intimacy, and focus in online critical ethnography. In M. D. Johns, S. S. Chen, & G. J. Hall (Eds.), *Online social research: Methods, issues, ethics* (pp. 63–80). New York: Peter Lang.

Leurs, K. (2009, April 30–May 2). *Be(com)ing cyber Mocro's: Digital media, migration and glocalized youth cultures.* Paper presented at the Texas A&M University Race & Ethnic Studies Institute Symposium: Race, Ethnicity, and (New) Media, Texas A&M University, College Station, TX.

Lotz, A. D., & Ross, S. M. (2004). Toward ethical cyberspace audience research: Strategies for using the Internet for television audience studies. *Journal of Broadcasting & Electronic Media Studies, 48*(3), 501–512.

Lu, J. (2009). *Software copyright and piracy in China.* Dissertation, Texas A&M University, College Station.

Lynd, R. S., & Lynd, H. M. (1956). *Middletown: A study in American culture.* New York: Harcourt, Brace. (Original work published in 1927)

MacKinnon, R.C. (2002). Punish the persona: Correctional strategies for the virtual offender. In S. G. Jones (Ed.), *Virtual culture: Identity and communication in cyber-society* (pp. 206–235). Thousand Oaks, CA: Sage. (Original work published 1997)

Mallapragada, M. (2009, April 30–May 2). *Desi webs: South Asian America, online cultures and the politics of race.* Paper presented at the Texas A&M University Race & Ethnic Studies Institute Symposium: Race, Ethnicity, and (New) Media, Texas A&M University, College Station, TX.

Mann, C., & Stewart, F. (2004). Introducing online methods. In S. N. Hesse-Biber & P. Leavy (Eds.), *Approaches to qualitative research: A reader on theory and practice* (pp. 367–401). New York: Oxford University Press.

Marcus, G. (1998). *Ethnography through thick and thin.* Princeton, NJ: Princeton University Press.

Markham, A. (1998). *Life online: Researching real experience in virtual space* (*Ethnographic Alternatives,* No. 6). Walnut Creek, CA: AltaMira Press.

Markham, A. (2004). Representation in online ethnographies: A matter of context sensitivity. In M. D. Johns, S. S. Chen, & G. J. Hall (Eds.), *Online social research: Methods, issues, ethics* (pp. 141–156). New York: Peter Lang.

Markham, A. (2005a). The methods, politics, and ethics of representation in online ethnography. In N. K. Denzin & Y. S. Lincoln (Eds.), *The SAGE handbook of qualitative methods* (3rd ed., pp. 793–820). Thousand Oaks, CA: Sage.

Markham, A. (2005b). "Go ugly early": Fragmented narrative and bricolage as interpretive method. *Qualitative Inquiry, 11*(6), 813–839.

Markham, A. N., & Baym, N. K. (2009). *Internet inquiry: Conversations about method.* Thousand Oaks, CA: Sage.

May, R. B. A. (2003). "Flirting with boundaries": A professor's narrative tale contemplating research of the wild side. *Qualitative Inquiry, 9*(3), 442–465.

May, R. B. A., & Patillo, M. (2000). Do you see what I see? Examining a collaborative ethnography. *Qualitative Inquiry, 6*(1), 65–87.

McPherson, T. (2000). I'll take my stand in Dixie-Net: White guys, the South, and cyberspace. In B. E. Kolko, L. Nakamura, & G. B. Rodman (Eds.), *Race in cyberspace* (pp. 117–132). New York: Routledge.

Millard, W. B. (1997). I flamed Freud: A case study in teletextual incendiarism. In D. Porter (Ed.), *Internet culture* (pp. 145–160). New York: Routledge.

Millet, K. (1973). *The prostitution papers.* New York: Avon.

Mitchell, W. J. (1999). *E-Topia: "Urban Life Jim, But Not as We Know It."* Cambridge: MIT Press.

Mizrach, S. (1996). Cyberanthropology. Retrieved August 18, 1999, from http://www.lastplace.com/page205.htm

Murguía, E., Tackett-Gibson, M., & Lessem, A. (Eds.). (2007). *Real drugs in a virtual world: Drug discourse and community online.* Lanham, MD: Lexington Books.

Nakamura, L. (2002). *Cyber types: Race, ethnicity, and identity on the Internet.* New York: Routledge.

Nakamura, L. (2009). Don't hate the player, hate the game: The racialization of labor in world of warcraft. *Critical Studies in Media Communication, 26*(2), 128–144.

Nieckarz, P. P., Jr. (2005). Community in cyber space?: The role of the Internet in facilitating and maintaining a community of live music collecting and trading. *City & Community, 4*(4), 403–424.

Nordt, M., Meisner, J., Dongaonkar, R., Quick, C. M., Gatson, S. N., Karadkar, U. P., & Furuta, R. (2007). eBat: A technology-enriched life sciences research community. *Proceedings of the American Society for Information Science & Technology, 43,* 1–25. Available at http://www3.interscience.wiley.com/journal/116327865/issue

Norris, P. (2004). The bridging and bonding role of online communities. In P. N. Howard & S. Jones (Eds.), *Society online: The Internet in context* (pp. 31–42). Thousand Oaks, CA: Sage.

O'Brien, J. (1997). Changing the subject. *Women and Performance: A Journal of Feminist Theory, 17.* Available at http://www.echonyc.com/~women/Issue17/

O'Brien, J. (1999). Writing in the body: Gender (re)production in online interaction. In M. A. Smith & P. Kollock (Eds.), *Communities in cyberspace* (pp. 76–104). New York: Routledge.

Ow, J. A. (2000). The revenge of the yellowfaced cyborg: The rape of digital geishas and the colonization of cyber-coolies in 3D realms' *Shadow warrior.* In B. E. Kolko, L. Nakamura, & G. B. Rodman, (Eds.), *Race in cyberspace* (pp. 51–68). New York: Routledge.

Parpart, L. (2003). "Action, chicks, everything": Online interviews with male fans of *Buffy the Vampire Slayer.* In F. Early & K. Kennedy (Eds.), *Athena's daughters: Television's new women warriors* (pp. 78–91). Syracuse, NY: Syracuse University Press.

Parrish, J. J. (2007). *Inventing a universe: Reading and writing Internet fan fiction.* PhD dissertation, University of Pittsburgh, Pittsburgh, PA.

Peterson, L. (2009a, April 30–May 2.). *Ewww—You got your social justice in my video game!* Paper presented at the Texas A&M University Race & Ethnic Studies Institute Symposium: Race, Ethnicity, and (New) Media, Texas A&M University, College Station, Texas.

Peterson, L. (2009b, April 30–May 2). *Talking about race in digital space.* Paper presented at the Texas A&M University Race & Ethnic Studies Institute Symposium: Race, Ethnicity, and (New) Media, Texas A&M University, College Station, Texas.

Porter, D. (1997). *Internet culture.* New York: Routledge.

Reid, R.A. (2009, April 30–May 2). *Harshin ur squeez: Visual rhetorics of anti-racist work in livejournal fandoms.* Paper presented at the Texas A&M University Race & Ethnic Studies Institute Symposium: Race, Ethnicity, and (New) Media, Texas A&M University, College Station, TX.

Rheingold, H. (2000). *The virtual community: Homesteading on the electronic frontier.* Reading, MA: Addison-Wesley. (Original work published 1993)

Richards, L. (2003). Fandom and ethnography. Available at http://www.searingidolatry.co.uk/lond/index2.html

Salaff, J. W. (2002). Where home is the office: The new form of flexible work. In B. Wellman & C. Haythornthwaite (Eds.), *The Internet in everyday life* (pp. 464–495). Malden, MA: Blackwell.

Seabrook, J. (1997). *Deeper: Adventures on the Net.* New York: Touchstone (Simon & Schuster).

Schmitz, J. (2002). Structural relations, electronic media, and social change: The public electronic network and the homeless. In S. Jones (Ed.), *Virtual culture: Identity & communication in cybersociety* (pp. 80–101). Thousand Oaks, CA: Sage. (Original work published 1997)

Sharf, B. (1997). Communicating breast cancer online: Support and empowerment on the Internet. *Women and Health, 26,* 65–84.

Sharf, B. (1999). Beyond netiquette: The ethics of doing naturalistic discourse research on the Internet. In S. G. Jones (Ed.), *Doing Internet research: Critical issues and methods for examining the Net* (pp. 57–74). Thousand Oaks, CA: Sage.

Shaw, D. F. (2002). Gay men and computer communication: A discourse of sex and identity in cyberspace. In S. G. Jones (Ed.), *Virtual culture: Identity and communication in cybersociety* (pp. 133–145). Thousand Oaks, CA: Sage. (Original work published 1997)

Shirky, C. (2002). Communities, audiences, and scale. Available at http://shirky.com/writings/community_scale.html

Shostak, M. (1981). *Nisa: The life and words of !Kung woman.* Cambridge, MA: Harvard University Press.

Silver, D. (2000). Margins in the wires: Looking for race, gender, and sexuality in the Blacksburg Electronic Village. In B. E. Kolko, L. Nakamura, & G. B. Rodman (Eds.) *Race in cyberspace* (pp. 133–150). New York: Routledge.

Smith, D. (1990). *Texts, facts, and femininity: Exploring the relations of ruling.* New York: Routledge.

Smith, K. M. C. (2004). "Electronic eavesdropping": The ethical issues involved in conducting a virtual ethnography. In M. D. Johns, S. S. Chen, & G. J. Hall (Eds.), *Online social research: Methods, issues, ethics* (pp. 223–238). New York: Peter Lang.

Stafford, N. (2002). *Bite me! An unofficial guide to the world of Buffy the vampire slayer.* Toronto, ON: ECW Press. (Original work published in 1998)

Stark, L. (2007). Victims in our own minds?: IRBs in myth and practice. *Law & Society Review, 41*(4), 777–786.

Stenger, J. (2006). The clothes make the fan: Fashion and online fandom when *Buffy the Vampire Slayer* goes to eBay. *Cinema Journal, 45*(4), 26–44.

Stern, M. J., & Dillman, D. A. (2006). Community participation, social ties, and use of the Internet. *City & Community, 5*(4), 409–424.

Stivale, C. J. (1997). Spam: Heteroglossia and harassment in cyberspace. In D. Porter (Ed.), *Internet culture* (pp. 133–144). New York: Routledge.

Tepper, M. (1997). Usenet communities and the cultural politics of information. In D. Porter (Ed.), *Internet culture* (pp. 39–54). New York: Routledge.

Thomas, J. (2004). Reexamining the ethics of Internet research: Facing the challenge of overzealous oversight. M. D. Johns, S. S. Chen, & G. J. Hall (Eds.), *Online social research: Methods, issues, ethics* (pp. 187–202). New York: Peter Lang.

Travers, A. (2000). *Writing the public in cyberspace: Redefining inclusion on the net.* Garland studies in American popular history and culture. New York: Garland Press.

Travers, M. (2009). New methods, old problems: A sceptical view of innovation in qualitative research. *Qualitative Research, 9*(2), 161–179.

Tulloch, J., & Jenkins, H. (1995). *Science fiction audiences: Watching* Doctor Who *and* Star Trek. New York: Routledge.

Turkle, S. (1995). *Life on the screen: Identity in the age of the Internet.* New York: Simon & Schuster.

Tuszynski, S. (2006). *IRL (in real life): Breaking down the binary of online versus offline social interaction.* PhD dissertation, Bowling Green State University, Bowling Green, OH.

Van Maanen, J. (2004). An end to innocence: The ethnography of ethnography. In S. N. Hesse-Biber & P. Leavy (Eds.), *Approaches to qualitative research: A reader on theory and practice* (pp. 427–446). New York: Oxford University Press.

Walstrom, M. K. (2004). "Seeing and sensing" online interaction: An interpretive interactionist approach to USENET support group research. In M. D. Johns, S. S. Chen, & G. J. Hall (Eds.), *Online social research: Methods, issues, ethics* (pp. 81–100). New York: Peter Lang.

Watson, N. (2003). Why we argue about virtual community: A case study of the Phish. Net fan community. In S. G. Jones (Ed.), *Virtual culture: Identity and communication in cybersociety* (pp. 102–132). Thousand Oaks, CA: Sage. (Original work published in 1997)

Whiteman, N. (2009). The de/stabilization of identity in online fan communities. *Convergence: The International Journal of Research into New Media Technologies, 15*(4), 391–410.

Williams, R. (2004). "It's about power": Executive fans, spoiler whores and capital in the *Buffy the Vampire Slayer* online fan community. *Slayage: The Online Journal of Buffy Studies,* 11–12.

Zickmund, S. (2002). Approaching the radical other: The discursive culture of cyberhate. In S. Jones *Virtual culture: Identity and communication in cybersociety* (pp. 185–205). Thousand Oaks, CA: Sage. (Original work published 1997)

Zweerink, A., & S. N. Gatson (2002). www.buffy.com: Cliques, boundaries, and hierarchies in an Internet community. In R. Wilcox & D. Lavery (Eds.), *Fighting the forces: What's at stake in Buffy the Vampire Slayer* (pp. 239–249). Lanham, MD: Rowman & Littlefield, pp. 239–249.

9

Analyzing Talk and Text

Anssi Peräkylä and Johanna Ruusuvuori

There are two much used but distinctively different types of empirical materials in qualitative research: interviews and "naturally occurring" materials. Interviews consist of accounts given to the researcher about the issues in which he or she is interested. The topic of the research is not the interview itself but rather the issues discussed in the interview. In this sense, research that uses "naturally occurring" empirical material is different; in this type of research, the empirical materials themselves (e.g., the tape recordings of mundane interactions, the written texts) constitute specimens of the topic of the research. Consequently, the researcher is in more direct touch with the very object that he or she is investigating.

Most qualitative research probably is based on interviews. There are good reasons for this. By using interviews, the researcher can reach areas of reality that would otherwise remain inaccessible such as people's subjective experiences and attitudes. The interview is also a very convenient way of overcoming distances both in space and in time; past events or faraway experiences can be studied by interviewing people who took part in them.

In other instances, it is possible to reach the object of research directly using naturally occurring empirical materials (Silverman, 2001). If the researcher is interested in, say, strategies used by journalists in interviewing politicians (e.g., Clayman & Heritage, 2002a), it might be advisable to tape-record broadcast interviews rather than to ask journalists to tell about their work. Or, if the researcher wants to study the historical evolvement of medical conceptions regarding death and dying, it might be advisable to study medical textbooks rather than to ask doctors to tell what they know about these concepts.

The contrast between interviews and naturally occurring materials should not, however, be exaggerated (see also Potter, 2004; Speer, 2002). There are types of research materials that are between these two pure types. For example, in *informal interviews that are part of ethnographic fieldwork,* and in *focus groups,* people describe their practices and ideas to the researcher in circumstances that are much closer to "naturally occurring" than are the circumstances in ordinary research interviews. Moreover, even "ordinary" interviews can be, and have been, analyzed as specimens of interaction and reasoning practices rather than as representations of facts or ideas outside the interview situation. As Susan Speer (2002) recently put it, "The status of pieces of data as natural or not depends largely on what the researcher intends to 'do' with them" (p. 513). Margaret Wetherell and Jonathan Potter (1992), for example, analyzed the ways in which interviewees use different linguistic and cultural resources in constructing their relation to racial and racist discourses. On the other hand, as David Silverman (2001) put it, no data—not even tape recordings—are "untouched by the researcher's hands" (p. 159; see also Speer, 2002, p. 516); the researcher's activity is needed, for example, in obtaining informed consent from the participants. The difference between researcher-instigated data and naturally occurring data should, therefore, be understood as a continuum rather than as a dichotomy.

This chapter focuses on one end of this continuum. It presents some methods that can be used in analyzing and interpreting tape-recorded interactions and written texts, which probably are the types of data that come closest to the idea of "naturally occurring."

Analyzing Texts

USES OF TEXTS AND VARIETY OF METHODS OF TEXT ANALYSIS

As Dorothy Smith (1974, 1990) and Paul Atkinson and Amanda Coffey (1997) have pointed out, much of social life in modern society is mediated by written texts of different kinds. For example, modern health care would not be possible without patient records; the legal system would not be possible without laws and other juridical texts; professional training would not be possible without manuals and professional journals; and leisure would not be possible without newspapers, magazines, and advertisements. Texts of this kind have provided an abundance of material for qualitative researchers.

In many cases, qualitative researchers who use written texts as their materials do not try to follow any predefined protocol in executing their analysis. By reading and rereading their empirical materials, they try to pin down their key themes and, thereby, to draw a picture of the presuppositions and meanings that constitute the cultural world of which the textual material is a specimen. An example of this kind of informal approach is Clive Seale's (1998) small but elegant case study on a booklet based on a broadcast interview with the British playwright Dennis Potter (pp. 127–131). The interviewee was terminally ill at the time of the interview. Seale showed how the interview conveys a particular conception of death and dying, characterized by intensive awareness of the imminent death and special creativity arising from it.

An informal approach may, in many cases, be the best choice as a method in research focusing on written texts. Especially in research designs where the qualitative text analysis is not at the core of the research but instead is in a subsidiary or complementary role, no more sophisticated text analytical methods may be needed. That indeed was the case in Seale's (1998) study, in which the qualitative text analysis complemented a larger study drawing mostly on interview and questionnaire materials as well as on theoretical work. In projects that use solely texts as empirical materials, however, the use of different kinds of analytical procedures may be considered.

The researchers can choose from many methods of text analysis. The degree to which they involve predefined sets of procedures varies; some of them do to a great extent, whereas in others the emphasis is more on theoretical presuppositions concerning the cultural and social worlds to which the texts belong. Moreover, some of these methods can be used in the research of both written and spoken discourse, whereas others are exclusively fitted to written texts. In what follows, we briefly mention a few text analytical methods and then discuss two a bit more thoroughly.

Semiotics is a broad field of study concerned with signs and their use. Many tools of text analysis have arisen from this field. The most prominent of them may be *semiotic narrative analysis.* The Russian ethnologist Vladimir Propp (1968) and the French sociologist Algirdas Julien Greimas (1966) developed schemes for the analysis of narrative structures. Initially their schemes were developed in fairy tales, but later they were applied to many other kinds of texts. For example, by using Greimas's scheme, primordial structural relations (e.g., subject vs. object, sender vs. receiver, helper vs. opponent) can be distilled from the texts. Jukka Törrönen (2000, 2003) used and developed further Greimasian concepts in analyzing newspaper editorials addressing alcohol policy, showing how these texts mobilize structural relations to encourage readers to take action to achieve particular political goals.

Another, more recent, trend in narrative analysis focuses on *narratives as practice within social interaction* rather than as text with an identifiable structure. In anticipation of the second half of this chapter (focusing on research on interaction), we will briefly introduce this new approach on narrative here. This new turn in narrative analysis lays emphasis on the multiple, fragmented, and situated nature of narrative (Hyvärinen et al., 2010). It investigates stories and storytelling as they operate within society. In this trend, context is not seen as a static setting but as multiple intersecting processes that are a resource for talk-in-interaction (De Fina & Georgakopoulou, 2008). Traditionally within the narrative field of study, the narratives that are investigated have been derived from interview data (Bamberg & Georgakopoulou, 2008). The focus has been on the *internal organization* of narratives—on the ways in which particular types of narrative organization are connected with factors such as gender, for example. Within the new trend, the focus has been turned more on the *external organization* of narratives, on the production of narratives in their immediate surroundings (Gubrium & Holstein, 2009, pp. vii–ix, 1–2). Narratives are analyzed as talk-in-interaction in varying contexts; on one hand, the focus is on the ways in which stories are told and shaped by other people and the surrounding context of the situation, and on the other hand, the focus is on the ways in which this context is shaped by the narrative tellings (De Fina & Georgakopoulou, 2008; Ochs & Capps, 2001, p. 2). To give an example, Michael Bamberg and Alexandra Georgakopoulou (2008) have analyzed the storytelling activities of 10-year-old boys in a group discussion as tools of identity work. Bamberg and Georgakopoulou's starting point is that narratives can be used as means to construct characters in space and further, positions relative to other participants of the situation (see also Sacks, 1974b). Thus, specific linguistic choices can be linked with larger social identities (Georgakopoulou, 2007, p. 13). Bamberg and Georgakopoulou (2008) show how 10-year-old boys juggle between two contrasting story lines (of being interested in girls and not being interested) in a focus group situation with an interviewer and three other boys. Their focus is on the discursive maneuvering of the boys between two master narratives that are dominant in the boys' peer group and on the development of their sense of self through this navigation process. The researchers point out that small stories that are told within changing situations can gradually amount to more constant ways of organizing life experience and result in life stories that form a sense of who we are.

The term *discourse analysis* (DA) may refer, depending on context, to many different approaches of investigation of written texts (and of spoken discourse as well). In the context of linguistics, DA usually refers to research that aims at uncovering the features of text that maintain coherence in units larger than the sentence (Brown & Yule, 1983). In social psychology, DA (or *discursive psychology*, as it has been called more recently) involves research in which the language use (both written and spoken) underpinning mental realities, such as cognition and emotion, is investigated. Here, the key theoretical presupposition is that mental realities do not reside "inside" individual humans but rather are constructed linguistically (Edwards, 1997; Potter, 2006; Potter & te Molder, 2005). *Critical discourse analysis* (CDA), developed by Norman Fairclough (1989, 1995) among others, constitutes yet another kind of discourse analytical approach in which some key concerns of linguistic and critical social research merge. Critical discourse analysts are interested in the ways in which texts of different kinds reproduce power and inequalities in society (see Wodak & Meyer, 2009). Liisa Tainio's (1999) study on the language of self-help communication guidebooks for married couples is one example of a CDA study. Tainio showed, for example, how in these texts the woman is expected to change for the communication problems to be solved, whereas the man is treated as immutable.

A *Foucauldian approach* to the analysis of texts, or *historical discourse analysis* (HDA) as it is sometimes called, focuses on tracing the interrelatedness of knowledge and power in studying historical processes through which certain human practices and ways of thinking have emerged. The term *analytics of government* (Dean, 1999; Meskus, 2009a; Rose, 1999) refers to a method of analysis where this type of research approach is in use. In the following, we will introduce an example of this approach.

ANALYZING THE GOVERNMENT OF HUMAN HEREDITY: A RESEARCH EXAMPLE

Many scholars working with written texts have drawn insights and inspiration from the work of Michel Foucault. (For examples of his own studies, see Foucault, 1973, 1977, 1978. For examples of accessible accounts of his theories and methods, see Dean, 1999; Kendall & Wickham, 1999; McHoul & Grace, 1993; Rose, 1999.) Foucault did not propose a definite set of methods for the analysis of texts; hence, the ways of analyzing and interpreting texts of scholars inspired by him vary. For all of them, however, a primary concern is, as Potter (2004) aptly put it, how a set of "statements" comes to constitute objects and subjects. The constitution of subjects and objects is explored in historical context—or, in Foucault's terms, through *archeology* and *genealogy.*

A recent example of this kind of historical approach is offered by Mianna Meskus' (2009b) research on the ways in which the rationale and technologies concerning heredity have evolved in Finnish medicine and health care. Meskus focuses on the development starting in the early 20th century during which concepts such as *eugenics* and *racial hygiene* were gradually replaced by the idea of

risk, and how the technologies for governing the sphere of heredity and reproduction changed respectively.

Meskus (2009b) investigates texts from the spheres of professional, political,
and lay discourses (medical articles, policy documents, committee reports,
guidebooks, and health magazines) tracing the interconnectedness of the
advancements in genetics, the changes in national population policy and the
practices of its implementation in health care. Her specific focus is on the technology of prenatal screening and the doctor-driven development during which
it was gradually extended to encompass all pregnant women.

Meskus distinguishes three phases or periods in the government of human
heredity. The first reaches from the beginning of the 20th century to the 1960s.
During that period, it was thought that people with mental illness or cognitive
impairment should be sterilized to enhance the "quality of population." In the
second phase, in the 1970s and 1980s, the focus of policy turned from the quality
of population to health. During this period, the state strongly invested in preventive health care, launching a nationwide system for health counseling. At the
same time, the chromosomal diagnosis of congenital and hereditary diseases was
implemented into clinical practices. At this stage, the concept of risk was attached
to pregnancy, and technologies (such as amniocentesis) were developed and
implemented to diagnose potential anomalies of the fetus in specific risk groups,
such as mothers older than 40. If anomalies were found and future parents
would so decide, abortion could be induced. In the third phase, starting in the
1990s, the development of genetics made available new tests that were relatively
easy to implement clinically. Meskus shows how, in this latter phase, prenatal
screening was adopted as a routine procedure for all pregnant mothers in
Finland, but in Sweden, for example, fetal diagnostics were only targeted at specific risk groups. The rationale was presented as providing a possibility of *choice
for parents* to control the health of their future baby. A central difference to the
practice in Sweden was that whereas in Finland all pregnant mothers were routinely offered the test, and therefore had to say yes or no, such a routine offer was
not made in Sweden, where the mothers were given information about hereditary diseases and could ask for the test on their own initiative, if they so decided.

Meskus points out how the development has advocated individual choice and
at the same time covered the social and economical contexts within which prenatal screening has emerged as a routine practice. Through all the three periods,
the procedures for managing the "quality" or health of the population with
regard to pregnancy or childbirth were connected with the health policy interests
in saving expenses of social and health care. However, the rationale of the doctors and geneticists who have advocated screening for all pregnant mothers has

centered around future parents' increasing possibilities to know about the health of their future children and to choose whether they are willing to manage with a disabled child.

Meskus concludes by referring to new ethical problems that have arisen with this "freedom to choose." As the awareness of health risks among the public has increased and their possibilities to choose have been promoted, parents' expectations concerning the health and normality of their future children have also increased, and in some cases beyond the limits offered by medicine. In practice, however, the freedom to choose brings parents against a very difficult choice between abortion and taking the risk that their baby may be disabled. This freedom entails a heavy burden of responsibility for pregnant mothers and their partners in case anomalies are found. Thus, Meskus shows how adoption of a medical technology, such as prenatal screening, that is seemingly based on neutral medical knowledge is actually a result of various historical, social, and political underpinnings and may further result in unexpected ethical dilemmas.

Meskus' method is Foucauldian in the sense that she examines historical (textual) entities and ways of thinking through concepts that are typical for the period and for the texts under investigation (Meskus, 2009b, p. 232). Drawing on ethnographic ideas, she describes her research object in various, changing contexts: in different types of texts during different periods of time, to make a synthesis. Her versatile data include medical articles, administrative documents, memos, and guidebooks, with focus on issues that are presented as problematic, and on interests and debates around these concerns. Having arranged the data thematically, Meskus examines particular dimensions present in the expert texts: How are *the entities of interest* (scientific facts about heredity) defined and described, what are the *standpoints and styles of reasoning and argumentation* (how heredity is made problematic and what solutions are presented to the problems), and how are *the target groups* (particular sections of the population) defined. This analysis is then drawn together from the historical point of view by tracing the *continuities and turning points in the historical approach to the focus of interest* (heredity). The overarching idea is the intertwining of texts and practices. Meskus' study efficiently shows how the medical "facts" on heredity are produced in particular kinds of societal climate where particular policy ideas, values, and needs are present. These, then, are reflected on the practices of the government of heredity during each period.

Meskus' historical and Foucauldian way of analyzing and interpreting texts offers one compact alternative for qualitative text analysis. We now turn to a quite different way of reading texts in qualitative research, that is, *membership categorization analysis* (MCA).

MEMBERSHIP CATEGORIZATION ANALYSIS

Whereas Meskus' historical analysis was concerned with how issues are defined as problems in the texts and how the styles of reasoning are reformed or stabilized in time and across different types of data, MCA is concerned about *the descriptive apparatus* that makes it possible to say whatever is said.

Before we start to examine MCA, we want to remind the reader about the wide range of applications that this approach has. In addition to the analysis of written texts, it can be used in the analysis of interviews (e.g., Nikander, 2002; Roca-Cuerbes, 2008) and in the analysis of naturally occurring talk (e.g., Butler & Weatherall, 2006; Stokoe, 2003). In the following, however, we focus on the text analytical applications.

The idea of membership categorization came from the American sociologist Harvey Sacks (1974b, 1992). *Description* was a key analytical question for Sacks; he was concerned about the conditions of description, that is, what makes it possible for us to produce and understand descriptions of people and their activities. As Silverman (2001) aptly put it, Sacks was concerned about "the apparatus through which members' descriptions are properly produced" (p. 139). This interest led Sacks to examine categorization.

People are usually referred to by using categories. The point of departure for MCA is recognition that at any event, a person may be referred to by using many alternative categories. As the authors of this chapter, we may also be referred to as academics, Finns, parents, sociologists, Europeans, University of Tampere alumni, and so forth. MCA is about the selection of categories such as these and about the conditions and consequences of this selection.

Sacks's (1974b) famous example is the beginning of a story written by a child: *The baby cried. The mommy picked it up.* There are two key categories in this story: "baby" and "mommy." Why are these categories used, and what is achieved by them? If the mommy happened to be a biologist by profession, why would the story not go like this: *The baby cried. The scientist picked it up* (Jayyusi, 1991, p. 238)? Why do we hear the story being about a baby and *its* mother and not just about any baby and any mother? MCA provides answers to questions such as these and offers a toolkit for analyzing various kinds of texts.

Sacks (1992) noted that categories form sets, that is, collections of categories that go together. Family is one such collection, and "baby," "mother," and "father" are some categories of it. "Stage of life" is another collection; it consists of categories such as "baby," "toddler," "child," and "adult." Now, "baby" could in principle be heard as belonging to both collections, but in the preceding little story we hear it as belonging to the "family" collection. This is because in hearing (or reading) descriptions where two or more categories are used, we orient to a rule according to which we hear them as being from the same collection if they indeed can be heard in that way. Therefore, in this case we hear "baby" and "mommy" being from the device "family" (p. 247).

Categories also go together with *activities.* Sacks used the term *category-bound activities* in referring to activities that members of a culture take to be "typical" of a category (or some categories) of people. "Crying" is a category-bound activity of a baby, just as "picking a (crying) baby up" is a category-bound activity of a mother. In a similar fashion, "lecturing" is a category-bound activity of a professor. Activities such as these can be normative; it is appropriate for the baby to cry and for the mother to pick it up, but it is not appropriate for an adult to cry (like a baby) or for a mother to fail to pick her crying baby up. *Standardized relational pairs* consist of two categories where incumbents of the categories have standardized rights and obligations in relation to each other, with "mother and baby" clearly being one pair, just as "husband and wife" and "doctor and patient" are common pairs. Moreover, the receivers of descriptions can and do infer from actions to categories and vice versa. By knowing actions, we infer the categories of the agents; by knowing categories of agents, we infer what they do.

Even on the basis of these fragments of Sacks's ideas (for more thorough accounts, see Lepper, 2000; Schegloff, 2007b; Silverman, 1998), the reader may get an impression of the potential that this account offers for the analysis of texts. Sacks's ideas are resources for the analysis of texts as sites for the production and reproduction of social, moral, and political orders. Merely by bearing in mind that there is always more than one category available for the description of a given person, the analyst always asks "Why this categorization now?"

Let us examine a brief example of MCA. Marc Rapley, David McCarthy, and Alec McHoul (2003) report a social psychological analysis on the news coverage of a mass killing in Tasmania in 1996 (on MCA of an equivalent case, see Eglin & Hester, 2003). Rapley et al. focus on the public categorizations of the gunman both by lay people and professionals and pay attention to the tension that is created in between the candidate category memberships that are assigned to the gunman, in both lay and professional accounts of the incident.

The authors make use of Sacks' idea of methods of categorization, where particular ties are inferred between categories of person and their category-bound activities—including the moral accountability of these activities. The authors observe how in lay accounts of the event the gunman is presented as *a psycho* or as *schizophrenic,* but also as *a young man dogged by tragedy.* When assigned to the category of *mentally ill,* the man is supposed to lose his sense of reality and is thus regarded as capable of doing unexpected and abnormal things—he is not accountable for his actions. Conversely, as a member of society, *a young man,* the man's deviant actions can be judged as wrong and immoral. Thus, on the one hand, his actions are explained in terms of otherness, as the workings of a madman who is not responsible of his doings, but on the other hand, he is described as a member of a shared social order, and in this way, as morally accountable for his actions.

Interestingly, the authors find that professional explanations for the incident are no less incongruent. Some experts describe the killer as having little intellectual capability and not insane, whereas others refer to him as possibly schizophrenic. This way, a similar tension between the moral accountability and non-accountability of the gunman's actions is created as in lay explanations of the incident. The psychiatrists and psychologists who examined the gunman finally agreed that he suffered from a personality disorder and was in the borderline range between intellectual disability and a "dull normal individual," but did NOT suffer from a serious mental illness that would have prevented him from knowing the difference between right and wrong. Thus, the expert explanation offered made use of lay categories situating the gunman in between mad and not mad, abnormal and normal, "not-us" and "us," which then allowed the gunman to be held morally (and legally) accountable for his actions.

Following Sacks, Rapley et al. point out how the way in which we categorize people does the work of explanation, and how this categorization work is inherently moral, even when it is done by professional experts. According to Rapley et al.'s analysis, the categorizations used in the media were organized to produce an account of the gunman that retained his status as a moral and accountable actor. In the case presented, the psychiatric (expert) categories were also harnessed to accomplish this possibility. In terms of membership categorization, the categorizations of the actor were tied to moral types to accomplish practical moral judgments. The actual scientific grounds for choosing the particular categories were left aside. Rapley et al. conclude that categories (also psychiatric ones) should be regarded as resources that people use to accomplish things, in this case, a moral verdict, rather than treating them as neutral scientific facts: categorization as a method of describing events and thus for producing moral accounts precedes and grounds other "technical," "clinical," or "scientific" judgments.

Because all description draws on categorization, MCA has wide applicability in the analysis of texts. The analysis of categorization gives the researcher access to the cultural worlds and moral orders on which the texts hinge. Importantly, however, categorization analysis is not *only* about specific cultures or moralities. In developing his concepts, Sacks was not primarily concerned about the "contents" of the categorizations; rather, he was concerned about the ways in which we use them (Atkinson, 1978, p. 194). Therefore, at the end of the day, membership categorization analysis invites the qualitative researcher to explore the conditions of action of description in itself.

Analyzing Talk

Face-to-face social interaction (or other live interaction mediated by phones and other technological media) is the most immediate and the most frequently experienced social reality. The heart of our social and personal being lies in the immediate contact with other humans. Even though ethnographic observation of face-to-face social interaction has been done successfully by sociologists and social psychologists, video and audio recordings are what provide the richest possible data for the study of talk and interaction today. Such recordings have been analyzed using the same methods that were discussed previously in the context of interpretation of written texts. CDA, MCA, and even Foucauldian DA have all their applications in researching transcripts based on video or audio recordings. However, as Erving Goffman (1983) pointed out, to be fully appreciated, the face-to-face social interaction also requires its own specific methods. The interplay of utterances and actions in live social interaction involves a complex organization that cannot be found in written texts. *Conversation analysis* (CA) is presented as a method specialized for analyzing that organization.

ORIGINS OF CONVERSATION ANALYSIS

CA is a method for investigating the structure and process of social interaction between humans. As their empirical materials, CA studies use video or audio recordings made from naturally occurring interactions. As their results, these studies offer qualitative (and sometimes quantitative) descriptions of interactional structures (e.g., turn taking, relations between adjacent utterances) and practices (e.g., telling and receiving news, making assessments).

CA was started by Sacks and his coworkers, especially Emanuel Schegloff and Gail Jefferson (1977), at the University of California during the 1960s. At the time of its birth, CA was something quite different from the rest of social science. The predominant way of investigating human social interaction was quantitative, based on coding and counting distinct, theoretically defined actions (see especially Bales, 1950). Erving Goffman (e.g., 1955) and Harold Garfinkel (1967) had challenged this way of understanding interaction with their studies that focused on the moral and inferential underpinnings of social interaction.

Drawing part of his inspiration from them, Sacks started to study qualitatively the real-time sequential ordering of actions—the rules, patterns, and structures in the relations between consecutive actions (Silverman, 1998). Schegloff (1992a) argued that Sacks made a radical shift in the perspective of social scientific inquiry into social interaction; instead of treating social interaction as a screen on which other processes (Balesian categories or moral and inferential processes) were projected, Sacks started to study the very structures of the interaction itself (Schegloff, 1992a, p. xviii).

BASIC THEORETICAL ASSUMPTIONS

In the first place, CA is not a theoretical enterprise but rather a very concretely empirical one. Conversation analysts make video or audio recordings of naturally occurring interactions, and they transcribe these recordings using a detailed notation system (see Appendix). They search, in the recordings and transcripts, for recurrent distinct interactive practices that then become their research topics. These practices can involve, for example, specific sequences (e.g., news delivery sequence consisting of "news announcement," "announcement response," "elaboration," and "assessment" [Maynard, 2003]) or specific ways of designing utterances (e.g., "oh"-prefaced answers to questions [Heritage, 1998]). Then, through careful listening, comparison of instances, and exploration of the context of them, conversation analysts describe in detail the properties and tasks that the practices have (e.g., "oh"-preface as marking a change in the epistemic state of its speaker, see Heritage, 1998).

However, through empirical studies—in an "inductive" way—a body of theoretical knowledge about the organization of conversation has been accumulated. The actual "techniques" in doing CA can be understood and appreciated only against the backdrop of these basic theoretical assumptions of CA. In what follows, I try to sketch some of the basic assumptions concerning the organization of conversation that arise from these studies. There are perhaps three most fundamental assumptions of this kind (see also Heritage, 1984, Chapter 8; Hutchby & Wooffitt, 1998), namely that (a) talk is action, (b) action is structurally organized, and (c) talk creates and maintains intersubjective reality.

Talk Is Action

As in some other philosophical and social scientific approaches, in CA talk is understood primarily as a vehicle of human action (Schegloff, 1991). The capacity of language to convey ideas is seen as being derived from this more fundamental task. In accomplishing actions, talk is seamlessly intertwined with (other) corporeal means of action such as gaze and gesture (Goodwin, 1981). Some CA studies have as their topics the organization of actions that are recognizable as distinct actions even from a vernacular point of view. Thus, conversation analysts have studied, for example, openings (Schegloff, 1968) and closings (Schegloff & Sacks, 1973) of conversations, assessments and ways in which the recipients agree or disagree with them (Goodwin & Goodwin, 1992; Pomerantz, 1984), storytelling (Mandelbaum, 1992; Sacks, 1974a), complaints (Drew & Holt, 1988), telling and receiving news (Maynard, 2003), and laughter (Glenn, 2003; Haakana, 2001; Jefferson, 1984). Many CA studies have as their topic actions that are typical in some institutional environment. Examples include diagnosis (Heath, 1992; Maynard, 1991, 1992; Peräkylä, 1998, 2002; ten Have, 1995) and physical examination (Heritage & Stivers, 1999) in medical consultations, questioning and answering practices in cross-examinations (Drew, 1992), ways of managing disagreements in news interviews (Greatbatch, 1992), and advice giving in a number of different environments (Heritage & Sefi, 1992; Silverman, 1997; Vehviläinen, 2001). Finally, many important CA studies focus on fundamental aspects of conversational organization that make any action possible. These include turn taking (Sacks, Schegloff, & Jefferson, 1974), repair (Schegloff, 1992c; Schegloff, Jefferson, & Sacks, 1977), and the general ways in which sequences of action are built (Schegloff, 2007a).

Action Is Structurally Organized

In the CA view, the practical actions that comprise the heart of social life are thoroughly structured and organized. In pursuing their goals, the actors have to orient themselves to rules and structures that only make their actions possible. These rules and structures concern mostly the relations between actions. Single acts are parts of larger, structurally organized entities. These entities may be called *sequences* (Schegloff, 2007a).

The most basic and the most important sequence is called the *adjacency pair* (Schegloff & Sacks, 1973). It is a sequence of two actions in which the first action ("first pair part"), performed by one interactant, invites a particular type of second action ("second pair part") to be performed by another interactant. Typical examples of adjacency pairs include question–answer, greeting–greeting, request–grant/refusal, and invitation–acceptance/declination. The relation between the first and second pair parts is strict and normative; if the second pair part does not come forth, the first speaker can, for example, repeat the first action or seek explanations for the fact that the second action is missing (Atkinson & Drew, 1979, pp. 52–57; Merritt, 1976, p. 329).

Adjacency pairs often serve as a core around which even larger sequences are built (Schegloff, 2007a). So, a *pre-expansion* can precede an adjacency pair, for example, in cases where the speaker first asks about the other's plans for the evening and only thereafter (if it turns out that the other is not otherwise engaged) issues an invitation. An *insert expansion* involves actions that occur between the first and second pair parts and makes possible the production of the latter, for example, in cases where the speaker requests specification of an offer or a request before responding to it. Finally, in *post-expansion,* the speakers produce actions that somehow follow from the basic adjacency pair, with the simplest example being "okay" or "thank you" to close a sequence of a question and an answer or of a request and a grant (Schegloff, 2007a).

Talk Creates and Maintains the Intersubjective Reality

CA has sometimes been criticized for neglecting the "meaning" of talk at the expense of the "form" of talk (Alexander, 1988, p. 243; Taylor & Cameron, 1987, pp. 99–107). This is, however, a misunderstanding, perhaps arising from the impression created by the technical exactness of CA studies. Closer reading of CA studies reveals that in such studies, talk and interaction are examined as a site where intersubjective understanding about the participants' intentions is created and maintained (Heritage & Atkinson, 1984, p. 11). As such, CA gives access to the construction of meaning in real time where the methods or "vehicles" of this construction are inseparable from what is constructed (see also the example of MCA earlier). But it is important to notice that the conversation analytical "gaze" focuses exclusively on meanings and understandings that are made public through conversational action and that it remains "agnostic" regarding people's intrapsychological experience (Heritage, 1984).

The most fundamental level of intersubjective understanding—which constitutes the basis for any other type of intersubjective understanding—concerns *the understanding of the preceding turn displayed by the current speaker.* Just like any turn of talk that is produced in the context shaped by the previous turn, it also displays its speaker's understanding of that previous turn (Atkinson & Drew, 1979, p. 48). Thus, in simple cases, when producing a turn of talk that is hearable as an answer, the speaker also shows that he or she understood the preceding turn as a question. Sometimes these choices can be crucial for the unfolding of the interaction and the social relation of its participants, for example, in cases where a turn of talk is potentially hearable in two ways (e.g., as an announcement or a request, as an informing or a complaint) and the recipient makes the choice in the next turn. In case the first speaker considers the understanding concerning his talk to be incorrect or problematic, as displayed in the second speaker's utterance, the first speaker has an opportunity to correct this understanding in the "third position" (Schegloff, 1992c), for example, by saying "I didn't mean to criticize you; I just meant to tell you about the problem."

Another important level of intersubjective understanding concerns the *context* of the talk. This is particularly salient in institutional interaction, that is, in interaction that takes place to accomplish some institutionally ascribed tasks of the participants (e.g., psychotherapy, medical consultations, news interviews) (Arminen, 2005; Drew & Heritage, 1992; Heritage, 2004). The participants' understanding of the institutional context of their talk is documented in their actions. As Emmanuel Schegloff (1991, 1992b) and Paul Drew and John Heritage (1992) pointed out, if the "institutional context" is relevant for interaction, it can be observed in the details of the participants' actions—in their ways of giving and receiving information, asking and answering questions, presenting arguments, and so forth. CA research that focuses on institutional interactions explores the exact ways in which the performers of different institutional tasks shape their actions to achieve their goals.

RESEARCH EXAMPLE

After these rather abstract considerations, let us consider a concrete example of CA research. A recent study by John Heritage and Geoffrey Raymond (2005) that focuses on the ways in which participants to an interaction manage their epistemic status, that is, their rights to know about the topic or target talked about. It has long been known in CA research that in describing events people also make explicit how they are able to know about the incident they are telling about, what sort of access they have to the incident (Sacks, 1992; Whalen & Zimmerman, 1990). Similarly, in telling stories or delivering news, people give primary rights to tell about an event to a person who has actually experienced the event (Maynard, 2003; Peräkylä, 1995; Pomerantz, 1984; Sacks, 1984). In their study "The Terms of Agreement," Heritage and Raymond (2005) describe how epistemic authority and subordination are constantly managed also in evaluating a common target in everyday talk and show some subtle and recurring methods with which this is done.

In CA terms, Heritage and Raymond's investigation concerns assessment sequences in conversation. Assessments are typically made in adjacency pairs, meaning that when one speaker assesses a target in conversation, the others orient to this first assessment as making relevant a second assessment. Heritage and Raymond maintain that by making the first assessment, the speaker simultaneously claims to have a primary right to evaluate the target. Thus, in making the first assessment, speakers orient to the possibility that the other participants have a better access to, or a closer relationship with, the assessed target. Heritage and Raymond show various cases in which speakers regulate these epistemic rights, such as by downgrading them in making the first assessment or by upgrading them in making the second assessment. Reaching agreement thus requires careful management of the participants' epistemic status: It inherently involves negotiation on epistemic rights, authority, and subordination.

The following two extracts from Heritage and Raymond's article show unmarked assessment sequences, where both participants orient to their right to assess the target as unproblematic:

```
(1)  [VIYMC 1:4]
1 J:    Let's feel the water. Oh, it...
2 R: -> It's wonderful. It's just right.
3       It's like bathtub water.


(2)  [NB:IV.7:-44]
1 A: -> Adeline's such a swell [gal
2 P:                           [Oh God, whadda
3       gal. You know
```

In these cases, both speakers in both assessment sequences have similar access to the target that they are assessing and treat their rights to assess the target as equal. If this is not the case, speakers have various ways to make this clear. The following two sequences show some ways in which the speakers of the *first assessment* may orient to their respective epistemic status. In extract 3, the speaker downgrades her epistemic rights with a *tag question*:

```
(3)  [Rah 14:2]
1 Jen:    Mm [I: bet they proud o:f the fam'ly.=
2 Ver:       [Ye:s.
3 Jen:-> =They're [a luvly family now ar'n't [they.
```

```
4 Ver:                    [°Mm:.°                        [They
5            are: yes ye[s.
6 Jen:                  [eeYe[s::,
7 Ver:                       [Yes,
8 Jen: Mm: All they need now is a little girl
9      tih complete i:t.
```

It is evident in the first two lines of the sequence that Vera has more information on the family in question as she answers Jennie's question concerning the family. In line 3, Jennie assesses the family as lovely, and downgrades her assessment with a tag question *aren't they*. This way she indicates that her co-participant has primary rights to assess the family, as she is the one who knows them better.

There are also methods to emphasize one's primary rights to assess a target. One such method is *negative interrogative* of which extract 4 shows a case:

```
(4) [SBL:2-1-8:5]
1 Bea: Wz las'night th'firs'time you met Missiz Kelly?
2       (1.0)
3 Nor: Me:t who:m?
4 Bea: Missiz Kelly?
5 Nor: ^Ye:s. hh[Yih kno] :w what<]
6 Bea:          [ Isn't ]she a cu]te little thi:ng?
```

In this extract, the interrogative syntax that Bea deploys in her first assessment at line 6 increases the relevancy of a response, the yes-no question structure predisposes the terms to be used in the response and that an agreeing response is expected. Through all these characteristics of the turn, Bea shows that her stance toward Mrs. Kelly is settled, she has an established acquaintance with her and has stronger rights to assess her than Norman.

Similarly, there are available for speakers of *the second assessment* to manage their epistemic status. One of these is the oh-preface. In the following extract (5) Ilene and Norman are talking about Norman's dog Trixie. The first assessment is in lines 9-10 and the second in line 11.

```
(5) [Heritage 1:11:4]
1 Ile: No well she's still a bit young though
2      isn't [she<ah me]an:=uh[:
```

```
 3 Nor:          [She : :]        [She wz a year:
         la:st wee:k.
 5 Ile: Ah yes. Oh well any time no:w [then.]
 6 Nor:                               [Uh: : :] : [m
 7 Ile:                                            [Ye: s.=
 8 Nor: =But she[:'s ( )           ]
 9 Ile:         [Cuz Trixie started] so
10      early [didn't sh[e,
11 Nor:       [°O h : : [ye:s.°=
12 Ile: =°Ye:h°=
```

In line 11, we see how oh-prefacing of the second assessment indexes the speaker's independent access to the target. This is achieved with the oh-prefaces change-of-state characteristics, indicating that Ilene's first assessment has made it relevant for Norman to review his previous, preexisting experience of the target (see Heritage, 2002).

Thus, various methods can be deployed in asserting primary or secondary rights to assess a certain target in conversation. Heritage and Raymond show how through these methods, while agreeing and disagreeing with assessments, participants also negotiate who knows better about the target of the assessment. This work is sometimes subtle and the participants establish mutual alignment, but it can also involve competition and even conflict. Heritage and Raymond conclude by stating that their results point at "a dilemma at the heart of agreement sequences." People seek to know what others think about a certain target, but they at the same time have to pay heed to each other's epistemic rights. Especially when the question is of personal matters (assessing somebody else's grandchildren or pets for example), people may have to engage in complicated face-saving procedures to solve this basic dilemma. The analysis points out how involvement in or detachment from social relationships is an issue that is deeply practical and present in our everyday talk: This is an issue that we have to manage to some extent whenever we engage in the act of assessing a target.

Heritage and Raymond's findings are a good example of the sort of research that is capable of unraveling the fine-tuned logic of face-to-face interaction and to uncover the embedded norms of conduct that are oriented to by the participants in managing their social relations. Their article depicts some ways in which people encode and argue for their epistemic status in interaction. The authors' results, however, are relevant beyond the sphere of everyday interactions. Epistemic relations between people in different statuses are at the heart of many institutions—such as medicine and education. Heritage and Raymond's study provides a baseline in relation to which it is possible to analyze how epistemic rights are managed in many institutional encounters.

RETHINKING THE PLACE OF MENTAL REALITIES

Some years ago, Martyn Hammersley (2003) instigated a debate concerning methodological foundations of conversation analysis. In particular, he criticized CA for refusing to acknowledge that various psychosocial features are not "observable" in the subjects' public actions or the immediate context of action, but nevertheless have bearing to these actions. Hammersley thus calls for more recognition for both psychological and social factors, which reside, as it were, "outside" the immediate interactional expression and context. The ways in which CA can address the social factors will be discussed at the conclusion of this chapter. Regarding the psychological realities, the recent research program outlined by N. J. Enfield and Stephen C. Levinson (2006) is of great interest. Levinson and his coworkers have brought together a key contemporary discussion in psychology on *theory of mind*, and the findings of conversation analysis. In result, they propose that the basic practices of social interaction involve a process of mutual "reading" of the mental states of the co-interactants.

Although CA traditionally has avoided references to mental states of the participants of interaction—for example by referring to *epistemic rights* rather than to *cognition*—for Enfield and Levinson (2006, p. 1), the interactants take part in a "shared mental world." This shared mental world involves the interactants' detailed expectations concerning each other's behavior and their understandings regarding each other's cognitions, intentions, and motives. It is a world that is shaped and maintained in and through the sequentially organized action.

Theory of mind is a cornerstone of conceptualization by Enfield and Levinson. This is not a "researcher's theory," but a basic competence of understanding the social world, shared by humans. It involves an ability to attribute to other persons a world of inner experience that is independent from the outer world and the observer's own experience—a world consisting of states such as beliefs, desires, and intentions (Premack, 1976).

According to Enfield and Levinson, theory of mind is in incessant use in social interaction. The use of theory of mind is normally automatic and unconscious. The interactants read each other's communicative intentions and respond to these (Enfield & Levinson, 2006, p. 5; Levinson, 2006a, p. 45). Interactants do not respond to other's behavior as such. Interaction requires interpretation of other's behavior: "mapping intentions or goals onto behaviour" (Levinson, 2006a, p. 45), whereby behavior is understood as intentional action. This process of interpretation, according to Levinson, involves "some kind of simulation of the other's mental world" (p. 45).

Levinson (2006a, 2006b) and Enfield (Enfield & Levinson, 2006), and the contributors to their recent collection (especially Schegloff, 2006) show how the practices identified by CA—adjacency pairs, pre-sequences, recipient design, repair—involve reciprocal and reflexive simulation of the mental states of the participants. Through the integration of CA and the research tradition on theory of mind, suggested by Enfield and Levinson, we can thus arrive at a conceptualization of interaction that preserves the conversation analytical findings, and yet does not call into question the relevancy of mental processes.

The reinterpretation of conversation analytical findings in the light of the psychological research traditions on theory of mind involves a new turn in the conceptualization of social interaction. The coming years will show whether this new conceptualization yields new kinds of empirical research designs and research results in CA.

Conclusion

In this chapter, we have introduced a number of qualitative research approaches that use language—text or talk—as data. Approaches like those that we have presented are sometimes criticized for their narrow focus, as investigating an arbitrary fracture of reality, a piece of text or a fragment of talk, that has no bearing on broader social issues (e.g., Hammersley, 2003). If we study language, do we neglect something else, which might be more important, at least in social and political terms? Does qualitative research on talk and text involve *merely* language, or can these approaches address broader social issues? To conclude this chapter, we compare some of the methods discussed for their relation to issues of *power* and *social change*. We focus on the three methods discussed most thoroughly: HDA, MCA, and CA. Our main conclusion will be that these methods are indeed potent in addressing broader social phenomena.

The HDA exemplified in this chapter by Meskus' work is most directly a method for investigating social change. Meskus showed us the evolvement of the management of human heredity in Finnish maternity health care. At the same time, her analysis of texts was about power—about the discourses given which certain decisions concerning the management of heredity were made and about the practices that were adopted as technologies of this management—as well as about the ways in which these developments concerned groups of individuals (in this case, mostly pregnant mothers). Meskus treated power here as a productive force—as something that calls realities into being rather than suppresses them.

The potential of MCA in dealing with questions pertaining to power and social change was well shown in Rapley et al.'s (2003) research where they demonstrated the deeply moral underpinnings of the use of categories that were neutral on the surface. The adoption and use of specific categories in social situations as well as in texts—the mere naming of a member as belonging to a certain category—simultaneously attributes specific obligations and refutations to the chosen category and thus also obliges the person in question. This was the case with the media struggle on the categorization of the gunman described by Rapley et al. MCA provides a method with which we can bring to the fore the subtle underpinnings of seemingly innocent language use: it shows how any categorization of a member or group in society involves their placement within certain moral space with regard to which their actions can be judged.

The relation of CA to broader social issues is more complex. CA that focuses on generic practices and structures of mundane everyday talk might seem irrelevant in power and social change. The research example we showed was about everyday casual conversations, the minute reality of which is perhaps far away from the large-scale questions of change in social, economic, and political structures. Michael Billig (1998) argued that this irrelevance may actually imply politically conservative choices. Even in researching institutional interaction, the fact that conversation analysts often focus on small details of video- or audio-recorded talk might seem to render their studies impotent for the analysis of social relations and processes *not* incorporated in talk (see also Hak, 1999).

From the CA point of view, two responses can be given to these criticisms. First, the significance of orderly organization of face-to-face (or other "live") interaction for *all* social life needs to be restated. No "larger-scale" social institutions could operate without the substratum of the interaction order. These institutions operate largely through questions, answers, assessments, accusations, accounts, interpretations, and the like. Hence, even when not focusing on hot social and political issues that we read about in the newspapers, CA is providing knowledge about the basic organizations of social life that make these issues, as well as their possible solutions and the debate about them, possible in the first place. The observation made by Heritage and Raymond, for instance, about the terms of agreement in social interaction makes it possible to suggest that such fine-tuned management of epistemic rights may lie behind various struggles for power and status at the workplace, in professional encounters, and so on. Further, CA research that is not explicitly framed around questions of power or status may, however, bring results that are relevant in discussing these topics. For instance, analyses of professional practices may bring forward covered ways of influencing clients to reach particular goals, which may then give reason to discuss the legitimacy or potential effects of these practices (see Clark, Drew, & Pinch, 2003, on sales encounters; Ruusuvuori, 2007, on homeopathic consultations).

Some CA research is more directly relevant for political and social concerns. For example, many CA studies have contributed to our understanding of the ways in which specific interactional practices contribute to the maintenance or change of the *gender system*. In these studies, gender and sexuality are treated as practical accomplishments rather than as "facts." Work by Candace West (1979) and Don Zimmerman (Zimmerman & West, 1975) on male–female interruptions is widely cited. More recently, Celia Kitzinger (2005) has shown how heterosexual speakers constantly allow their heterosexuality to be inferred in their talk and how this "both reflects and constructs heteronormativity" (p. 222; see also Kitzinger, 2000; Kitzinger & Kitzinger, 2007). In a somewhat more linguistic CA study, Tainio (2002) explored how syntactical and semantic properties of utterances are used in the construction of heterosexual identities in elderly couples' talk. Studies such as these (for an overview, see McIlvenny, 2002) also amply demonstrate the *critical* potential of CA. A different CA study on social change was offered in Steven Clayman and John Heritage's (2002b) work on question design in U.S. presidential press conferences. By combining qualitative and quantitative techniques, Clayman and Heritage showed how the relative proportions of different types of journalist questions, exhibiting different degrees of "adversarialness," have changed over time. As such, they explored the historical change in the U.S. presidential institution and media. A further example of a critical potential of a study that combines CA and statistical methods is Tanya Stivers and Asifa Majid's (2007) research on implicit race bias in asking questions in pediatric consultations. Stivers and Majid's study shows that parental race and education have a significant effect on whether doctors select children to answer questions. Thus, at least to scholars using CA or MCA in their analyses of the everyday world, these methods offer ample critical perspectives for inquiry of social life.

Dorothy Smith (among others) has criticized the Goffmanian approach (adopted in CA and MCA) to social interaction as a self-sufficient object of study of its own. She argues that treating the everyday world of social interaction as such an object isolates it from its context of broader forms of organization and makes it appear self-contained (Grahame, 1998). Smith (1987, pp. 152–154) maintains that local social organization is generated by social relations external to the local setting and that these social relations cannot be adequately grasped by investigating the local setting only. It seems to us, however, that the way in which CA is able to provide for detailed descriptions of the organization of the world of social interaction (such as the terms of agreement for instance) could rather be seen as one step further in uncovering the mechanisms through which social relations operate. Further, the new trends such as Kitzinger's feminist CA (2000, 2005) or Stivers & Majid's analysis of race bias in pediatric consultations (2007) show that in principle there is nothing in the actual method that would prevent combining its results with further investigations of the research object with other methods—to gain a more comprehensive view of it.

Thus, our conclusion is, qualitative research on text and talk is not only about language. The observations made by methods on text and talk provide one avenue to understanding social structures, as well as individual actions.

Appendix

The Transcription Symbols in CA

[	Starting point of overlapping speech
]	End point of overlapping speech
(2.4)	Silence measured in seconds
(.)	Pause of less than 0.2 seconds
↑	Upward shift in pitch
↓	Downward shift in pitch
word	Emphasis
wo:rd	Prolongation of sound
°word°	Section of talk produced in lower volume than the surrounding talk
WORD	Section of talk produced in higher volume than the surrounding talk
w#ord#	Creaky voice
£word£	Smile voice
wo(h)rd	Laugh particle inserted within a word
wo-	Cut off in the middle of a word
word<	Abruptly completed word
>word<	Section of talk uttered in a quicker pace than the surrounding talk
<word>	Section of talk uttered in a slower pace than the surround talk
(word)	Section of talk that is difficult to hear but is likely as transcribed
( )	Inaudible word
.hhh	Inhalation
hhh	Exhalation
.	Falling intonation at the end of an utterance
?	Rising intonation at the end of an utterance
,	Flat intonation at the end of an utterance
word.=word	"Rush through" without the normal gap into a new utterance.
((word))	Transcriber's comments

Source: Adapted from Drew & Heritage (Eds.). (1992). *Talk at work: Interaction in institutional settings.* Cambridge, UK: Cambridge University Press.

References

Alexander, J. (1988). *Action and its environments: Toward a new synthesis.* New York: Columbia University Press.

Arminen, I. (2005). *Institutional interaction: Studies of talk at work.* Aldershot, UK: Ashgate.

Atkinson, J. M. (1978). *Discovering suicide: Studies in the social organization of sudden death.* London: Macmillan.

Atkinson, P., & Coffey, A. (1997). Analysing documentary realities. In D. Silverman (Ed.), *Qualitative research: Theory, method, and practice* (pp. 45–62). London: Sage.

Atkinson, J. M., & Drew, P. (1979). *Order in court: The organization of verbal interaction in judicial settings.* London: Macmilllan.

Bales, R. F. (1950). *Interaction process analysis: A method for the study of small groups.* Reading, MA: Addison-Wesley.

Bamberg, M., & Georgakopoulou, A. (2008). Small stories as a new perspective in narrative and identity analysis. *Text & Talk, 28*(3), 377–396.

Billig, M. (1998). Whose terms? Whose ordinariness? Rhetoric and ideology in conversation analysis. *Discourse & Society, 10,* 543–558.

Brown, G., & Yule, G. (1983). *Discourse analysis.* Cambridge, UK: Cambridge University Press.

Butler, C., & Weatherall, A. (2006). "No, we're not playing families": Membership categorization in children's play. *Research on Language and Social Interaction, 39*(4), 441–470.

Clark, C., Drew, P., & Pinch, T. (2003). Managing prospect affiliation and rapport in real-life sales encounters. *Discourse Studies, 5*(1), 5–31.

Clayman, S., & Heritage, J. (2002a). *The news interview: Journalists and public figures on the air.* Cambridge, UK: Cambridge University Press.

Clayman, S., & Heritage, J. (2002b). Questioning presidents: Journalistic deference and adversarialness in the press conferences of Eisenhower and Reagan. *Journal of Communication, 52,* 749–775.

De Fina, A., & Georgakopoulou, A. (2008). Introduction: Narrative analysis in the shift from texts to practices. *Text & Talk, 23*(3), 275–281.

Dean, M. (1999). *Governmentality: Power and rule in modern society.* London: Sage.

Drew, P. (1992). Contested evidence in courtroom cross-examination: The case of a trial for rape. In P. Drew & J. Heritage (Eds.), *Talk at work: Interaction in institutional settings* (pp. 470–520). Cambridge, UK: Cambridge University Press.

Drew, P., & Heritage, J. (1992). Analyzing talk at work: An introduction. In P. Drew & J. Heritage (Eds.), *Talk at work: Interaction in institutional settings* (pp. 3–65). Cambridge, UK: Cambridge University Press.

Drew, P., & Holt, E. (1988). Complainable matters: The use of idiomatic expression in making complaints. *Social Problems, 35,* 398–417.

Edwards, D. (1997). *Discourse and cognition.* London: Sage.

Eglin, P., & Hester, S. (2003). *The Montreal massacre: A story of membership categorization analysis.* Waterloo, ON: Wilfred Laurier University Press.

Enfield, N. J., & Levinson, S. (2006). Introduction: Human sociality as a new interdisciplinary field. In N. J. Enfield & S. C. Levinson (Eds.), *Roots of human sociality: Culture, cognition and interaction* (pp. 1–34). New York: Berg.

Fairclough, N. (1989). *Language and power.* London: Longman.

Fairclough, N. (1995). *Media discourse.* London: Edward Arnold.

Foucault, M. (1973). *The birth of the clinic: An archaeology of medical perception.* New York: Pantheon.

Foucault, M. (1977). *Discipline and punish: The birth of the prison.* London: Allen Lane.

Foucault, M. (1978). *The history of sexuality: Vol. 1. An introduction.* New York: Pantheon.

Garfinkel, H. (1967). *Studies in ethnomethodology.* Englewood Cliffs, NJ: Prentice Hall.

Georgakopoulou, A. (2007). *Small stories, interaction and identities.* Amsterdam: John Benjamins.

Glenn, P. (2003). *Laughter in interaction.* Cambridge, UK: Cambridge University Press.

Goffman, E. (1955). On face work. *Psychiatry, 18,* 213–231.

Goffman, E. (1983). The interaction order. *American Sociological Review, 48,* 1–17.

Goodwin, C. (1981). *Conversational organization: Interaction between speakers and hearers.* New York: Academic Press.

Goodwin, C., & Goodwin, M. H. (1992). Assessments and the construction of context. In A. Duranti & C. Goodwin (Eds.), *Rethinking context: Language as interactive phenomenon* (pp. 147–190). Cambridge, UK: Cambridge University Press.

Grahame, P. R. (1998). Ethnography, institutions, and the problematic of the everyday world. *Human Studies, 21,* 347–360.

Greatbatch, D. (1992). On the management of disagreement between news interviewees. In P. Drew & J. Heritage (Eds.), *Talk at work: Interaction in institutional settings* (pp. 268–302). Cambridge, UK: Cambridge University Press.

Greimas, A. J. (1966). *Semantique structurale.* Paris: Larousse.

Gubrium, J., & Holstein, J. (2009). *Analyzing narrative reality.* Thousand Oaks, CA: Sage.

Haakana, M. (2001). Laughter as a patient's resource: Dealing with delicate aspects of medical interaction. *Text, 21,* 187–219.

Hak, T. (1999). "Text" and "con-text": Talk bias in studies of health care work. In S. Sarangi & C. Roberts (Eds.), *Talk, work, and institutional order* (pp. 427–452). Berlin, Germany: Mouton de Gruyter.

Hammersley, M. (2003). Conversation analysis and discourse analysis: Methods or paradigms. *Discourse and Society, 14*(6), 751–781.

Heath, C. (1992). The delivery and reception of diagnosis in the general-practice consultation. In P. Drew & J. Heritage (Eds.), *Talk at work: Interaction in institutional settings* (pp. 235–267). Cambridge, UK: Cambridge University Press.

Heritage, J. (1984). *Garfinkel and ethnomethodology.* Cambridge, UK: Polity Press.

Heritage, J. (1998). Oh-prefaced responses to inquiry. *Language in Society, 27*(3), 291–334.

Heritage, J. (2002). Oh-prefaced responses to assessments: A method of modifying agreement/disagreement. In C. Ford, B. Fox, & S. Thompson (Eds.), *The language of turn and sequence* (pp.196–224). New York: Oxford University Press.

Heritage, J. (2004). Conversation analysis and institutional talk. In R. Sanders & K. Fitch (Eds.), *Handbook of language and social interaction* (pp. 103–146). Mahwah, NJ: Lawrence Erlbaum.

Heritage, J., & Atkinson, J. M. (1984). Introduction. In J. M. Atkinson & J. Heritage (Eds.), *Structures of social action* (pp. 1–15). Cambridge, UK: Cambridge University Press.

Heritage, J., & Raymond, G. (2005). The terms of agreement: Indexing epistemic authority and subordination in talk-in-interaction. *Social Psychology Quarterly, 68*(1), 15–38.

Heritage, J., & Sefi, S. (1992). Dilemmas of advice: Aspects of the delivery and reception of advice in interactions between health visitors and first-time mothers. In P. Drew & J. Heritage (Eds.), *Talk at work: Interaction in institutional settings* (pp. 359–417). Cambridge, UK: Cambridge University Press.

Heritage, J., & Stivers, T. (1999). Online commentary in acute medical visits: A method for shaping patient expectations. *Social Science and Medicine, 49*, 1501–1517.

Hutchby, I., & Wooffitt, R. (1998). *Conversation analysis: Principles, practices, and applications.* Cambridge, UK: Polity Press.

Hyvärinen, M., Hydén, L-C., Saarenheimo, M., & Tamboukou, M. (2010). Beyond narrative coherence: An introduction. In M. Hyvärinen, L-C. Hydén, M. Saarenheimo, & M. Tamboukou (Eds.) *Beyond narrative coherence: Studies in narrative 11.* Amsterdam: John Benjamins.

Jayyusi, L. (1991). Values and moral judgment: Communicative praxis as moral order. In G. Button (Ed.), *Ethnomethodology and the human sciences* (pp. 227–251). Cambridge, UK: Cambridge University Press.

Jefferson, G. (1984). On the organization of laughter in talk about troubles. In J. M. Atkinson & J. Heritage (Eds.), *Structures of social action* (pp. 346–369). Cambridge, UK: Cambridge University Press.

Kendall, G., & Wickham, G. (1999). *Using Foucault's methods.* London: Sage.

Kitzinger, C. (2000). Doing feminist conversation analysis. *Feminism & Psychology, 10*, 163–193.

Kitzinger, C. (2005). Speaking as a heterosexual: (How) does sexuality matter for talk-in-interaction. *Research on Language and Social Interaction, 38*(3), 221–265.

Kitzinger, C., & Kitzinger, S. (2007). Birth trauma: Talking with women and the value of conversation analysis. *British Journal of Midwifery, 15*(5), 256–264.

Lepper, G. (2000). Categories in text and talk. *A practical introduction to categorization analysis.* Introducing Qualitative Methods Series. London: Sage.

Levinson, S. (2006a). On the human "interaction engine." In N. J. Enfield & S. C. Levinson (Eds.), *Roots of human sociality: Culture, cognition and interaction* (pp. 39–69). New York: Berg.

Levinson, S. (2006b). Cognition at the heart of human interaction. *Discourse Studies, 8*(1), 85–93.

Mandelbaum, J. (1992). Assigning responsibility in conversational storytelling: The interactional construction of reality. *Text, 13,* 247–266.

Maynard, D. W. (1991). Interaction and asymmetry in clinical discourse. *American Journal of Sociology, 97,* 448–495.

Maynard, D. W. (1992). On clinicians co-implicating recipients' perspective in the delivery of diagnostic news. In P. Drew & J. Heritage (Eds.), *Talk at work: Interaction in institutional settings* (pp. 331–358). Cambridge, UK: Cambridge University Press.

Maynard, D. W. (2003). *Bad news, good news: Conversational order in everyday talk and clinical settings.* Chicago: University of Chicago Press.

McHoul, A. W., & Grace, A. (1993). *A Foucault primer: Discourse, power, and the subject.* Melbourne, Australia: Melbourne University Press.

McIlvenny, P. (2002). *Talking gender and sex.* Amsterdam: John Benjamins.

Merritt, M. (1976). On questions following questions (in service encounters). *Language in Society, 5,* 315–357.

Meskus, M. (2009a). Governing risk through informed choice: Prenatal testing in welfarist maternity care. In S. Bauer & A. Wahlberg (Eds.), *Contested categories: Life sciences in society* (pp. 49–68). Farnham, UK: Ashgate.

Meskus, M. (2009b). *Elämän tiede.* Tampere, Finland: Vastapaino.

Nikander, P. (2002). *Age in action: Membership work and stage of life categories in talk.* Helsinki: Finnish Academy of Science and Letters.

Ochs, E., & Capps, L. (2001). *Living narrative. Creating lives in everyday storytelling.* Cambridge, MA: Harvard University Press.

Peräkylä, A. (1995). *AIDS counselling; Institutional interaction and clinical practice.* Cambridge, UK: Cambridge University Press.

Peräkylä, A. (1998). Authority and accountability: The delivery of diagnosis in primary health care. *Social Psychology Quarterly, 61,* 301–320.

Peräkylä, A. (2002). Agency and authority: Extended responses to diagnostic statements in primary care encounters. *Research on Language and Social Interaction, 35,* 219–247.

Pomerantz, A. (1984). Agreeing and disagreeing with assessments: Some features of preferred/dispreferred turn shapes. In J. M. Atkinson & J. Heritage (Eds.), *Structures of social action: Studies in conversation analysis* (pp. 67–101). Cambridge, UK: Cambridge University Press.

Potter, J. (2004). Discourse analysis as a way of analysing naturally occurring talk. In D. Silverman (Ed.), *Qualitative research: Theory, method, and practice* (2nd ed., pp. 200–201). London: Sage.

Potter, J. (2006). Cognition and conversation. *Discourse Studies, 8*(1), 131–140.

Potter, J., & te Molder, H. (2005). Talking cognition: Mapping and making the terrain. In H. te Molder & J. Potter (Eds.), *Conversation and cognition* (pp. 1–54). Cambridge, UK: Cambridge University Press.

Premack, D. (1976). Language and intelligence in ape and man. *American Scientist, 64*(4) 674–683.

Propp, V. I. (1968). *Morphology of the folktale* (rev. ed., L. A. Wagner, Ed.). Austin: University of Texas Press.

Rapley, M., McCarthy, D., & McHoul, A. (2003). Mentality or morality? Membership categorization, multiple meanings and mass murder. *British Journal of Social Psychology, 42,* 427–444.

Roca-Cuerbes, C. (2008). Membership categorization and professional insanity ascription. *Discourse Studies, 10*(4), 543–570.

Rose, N. (1999). *Powers of freedom: Reframing political thought.* Cambridge, UK: Cambridge University Press.

Ruusuvuori, J. (2007). Managing affect: Integration of empathy and problem-solving in health care encounters. *Discourse Studies, 9*(5), 597–622.

Sacks, H. (1974a). An analysis of the course of a joke's telling in conversation. In R. Bauman & J. Sherzer (Eds.), *Explorations in the ethnography of speaking* (pp. 337–353). Cambridge, UK: Cambridge University Press.

Sacks, H. (1974b). On the analysability of stories by children. In R. Turner (Ed.), *Ethnomethodology* (pp. 216–232). Harmondsworth, UK: Penguin.

Sacks, H. (1992). *Lectures on conversation* (Vol. 1, G. Jefferson, Ed., with an introduction by E. Schegloff). Oxford, UK: Blackwell.

Sacks, H., Schegloff, E., & Jefferson, G. (1974). A simplest systematics for the organization of turn-taking for conversation. *Language, 50,* 696–735.

Schegloff, E. A. (1968). Sequencing in conversational openings. *American Anthropologist, 70,* 1075–1095.

Schegloff, E. A. (1991). Reflection on talk and social structure. In D. Boden & D. Zimmerman (Eds.), *Talk and social structure* (pp. 44–70). Cambridge, UK: Polity Press.

Schegloff, E. A. (1992a). Introduction. In G. Jefferson (Ed.), *Harvey Sacks: Lectures on conversation: Vol. 1. Fall 1964–Spring 1968.* Oxford, UK: Blackwell.

Schegloff, E. A. (1992b). On talk and its institutional occasion. In P. Drew & J. Heritage (Eds.), *Talk at work: Interaction in institutional settings* (pp. 101–134). Cambridge, UK: Cambridge University Press.

Schegloff, E. A. (1992c). Repair after next turn: The last structurally provided defense of intersubjectivity in conversation. *American Journal of Sociology, 98,* 1295–1345.

Schegloff, E. A. (2006). Interaction: The infrastructure for social institutions, the natural ecological niche for language, and the arena in which culture is enacted. In N. J. Enfield & S. C. Levinson (Eds.), *Roots of human sociality: Culture, cognition and interaction* (pp. 70–98). New York: Berg.

Schegloff, E. A. (2007a). *Sequence organization.* Cambridge, UK: Cambridge University Press.

Schegloff, E. A. (2007b). A tutorial on membership categorization. *Journal of Pragmatics, 39,* 462–482.

Schegloff, E. A., Jefferson, G., & Sacks, H. (1977). The preference for self-correction in the organization of repair in conversation. *Language, 53,* 361–382.

Schegloff, E. A., & Sacks, H. (1973). Opening up closings. *Semiotica, 8,* 289–327.

Seale, C. (1998). *Constructing death: The sociology of dying and bereavement.* Cambridge, UK: Cambridge University Press.

Silverman, D. (1997). *Discourses of counselling.* London: Sage.

Silverman, D. (1998). *Harvey Sacks: Social science and conversation analysis.* Cambridge, UK: Polity Press.

Silverman, D. (2001). *Interpreting qualitative data: Methods for analyzing talk, text, and interaction* (2nd ed.). London: Sage.

Smith, D. (1974). The social construction of documentary reality. *Sociological Inquiry, 44,* 257–268.

Smith, D. (1987). *The everyday world as problematic: A feminist sociology.* Toronto, ON: University of Toronto Press.

Smith, D. (1990). *The conceptual practices of power.* Toronto: University of Toronto Press.

Speer, S. (2002). "Natural" and "contrived" data: A sustainable distinction. *Discourse Studies, 4,* 511–525.

Stivers, T., & Majid, A. (2007). Questioning children: Interactional evidence of implicit bias in medical interviews. *Social Psychology Quarterly, 70*(4), 424–441.

Stokoe, E. (2003). Mothers, single women and sluts: Gender, morality and membership categorization in neighbour disputes. *Feminism & Psychology, 13*(3), 317–344.

Tainio, L. (1999). Opaskirjojen kieli ikkunana suomalaiseen parisuhteeseen. *Naistutkimus, 12*(1), 2–26.

Tainio, L. (2002). Negotiating gender identities and sexual agency in elderly couples' talk. In P. McIlvenny (Ed.), *Talking gender and sexuality* (pp. 181–206). Amsterdam: John Benjamins.

Taylor, T. J., & Cameron, D. (1987). *Analyzing conversation: Rules and units in the structure of talk.* Oxford, UK: Pergamon.

Törrönen, J. (2000). The passionate text: The pending narrative as a macrostructure of persuasion. *Social Semiotics, 10*(1), 81–98.

Törrönen, J. (2003). The Finnish press' political position on alcohol between 1993 and 2000. *Addiction, 98*(3), 281–290.

ten Have, P. (1995). Disposal negotiations in general practice consultations. In A. Firth (Ed.), *The discourse of negotiation: Studies of language in the workplace* (pp. 319–344). Oxford, UK: Pergamon.

Vehviläinen, S. (2001). Evaluative advice in educational counseling: The use of disagreement in the "stepwise entry" to advice. *Research on Language and Social Interaction, 34,* 371–398.

West, C. (1979). Against our will: Male interruption of females in cross-sex conversation. *Annals of the New York Academy of Science, 327,* 81–97.

Wetherell, M. (1998). Positioning and interpretative repertoires: Conversation analysis and post-structuralism in dialogue. *Discourse & Society, 9,* 387–412.

Wetherell, M., & Potter, J. (1992). *Mapping the language of racism: Discourse and the legitimation of exploitation.* London: Harvester.

Whalen, M., & Zimmerman, D. (1990). Describing trouble: Practical epistemology in citizen calls to the police. *Language in Society, 19,* 465–492.

Wodak, R., & Meyer, M. (2009). Critical discourse analysis: History, agenda, theory and methodology. In R. Wodak & C. Meyer (Eds.), *Methods of critical discourse analysis* (pp. 1–33). London: Sage.

Zimmerman, D. H., & West, C. (1975). Sex roles, interruptions, and silences in conversation. In B. Thorne & N. Henley (Eds.), *Language and sex: Difference and dominance* (pp. 105–129). Rowley, MA: Newbury House.

10

Focus Groups

Contingent Articulations of Pedagogy, Politics, and Inquiry

George Kamberelis and Greg Dimitriadis

As traditional research demarcations collapse and new questions and issues arise (as evidenced by the evolution of the *Handbook of Qualitative Inquiry* across four editions), focus groups offer a particularly fruitful method for "thinking through" qualitative research today. Basically, focus groups are collective conversations or group interviews. They can be small or large, directed or nondirected. Focus groups have been used for a wide range of purposes during the past century or so. The U.S. military (e.g., Robert Merton), multinational corporations (e.g., Proctor & Gamble), Marxist revolutionaries (e.g., Paulo Freire), literacy activists (e.g., Jonathan Kozol), and three waves of feminist scholar-activists (e.g., Esther Madriz), among others, have all used focus groups to help advance their concerns and causes.

In the last edition of this handbook, we argued that focus group research exists at the intersection of pedagogy, activism, and interpretive inquiry. We also argued that researchers are typically strategic in configuring these intersections. In this chapter, we build upon and extend that work: (a) by troubling the idea that the intersection of pedagogy, activism, and inquiry is always or primarily strategic and (b) by exploring both new possibilities of and new dangers faced by focus group research in the current social and political climate, especially in relation to debates around the politics of evidence. To accomplish these goals, we engage in two related pragmatic/rhetorical moves. First, we reimagine focus group work as almost always multifunctional. Second, we situate focus group work within a performative idiom. Before we revivify and expand our earlier discussions of focus group work, we describe each of these moves.

Multifunctionality and Focus Groups

Multifunctionality has become an increasingly important construct used to explain complexity and contingency within many different disciplines. In linguistics, for example, it has long been known that many different linguistic functions (e.g., referential, conative, phatic, poetic) almost always operate simultaneously, with one function typically assuming a dominant role (e.g., Jakobson, 1960). In contemporary agriculture research, *multifunctionality* refers to the benefits beyond food production and trade that result from agricultural policies. Such benefits include such things as landscape preservation and increasing rural employment opportunities.

Inspired by Laurel Richardson's (2000) image of the crystal as productive for mapping the changing complexity of the lives of her research participants and her own life as a sociologist, we find the image of the prism to be useful for revisioning the primary functions of focus group work (pedagogy, politics, and inquiry), as well as the relations between and among them. A prism is a transparent optical element with flat, polished surfaces that can both refract and reflect light. The most common use of the term *prism* refers to a triangular prism—one that has a triangular base and three clear rectangular surfaces. When viewed from different angles, one can see more or less of each of its three surfaces. From some angles, one surface is completely and directly visible with the other two surfaces partially and obliquely visible. From other angles, two surfaces are completely visible with the third surface visible but obliquely and in the distance. Importantly, however, from every angle of vision, at least some of every surface is visible. Additionally, from some angles prisms break up light into its constituent spectral colors whereas from other angles they act like mirrors, reflecting all or almost all approaching light back toward its source. Similarly, all three focus group functions are always at work simultaneously, they are all visible to the researcher to some extent, and they all both refract and reflect the substance of focus group work in different ways.

Before saying more about the complex relations among the three primary functions of focus group work, and even though the meanings of each function may be (or appear to be) self-explanatory, we first briefly discuss how we have defined each function for our work here. The pedagogic function basically involves collective engagement designed to promote dialogue and to achieve higher levels of understanding of issues critical to the development of a group's interests and/or the transformation of conditions of its existence. In Paulo Freire's (1970/1993) *Pedagogy of the Oppressed,* for example, it is a matter of "reading the word" to better read the world. Among other things, this means asking and answering questions such as the following: What social facts are portrayed in a message as if they were perfectly "natural" or "normal"? Whose positions, interests, and values are represented in the message? Whose positions, interests, and values are absent or silent? Are any positions, interests, or values ridiculed, vilified, or demonized? How is the message trying to position its readers/ viewers in relation to its messages? How does this message do its work through the use of specific textual features and specific arrangements of these features?

Although not necessarily, the political function of focus group work often builds on the pedagogic function. The primary goal of the political function is to transform the conditions of existence for particular stakeholders. Activism (or enacting the political function) can grow out of a wide variety of political orientations; it typically constitutes a response to conditions of marginalization or oppression; the goal of the political function is usually to transform these conditions, making them more democratic, and it may be enacted in a variety of ways including consciousness-raising activities; writing editorials or manifestos; participating in campaigns, public marches, or strikes; boycotting products or services; lobbying government agencies; or simply adjusting one's needs and desires or changing one's lifestyle. In a recent interview (Kreisler, 2002), linguist and political activist Noam Chomsky cited several key moments of political activism in history that he argues literally changed the world: the Lowell factory girls' protest in the 1850s that catalyzed the labor movement in the United States; the antiwar, civil rights, and feminist movements of the 1960s; and the efforts of journalists, artists, and public intellectuals in Turkey fighting censorship today through acts of civil disobedience in their everyday professional work. Less obvious, more local forms of activism are also in evidence everywhere all the time— whether in neighborhoods, schools, or workplaces. Indexing both the nature and the importance of the political function, Chomsky noted that all effective political accomplishments "got there by struggle, common struggle by people who dedicated themselves with others, because you can't do it alone, and made [this] a much more civilized country. It was a long way to go, and that's not the first time it happened. And it will continue" (2002, Activism, para. 7).

Research (or inquiry) is perhaps the function most typically associated with focus group research. Yet, it is a slippery term with a long and contested history. At least since the Enlightenment, inquiry has been associated with the so-called hard sciences. From this perspective, reality and knowledge are *a priori* givens. The primary goals of inquiry are to explain, predict, and control both natural and social phenomena. And inquiry operates according to a correspondence theory of truth (one-to-one mapping of representations onto reality). Since the "interpretive turn," the nature and scope of inquiry have expanded considerably. Within this perspective, reality is considered to be (at least partially) socially constructed and thus changing and changeable. Knowledge is seen as partial and perspectival. The primary goal of inquiry within this view is to achieve richer, thicker, and more complex levels of understanding. And inquiry operates according to a logic of argumentation with the argument most well supported by evidence and warrants holding the day. Even more recently, inquiry has been shown to be messy, dirty, thoroughly imbricated within colonial and neocolonial impulses, and in need of retooling from the ground up to be more praxis-oriented and democratizing (Denzin & Lincoln, 2005). Based on the emergence of focus group research as a way to answer *how* and *why* questions that remained unanswered by positivistic quantitative methods, our working definition of the inquiry function is most closely aligned with that of the "interpretive turn" and especially the Chicago School of Sociology. The primary goal of inquiry from this perspective is to generate rich, complex, nuanced, and even contradictory accounts of how people ascribe meaning to and interpret their lived experience with an eye toward how these accounts might be used to affect social policy and social change. Clearly, we are already signaling that the boundaries between and among inquiry, pedagogy, and politics within focus group work are porous.

In this regard, these three functions are seldom related in simple, unproblematic ways. Political interventions, for example, do not necessarily emerge from inquiry. And when they do, this often occurs in unexpected or unintended ways. Similarly, pedagogy is not always central to activist work, but it can be and often is. Within any given project, these different dimensions or functions of focus group work emerge and interact in distinct and often disjunctive ways, eventually resulting in some unique interactive stabilization. We will touch on this idea of disjunctive emergence in our discussions of different lines of work within which one or another of these three functions has been framed as dominant. Toward the end of the chapter, we will address this issue more thoroughly and more directly when we discuss the performative nature of our own and our students' work. That said, we now discuss the efficacy of reframing focus group work within a performative idiom.

Focus Groups and/in the Performative Turn

Long connected with theater and elocution, performance has more recently emerged as basic, ontological, but inherently contested concept. "Performance is a contested concept because when we understand performance beyond theatrics and recognize it as fundamental and inherent to life and culture we are confronted with the ambiguities of different spaces and places that are foreign, contentious, and often under siege" (Madison & Hamera, 2006, p. xii). In moving across the academy, this turn to performance has posed new questions about our understandings of texts, practices, identities, and cultures. The turn to performance has also allowed us to see the world as always already in motion. Such a notion of performance gives us nowhere to hide in our responsibilities for the work we do. More specifically, we are forced to see the routine as ambiguous, as foreign, as contentious, and as often under siege.

This turn to performance has also created powerful spaces for thinking about emergent methodologies, those that "explore new ways of thinking about and framing knowledge construction," remaining ever-conscious of the links among epistemologies, methodologies, and the techniques used to carry out empirical work (Hesse-Biber & Leavy, 2006, pp. xi–xii). From this perspective, inquiry (and especially qualitative inquiry) is no longer a discrete set of methods we deploy functionally to solve problems defined *a priori*. Instead, we must question the reification of particular methods that has so marked the emergence of qualitative inquiry as a transdisciplinary field of inquiry (Kamberelis & Dimitriadis, 2005).

New Challenges Facing Focus Group Work

Guided by commitments to multifunctionality and a performative idiom, our primary goal in this chapter is to reimagine the roles of focus groups in qualitative inquiry from the ground up. Our approach is thus conceptual and transdisciplinary. Only occasionally and in passing do we discuss procedural and practical issues related to selecting focus group members, facilitating focus group discussion, or analyzing focus group transcripts. Many texts are available for readers who are looking for this kind of treatment (e.g., Barbour, 2008; Bloor et al., 2001; Krueger & Casey, 2008; Morgan, 1998; Schensul et al., 1999; Stewart, Shamdasani, & Rook, 2006). Instead, we both explore and attempt to move beyond recent historical and theoretical treatments of focus groups as "instruments" of qualitative research. In doing so, we try to show how, independent of their intended purposes, focus groups are almost always multivalent and contingent articulations of instructional, political, and empirical practices and effects. Focus groups thus offer unique insights into the possibilities of critical inquiry as deliberative, dialogic, democratic practice that is always already engaged in and with real-world problems and asymmetries in the distribution of economic, cultural, and social capital (e.g., Bourdieu & Wacquant, 1992).

Because the performative turn has decentered the research act—creating spaces that *de facto* collapse demarcations between and among research, pedagogy, and activism—reimagining qualitative inquiry largely involves seeing it more as a matter of asking and dwelling in new questions that are not necessarily answerable in finalizable ways. Although we look to start a discussion about the ways different strategies and practices can coalesce in productive and synergistic ways, we do not advocate an "anything goes" position. The specific competencies required by each dimension of focus group work—not to mention the articulation of multiple dimensions—demands specific sets of skills that are not easily or readily transferred from one dimension to another.

Our orientation to focus group work thus constitutes a productive challenge, encouraging a new angle of vision (among other things) on the politics of evidence. Mindful of the best impulses of the sociology of knowledge and the attendant co-implication of knowledge and power, the new politics of evidence, we believe, must attend to the specificity and autonomy of evidence in new ways. Recognizing that evidence never "speaks for itself," a key task today is finding ways to use evidence to challenge how we are situated and to help us develop new avenues of thought and practice. By locating focus groups within a performative idiom and at the intersection of research, pedagogy, and politics, we are provided no "alibis" for our work. Thus, for example, we cannot attend to the political dimension of our work without attending to the traditional empirical dimensions. And we cannot attend to either without attending to the ways our work circulates pedagogically. Focus group work is thus inevitably prismatic, with all three faces of the prism visible to some extent no matter which face we fix on or how direct our gaze.

Jean-Paul Sartre's notion of "bad faith" is instructive with regard to the reenvisaging the politics of evidence. By "bad faith," Sartre meant all the ways we refuse our basic, human freedoms through recourse to received and static ideas, beliefs, and roles. "Bad faith," Sartre wrote, "implies in essence the unity of a *single* consciousness" (2001, p. 208). Through bad faith, according to Stephen Priest, "we masquerade as fixed essences by the adoption of hypocritical social roles and inert value systems" (in Sartre, 2001, p. 204). To be in bad faith is to remain mired in either simple "facticity" or "transcendence"—to believe either that the empirical world is "as it is" and that we cannot move beyond it or to believe that we can move beyond our circumstances by simple force of will and imagination alone (Solomon, 2006). Either option lets us "off the hook" both for engaging our particular realities and circumstances and for imaginatively looking beyond them toward a broader "state" of human freedom. Either option robs us of our fundamental responsibilities to our fellow human beings.

The implications for how we live the politics of evidence are key here. As David Denter (2008) noted, a cornerstone of bad faith is the willingness to be "persuaded by weak evidence" (p. 84). That is, to arrive at conclusions *a priori* and then to search for evidence to support them. This means lowering one's "evidentiary standard[s]" in favor of one's preconceived dispositions (p. 84). In Sartre's own words, this approach to evidence is one that does not "*demand too much,*" that has a firm resolution "to count itself satisfied when it is barely persuaded, to force itself in decisions to adhere to uncertain truths" (Sartre quoted in Denter, 2008, p. 85). This impulse toward early and easy closure—to willfully "force" ourselves to accept evidence in service of positions we hold over time—is a cornerstone of "bad faith."

A new politics of evidence must avoid approaches to evidence that work either in the service of transcendent *a priori* ideals or brute empirical reductionism. We have seen both forms taken to extremes during the past decade or so, when evidence has been invalidated or discarded when not in service of neoconservative or progressive ideologies or when only the most reductive forms of "evidence-based" scholarship has been encouraged, funded, or published. In the end, we argue that focus groups have unique affordances that allow researchers to dwell in an evidentiary middle space, gathering empirical material while engaging in dialogues that help avoid premature consolidations of their understandings and explanations. This is a starting point for a new approach to evidence that respects the particularities and autonomies of evidence without assuming that evidence can ever speak for itself.

In short, the broader conception of focus group work we discuss in this chapter offers a useful intervention into debates around evidence. On the one hand, the collective nature of focus group discussions can help avoid the temptation to be too easily or quickly persuaded by weak evidence. Although groups can certainly reach consensus too easily—a point we will take up at the end of this chapter—focus group discussions allow us both to moderate and to calibrate this danger. On the other hand, a more expansive treatment of focus groups allows us to reflect continually on the particular limits of our methodological strategies.

By destabilizing how we understand focus groups—locating them at contingent intersections of research, pedagogy, and activism—we continually work against the tendency to reify our methodological strategies. Approaching focus groups in this way allows us to see our empirical material as always already refracted through multiple and often quite distinct prismatic faces, giving us more and more acute perspectives on the data we generate from them and how we interpret these data.

Focus Groups as Pedagogical, Political, and Research Practice

THE PEDAGOGICAL SURFACE OF FOCUS GROUP WORK: PAULO FREIRE AND BEYOND

In this section, we highlight how focus groups have been important pedagogical sites and instruments throughout history. Acknowledging that there are a plethora of historical examples of pedagogically motivated focus groups— from dialogues in the 5th-century BC Athenian Square to early African American book clubs to union-sponsored "study circles" to university study groups—we analyze the focus groups cultivated by Freire in Brazil to illustrate their pedagogical dimensions. Through analyses of these exemplars, we show how collective critical literacy practices were used to address local politics and concerns for social justice. Among other things, we foreground the ways in which Freire worked *with* people and not *on* them, thus modeling an important praxis disposition for contemporary educators and qualitative researchers (e.g., Barbour & Kitzinger, 1999). Pedagogy, in Freire's work, was the dominant function of focus groups. However, inquiry always nourished pedagogy, and pedagogy was seen as useful only to the extent that it mobilized activist work.

Freire's work was intensely practical as well as deeply philosophical. His most famous book, *Pedagogy of the Oppressed* (1970/1993), can be read as equal parts social theory, philosophy, and pedagogical method. His claims about education are foundational, rooted both in his devout Christian beliefs and his commitment to Marxism. Throughout *Pedagogy of the Oppressed*, Freire argued that the goal of education is to begin to name the world, to recognize that we are all "subjects" of our own lives and narratives, not "objects" in the stories of others. We must acknowledge the ways in which we, as human beings, are fundamentally charged with producing and transforming reality together. He argued further that those who do not acknowledge this, those who want to control and oppress, are committing a kind of epistemic violence.

Freire often referred to oppressive situations as *limit situations*—situations that people cannot imagine themselves beyond. Limit situations naturalize people's sense of oppression, giving it a kind of obviousness and immutability. As particularly powerful ideological state apparatuses, schools, of course, play a big role in this naturalization process. Freire argued that most education is based on the *banking model* where educators see themselves as authoritative subjects, depositing knowledge into their students, their objects. This implies an Enlightenment worldview, where subject and object are *a priori* independent of each other, and where subjects are objectified and thus dehumanized. Among other things, the banking model of education implies that "the teacher teaches and the students are taught" and that "the teacher knows everything and the students know nothing" (1970/1993, p. 54). The model operates according to monologic rather than dialogic logics, serving the interests of the *status quo* and functioning to promote business as usual rather than social change. As problematic as it is, the banking model provides the epistemological foundation for most contemporary educational institutions and practices.

In the place of a banking model of education, Freire offered an alternative model that was based on the elicitation of words (and concomitant ideas) that are fundamentally important in the lives of the people for whom educational activities are designed. He called these words *generative words*. He spent long periods in communities trying to understand community members' interests, investments, and concerns to elicit comprehensive sets of generative words. These words were then used as starting points for literacy learning, and literacy learning was deployed in the service of social and political activism. More specifically, generative words were paired with pictures that represented them and then interrogated by people in the community who used the terms both for what they revealed and concealed with respect to the circulation of multiple forms of capital. Freire encouraged the people both to explore how the meanings and effects of these words functioned in their lives and to conduct research on how their meanings and effects did (or could) function in different ways in different social and political contexts. The primary goal of these activities was to help people feel in control of their words and to be able to use them to exercise power over the material and ideological conditions of their own lives. Thus, Freire's literacy programs were designed not so much to teach functional literacy but to raise people's critical consciousness (*conscientization*) and to encourage them to engage in "praxis" or critical reflection inextricably linked to political action in the real world. He was clear to underscore that praxis is never easy and always involves power struggles, often violent ones.

That Freire insisted that the unending process of emancipation must be a collective effort is far from trivial. Central to this process is a faith in the power of dialogue. Importantly, dialogue for Freire was defined as collective reflection and action. He believed that dialogue, fellowship, and solidarity are essential to human liberation and transformation. "We can legitimately say that in the process of oppression someone oppresses someone else; we cannot legitimately say that in the process of revolution, someone liberates someone else, nor yet that that someone liberates himself, but rather that men in communion liberate each other" (1970/1993, p. 103). Only dialogue is capable of producing critical consciousness and praxis. Thus, all educational programs (and especially all language and literacy programs) must be dialogic. They must be spaces wherein "equally knowing subjects" (p. 31) engage in collective struggle in efforts to transform themselves and their worlds.

Within Freireian pedagogies, the development and use of generative words and phrases and the cultivation of *conscientization* are enacted in the context of locally situated "study circles" (or focus groups). The goal for the educator within these study circles is to engage, with people, in their lived realities, producing and transforming them. Again, for Freire, this kind of activity was part and parcel of literacy programs always already grounded in larger philosophical and social projects, those concerned with how people might more effectively "narrate" their own lives. In the context of these study circles, educators immerse themselves in the communities to which they have committed themselves. They try to enter into conversations, to elicit generative words and phrases together with their participants, and then to submit these words and phrases to intense reflection—presentation and re-presentation—to bring into relief lived contradictions that can then be acted upon.

To illustrate this kind of problem-posing education rooted in people's lived realities and contradictions, Freire created many research programs with participants, including one designed around the question of alcoholism. Because alcoholism was a serious problem in the city, a researcher showed an assembled group a photograph of a drunken man walking past three other men talking on the corner and asked them to talk about what was going on in the photograph. The group responded, in effect, by saying that the drunken man was a hard worker, the only hard worker in the group, and he was probably worried about his low wages and having to support his family. In their words, "he is a decent worker and a souse like us" (1970/1993, p. 99). The men in the study circle seemed to recognize themselves in this man, noting both that he was a "souse" but also situating his drinking in a politicized context. Alcoholism was "read" as a response to oppression and exploitation. The group went on to discuss these issues. This example of problem-posing pedagogy is quite different from (and we would argue much more effective than) a more didactic approach such as "character education," which would more likely involve "sermonizing" to people about their failings. Problem-posing education is proactive and designed to allow the people themselves to identify and generate solutions to the problems they face. The goal is to decode images and language in ways that eventually lead to questioning and transforming the material and social conditions of existence. Freire offered other examples as well, including showing people different (and contradictory) news stories covering the same event. In each case, the goal of problem–posing pedagogy is to help people understand the contradictions they live and to use these understandings to change their worlds.

In sum, focus groups have always been central to the kinds of radical pedagogies that have been advocated and fought for by such intellectual workers as Freire and his many followers (e.g., Henry Giroux, Joe Kincheloe, Jonathan Kozol, Peter McLaren). Organized around generative words and phrases and usually located within unofficial spaces, focus groups become sites of and for collective struggle and social transformation. As problem-posing formations, they operate locally to identify, interrogate, and change specific lived contradictions that have been rendered invisible by hegemonic power and knowledge regimes. Focus groups' operation also functions to reroute the circulation of power within hegemonic struggles and even to redefine what power is and how it works. Perhaps most importantly for our purposes here, the impulses that motivate focus groups in pedagogical domains or for pedagogical functions have important implications for reimagining and using focus groups as resources for constructing "effective histories" within qualitative research endeavors in the "seventh moment."

Although we have highlighted the pedagogical role of Freire's use of study circles, pedagogy is only a contingently situated function. That is, the three functions noted earlier can—and indeed, always have been—implicated in each other. Freire's study circles are excellent examples. Though designed as pedagogical activities, they were also and inextricably linked to activist-based and research-oriented activities. Recall that a starting point for Freire's work was to investigate and unearth the key generative phrases that indexed key social problems in the Brazilian communities in which Freire worked—clearly a form of research. And of course, his pedagogy was entirely entwined with an activist agenda—helping rural Brazilians learn to decode and then transform the world around them, especially its systemic oppressions.

In addition, the pedagogical uses of "focus groups" highlight several of the themes that run throughout this chapter, including those around the politics of evidence. The banking model of education, for example, draws broadly on what Sartre called "bad faith"—the recourse to static roles and stances defined *a priori*. As Freire repeatedly emphasized, such a model refuses our basic human freedoms, including the nature and effects of "authentic dialogue" which clearly is at the core of all of his work. When we adopt static roles, we refuse a transformative engagement with the world, opting instead for premature closure on key topics and issues. In contrast, the kind of pedagogically inflected focus groups advocated by Freire afford (even require) opportunities to engage with the world and with others in good faith.

THE POLITICAL SURFACE OF FOCUS GROUP WORK: CONSCIOUSNESS-RAISING GROUPS AND BEYOND

In this section, we offer descriptions and interpretations of focus groups in the service of radical political work designed within social justice agendas. In particular, we focus on how the consciousness-raising groups (CRGs) of second- and third-wave feminism have been deployed to mobilize empowerment agendas and to enact social change. This work complements and extends the explicitly pedagogical work we just discussed, especially in its active investment in community empowerment agendas and its commitment to praxis. It also provides important insights relevant for reimagining the possibilities of focus group activity within qualitative research endeavors. Where Freire's primary goal was to use literacy (albeit broadly defined) to mobilize oppressed groups to work against their oppression through praxis, the primary goal of the CRGs of second- and third-wave feminism was to build theory from the lived experiences of women that could contribute to their emancipation.

In our discussion of CRGs here, we draw heavily on Esther Madriz's retrospective analyses of second-wave feminist work as well as her own third-wave feminist empirical work. In both of these endeavors, Madriz focused on political (and politicized) uses of focus groups within qualitative inquiry, demonstrating that there has been a long history of deploying focus groups in consciousness-raising activities and for promoting social justice agendas within feminist and womanist traditions. Importantly, as forms of collective testimony, focus group participation has often been empowering for women, especially women of color (2000, p. 843). This is the case for several reasons. Focus groups decenter the authority of the researcher, allowing women safe spaces to talk about their own lives and struggles. These groups also allow women to connect with each other collectively, to share their own experiences, and to "reclaim their humanity" in a nurturing context (p. 843). Often, Madriz noted, women themselves take these groups over, reconceptualizing them in fundamental ways and with simple yet far-reaching political and practical consequences. In this regard, Madriz argued, "Focus groups can be an important element in the advancement of an agenda of social justice for women, because they can serve to expose and validate women's everyday experiences of subjugation and their individual and collective survival and resistance strategies" (p. 836). "Group interviews are particularly suited for uncovering women's daily experience through collective stories and resistance narratives that are filled with cultural symbols, words, signs, and ideological representations that reflect different dimensions of power and domination that frame women's quotidian experiences" (p. 839). As such, these groups constitute spaces for generating collective "testimonies," and these testimonies help both individual women and groups of women find or produce their own unique and powerful "voices."

As Madriz and others have noted, focus groups have multiple histories within feminist lines of thought and action. Soon after slavery ended in the United States, for example, churchwomen and teachers gathered to organize political work in the South (e.g., Gilkes, 1994). Similarly, early 20th–century "book clubs" were key sites for intellectual nourishment and political work (e.g., Gere, 1997). Mexican women have always gathered in kitchens and at family gatherings to commiserate and to work together to better their lives (e.g., Behar, 1993; Dill, 1994). And in 1927, Chinese women working in the San Francisco garment industry held focus group discussions to organize against their exploitation, which eventually led to a successful strike (e.g., Espiritu, 1997). Although we do not unpack these and other complex histories in this chapter, we do offer general accounts of the nature and function of focus groups within second- and third-wave feminism in the United States. These accounts pivot on the examination of several key original manifesto-like texts generated within the movement, which we offer as synecdoches of the contributions of a much richer, more complex, contradictory, and intellectually and politically "effective" set of histories.

Perhaps the most striking realization that emerges from examining some of the original texts of second-wave feminism are the explicitly self-conscious ways in which women used focus groups as "research" to build "theory" about women's everyday experiences and to deploy theory to enact political change. Interestingly but not surprisingly, this praxis-oriented work was dismissed by male radicals at the time as little more than "gossip" in the context of "coffee klatches." Ironically, this dismissal mirrors the ways in which qualitative inquiry is periodically dismissed for being "soft" or "subjective" or "nonscientific." Nevertheless, second-wave feminists persisted in building theory from the "standpoint" of women's lived experiences, and their efforts eventually became a powerful social force in the struggle for equal rights.

In many respects, the CRGs of second-wave feminism helped set the agenda for the next generation of feminist activism. As Hester Eisenstein (1984) noted, these groups helped bring personal issues in women's lives to the forefront of political discourse. Abortion, incest, sexual molestation, and domestic and physical abuse, for example, emerged from these groups as pressing social issues around which public policy and legislation had to be enacted. Importantly, these issues had previously been considered too personal and too intensely idiosyncratic to be taken seriously by men at the time, whether they were scholars, political activists, or politicians. By finding out which issues were most pressing in women's lives, CRGs were able to articulate what had previously been considered individual, psychological, and private matters to the agendas of local collectives and eventually to social and political agendas at regional and national levels.

Working within the movement(s) of third-wave feminism, Madriz used focus groups in powerful ways, some of which are evidenced in her 1997 book, *Nothing Bad Happens to Good Girls: Fear of Crime in Women's Lives*. In this book, Madriz discussed all the ways in which the fear of crime works to produce an insidious form of social control on women's lives. Fear of crime produces ideas and dispositions about what women "should" and "should not" do in public to protect themselves, enabling debilitating ideas about what constitutes "good girls" versus "bad girls" and severely constraining the range of everyday practices available to women.

With respect to research methods, Madriz called attention to the fact that most research findings on women's fear of crime had previously been generated from large survey studies of both men and women. This approach, she argued, severely limits the range of thought and experience that participants are willing to share and thus leads both to inaccurate and partial accounts of the phenomenon. In other words, it is hard to get people—women in particular—to talk about such sensitive topics as their own fears of assault or rape in uninhibited and honest ways in the context of oral or written surveys completed alone or in relation to a single social scientist interviewer. This general problematic is further complicated by differences in power relations between researchers and research participants that obtain as a function of age, social class, occupation, language proficiency, race, and so on.

To work against the various alienating forces that seem inherent in survey research and to collect richer and more complex accounts of experience with greater verisimilitude, Madriz used focus groups, noting that these groups provided a context where women could support each other in discussing their experiences of and fears and concerns about crime. Indeed, these groups do mitigate the intimidation, fear, and suspicion with which many women approach the one-on-one interview. In the words of one of Madriz's participants, "When I am alone with an interviewer, I feel intimidated, scared. And if they call me over the telephone, I never answer their questions. How do I know what they really want or who they are?" (1997, p. 165). In contrast, focus groups afford women much safer and more supportive contexts within which to explore their lived experiences and the consequences of these experiences with other women who will understand what they are saying intellectually, emotionally, and viscerally.

This idea of safe and supportive spaces ushers in another important dimension of focus group work within third-wave feminist research, namely the importance of constituting groups in ways that mitigate alienation, create solidarity, and enhance community building. To achieve such ends, Madriz argued for the importance of creating homogenous groups in race, class, age, specific life experiences, and so on.

In relation to this point, CRGs of second-wave feminism suffered from essentializing tendencies (whether politically strategic or not) that ended up glossing the many, different, and even contradictory experiences of many women and groups of women under the singular sign of the homogenous "woman." More importantly and more problematically, this sign was constructed largely from the lived experiences of White middle-class women. Acknowledging the need to see and to celebrate more variability in this regard, third-wave feminist researchers refracted and multiplied the "standpoints" from which testimonies might flow and voices might be produced. Although many held onto the post-positivist ideal of "building theory" from lived experience, researchers such as Madriz pushed for theory that accounted more fully for the local, complex, and nuanced nature of lived experience, which is always already constructed within intersections of power relations produced by differences between and among multiple social categories (e.g., race, ethnicity, national origin, class, gender, age, sexual orientation, etc.). In the end, a primary goal of focus group activity within third-wave feminist research is not to offer prescriptive conclusions but to highlight the productive potentials (both oppressive and emancipatory) of particular social contexts (with their historically produced and durable power relations) within which such prescriptions typically unfold. In this regard, Madriz's work is a synecdoche for third-wave feminist work more broadly conceived—particularly work conducted by women of color such as Dorinne Kondo, Smadar Lavie, Ruth Behar, Aiwa Ong, and Lila Abu-Lughod.

The nature and functions of CRGs within second- and third-wave feminism offer many important insights into the potentials of focus group work. Building on Madriz's political reading of focus groups, and more specifically on the constructs of *testimony* and *voice*, we now highlight some of these potentials. One key purpose of focus groups within feminist work has been to elicit and validate collective testimonies and group resistance narratives. Such testimonies and narratives have been used by women (and could be used by any subjugated group) "to unveil specific and little-researched aspects of women's daily existences, their feelings, attitudes, hopes, and dreams" (Madriz, 2000, p. 836). Another key emphasis of focus groups within feminist and womanist traditions has been the discovery or production of *voice*. Because focus groups often result in the sharing of similar stories of everyday experience, struggle, rage, and the like, they often end up validating individual voices that had previously been constructed within and through mainstream discourses as idiosyncratic, selfish, and even evil. Because they foreground and exploit the power of testimony and voice, focus groups can become sites for overdetermining collective identity as strategic political practice—to create a critical mass of visible solidarity that seems a necessary first step toward social and political change.

Focus groups within feminist and womanist traditions have also mitigated the Western tendency to separate thinking and feeling, thus creating possibilities for reimagining knowledge as distributed, relational, embodied, and sensuous. Viewing knowledge in this light brings into relief the complexities and contradictions that are always involved in field work. It also brings into view the relations between power and knowledge and thus insists that qualitative research is always already political—implicated in social critique and social change.

Either from necessity or for strategic purposes, feminist work has always taken the constitutive power of *space* into account. To further work against asymmetrical power relations and the processes of "othering," meetings are almost always held in safe spaces where women feel comfortable, important, and validated. This is a particularly important consideration when working with women who have much to lose from their participation such as undocumented immigrants, victims of abuse, or so-called deviant youth.

Finally, the break from second-wave to third-wave feminism both challenged the monolithic treatment of difference under the sign of "woman" that characterized much of second-wave thinking and highlighted the importance of creating focus groups that are relatively "homogeneous" with respect to life histories, perceived needs, desire, race, social class, region, age, and so forth because such groups are more likely to achieve the kind of solidarity and collective identity requisite for producing "effective histories" (Foucault, 1984). Although coalition building across more heterogeneous groups of women may be important in some instances, focused intellectual and political work is often most successful when enacted by people with similar needs, desires, struggles, and investments.

Such work does justice to the unique and often extremely complex vantage points of (often) subordinated groups. According to Patricia Hill Collins (1991), for example, African American women have often been expected to speak either from the vantage point of "woman" or "African American." Historically, these positions have spoken to the needs and concerns of "White women" and "Black men" respectively. For Collins, it is critical to do justice to and to acknowledge the ways Black women have their own needs, concerns, and experiences, which need to be addressed in their specificity. In this regard, she argued for what she calls "standpoint epistemologies" or knowledge frameworks generated from specific vantage points. The kind of focus group work envisioned and enacted by Madriz and other third-wave feminist researchers goes a long way toward imagining, enabling, and constructing such knowledge frameworks.

Yet, focus groups also allow us to challenge the limits of such knowledge claims. At their most reductive extreme, standpoint epistemologies essentialize the truth claims of particular subjects and create an imaginary kind of collective experience. Additionally, celebrating and generalizing situated individual experience can degenerate very quickly into a kind of uncritical relativism—an "anything goes" approach to knowledge that privileges individual biography and history in ways that reduce knowledge claims only to questions of power. Focus groups provide an important potential corrective here, allowing for both a collective articulation of particular subject positions, as discussed earlier, while opening them to contestation. In other words, focus groups allow people to speak in both collective and individual voices—creating space for traditionally marginalized groups to articulate their particular experience while allowing people to argue and disagree and ultimately produce what Michelle Fine calls "strong objectivity" (more on this later).

Politicized forms of focus group work are perhaps best evidenced today in various participatory action research (PAR) projects. In the United States, Fine has helped form various "research collectives" with youth at the City University of New York (CUNY) Graduate Center during the past several years, around several key contemporary issues (Cammarota & Fine, 2008). For example, Fine brought together multiethnic groups of suburban and urban high schools for *Echoes of Brown,* a study of the legacies of *Brown v. Board of Education.* Originally a study of the so-called achievement gap, the framework soon shifted, largely because of the focus group–like sessions that drew the participants together: "At our first session, youth from six suburban high schools and three urban high schools immediately challenged the frame of our research" (Torre & Fine, 2006, p. 273). After discussion, the framework changed from one of the "achievement gap"—a construct the youth felt put too much of the onus on themselves—to the "opportunity gap."

These research collectives create spaces for youth to challenge themselves and others in ongoing dialogue—a key affordance of focus group work, as noted earlier. "As we moved through our work, youth were able to better understand material, or to move away from experiences that were too uncomfortable, or to make connections across seemingly different positions" (Torre & Fine, 2006, p. 276). Ultimately, these youth were able to carry out both empirical projects around "push out rates" and disciplinary practices in schools as well as to produce powerful individual and collective testimonies about their own perspectives on and experiences of schooling, 50 years after *Brown*. Key here was the PAR "under construction" principle, the idea that opinions, ideas, beliefs, and practices are always expected to change and grow (Torre & Fine, 2006, p. 274). See Julio Cammarota and Michelle Fine (2008) for additional examples of this principle at work.

Fine and others have done their work largely in the United States, but Torre and Fine link PAR explicitly to histories of worldwide political struggle. "Based largely on the theory and practice of Latino activist scholars, PAR scholars draw from neo-Marxist, feminist, queer, and critical race theory . . . to articulate methods and ethics that have local integrity and stretch topographically to site/cite global patters on domination and resistance" (2006, p. 271). They call particular attention to Colombian sociologist Fals Borda, whom many consider the "founder" of PAR. In so doing, Torre and Fine underscore the international scope of focus group work, particularly around their political uses.

Indeed, if we look elsewhere around the world, we quickly realize that the original impulses of feminist consciousness-raising work have been taken up and re-inflected in multiple ways for many purposes within various PAR initiatives. In Australia, for example, the "Deadly Maths Consortium" created by Thomas Cooper and Annette Barturo is a PAR project that has been quite effective in improving mathematics learning among indigenous peoples (e.g., Cooper et al., 2008). In New Zealand, Russell Bishop has worked both tirelessly and very successfully to enact PAR initiatives designed to create positive change in classrooms, curricula, schools, and education policy based on caring relationships where power is shared among self-determining individuals within non-dominating relations of interdependence. Within his PAR focus groups, where cultural traditions are honored, learning is dialogic, and participants are connected to one another through the establishment of a common vision for what constitutes excellence in educational outcomes—all characteristics that are paramount to the educational performance of Maori students (e.g., Bishop et al., 2006). And indigenous scholars in the United States have used various forms of collaborative and participatory action research to work against the effects of colonization and to pursue their own liberation collectively and systematically (e.g., Grand, 2004; Wilson & Yellow Bird, 2005).

We have highlighted here the political function of focus groups—the ways these groups allow participants to coalesce around key issues, coproducing knowledges and strategies for transcending their circumstances. As noted throughout, however, other functions are embedded in these practices as well. For example, the theory building we emphasized relies on the kinds of critical, pedagogical practices associated with Freire and others. (Torre and Fine also explicitly link PAR to the work of Freire). The interactions between participants in consciousness-raising and other feminist groups, for example, are deeply pedagogical, as knowledge is co-created in situated and dialogic ways. Finally, these groups often engage in inquiry, especially inquiry focused on understanding asymmetrical power relations that render both women and particular groups of women as inferior in any number of ways. Although they have often been caricatured as uncritical support groups, consciousness-raising and other feminist groups have always been intensely concerned with producing new and useful knowledge about issues such as domestic violence or rape or workplace marginalization that were often broadly misconstrued within "official knowledges." And the PAR work we have mentioned continues to build on and extend the productive linkages among pedagogy, politics, and inquiry.

Fine's notion of "strong objectivity" is helpful for this discussion. According to Fine, we must work toward new forms of objectivity informed by the insights and advances of critical scholarship—particularly scholarship about the "situatedness" of all knowledge. For Fine, this reflection can be a source of better, more honest, and more "objective" accounts of our work. Drawing on the work of Sandra Harding, Fine argues that "strong objectivity" is "achieved when researchers work aggressively through their own positionality, values, and predispositions, gathering as much evidence as possible, from many distinct vantage points, all in an effort not to be guided, unwittingly, by predispositions and the pull of biography" (Fine, 2006, p. 89). Such an approach helps researchers become more aware of potential "blind spots" that they may "import, wittingly and not, to their studies." Such work can be usefully done in "work groups," where empirical material can be discussed, pulled apart, and cleared of the "fog of unacknowledged subjectivities." These work groups seem to share the best impulses of focus groups, as participants forge new kinds of understandings and try to avoid premature closure.

In sum, the various practices and insights of second- and third-wave feminist and the various trajectories they have spawned (notably PAR) move us further down the road of imagining and enacting: (a) a commitment to morally sound, praxis-oriented research, (b) the strategic use of eclectic constellations of theories, methods, and research strategies, (c) the cultivation of dialogic relationships in the field, (d) the production of polyvocal non-representational texts, and (e) the conduct of mindful inquiry attuned to what is sacred in and about life and text.

The Inquiry Surface of Focus Group Work: From Positivism to Poststructuralism and Beyond

Interest in focus groups in the social sciences has ebbed and flowed during the past 60 or so years. In many respects, the first really visible use of focus groups for conducting social science research may be traced back to the work of Paul Lazarsfeld and Robert Merton. Their focus group approach emerged in 1941, as the pair embarked on a government-sponsored project to assess media effects on attitudes toward America's involvement in World War II. Working within the Office of Radio Research at Columbia University, they recruited groups of people to listen and respond to radio programs designed to boost "morale" for the war effort (e.g., Merton, 1987, p. 552). Originally, the pair asked participants to push buttons to indicate their satisfaction or dissatisfaction with the content of the radio programs. Because the data yielded from this work could help them answer "what" questions but not "why" questions about participants' choices, they used focus groups as forums for getting participants to explain why they responded in the ways that they did. Importantly, Lazarsfeld and Merton's use of focus groups strategies for data collection always remained secondary to (and less legitimate than) the various quantitative strategies they also used. In other words, they used focus groups in exploratory ways to generate new questions that could be operationalized in quantitative work or simply to complement or annotate the findings yielded from their mostly large-scale survey studies.

In philosophy of science terms, the early use of focus groups as resources for conducting research was highly conservative in nature. This is not at all surprising when we consider that Lazarsfeld and Merton's work was funded by the military and included "interviewing groups of soldiers in Army camps about their responses to specific training films and so-called morale films" (Merton, 1987, p. 554). Their research also included many other media reception studies on topics such as why people made war bond pledges or how people responded to government-sponsored advertisements. The goal of most of this work was use knowledge about people's beliefs and decision-making processes to develop increasingly effective forms of propaganda—inquiry in the service of politics.

Although both their goals and the techniques merit harsh criticism (especially from progressive and radical camps), two key ideas from Lazarsfeld's and Merton's work have become central to the legacy of using focus groups within qualitative research: (a) capturing people's responses in real space and time in the context of face-to-face interactions and (b) strategically "focusing" interview prompts based on themes that are generated in these face-to-face interactions and that are considered particularly important to researchers.

The kind of focus group research conducted by scholars such as Lazarsfeld and Merton continued as a powerful force within corporate-sponsored market research, but it all but disappeared within the field of sociology in the middle-part of the 20th century, only to reemerge in the early 1980s in the form of "audience analysis" research. When it did reemerge, it was no longer wed to (or used in the service of) predominantly quantitative-oriented research, a fact that Merton bemoaned: "One gains the impression that focus-group research is being mercilessly misused as quick-and-easy claims for the validity of the research are not subjected to further, quantitative test . . ." (Merton, 1987, p. 557).

Criticisms such as these notwithstanding, audience analysis research was and is decidedly interpretive and increasingly dialogic and emancipatory. Its primary goal is to understand the complexities involved in how people understand and interpret media texts. Its methods are almost exclusively qualitative. In contrast to Lazarsfeld's and Merton's work, which focused on expressed content, audience analysis researchers typically focus on group dynamics, believing that the meanings constructed within groups of viewers are largely socially constructed. In a groundbreaking audience analysis study, for example, David Morley (1980) attempted to chart all the various ways in which groups of viewers from different social and economic classes responded to the popular television show, *Nationwide*. He conducted content analyses of many episodes of the show which included focus group interviews with people who had just watched these episodes, and he compared their responses with his analysis of the show's content. Working from within a social constructionist framework (e.g., Berger & Luckmann, 1966), Morley's use of focus groups was strategic: "The choice to work with groups rather than individuals . . . was made on the grounds that much individually based interview research is flawed by a focus on individuals as social atoms divorced from their social context" (1980, p. 97). For Morley and other scholars interested in audience reception practices, focus groups are invaluable because they afford insights into how meanings get constructed *in situ,* and thus allow researchers "to discover how interpretations were collectively constructed through talk and the interchange between respondents in the group situation—rather than to treat individuals as the autonomous repositories of a fixed set of individual 'opinions' isolated from their social context" (p. 97).

Janice Radway also used focus groups to great effect in her pioneering research on the reading practices of romance novel enthusiasts that resulted in her 1984 book, *Reading the Romance*. The research took place in and around a local bookstore, and Radway's participants included the storeowner and a group of 42 women who frequented the store and were regular romance readers. Like Morley, Radway developed a mixed-method research design that included text analysis and focus group interviews. Assisted by the bookstore owner (Dot), Radway was able to tap into the activity dynamics of existing networks of women who were avid romance novel readers. These women interacted frequently with Dot about newly published novels, and they interacted with each other as well. Radway simply "formalized" some of these ongoing social activities to generate a systematic and rich store of information about the social circumstances, specific reading practices, attitudes, reading preferences, and multiple and contradictory functions of romance reading among the women she studied. She took her cues about what books to read and what issues to focus discussions around from Dot and her other participants. She read all of the books that her participants read. She talked with many of them informally whenever they were at the bookstore together. And she conducted formal focus groups.

Among other things, Radway noted the importance of group dynamics in how different romance novels were interpreted and used. Even though the novels themselves were read privately, sharing their responses to the novels both in informal conversations and formal focus group discussions was very important to the women. Radway also came to understand how important belonging to a reading group was for mitigating the stigma often associated with the practice of reading romance novels: "Because I knew beforehand that many women are afraid to admit their preference for romantic novels for fear of being scorned as illiterate or immoral, I suspected that the strength of numbers might make my informants less reluctant about discussing their obsession" (1984, p. 252). Finally, the ways in which Radway positioned herself within the reading groups was crucial. She noted, for example, that when she was gently encouraging and when she backgrounded her own involvement, "the conversation flowed more naturally as the participants disagreed among themselves, contradicted one another, and delightedly discovered that they still agreed about many things" (p. 48).

All of the various strategies that Radway deployed helped to mobilize the collective energy of the group and to generate kinds and amounts of data that are often difficult, if not impossible, to generate through individual interviews and even observations. Additionally, these strategies—and participation in the focus groups themselves—helped to build a stronger and more effective collective with at least local political teeth. Radway concluded her book-length treatment of her romance novel project with a hopeful yet unfinalized call to praxis, noting, "It is absolutely essential that we who are committed to social change learn not to overlook this minimal but nonetheless legitimate form of protest. . . . and to learn how best to encourage it and bring it to fruition" (1984, p. 222)

If Radway began to outline the political, ethical, and praxis potentials of focus groups within qualitative inquiry, Patti Lather attempted to push the "limit conditions" of such work even further. In their book, *Troubling the Angels,* for example, Lather and Chris Smithies (1997) explored the lives, experiences, and narratives of 25 women living with HIV/AIDS. The book is filled with overlapping and contradictory voices that grew out of five years of focus group interviews conducted within different "support groups" in five major cities in Ohio. Lather and Smithies met and talked with their women participants at birthday parties and holiday get-togethers, hospital rooms and funerals, baby showers and picnics. Group dynamics among these women were unpredictable, emotionally charged (even ravaging), and changed constantly across the project. In what she calls a "postbook," Lather (2001, p. 210) acknowledged experiencing at least two "breakdowns" as she bore witness to the women's experiences and stories. Insofar as "breakdowns" are central to human understanding (Heidegger, 1927/1962), clearly these groups were surfaces of or for inquiry and pedagogy for researchers and research participants alike.

In both "strategic" and "found" ways, more organized occasions for "collecting data" constantly blurred into the "practices of everyday life" (deCerteau, 1984). Among other things, this social fact transformed the very nature of the focus groups these researchers conducted, rendering them more like rich and powerful conversations among people who cared deeply for each other. Yet Lather and Smithies were careful to work against the tendency to sentimentalize or romanticize their roles or their work by enacting what Lather (2001, p. 212) referred to as a "recalcitrant rhetoric" to counteract tendencies toward *verstehen* or simple empathy. Lather and Smithies tried to remain aware that the goals and rewards of their involvement in the groups were very different from the goals and rewards of their research participants. Their participants, for example, wanted to produce a "K-Mart" book, a collection of autobiographies or autoethnographies of "lived experience." Lather and Smithies were more interested in theorizing their participants' experiences and foregrounding the political (especially micropolitical) dimensions and effects of these experiences. According to Lather, these competing goals were constantly negotiated in focus groups. This pedagogic and political activity resulted in producing a book that embodies a productive, if uncomfortable/uncomforting tension between the two competing goals.

Although much of this book is devoted to troubling the waters of ethnographic representation, the experience of conducting fieldwork primarily through focus groups also troubled the waters of research practice. In this regard, Lather and Smithies integrated sociological, political, historical, therapeutic, and pedagogical practices and discourses in their work with the women they studied. In her postbook, for example, Lather claims to have looked constantly for "the breaks and jagged edges of methodological practices from which we might draw useful knowledge for shaping present practices of a feminist ethnography in excess of our codes but, still, always already forces already active in the present" (2001, pp. 200–201).

One of the most interesting sections of the book for our purposes in this chapter is one in which Lather and Smithies cultivate what they call a "methodology of getting lost":

> At some level, the book is about getting lost across the various layers and registers, about not finding one's way into making a sense that maps easily onto our usual ways of making sense. Here we all get lost: the women, the researchers, the readers, the angels, in order to open up present frames of knowing to the possibilities of thinking differently. (Lather & Smithies, 1997, p. 52)

Although these reflections refer to the book itself rather than the process of conducting the research that led to it, they apply equally well to working with research participants in the field in the sense that the reflections index the political, pedagogical, and ethical dimensions of all practices and all knowledge. For example, Lather and Smithies refused to position themselves as grand theorists and to interpret or explain the women's lives to them. Instead, they granted "weight to lived experience and practical consciousness by situating both researcher and researched as bearers of knowledge while simultaneously attending to the 'price' we pay for speaking out of discourses of truth, forms of rationality, effects of knowledge, and relations of power" (Lather 2001, p. 215). Through their tactical positioning, Lather and Smithies both challenged the researcher's right to know and interpret the experiences of others while they interrupted and got in the way of their participants' attempts to narrate their lives through a kind of innocent ethnographic realism where their voices simply spoke for themselves in some way (e.g., reading AIDS as the work of God's will).

Additionally, Lather and Smithies acknowledged their impositions and admitted that a different kind of book—a K-Mart book—might have pleased their participants more. But such a book would have taken Lather and Smithies outside their own predilections and perhaps competencies as researchers, and is thus a task easier stated than accomplished. A K-Mart book has never been written, and Lather's (2007) follow-up to *Troubling the Angels* is even more theoretical than the original volume, highlighting the difficulties of accomplishing multiple interpretive tasks and embodying multiple voices simultaneously.

The various relational and rhetorical tactics enacted by Lather and Smithies bring to light the very complicated and sometimes troubling micro-politics that are part and parcel of research practice in the seventh, eighth, and ninth moments of qualitative inquiry (Denzin & Lincoln, 2005)—whether we are willing to see and enact these micro-politics in our own work. Lather and Smithies remind us constantly that there are no easy separations between "researcher" and "researched"; that research itself is always already relational, political, pedagogical, and ethical work; and that we have no alibis for thinking and acting otherwise lest we follow one or another path of "bad faith." There is no privileged place from which to experience and to report on experiences objectively. Only positions in dialogue. And even then, the issue of whose positions get foregrounded and whose get backgrounded remains a bit of a black hole that challenges the limits of dialogue, transparency, and self-reflexivity, which are inevitably and forever threatened by the possible (and usually invisible) reemergence of "bad faith." Notwithstanding our critique here, more than most other research of which we are aware, Lather and Smithies' work offers us ways to think about research that transcends and transforms the potentials of using focus groups for revisioning epistemology, interrogating the relative purchase of both lived experience and theory, reimagining ethics within research practice, and enacting field work in ways that are more attuned to its spiritual, even sacred, dimensions. And perhaps even more than this, the weaknesses and limitations of Lather and Smithies's work index the many experiential, epistemological, ethical, theoretical, and all-too-human challenges we still face in conducting seventh, eighth, and ninth moment qualitative inquiry (Denzin & Lincoln, 2005). In this regard, focus groups surface the dialogic possibilities inherent in but often thwarted both in everyday social life and in research practice. What happens in focus groups can help researchers work against premature consolidation of their understandings and explanations, thus signaling the limits of reflexivity and the importance of intellectual/empirical modesty as forms of ethics and praxis. Such modesty can allow researchers to engage at least partially in "doubled practices" where we *both* listen to the attempts of others as they make sense of their lives *and* also resist the seductive qualities of "too easy" constructs such as "voice" or "faith" by recognizing and showing how experience itself (as well as our accounts of it) are always constituted within one or another "grand narrative" (Lather, 2001, p. 218). No less than life itself, doing social science has no guarantees.

Focus Groups as Contingent, Synergistic Articulations

We'd like now to highlight what we view as some of the more productive possibilities and some of the more serious dangers in conducting focus group research. Framing focus groups as contingent and often synergistic articulations of research, pedagogy, and politics seems to allow a clearer understanding of both.

First, a reconceptualized notion of focus groups can work to avoid premature closure at the institutional level. To return to the earlier discussion, if done in "bad faith," with an eye toward early closure, such groups scaffold "group think," registering and generating false notions of cohesion. For example, a certain narrow notion of focus group work has been used to construct notions of singular "publics" in popular political discussions. Recall, for example, the ways focus groups were used to gauge responses instantly during the 2008 presidential debates on CNN. This kind of brute empiricism—responses were gathered instantly and often immediately quantified on a modified sliding scale—was used to construct notions of what a supposed cross-section of Americans thought about the candidates. This impulse toward early closure and consolidation in focus group work can lead to the construction of construct *communities* that are facile and can be readily used toward any number of political ends. Understanding focus groups as contingent, synergistic articulations can help mitigate this problem.

Additionally, a more robust and complex version of focus groups can be used to resist local, institutional closure. Writing about the specificity of feminism (a movement we discussed above), Ellen Messer-Davidow (2002) writes, "To launch any feminist-studies project (whether it is to be located in the academy, the community, or both), individuals have to take collective action, and to take collective action they have to form a collective identity. Collective identity is not a conceptual product, like a job description, that individuals discuss, write up, and perform; it is the practical work of producing linkages among themselves while they negotiate their project's forms, objectives, and strategies" (p. 124). The practical work of producing and negotiating linkages was evidenced (in part) in the CRGs that were a part of second-wave feminism. As she shows, however, the academic incorporation of feminism was accomplished by a certain kind of institutional "formatting" that took up the smoother contours of the movement, producing an ever-proliferating meta-discourse with its own questions, rules, and feedback relays (p. 207). Keeping the multiple genealogies of focus groups in mind—including their co-implicated but distinct trajectories in research, pedagogy, and activism—might allow us to resist such institutional closure and reengage with a new and more productive version of the politics of evidence.

Second, although focus groups are becoming a larger part of public discourse, they are increasingly under new kinds of surveillance from within the academy (from institutional review boards [IRBs], funding agencies, publication venues, etc.). Ironically perhaps, the deployment of focus groups in the public sphere seems to have revivified and magnified the dangers of long-standing concerns about issues such as *anonymity*. Indeed, anonymity has been a long-standing cornerstone of academic research—in particular, the ability of research participants to choose not to be identified in research reports or to have sensitive, personal information kept confidential. This kind of anonymity can usually be preserved in one-on-one interviews if the interviewer adheres to given protocols. Yet, in a group setting, trust and a commitment to confidentiality are more widely distributed. Indeed, the distribution of trust, as well as knowledge and experience, constitutes part of the power of focus groups. Yet, it also embodies their potential dangers. This paradox has surfaced repeatedly in our own work and the work of our students.

Greg Dimitriadis, for example, has served as major advisor and committee member for two doctoral students who used focus groups as a major tool for collecting empirical material. One student, Dr. Getnet Tizazu Fetene, studied attitudes toward HIV/AIDS among college-aged youth in Ethiopia. The second student, Dr. Touorouzou Some, investigated attitudes toward university cost-sharing among college-aged youth in Burkina Faso. Both projects were flagged by the IRB as potentially "high risk" endeavors, even though both students had been proactive in arguing that these very commonly discussed topics were not likely to cause undue stress among participants. The question of anonymity was central among the IRB's concerns. Originally, some suggested that one-on-one interviews should be conducted instead of focus groups. The logic was sound. Even if the researcher told members of the group that information shared during these sessions must remain confidential, they could not guarantee it. So why take the risk?

What was really at issue became clearer when Dimitriadis talked with the IRB. Unfamiliar with focus group work, some members thought focus groups were simply a way to conduct multiple interviews simultaneously—almost as a time-saving measure. Dimitriadis had to provide information about focus groups—including the fact that participants often feel more comfortable in groups, thereby diminishing the possibility of personal vulnerability and risk. He also had to make the point that some kinds of information are more likely to emerge from focus group discussions (as opposed to one-on-one interviews) including (and perhaps especially) information about sex and sexuality. Although the question of anonymity remained a thorny one to the IRB, it was reconstructed (and thus resolved) in the following way: The potential risk of participants breaking anonymity in focus groups was outweighed by the potential information that could only be gleaned from group interviews. Importantly, this demanded educating powerful administrators not entirely familiar with this methodological tool about its particular benefits—an interesting twist on the pedagogic function we have addressed in this chapter.

The point is worth underscoring. As is well documented by now (see this volume), IRBs can be problematic institutions for qualitative researchers because they are often targeted toward positivist and medical kinds of research. It is important to remember, however, that these boards are always balancing potential "risk/reward" ratios when approving this work. For example, such ratios are an explicit concern when, say, approaching clinical tests for a new drug. Qualitative researchers can often appropriate this language when "road bumps" such as this one around anonymity emerge. Such boards often have to be educated (quite literally) about different data collection techniques and have the potential benefits both to the study and the field explained. These can then be explicitly balanced against potential risks such as this one around anonymity. Such an approach, we think, is more useful than simply stating (again) that these boards "don't get it." It is often a question of moving across different language fields.

The rewards for this project on HIV/AIDS in Ethiopia were profound and highlight many of the issues thread throughout. To begin with, Fetene was *not* able to secure one-on-one interviews with his participants—a technique he hoped to use to complement his focus groups. As he reported, many of the students were reluctant (even unwilling) to discuss such sensitive material with a partial stranger in a close, interpersonal setting. This response defied the position of the IRB, which assumed one-on-one interviews would offer a more comfortable, less stressful interviewing context. Perhaps more importantly, Fetene's the empirical material yielded from the focus groups proved highly revealing, in ways that personally challenged him and his co-researcher Dr. Muluemebet Zenebe (who conducted the groups with young women). In particular, many of these young people—specifically, the young women—talked very openly about their romantic relationships, astonishing both researchers and forcing them to reevaluate their own beliefs and understandings about the culture in which they both grew up and lived. From a traditionally conservative culture, Fetene was initially surprised by how openly these young Ethiopian men talked about sex. His female co-researcher initially assumed these men were just trying to "show off" for each other—until she conducted focus groups with a group of young women. To her self-proclaimed astonishment, these discussions largely mirrored the discussions among the young men. This "evidence" forced both researchers to reconsider and revise long-held assumptions about their own culture and society.

Recall the discussions of "bad faith" and the politics of evidence we presented earlier in the chapter. Focus groups can be powerful sites or tools for interrupting and taking us beyond our own calcified positions—the temptation to be persuaded by weak evidence or *a priori* beliefs. In this case, focus group evidence proved transformative in moving both researchers past their own beliefs about Ethiopian youth and sexuality and the culture in which they were both so deeply immersed. Moreover, these discussions challenged the ways in which the global discourse around HIV/AIDS is presently constituting itself. Although much of this discourse has assumed that a lack of "knowledge" about safe sex is a key issue, these focus groups disrupted such assumptions, with young people stating again and again that they knew about the importance (for example) of condom use. These youth raised other key issues, including changing mores around sex. Again, and importantly, the focus group interviewing context was central to the emergence of these knowledges and insights and for disrupting the kind of "commonsense" closure that often surrounds discussions of so-called sensitive topics. Also worth noting here is that a project that began focused primarily on *inquiry* quickly took on communitarian, political, and pedagogical valences for researchers and research participants alike.

Finally, we would like to say a bit more about the synergistic potential of focus group work. This potential was realized in highly visible ways in a project conducted by one of George Kamberelis's students, Graciana Astazarian. The project focused on the experiences and needs of recent Mexican American immigrants to a small community in the midwestern United States. Largely because it had an abundance of good manufacturing jobs, Mexican American immigrants were moving to this community in large numbers. However, because the influx of new immigrants was happening so fast, little or no infrastructure for supporting the health, education, transportation, employment, linguistic, and cultural needs of these people existed. Astazarian's project focused on understanding these needs. She conducted focus groups with small groups of women in a variety of contexts—homes, community centers, churches, and even the waiting line at the Latino Coalition office. Several issues emerged from the focus groups as particularly important problems for the women interviewed: learning English, transportation, language barriers in school and health care settings, and discrimination at work. We focus on the discussions of two of these problems—English language learning and transportation—for the ways in which they draw out the synergistic potential afforded by focus group work. Indeed, discussions about these (and other) problems almost always surfaced a good deal of complexity, nuance, and contradiction.

Many factors contributed to problems with English language learning among these new immigrants—from biological ones (learning disabilities) to life historical ones (bad school experiences) to social ones (linguistic and cultural imperialism) to educational ones (poor instructors and instructional materials) to economic ones (the cost of instruction). Discussing these various factors created tremendous solidarity among the participants. These discussions also surfaced some of the hidden, macro-level factors such as linguistic and cultural imperialism, which both surprised and gratified group members.

Astazarian's focus groups generated considerable political synergy around the issue of English language learning. Several participants created a manifesto of English language learning needs and desires that included: (a) having more opportunities for adult education; (b) having more financial aid for English classes; (c) having ESL classes at night and not just during the day; (d) having ESL classes that were dynamic, fun and encouraged oral communication; (e) creating different levels of classes to meet the different levels and needs of students; (f) having amnesty for undocumented immigrants; and (g) having more bilingual workers at most community agencies.

This group of participants also lobbied the Latino Coalition and other advocacy agencies to push for more translators in hospitals and clinics. Group members composed a letter to the editor of the local newspaper about the need for translation services in these sites. And they assembled and distributed an information sheet about the documentation required to open a bank account at most local banks. Within two years, and largely motivated by this focus group work, many positive changes occurred in the community. The nature and scope of ESL classes available in the community changed considerably and along the lines suggested. The Community Health Clinic hired three bilingual staff members. The Industrial Federal Credit Union hired five bilingual tellers.

Transportation to work, school, health care facilities, and so on was another key problem faced by these new immigrants. Public transportation was both scarce and unreliable. Underground car services run by entrepreneurial Mexican American men were expensive and unreliable. In discussing these problems, participants surfaced even more serious problems such as sexism and economic exploitation within the Mexican American community. They went on to talk about the fracturing effects these forces had on community solidarity. Within weeks of the initial discussion of this transportation problem, a group of women created a co-op ride sharing system. This system grew and became more efficient over time. Among other things, the co-op forced mercenary drivers to lower their fees.

Participants also instigated discussions of sexism that emerged in the initial focus group sessions, especially the oppression resulting because many husbands discouraged (even prevented) their wives from getting licenses. In about a year, women who had licenses began to teach women who didn't have licenses how to drive and arranged for them to take their driving tests.

As these examples show, a contingent and unpredictable potential for synergy exists within focus group work. This synergy often constitutes "breakdowns" (Heidegger, 1927/1962) that disclose complexities, nuances, and contradictions embodied in "lived experience." It often indexes social and economic forces such as linguistic imperialism, economic exploitation, and sexism that often get glossed or explained away by one or another cultural logic—thus introducing new versions of the politics of evidence that mitigate the effects of "bad faith" (Sartre, 2001) and allow neither researchers nor research participants any alibis for their actions. These positive potentials are, of course, accompanied by attendant dangers. Given how power operates within relations of dominance and oppression, naming and talking back to imperialism or sexism can have serious, even devastating, consequences. Indeed, the participants in this project faced such consequences in their marriages, in the Mexican American community, in the workplace, and in the community at large. Finally, and notwithstanding such dangers, synergy can motivate the kinds political and pedagogic activity required for (a) connecting social science and social purpose; (b) encouraging and celebrating local, indigenous social sciences; and (c) decolonizing the academy within the contemporary imperatives of qualitative inquiry (Denzin & Lincoln, 2005, pp. 117–124).

Final Comments

Focus group research is a key site where pedagogy, politics, and inquiry intersect and interanimate each other. Because of their synergistic potentials, focus groups often produce data that are seldom produced through individual interviewing and observation and thus yield particularly powerful knowledges and insights. Specifically, the synergy and dynamism generated within homogeneous collectives often reveal unarticulated norms and normative assumptions. They also take the interpretive process beyond the bounds of individual memory and expression to mine historically sedimented collective memories and desires.

The unique potentials of focus group research are most fully realized when we acknowledge and exploit their multifunctionality. To return to the metaphor with which we opened this chapter, this kind of multifunctionality can best be imagined as a prism. That is, the three sides of this prism—pedagogy, politics, and research—are always implicated in and productive of each other. One surface of the prism may be most visible at any particular moment, but the others are always also visible, refracting what is brought to light in multiple and complex directions. How we choose to "hold" this imaginary prism at any moment in time has important consequences both for what we see and what we do with what we see.

In addition to enhancing the kinds and amounts of empirical material yielded from a qualitative study, focus group work also foregrounds the importance both of content and of expression because it capitalizes on the richness and complexity of group dynamics. Acting somewhat like magnifying glasses, focus groups induce social interactions akin to those that occur in everyday life but with greater intensity. More than observations and individual interviews, focus groups afford researchers access to social-interactional dynamics that produce particular memories, positions, ideologies, practices, and desires among specific groups of people. Focus groups also allow the researcher to see the complex ways people position themselves in relation to each other as they process questions, issues, and topics in focused ways. These dynamics, themselves, become relevant "units of analyses" for study.

If taken seriously, these dynamics help us to avoid premature closure on our understandings of the particular issues and topics we explore. They challenge us to avoid being persuaded too easily and too early by weak evidence. Although certainly not a simple solution to the complexities involved in the new politics of evidence we face, the way we have reconceptualized focus groups discourages us from ever being too comfortable in our understandings and insights. Understanding focus groups and their dynamics through multiple angles of vision forces us always to see the world in new and unexpected ways. We remain less tempted by the lures of simple facticity or transcendence—pulled always to see our empirical material in new and more rigorous ways.

In addition, focus groups function to decenter the role of the researcher. As such, focus groups can facilitate the democratization of the research process, allowing participants more ownership over it, and promoting more dialogic interactions and the joint construction of more polyvocal texts. These social facts were brought into relief by the feminist work conducted by Madriz, Radway, and Lather and Smithies that we discussed earlier. Although also functioning as sites for consolidating collective identities and enacting political work, focus groups allow for the proliferation of multiple meanings and perspectives, as well as interactions between and among them. Because focus groups get multiple perspectives on the table, they help researchers and research participants alike realize that both the interpretations of individuals and the norms and rules of groups are inherently situated, provisional, contingent, unstable, and thus changeable. In this regard, focus groups help us move toward constructing a "methodology of getting lost" and toward enacting "doubled practices" (Lather, 2001), which seem necessary first steps toward conducting eighth and ninth moment qualitative research.

Echoing Antonio Gramsci, we conclude that the "we" enabled by focus groups has "no guarantees." With no guarantees, focus groups must operate according to a hermeneutics of vulnerability (Clifford, 1988). Clifford developed the construct of a "hermeneutics of vulnerability" to discuss the constitutive effects of relationships between researchers and research participants on research practice and research findings. A hermeneutics of vulnerability foregrounds the ruptures of fieldwork, the multiple and contradictory positionings of all participants, the imperfect control of the researcher, and the partial and perspectival nature of all knowledge. Among the primary tactics for achieving a hermeneutics of vulnerability, according to Clifford, is the tactic of self-reflexivity, which may be understood in at least two senses. In the first sense, self-reflexivity involves making transparent the rhetorical and poetic work of the researcher in representing the object of her or his study. In the second (and, we think, more important) sense, self-reflexivity refers to the efforts of researchers and research participants to engage in acts of self-defamiliarization in relation to each other. In this regard, Elspeth Probyn (1993) discussed how the fieldwork experience can engender a virtual transformation of the identities of both researchers and research participants even as they are paradoxically engaged in the practice of consolidating them. This is important theoretically because it allows for the possibility of constructing a mutual ground between researchers and research participants even while recognizing that the ground is unstable and fragile. Self-reflexivity in this second sense is also important because it encourages reflection on interpretive research as the dual practice of knowledge gathering and self-transformation through self-reflection and mutual reflection with the other. Finally, as Lather (2001, 2007) has shown, even self-reflexivity has serious limits with respect to working against the triple crisis of representation, legitimation, and praxis. Indeterminacies always remain. Allowing ourselves to dwell in (and even celebrate) these indeterminacies—the truly prismatic nature of things worth studying—may be the best way to move down the roads of qualitative research practice and theory building at this particular historical juncture.

References

Barbour, R. (2008). *Doing focus groups.* Thousand Oaks, CA: Sage.

Barbour, R., & Kitsinger, J. (1999). *Developing focus group research.* Thousand Oaks, CA: Sage.

Behar, R. (1993). *Translated woman: Crossing the border with Esperanza's story.* Boston: Beacon Press.

Berger, P., & Luckmann, T. (1966). *The social construction of reality.* New York: Doubleday.

Bishop, R., Berryman, M., Cavanagh, T., Teddy, L., & Clapham, S. (2006). *Te Kotahitanga Phase 3 Whakawhanaungatanga: Establishing a culturally responsive pedagogy of relations in mainstream secondary school classrooms.* Wellington: New Zealand Ministry of Education.

Bloor, M., Frankland, J., Thomas, M., & Robson, K. (2001). *Focus groups in social research.* Thousand Oaks, CA: Sage.

Bourdieu, P., & Wacquant, L. J. D. (1992). *An invitation to reflexive sociology.* Chicago: University of Chicago Press.

Cammarota, J., & Fine, M. (Eds.). (2008). *Revolutionizing education.* New York: Routledge.

Chomsky, N. (2002). Activism, anarchy, and power: Noam Chomsky interviewed by Harry Kreisler. *Conversations with history,* March 22, 2002. Retrieved from http://www.chomsky.info/interviews/20020322.htm

Clifford, J. (1988). *The predicament of culture.* Cambridge, MA: Harvard University Press.

Collins, P. H. (1991). *Black feminist thought: Knowledge, consciousness and the politics of empowerment.* New York: Routledge.

Cooper, T. J., Baturo, A. R., Duus, E. A., & Moore, K. M. (2008). Indigenous vocational students, culturally effective communities of practice and mathematics understanding. In O. Figueras, J. L. Cortina, S. Alatorre, T. Rojano, & A. Sepulveda (Eds.), *Proceedings of the 32nd Annual Conference of the International Group for the Psychology of Mathematics Education* (pp. 378–384). Morelia, Mexico: PME.

deCerteau, M. (1984). *The practice of everyday life* (S. F. Rendall, Trans.). Berkeley: University of California Press.

Denter, D. (2008). *Sartre explained.* Chicago: Open Court.

Denzin, N. K., & Lincoln, Y. S. (2005). Epilogue: The eighth and ninth moments—|qualitative research in/and the fractured future. In N. K. Denzin & Y. S. Lincoln (Eds.), *The SAGE handbook of qualitative research* (3rd ed., pp. 1115–1126). Thousand Oaks, CA: Sage.

Dill, B. T. (1994). Fictive kin, paper sons, and compadrazgo: Women of color and the struggle for family survival. In M. B. Zinn & B. T. Dill (Eds.), *Women of color in U.S. society* (pp. 149–169). Philadelphia: Temple University Press.

Eisenstein, H. (1984). *Contemporary feminist thought.* New York: Macmillan.

Espiritu, Y. L. (1997). *Asian women and men: Labor, laws, and love.* Thousand Oaks, CA: Sage.

Fine, M. (2006). Bearing witness: Methods for researching oppression and resistance. *Social Justice Research, 19*(1), 83–108.

Foucault, M. (1984). Nietzsche, genealogy, and history. In P. Rabinow (Ed.), *The Foucault reader* (pp. 76–100). New York: Pantheon Books.

Freire, P. (1993). *Pedagogy of the oppressed.* New York: Continuum. (Original work published in 1970)

Gere, A. R. (1997). *Writing groups: History, theory, and implications.* Carbondale: Southern Illinois University Press.

Gilkes, C. T. (1994). "If it wasn't for the women . . .": African American women, community work, and social change. In M. B. Zinn & B. T. Dill (Eds.), *Women of color in U.S. society* (pp. 229–246). Philadelphia: Temple University Press.

Grand, S. (2004). *Red pedagogy: Native America social and political thought.* Lanham, MD: Rowman & Littlefield.

Heidegger, M. (1962). *Being and time* (J. Macquarrie & E. Robinson, Trans.). San Francisco: HarperSanFrancisco. (Original work published in 1927)

Hesse-Biber, S., & Leavy, P. (Eds.). (2006). *Handbook of emergent methods.* Thousand Oaks, CA: Sage.

Jakobson, R. (1960). Concluding statement: Linguistics and poetics. In T. A. Sebeok (Ed.), *Style in language.* Cambridge: MIT Press.

Kamberelis, G., & Dimitriadis, G. (2005). *On qualitative inquiry: Approaches to language and literacy research.* New York: Teachers College Press.

Kreisler, H. (2002). Activism, anarchism, and power: Conversation with Noam Chomsky, linguist and political activist. University of California at Berkeley, Institute of International Studies, Conversation with History Series. Retrieved August 1, 2009, from http://globetrotter.berkeley.edu/people2/Chomsky/chomsky-con0.html

Kreuger, R. A., & Casey, M. A. (2008). *Focus groups: A practical guide for applied research* (4th ed.). Thousand Oaks, CA: Sage.

Lather, P. (2001). Postbook: Working the ruins of feminist ethnography. *Signs: Journal of Women in Culture and Society, 27*(1), 199–227.

Lather, P. (2007). *Getting lost: Feminist efforts toward a double(d) science.* Albany: SUNY Press.

Lather, P., & Smithies, C. (1997). *Troubling the angels: Women living with HIV/AIDS.* Boulder, CO: Westview Press.

Madison, D., & Hamera, J. (2006). Introduction. In D. Madison & J. Hamera (Eds.), *The SAGE handbook of performance studies* (pp. xi–xxv). Thousand Oaks, CA: Sage.

Madriz, E. (1997). *Nothing bad happens to good girls: Fear of crime in women's lives.* Berkeley: University of California Press.

Madriz, E. (2000). Focus groups in feminist research. In N. K. Denzin & Y. S. Lincoln (Eds.), *Handbook of qualitative research* (2nd ed., pp. 835–850). Thousand Oaks, CA: Sage.

Merton, R. (1987). The focused group interview and focus groups: Continuities and discontinuities. *Public Opinion Quarterly, 51,* 550–566.

Messer-Davidow, E. (2002). *Disciplining feminism.* Durham, NC: Duke University Press.

Morgan, D. L. (1998). *The focus group guidebook*. Thousand Oaks, CA: Sage.

Morley, D. (1980). *The* Nationwide *audience*. London: British Film Institute.

Probyn, E. (1993). *Sexing the self: Gendered positions in cultural studies*. London: Routledge.

Radway, J. (1984). *Reading the romance: Women, patriarchy, and popular literature*. Durham, NC: University of North Carolina Press.

Richardson, L. (2000). Writing: A method of inquiry. In N. K. Denzin & Y. S. Lincoln (Eds.), *Handbook of qualitative research* (2nd ed., pp. 923–948). Thousand Oaks, CA: Sage.

Sartre, J. (2001). *Basic writings*. New York: Routledge.

Schensul, J. J., LeCompte, M. D., Nastasi, B. K., & Borgatti, S. P. (1999). *Enhanced ethnographic methods: Audiovisual techniques, focused group interviews, and elicitation techniques*. Walnut Creek, CA: AltaMira Press.

Solomon, R. (2006). *Dark feelings, grim thoughts: Experience and reflection in Camus and Sartre*. New York: Oxford University Press.

Stewart, D. W., Shamdasani, P. N., & Rook, D. (2006). *Focus groups: Theory and practice*. Thousand Oaks, CA: Sage.

Torre, M., & Fine, M. (2006). Researching and resisting. In S. Ginwright, P. Nogurea, & J. Cammarota (Eds.), *Beyond resistance* (pp. 269–283). New York: Routledge.

Wilson, W. A., & Yellow Bird, M. (2005). *For indigenous eyes only: A decolonization handbook*. Santa Fe, NM: School of American Research Press.

Part II

The Art and Practices of Interpretation, Evaluation, and Representation

In conventional terms, Part V of the *Handbook* signals the terminal phase of qualitative inquiry. The researcher and evaluator now assess, analyze, and interpret the empirical materials that have been collected. This process, conventionally conceived, implements a set of analytic procedures that produces interpretations that are then integrated into a theory, or put forward as a set of policy recommendations. The resulting interpretations are assessed in terms of a set of criteria, from the positivist or postpositivist traditions, including validity, reliability, and objectivity. Those interpretations that stand up to scrutiny are put forward as the findings of the research.

The contributors to Part V explore the art, practices, and politics of interpretation and evaluation, and representation. In so doing, they return to the themes of Part I—asking, that is, *how the discourses of qualitative research can be used to help create and imagine a free democratic society*. In returning to this question, it is understood that the processes of analysis, evaluation, and interpretation are neither terminal nor mechanical. They are like a dance—to invoke the metaphor used by Valerie Janesick (2010)—a dance informed at every step of the way by a commitment to this civic agenda. The processes that define the practices of interpretation and representation are always ongoing, emergent, unpredictable, and unfinished. They are always embedded in an ongoing historical and political context. As argued throughout this volume, in the United States, neoconservative discourse in the educational arena (No Child Left Behind, National Research Council) privileges experimental criteria in the funding, implementation, and evaluation of scientific inquiry. Many of the authors in this volume observe that this creates a chilling climate for qualitative inquiry.

We begin by assessing a number of criteria that have been traditionally (as well as recently) used to judge the adequacy of qualitative research. These criteria flow from the major paradigms now operating in this field, as well from standards set by governmental agencies.

Evidence, Criteria, Policy, and Politics

Torrance (Chapter 11, this volume) reviews the debates surrounding qualitative research and social policy, especially in the United Kingdom, the United States, Australia, and New Zealand. Often this discourse has marginalized qualitative inquiry, claiming that it is of low quality, and holding up experimental design as the preferred scientific protocol. There is a worldwide movement to reassert empiricist, technicist approaches to the production of evidence for policy-making purposes. This move undercuts previous policies, which endorsed a hands-off approach to the public funding of university-based science. Today, in too many places, social science is expected to serve short-term government policy, economic development, and educational achievement.

Torrance reviews the major criticism of the experimental, RCT (randomized controlled trial) model. Too often there are not clear-cut effects that can be connected to the experimental treatment condition. In response, some investigators have moved to mixed method designs, while others resort to meta-reviews, arguing that evidence to inform policy should be accumulated across studies. Meta-reviews raise the issue of criteria of quality, and there are competing quality appraisal checklists that can be deployed.

In response to these governmental initiatives, various professional associations have developed their own criteria (see Denzin, Chapter 16, this volume, for a review). These discussions of quality revolve around issues of engagement, deliberation, ethics, and desires to reconnect critical inquiry to democratic processes.

We live in an age of relativism. In the social sciences today, there is no longer a God's-eye view that guarantees absolute methodological certainty; to assert such is to court embarrassment. Indeed, there is considerable debate over what constitutes good interpretation in qualitative research. Nonetheless, there seems to be an emerging consensus that all inquiry reflects the standpoint of the inquirer, all observation is theory-laden, and there is no possibility of theory-free knowledge. We can no longer think of ourselves as neutral spectators of the social world.

Consequently, few speak in foundational terms. Before the assault of methodological conservativism, relativists would calmly assert that no method is a neutral tool of inquiry, and hence the notion of procedural objectivity could not be sustained. Anti-foundationalists thought the days of naïve realism and naïve positivism were over. In their place stand critical and historical realism, and various versions of relativism. The criteria for evaluating research have become relative, moral, and political.

There are three basic positions on the issue of evaluative criteria: foundational, quasi-foundational, and non-foundational. There are still those who think in terms of a *foundational* epistemology. They would apply the same criteria to qualitative research as are employed in quantitative inquiry, contending that there is nothing special about qualitative research that demands a special set of evaluative criteria. As indicated in our introduction to Part II, the positivist and postpositivist paradigms apply four standard criteria to disciplined inquiry: internal validity, external validity, reliability, and objectivity. The use of these criteria, or their variants, is consistent with the foundational position.

In contrast, *quasi-foundationalists* approach the criteria issue from the standpoint of a non-naïve, neo- or subtle realism. They contend that the discussion of criteria must take place within the context of an ontological neorealism and a constructivist epistemology. They believe in a real world that is independent of our fallible knowledge of it. Their constructivism commits them to the position that there can be no theory-free knowledge. Proponents of the quasi-foundational position argue that a set of criteria unique to qualitative research needs to be developed. Hammersley (1992, p. 64; also 1995, p. 18; 2008; see also Wolcott, 1999, p. 194) is a leading proponent of this position. He wants to maintain the correspondence theory of truth, while suggesting that researchers assess a work in terms of its ability to (1) generate generic/formal theory; (2) be empirically grounded and scientifically credible; (3) produce findings that can be generalized, or transferred to other settings; and (4) be internally reflexive in terms of taking account of the effects of the researcher and the research strategy on the findings that have been produced.

Hammersley (2008) reduces his criteria to three essential terms: plausibility (is a claim plausible), credibility (is the claim based on credible evidence), and relevance (what is the claim's relevance for knowledge about the world). Of course, these terms require social judgments. They cannot be assessed in terms of any set of external or foundational criteria. Their meanings are arrived at through consensus and discussion in the scientific community. Within Hammersley's model, there is no satisfactory method for resolving this issue of how to evaluate an empirical claim.

For the non-foundationalists, relativism is not an issue. They accept the argument that there is no theory-free knowledge. Relativism, or uncertainty, is the inevitable consequence of the fact that as human beings we have finite knowledge of ourselves, and the world we live in. Non-foundationalists contend that the injunction to pursue knowledge cannot be given epistemologically; rather, the injunction is moral and political.

Accordingly, the criteria for evaluating qualitative work are also moral and fitted to the pragmatic, ethical, and political contingencies of concrete situations. Good or bad inquiry in any given context is assessed in terms of criteria that flow from a feminist, communitarian moral ethic of empowerment, community, and moral solidarity. Returning to Clifford Christians (Chapter 4 volume 1), this moral ethic calls for research rooted in the concepts of care, shared governance, neighborliness, love, and kindness. Further, this work should provide the foundations for social criticism and social action.

In an ideal world, the anti- or non-foundational narrative would be uncontested. But such is not the case. We continue to live in dark days.

Interpretive Adequacy in Qualitative Research

Altheide and Johnson (Chapter 12) call their approach to interpretive adequacy "analytical realism"; that is, there is a real world that we interact with. We create meaning in this world through interaction. They discuss how analytical realism can be used to enhance the credibility, relevance, and importance of qualitative methods and interpretive materials. All knowledge is contextual and partial. Evidence is a part of a communication process. This interactional process "symbolically joins an actor, an audience, a point of view, and . . . claims about the relations between two or more phenomena." This view of evidence-as-process is termed the "evidentiary narrative." It is shaped "by symbolic filters, including distinct epistemic communities, or collective meanings, standards, and criteria that govern sanctioned action."

They discuss how this view of evidence has been framed in clinical and policy studies, in action research, and in performance and autoethnography. Various forms of validity—successor, catalytic, interrogated, transgressive, imperial, ironic, situated—are discussed. They offer a hyphenated model—validity-as-culture, -as-ideology, -as-gender, -as-language, -as-relevance, -as-standards, -as-reflexive-accounting, and -as-marketable-legitimacy.

Their model of evidentiary narrative shows how evidence is not about facts, but about narrative. Their ethnographic ethic enacts this model of evidence, connecting it to relationships between the observer, the observed, the setting, the reader, and the written text. Their goal is not to offer a checklist for assessing quality or validity. They open their text with a quote from the artist Paul Klee—"A line is a dot that went for a walk." Their task, they contend, is "to continue pushing the line in new directions to illuminate our humanity and our communicative worlds."

Analysis and Representation

Laura Ellingson (Chapter 13) offers a continuum—right, left, middle—approach to the analysis and representation of qualitative materials. On the far right, there is an emphasis on valid, reliable knowledge generated by neutral researchers using rigorous methods to generate Truth. This is the space of postpositivism. At the left end of the continuum, researchers value humanistic, openly subjective knowledge—autoethnography, poetry, video, stories, narratives, photography, drama, painting. Truths are multiple, ambiguous; literary standards of truthfulness replace those of positivism. In the middle is work that offers description, exposition, analysis, insight, and theory, blending art and science, and often transcending these categories. First-person voice is used, scholars seek intimate familiarity with their textual materials, and grounded theory and multiple methods may be employed.

Ellingson offers a series of writing/stretching exercises, a process she calls "wondering." It asks the researcher to think seriously and freely about their empirical materials, their inquiry topics, the audiences for their work, the pleasures they derive from their project, their identities as writers, and the writing genres they feel most comfortable with.

Multigenre crystallization is Ellingson's postmodern-influenced approach to triangulation. Crystallization combines multiple forms of analysis and genres of representation into a coherent text. Crystallization seeks to produce thick, complex interpretation. It utilizes more than one writing genre. It deploys multiple forms of analysis, reflexively embeds the researcher's self in the inquiry process, and eschews positivist claims to objectivity. Crystallization features two primary types: those *integrated* into a single text, and those that are *dendritic,* involving multiple textual formations. Guerilla scholarship moves back and forth across both types of crystallization, and engages different methods, genres, paradigms, and ideologies, always in the name of social justice.

Ellingson predicts a sharp rise in the next decade in the number of researchers who are willing to take up her view of the qualitative continuum in pursuit of socially engaged programs. So do we.

Post Qualitative Research

St.Pierre (Chapter 14) calls for the resurgence of postmodernism, a philosophically informed inquiry that will resist calls for scientifically based forms of research (SBR). In so doing, she also offers a powerful postmodern critique of conventional humanistic qualitative methodology. (Her reading of the SBR discourse complements Torrance's critique of this movement.)

She convincingly argues that it is time for qualitative inquiry to reinvent itself, to put under erasure all that has been accomplished, so that something different can be done, a "rigorous reimagining of a capacious science that cannot be defined in advance and is never the same again." Thus does she take up the "posts"—postmodernism, poststructuralism—offering a valuable history of each discourse. She introduces the concepts of haecceity, assemblage, and entanglement to deconstruct the humanist concept of human being. She notes, though, that it is difficult to escape the concept of "I."

Drawing on her own research, she shows how deconstruction can work, from transgressive data, to understanding that writing is always analysis. Writers interpret as they write, so writing is a form of inquiry, a way of making sense of the world. Writing as a method of inquiry coheres with the development of ethical selves. St.Pierre troubles conventional understandings of ethics. Drawing on Derrida and Deleuze, she places ethics under deconstruction: "What happens when we cannot apply the rules?" We must not be unworthy of what happens to us. We struggle to be worthy, to be willing to be worthy. We seek a writing space that goes beyond the "posts," to reach into the future.

Qualitative Research and Technology

Davidson and di Gregorio (Chapter 15) note that in the 1980s, as qualitative researchers began to grapple with the promise of computers, a "handful of innovative researchers created the first generation of what became known as CAQDAS (Computer Assisted Qualitative Data Analysis Software)," or QDAS (Qualitative Data Analysis Software), as they refer to it in their chapter. Initially, these software packages were used for simple text retrieval tasks. They quickly expanded into comprehensive all-in-one-packages that offered qualitative researchers a suite of digital tools that could be used to store, organize, analyze, represent, and transport qualitative materials.

Three decades later, with the explosion of the Internet and the emergence of web-based tools known as Web 2.0, or Web 3.0, QDAS is on the brink of a new wave of developments. These developments are multimodal, visually attractive, easier to learn, less expensive, and more socially connected. Yet despite this fact, QDAS is used by a small minority of qualitative researchers. There is still a lack of institutional understanding and support for the tools. The major initiatives in qualitative inquiry have not taken up these technologies.

But qualitative research and computer technology are in the midst of a revolution. This chapter sets the historical context for understanding these developments. Their six-stage model of QDAS development is fitted to our eight-stage model: traditional, modernist, blurred genres, crisis of representation, postmodernism, post-experimental, methodologically contested present, a fractured future. Key texts (grounded theory) and QDAS in each of their six stages are identified.

In 1989, the first international conference on qualitative computing was held at the University of Surrey, in the United Kingdom. In 1994, the Economic and Social Research Council (ESRC) in Great Britain funded the CAQDAS networking project. In 1995, Sage Publications agreed to market QSR: Qualitative Social Research International's NUD*IST package. By the end of the 1990s, three major QDAS packages came to dominate: ATLAS.ti, MAXQDA, and NVivo.

In the recent past, concern shifted to teaching with QDAS, developments of the E-project, and international conferences exploring new frontiers with Web 2.0. These frontiers include the electronic future, the rapid growth of media and social networking technologies on the Internet: wikis, YouTube, Flickr, Twitter, Facebook, and so forth. Ethical issues continue, as Gatson discussed in Chapter 31, many taken up by the Association of Internet Researchers. As we move to QDAS 2.0, how can we ensure that web-based storage systems have the security we need?

The Politics of Evidence

Denzin's chapter (Chapter 16) reviews the by now all-too-familiar arguments about policy, SBR, and the politics of evidence. He reviews state- and discipline-sponsored standards and criteria for qualitative work. He criticizes recent efforts by the American Education Research Association to offer a set of standards for reporting on humanities-oriented research. He notes the multiple points of tension within the qualitative inquiry community: Interpretivists dismiss postpositivists. Poststructuralists dismiss interpretivists, and postinterpretivists dismiss the interpretivists. Global efforts to impose a new orthodoxy on critical social science inquiry must be resisted.

Writing Into Position

Pelias (Chapter 17) argues that the writerly self is a performance. In the moment of composition, the I comes into existence. Writing becomes a form of inquiry, a form of self-realization. Writing functions as way of moving the individual forward, into poetic, narrative spaces. Evocative, reflexive, embodied practices allow the I to position him- or herself in partisan places. The three major sections of Pelias's chapter interrogate these strategies for composition and evaluation. Each writing position, each writing strategy, poeticizes the researcher's body, locates it in a story, a narrative, which is all that we have.

Reflexive writers write about their complicity in the problems they interrogate, inviting others to interrogate their own actions, seeking, perhaps, a new, more utopian democratic space. Qualitative researchers always write from a location of corporeal presence. As Spry argues in Chapter 7, they write from the site of the body, the body in pain, the abused body, the damaged body. They write to make the world a better place; they write in the hope of dialogue, of new possibilities. We sit at our desks trying, trying.

Policy and Qualitative Evaluation

Program evaluation, as an applied science, is a major site of qualitative research. Evaluators are interpreters, and they do their work in socio-political contexts. Their texts tell stories. These stories are inherently moral and political, and relational. For Abma and Widdershoven (Chapter 18), evaluation is a relationally responsible practice. In their work, evaluators enact a shared understanding of what it means to be an evaluator and do evaluative work.

They offer a history of this field, which complements House's (2005) narrative. The field has moved from faddish experimental, social engineering, and quantitative evaluation studies (1960s), to small-scale qualitative studies, to meta-analyses and program theory. A move from a model of value-free inquiry to committed social justice projects, and back again, is also part of this history. In the 1980s, evaluation moved away from quantitative methods and value-free studies, toward qualitative studies focused on stakeholders, social justice concerns, and participatory techniques.

The qualitative evaluator makes judgments, based on values, ethics, methodologies, stakeholders' accounts, and contextual understandings. The evaluator develops evaluations that are in between advocacy and critique, midway between "antipathy and sympathy . . . an Aristotelian middle-ground position." Abma and Widdershoven's evaluator is a wise judge who understands that evaluation is a political practice; "it has unequal consequences for various stakeholders in the evaluation." There is a desire to empower people. They review feminist, transformative, democratic, participatory, critical, social justice, and fourth and fifth evaluation traditions—evaluation for understanding and evaluation for social critique and transformation—that advance these positions.

Qualitative evaluation is holistic, dialogical, and emergent. It evolves through closely connected stages or phases. It starts with hearing marginalized voices, then placing these voices in dialogue with one another. The evaluator empowers those who are heard, and creates a safe space for dialogue and inclusion. The authors present a case study from the field of psychiatry to illustrate their ideas, which they call "interactive evaluation." The challenge of ensuring that positive cultural change endures remains.

Conclusion

The readings in Part V affirm our position that qualitative research has come of age. Topics that were contained within the broad grasp of the positivist and postpositivist epistemologies are now surrounded by multiple discourses. There are now many ways in which to write, read, assess, evaluate, and apply qualitative research texts. Even so, there are pressures to turn back the clock. This complex field invites reflexive appraisal, the topic of Part VI—the future of qualitative research.

References

Hammersley, M. (1992). *What's wrong with ethnography?* London: Routledge.

Hammersley, M. (1995). *The politics of social research.* London: Sage.

Hammersley, M. (2008). *Questioning qualitative inquiry: Critical essays.* London: Sage.

House, E. (2005). Qualitative evaluation and changing social policy. In N. K. Denzin & Y. S. Lincoln (Eds.), *The SAGE handbook of qualitative research* (3rd ed., pp. 1069–1082). Thousand Oaks, CA: Sage.

Janesick, V. (2010). *"Stretching" exercises for qualitative researchers.* Thousand Oaks, CA: Sage.

Wolcott, H. F. (1999). *Ethnography: A way of seeing.* Walnut Creek, CA: AltaMira Press.

Qualitative Research, Science, and Government

Evidence, Criteria, Policy, and Politics

Harry Torrance

The debate about how educational research and, more generally, social research, might better serve policy has been continuing for more than a decade now. It is not a new debate, and has been revisited many times since the inception of educational and social research as established university-based activities (e.g., Lagemann, 2000; Nisbet & Broadfoot; 1980; Weiss, 1972, 1980). However, it has been addressed with new vigor since the late 1990s as successive governments in the USA, the UK, and elsewhere have looked for better value for money from research, and more particularly looked for legitimating and supportive endorsements of their policies. The debate carries particular import for those working in what might be termed the broad field of "qualitative inquiry," since it has tended to privilege so-called 'scientific' approaches to educational and social research, by which is meant empirical investigations of educational activities and innovations, oriented to the identification of causality, explanation, and generalization (e.g., National Research Council, 2002). Implicitly, therefore, and sometimes quite explicitly, qualitative approaches to research are marginalized. The debate seems to reflect both long-term changes in what we might call the "terms of trade" between science and policy, along with more specific short-term jockeying for position amongst particular researchers and government officials/advisers at a particular point in time. This chapter will attempt briefly to review the background to the debate before examining some of its key elements in more detail and reflecting on its implications for the field of qualitative research and its relationship to policy.

The intensity and focus of the current debate in the UK can be dated from a speech in 1996 by David Hargreaves (then Professor of Education at Cambridge University) to the Teacher Training Agency (TTA—a government agency regulating teacher training). Hargreaves (1996) attacked the quality and utility of educational research, arguing that such research should produce an "agreed knowledge base for teachers" (p. 2) that "demonstrates conclusively that if teachers change their practice from X to Y there will a significant and enduring improvement in teaching and learning" (p. 5). Subsequent government-sponsored reviews and reports took their lead from this speech and produced what might be termed a mainstream policy consensus that the quality of educational research was low, particularly because so many studies were conducted on a small scale and employed qualitative methods, and therefore "something had to be done" (Hillage, Pearson, Anderson, & Tamkin, 1998; Tooley & Darby, 1998; Woodhead, 1998). That such claims were disputed need not detain us here (but see for example Hammersley, 1997, 2005; MacLure, 2003). It is worth noting, however, that subsequent analyses of papers published by the *British Educational Research Journal,* the leading UK journal of the British Educational Research Association, and of educational research projects funded by the UK Economic and Social Research Council (ESRC), demonstrated that critics had misrepresented the field and that in fact a wide range of methods were and are employed in British educational research, including-large scale quantitative analysis, experimental design, and mixed methods (Gorard & Taylor, 2004; Torrance, 2008).

The parallel intervention to Hargreaves in the USA is probably the National Research Council report (2002) "Scientific Research in Education," though this in turn was produced in response to already extant policy debate and legislation identifying what would be defined as "research" for purposes of federal funding—specifically the Reading Excellence Act, 1999, and the No Child Left Behind Act, 2001 (see Baez & Boyles, 2009, pp. 5 ff., for illustration and discussion of these acts). A huge literature has been prompted by this legislation, subsequent attempts to delineate the boundaries of "scientific research in education" and responses to those attempts, and again, it is not my purpose to review it further here (see, e.g., *Educational Researcher,* 2002, vol. 31, no. 8; *Qualitative Inquiry,* 2004, vol. 10, no. 1; *Teachers College Record,* 2005, vol. 107, no. 1). However, one quotation from this debate is worth highlighting, since in many respects it summarizes the "scientific" case, particularly the case for using not just a broadly quantitative empirical approach, but a specifically experimental design. Thus, Robert Slavin (2002), a leading proponent of the scientific method in the USA and recently appointed Director of the Institute for Effective Education at the University of York, UK, argues that "the experiment is the design of choice for studies that seek to make causal conclusions, and particularly for evaluations of educational innovations" (p. 18.). And, in a turn of phrase that is directly reminiscent of Hargreaves's (1996) speech, Slavin suggests that policy makers want to know "if we implement Program X instead of Program Y, or instead of our current program, what will be the likely outcomes for children?" (p. 18).

Here, then, is the essential focus of, and apparent justification for, the current debate. Educational research, and especially, qualitative approaches to educational research, has not provided a sufficiently cumulative and robust evidence base for the development of educational policy and practice, and in particular has not produced sufficient experimental data to allow policy makers to evaluate policy alternatives.

However, it is important to recognize that these criticisms are not restricted to the USA and/or UK policy contexts, nor indeed are they restricted to educational research. Reviews of and attacks on the quality of educational research, and particularly the quality of qualitative educational research, have similarly impacted debate in Australia and New Zealand (Cheek, 2007; Middleton, 2009; Yates, 2004), and are beginning to emerge in the European Union (Besley, 2009; Bridges, 2005, 2009; Brown, 2003). Overall, and to reiterate, the argument has been that educational research is too often conceived and conducted as a "cottage industry": producing too many small-scale, disconnected, non-cumulative studies that do not provide convincing explanations of educational phenomena or how best to develop teaching and learning. There is no cumulative or informative knowledge base in the field, and it is characterized as being of both poor quality and limited utility. Similar critiques have been leveled against social research more generally. In a speech to the ESRC in 2000, titled "Influence or Irrelevance" the then Secretary of State for Education, David Blunkett (2000), asserted that

> often in practice we have felt frustrated by a tendency for research . . . to address issues other than those directly relevant to the political and policy debate. . . . Many feel that too much social science research is inward-looking, too piecemeal, rather than helping to build knowledge in a cumulative way, and fails to focus on the key issues of concern to policy-makers, practitioners and the public, especially parents. (p. 1)

In an attempt to address such political concerns, the Campbell Collaboration, a direct parallel to the Cochrane Collaboration in medical research, seeks to review and disseminate social science knowledge for policy makers through what it terms "systematic reviews" (Davies & Boruch, 2001; Wade, Turner, Rothstein, & Lavenberg, 2006). I will return to systematic reviewing below, but for the moment my point is that while the legislative concern to promote "scientific research in education" is a fairly specific American phenomenon, as is the particular focus on experimental design, this sits in a much broader international context of concern about the nature and purpose of social research and its relationship to policy. Such concerns reflect both the topics and methods of inquiry. Educational research, qualitative approaches to educational research, but also qualitative approaches to social research more generally have all come in for criticism and, taken together, suggest that qualitative inquiry is facing a global movement to reassert broadly empiricist and technicist approaches to the generation and accumulation of social scientific "evidence" for policy making. The focus, worldwide, is on seeking evidence to inform policy making, particularly evidence about "what works." Elements of such a movement will differ in their origins, orientations, and specific national aspirations. But equally they do seem to represent a concerted attempt to impose (or perhaps reimpose) scientific certainty and a form of center-periphery, research, development, dissemination (RDD) system management on an increasingly complex and uncertain social world.

Long-Term Trends: Whither/Wither Science and Government?

Part of the backcloth to the current debate is the uncertain status and legitimacy of both science and government at the present time. The role, purpose, and utility of science and scientific research is less agreed upon and less secure than it once was, and with respect to this, just as educational research can be seen to be situated in a wider debate about social research, so social research can be seen to be located in a wider debate about scientific research and the role of science in society. In the UK, for most of the 20th century, the relationship between science and government was determined by the so-called "Haldane principle" (after Viscount Haldane, an influential liberal politician who chaired the committee that articulated the principle in 1918). This settlement essentially resolved that university-based science would be funded from the public purse to pursue fundamental research, which would in turn produce unpredictable, but nevertheless substantial, long-term scientific and technical benefit—i.e., "basic" research would, over time, produce the platform for more "applied" technological developments and benefits. This was even characterized as the creation and operation of the "independent republic of science" by Michael Polyani (1962, as cited in Boden, Cox, Nedeva, & Barker, 2004). It has its direct parallel in the United States with the publication of Vannevar Bush's "Science: The Endless Frontier" (1945). This argued, on the back of scientific successes apparent in the Second World War, for the federal government to significantly expand support for scientific research on the basis of a similarly "arms length" linear model of "basic" research eventually leading to technological benefit (e.g., Greenberg, 2001, Chapter 3). More recently, however, government calls for much more short-term responsiveness and utility have pervaded policy debates and aspirations on both sides of the Atlantic and elsewhere—e.g., the Clinton focus on science and technology policy in the 1990s (Greenberg, 2001), and the current UK government concern to document and evaluate the "impact" of research through its new Research Excellence Framework (Department for Business, Innovations, and Skills [DBIS], 2009; Higher Education Funding Council for England [HEFCE], 2009), the successor to the Research Assessment Exercise (Torrance, 2006). Science in general, and social science in particular, is now expected to serve government policy and economic development very directly. This clearly begs questions about how to define quality and utility.

Equally, however, government itself is under pressure to "deliver," especially in areas of public policy. Since the first oil crisis of the 1970s put severe pressure on public spending, especially in the UK, and with the development and implementation of monetarist critiques of government spending in the 1980s, and the collapse of the Soviet Communist Bloc in 1989, there has developed a severe crisis of confidence and legitimation with respect to the role of government itself, especially with regard to the provision of public services: Are they really needed? If so, could they be better and more efficiently provided by other mechanisms and stakeholders? What reasons are there for state intervention in the lives of ordinary citizens? In this respect, government demand for "evidence" is as much a demand for material to justify its own existence, as it is a demand for the evaluation of particular policy alternatives. What is at stake is the legitimacy of policy intervention *per se*.

Experimentalism: Part of the Solution or Part of the Problem?

Advocates of experimental design have inserted themselves into this uncertain nexus. Given such uncertainty, it is understandable that governments and policy makers will look to research for assistance. Research, or more generally, "science," is still largely regarded as independent of government and thus able, at least in principle, to provide disinterested evidence for both the development and evaluation of policy, despite recent moves toward the development of a closer and more utilitarian relationship. To reiterate, "if we implement Program X instead of Program Y, or instead of our current program, what will be the likely outcomes for children?" (Slavin, 2002, p. 18). The attraction of the sort of evidence that Hargreaves (1996) and Slavin claim can and should be provided is easy to appreciate. It sounds seductively simple. When charged with dispensing large amounts of public money for implementing programs and supporting research, one can understand that policy makers might value this sort of help—at least as long as the answers to the questions posed are clear and not too radical or expensive.

But here's the rub—the answers to questions of public policy and program evaluation are often not very clear (nor indeed are the questions sometimes). More circumspect proponents of experimental methods, specifically randomized controlled trials (RCTs), acknowledge that in order for a causal relationship to be established, even within the narrow terms of an RCT, very specific questions have to be asked. Thus, for example, Judith Gueron (2002) argues that while "random assignment . . . offers unique power in answering the 'Does it make a difference?' question" (p. 15), it is also the case that "[t]he key in large-scale projects is to answer a few questions well" (p. 40). In the same edited volume of papers, produced from a conference convened to promote "Randomized Trials in Education Research," Thomas Cook and Monique Payne (2002) agree that

> most randomized experiments test the influence of only a small subset of potential causes of an outcome, and often only one . . . even at their most comprehensive, experiments can responsibly test only a modest number of the possible interactions between treatments. So, experiments are best when a causal question involves few variables [and] is sharply focused. (p. 152)

What these observations mean is that RCTs can be very good at answering very specific questions and attributing cause in a statistically descriptive (i.e., observable) way. What they cannot do is produce the questions in the first place: That depends on much prior, often qualitative, investigation, not to mention value judgments about what is significant in the qualitative data and what problem might be addressed by a particular program intervention. Nor can RCTs provide an explanation of *why* something has happened (i.e., the causal mechanisms at work). That, likewise, will depend on much prior investigation and, if possible, parallel qualitative investigation of the phenomenon under study, to inform the development of a theory about what the researchers think may be happening. Without a reasonable understanding of why particular outcomes have occurred, along with identifying the range of unintended consequences that will almost inevitably accompany an innovation, it is very difficult to generalize such outcomes and implement the innovation with any degree of success elsewhere. A good example of such problems is provided by California's attempt to implement smaller class sizes off the back of the apparent success of the Tennessee "STAR" evaluation. The Tennessee experiment worked with a sample, whereas California attempted statewide implementation, creating more problems than they solved by creating teacher shortages, especially in poorer neighborhoods in the state. There simply weren't enough well-qualified teachers available to reduce class size statewide, and those that were tended to move to schools in richer neighborhoods when more jobs in such schools became available (see Grissmer, Subotnik, & Orland, 2009).

Interestingly in this respect, Cook and Payne (2002) continue,

> The advantages of case study methods are considerable . . . we value them as adjuncts to experiments. . . . Case study methods complement experiments when . . . it is not clear how successful program implementation will be, why implementation shortfalls may occur, what unexpected effects are likely to emerge, how respondents interpret the questions asked of them, [and] what the causal mediating processes are . . . qualitative methods have a central role to play in experimental work. (p. 169)

One is tempted to ask, "So what's all the fuss about?" Why is some RCT advocacy so strident and exclusive? Of course, different researchers will vary in the importance they give to qualitative methods, and it is irritating to have qualitative methods reduced to an "adjunct" or a "complement" to experimental approaches, or as some activity to be undertaken before the "real" scientific work begins (see Shavelson, Phillips, Towne, & Feuer, 2003, p. 28). But it does seem as though those whose work actually involves the conduct of social science experiments have a well-informed view of the strengths of qualitative research, along with clear understandings of the limitations of experiments, as opposed to those who just engage in uninformed criticism of qualitative methods and advocacy for RCTs.[1]

There is not enough space here to go into all the potential problems of conducting randomized experiments in the "natural" (as opposed to laboratory) setting of the school or the classroom. Extensive philosophical and practical critiques (and rejoinders) about the nature of causality and the place of RCTs in understanding social interaction and evaluating human services have been published by Erickson and Gutierrez (2002), Howe (2004), and Maxwell (2004), among many others. Indeed, practitioners such as Gueron (2002) and Cook and Payne (2002), cited above, provide comprehensive accounts of the challenge of undertaking experiments "in the field." The real problem with experimental methods, however, is that even if conducted as effectively as possible, they often don't actually answer the "Does it make a difference?" question. Already, accounts of disappointing results are starting to appear in the press:

> Like a steady drip from a leaky faucet, the experimental studies being released this school year by the federal Institute of Education Sciences are mostly producing the same results: "No effects," "No effects," "No effects."
>
> The disappointing yield is prompting researchers, product developers, and other experts to question the design of the studies, whether the methodology they use is suited to the messy real world of education, and whether the projects are worth the cost, which has run as high as $14.4 million in the case of one such study. (Viadero, 2009, p. 1)

We should not be surprised. It was precisely the confounding problems of diverse implementation and interaction effects that produced so many "no significant difference" results in the 1960s in the context of curriculum evaluation studies. Reflections on such results prompted the development and use of qualitative methods in evaluation studies in the first place, in the1970s and 1980s (Cronbach, 1975; Cronbach & Associates, 1980; Guba & Lincoln, 1981, 1989; Hamilton, Jenkins, King, MacDonald, & Parlett, 1976; Stake, 1967, 1978; Stenhouse, 1975; Stenhouse, Verma, Wild, & Nixon, 1982). Indeed, in one mixed method study of the "problems and effects of teaching about race relations" (as issues of race were called in the UK in those days), it was reported that 60% of the sample student population became less racially prejudiced as measured by attitude tests after following a particular program, but 40% became *more* prejudiced—as the author himself mused, what on earth is one supposed to do with such a result (Stenhouse et al., 1982)?

Beyond Single Studies: Systematic Reviewing

The response of those interested in unpacking the sort of dilemma highlighted above would probably be to conduct further detailed investigation of the program as implemented, and indeed, Stenhouse and his team (Stenhouse et al., 1982) did conduct other investigations, including an "action research" approach to the development of the program. Similar mixed methods evaluation studies are often funded in the UK as those stakeholders with an interest in the development—local authorities (i.e., school districts), head teachers (principals), school governors, and so forth—seek maximum information about the effects of an intervention, not just a one-off research result about whether or not it "works" (e.g., Somekh et al., 2007).

However, a different approach has been advanced by those committed to experimental design but who acknowledge the potential weakness of relying on single studies—that of so-called "systematic reviewing." Advocates of systematic reviewing argue that evidence to inform policy should be accumulated across studies, but not just any studies, rather, only those that pass strict tests of quality. And those tests of quality have until relatively recently involved focusing on large-scale samples and, ideally, experimental designs (Gough & Elbourne, 2002; Oakley 2000, 2003). The case for developing systematic reviewing is based on transparency of process and clear criteria for including and excluding studies from the review. The case derives from critiques of so-called "narrative reviewing," which, it is claimed, focuses on summarizing findings, in relation to a particular argument, rather than reviewing the whole field dispassionately and "systematically" so that the reader can be confident that all relevant prior knowledge in a field has been included and summarized. Arguments in favor of conducting such reviews reflect the critiques of social and educational research outlined earlier: that the findings of empirical studies are often too small-scale, non-cumulative, or contradictory to be useful. Advocates are closely associated with the Cochrane Collaboration in medical and health care research and the Campbell Collaboration in social science, both of which favor the accumulation and dissemination of research findings based on scientific methods, particularly randomized controlled trials. As such, systematic reviewing is very much located within the international "evidence-based policy and practice" movement (Davies, 2004; Davies & Boruch, 2001; see also Mosteller & Boruch, 2002, p. 2, for evidence of the close networking of this international movement).

The original criteria of quality employed by systematic reviewing clearly derived from the medical model, but it is interesting to note that even as some researchers started to argue the relevance of an RCT-based medical model to educational and social research in the UK, it was already being subject to criticism in the field of medicine itself. Medical researchers understood that many issues of patient treatment and care require the design of qualitative as well as quantitative studies, and substantial subsequent developments have tried to find ways of integrating the findings of qualitative studies into systematic reviews (e.g., Barbour & Barbour, 2003; Dixon-Woods, Booth, & Sutton, 2007; Dixon-Woods, Fitzpatrick,

& Roberts, 2001). Sometimes this has led to the rather absurd deployment of Bayesian statistics to incorporate qualitative data into quantitative estimates of effects—essentially transforming expert judgment of qualitative studies into numerical indicators by rank-ordering the importance of key variables discernable from qualitative studies. The rank-ordered expert judgments of quality are then rendered into probabilities (of which variables are likely to be most important) and included in quantitative meta-analyses. This seems to do little more than add a spurious mathematical accuracy (to three decimal points in Roberts, Dixon-Woods, Fitzpatrick, Abrams, & Jones, 2002) to what would be far better left as "expert" judgment. At least we can be appropriately skeptical of expert judgment, precisely because it is usually expressed in narrative form, even if we might also regard it as the best available evidence in the circumstances. Nevertheless, such developments indicate that qualitative data are appreciated as important in understanding the conduct and impact of medical processes and treatments.

The original "hard line" position of systematic reviewing in social research has now been significantly modified, as it has encountered considerable skepticism over the last 10 years in the UK (Hammersley, 2001; MacLure; 2005; cf. also Oakley's 2006 response, and Hammersley's 2008 rejoinder). Work is now underway to integrate different kinds of research findings, including those of qualitative research, into such reviews. This involves attempts to appraise the quality and thus the "warrant" of individual qualitative research studies and their findings: Are they good enough to be included in a systematic review or not? Once again, however, this can lead toward absurdity rather than serious synthesis as the complexity of qualitative work is rendered into an amenable form for instant appraisal. Thus, for example, Attree and Milton (2006) report on a "Quality Appraisal Checklist . . . [and its associated] quality scoring system . . . [for] "the quality appraisal of qualitative research" (p. 125). Studies are scored on a 4-point scale:

A No or few flaws

B Some flaws

C Considerable flaws, study still of some value

D Significant flaws that threaten the validity of the whole study (p. 125)

Only studies rated A or B were included in the systematic reviews that the authors conducted, and in the paper they attempt to exemplify how these categories are operationalized in their work. But their descriptions beg many more questions than they answer. The above scale simply provides a reductionist checklist of mediocrity. Even the most stunning and insightful piece of qualitative work can only be categorized as having "No or few flaws."

To try to be fair to the authors, they indicate that

> the checklist was used initially to provide an overview of the robustness of qualitative studies . . . to balance the rigor of the research with its importance for developing knowledge and informing policy and practice. (Attree & Milton, 2006, p. 119)

But this is precisely the point at issue with respect to using research to inform policy: Standards and checklists *cannot* substitute for informed judgment when it comes to balancing the rigor of the research against its potential contribution to policy. This *is* a matter of judgment, both for researchers and for policy makers.

Impact on Qualitative Research: Setting Standards to Control Quality

Many other criticisms could be directed at systematic reviewing in addition to its apparent disdain for qualitative evidence. For example, it is also very expensive and inefficient in terms of time and material resources, given the little it often delivers in terms of actual "findings." The results of systematic reviews can take many months to appear, and policy makers in England are as likely to ask for very rapid reviews of research to be conducted over a few days or weeks, and possibly assembled via an expert seminar, as to commission longer-term systematic reviews (Boaz, Solesbury, & Sullivan, 2004, 2007). However, the more general issue for this chapter is the impact of the "scientific evidence movement" on qualitative research, and the above checklist produced by Attree and Milton (2006) well illustrates the contortions that some qualitative researchers are starting to go through, in order to maintain the visibility of their work in the context of this movement.

A major response to the evidence movement has been for organizations and associations to start trying to "set standards" in qualitative research, and indeed in educational research more generally, to reassure policy makers about the quality of qualitative research and to reassert the contribution that qualitative research can (and should) make to government-funded programs. However, the field of qualitative research, or qualitative inquiry, is very broad, involving large numbers of researchers working in different countries, working in and across many different disciplines (anthropology, psychology, sociology, etc.), different applied research and policy settings (education, social work, health studies, etc.), and different national environments with their different policy processes and socioeconomic context of action. It is not at all self-evident that reaching agreement across such boundaries is desirable, even if it were possible. Different disciplines and contexts of action produce different readings and interpretations of apparently common literatures and similar issues. It is the juxtaposition of these readings, the comparing and contrasting within and across boundaries, that allows us to learn about them and reflect on our own situated understandings of our own contexts. Multiplicity of approach and interpretation, and multivocalism of reading and response, are the basis of quality in the qualitative research community and, it might be argued, in the advancement of science more generally. The key issue is to discuss and explore quality across boundaries, thereby continually to develop it, not fix it, as at best a good recipe and at worst a narrow training manual.

Nevertheless, various attempts at "setting standards" are now being made, often, it seems, with the justification of "doing it to ourselves, before others do it to us" (Cheek, 2007; see also the discussion by Moss et al., 2009). In England, independent academics based at the National Centre for Social Research (a not-for-profit consultancy organization) were commissioned by the Strategy Unit of the UK government Cabinet Office to produce a report on "Quality in Qualitative Evaluation: A Framework for Assessing Research Evidence" (Cabinet Office, 2003a). The rationale seems to have been that UK government departments are increasingly commissioning policy evaluations in the context of the move toward evidence-informed policy and practice and that guidelines for judging the quality of qualitative approaches and methods were considered to be necessary.

The report is in two parts: a 17-page summary, including the "Quality Framework" itself (Cabinet Office, 2003a), and a 167-page full report (Cabinet Office, 2003b), including discussion of many of the issues raised by the framework. The framework is a guide for the commissioners of research when drawing up tender documents and reading reports, but it is also meant to influence the conduct and management of research and the training of social researchers (Cabinet Office, 2003a, p. 6). However, the short "Quality Framework" begs many questions, while the full 167-page report reads like an introductory text on qualitative research methods. Paradigms are described and issues rehearsed, but all are resolved in a bloodless, technical, and strangely old-fashioned counsel of perfection. The reality of doing qualitative research and indeed of conducting evaluation, with all the contingencies, political pressures, and decisions that have to be made, is completely absent. Thus, in addition to the obvious need for "Findings/conclusions [to be] supported by data/evidence" (Cabinet Office, 2003b, p. 22), qualitative reports should also include

> Detailed description of the contexts in which the study was conducted; (p. 23)
> Discussions of how fieldwork methods or settings may have influenced data collected; (p. 25)
> Descriptions of background or historical developments and social/organizational characteristics of study sites; (p. 25)
> Description and illumination of diversity/multiple perspectives/alternative positions; (p. 26)
> Discussion/evidence of the ideological perspectives/values/philosophies of the research team. (p. 27)

And so on and so forth, the document continues across a total of six pages and 17 quality "appraisal questions."

No one would deny that these are important issues for social researchers to take into account in the design, conduct, and reporting of research studies. However, simply listed as such, they comprise a banal and inoperable set of standards that beg all the important questions of conducting and writing up qualitative fieldwork. Everything cannot be done; *choices* have to be made: How are they to be made, and how are they to be justified?

To be more positive for a moment, and note the arguments that might be put forward in favor of setting standards, it could be argued that if qualitative social and educational research is going to be commissioned, then a set of standards that can act as a bulwark against commissioning inadequate or underfunded studies in the first place ought to be welcomed. It might also be argued that this document at least demonstrates that qualitative research is being taken seriously enough within government to warrant a guidebook being produced for civil servants. This might then be said to confer legitimacy on civil servants who want to commission qualitative work; on qualitative social researchers bidding for such work; and indeed on social researchers more generally, who may have to deal with local research ethics committees (RECs; IRBs in the USA), which are predisposed toward a more quantitative natural science model of investigation. But should we really welcome such "legitimacy"? The dangers on the other side of the argument, as to whether social scientists need or should accede to criteria of quality endorsed by the state, are legion. In this respect, it is not at all clear that, *in principle,* state endorsement of qualitative research is any more desirable than state endorsement of RCTs.

Similar guidelines and checklists are starting to appear in the USA. Thus, for example, Ragin, Nagel, and White (2004) report on a "Workshop on Scientific Foundations of Qualitative Research," conducted under the auspices of the National Science Foundation and with the intention of placing "qualitative and quantitative research on a more equal footing . . . in funding agencies and graduate training programs" (p. 9). The report argues for the importance of qualitative research and thus advocates funding qualitative research *per se,* but equally, by articulating the "scientific foundations" it is arguing for the commissioning of not just qualitative research, but "proper" qualitative research. Thus, for example, they argue that

> Considerations of the scientific foundations of qualitative research often are predicated on acceptance of the idea of "cases." . . . No matter how cases are defined and constructed, in qualitative research they are studied in an in-depth manner. Because they are studied in detail their number cannot be great. (pp. 9–10)

This is interesting and provocative with respect to the idea of standards perhaps acting as a professional bulwark against commissioning inadequate or underfunded studies: A quick and cheap survey by telephone interview would not qualify as high-quality "scientific" qualitative research. But when it comes to the basic logic of qualitative work, Ragin et al. (2004) do not get much further than arguing for a supplementary role for qualitative methods:

> Causal mechanisms are rarely visible in conventional quantitative research . . . they must be inferred. Qualitative methods can be helpful in assessing the credibility of these inferred mechanisms. (p. 15)

In the end, Ragin et al.'s (2004) "Recommendations for Designing and Evaluating Qualitative Research" also conclude with another counsel of perfection:

> These guidelines amount to a specification of the *ideal* qualitative research proposal. A strong proposal should include as many of these elements as feasible. (p. 17, emphasis original)

But again, that's the point: What is *feasible* (and relevant to the particular investigation) is what is important, not what is ideal. How are such crucial choices to be made? Once again, "guidelines" and "recommendations" end up as no guide at all; rather, they are a hostage to fortune whereby virtually any qualitative proposal or report can be found wanting.

A potentially much more significant example of this tendency is the American Educational Research Association (AERA) *Standards for Reporting on Empirical Social Science Research in AERA Publications* (2006). The *Standards* comprise eight closely typed double-column pages and include "eight general areas" (p. 33) of advice, each of which is subdivided into a total of 40 subsections, some of which are subdivided still further. Yet only one makes any mention of the fact that research findings should be interesting or novel or significant, and that is the briefest of references under "Problem Formulation," which we are told should answer the question of "why the results of the investigation would be of interest to the research community" (p. 34). Intriguingly, whether the results might be of interest to the *policy* community is not mentioned as a criterion of quality.

As is typical of the genre, the *Standards* include an opening disclaimer that

> The acceptability of a research report does not rest on evidence of literal satisfaction of every standard. . . . In a given case there may be a sound professional reason why a particular standard is inapplicable. (p. 33)

But once again, this merely restates the problem rather than resolves it. The *Standards* may be of help in the context of producing a book-length thesis or dissertation, but no 5,000-word journal article could meet them all. Equally, however, even supposing that they could all be met, the article might still not be worth reading. It would be "warranted" and "transparent," which are the two essential standards highlighted in the preamble (p. 33), but it could still be boring and unimportant.

It is also interesting to note that words such as *warrant* and *transparency* raise issues of trust. They imply a concern for the very existence of a substantial data set as well as how it might be used to underpin conclusions drawn. Yet the issue of trust is only mentioned explicitly once, in the section of the *Standards* dealing with "qualitative methods": "It is the researcher's responsibility to show the reader that the report can be trusted" (AERA, 2006, p. 38). No such injunction appears in the parallel section on "quantitative methods" (p. 37); in fact, the only four uses of the actual word *warrant* in the whole document all occur in the section on "qualitative methods" (p. 38). The implication seems to be that quantitative methods really are trusted—the issue doesn't have to be raised—whereas qualitative methods are not. Standards of probity are only of concern when qualitative approaches are involved.

Capacity Building, Professionalization, and the Retreat Into "Science"

One response to the above examples of standards and guidelines is simply to accept them at face value. As I have already noted, in many respects they are unremarkable, and one of the key weaknesses that I have identified (i.e., their attempt at comprehensiveness) could even be used as a teaching device—for example, by asking students to identify which issues might *actually* be more or less important in the design of a particular study. And yet such documents carry more import than this—they also legitimate a particular delineation and control of the discourse surrounding qualitative research. In so doing, and in combination with other interventions such as the increasing reach of ethics committees and government regulation of research activity (Department of Health, 2005; Lincoln & Tierney, 2004; Torrance, 2006), they are beginning to change the very social relations of research and the ways in which issues of research quality have hitherto been addressed. Pursuing and developing quality in qualitative research has involved reading key sources iteratively and critically, in the context of designing and conducting a study, and discussing the implications and consequences with doctoral supervisors, or colleagues or project advisory groups. *Setting* standards in qualitative research, however, is a different enterprise. It implies the identification of universally appropriate and applicable procedures, which in turn involves documentary and institutional realization and compliance.

Much of the activity associated with such moves also now goes under the heading of "capacity building," certainly in the UK. As the government seeks to concentrate research resources in a smaller number of universities and extract maximum economic and social value from them, "centers of excellence" are being promoted, along with a concomitant obligation for the centers to link with and train in standard procedures those left stranded outside them (Department for Business, Innovations, and Skills, 2009; ESRC, 2005, 2009; National Centre for Research Methods, n.d.; Torrance, 2006). Similar aspirations also seem to be emerging in the USA (Eisenhart & DeHaan, 2005; NRC, 2005). It seems, then, that what is going on here is a struggle over the political economy and bureaucratic institutionalization of social research. What we are witnessing is a crucial moment in the continuing professionalization of social research. Governments are looking to control and quality-assure the process of social research and in so doing are treating researchers as an almost directly employed category of government worker in the "nationalized industry" of knowledge production. This in turn provides threats and opportunities for researchers as they seek to position themselves as both independent and autonomous sources of disinterested (i.e., scientific) advice, but nevertheless trustworthy professionals who can be relied upon to focus on topics of interest to policy and deliver a high-quality product.

Thus, some researchers are attempting to respond to the pressure of policy and the evidence movement by producing defensive documents that emphasize the need for professional standards and self–regulation (i.e., the AERA *Standards* above). In so doing, they appeal to and attempt to reassert the independence of "science" and the scientific community as a self-regulating group which, while broadly inclusive, nevertheless has clear boundaries and not only can define and protect standards, but *will*. Other researchers are seeing opportunities to redefine the field and their place within it (i.e., their status and access to research funding). This is similarly being pursued by an appeal to science, but it involves a much more exclusive, elitist, and static interpretation of science—defined by method, rather than broad approach, and by association with other more specifically social science disciplines such as psychology, political science, and economics. However, this latter group seems increasingly out of step with government demands for utility (namely, the problems created by results that simply show "no effects"), and thus it would appear that they are deploying the rhetoric of science as part of an internal struggle with other researchers, rather than in any direct response to the supposed needs of government (see also Baez & Boyles, 2009, for a longer-term analysis of such trends).

Science Is Not Enough: Toward a Different Approach

Interestingly, just as we've been here before with respect to 1960s/1970s disillusionment with research results that constantly showed "no significant difference," so we've been here before with respect to the response of the research community. Barry MacDonald (1974/1987) identified similar tensions over what role the research community should play in evaluating educational innovations. He identified three ideal types of approaches to evaluation—*autocratic, bureaucratic,* and *democratic,* aligning autocratic with scientific research, bureaucratic with confidential technical collaboration, and democratic with providing information for the widest possible public audience:

> Autocratic evaluation is a conditional service to . . . government. . . . It offers external validation of policy in exchange for compliance with its recommendations . . . the evaluator . . . acts as expert adviser. . . .

> Bureaucratic evaluation is an unconditional service to ... government. ...
> The evaluator ... acts as a management consultant [and] the report is
> owned by the bureaucracy and lodged in its files. ... Democratic evaluation
> is an information service to the whole community about the characteristics
> of an educational program. ... The democratic evaluator recognises value
> pluralism and seeks to represent a range of interests ... techniques of data
> gathering and presentation must be accessible to non-specialist audiences.
> (pp. 44–45)

Of course, times change and the parallels with current debates are not exact.
In particular, the obviously favored stance of "democratic evaluation" still presupposes that data can be gathered and interests represented in a fairly straightforward, realist fashion. Such aspirations would be more complex to accomplish
now. Yet such a formulation also resonates with contemporary issues around
stakeholder involvement, voice, and the engagement of a wider community in
deciding which research questions are important to ask and how best to try to
answer them.

It is now widely recognized from many different perspectives, including that
of the empowerment of research subjects on the one hand, and policy relevance
and social utility on the other, that an assumption of scientific disinterest and
independence is no longer sustainable. Other voices must be heard in the debate
over scientific quality and merit, particularly in an applied, policy-oriented field
such as education. Thus, for example, Gibbons el al. (1994) distinguish between
what they term Mode 1 and Mode 2 knowledge, with Mode 1 knowledge deriving
from what might be termed the traditional academic disciplines, and Mode 2
knowledge deriving from and operating within "a context of application":

> [I]n Mode 1 problems are set and solved in a context governed by the,
> largely academic, interests of a specific community. By contrast, Mode 2
> knowledge is carried out in a context of application. (p. 3)

Such knowledge is "transdisciplinary ... [and] involves the close interaction of
many actors throughout the process of knowledge production" (p. vii). In turn,
quality must be "determined by a wider set of criteria which reflects the
broadening social composition of the review system" (p. 8).

The language employed by Gibbons et al. (1994) and the assumed context of
operation very much reflect an engineering/technology-transfer type set of
activities, but they also mirror a far wider set of concerns with respect to redefining the validity and social utility of research. There is a clear orientation toward

the co-creation of knowledge through collaborative problem-solving action—rather than the discovery of knowledge through centralized, "expert" experimental investigation, which then gets disseminated to "practitioners" at the periphery. Ideas about the co-creation of knowledge link with deliberative and empowerment models of evaluation (Fetterman, 2001; House & Howe, 1999), which in turn owe something to MacDonald's (1974/1987) original notion of "democratic evaluation" (explicitly so, in House & Howe's case). The concept of "Mode 2 knowledge" also reflects something of the arguments around indigenous knowledge (Smith, 2005) and the many articulations and interrogations of how to identify and represent different "voices" in research (e.g., Alcoff, 1991; Fielding, 2004; Goodley, 1999; Jackson & Mazzei, 2009). Such arguments, coalescing into a diverse, contested, but nevertheless highly provocative and promising constellation of issues around the validity, utility, and ethics of social research, also bring us to the very limit of what it is currently possible to think about the relationship of qualitative inquiry to science, policy, and democracy. The challenge we face is how to sustain the tension between interrogating and reconceptualizing problems—"thinking the new"—while also addressing the "here and now" of the enduring social and political issues that face our society (see Lather, 2004, and Lather's contribution to Moss et al., 2009). The issue is how to reconcile the (research) need to investigate and comprehend complexity with the (policy) urge to simplify and act. To invert Marx, policy makers seek to change the world, but first they need to try to understand it, while involving others in both processes.

The scholarly retreat into trying to define the "scientific" merit of qualitative research simply in terms of theoretical and methodological standards, rather than in wider terms of social robustness and responsiveness to practice, seems to betray a defensiveness and loss of nerve on the part of the scholarly community. We need to acknowledge and discuss the imperfections of what we do, rather than attempt to legislate them out of existence. We need to embody and enact the deliberative process of academic quality assurance, in collaboration with research participants, not subcontract it to a committee. Assuring the quality of research, and particularly the quality of qualitative research, must be conceptualized as a vital and dynamic process that is always subject to further scrutiny and debate. The process cannot be ensconced in a single research method or a once-and-for-all set of standards. Furthermore, it should be oriented toward risk taking and the production of new knowledge, including the generation of new questions (some of which may derive from active engagement with research respondents and policy makers) rather than supplication, risk aversion, and the production of limited data on effectiveness for a center-periphery model of system maintenance ("what works").

What this means for the actual conduct of social research, particularly qualitative research, over the medium to long term is still difficult to say, but various modest examples are emerging in the UK. These involve designing studies with collaborating sponsors and participants, including policy makers and those "on the receiving end" of policy, and talking through issues of validity, warrant, appropriate focus, and trustworthiness of the results, rather than trying to establish all of the parameters in advance (see, e.g., James, 2006; Pollard, 2005; Somekh & Saunders, 2007; Somekh et al., 2007; Torrance et al., 2005; Torrance & Coultas, 2004). It can also involve new forms of dissemination and intellectual engagement with participants, rather than the simple reporting of "research findings" (MacLure, Holmes, MacRae, & Jones, 2010).

The process is not without its problems or critics, especially with respect to issues of co-option into a too closely defined "bureaucratic" agenda—policy makers and sponsors usually being rather more powerful than research participants. But in essence, the argument is that if research is to engage critically with policy and practice, then research and policy making must progress, both theoretically and chronologically, in tandem. Neither can claim precedence in the relationship. Research should not simply "serve" policy; equally, policy cannot simply "wait" for the results of research. And just as participant and practitioner perspectives (often called research "end-users" by policy makers) may be used by policy to attempt to discipline the research agenda pursued by researchers, equally, such perspectives can be used to critically interrogate policy. Research will encompass far more than simply producing policy-relevant findings; policy making will include far more than simply disseminating and acting upon research results. Where research and policy do cohere, the relationship should be pursued as an iterative one, with gains on both sides.

Ultimately, the issue revolves around whether or not quality is protected and advanced by compliance with a particular set of standards, or by the process of open democratic engagement and debate. Governments, and some within the scholarly community itself, seem to be seeking to turn educational research into a technology that can be applied to solving short-term educational problems, thereby also entrenching the power of the expert in tandem with the state. An alternative vision proposes research as a system of reflective and engaged enquiry that might help practitioners and policy makers think more productively about the nature of the problems they face and how they might be better addressed. And in fact, the latter process will be as beneficial to policy as to research. Producing research results takes time, and, as we have seen above, such results are unlikely to be unequivocal. Drawing policy makers and practitioners into a discussion of these issues will improve the nature of research questions and research design, while also signaling to them that the best evidence available is unlikely ever to be definitive—it should inform and educate judgment, but it cannot supplant judgment, nor should it.

Both the concept and the practice of science and government are under severe pressure at present, and ironically, despite all the recent criticisms of qualitative research, it is qualitative research that is best placed to recover and advance new forms of science and government, precisely because it rests on direct engagement with research participants. Many recent discussions of quality in qualitative research revolve around issues of engagement, deliberation, ethical process, and responsiveness to participant agendas, along with the need to maintain a critical perspective on both the topic at hand and the power of particular forms of knowledge (Lincoln, 1995; Schwandt, 1996; Lather, 2004; Smith, 2005). It is these strengths of a qualitative approach that are needed to reinvigorate the research enterprise and reconnect it with democratic processes.

Note

1. See Grissmer, Subotnik, and Orland (2009) for another illustration of the significance of qualitative data in focusing research questions and modifying the analyses of an experimental study of housing provision.

References

Alcoff, L. (1991, Winter). The problem of speaking for others. *Cultural Critique,* 5–32.

American Educational Research Association. (2006). Standards for reporting on empirical social science research in AERA publications. *Educational Researcher, 35*(6), 33–40.

Attree, P., & Milton, B. (2006). Critically appraising qualitative research for systematic reviews: Defusing the methodological cluster bombs. *Evidence and Policy, 2*(1), 109–126.

Baez, B., & Boyles, D. (2009). *The politics of inquiry: Education research and the "culture of science."* Albany: State University of New York Press.

Barbour, R., & Barbour, M. (2003). Evaluating and synthesizing qualitative research: The need to develop a distinctive approach. *Journal of Evaluation in Clinical Practice, 9*(2), 179–185.

Besley, T. (Ed.). (2009). *Assessing the quality of educational research in higher education: International perspectives.* Rotterdam, The Netherlands: Sense Publishers.

Blunkett, D. (2000). Influence or irrelevance: Can social science improve government? Speech to the Economic and Social Research Council (ESRC). (Reprinted in *Research Intelligence, 71,* British Educational Research Association, and *Times Higher Education* 2000, February 4, 2000.) Available at http://www.timeshighereducation.co.uk/story.asp?storyCode=150012&sectioncode=26

Boaz, A., Solesbury, W., & Sullivan, F. (2004). *The practice of research reviewing 1: An assessment of 28 review reports.* London: UK Centre for Evidence-Based Policy and Practice, Queen Mary College.

Boaz, A., Solesbury, W., & Sullivan, F. (2007). *The practice of research reviewing 2: Ten case studies of reviews.* London: UK Centre for Evidence-Based Policy and Practice, Queen Mary College.

Boden, R., Cox, D., Nedeva, M., & Barker, K. (2004) *Scrutinising science: The Changing UK government of science.* London: Palgrave.

Bridges, D. (2005, December 16). *The international and the excellent in educational research.* Paper prepared for the Challenges of the Knowledge Society for Higher Education Conference, Kaunas, Lithuania.

Bridges, D. (2009). Research quality assessment in education: Impossible science, possible art? *British Educational Research Journal, 35*(4), 497–517.

Brown, S. (2003, September 17). *Assessment of research quality: What hope of success?* Keynote address to European Educational Research Association annual conference, Hamburg, Germany.

Bush, V. (1945, July). *Science: The endless frontier.* A report to the president by Vannevar Bush, Director of the Office of Scientific Research and Development. Washington, DC: U.S. Government Printing Office. Available at http://www.nsf.gov/od/lpa/nsf50/vbush1945.htm

Cabinet Office. (2003a). *Quality in qualitative evaluation: A framework for assessing research evidence* [Summary]. London: Author.

Cabinet Office. (2003b). *Quality in qualitative evaluation: A framework for assessing research evidence* [Full report]. London: Author.

Cheek J. (2007). *Qualitative inquiry, ethics, and the politics of evidence. Qualitative Inquiry, 13*(8), 1051–1059.

Cook, T., & Payne, M. (2002). Objecting to the objections to using random assignment in educational research. In F. Mosteller & R. Boruch (Eds.), *Evidence matters: Randomized trials in education research* (pp. 150–178). Washington, DC: Brookings Institution Press.

Cronbach, L. (1975). Beyond the two disciplines of scientific psychology. *American Psychologist, 30,* 116–127.

Cronbach, L., & Associates. (1980). *Toward reform of program evaluation.* San Francisco: Jossey-Bass.

Davies, P. (2004). Systematic reviews and the Campbell Collaboration. In G. Thomas & R. Pring (Eds.), *Evidence-based practice in education* (pp. 21–33). Maidenhead, UK: Open University Press.

Davies, P., & Boruch, R. (2001). The Campbell Collaboration. *British Medical Journal, 323,* 294–295.

Department for Business, Innovations, and Skills. (2009). *Higher ambitions: The future of universities in a knowledge economy.* Available at http://www.bis.gov.uk/policies/higher-ambitions

Department of Health. (2005). *Research governance framework for health and social care* (2nd ed.). London: Author.

Dixon-Woods, M., Booth, A., & Sutton, A. (2007). Synthesizing qualitative research: A review of published reports. *Qualitative Research, 7*(3), 375–422.

Dixon-Woods, M., Fitzpatrick, R., & Roberts, K. (2001). Including qualitative research in systematic reviews: Opportunities and problems. *Journal of Evaluation in Clinical Practice, 7*(2), 125–133.

Economic and Social Research Council. (2005). *Postgraduate training guidelines.* Available at http://www.esrcsocietytoday.ac.uk/ESRCInfoCentre/Images/Postgraduate_Training_Guidelines_2005_tcm6-9062.pdf

Economic and Social Research Council. (2009). *Capacity building clusters.* Available at http://www.esrcsocietytoday.ac.uk/ESRCInfoCentre/research/CapacityBuilding-Clusters/index.aspx

Eisenhart, M., & DeHaan, R. (2005). Doctoral preparation of scientifically based education researchers. *Educational Researcher, 34*(4), 3–13.

Erickson, F., & Gutierrez, K. (2002). Culture, rigor, and science in educational research. *Educational Researcher, 31*(8), 21–24.

Fetterman, D. (2001). *Foundations of empowerment evaluation.* Thousand Oaks, CA: Sage.

Fielding, M. (2004). Transformative approaches to student voice: Theoretical underpinnings, recalcitrant realities. *British Educational Research Journal, 30*(2), 295–311.

Gibbons, M., Limoges, C., Nowotny, H., Schwartzman, S., Scott, P., & Trow, M. (1994). *The new production of knowledge.* Thousand Oaks, CA: Sage.

Goodley, D. (1999). Disability research and the "researcher template": Reflections on grounded subjectivity in ethnographic research. *Qualitative Inquiry, 5*(1), 24–46.

Gorard, S., & Taylor, C. (2004). *Combining methods in educational and social research.* Maidenhead, UK: Open University Press.

Gough, D., & Elbourne, D. (2002) Systematic research synthesis to inform policy, practice, and democratic debate. *Social Policy and Society, 1*(3), 225–236.

Greenberg, D. (2001). *Science, money, and politics* Chicago: University of Chicago Press.

Grissmer, D., Subotnik, R., & Orland, M. (2009). *A guide to incorporating multiple methods in randomized controlled trials to assess intervention effects.* Available at http://www.apa.org/ed/schools/cpse/activities/mixed-methods.aspx

Guba, E., & Lincoln, Y. (1981). *Effective evaluation: Improving the usefulness of evaluation results through responsive and naturalistic approaches.* San Francisco: Jossey-Bass.

Guba, E., & Lincoln, Y. (1989). *Fourth generation evaluation.* Newbury Park, CA: Sage.

Gueron, J. (2002). The politics of random assignment: Implementing studies and affecting policy. In F. Mosteller & R. Boruch (Eds.), *Evidence matters: randomized trials in education research* (pp. 15–49). Washington, DC: Brookings Institution Press.

Hamilton, D., Jenkins, D., King, C., MacDonald, B., & Parlett, M. (1976). *Beyond the numbers game.* London: Macmillan.

Hammersley, M. (1997). Educational research and teaching: A response to David Hargreaves' TTA lecture. *British Educational Research Journal, 23*(2), 141–161.

Hammersley, M. (2001). On systematic reviews of research literature: A narrative response. *British Educational Research Journal 27*(4), 543–554.

Hammersley, M. (2005). The myth of research-based practice: The critical case of educational inquiry. *International Journal of Social Research Methodology, 8*(4), 317–330.

Hammersley, M. (2008). Paradigm war revived? On the diagnosis of resistance to randomized controlled trials and systematic review in education. *International Journal of Research and Method in Education, 31*(1), 3–10.

Hargreaves, D. (1996). *Teaching as a research-based profession.* Teacher Training Agency 1996 Annual Lecture. London: Teacher Training Agency.

Higher Education Funding Council for England. (2009). *Research Excellence Framework.* Bristol, UK: Author.

Hillage, J., Pearson, R., Anderson, A., & Tamkin, P. (1998). *Excellence in research on schools* (DfEE Research Report 74). London, Department for Education and Employment.

House, E., & Howe, K. (1999). *Values in evaluation and social research.* Thousand Oaks, CA: Sage.

Howe, K. (2004). A critique of experimentalism. *Qualitative Inquiry, 10*(1), 42–61.

Jackson, A., & Mazzei, L. (Eds.). (2009). *Voice in qualitative inquiry.* London: Routledge.

James, M. (2006). Balancing rigor and responsiveness in a shifting context: Meeting the challenges of educational research. *Research Papers in Education, 21*(4), 365–380.

Lagemann, E. (2000). *An elusive science: The troubling history of education research.* Chicago: University of Chicago Press.

Lather, P. (2004). This IS your father's paradigm: Government intrusion and the case of qualitative research in education. *Qualitative Inquiry, 10*(1), 15–34.

Lincoln, Y. (1995). Emerging criteria for quality in qualitative and interpretive research. *Qualitative Inquiry, 1*(3), 275–289.

Lincoln, Y., & Tierney, W. (2004). Qualitative research and institutional review boards. *Qualitative Inquiry, 10*(2), 219–234.

MacDonald, B. (1987). Evaluation and the control of education. In R. Murphy & H. Torrance (Eds.), *Evaluating education: Issues and methods.* London: Harper & Row. (Reprinted from *Innovation, evaluation, research and the problem of control,* pp. 9–22 [SAFARI Interim Papers], by B. MacDonald & R. Walker, Eds., 1974, Norwich: UK: University of East Anglia, Centre for Applied Research in Education.

MacLure, M. (2003). *Discourse in education and social research.* Maidenhead, UK: Open University Press.

MacLure, M. (2005). Clarity bordering on stupidity: Where's the quality in systematic review? *Journal of Education Policy, 20*(4), 393–416.

MacLure, M., Holmes, R., MacRae, C., & Jones, L. (2010). Animating classroom ethnography: Overcoming video-fear. In L. Mazzei & K. McCoy (Eds.), Thinking with

Deleuze in qualitative research [Special issue]. *International Journal of Qualitative Studies in Education, 23*(5), 543–556.

Maxwell, J. (2004). Causal explanation, qualitative research, and scientific enquiry in education. *Educational Researcher, 33*(2), 3–11.

Middleton, S. (2009). Becoming PBRF-able: Research assessment and education in New Zealand. In T. Besley (Ed.), *Assessing the quality of educational research in higher education: International perspectives* (pp. 193–208). Rotterdam, The Netherlands: Sense Publishers.

Moss, P., Phillips, D., Erickson, F., Floden, R., Lather, P., & Schneider, B. (2009). Learning from our differences: A dialogue across perspectives on quality in education research. *Educational Researcher, 38*(7), 501–517.

Mosteller, F., & Boruch, R. (Eds.). (2002). *Evidence matters: Randomized trials in education research.* Washington, DC: Brookings Institution Press.

National Centre for Research Methods. (n.d.). *A strategic framework for capacity building within the ESRC National Centre for Research Methods (NCRM).* Available at http://www.ncrm.ac.uk/TandE/capacity/documents/NCRMStrategicFrameworkForCapacityBuildingMain.pdf

National Research Council. (2002). *Scientific research in education.* Washington, DC: Author.

National Research Council. (2005). *Advancing scientific research in education.* Washington, DC: Author.

Nisbet, J., & Broadfoot, P. (1980). *The impact of research on policy and practice in education.* Aberdeen, Scotland: Aberdeen University Press.

Oakley, A. (2000). *Experiments in knowing.* Cambridge, UK: Polity Press.

Oakley A. (2003). Research evidence, knowledge management and educational practice: Early lessons from a systematic approach. *London Review of Education, 1*(1), 21–33.

Oakley, A. (2006). Resistances to new technologies of evaluation: Education research in the UK as a case study. *Evidence and Policy, 2*(1), 63–88.

Pollard, A. (2005). Challenges facing educational research. *Educational Review, 58*(3), 251–267.

Ragin, C., Nagel, J., & White, P. (2004). *Workshop on scientific foundations of qualitative research.* Available at http://www.nsf.gov/pubs/2004/nsf04219/start.htm

Roberts, K., Dixon-Woods, M., Fitzpatrick, R., Abrams, K., & Jones, D. (2002). Factors affecting uptake of childhood immunization: A Bayesian synthesis of qualitative and quantitative evidence. *The Lancet, 360,* 1596–1599.

Schwandt, T. (1996). Farewell to criteriology. *Qualitative Inquiry 2*(1), 58–72.

Shavelson, R., Phillips, D., Towne, L., & Feuer, M. (2003). On the science of education design studies. *Educational Researcher, 32*(1), 25–28.

Slavin, R. (2002). Evidence-based education policies: Transforming educational practice and research. *Educational Researcher, 31*(7), 15–21.

Smith, L. (2005). On tricky ground: Researching the native in the age of uncertainty. In N. K. Denzin & Y. S. Lincoln (Eds.), *The SAGE handbook of qualitative research* (3rd ed., pp. 85–107). Thousand Oaks, CA: Sage.

Somekh, B., & Saunders, L. (2007). Developing knowledge through intervention: Meaning and definition of "Quality" in research into change. *Research Papers in Education, 22*(2), 183–197.

Somekh, B., Underwood, J., Convery, A., Dillon, G., Jarvis, J., Lewin, C., et al. (2007). *Final report of the evaluation of the ICT Test Bed Project.* Coventry, UK: Becta.

Stake, R. (1967). The countenance of educational evaluation. *Teachers' College Record,* 68, 523–540.

Stake, R. (1978). The case study method in social inquiry. *Educational Researcher, 7*(2), 5–8.

Stenhouse, L. (1975). *An introduction to curriculum research and development.* London: Heineman.

Stenhouse, L., Verma, G., Wild, R., & Nixon, J. (1982). *Teaching about race relations: Problems and effects.* London: Routledge.

Tooley, J., & Darby, D. (1998). *Educational research: A critique.* London: Office for Standards in Education.

Torrance, H. (2006). Research quality and research governance in the United Kingdom: From methodology to management. In N. K. Denzin & M. Giardina (Eds.), *Qualitative inquiry and the conservative challenge* (pp. 127–148). Walnut Creek, CA: Left Coast Press.

Torrance, H. (2008). *Overview of ESRC research in education: A consultancy commissioned by ESRC: Final report.* Available at http://www.sfre.ac.uk/uk/

Torrance, H., Colley, H., Ecclestone, K., Garratt, D., James, D., & Piper, H. (2005). *The impact of different modes of assessment on achievement and progress in the learning and skills sector.* London: Learning and Skills Research Centre.

Torrance, H., & Coultas, J. (2004). *Do summative assessment and testing have a positive or negative effect on post-16 learners' motivation for learning in the learning and skills sector?* London: Learning and Skills Research Centre.

Viadero, D. (2009, April 1). "No effects" studies raising eyebrows. *Education Week.* Available at http://www.projectcriss.com/newslinks/Research/MPR_EdWk--NoEffectsArticle.pdf

Wade, C., Turner, H., Rothstein, H., & Lavenberg, J. (2006). Information retrieval and the role of the information specialist in producing high-quality systematic reviews in the social, behavioral, and education sciences. *Evidence and Policy, 2*(1), 89–108.

Weiss, C. (1972). *Evaluating action programs.* Boston: Allyn & Bacon.

Weiss, C. (1980). *Social science research and decision-making.* New York: Columbia University Press.

Woodhead, C. (1998, March 20). Academia gone to seed. *New Statesman,* pp. 51–52.

Yates, L. (2004). *What is quality in educational research?* Buckingham, UK: Open University Press.

12

Reflections on Interpretive Adequacy in Qualitative Research

David L. Altheide and John M. Johnson

A line is a dot that went for a walk.

—Paul Klee

O ver 15 years ago, we published "Criteria for Assessing Interpretive Validity in Qualitative Research" (Altheide & Johnson, 1994). In this work, we continued the development of our ideas about qualitative research, many of which were developed during a long series of professional meetings in the 1980s. Our animating questions were how interpretive methodologies should be judged by readers (audiences) who share the perspective that how knowledge is acquired, organized, interpreted, and presented is relevant for the substance of those claims. We presented our ideas about how to make the claims and narratives of qualitative research more trustworthy to readers and audiences. We called our approach "analytic realism," to identify how reflexive and interpretive methods could be presented to enhance their credibility, relevance, and importance.

Much has happened in the world of qualitative methods during the last two decades, and important questions and issues now span many new disciplines, venues, arenas, perspectives, theories, and problem areas. Methodological issues once considered relevant for only a minority of anthropologists and sociologists are now discussed (and disputed) in many other disciplines, especially education, policy studies, the health sciences, gender studies, communication, cultural studies, justice studies, and others. Many new models of representation and inter-pretation have arisen during this period, including those from advocates for link-ing qualitative research to justice values, issues, and agendas. Performative writing and performance ethnography emerge as new positions, and advocates for stand-point epistemologies cross disciplinary boundaries. A robust debate about using cyberspace for research generates new issues and perspectives. In the context of this creative flux, conservative countermovements emerge to standardize or nor-malize the practice and evaluation. In the United States, a scientifically based research (SBR) countermovement has arisen, also called scientific inquiry in edu-cation (SIE), and this is joined by similar movements in the United Kingdom, called the research assessment exercise (RAE), or in Australia the research quality framework (RQF). Two reports by the U.S. National Science Foundation have proven especially troublesome and problematic for American scholars (Lamont & White, 2009; Ragin, Nagel, & White, 2004). These movements have generated heated debates about "the politics of evidence," and inspired claims about qualita-tive inquiry being "under fire" by these state-sponsored efforts to constrain and control the criteria of scientific inquiry (Denzin, 2009).

Our advocacy of analytic realism in the 1994 paper was intended to align our efforts with philosophical realism, arguably the dominant philosophical position in the social sciences for many decades. The basic idea of realism is that there is a real world with which we act and interact (an "obdurate" world in the words of George Herbert Mead), that individuals and groups create meaning in this world, and that while our theories, concepts, and perspectives may approach some kind of valid understanding, they cannot and do not exhaust the phenom-ena of our interest. All theories, concepts, and findings are grounded in values and perspectives; all knowledge is contextual and partial; and other conceptual schemas and perspectives are always possible. We are heartened that many other scholars have advanced some related version of this perspective, such as "critical realism" (Bhaskar, 1979; Harré & Madden, 1975; Manicas & ebrary, Inc. 2006; Maxwell, 2008), "experimental realism" (Lakoff, 1987), "subtle realism" (Emerson, Fretz, & Shaw, 1995; Hammersley, 1992), "ethnographic realism" (Lofland, 1995), "innocent realism" (Haak, 2003), "natural realism" (Putnam, 1999), and "emergent realism" (Henry, Julnes, & Mark, 1998). These different versions of realism share certain basic ideas: that human social life is meaningful, and that it is essential to take these meanings into account in our explanations, concepts, and theories; furthermore, to grasp the importance of the values, emotions, beliefs, and other meanings of cultural members, it is imperative to embrace an interpretivist approach in our scientific and theoretical work. According to Maxwell (2008), these versions of realism reflect an ontological realism while simultaneously accepting a form of epistemological constructionism and relativity. They oppose the radical constructivist view, which denies the existence of any reality apart from our constructions of it (or them). This kind of realist perspective has proven very valuable in grasping the relationship(s) between the meanings and perspectives of cultural members and the social contexts in which they are embedded, and especially for understanding conflicts or differences in meanings for actors located in the same situation or context.

When knowledge and evidence are viewed from a symbolic interactionist perspective, evidence is seen *as part of a communication process that symbolically joins an actor, an audience, a point of view, assumptions, and claims about the relations between two or more phenomena.* This view of evidence-as-process is termed the "evidentiary narrative," and draws attention to the ways in which credible information and knowledge are buffeted by symbolic filters, including distinctive "epistemic communities," or collective meanings, standards, and criteria that govern sanctioned action (see Altheide, 2008). It is heartening to see that numerous qualitative researchers in a number of these epistemic communities have made impressive strides in addressing their validity issues within their own perspectives, and have developed many useful ideas to create more trustworthy knowledge to be shared with other audiences. We briefly review some of these developments as a prelude to saying how this has changed our views in recent years.

Framing Validity Issues in Interpretive Research

There are many ways to use, practice, promote, and claim qualitative research, and in each there is a proposed or claimed relationship between some field of human experience, a form of representation, and an audience. Researchers and scholars in each of these areas have been grappling with issues of truth, validity, verisimilitude, credibility, trustworthiness, dependability, confirmability, and so on. What is valid for clinical studies or policy studies may not be adequate or relevant for ethnography or autoethnography or performance ethnography. We return to this point later.

CLINICAL STUDIES

In recent years, researchers in several clinical fields have utilized qualitative methods to grasp and articulate invisible or taken-for-granted realities they experience in clinical settings. Miller and Crabtree (2005) write,

Qualitative clinical researchers bring several power perspectives to the clinical encounter that help surface the unseen and the unheard and also add depth to what is already present. These include understanding disease as a cultural construction . . . possessing knowledge of additional medical models such as biopsychosocial and humanistic models, homeopathy, and non-Western models that include traditional Chinese, Ayurvedic, and shamanism, and recognizing the face and importance of spirituality in human life. (p. 612)

Clinical practitioners who utilize observational, narrative, or discourse methods are seeking to articulate standards of validity (or truthfulness) that can be shared with others in their field, and hence are subject to independent tests and verification. Of these efforts, Rolfe (2004) writes,

[For some,] validity and reliability [in clinical studies] are achieved when the researcher rigorously follows a number of verification strategies in the course of the research process. "Together, all these verification strategies incrementally and interactively contribute to and build reliability and validity, thus ensuring rigor. Thus, the rigor of qualitative inquiry should be beyond question, beyond challenge, and provide pragmatic *scientific evidence* that *must* be integrated into our developing knowledge base" [Morse et al., 2002, emphasis added by Rolfe]. This statement of intent exemplifies very strongly the aspirations of some qualitative researchers to the values, approaches, terminologies, and hence, to the certainties of the "hard" sciences. Rigor is clearly the key to success. . . . [But others] argue that issues of validity in qualitative studies should be linked not to "truth" or "value," as they are for the positivists, but rather to "trustworthiness," which becomes a matter of persuasion whereby the scientist is viewed as having made those practices visible, and therefore, auditable. (p. 305)

These comments illustrate the ongoing debates of the *evidence-based practice movement* in clinical studies, where for many years now qualitative practitioners and researchers have been discussing the applicability of such ideas as truth, validity, reliability, trustworthiness, and so on. While many anthropologists or sociologists who practice qualitative research might be primarily motivated to make fundamental contributions to the basic knowledge of their disciplines, or contributions to a substantive problem area, those who practice qualitative methods in clinical studies typically intend a different audience, those interested in advancing effective clinical practice. These comments illustrate that there is a diversity of purposes that animate qualitative research, and that criteria of usefulness in research are tied to these practical purposes and disciplinary/occupational values.

POLICY STUDIES

Qualitative research is increasingly used in policy studies, where the intention is to study how various actors bring and make meaning in actual concrete settings, and the consequences of these actions. The goals of this type of research are crisply stated by Hammersley (2005): "Qualitative policy research is aimed at having an impact on current programs and practices" (p. 3). The focus here can be on the impact or consequences of policy, but additionally the processes of how official law or policies are translated and interpreted, from the heights of inception down to the points of implementation, to the "street-level" realities. There is little doubt that qualitative research can be more flexible than traditional quantitative research, and has the potential to adjust research agendas to meet changing demands in the field. While the focus of quantitative research is usually on "outcome measures," or metrics, qualitative research has the potential to study the complex social and bureaucratic processes whereby laws and policies are actually implemented in daily life. In the United Kingdom, central policy makers have proposed their own set of standards for what they expect of qualitative research in these areas (Cabinet Office, 2003). These should include a detailed description of the contexts in which the study was conducted, a discussion of how fieldwork settings or methods may have influenced data collection, descriptions of background or historical developments and social/organizational characteristics of study sites, description and illumination of diversity/multiple perspectives or positions, and discussion/evidence of the ideological perspectives/values/philosophies that guide the researcher or research team (see Torrance, 2007, pp. 55–79).

The tensions and debates in policy studies mirror those in other areas; some feel that validity or truth is better served by affirming a set of research standards (such as those offered by the UK Cabinet Office above), whereas others think that truth is better served by making comparative assessments between studies, over time, and between diverse settings. Harry Torrance (2007) writes,

Assuring the quality of research, and particularly the quality of qualitative research in the context of policy making, must be conceptualized as a vital and dynamic process that is always subject to further scrutiny and debate. The process cannot be ensconced in a single research method or a once-and-for-all set of standards. (p. 73)

Others in the policy field also affirm the necessity for comparing research reports with prior reports, and for comparing settings with other settings (Hammersley, 1992). This is a common theme in what is now called "the new public management movement," which seeks greater transparency and clarity of the policy-making and policy-implementation processes. This suggests a dual approach to the issue of validity: certain expectations for the researcher or research team to show readers the grounds for trusting their report, on the one hand, in conjunction with a measured and realistic skepticism by readers, on the other hand, to place the claims of any given research report in a context of many other reports, even one's life experiences.

ACTION RESEARCH

Action research or participatory action research is another emergent form of qualitative research, which usually involves one researcher or a research team in the field, participating with societal members to produce social change or implement a social policy or organized response to a problem. Kemmis and McTaggart (2005) propose their vision of this kind of research:

Through participatory action research, people can come to understand that—and how—their social and educational practices are located in, and are the product of, particular material, social, and historical circumstances that *produced* them and by which they are *produced* in everyday social interaction in a particular setting. By understanding their practices as the product of particular circumstances, participatory action researchers becomes alert to clues about how it may be possible to *transform* the practices they are producing and reproducing through their current ways of working. (p. 565, emphasis original)

Social action researchers do not deny the relevance or importance of foundational or basic knowledge, but often insist that they seek experiential knowledge as well, often expressing the hope that theory and pragmatics together can achieve a whole that is greater than its parts. To provide grounds for trusting participatory action research, Ladkin (2004) proposes that research done in this vein should include accounts to demonstrate emergence and enduring consequences of actions or policies, accounts of how the research dealt with pragmatic issues of practice and practicing, accounts of how the research deals with questions of significance, and accounts showing how the research considers a number of different ways of knowing. While it would be easy to criticize Ladkin's proposals as being very abstract and insubstantial, or for emphasizing certain things (like the consequences) that are not within the control of the researcher or research team, our main point here is to show that those working in this vein are struggling with issues of truthfulness and validity, and seek to engage this debate within the confines of their own expertise.

AUTOETHNOGRAPHY AND EXPRESSIVE FRAMES

A diversity of current research seeks to break down the prior barriers between subject and object, between the knower and the known, between the self and the social, between the spiritual and the empirical, and between the writer and the audience. Autoethnography is only one of several names given to this emerging enterprise, and autoethnographers commonly seek to integrate the storyteller and the story. Laurel Richardson (1997) says that "writing stories about our 'texts' is a way of making sense of and changing our lives" (p. 5). Carolyn Ellis (2009) seeks to "open up conversations about emotions in romantic and family relationships" (p. 17). She additionally says,

> Thus, reexamining the events we have lived through and the stories we have told about them previously allows us to expand and deepen our understandings of the life we have led, the culture in which we have lived, and the work we have done. This review provides new possibilities for understanding ourselves and keeps us from remaining stuck in the interpretations we have settled on in the past. (p. 13)

On many occasions, autoethnographers grapple with the issue of "memory," and how to contextualize or re-contextualize people and events from long ago. This issue is larger than the vagaries of remembering empirical facts, because it includes the many issues of interpretation and perspective. On the standards involved in this kind of research, Bochner (2007) states,

> Of course, my gravest obligation is not to lie. But the space between lying and telling the truth can be vast. If telling the truth is merely saying what I remember, then I have set the bar of obligation extremely low. Once the

past was there, now it is gone. I want to be faithful to the past, but what I remember of my history is anchored by what summons me *now* to remember, and my memory is, in part, a response to what inspired my recollections. (p. 198, emphasis original)

For many of its practitioners, autoethnography becomes a disciplined way to interrogate one's memory, to contextualize or re-contextualize empirical facts or memories within interpretations or perspectives that "make sense" of them in new or newly appreciated ways. Many of these studies deal with intimate and family relations, and commonly seek to make explicit what is usually taken for granted within these relationships, the many seen-but-unspoken or known-but-not-acknowledged complexities of our lives. In some autoethnographic studies, the time frame of interest is longer than that of a traditional, observational ethnography, which might take as long as 10 years between the time of inception and the time of the final report; many autoethnographers seek to elucidate the changes in meaning or perspective over many years, even decades, where the long passage of time itself produces new or altered understandings of past "facts."

Performance ethnography and expressive artists often share the autoethnographer's desire to explore and communicate the deeply personal or taken-for-granted aspects of personal or daily life, but in addition they often seek to engage their audience in a more direct manner, often seeking to evoke an emotional response. This may be done with acted performances, poems, photography, multimedia collages, or readings. Szto, Furman, and Langer (2005) write,

The photographer is an ethnographer in this sense [of trying to capture a subject's reality]. You try to capture the context. You have to take poetic license and select context. . . . In the role of researcher, the poet must engage in conscious and constant self-exploration. When he (or she) writes about a subject in front of himself (herself), or when he (she) is reducing data from narratives, he (she) has to be very clear to stay faithful to the data. His (her) notes serve as both data to be worked with, as well as ethnographic notes that explore their reactions. Many times, these biases should be presented so the readers can decide for themselves how to interpret the poem. The first allegiance of the researcher, as poet, has to be to the subject's experience. In a sense, there are two types of poems for the researcher. There are poems in which they merely present the subjects' experience as accurately as possible, hopefully utilizing their words, and then there are interpretive poems, in which they deconstruct the meaning of the experience and consciously allow for interpretation. (p. 139)

There is great diversity of qualitative research, and there is diversity in the ways to justify or legitimize each of the above approaches. While these approaches differ, they also share an ethical obligation to make public their claims, to show the reader, audience, or consumer why they should be trusted as faithful accounts of some phenomenon. Moreover, each of these approaches reflects the context and purposes for the practitioners and audiences, including clients. The pragmatic utility of validity as "good for our present intents and purposes" cuts through all of the methodological approaches and authoritative claims. In other words, whether it is truthful, accurate, on the mark, and so forth is framed by an ecology of knowing tied to practices and intentions, and ultimately, "our justifications" for using this method. What is common to each of these approaches, and by implication all forms of inquiry, is a *process* of acquiring information, organizing it as data, and then analyzing and interpreting those data with the help of refractive (conceptual, theoretical, perhaps political) lenses.

We have noted that validity has been referred to many ways, including successor validity, catalytic validity, interrogated validity, transgressive validity, imperial validity, simulacra/ironic validity, situated validity, and voluptuous validity (see, e.g., Atkinson, 1990; Atkinson, 1992; Guba, 1990; Hammersley, 1990, 1992; Lather, 1993; Wolcott, 1990). Our effort to clarify the logic-in-use by many qualitative researchers suggested that a heuristic view of "hyphenated validity" could help clarify the methodological discourse at the time (early 1990s).

TYPES OF VALIDITY

Validity-as-culture (VAC) is well known to social science students. A basic claim is that the ethnographer reflects, imposes, reproduces, writes, and then reads their cultural point of view for the "others." Point of view is the culprit in validity. The solution includes efforts to include more points of view, including reassessing how researchers view the research mission and the research topic. Atkinson (1992, p. 34 ff.) suggests that ethnographies can be mythologized: "But the sense of class continuities is hardly surprisingly stronger in the British genre than in the American which is more preoccupied with a sense of place."

Validity-as-ideology (VAI) is very similar to VAC, except the focus is on the certain specific cultural features involving social power, legitimacy, assumptions about social structure, e.g., subordinate/superordinate.

Validity-as-gender (VAG), like the previous two, focuses on taken-for-granted assumptions made by "competent" researchers in carrying out their conceptual and data collection tasks, including some issues about power and domination in social interaction. One concern is that these asymmetrical aspects of social power may be normalized and further legitimated.

Validity-as-language/text (VAL) resonates with all that have come before, particularly how cultural categories and views of the world, as implicated in language, and more broadly, "discourse," restricts decisions and choices by how things are framed.

Validity-as-relevance/advocacy (VAR) stresses the utility and "empowerment" of research to benefit and uplift those groups often studied, relatively powerless people, e.g., the poor, peasants, etc.

Validity-as-standards (VAS) asserts that the expectation about a distinctive authority for science, or the researchers legitimized by this "mantle of respectability," is itself suspect, and that truth-claims are so multiple as to evade single authority or procedure. In the extreme case, science ceases to operate as a desirable model of knowledge, because it is, after all, understanding rather than codified, theoretically integrated information—as knowledge—that is to be preferred. (Altheide & Johnson, 1994, p. 488)

These approaches to validity, while certainly not definitive, reflected the purpose and audiences for research approaches and applications. The subtext was openness and engagement. Notwithstanding intense debates that occurred among the practitioners, the tone was inclusive and the spirit was to not overlook important segments of, say, audiences that might not be so well served by unintended limitations of the generation of knowledge. Informed by our basic assumption that *the social world is an interpreted world, not a literal world, always under symbolic construction, with emphasis on awareness of the process of the ethnographic work,* we offered another inclusive view: validity-as-reflexive-accounting (VARA), which places the researcher, the topic, and the sense-making process in interaction.

We identified these hyphenated validities (above) as illustrations of the range of attention the "problem of validity" has received. But another standard for validity has appeared. The SBR, SIE, and RAE movements noted above represent examples of an expanded context of control involving disparate audiences with oversight interests in corralling and regulating qualitative research in accordance with conventional formats of communication and regulation, and ultimately legitimacy associated with more positivistic methodology. This has led to a new version of validity, validity-as-marketable-legitimacy (VAML), which refers to the negotiated order of socially sanctioned (and respectable) research methodology.

This latest version of validity is being promoted for bureaucratic, rational, and organizational purposes and not to enhance inquiry, creativity, or discovery, but rather, accountability, as in; Funding this is warranted according to our "guidelines"; therefore no individual will be accountable for any errors, and so forth (Denzin, 2010; Kvale & Brinkmann, 2008). An unintended consequence of VAML is to dampen the creative search for varied forms of truth and relevant search. Openness and the tremendous success of the explorations of various approaches to qualitative work across many disciplines have, paradoxically, contributed to its utility, use, and imposed limitations for practical purposes. In recent years, the debate has intensified and changed, as qualitative research has become more accepted for funding and "practical" applications, e.g., policy research. One interpretation is that qualitative research is now in the marketplace of ideas, where the coinage is not just intellectual prowess, but actual coin. The approaches to validity that we delineated were consistent with the pursuit of truth and a logic of discovery. However, the success of varied approaches to qualitative research has opened up market possibilities not only for publication and teaching, but also for funding and sponsored projects that are accountable to administrators and overseers of agencies and organizations that must answer to other scientific and political constituencies. The standardization and reduction of an array of approaches leads to more than smoothing out sharp edges; domains become sacrificed for the sake of an established lexicon, rhetoric, and narrative of authorized knowing, ultimately as "objective." The push to the linear criteria and decision making—recall Klee's dot that went for a walk!—means that approved criteria and checklists of acceptability and standardization matter. We will say a bit more about this later in the essay after discussing the complexities of evidence and the importance of tacit knowledge in understanding the social construction of reality. For now, we wish to emphasize that the standardization of qualitative work is also risk avoidance and demonstrates a "risk society" approach to solving the problem of evaluating research, and so forth (Erikson & Doyle, 2003). However, evidence is not that simple.

THE PROBLEM OF EVIDENCE

Much of the foregoing discussion rests on an understanding of "evidence," or agreed-upon—or potentially agreeable—information that would serve as a basis or foundation. There is a rich literature on the control of information, research subjects, and topics (Van den Hoonaard, 2002), as well as the politics of evidence (Altheide, 2008; Denzin & Giardina, 2008). Evidence and facts are similar but not identical. We can often agree on facts, e.g., there is a rock, it is harder than cotton candy. Evidence involves an assertion that some facts are relevant to an argument or claim about a relationship. Since a position in an argument is likely tied to an ideological or even an epistemological position, evidence is not completely bound by facts, but is more problematic and subject to disagreement. Indeed, until the 1990s, most qualitative research was not taken seriously by many sociologists, and was regarded as second-rate social science; editors and reviewers for the discipline's major journals would rarely publish qualitative reports. The basic problem, of course, was that qualitative research, with exceptions, was not regarded as being based on data; quotes and observations were not regarded as appropriate evidence, especially if there were not a large enough number or "N" of these, thus rendering qualitative claims as akin to quantitative estimates. The situation was so dire that several groups of qualitative researchers started their own journals, including *Urban Life* (later, *Journal of Contemporary Ethnography*), *Symbolic Interaction,* and *Qualitative Sociology.* In 2011—as this handbook attests—the situation has much improved, as qualitative methods, data, and "evidence" have come to be more accepted. Yet, as the foregoing discussion indicates, there remains a kind of impatience with the wide-ranging epistemologies that certain interest groups want to compartmentalize and regulate.

The problem that sociologists have with conflicts over evidence, however, is minimal compared to the nonacademic settings. When the president of the United States uses rhetoric and photographs to demonstrate/show that Iraq had weapons of mass destruction (WMD) and therefore should be invaded in order to keep the world safe, and when this "proof" turns out to be false, then it is even more important that evidence be examined and critically analyzed. Accordingly, qualitative researchers have focused on evidence and its social contexts (Denzin & Giardina, 2008).

We wish to stress that communication strategies, formats, and paradigmatic boundaries can cloud our vision. The symbolic meaning filters that are called forth all stem from various memberships. Ultimately, evidence is bound up with our identity in a situation. The multiple memberships we hold in various epistemic communities are situationally shuffled and joined for a particular purpose (e.g., when an assumption or value is challenged or called into question). An "evidentiary narrative" emerges from a reconsideration of how knowledge and belief systems in everyday life are tied to epistemic communities that provide perspectives, scenarios, and scripts that reflect symbolic social and moral orders.

> An "evidentiary narrative" symbolically joins an actor, an audience, a point of view (definition of a situation), assumptions, and a claim about a

relationship between two or more phenomena. If any of these factors are not part of the context of meaning for a claim, it will not be honored, and thus, not seen as evidence. Moreover, only the claim is discursive, or potentially problematic, but it need not be so. (Altheide, 2009, p. 65)

The idea is that evidence is not about facts per se, but is about an argument, a narrative that is appropriate for the purpose-at-hand. That means it is contextualized and part of a bounded project, with accompanying assumptions, criteria, rules of membership, participation, and so on.

From a sociology-of-knowledge perspective, the active reception of a point "of information" is contingent on the "media logic" of legitimacy (acceptability) of the information source, the technology, medium, format and logic through which it is delivered (Altheide & Snow, 1979). What is meant by "evidence" can be viewed as "information that is filtered by various symbolic filters and nuanced meanings compatible with membership" (Altheide, 2009, p. 65). Only then can the information be interpreted as evidence in juxtaposition with an issue, problem, or point of contention. Conversely, information that is not suitably configured and presented is likely to be resisted, if not rebuffed, within a prevailing discourse.

Earlier we argued (Altheide & Johnson, 1994) that a more encompassing view of the ethnographic enterprise would take into account the process by which the ethnography occurred, which must be clearly delineated, including accounts of the interaction between the context, researcher, methods, setting, and actors. The broad term that we offered, "analytic realism," is based on the view that the social world is an interpreted world, not a literal world, always under symbolic construction (even deconstruction!). We can also apply this perspective to understand how situations in everyday life are informed by social contexts and uses of evidence. This application illuminates the process by which evidence is constituted. We can now see how any effort to standardize and limit qualitative research criteria is doomed to failure and irrelevance. As long as the core of qualitative research is extended to more specific audiences and uses, criteria for validity will be linked with the evidence appropriate for specific tastes and uses. It is useful, then, to consider the following elements of what we termed "an ethnographic ethic" (Altheide & Johnson, 1994, p. 489) when trying to understand evidence that is stated or affirmed in a situation:

(1) The relationship between what is observed (behaviors, rituals, meanings) and the larger cultural, historical, and organizational contexts within which the observations are made (the substance);

(2) The relationship between the observer, the observed, and the setting (the observer);

(3) The issue of perspective (or point of view), whether that of the observer or the member(s), used to render an interpretation of the ethnographic data (the interpretation);

(4) The role of the reader in the final product (the audience); and

(5) The issue of representational, rhetorical, or authorial style used by the author(s) to render the description or interpretation (the style).

Each of these areas includes questions or issues that must be addressed and pragmatically resolved by any particular observer in the course of his or her research. As originally formulated, these five dimensions of qualitative research include problematic issues pertaining to validity. Indeed, we argued that the "ethnographic ethic" calls for ethnographers to substantiate their interpretations and findings with a reflexive account of themselves and the process(es) of their research (Altheide & Johnson, 1993).

The evidentiary narrative is built on several arrays of meaning: what we know, who we are, and what we consider as evidence of either our most basic assumptions (e.g., that there is order in the world), or a specific claim about part of that order (e.g., my beliefs are legitimate and truthful). Prior to delving into a solution, let's attempt an overview of the problem. We live as social beings and are accountable to some people but not others. Why do we accept certain claims but reject others, and what would lead us to change our minds? In the modern era, this involved scientific authority about certain empirical truths that were based on "data" as evidence, or as a kind of fact-guided proof. The modernist project relied on rationality, including some formal rules of logic grounded in an objective view of things. This view has been seriously questioned by extensive research and writings encompassing such approaches as ethnomethodology, phenomenology, existential sociology, symbolic interactionism, feminism, literary criticism, performance studies, and autoethnography, to name a few (Denzin & Lincoln, 1994). These approaches contributed to the "reflexive turn" in the social sciences, and the examination of how the research process, including the "act of writing" partially produces the research result (Marcus & Clifford, 1986; Van Maanen, 1988).

The reflexive turn is central to the problem of evidence, not just why people believe "crazy things" and won't easily consider evidence that would lead them to reject such beliefs, but more basically, why—and how—do researchers and scientists accept information as evidence for a particular matter? The subject matter under investigation still matters, but mainly as a "product" that is socially constructed.

Efforts like SBR and SIE referred to above attempt to formulate what qualitative research should look like, in terms of criteria and checklists, but such efforts are risky, since this is likely to be mainly regulative but not constitutive of the process that gave rise to the innovations in the first place. The upshot is nothing less than treating ethnography and qualitative research as a commodity—a product—to be bought and sold in a market, but this market, like all markets, is reflexive of the process and interest that gives rise to all markets. Nico Stehr's (2008) insights about knowledge markets are instructive:

> [W]hen viewed from a contemporary sociological perspective—and this is the much more common and developed critique—markets are not so much responsible for widespread affluence; rather, they represent a rather harsh, impersonal institution that has put into practice what major classical sociological theorists have always anticipated and, of course, feared. From this perspective market relations are nothing but power relations. Market relations are a form of pure power relationship, pitting the owners of the means of production against the owners of labor power. (p. 85)

The power relations inherent in funding agencies and sanctioning boards that sanctify appropriate methodology can, perhaps unintentionally, purge qualitative research of the subtle but important distinctions noted above.

The creative logic-in-use of scientific discovery that has shaped much of qualitative inquiry and development is pushed aside as qualitative research becomes recast as "expertise" and becomes a resource for knowledge producers to employ for practical purposes and for diverse audiences with limited understanding (and interest) in the complexities of qualitative research, including varieties of validity. Steven Fuller (2008) argues that historically, science and expertise have been antithetical forms of knowledge, with the former associated with creativity and contemplation, and in a sense, examining the nature and realms of order and possibilities, while the latter was more associated with application, and "doing" practical things. Focusing on research in science technological studies (STS), he asserts,

> Science and expertise are historically opposed ideas: The former evokes a universalistic ideal meant to be pursued in leisure, while the latter consists of particular practices pursued to earn a living. However, expertise can

serve the universalistic ideal of science by undermining the authority of other expertises that would cast doubt on the viability of this ideal. Put bluntly, expertise is "progressive" only when it serves as the second moment of a Hegelian dialectic. . . . I see the modern university—specifically through its teaching function—as the place where this moment most often happens. (p. 115)

Fuller's concern is to save inquiry, exploration, and discovery as process from a steamrolling rhetoric and organizational push for completion and results that can flatten subtleties as useful products and procedures. This issue is apparent in current discussions about the nature and uses of evidence.

The Evidentiary Narrative as Process

We began with the quote from Klee, about a dot that went for a walk, and before one realizes, there is a line. The qualitative researcher shows us a "line" by describing and telling about the meanings in order to make them visible. Because of the reflexivity of all research and the indexicality of all communication, this is often problematic. The nature and meaning of a person's experience is not isomorphic with the researcher's account of that experience. As Schutz (1967) noted, the lifeworld is a world interpreted by social actors. These are first-order cognitions and constructs; the social scientist or qualitative research must interpret the actors' meanings and provide second-order constructs and accounts. As noted above, these second-order constructs are made within a social/cultural/historical context, with an intended audience. Our emphasis here is on the ways audience members might critically assess research reports or other representations in order to apply their criteria of validity, adequacy, or truthfulness. Some of the dimensions we will here examine are basic, yet they provide tools to assist us in assessing qualitative research. This raises the issue of the transparency of qualitative research, the ways used by researchers to "connect the dots" of their efforts, from inception to final report or representation. It is not possible to have complete or total transparency, again because of the inherent reflexivity and indexicality of the research process itself, yet most qualitative reports contain guidance about the relatedness of the observations, findings, claims, explanations, or conclusions.

Practitioners of qualitative methods routinely encounter certain problems and issues in the conduct of their observations, experiences, or research. While many of these problems and issues are legendary in traditional social science ethnography, rather than drawing on these well-known examples from classical observational research, we will use illustrations from an exceptional recent autoethnography, H. Lloyd (Bud) Goodall's book *A Need to Know: The Clandestine History of a CIA Family* (2006), which reports his experiences as a child growing up in a family governed by secrecy and paranoia, and routinely under the surveillance of the U.S. government. Only upon the death of his father did Goodall learn that he had been a CIA operative. Bud's subsequent impassioned quest for answers about his father's work, life, and commitments provided some clarity about family history, his mother's illness, and numerous moves, as well as documenting the institutional and organizational contexts for real family events, personal lives, and a young boy's fears and insecurities. Bud Goodall's problem was solved through careful weaving of subtle and tacit knowledge of real-life events that were constructively revealed by replaying narratively shaped memories, and checking these against new interpretations gleaned from various documents about his family history, including a Bible, a diary, and his father's agency codebook, *The Great Gatsby*.

We draw on this extraordinary project to illuminate the sometimes circular path of the dimensions of qualitative inquiry.

We argue that in one form or another, qualitative research, especially ethnography, involves some data collection, analysis, and interpretation, although these may not always be as apparent and transparent as a reader may desire. Indeed, a distinctive aspect of qualitative research designs that emerge from lived experience is the blurring of data collection and analysis, since the latter often informs what new data or examples/comparisons to seek out, clarify, and compare. For example, Professor Goodall (2006) began with his personal experiences, but later came to rely on various documents, including photographs, family and military records, and so forth, for more information. All research involves collecting, organizing, analyzing, and interpreting data. Sometimes this involves recognizing that we have something worthwhile, and then finding out what it is. The most basic concern is perhaps an epistemological one: How do we know? But this involves several features of the "knowing process," including what is it that we know, how did we learn or come to know something about it, and how do we make sense of this? We are not suggesting any particular approach, mode, or representation for these activities, but only that they help distinguish a social science "telling" or "accounting" from other genres.

Qualitative research should provide a window for a critical reading, or at the very least, permit an informed reader's queries about what is being read, or seen, or heard. Our position is that any claim for veracity, validity, adequacy, or truthfulness turns on the transparency of these dimensions, and their personal relevance, pertinence, and significance for the audience member (e.g., reader, listener, viewer). Transparency promotes empathic and sympathetic understanding and participation between the author and the audience. We wish to stress, then, that it is not enough to "like" a research account/narrative, but that for social science purposes, such "liking" can be linked to these dimensions.

The power of extensive involvement with the lifeworld one is experiencing is apparent from journalistic accounts as well. Journalists do not have a method as such. They inquire and search out leads for a story. Their main connection to a kind of realism is to have "facts checked" by someone else, which often involves someone finding out if a person actually told the journalist something, but not whether what that person said was actually true. While social scientists operate with a theoretical orientation that guides data collection and interpretation, being close to the data, the actual experience, is critical for understanding. Journalists are often closer to the action, and their descriptions provide great insight, even though their rendering is less theoretically guided and informed. This can be seen with journalist Roberto Saviano's (2007) statement of how he knows about the corruption of the Camorra, Italy's brutal criminal organization that dominates commerce in southern Italy. In describing his familiarity with the criminal control of the cement industry, Saviano states,

> I know and I can prove it. I know how economies originate and where they get their odor. The odor of success and victory. I know what sweats of profit. I know. And the truth of the war takes no prisoners because it devours everything and turns everything into evidence. It doesn't need to drag in cross-checks or launch investigations. It observes, considers, looks, listens. . . . The proofs are not hidden in some flash drive concealed in a hole in the ground. I don't have compromising videos hidden in a garage in some inaccessible mountain village. Nor do I possess copies of secret service documents. The proofs are irrefutable because they are partial, recorded with my eyes, recounted with words, and tempered with emotions that have echoed off iron and wood. I see, hear, look, talk, and in this way I testify, an ugly word that can still be useful when it whispers, "It's not true," in the ear of those who listen to the rhyming lullabies of power. The truth is partial; after all, if it could be reduced to an objective formula, it would be chemistry. I know and I can prove it. And so I tell. About these truths. (p. 213)

We wish to emphasize that those portions of experience that are the basis for a particular project, argument, or account need to be available or at least be a point of reference for the reader or audience. What, for example, was the basis for a claim or explanation or rendering or narrative with which we are engaged? Is it personal experience (e. g., biographical), a critical event/experience shared with others, an observation—or series of observations such as an extended ethnography, informal or formal interviews, reflections on documentary "evidence" or accounts, and so on? Even if the critical insight is personal, emergent from a creative consciousness, is the referent in any sense actual, and if not, in what ways is it connected to the lifeworld presumably shared by readers, viewers, or listeners? An example is insights about metaphors of life or how identities are shaped by popular culture. Saviano (2007) reports how dominant Camorra leaders mimic Hollywood bad guys as part of a lifestyle of domination and control:

> Camorra villas are pearls of cement tucked away on rural streets, protected by walls and video cameras. There are dozens and dozens of them. Marble and parquet, colonnades and staircases, granite fireplaces with the boss's initials. One, the most sumptuous, is particularly famous, or perhaps it has merely generated the most legends. Everyone calls it Hollywood. Just saying the word makes you understand why. . . . Walter Schiavone's villa really does have a link to Hollywood. People in Casal di Principe say the boss told his architect he wanted a villa just like Tony Montana's, the Miami Cuban gangster in *Scarface*. He'd seen the film countless times and it had made a deep impression in him, to the point that he came to identify with the character played by Al Pacino. With a bit of imagination, Schiavone's hollowed face could actually be superimposed on the actor's. The story has all the makings of a legend. People say Schiavone even gave his architect a copy of the film; he wanted the Scarface villa, exactly as it was in the movie. (pp. 344–345)

Many insights found in qualitative research originate in a researcher's personal experience. A bit later in the chapter, we discuss the importance of tacit knowledge. As we move from insights or hunches to more robust claims-making, we run into the issue of sampling, that is, how cases were selected. Qualitative researchers do not discount research from small samples, even a sample of one—a case—but it is helpful if this information is available. Indeed, we could say that most ideas—no matter what method is used to develop them—are not disconnected from personal experience. But there is more to it. Unless it is clear that the account being offered is completely idiosyncratic or unique, then we also would like to know how a "case" was selected, as well as whether other cases were examined, other comparisons made, and if not, are others implied or suggested?

In other words, qualitative researchers are trying to make statements about the world of experience such as how things are organized and the consequences of this action. We do not know of a single piece of research in which the researcher avowed that the work being examined was not relevant for anything, any situation, context, application, and the like. The relevance might be limited, but the work matters because it is assumed to shed some light on a specific or related problem that goes beyond the particular case being illuminated, referred to, or scrutinized. Again, Roberto Saviano's (2007) account of the banality of fear and intimidation illustrates the taken-for-granted moral order dictated by the Camorra. Here, he discusses the violation of the code of morality by a witness to a street killing, who was willing to testify. And there were consequences for this brave woman:

> It wasn't testifying in itself that generated such fear, or her identifying a killer that caused such a scandal. The logic of Omerta isn't so simple. What made the young teacher's gesture scandalous is that she considered being able to testify something natural, instinctive, and vital. In a land where [lying] is considered to be what gets you something and [truth] what makes you lose, living as if you actually believe truth can exist is incomprehensible. So the people around you feel uncomfortable, undressed by the gaze of one who has renounced the rules of life itself, which they have fully accepted. (pp. 279–280)

Saviano's gathering of various examples for his story provides data for other investigators, criminal and sociological.

The expanded focus to other types of data is well illustrated with Goodall's (2006) experience, which began with his own family, but he subsequently branched out to explore how CIA operatives were dealt with by the government, how their families were treated, and so on.

> I didn't go into this research project believing that I would be able to discover the "truth" about my father's clandestine career, or even about the meaning of my family's cold war life. I hoped for something less grand. I hoped to find an adequate, even if partial, explanation for what happened to us, and why. (p. 24)

This work involved interviews, historical records and other documents, and even connections with other social science literature, but he was able to relate a unique case—his family—with other cases, and was able to track how organizational practices and cultures—including the unique culture of the CIA—and how it contributed to family dysfunction, on the one hand, but also foreign policy missteps, on the other.

Moreover, it is clear from Goodall's (2006) excellent monograph what the different sources of data were, how they were interwoven, and the reader is given a good understanding of how his subsequent interpretations and conclusions are more or less closely tied to the various data, while other considerations may be a bit more speculative and less data bound.

Saviano (2007) understands what any ethnographer might, but the way that he knows is not transparent, partly because, as a journalist, he answers to a different epistemological canon. Yet, it is compelling enough to motivate researchers to know as much as he does, but to be able to offer an account of how we know what we claim. Listen to his testament of authenticity in the final pages of his riveting book:

> I was born in the land of the Camorra, in the territory with the most homicides in Europe, where savagery is interwoven with commerce, where nothing has value except what generates power. Where everything has the taste of a final battle. It seemed impossible to have a moment of peace, not to live constantly in a war where every gesture is a surrender, where every necessity is transformed into weakness, where everything needs to be fought for tooth and nail. In the land of the Camorra, opposing the clans is not a class struggle, an affirmation of a right, or a expropriation of one's civic duty. It's not the realization of one's honor or the preservation of one's pride. . . . To set oneself against the clans becomes a war of survival, as if existence itself—the food you eat, the lips you kiss, the music you listen to, the pages you read—were merely a way to survive, not the meaning of life. Knowing is thus no longer a sign of moral engagement. Knowing—understanding—becomes a necessity. (pp. 300–301)

While we are convinced, ethnography must provide more to maintain authority.

We have addressed mainly personal experiences and very close—if not biographical—observations and recollections to this point. But the same logic about the veracity and relevance of a report resonates with various kinds of interviews, additional observations, and even documents. Again, it is not our intent here to say which is better or which ones you should trust more than the others, but we mainly want to emphasize that the reader/listener/viewer should be able to discern what was used in general, as well as in specific instances. Any audience member will discern his or her own criteria for being "convinced" or "skeptical" of the connection between what is being reported and its avowed source. But the main concern is that the connection be apparent, and to the extent possible, transparent. This can even be aided by adding a methodological appendix in which parts of the research process are delineated, which we address shortly below, or even an occasional footnote.

These general principles of transparency can be applied to data analysis as well. Data analysis seems self-evident in some first-person qualitative reports, but it is seldom as straightforward as it seems. The popular applications of "grounded theory" provide one rationale for coding and comparison, but there are other modes of comparison as well. The skilled writer can weave in the creative processes of data explication, comparison, and triangulation that are usually involved in qualitative reports, while in other instances it is helpful to have a section (e.g., footnote) delineating "what I did" and "how I came up with this." Again, Goodall's (2006) use of official government records about his father's bogus job descriptions clearly illustrated the pervasive bureaucratic duplicity and lies, even when he was trying to understand his deceased father's life, troubles, and perspective. His use of these materials helped make an organizational bureaucratic process of duplicity more visible. The challenge of making our research approach visible underlies validity issues.

Tacit Knowledge and an Ecology of Understanding

Good ethnographies display tacit knowledge. We focus on the dimensions of "an ecology of understanding." Contextual, taken-for-granted, "tacit knowledge" plays a constitutive role in providing meaning. Goodall (2006) reports some bewilderment as a child about what his father did for a living, and where he would disappear to for weeks at a time. His parents' answer, "It's complicated," would be given to other queries over the years. Social life is spatially and temporally ordered through experiences that cannot be reduced to spatial boundaries, as numerous forms of communication attempt to do, especially those based on textual and linear metaphors. More specifically, experience is different from words and symbols about those experiences. Words are always poor representations of the temporal and evocative lifeworld. Words and texts are not the primary stuff of the existential moments of most actors in what Schutz (1967) termed the "natural attitude." They are very significant for intellectuals and wordsmiths who claim to represent such experiences. Yet, as those word-workers have come to rely on and substitute words and other texts for the actual experiences, their procedures of analysis have been reified to stand for the actual experience. Therein lies much of the problem that some have termed the "crisis in representation."

Capturing members' words alone is not enough for ethnography. If it were, ethnographies would be replaced by interviews. Goodall (2006) could not simply have told his story to an interviewer, because part of the story was not clear to him until he reflected more on his past, sought other information sources, compared different versions of events, and pieced the meanings together into a coherent narrative. His book, in other words, is not the foundation of his story, but is actually part of the method he used in discovering, selecting, and interpreting experiences. Good ethnographies, like Goodall's, reflect tacit knowledge, the largely unarticulated, contextual understanding that is often reflected in nods, silences, humor, and naughty nuances. This is the most challenging dimension of ethnography, and gets to the core of the members' perspective, or for that matter, the subtleties of membership itself. As Laura Nader (1993) suggests, this is the stuff of ethnography: "Anthropology is a feat of empathy and analysis" (p. 7). But, without doubting the wisdom of Professor Nader, it is necessary to give an accounting of how we know things, what we regard and treat as empirical materials—the experiences—from which we produce our second (or third) accounts of "what was happening."

Reflexive Accounting for Substance

As we learn more about other significant and essentially invariable dimensions of settings, such as hierarchical organization, these are added. In order to satisfy the basic elements of the ethnographic ethic, the following "generic" topics can be found in ethnographic reports. Goodall's (2006) descriptions of his mother's practiced attempts to appear more sophisticated and the tensions and problems that this created are apt illustrations. After noting that his mother's modest West Virginia childhood hardly prepared her for the duties and cultural performances of a vice consul's wife, often before the critical eye of Ambassador to Italy Clare Boothe Luce, we read the following:

> Embassy social gatherings were an American cultural performance. They relied heavily on appearances and the careful cultivation of approved patterns of perceptions. My mother was given detailed instruction on appropriate behavior at social functions during a State Department orientation for spouses. . . . She also had been coached on conversation. She knew how

to appear interested in a topic when she was uninterested in it; how to deflect talk when confronted with an unwanted question or merely something tedious or dull; how to appear happy and energetic when she felt tired and unhappy; and how to appear helpless or clueless to get out of trouble if the case required it. (p. 141)

There is a distinction to be drawn between interesting, provocative, and insightful accounts of ethnographic research, on the one hand, and high-quality ethnographic work. Given our emphasis on the reflexive nature of social life, it will not surprise the reader that we prefer those studies that enable the ethnographic audience to symbolically engage the researcher and enter through the research window of clarity (and opportunity). While no one is suggesting a "literal" accounting, our work and that of many others suggests that the more a reader (audience member) can engage in a symbolic dialogue with the author about a host of routinely encountered problems that compromise ethnographic work, the more our confidence increases. Good ethnographies increase our confidence in the findings, interpretations, and accounts offered.

Accounting for Ourselves

A key part of the ethnographic ethic is how we account for ourselves. Good qualitative research—and particularly ethnographies—shows the hand of the ethnographer. The effort may not always be successful, but there should be clear "tracks" that the attempt has been made. We are in the midst of a rediscovery that social reality is constructed by human agents—even social scientists—using cultural categories and language in specific situations or contexts of meaning. This interest is indeed welcomed because it gives us license to do yet another elucidation of the "concept of knowing."

Our collective experience in reading a literature spanning more than 50 years, along with our own work on numerous topics and projects, suggests that there is a minimal set of problem areas that are likely to be encountered in most studies. We do not offer a solution to the problems that will follow, but only suggest that these can offer a focus for providing a broader and more complete account of the reflexive process through which something is understood (Altheide, 1976; Denzin, 1991; Douglas, 1976; Johnson, 1975). Such information enables the reader to engage the study in an interactive process that includes seeking more information and contextualizing findings, reliving the report as the playing out of the interactions between the researcher, the subjects, and the topic in question.

The idea for the critical reader of an ethnography is to ask whether or not any of the basic issues of data collection and analysis were likely to have been relevant problems, were they explicitly treated as problematic by the researcher, and if so, how were they addressed, resolved, compromised, avoided, and so forth. Because these dimensions of ethnographic research are so pervasive and important for obtaining truthful accounts, they should be implicitly or explicitly addressed in the report. Drawing on such criteria enables the ethnographic reader to approach the ethnography interactively and critically, and to ask what was done, how it was done, what are the likely and foreseen consequences of the particular research issue, and how was it handled by the researcher. These dimensions represent one range of potential problems likely to be encountered by an ethnographer.

No study avoids all of these problems, although few researchers give a reflexive account of their research problems and experience. One major problem is that the phenomenon of our interest reflects multiple perspectives; there are usually a multiplicity of modes of meanings, perspectives, and activities, even in one setting. Indeed, this multiplicity is often unknown to many of the official members of the setting. Thus, one does not easily "become the phenomenon" in contemporary life. As we strive to make ourselves, our activities and claims, more accountable, a critical feature is to acknowledge our awareness of a process that may actually impede and prevent our adequate understanding of all relevant dimensions of an activity.

Our experience suggests that the subjects of ethnographic studies are invariably temporally and spatially bounded. That the range of activities under investigation occurs in time and space (which becomes a "place" when given a meaning) provides one anchorage, among many others, for penetrating the hermeneutic circle. One feature of this knowledge, of course, is its incompleteness, its implicit and tacit dimensions. The qualitative researcher seeks to draw on the tacit dimension in order to make meanings and order more explicit, and in a sense, more visible. Our subjects always know more than they can tell us, usually even more than they allow us to see; likewise, we often know far more than we can articulate. Even the most ardent social science wordsmiths are at a loss to transform the nuances, subtleties and the sense of the sublime into symbols! For this reason, we acknowledge the realm of tacit knowledge, the ineffable truths, unutterable partly because they are between meanings and actions, the glue that separates and joins human intentionality to more concretely focused symbols of practice. As we have stressed, the key issue is not to capture the informant's voice, but to elucidate the experience that is implicated by the subjects in the context of their activities as they perform them, and as they are understood by the ethnographer. Harper's (1987) explanation of how he used photography in a study of a local craftsman illustrates this intersection of meaning:

> The key, I think, is a simple idea that is the base of all ethnography. I want to explain the way Willie has explained to me. I hope to show a small social world that most people would not look at very closely. In the process I want to tell about some of the times between Willie and me, thinking that at the root of all sociology there are people making connections, many like ours. (p. 14)

One approach to making ourselves more accountable and thereby sharing our experience and insights more fully with readers, is to locate inquiry within the process and context of actual human experience. Our experience suggests that researchers should accept the inevitability that all statements are reflexive, and that the research act is a social act. Indeed, that is the essential rationale for research approaches grounded in the contexts of experience of the people who are actually involved in their settings and arenas.

Studies of popular culture and symbolic reality construction are, for some people, ethnographically on the edge; the lifeworlds under investigation are experiential, but representational of entertainment-oriented media personas and styles. Considerable care must be taken to show something of the process, the contexts of understanding and the social relationships connecting the symbolic to the actual or the real, as in everyday life discipline, language, and actions involving enforcement and resistance.

Recent work employing *qualitative document analysis* (also referred to as "ethnographic content analysis") illustrates the application of an ethnographic ethic and tacit knowledge where the emphasis is on discovery and description, including searching for contexts, underlying meanings, patterns, and processes, rather than mere quantity or numerical relationships between two or more variables. Michael Coyle's (2007) study of "The Language of Justice" examined numerous documents, including dictionaries, to trace the etiology of the terms *victim*— especially *innocent victim*—and *evil*. His focus was the penetration of these terms into public discourse about crime and punishment, including the popular phrase "tough on crime" that was widely used by moral entrepreneurs and politicians.

Chris Schneider (2008) drew on a lifelong interest and study of popular music to track how digitized and embedded technologies can simultaneously resist and assist authority and social control. His examination of a range of documents, especially popular music (e.g., rap music), as well as school contexts for controlling students' use of interactive portable technology (e.g., cell phones, iPods), illuminated how the communication of control is embedded in products marketed for entertainment.

Similarly, as Tim Rowlands (2010) has masterfully shown, the world of virtual experience and reality can be investigated, described, and rendered theoretically through intensive fieldwork in cyberspace. As with Coyle's and Schneider's studies, Rowlands' personal experience was significant in providing resources and questions to uncover data; years of experience as a serious player of various "computer games" opened up experiences with other players and provided opportunities for informal interviews to clarify the semiotic scenarios of, for example, *EverQuest,* that could be conceptually treated as exploration of one virtual utopia. What were the rules, Rowlands asked, what were the underlying assumptions of order, and above all, what does justice look like in virtual space? He found violence and the iconography of violence, but also a technologically rendered cosmology of alienated confrontations as task completion for role fulfillment that players recognized and pursued as pastimes of boredom, fun, work, and as an inevitable feature of the computer environment that reflected a capitalistic order. Examining the evidence within the confines of interpretive validity suggests, "MMOs [massive multiplayer online games] such as *EverQuest* serve in important ways to shape our understanding of what virtual worlds currently are" (p. 369).

Let us bring the parts of the argument closer together. Evidence is a feature of the interaction between an audience, a claim, and practical epistemologies of everyday life. Whether evidence is convincing follows along the same lines; is the evidence "good enough," or is there enough evidence relevant to the topic? The key question is, what is relevant for the topic or question under investigation? A reader's (listener's) perspective about what is "evidence" is informed by biography, culture, and so forth.

Conclusion

The great artist Paul Klee, who stated that a line is a dot that went for a walk, could enjoy the task of trying to capture the intersection of many lines—borne of numerous dots—that are heading in different directions. We seek, among other things, to understand the nature, process, and consequences of social interaction, on the one hand, and how this promotes individual and joint renderings of a definition of a situation, on the other hand. A positivistic view of validity works fine in a different social universe where there are not multiple perspectives, vastly different methods and materials with which to work, and myriad uses and audiences. But that is not our social research world. The social world and its human actors make and interpret meanings through an interaction process that contributes to the construction, reification, and resistance of social reality. Any method that obliterates the essential role of emergence, negotiation, and tacit knowledge will not be valid. And any effort to remake this world to comply with an idealized model is folly, will lack credibility, and is doomed to failure. Our overview of validity issues in qualitative research, with a focus on ethnographic reports, suggests that a proper set of standards or criteria for assessing validity entails considering the place of evidence in an interaction process between the researcher, the subject matter (phenomenon to be investigated), the intended effect or utility, and the audience for which the project will be evaluated and assessed.

We continue to hold that focusing on the process of investigation and communicating that process, the problems and solutions encountered in accessing, collecting, analyzing, and interpreting data—to the best of our ability—is quite consistent with analytic realism, or the general notion that the social world is an interpreted one. We are not opposed to using evidence, but prefer that the spirit of the evidentiary narrative be considered.

We do not intend to leave the question of validity completely open-ended. There are parameters, and the criteria and process can become tighter within the community of scholars who employ certain methods and criteria. While we do not recommend "recipe" methods, we have offered several "lists" of items to consider when focusing on the presentation of research problems and solutions in a given project (Altheide & Johnson, 1994). For example, many approaches to interviewing (e.g., focused, life history, etc.), ethnography (e.g., grounded theory), and document analysis (qualitative content analysis) have developed criteria and procedures for optimal work. But our task is not to refine and squeeze the novelty and richness out of experience in favor of some bygone notion of rigor and efficiency, nor is it to make sure that creative problem solving and discovery are compromised in order to dot the i's and cross the t's. We want to see more dots flourish and evolve into creative insights. Our task is to continue pushing the line in new directions to illuminate our humanity and communicative worlds.

References

Altheide, D. L. (1976). *Creating reality: How TV news distorts events.* Beverly Hills, CA: Sage.

Altheide, D. L. (2008). The evidentiary narrative: Notes toward a symbolic interactionist perspective about evidence. In N. K. Denzin & M. D. Giardina (Eds.), *Qualitative inquiry and the politics of evidence* (pp. 137–162). Walnut Creek, CA: Left Coast Press.

Altheide, D. L. (2009). *Terror post 9/11 and the media*. New York: Peter Lang.

Altheide, D. L., & Johnson, J. M. (1993). The ethnographic ethic. In N. K. Denzin (Ed.), *Studies in symbolic interaction* (pp. 95–107). Greenwich, CT: JAI Press.

Altheide, D. L., & Johnson, J. M. (1994). Criteria for assessing interpretive validity in qualitative research. In N. K. Denzin & Y. S. Lincoln (Eds.), *Handbook of qualitative research* (pp. 485–499). Newbury Park, CA: Sage.

Altheide, D. L., & Snow, R. S. (1979). *Media logic*. Beverly Hills, CA: Sage.

Atkinson, P. (1990). *The ethnographic imagination: Textual constructs of reality*. New York: Routledge.

Bhaskar, R. (1979). *The possibility of naturalism: A philosophical critique of the human sciences*. Brighton, UK: Harvester.

Bochner, A. P. (2007). Notes toward an ethics of memory in autoethnographic inquiry. In N. K. Denzin & M. D. Giardina (Eds.), *Ethical futures in qualitative research: Decolonizing the politics of knowledge* (pp. 197–208). Walnut Creek, CA: Left Coast Press.

Cabinet Office. (2003). *Quality in qualitative evaluation: A framework for assessing research evidence* [Full report]. London: Author.

Coyle, M. J. (2007). *The language of justice: Exposing social and criminal justice discourse*. Unpublished doctoral dissertation, School of Justice and Social Inquiry, Arizona State University, Tempe.

Denzin, N. K. (2009). *Qualitative inquiry under fire*. Walnut Creek, CA: Left Coast Press.

Denzin, N. K. (2010). A qualitative stance: Remembering Steinar Kvale (1938–2008). *International Journal of Qualitative Studies in Education, 23*(2), 125–127.

Denzin, N. K., & Giardina, M. D. (Eds.). (2008). *Qualitative inquiry and the politics of evidence*. Walnut Creek, CA: Left Coast Press.

Denzin, N. K., & Lincoln, Y. S. (Eds.). (1994). *Handbook of qualitative research*. Newbury Park, CA: Sage.

Douglas, J. D. (1976). *Investigative social research: Individual and team field research*. Beverly Hills, CA: Sage.

Ellis, C. (2004). *The ethnographic I*. Walnut Creek, CA: AltaMira Press.

Ellis, C. (2009). *Revision: Autoethnographic reflections on life and work*. Walnut Creek, CA: Left Coast Press.

Emerson, R. M., Fretz, R. I., & Shaw, L. L. (1995). *Writing ethnographic fieldnotes*. Chicago: University of Chicago Press.

Erikson, R. V., & Doyle, A. (2003). *Risk and morality*. Toronto, ON, Canada: University of Toronto Press.

Fuller, S. (2008). Science democratized—Expertise decommissioned. In N. Stehr (Ed.), *Knowledge and democracy* (pp. 105–117). New Brunswick, NJ: Transaction.

Goodall, H. L., Jr. (2006). *A need to know: The clandestine history of a CIA family*. Walnut Creek, CA: Left Coast Press.

Guba, E. G. (1990). Subjectivity and objectivity. In E. W. Eisner & A. Peshkin (Eds.), *Qualitative inquiry in education* (pp. 74–91). New York: Teachers College Press.

Haak, S. (2003). *Defending science—within reason.* Amherst, NY: Prometheus.

Hammersley, M. (1990). *Reading ethnographic research.* London: Longman.

Hammersley, M. (1992). *What's wrong with ethnography? Methodological explorations.* London & New York: Routledge.

Hammersley, M. (2005). The myth of research-based practice: The critical case of educational inquiry. *International Journal of Social Research Methodology, 8*(4), 317–330.

Harper, D. (1987). *Working knowledge: Skill and community in a small shop.* Berkeley: University of California Press.

Harré, R., & Madden, E. (1975). *Causal powers.* Oxford, UK: Basil Blackwell.

Henry, G., Julnes, G. J., & Mark, M. (Eds.). (1998). *Realist evaluation.* San Francisco: Jossey-Bass.

Johnson, J. M. (1975). *Doing field research.* New York: Free Press.

Kemmis, S., & McTaggart, R. (2005). Participatory action research: Communicative action in the public sphere. In N. K. Denzin & Y. S. Lincoln (Eds.), *The SAGE handbook of qualitative research* (3rd ed., pp. 599–603). Thousand Oaks, CA: Sage.

Kvale, S., & Brinkmann, S. (2008). *InterViews: Learning the craft of qualitative research interviewing.* Thousand Oaks, CA: Sage.

Ladkin, D. (2004). Action research. In C. Sale, G. Gobo, J. F. Gubrium, & D. Silverman (Eds.), *Qualitative research practice* (pp. 536–48). New York: Routledge.

Lakoff, G. (1987). *Women, fire, and other dangerous things: What categories reveal about the mind.* Chicago: University of Chicago Press.

Lamont, M., & White, P. (2009). *Workshop on interdisciplinary standards for systematic qualitative research.* Washington, DC: National Science Foundation.

Lather, P. (1993). Fertile obsession: Validity after poststructuralism. *Sociological Quarterly, 34,* 673–93.

Lofland, J. (1995). Analytic ethnography. *Journal of Contemporary Ethnography, 24*(1), 30–67.

Mancias, P. T., & ebrary, Inc., 2006. *A realist philosophy of social science explanation.* Cambridge, UK: Cambridge University Press.

Marcus, G. E., & Clifford, J. (1986). *Writing culture: The poetics and politics of ethnography.* Berkeley: University of California Press.

Maxwell, J. A. (2008). The value of a realist understanding of causality for qualitative research. In N. K. Denzin & G. D. Giardina (Eds.), *Qualitative inquiry and the politics of evidence* (pp. 163–181). Walnut Creek, CA: Left Coast Press.

Miller, W. L., & Crabtree, B. F. (2005). Clinical research: Participatory action research. In N. K. Denzin & Y. S. Lincoln (Eds.), *The SAGE handbook of qualitative research* (3rd ed., pp. 605–639). Thousand Oaks, CA: Sage.

Nader, L. (1993). Paradigm busting and vertical linkage. *Contemporary Sociology, 33,* 6–7.

Putnam, H. (1999). *The threefold cord: Mind, body, and the world.* New York: Columbia University Press.

Ragin, C., Nagel, J., & White, P. (2004). *Workshop on scientific foundations of qualitative research.* Washington, DC: National Science Foundation.

Richardson, L. (1997). *Fields of play.* New Brunswick, NJ: Rutgers University Press.

Rolfe, G. (2004). Validity, trustworthiness, and rigor: Quality and the idea of qualitative research. *Journal of Advanced Nursing, 53*(3), 304–310.

Rowlands, T. E. (2010). *Empire of the hyperreal.* Unpublished doctoral dissertation, School of Social Transformation, Arizona State University, Tempe.

Saviano, R. (2007). *Gomorrah.* New York: Farrar, Straus and Giroux.

Schneider, C. J. (2008). *Mass media, popular culture and technology: Communication and information formats as emergent features of social control.* Unpublished doctoral dissertation, School of Justice and Social Inquiry, Arizona State University, Tempe.

Schutz, A. (1967). *The phenomenology of the social world.* Evanston, IL: Northwestern University Press.

Stehr, N. (2008). *Moral markets.* Boulder, CO: Paradigm.

Szto, P., Furman, R., & Langer, C. (2005). Qualitative research in sociology in Germany and the U.S. *Focus: Qualitative Social Work, 4*(2), 135–156.

Torrance, H. (2007). Building confidence in qualitative research: Engaging the demands of policy. In N. K. Denzin & M. D. Giardina (Eds.), *Qualitative inquiry and the politics of evidence* (pp. 55–79). Walnut Creek, CA: Left Coast Press.

Van den Hoonaard, W. C. (2002). *Walking the tightrope: Ethical issues for qualitative researchers.* Toronto, ON, Canada: University of Toronto Press.

Van Maanen, J. (1988). *Tales of the field: On writing ethnography.* Chicago: University of Chicago Press.

Wolcott, H. F. (1990). On seeking—and rejecting—validity in qualitative research. In E. W. Eisner & A. Peshkin (Eds.), *Qualitative inquiry in education: The continuing debate* (pp. 121–152). New York: Teachers College Press.

Analysis and Representation Across the Continuum

Laura L. Ellingson

[Researchers] do jump across traditions, we do straddle metatheoretical camps, and (unfortunately) we do let paradigmatic "definitions" constrain our work. . . . [I want to] allow for comfortable jumps and straddles and to loosen some of these constraints.

—K. I. Miller (2000, p. 48)

In the interest of loosening some of the unproductive methodological constraints highlighted by K. I. Miller (2000), I encourage qualitative researchers to consider jumping and straddling multiple points across the field of qualitative methods—consciously, actively, and creatively. Large qualitative projects provide ample opportunity for producing a series of analyses and interpretations that subdivides findings, not only according to logical topic segments, but also with regard to embodying a range of artistic, expository, and social scientific writing genres or other representational media. Yet too often researchers learn and embrace a handful of strategies and settle into comfortable methodological ruts. Such complacency is not limited to practitioners of more traditional, social scientific forms of qualitative research; singular devotion to autoethnographic, narrative, and other artistic approaches may be just as slavish. I go beyond supporting multiple methods research strategies to advocate the use of multiple

methods of analysis and representation that span artistic and scientific epistemologies, or ways of knowing.

For the purposes of this chapter, analysis of data or other assembled empirical
materials will be understood as the process of separating aggregated texts (oral,
written, or visual) into smaller segments of meaning for close consideration,
reflection, and interpretation. Forming representations will mean rendering
intelligible accounts of analyses, such as through construction of themes or patterns; transformation of journal entries or transcripts into narratives; or explication of an individual account using a particular theoretical lens. Of course, the
processes of analysis and representation overlap throughout the duration of a
qualitative project; for example, the production of ethnographic fieldnotes
involves both selection of details of an encounter or setting to document (i.e.,
analysis) and generation of a representation of that analysis (the written notes).

In this chapter, I make the case for qualitative methods to be conceptualized
as a continuum anchored by art and science, with vast middle spaces that
embody infinite possibilities for blending artistic, expository, and social scientific
ways of analysis and representation (Ellis & Ellingson, 2000; Potter, 1996). Such
an approach moves past the tendency to understand art and science as dichotomies (i.e., mutually exclusive, paired opposites) by illuminating research and
representational options that fall between these two poles. To begin, I review
traditional and current ways of straddling points of the continuum within
research projects. I then offer a guide to being conscious about the interpretive
process of selecting methods and genres, and describe three promising strategies
for deliberate endeavors to traverse the qualitative continuum.

A Continuum Approach

EMBRACING A CONTINUUM

Dichotomous thinking remains pervasive within methodological debates:
"[D]ifferences have been cast in terms of binaries. . . . All are distinguished
by virtue of what they are not" (Gergen, 1994, p. 9). Nowhere are dualisms
evidenced more strongly than in the quantitative/qualitative divide. Even within
the qualitative field itself, polarities mark the differences between interpretivists
and realists (Anderson, 2006; Atkinson, 2006; Ellis & Bochner, 2006). On the
one hand, qualitative social scientists often rely on appeals to an authoritative tradition to disparage what they characterize as the subjective, messy,

nongeneralizable work of the "navel-gazers" to their left, reifying the natural primacy of "hard" over "soft" ways of knowing. On the other hand, artistic/ interpretive researchers may construct traditional social scientists as deluded positivists obsessed with the mythical gods of objectivity, validity, and reliability, in order to legitimate creative analytic approaches to analysis and representation (Richardson, 2000). Moving beyond defining artistic approaches as "not science" and social science as "not art" takes some generative thinking. Many qualitative researchers, if not most, will affirm that art and science are ends of a continuum, not a dichotomy; yet in practice, the use of the methodological "other" to legitimate our particular methodological and paradigmatic preferences leads to a reification of dichotomous ways of conceptualizing and writing about qualitative research practices.

A continuum approach to mapping the field of qualitative methodology constructs a nuanced range—or broad spectrum—of possibilities to describe what traditionally have been socially constructed as dichotomies such as art/science, hard/soft, and qualitative/quantitative (Potter, 1996). Significantly, the continuum is made up primarily of a vast and varied middle ground, with art and science representing only the extreme ends of the methodological and representational range, rather than each constituting half of the methodological ground. Such middle-ground approaches need not represent compromise or a lowering of artistic or scientific standards. Rather, they can signal innovative approaches to sense making and representation.

Building upon Ellis's (2004) representation of the two ends of the qualitative continuum (i.e., art and science) and the analytic mapping of the continuum developed in Ellis and Ellingson (2000), I envision the continuum as having three main areas, with infinite possibilities for blending and moving among them (Ellingson, 2009). As exemplified in Figure 13.1, the goals, questions posed, methods, writing styles, vocabularies, role(s) of researchers, and criteria for evaluation vary across the continuum as we move from a realist/positivist social science stance on the far right, through a social constructionist middle ground, to an artistic/interpretive paradigm on the left. Each of these general approaches offers advantages and disadvantages, and they are not mutually exclusive. Moreover, no firm boundaries exist to delineate the precise scope of left/middle/ right; these reflect ideal types only. Furthermore, terms of demarcation and description used throughout the continuum (e.g., interpretive, postpositivist) are suspect and contestable; use of key terminology in qualitative methods remains dramatically inconsistent across disciplines, paradigms, and methodological communities, with new terms arising continually (Gubrium & Holstein, 1997). At any point on the qualitative continuum, a set of assumptions about epistemology (i.e., about what knowledge is and what it means to create it) influences choices surrounding the collection of empirical materials and analysis methods, which in turn tend to foster (but do not require) particular forms of representation.

I now sketch the right, left, and middle areas of the continuum, along with a brief review of both traditional and more contemporary approaches to spanning the boundaries among those areas.

RIGHT/SCIENCE

At the far right of the qualitative continuum (see Figure 13.1), emphasis on valid and reliable knowledge, as generated by neutral researchers utilizing the scientific method to discover universal Truth, reflects an epistemology commonly referred to as positivism (Warren & Karner, 2010). Historically, social scientists understood positivism as reflected in a "realist ontology, objective epistemology, and value-free axiology" (K. I. Miller, 2000, p. 57). Few, if any, qualitative researchers currently subscribe to an absolute faith in positivism, however. Many postpositivists, or researchers who believe that achievement of objectivity and value-free inquiry are not possible, nonetheless embrace the goal of production of generalizable knowledge through realist methods and minimization of researcher bias, with objectivity as a "regulatory ideal" rather than an attainable goal (Guba & Lincoln, 1994). In short, postpositivism does not embrace naive belief in pure scientific truth; rather, qualitative research conducted in a strict postpositivist tradition utilizes precise, prescribed processes and produces social scientific reports that enable researchers to make generalizable claims about the social phenomenon within particular populations under examination.

Postpositivists commonly utilize qualitative methods that bridge quantitative methods, in which researchers conduct an inductive analysis of textual data, form a typology grounded in the data (as contrasted with a preexisting, validated typology applied to new data), use the derived typology to sort data into categories, and then count the frequencies of each theme or category across data. Such research typically emphasizes validity of the coding schema, inter-coder reliability, and careful delineation of procedures, including random or otherwise systematic sampling of texts. Content analyses of media typify this approach. For example, Feng and Wu (2009) derived a typology of values represented in advertisements in a Chinese Communist Party newspaper, which they used to code their samples from the years 1980 and 2002. They then compared the frequency

Figure 13.1 Qualitative Continuum

Writing

- Use of first-person voice
- Literary techniques
- Stories
- Poetry/poetic transcription
- Multivocal, multigenre texts
- Layered accounts
- Experiential forms
- Personal reflections
- Open to multiple interpretations

- Use of first-person voice
- Incorporation of brief narratives in research reports
- Use "snippets" of participants' words
- Usually a single interpretation, with implied partiality and positionality
- Some consideration of researcher's standpoint(s)

- Use of passive voice
- "View from nowhere" (Haraway, 1998)
- Claim single authoritative interpretation
- Meaning summarized in tables and charts
- Objectivity and minimization of bias highlighted

Researcher

- Researcher as the main focus, or as much the focus of research as other participants

- Participants are main focus, but researcher's positionality is key to forming findings

- Researcher is presented as irrelevant to results

Vocabularies

- Artistic/Interpretive: inductive, personal, ambiguity, change, adventure, improvisation, process, concrete details, evocative experience, creativity, aesthetics

- Social Constructionist/Postpositivist: inductive, emergent, intersubjectivity, process, themes, categories, thick description, co-creation of meaning, social construction of meaning, standpoint, ideology (e.g., feminism, postmodernism, Marxism)

- Positivist: deductive, tested, axioms, measurement, variables, manipulation of conditions, control, predication, generalizability, validity, reliability, theory driven

Criteria

- Do stories ring true, resonate, engage, move?
- Are they coherent, plausible, interesting, aesthetically pleasing?

- Flexible criteria
- Clarity and openness of processes
- Clear reasoning and use of support
- Evidence of researcher's reflexivity

- Authoritative rules
- Specific criteria for data, similar to quantitative
- Proscribed methological processes

(Continued)

(Continued)

Qualitative Continuum

	Art/Impressionist	Middle-Ground Approaches	Science/Realist
Goals	To unravel accepted truths To construct personal truths To explore the specific To generate art	To construct situated knowledges To explore the typical To generate description and understanding To trouble the taken-for-granted To generate pragmatic implications for practitioners	To discover objective truth To generalize to larger population To explain reality "out there" To generate scientific knowledge To predict and control behavior
Questions	How do we/can we cope with life? What other ways can we imagine? What is unique about my or another's experience?	How do participants understand their world? How do the participants and author co-construct a world? What are the pragmatic implications of research?	What does it mean from the researcher's point of view? What is the relationship among factors? What behaviors can be predicted?
Methods	Autoethnography Interactive interviewing Participant observation Performance Sociological introspection Visual arts	Semistructured interviewing Focus groups Participant observation/ethnography Thematic, metaphoric, and narrative analysis Grounded theory Case studies Participatory action research Historical/archival research	Coding textual data Random sampling Frequencies of behaviors Measurement Surveys Structured interviews

of messages reflecting values considered "hedonistic" with those messages reflecting utilitarian values, thus evaluating the overall appeals in the newspaper (see also Kuperberg & Stone, 2008). This type of analysis can also utilize textual data generated by researchers and participants, such as transcribed interviews, focus groups, or participant journals. Bruess and Pearson's (1997) study of interpersonal rituals between heterosexually married couples and both single-sex and cross-sex adult friends is illustrative. In interviews and in written accounts solicited from participants, researchers collected descriptions of everyday rituals that affirm our bonds to significant others. They conducted an inductive analysis, then counted frequencies and used chi-square tests to determine significance of differences between friends and married couples (see also Cousineau, Rancourt, & Green, 2006; Güven, 2008).

Other postpositivist qualitative research modeled similar research processes, but without quantification of themes or categories. Glaser and Strauss (1967) supported their original formulation of grounded theory methods with positivist claims of inductively deriving themes that "emerge" from the data, ensuring validity as long as researchers correctly employed the method. Adopting the language of science, they did not require counting of themes, but they emphasized detailed analytical procedures and a detached, scholarly voice, generating research reports quite similar to statistical reports (e.g., Kwok & Sullivan, 2007).

Another way postpositivist researchers support ideals of objectivity is to highlight issues of data collection while glossing over details of analysis and omitting any acknowledgment of researchers' role in sense making. Such an approach assumes a shared understanding of data analysis procedures and a relatively impartial researcher. Contemporary realist ethnographers sometimes follow this model of understanding and reporting their analytic processes with few or no details in favor of devoting more space to documentation of findings; see for example Brooks and Bowker's (2002) study of play in the workplace (see also Meyer, 2004).

LEFT

At the left end of the continuum, researchers value humanistic, openly subjective knowledge, such as that embodied in stories, poetry, photography, and painting (Ellis, 2004). Researchers may study their own lives and/or those of intimate others, community members, or strangers. Among the artistic/interpretivists, truths are multiple, fluctuating, and ambiguous. Autoethnographers, performance studies scholars, and others engaged in such practices embrace aesthetics and evocation of emotion and identification as equally or even more important than illumination of a particular topic (Richardson, 2000). Literary standards of truthfulness in storytelling (i.e., verisimilitude) replace those of social scientific truth (Ellis, 2004). Like all art, creative social science representations enable us to learn about ourselves, each other, and the world through encountering the unique lens of a person's (or a group's) passionate rendering of reality into a moving, aesthetic expression of meaning. At its best, art sparks compassion and inspires people to nurture themselves, their communities, and the world.

Analysis and representation merge to a great degree as art is produced, based upon experiences or empirical materials. A tremendous variety of artistic practices exists, with new forms continually arising; I review some of the most common here. *Autoethnography* is research, writing, story, and method that connect the autobiographical to the cultural, social, and political through the study of a culture or phenomenon of which one is a part, integrated with relational and personal experiences (Ellingson & Ellis, 2008). Autoethnographers typically produce emotionally evocative accounts, such as Lee's (2006) autoethnography of her grief following a loved one's suicide (see also Defenbaugh, 2008; Kiesinger, 2002; Lindemann, 2009; Rambo, 2005, 2007; Secklin, 2001). *Narratives* constructed from fieldnotes, interview transcripts, personal experiences, or other empirical materials enable readers to think with and feel with a story, rather than explicitly analyzing its meaning (Frank, 1995). Parry (2006) constructed short stories based upon her interviews with women negotiating pregnancy, birth, and midwifery (see also Abu-Lughod, 1993; Drew, 2001; Tillmann-Healy, 2001; Trujillo, 2004). The creative analytic practice of *poetic representation* of findings provides rich modes for artistic expression of research (Faulkner, 2007, 2010; Richardson, 1992a, 1992b, 1993, 2000). Variations include research poetry that represents a fieldwork experience in India (Chawla, 2006), investigative poetry critiquing the U.S. prison-industrial complex (Hartnett, 2003), and hybrid poems exploring issues of culture and identity (Prendergast, 2007; see also Austin, 1996; González, 1998). Many *video* representations of empirical materials involve participatory methods, ideally empowering participants to act on their own behalf, as reflected in a project designed to highlight the voices of parents of children in Head Start programs (McAllister, Wilson, Green, & Baldwin, 2005; see also Carlson, Engebretson, & Chamberlain, 2006; Nowell, Berkowitz, Deacon, & Foster-Fishman, 2006; Singhal, Harter, Chitnis, & Sharma, 2007; White, 2003). Many researchers create live *performances* based on autoethnography, ethnographic fieldnotes, or interviews that engage audiences and invite them to connect to and empathize with others (Spry, 2001). One research team developed a dramatic production exploring personhood in patients with Alzheimer's disease that is used as a teaching tool with medical students (Kontos & Naglie, 2007; see also Gray & Sinding, 2002; Mienczakowski, 1996, 2001).

MIDDLE

Enlarging, illuminating, and bolstering the middle ground of qualitative inquiry has been and remains my particular quest as a qualitative methodologist. I am most at home in what I have come to understand as the middle ground—not a fence-sitting, ambivalent, or commitment-phobic place, but a rich, varied, and complex location. In the middle sits not merely work that is "not art" or "not science," but also work that offers description, exposition, analysis, insight, theory, and critique, blending elements of art and science or transcending the categories.

In the middle ground, qualitative researchers adopt social constructionist or postmodernist-influenced perspectives of meaning as intersubjective and co-created, but also as retaining emphasis on the significance of commonalties and connections across the objects of analysis (Ellingson, 2009). Middle-ground work often concerns the construction of patterns, e.g., themes, categories, and portrayals, as well as practicalities, e.g., applied research, recommendations for action, empowerment of marginalized groups (Ellis & Ellingson, 2000). First-person voice departs from the passive voice that characterizes positivist work, moving away from objectivity and toward intersubjectivity, but not all the way to avowed subjectivity of art. Researchers acknowledge claims of truth as contingent upon (among other things) the politics of research funding, indeterminacy of language in which authors express claims, and fallibility of human sense making. Rather than apologizing for being subjective or ignoring the ways in which researchers construct findings, middle-ground qualitative researchers often reflect upon their standpoints to shed light on how their race, class, gender, dis/ability, sexuality, and other identities and experiences shape research processes and results (Ellingson, 1998). Rigor, depth of analysis, and reflexivity constitute important criteria for evaluating claims of middle-ground qualitative research (Fitch, 1994).

Qualitative researchers in the middle ground achieve "intimate familiarity" with their textual materials by rereading them many times, making notes on emergent trends, and then constructing themes or patterns concerning aspects of the culture (Strauss & Corbin, 1998; Warren & Karner, 2010). Charmaz (2000, 2005, 2006) situates grounded theory methods within social constructionist theory, developing the constructed nature of all knowledge claims as arising out of relationships; thus, meaning resides not in people or in texts, but *between* them. One such study parses the meanings of emotional strain on palliative cancer nurses (Sandgren, Thulesius, Fridlund, & Petersson, 2006; see also Bergen, Kirby, & McBride, 2007; Ellingson, 2007; Larsen, 2006; Low, 2004; Miller-Day & Dodd, 2004; Montemurro, 2005; Sacks & Nelson, 2007; Wilson, Hutchinson, & Holzemer, 2002; Zoller, 2003). Similar middle-ground forms of analysis include "deriving themes" (Apker, 2001; Meyer & O'Hara, 2004) and narrative analysis (Goodier & Arrington, 2007; Riessman, 2008; Vanderford, Smith, & Olive, 1995). These middle-ground forms of analysis rely almost exclusively on traditional research report format for representation, but some researchers have begun to find unique ways of complementing reports with creative analytic representations, as I discuss below.

STRADDLING THE CONTINUUM: TRADITIONAL APPROACHES

Traditionally, researchers triangulate by employing multiple quantitative and qualitative methods or measures to capture more effectively the truth of a social phenomenon (Lindlof & Taylor, 2002). In positivist and (some) postpositivist research, triangulation or multiple methods design involves an attempt to get closer to the truth by bringing together multiple forms of data and analysis to clarify and enrich a report on a phenomenon (e.g., Creswell & Clark, 2006). Hence, while methods may complement and even contrast in terms of procedures (e.g., interviews and numerical surveys), the epistemological underpinnings are consistent, with both upholding positivist or postpositivist goals of generalization and prediction. While such work often includes both qualitative and quantitative data or a range of different qualitative data or statistical measurements combined into a single report, manuscripts tend to reflect traditional writing conventions and do not include artistic or creative genres. Scott and Sutton (2009), for instance, utilized open-ended and quantitative surveys and interviews to explore relationships between teachers' emotions and practice change during and following participation in a series of professional development workshops (see also Castle, Fox, & Souder, 2006; Hodgkin, 2008; O'Donnell, Lutfey, Marceau, & McKinlay, 2007).

STRADDLING THE CONTINUUM: CONTEMPORARY APPROACHES

Endless numbers of innovative ways to blend or transcend art and science in qualitative collection of empirical materials, analysis, and representation exist, with more being developed all the time. Hybrids may integrate inductive/ grounded theory analysis with other methods of representation, such as photography in a study of quality of life among African American breast cancer survivors (López, Eng, Randall-David, & Robinson, 2005) or participatory action research techniques employed by researchers exploring female childhood sexual abuse survivors' experiences with physical therapy (Teram, Schachter, & Stalker, 2005). Another way to overtly blend the voices of art and science is to weave them into a single representation. *Layered accounts* move back and forth between academic prose and narrative, poetry, or other art, revealing their constructed nature through the juxtaposition of social science and artistic ways of knowing (Ronai, 1995). Layered accounts often connect personal experiences to theory, research, and cultural critique or to discussions of methodological matters. As such, Jago's (2006) essay incorporates narratives to illustrate the experience of growing up with an absent father (see also Markham, 2005; Saarnivaara, 2003; Tracy, 2004).

Another current approach to straddling methodological camps is to reach out to multiple audiences outside of the academy with research findings (Fine, Weis, Weseen, & Wong, 2000). For example, Hecht and Miller-Day (2007) detailed their project that collected narratives from adolescents about their substance abuse experiences and conducted systematic analyses, which were published in an academic research journal. At the same time, the authors transformed their findings into dramatic performances and into a substance abuse prevention curriculum that clearly reflected artistic and pedagogical forms of representation far different from their scholarly report. I continue my discussion of reaching multiple audiences later in this chapter. At this point, I engage the decision-making processes involved in considering opportunities for analysis and representation across the qualitative continuum.

Engaging Interpretive Processes: Some Strategies for Successfully Navigating the Continuum

Now that I have stated my case for constructing qualitative methods as a continuum and urged researchers to navigate the possibilities for analysis and interpretation in a fluid and diverse way, I offer some suggestions for how to think about and move through a qualitative project. This is an answer (albeit not *the* answer) to the perennial question by students and practitioners of qualitative methods during and after they have collected a rich, intriguing set of empirical materials: What do I *do* with all this *stuff?* No substitute exists for wading through the interpretive process oneself, and each project holds unique opportunities and constraints. Yet qualitative researchers and students share many common experiences, obstacles, and decision points as we navigate our projects. For those who decide to cross the qualitative continuum instead of limiting themselves to one location, I offer some suggestions for how to do it, either when moving within a single project or across different projects. Many of these strategies were inspired by and overlap with reflexive exercises offered by other methodologists (see Janesick's [2006] "stretching exercises" and Richardson's [2000] writing exercises). I tuned these strategies to the challenges and opportunities of deliberately choosing to adopt more than one epistemological, analytical, and/or representational position on the continuum (Ellingson, 2009). Please consider the order to be flexible, and freely pick and choose which seem applicable to a particular project.

I encourage researchers to wonder, target audiences, strategically select material, consider format, keep the forest and the trees, acknowledge mutual influence, make each piece count, be pragmatic, and own the process.

WONDER

In addition to reading relevant methodological, theoretical, and topic-specific materials, I also suggest that researchers explore their goals in a process I call *wondering*. To prepare, explore the answers you generate to the following questions in deciding which points of the continuum will manifest within a project. I heartily encourage journaling or freewriting on these topics, using writing as a method of inquiry to open up possibilities (Richardson, 2000).

Empirical Materials/Analysis

- What cases, events, stories, or details come to mind immediately when I think about my data or other empirical materials?

- What have I learned about my materials by immersing myself in them?

- What contradictions, inconsistencies, or exceptions to the rules do I notice in my empirical materials?

- How does my identity relate to my work? How do my age, gender, race/ethnicity, nationality, abilities and disabilities, special talents, formative experiences, etc., shape how I understand my participants?

- How do I think my participants perceive me?
- What have my participants taught me about their worlds? About mine?
- How is power revealed and concealed in my empirical materials?
- How am I complicit with systems of power in my empirical materials and analyses?
- What truths seem to be missing from the preliminary analyses and accounts I have worked on?

Topics

- What are the key content claims I want to make about my topic?
- What patterns do I wish to explore?
- What is/are my thesis statement(s) for this project?
- What political implications of my project do I want to explore?
- What pragmatic suggestions for improving the world have I developed? Or in what areas do I detect a need for improvement that I might be able to shed light on with my study?
- What questions do I still have about my setting, participants, and processes?

Audiences

- What academic audiences do I want to reach with my work?
- What community, lay, or popular audiences could benefit from my findings?
- What would my favorite auntie [insert friend/relative of your choice] want to know about this topic?
- What nonprofit or government agencies could benefit from my project?
- What policies could be improved using ideas from my project?
- Sharing with which audiences would bring me the most satisfaction? Why?

Researcher Desire

- What is my favorite thing about my empirical materials? What makes me smile when I think of it? What makes me cry? What makes me angry?

- What would be fun to write?
- What process issues or ideas come up in my journaling that intrigue me?
- What strong emotions do I have about my participants, their stories, and our relationships?
- Whose research do I admire? Why?
- What about my study embarrasses me or makes me feel self-conscious? Why?
- What am I most proud of in my empirical materials?
- If one of my mentors asked me about my project, what would I want to tell her or him?

Genres

- What new forms would I like to experiment with?
- What types of writing am I good at?
- What non-written forms could I use to collect or represent my empirical materials?
- What genres do I enjoy reading? Why?
- With what genres are my participants most familiar and comfortable?
- What texts could I produce that would benefit my participants?
- How do accounts I have written or produced (e.g., fieldnotes, transcripts, photographs, e-mails, memos) shape each other? (adapted from Ellingson, 2009, pp. 75–77)

Any manuscript or representation requires innumerable decisions about content, language, and style. The freedom of moving beyond a single method or form of representation makes this process exponentially more complex, but also invigorating. Wondering enables researchers to explore options throughout the duration of qualitative projects as new opportunities, insights, and relationships develop. I urge researchers to set aside time for wondering and (re)answer questions throughout their collection of materials, analysis, and writing and producing art in other media (Fine et al., 2000).

TARGET AUDIENCES

One way to divide up findings at multiple points along the continuum is to judge what would most appeal to different audiences to whom a project has relevance, and then to produce pieces accordingly. Qualitative researchers segment audiences based on methodologies, (sub)topics, disciplines, publication outlets (e.g., academic journals, newsletters, websites, newspapers), policy makers, practitioners, community organizations, and other stakeholders. For instance, a researcher could publish an artistic, evocative, layered account in *Qualitative Inquiry* to reach an audience of ethnographers and interpretive qualitative researchers from sociology, communication, anthropology, and education; a grounded theory analysis in *Journal of Applied Communication Research* to reach organizational, interpersonal, and group communication scholars; a content analysis or a case study in *Qualitative Health Research* to reach qualitative research scholars in nursing, medicine, social work, medical sociology, medical anthropology, and health communication; and an article summarizing her or his research and offering recommendations to benefit practitioners who read a relevant professional newsletter or trade magazine.

STRATEGICALLY SELECT MATERIAL

Any qualitative researcher blessed with a rich body of empirical materials faces the challenge of deciding which theories and research to cite, of selecting examples with which to illustrate analytic themes, and of choosing specific incidents about which to write narratives. First, consider the research questions or issues to be addressed and the genre(s) to be used in the project. Reflect on the main point or thesis statement, and then make sure that every example or incident chosen clearly embodies one or more of these messages. Second, select particularly telling or evocative moments, quotes, or examples for lengthier representation in narrative or poetic writing, and keep the exemplars and instances that are representative but more easily broken into snippets to illustrate themes for analytic accounts. Planning ahead about which stories or incidents to develop narratively avoids boring and unhelpful repetition of the same incidents in both artistic representations and more social scientific pieces. Next, think in terms of which stories (or poems, photographs, etc.) can be shared and commented upon with a manageable amount of background information. Oftentimes qualitative researchers find themselves in the position of not being able to include a narrative or scene in an article because it would not make sense to readers unfamiliar with other aspects of their empirical materials, and insufficient space exists to fully contextualize the interaction. Similarly, some examples, taken out of context and serving as one of only a few representations of participants in a manuscript, may characterize participants in ways not intended or supported. Thus, choice of examples should be based in part on their comprehensiveness and their transportability. Finally, when writing systematic qualitative analyses, endeavor to illustrate themes with examples from different types of materials (e.g., transcripts, fieldnotes, organizational documents) and from a range of participants. Incorporating variety in this way when possible adds richness and interest to findings.

CONSIDER FORMAT

Perhaps the primary formatting concern for those who want to straddle the continuum within a single representation is to ensure that chosen formats embody the purpose of the article or other representation. That is, the form should reinforce the content, providing another kind of evidence or support for the main argument or another answer to a research question. A second formatting concern centers on choosing a structure that enables both showing *and* telling about a phenomenon in an effective manner. These goals are not mutually exclusive, of course; stories can also tell, and analysis can show in the midst of explication. However, accounts that combine more than one approach along the continuum should embody balanced portrayals: show *and* tell, talk *and* listen, move forward *and* step back, portray the personal *and* the political. Try to formulate a text or series of texts that provides not just multiple perspectives but a range of perspectives—group, societal, individual, dyadic, critical, appreciative, and so on. Resist limited notions of abstract or universal "fairness" or "equity" and instead think about what balance best serves the goals of the particular project.

Many authors now rely on some variant of the layered account that alternates narrative and academic prose in order to straddle constructionist (middle ground) and artistic epistemologies (Ronai, 1995). The best layered accounts show a world through particularly evocative accounts while also telling analytical arguments about theory and research. Magnet (2006), for example, alternates narratives of conversations from her life with theoretically informed critiques of her own White privilege as it informs and is informed by a dominant culture of racial oppression. The author presents a balance of showing and telling that does not necessarily accord equal length to each style but instead ensures a symbiotic relationship between the styles that serves to illuminate the central point of the article. One final formatting caution: Researchers should keep in mind the risks of reader fatigue; some very fragmented or overly complex text formats, while effective for highly motivated readers, can lose their luster over the course of a lengthy text. Avoid making mere novelty of format its own goal and instead make choices that enable readers to comprehend and engage material as fully as possible.

KEEP THE FOREST AND THE TREES

As researchers make decisions about where on the continuum to situate different parts of a project, in what form, and for what purposes, it is wise to keep in mind the project's larger picture. I find this wider purpose difficult to keep in my head when immersed in a study; moving back and forth among the concrete details of narratives, the analytic perspective involved in constructing patterns, and paradigmatic/ideological goals presents a significant challenge. Yet that big picture view remains critical to the construction of a meaningful project involving multiple epistemologies. To illustrate, consider several aspects of my big picture for the ethnographic exploration of a dialysis unit (Ellingson, 2007, 2008): my overall paradigm of social constructionism, my feminist commitments to praxis and critique of power, and my pragmatic goal of the transformation of the medical establishment into a more humane and just environment for employees, patients, and their loved ones. Collectively, these goals constitute a big picture of my project, and I work to ensure that each piece I produce adds to the picture—aesthetically, conceptually, and ethically.

ACKNOWLEDGE MUTUAL INFLUENCE

I advise researchers traversing the qualitative continuum to continually reflect on how writing or creating in one genre impacts representation in other genres; multidimensional thinking may arise, as each genre offers a different way of knowing about a topic. As we move back and forth among (for instance) constructing narratives, writing personal reflections, and inductively deriving analytical categories and processes, we play with the constraints of various genres and epistemologies by allowing each to inspire and shape the others. That is, we place the modes of thinking and writing into conversation with one another. After composing narrative, we could go back to a typology of themes and rethink how a narrative does and does not fit neatly within the categories. Narratives also focus attention on some events and divert attention from others. Ordering events constructs meaning(s) for them, and these subsequent meanings may affect the analytical process as well. The reflexive relationship among different forms of analysis and artistic representation is one of the benefits of exploring multiple points on the continuum, and I encourage others to explore how their representational practices (writing, filming, painting, performing, and so on) and analysis processes mutually influence one another.

MAKE EACH PIECE COUNT

Another helpful strategy for crossing the continuum is to make certain that each piece of a qualitative project provides some rich material and unique argument that differs in important ways from any other representations. That does not mean we should not refer to any of the same ideas, literature, methods, or theory in more than one representation, but that we be able to point to and articulate (ideally in a single sentence) the unique contribution of each piece. Moreover, I urge readers to take advantage of the particular opportunities and constraints of each genre, outlet, or medium by choosing wisely which points to make in which form. For example, trying to accomplish the goal of showing individuals' suffering, while (probably) possible within the boundaries of a traditional scholarly journal article, may be better suited to a performance or a series of poems. Tracy's (2000) study of communication and emotion provides an excellent illustration: In a mainstream journal, she published a scholarly analysis of emotional labor of social directors on a cruise ship. This same project yielded a case study included in a volume of organizational cases intended for use by students in organizational communication courses (Tracy, 2006). Then, she authored a script, performed, and acted as a consultant to the director of an ethnodrama, presented as a live performance that offered an embodied representation of the personal and professional rewards and costs of such work for her participants (Tracy, 2003). Each of these forms represented different points on the qualitative continuum, aptly reflected their content, and offered a significant contribution to the body of knowledge on emotion work.

BE PRAGMATIC

In service of the goal of completing pieces of projects that reflect multiple points of the continuum, be strategic; divide materials in ways that fit with opportunities to complete work in a timely manner. The great ideas for articles that we never get around to finishing do no service to anyone; looming deadlines prompt us to complete representations. I urge researchers to shape pieces of their work to calls for submissions to edited collections, conference panels, special issues of journals, or other fora, if/as suitable calls appear. While I concede the possibility of going to extremes by "retreading" work or making the same basic argument over and over without adding any new insights, I find such intellectual laziness relatively rare. Most of us segment our qualitative studies and adapt portions of our analyses and representations to multiple audiences because we spent years and countless hours collecting and conducting them, and they are *rich*. We cannot hope to come close to exhausting our empirical materials, and so we produce legitimate and often highly valuable scholarship by drawing fresh water from already drilled wells. Pragmatism underlies the decision making of prolific qualitative researchers, and upholding this value may encourage researchers to complete pieces reflecting diverse points on the qualitative continuum.

OWN THE PROCESS

A final suggestion for crossing the continuum is that as researchers we should be absolutely clear about what we did (and did not) do in our projects. This includes collection of empirical materials, analysis techniques, and especially choices about constructing representations. Terminology and practices vary widely among qualitative methodologists, even within the same discipline, and detailed methodological accounts are crucial (Potter, 1996). For example, I explained how I constructed the "day in the life" ethnographic narrative of an interdisciplinary geriatric oncology clinic:

> [T]o construct a day, I have taken liberties with chronology, condensing into a single day events that actually happened at different times during my fieldwork. I used the narrative convention of time frame (a day) to provide a sense of plot movement and improve clarity for readers. While faithfully representing the interactions I observed, I altered minor details of an inter-action in service of constructing a view of the clinic that reflects the team and the people it serves in an intelligible or comprehensible manner. In addition to the chronology changes, I made two other types of changes. (Ellingson, 2005, p. 16)

By explaining my process, I help alleviate suspicions that I took an "anything goes," sloppy attitude toward constructing my representation. While some colleagues may not like or approve of some methods or genres regardless of how they are explained, concise, explicit details of analytical and representational processes make it more difficult for them to dismiss choices as careless or random. Accounting for each element of our research processes (possibly in an appendix or endnote) constitutes an important nod toward methodological rigor. As many have posited, engaging in creative or other boundary-blurring work should be no less rigorous, exacting, and subject to standards of peer evaluation (e.g., Denzin & Lincoln, 2005).

Moreover, such methodological road maps assist others who may seek to follow. One of my persistent criticisms of qualitative researchers is their unwillingness or inability (due to space constraints) to represent the mistakes and misdirections that characterize real research; we neaten it up to sound credible and get published. I believe that few qualitative researchers deliberately lie, but we often commit the sin of omission. I find this representational practice particularly problematic when some of the audience for our work—students and those new to our methodologies or a particular genre, in particular—find themselves shocked when in the field or conducting an interview and all goes much less smoothly than it was "supposed to go." While these processes inevitably reflect individual personalities and circumstances, many commonalities of experience exist and deserve to be shared among the qualitative community. Researchers need models of how to negotiate uncomfortable circumstances, whether in the field or in our offices writing (or producing) representations.

Where to From Here?

Jumping, straddling, and loosening barriers among qualitative methodologies constitute high priorities for me. Straddling the continuum in creative ways provides a means of enlarging the possibilities and impact of qualitative research. In the final section of this chapter, I discuss three promising paths to navigating the qualitative continuum—engaging a multigenre crystallization framework (Ellingson, 2009), pursuing social justice work (Denzin & Giardina, 2009), and adopting "guerilla scholarship" strategies to enlarge editorial and generic boundaries (Rawlins, 2007)—and conclude with a look toward the next decade of traversing the qualitative continuum.

POSSIBILITIES OF MULTIGENRE CRYSTALLIZATION

In order to encourage boundary-spanning work along the qualitative continuum, I champion a postmodern-influenced approach to triangulation I term *crystallization*, building upon Richardson's (2000) work. Richardson invoked the crystal as an alternative metaphor to the two-dimensional, positivist image of a triangle as the basis for methodological rigor and validity. I further articulated this alternative to triangulation, which I defined as follows:

> Crystallization combines multiple forms of analysis and multiple genres of representation into a coherent text or series of related texts, building a rich

and openly partial account of a phenomenon that problematizes its own construction, highlights researchers' vulnerabilities and positionality, makes claims about socially constructed meanings, and reveals the indeterminacy of knowledge claims even as it makes them. (Ellingson, 2009, p. 4)

Crystallization thus serves to promote multiple perspectives on topics, while destabilizing those same claims, yielding a postmodern form of validity (see also Janesick, 2000, p. 392; Saukko, 2004, p. 25). Several principles further clarify the approach.

First, as with any qualitative approach, crystallization seeks to *produce knowledge about a particular phenomenon through generating a deepened, complex interpretation.* All good qualitative research should provide an in-depth understanding of a topic through "thick description" (Geertz, 1973). But crystallization provides another way of achieving depth, through not only the compilation of many details but also the juxtaposition of contrasting modes of organizing, analyzing, and representing those revealing details. Second, crystallization *utilizes forms of analysis or ways of producing knowledge across multiple points of the qualitative continuum,* generally including at least one middle-ground (constructivist) or middle-to-right (postpositivist) analytic method and one interpretive, artistic, performative, or otherwise creative approach. Third, crystallized texts *include more than one genre of writing or representation.* Crystallization depends upon segmenting, weaving, blending, or otherwise drawing upon two or more genres, media, or ways of expressing findings. The slipperiness of generic categories notwithstanding, crystallized texts (and crystallized series of separate texts) draw much of their strength from their willful crossing of epistemological boundaries. A fourth principle is that crystallized texts *feature a significant degree of reflexive consideration of the researcher's self* in the process of research design, collection of empirical materials, and representation. Depending upon the researcher's goals, explicit evidence of authorial reflexivity may be subtle, explicit, or creatively manifested. Fifth, crystallization *eschews positivist claims to objectivity and a singular, discoverable truth and embraces, reveals, and even celebrates knowledge as inevitably situated, partial, constructed, multiple, and embodied.* It brings together multiple methods *and* multiple genres simultaneously to enrich findings *and* to demonstrate the inherent limitations of all knowledge; each partial account complements the others, providing pieces of the meaning puzzle but never completing it, marking the absence of the completed image. At the same time that we surrender objectivity and singular truth, we can still make claims to know, recommendations for action, pragmatic suggestions for improvement, and theoretical insights. Although the terminology of crystallization is not yet widely used, some researchers already engage in practices that reflect these principles.

Crystallization features two primary types: integrated and dendritic. *Integrated crystallization* refers to multigenre texts that reflect the above principles in a single, coherent representation (e.g., a book, a performance) and take one of two basic forms: woven, in which small pieces of two or more genres are layered together in a complex blend; or patched, in which larger pieces of two or more genres are juxtaposed to one another in a clearly demarcated, sequential series. An outstanding exemplar of woven crystallization is Thorp's (2006) book about a participatory action project involving creating and caring for a garden at a diverse, under-resourced primary school that serves urban children, the majority of whom live in or skirt the edges of poverty. The book combines photographs, fieldnotes, poems, and analytic prose generated by the researcher with digital images of children's journals, drawings, and diagrams, artfully jumbled together in a pastiche. In an exploration of backstage teamwork among members of an interdisciplinary geriatric oncology team, I highlighted the constructed nature of accounts via patched crystallization, placing genres next to each other in a series of chapters—ethnographic narrative, grounded theory analysis, autoethnography, and feminist critique—in order to show how all accounts inevitably invoked authorial power (Ellingson, 2005; see also Bach, 2007; Lather & Smithies, 1997; D. L. Miller, Creswell, & Olander, 1998).

Dendritic crystallization refers to the ongoing and dispersed process of making meaning through multiple forms of analysis and multiple genres of representation without (or in addition to) combining genres into a single text. A particular benefit of conceptualizing the production of a series of separate representations as collectively constituting a form of postmodern methodological triangulation is scholarly legitimacy and support for academics to reach multiple audiences within and outside the academy while earning scholarly credit for work often considered to be "only" professional service. A compelling description of a research project incorporating dispersed representations that reflect multiple points on the continuum is found in Miller-Day's (2008) essay describing her study of low-wage working mothers and the personal and family challenges facing households classified as living in poverty, which included a community performance that Miller-Day argues persuasively is as significant as academic representations of findings (see also Lieblich, 2006).

PROMOTING SOCIAL JUSTICE ACROSS THE QUALITATIVE CONTINUUM

Much of the practice of ethnography and other qualitative methods remains rooted in the passion for exposing and addressing injustice that characterized the

Chicago School, many members of which explored marginalized groups in urban settings (see Lindlof & Taylor, 2002; Warren & Karner, 2010). Conquergood (1995) argued that research is always political, potentially revolutionary, and never neutral: Researchers "must choose between research that is 'engaged' or 'complicit.' By engaged I mean clear-eyed, self-critical awareness that research does not proceed in epistemological purity or moral innocence" (p. 85). Researchers cannot remain uninvolved—to refuse to advocate or to assist is to reinforce existing power relations, not to remain impartial. Calls to socially engaged work proliferate across the social sciences (e.g., Denzin & Giardina, 2009; Denzin & Lincoln, 2005; Frey & Carragee, 2007; Harter, Dutta, & Cole, 2009), often under the rubric of applied (Frey & Cissna, 2009), translational (Zerhouni, 2005), participatory action (Wang, 1999), or feminist (Hesse-Biber, 2007) research processes. I encourage readers to think of their work as always already political in its practices and implications and to use multiple modes of analysis and representation to highlight the material and ideological implications of their research practices and findings.

By consciously crossing the qualitative continuum to make the most of our rich empirical materials, we can produce written, oral, visual, and multimedia accounts that meet specific needs and interests of diverse audiences. To reach practitioners, policy makers, social commentators, and other stakeholders, we must engage in meaningful dialogue—a process that requires us to listen as much as (or more than) we speak. When we bring our ideas and willingness to collaborate to divergent academic disciplines (Parrott, 2008) and to the general public, we act as scholars and as public intellectuals who "embody and enact moral leadership" (Papa & Singhal, 2007, pp. 126–127; see also Brouwer & Squires, 2003; Giroux, 2004). When we speak out, we move beyond the important work of knowledge creation and theory building to apply our scholarly resources to benefit people more directly. The more varied our methodological toolbox, the more opportunities we have to creatively address social inequities and work for positive change—for example, through mixed methods research design (Mertens, 2007; Sosulski & Lawrence, 2008), visual and participatory methods such as photovoice (Singhal et al., 2007), and multigenre representation of research (Ellingson, 2009).

ENLARGING EDITORIAL BOUNDARIES: THE PRACTICE OF GUERILLA SCHOLARSHIP

Those of us who feel passionately that our work holds the potential to help people, to promote social justice, to shed light on complex problems, and to significantly influence our disciplines need to make sure important work that serves those goals gets done and published (or otherwise shared). If that goal requires being subtle (or even sneaky), so be it. In order to reach our intended audiences, some work may have to accommodate conventions that may not fit comfortably with postmodern, feminist, or narrative sensibilities, but which currently constitute the cost of admission to disciplinary ground. Rawlins (2007) explains that he resorted to fitting his work within the boundaries of traditional social scientific journal conventions by

> aping its trappings, writing style, and subdivisions . . . in order to *pass* as a serious researcher. I call such activity *guerilla scholarship*. It is necessary when certain ways of knowing are stringently enforced to the exclusion and neglect of others. The stated and unstated regimes of certain journals require these kinds of accoutrements. (p. 59, emphasis original)

Conversely, some work that closely follows traditions of (post)positivism may find that journals devoted to artistic/interpretive or "creative analytic" work (Richardson, 2000) reject the work for its apparent adherence to values that they reject. Likewise, practitioners may have jargon and communication norms that must be met to gain entry to their trade publications, or community organizations may request to have all theory, concepts, and findings translated into laypeople language. Given that no innocent or neutral portrayal is possible in any genre or medium, I consider adopting varied presentational norms that span the qualitative continuum in order to access particular outlets to be well within the boundaries of ethically sound practice. Indeed, to refuse to adapt to such conventions may just as easily reflect arrogance as integrity.

Another form of guerilla scholarship I suggest is to cite within an article multiple other works that reflect different methods, genres of representation, ideologies, or even paradigms (Ellingson, 2009). For example, Harter, Norander, and Quinlan (2007) dared to cite their research group's narratives written for a nonprofit agency's website (Harter, Norander, & Young, 2005) and a newspaper article (Novak & Harter, 2005) in a scholarly article on public intellectualism and activism published in a mainstream journal. Who knows what unsuspecting reader might follow the trail of cites straight into a forest of new practices that could broaden her or his horizons. Reference sections fulfill this function, of course, but footnotes, epigraphs, highlighted quotes in an essay or report, and interludes or other disruptive discourses can all be places to invoke the methodological or representational Other and lure the audience into new fields of play. Methods sections also offer good places to highlight connections; when I discuss analysis, I sometimes engage in guerilla scholarship by discussing the mutual influence of other pieces of my larger project with the one I documented in that method section. I urge qualitative scholars to share (or at least hint at) work from disparate areas of the qualitative continuum—that is, mention performances of findings when reporting the process of producing an inductive typology; in a performance playbill or flyer, add a note about reports based on the same data. We can also push the envelope through footnotes and the occasional provocative or creative phrase here and there that challenges the standards of acceptability in a publication outlet and thus subversively broaden the horizons of the publication and, by extension, our disciplines.

Conclusion

My passion for meandering across the qualitative continuum grows every year as I encounter the outstanding work of colleagues across the social sciences, education, and health and human services fields, and as I continue to stretch my own capabilities and interests into new areas. In the coming decade, I foresee a sharp rise in the number of researchers who willingly employ methods that span significant areas of the qualitative continuum in their efforts to address critical issues through socially engaged research programs. By this I mean not simply that some researchers will add some quantitative measures to highly structured qualitative content analyses or complement narratives with performances, but that the methodological lions and lambs shall lie down together peacefully in the form of stories tied to statistics, typologies interwoven with photographs, and community reports accompanied by poststructuralist critiques. I sense that such practices shall be, if not widespread, at least not uncommon. Structures and institutions change more slowly, and I hold out somewhat less hope that doctoral training programs will readily adapt to methodological and representational plurality that truly crosses epistemological boundaries within a given candidate's program of study in the same period of time. Still, the link between nimble navigation of the qualitative continuum and the pursuit of positive social change is clear, and it will undoubtedly prove irresistible to more and more researchers.

I am not naive; of course no researcher can achieve excellence in all forms of qualitative analysis and representation. We all have analytical strengths and weaknesses, individual standpoints and disciplinary predispositions, ideological commitments and artistic impulses. I encourage respect for the complexities and rigors of every art form and analytical technique, but I reject fear of the unknown and methodological prejudice inherited through our academic family lineages. K. I. Miller (2000) warned that too much emphasis on categorizing types of researchers or research orientations can serve to constrain researchers into thinking and acting in accordance with their perceptions of their researcher type rather than pursuing whichever important research questions interest them through whichever methods (and representational forms) best enable the pursuit of answers. I have thus provided what I hope are some useful questions and strategies for those who resist or want to resist unproductive limits on the ongoing navigation of the qualitative continuum.

References

Abu-Lughod, J. L. (1993). *Writing women's worlds: Bedouin stories.* Berkeley: University of California Press.

Anderson, L. (2006). Analytic autoethnography. *Journal of Contemporary Ethnography, 35*(4), 373–395.

Apker, J. (2001). Role development in the managed care era: A case of hospital-based nursing. *Journal of Applied Communication Research, 29,* 117–136.

Atkinson, P. (2006). Rescuing autoethnography. *Journal of Contemporary Ethnography, 35,* 400–404.

Austin, D. A. (1996). Kaleidoscope: The same and different. In C. Ellis & A. P. Bochner (Eds.), *Composing ethnography* (pp. 206–230). Walnut Creek, CA: AltaMira Press.

Bach, H. (2007). *A visual narrative concerning curriculum, girls, photography, etc.* Walnut Creek, CA: Left Coast Press.

Bergen, K. M., Kirby, E., & McBride, M. C. (2007). "How do you get two houses cleaned?" Accomplishing family caregiving in commuter marriages. *Journal of Family Communication, 7,* 287–307.

Brooks, L. J., & Bowker, G. (2002). Playing at work: Understanding the future of work practices at the Institute for the Future. *Information, Communication & Society, 5,* 109–136.

Brouwer, D. C., & Squires, C. R. (2003). Public intellectuals, public life, and the university. *Argumentation and Advocacy, 39,* 201–213.

Bruess, C. J. S., & Pearson, J. C. (1997). Interpersonal rituals in marriage and adult friendship. *Communication Monographs, 64,* 25–45.

Carlson, E. D., Engebretson, J., & Chamberlain, R. M. (2006). Photovoice as a social process of critical consciousness. *Qualitative Health Research, 16,* 836–852.

Castle, S., Fox, R. K., & Souder, K. O. (2006). Do professional development schools (PDSS) make a difference? A comparative study of PDS and non-PDS teacher candidates. *Journal of Teacher Education, 57,* 65–80.

Charmaz, K. (2000). Grounded theory: Objectivist and constructivist methods. In N. K. Denzin, & Y. S. Lincoln (Eds.), *The SAGE handbook of qualitative research* (2nd ed., pp. 509–535). Thousand Oaks, CA: Sage.

Charmaz, K. (2005). Grounded theory in the 21st century: A qualitative method for advancing social justice research. In N. K. Denzin & Y. S. Lincoln (Eds.), *The SAGE handbook of qualitative research* (3rd ed., pp. 507–535). Thousand Oaks, CA: Sage.

Charmaz, K. (2006). *Constructing grounded theory: A practical guide through qualitative analysis.* Thousand Oaks, CA: Sage.

Chawla. D. (2006). The bangle seller of Meena Bazaar. *Qualitative Inquiry, 12*(6), 1135–1138.

Conquergood, D. (1995). Between rigor and relevance: Rethinking applied communication. In K. N. Cissna (Ed.), *Applied communication in the 21st century* (pp. 79–96). Mahwah, NJ: Lawrence Erlbaum.

Cousineau, T. M., Rancourt, D., & Green, T. C. (2006). Web chatter before and after the Women's Health Initiative results: A content analysis of on-line menopause message boards. *Journal of Health Communication, 11,* 133–147.

Creswell, J. W., & Clark, V. L. P. (2006). *Designing and conducting mixed methods research.* Thousand Oaks, CA: Sage.

Defenbaugh, N. (2008). "Under erasure": The absent "ill" body in doctor–patient dialogue. *Qualitative Inquiry, 14,* 1402–1424.

Denzin, N. K., & Giardina, M. D. (2009). *Qualitative inquiry and social justice.* Walnut Creek, CA: Left Coast Press.

Denzin, N. K., & Lincoln, Y. S. (2005). Introduction: The discipline and practice of qualitative research. In N. K. Denzin & Y. S. Lincoln (Eds.), *The SAGE handbook of qualitative research* (3rd ed., pp. 1–32). Thousand Oaks, CA: Sage.

Drew, R. (2001). *Karaoke nights: An ethnographic rhapsody.* Walnut Creek, CA: AltaMira Press.

Ellingson, L. L. (1998). "Then you know how I feel": Empathy, identification, and reflexivity in fieldwork. *Qualitative Inquiry, 4,* 492–514.

Ellingson, L. L. (2005). *Communicating in the clinic: Negotiating frontstage and backstage teamwork.* Cresskill, NJ: Hampton Press.

Ellingson, L. L. (2007). The performance of dialysis care: Routinization and adaptation on the floor. *Health Communication, 22,* 103–114.

Ellingson, L. L. (2008). Patients' inclusion of spirituality within the comprehensive geriatric assessment process. In M. Wills (Ed.), *Spirituality and health communication* (pp. 67–85). Cresskill, NJ: Hampton Press.

Ellingson, L. L. (2009). *Engaging crystallization in qualitative research: An introduction.* Thousand Oaks, CA: Sage.

Ellingson, L. L., & Ellis, C. (2008). Autoethnography as constructionist project. In J. A. Holstein, & J. F. Gubrium (Eds.), *Handbook of constructionist research* (pp. 445–465). New York: Guilford Press.

Ellis, C. (2004). *The ethnographic I: A methodological novel about autoethnography.* Walnut Creek, CA: AltaMira.

Ellis, C., & Bochner, A. P. (2006). Analyzing analytic autoethnography: An autopsy. *Journal of Contemporary Ethnography, 35*(4), 429–449.

Ellis, C., & Ellingson, L. L. (2000). Qualitative methods. In E. F. Borgatta & R. J. V. Montgomery (Eds.), *Encyclopedia of Sociology* (2nd ed., Vol. 4, pp. 2287–2296). New York: Macmillan Library Reference.

Faulkner, S. L. (2007). Concern with craft: Using Ars Poetica as criteria for reading research poetry. *Qualitative Inquiry, 13*(2), 218–234.

Faulkner, S. L. (2010). *Poetry as method: Reporting research through verse.* Walnut Creek, CA: Left Coast Press.

Feng, J., & Wu, D. D. (2009). Changing ideologies and advertising discourses in China: A case study of *Nanfang Daily. Journal of Asian Pacific Communication, 19,* 218–238.

Fine, M., Weis, L., Weseen, S., & Wong, L. (2000). For whom? Qualitative research, representation, and social responsibilities. In N. K. Denzin, & Y. S. Lincoln (Eds.), *Handbook of qualitative research* (2nd ed., pp. 107–132). Thousand Oaks, CA: Sage.

Fitch, K. L. (1994). Criteria for evidence in qualitative research. *Western Journal of Communication, 58,* 32–38.

Frank, A. W. (1995). *The wounded storyteller: Body, illness, and ethics.* Chicago: University of Chicago Press.

Frey, L. R., & Carragee, K. M. . (2007). *Communication activism, vol. 1: Communication for social change.* Cresskill, NJ: Hampton Press.

Frey, L. R., & Cissna, K. (Eds.). (2009). *Handbook of applied communication research.* New York: Routledge.

Geertz. C. (1973). *The interpretation of cultures.* New York: Basic Books.

Gergen, K. J. (1994). *Realities and relationships: Soundings in social construction.* Cambridge, MA: Harvard University Press.

Giroux, H. A. (2004). Cultural studies, public pedagogy, and the responsibility of intellectuals. *Communication and Critical/Cultural Studies, 1*(1), 59–79.

Glaser, B., & Strauss, B. (1967). *The discovery of grounded theory: Strategies for qualitative research.* Chicago: Aldine.

González, M. C. (1998). Painting the white face red: Intercultural contact presented through poetic ethnography. In J. Martin, T. Nakayama, & L. Flores (Eds.), *Readings in cultural contexts* (pp. 485–495). Mountain View, CA: Mayfield.

Goodier, B. C., & Arrington, M. I. (2007). Physicians, patients, and medical dialogue in the NYPD Blue prostate cancer story. *Journal of Medical Humanities, 28*(1), 45–58.

Gray, R., & Sinding, C. (2002). *Standing ovation: Performing social science research about cancer.* Walnut Creek, CA: AltaMira Press.

Guba, E. G., & Lincoln, Y. S. (1994). Competing paradigms in qualitative research. In N. K. Denzin & Y. S. Lincoln (Eds.), *Handbook of qualitative research* (pp. 105–117). Thousand Oaks, CA: Sage.

Gubrium, J. F., & Holstein, J. A. (1997). *The new language of qualitative method.* New York: Oxford University Press.

Güven, B. (2008). Experience, instruction, and social environment: Fourth and fifth grade students' use of metaphor. *Social Behavior and Personality, 36,* 743–752.

Harter, L. M., Dutta, M., & Cole, C. (Eds.). (2009). *Communicating for social impact.* Cresskill, NJ: Hampton Press.

Harter, L. M., Japp, P. M., & Beck, C. (Eds.). (2005). *Narratives, health, and healing: Communication theory, research, and practice.* Mahwah, NJ: Lawrence Erlbaum.

Harter, L. M., Norander, S., & Quinlan, M. M. (2007). Imaginative renderings in the service of renewal and reconstruction. *Management Communication Quarterly, 21,* 105.

Harter, L. M., Norander, S., & Young, S. (2005). *Collaborative art: Cultivating connections between self and other.* Available at http://www.passionworks.org/articles

Hartnett, S. J. (2003). *Incarceration nation: Investigative prison poems of hope and terror.* Walnut Creek, CA: AltaMira Press.

Hecht, M. L., & Miller-Day, M. (2007). The Drug Resistance Strategies Project as translational research. *Journal of Applied Communication Research, 35,* 343–349.

Hesse-Biber, S. N. (Ed.). (2007). *Handbook of feminist research: Theory and praxis.* Thousand Oaks, CA: Sage.

Hodgkin, S. (2008). Telling it all: A story of women's social capital using a mixed methods approach. *Journal of Mixed Methods Research, 2*(3), 296–316.

Jago, B. (2006). A primary act of imagination: An autoethnography of father-absence. *Qualitative Inquiry, 12,* 398–426.

Janesick, V. J. (2000). The choreography of qualitative research design: Minuets, improvisations, and crystallization. In N. K. Denzin & Y. S. Lincoln (Eds.), *Handbook of qualitative research* (2nd ed., pp. 379–399). Thousand Oaks, CA: Sage.

Kiesinger, C. (2002). My father's shoes: The therapeutic value of narrative reframing. In A. Bochner & C. Ellis (Eds.), *Ethnographically speaking: Autoethnography, literature, and aesthetics* (pp. 95–114). Walnut Creek, CA: AltaMira Press.

Kontos, P. C., & Naglie, G. (2007). Expressions of personhood in Alzheimer's disease: An evaluation of research-based theatre as a pedagogical tool. *Qualitative Health Research, 17*(6), 799–811.

Kuperberg, A., & Stone, P. (2008). The media depiction of women who opt out. *Gender & Society, 22,* 497–517.

Kwok, C., & Sullivan, G. (2007). The concepts of health and preventive health practices of Chinese-Australian women in relation to cancer screening. *Journal of Transcultural Nursing, 18*(2), 118–126.

Larsen, E. A. (2006). A vicious oval. *Journal of Contemporary Ethnography, 35,* 119–147.

Lather, P., & Smithies, C. (1997). *Troubling the angels: Women living with HIV/AIDS.* Boulder, CO: Westview Press.

Lee, K. V. (2006). A fugue about grief. *Qualitative Inquiry, 12,* 1154–1159.

Lieblich, A. (2006). Vicissitudes: A study, a book, a play: Lessons from the work of a narrative scholar. *Qualitative Inquiry, 12,* 60–80.

Lindemann, K. (2009). Cleaning up my (father's) mess: Narrative containments of "leaky" masculinities. *Qualitative Inquiry, 16,* 29–38.

Lindlof, T. R., & Taylor, B. C. (2002). *Qualitative communication research methods* (2nd ed.). Thousand Oaks, CA: Sage.

López, E., Eng, E., Randall-David, E., & Robinson, N. (2005). Quality-of-life concerns of African American breast cancer survivors within rural North Carolina: Blending the techniques of photovoice and grounded theory. *Qualitative Health Research, 15,* 99–115.

Low, J. (2004). Managing safety and risk: The experiences of people with Parkinson's disease who use alternative and complementary therapies. *Health, 8,* 445–463.

Magnet, S. (2006). Protesting privilege: An autoethnographic look at whiteness. *Qualitative Inquiry, 12,* 736–749.

Markham, A. N. (2005). "Go ugly early": Fragmented narrative and bricolage as interpretive method. *Qualitative Inquiry, 11*(6), 813–839.

McAllister, C. L., Wilson, P. C., Green, B. L., & Baldwin, J. L. (2005). "Come and take a walk": Listening to Early Head Start parents on school-readiness as a matter of child, family, and community health. *American Journal of Public Health, 95,* 617–625.

Mertens, D. M. (2007). Transformative paradigm: Mixed methods and social justice. *Journal of Mixed Methods Research, 1,* 212–225.

Meyer, M. (2004). From transgression to transformation: Negotiating the opportunities and tensions of engaged pedagogy in the feminist organizational communication classroom. In P. M. Buzzanell, H. Sterk, & L. H. Turner (Eds.), *Gender in applied communication contexts* (pp. 195–213). Thousand Oaks, CA: Sage.

Meyer, M., & O'Hara, L. S. (2004). When they know who we are: The National Women's Music Festival comes to Ball State University. In P. M. Buzzanell, H. Sterk, & L. H. Turner (Eds.), *Gender in applied communication contexts* (pp. 3–23). Thousand Oaks, CA: Sage.

Mienczakowski, J. (1996). An ethnographic act: The construction of consensual theatre. In C. Ellis & A. P. Bochner (Eds.), *Composing ethnography: Alternative forms of qualitative writing* (pp. 244–264). Walnut Creek, CA: AltaMira.

Mienczakowski, J. (2001). Ethnodrama: Performed research—Limitations and potential. In P. Atkinson, A. Coffey, S. Delamont, J. Lofland, & L. Lofland (Eds.), *Handbook of ethnography* (pp. 468–476). Thousand Oaks, CA: Sage.

Miller, D. L., Creswell, J. W., & Olander, L. S. (1998). Writing and retelling multiple ethnographic tales of a soup kitchen for the homeless. *Qualitative Inquiry, 4*(4), 469–491.

Miller, K. I. (2000). Common ground from the post-positivist perspective: From "straw-person" argument to collaborative coexistence. In S. R. Corman & M. S. Poole (Eds.), *Perspectives on organizational communication: Finding common ground* (pp. 47–67). New York: Guilford Press.

Miller-Day, M. A. (2008). Performance matters. *Qualitative Inquiry, 14*(8), 1458–1470.

Miller-Day, M. A., & Dodd, A. H. (2004). Toward a descriptive model of parent–offspring communication about alcohol and other drugs. *Journal of Social and Personal Relationships, 21*(1), 69–91.

Montemurro, B. (2005). Add men, don't stir. *Journal of Contemporary Ethnography, 34,* 6–35.

Novak, D. R., & Harter, L. M. (2005, June 14–18). Blues fest showcase world's best. *StreetWise,* pp. 1–2.

Nowell, B. L., Berkowitz, S. L., Deacon, Z., & Foster-Fishman, P. (2006). Revealing the cues within community places: Stories of identity, history, and possibility. *American Journal of Community Psychology, 37,* 29–46.

O'Donnell, A. B., Lutfey, K. E., Marceau, L. D., & McKinlay, J. B. (2007). Using focus groups to improve the validity of cross-national survey research: A study of physician decision making. *Qualitative Health Research, 17,* 971–981.

Papa, M. J., & Singhal, A. (2007). Intellectuals searching for publics: Who is out there? *Management Communication Quarterly, 21,* 126–136.

Parrott, R. (2008). A multiple discourse approach to health communication: Translational research and ethical practice. *Journal of Applied Communication Research, 36,* 1–7.

Parry, D. C. (2006). Women's lived experiences with pregnancy and midwifery in a medicalized and fetocentric context: Six short stories. *Qualitative Inquiry, 12,* 459–471.

Potter, W. J. (1996). *An analysis of thinking and research about qualitative methods.* Mahwah, NJ: Lawrence Erlbaum.

Prendergast, M. (2007). Thinking narrative (on the Vancouver Island ferry): A hybrid poem. *Qualitative Inquiry, 13,* 743.

Rambo, C. (2005). Impressions of Grandmother: An autoethnographic portrait. *Journal of Contemporary Ethnography, 34,* 560–585.

Rambo, C. (2007). Handing IRB an unloaded gun. *Qualitative Inquiry, 13,* 353–416.

Rawlins, W. K. (2007). Living scholarship: A field report. *Communication Methods and Measures, 1,* 55–63.

Richardson, L. (1992a). The consequences of poetic representation: Writing the other, rewriting the self. In C. Ellis & M. G. Flaherty (Eds.), *Investigating subjectivity: Research on lived experience* (pp. 125–140). Thousand Oaks, CA: Sage.

Richardson, L. (1992b). The poetic representation of lives: Writing a postmodern sociology. *Studies in Symbolic Interaction, 13,* 19–29.

Richardson, L. (1993). Poetics, dramatics, and transgressive validity: The case of the skipped line. *Sociological Quarterly, 35,* 695–710.

Richardson, L. (2000). Writing: A method of inquiry. In N. K. Denzin & Y. S. Lincoln (Eds.), *Handbook of qualitative research* (2nd ed., pp. 923–943). Thousand Oaks, CA: Sage.

Riessman, C. K. (2008). *Narrative methods for the human sciences.* Thousand Oaks, CA: Sage.

Ronai, C. R. (1995). Multiple reflections on childhood sex abuse: An argument for a layered account. *Journal of Contemporary Ethnography, 23,* 395–426.

Saarnivaara, M. (2003). Art as inquiry: The autopsy of an [art] experience. *Qualitative Inquiry, 9*(4), 580–602.

Sacks, J. L., & Nelson, J. P. (2007). A theory of nonphysical suffering and trust in hospice patients. *Qualitative Health Research, 17,* 675–689.

Sandgren, A., Thulesius, H., Fridlund, B., & Petersson, K. (2006). Striving for emotional survival in palliative cancer nursing. *Qualitative Health Research, 16*(1), 79–96.

Saukko, P. (2004). *Doing research in cultural studies: An introduction to classical and new methodological approaches.* Thousand Oaks, CA: Sage.

Scott, C., & Sutton, R. E. (2009). Emotions and change during professional development for teachers. *Journal of Mixed Methods Research, 3*(2), 151–171.

Secklin, P. L. (2001). Multiple fractures in time: Reflections on a car crash. *Journal of Loss and Trauma, 6*(4), 323–333.

Singhal, A., Harter, L. M., Chitnis, K., & Sharma, D. (2007). Participatory photography as theory, method, and praxis: Analyzing an entertainment-education project in India. *Critical Arts, 21*(1), 212–227.

Sosulski, M. R., & Lawrence, C. (2008). Mixing methods for full-strength results. *Journal of Mixed Methods Research, 2*(2), 121–148.

Spry, T. (2001). Performing autoethnography: An embodied methodological praxis. *Qualitative Inquiry, 7*(6), 706–732.

Strauss, A., & Corbin, J. (1998). *Basics of qualitative research: Techniques and procedures for developing grounded theory* (2nd ed.). Thousand Oaks, CA: Sage.

Teram, E., Schachter, C. L., & Stalker, C. A. (2005). The case for integrating grounded theory in participatory action research: Empowering clients to inform professional practice. *Qualitative Health Research, 15*, 1129–1140.

Thorp, L. (2006). *Pull of the earth: Participatory ethnography in the school garden.* Walnut Creek, CA: AltaMira Press.

Tillmann-Healy, L. (2001). *Between gay and straight: Understanding friendship across sexual orientation.* Walnut Creek, CA: AltaMira Press.

Tracy, S. J. (2000). Becoming a character for commerce: Emotion labor, self subordination, and discursive construction of identity in a total institution. *Management Communication Quarterly, 14*, 90–128.

Tracy, S. J. (2003). *Navigating the cruise—A trigger script ethnodrama.* Tempe: The Hugh Downs School of Human Communication's Empty Space Theater, Arizona State University.

Tracy, S. J. (2004). The construction of correctional officers: Layers of emotionality behind bars. *Qualitative Inquiry, 10*(4), 509–533.

Tracy, S. J. (2006). Navigating the limits of a smile: Emotion labor and concertive control on a cruise ship. In J. Keyton & P. Shockley-Zalabak (Eds.), *Case studies for organizational communication: Understanding communication processes* (2nd ed., pp. 394–407). Los Angeles: Roxbury.

Trujillo, N. (2004). *In search of Naunny's grave: Age, class, gender, and ethnicity in an American family.* Walnut Creek, CA: AltaMira Press.

Vanderford, M. L., Smith, D. H., & Olive, T. (1995). The image of plastic surgeons in news media coverage of the silicone breast implant controversy. *Plastic and Reconstructive Surgery, 96*(3), 521–538.

Wang, C. C. (1999). Photovoice: A participatory action research strategy applied to women's health. *Journal of Women's Health, 8*(2), 185–192.

Warren, C. A. B., & Karner, T. X. (2010). *Discovering qualitative methods: Field research, interviews, and analysis* (2nd ed.). Los Angeles: Roxbury.

White, S. A. (2003). Introduction: Video power. In S. A. White (Ed.), *Participatory video: Images that transform and empower* (pp. 17–30). Thousand Oaks, CA: Sage.

Wilson, H. S., Hutchinson, S. A., & Holzemer, W. L. (2002). Reconciling incompatibilities: A grounded theory of HIV medication adherence and symptom management. *Qualitative Health Research, 12*(10), 1309–1322.

Zerhouni, E. A. (2005). Translational and clinical science: Time for a new vision. *New England Journal of Medicine, 353,* 1621–1623.

Zoller, H. M. (2003). Health on the line: Identity and disciplinary control in employee occupational health and safety discourse. *Journal of Applied Communication Research, 31*(2), 118–139.

14

Post Qualitative Research

The Critique and the Coming After

Elizabeth Adams St.Pierre

This chapter about *post* qualitative research may come both too late and too soon. I know it comes too late because I began to write it over 20 years ago, in 1995, in my first qualitative research report, my dissertation (St.Pierre, 1995). It may come too soon because qualitative research is still under a deliberate, naive, and crude attack as it has been since the beginning of the 21st century. With that in mind, I acknowledge the slippery politics of my critique. However, I am weary both of defending an overdetermined qualitative inquiry I find increasingly limited and also of the always already failed romance of trying to "talk across differences" (see, for example, Moss et al., 2009) with people who haven't kept up; are "paradigms behind" (Patton, 2008, p. 269); and have for over half a century, it seems, not read and/or engaged the linguistic turn, the cultural turn, the interpretive turn, the narrative turn, the historical turn, the critical turn, the reflexive turn, the rhetorical turn, the postmodern turn, and others. With Spivak (1993), I cannot see why "people who do not have the time to learn should organize the construction of the rest of the world" (p. 187).

Before providing a postmodern critique of what I call in this chapter *conventional humanist qualitative methodology,* I will sketch the political context in which this chapter is written, one in which both postmodernism and qualitative methodology have been rejected by "science."

THE CONTEXT OF SCIENTIFICALLY BASED RESEARCH

Qualitative research in education in the United States has taken a beating since 2002 when the U.S. No Child Left Behind Act took effect and the National

Research Council (NRC) (2002) published its report, *Scientific Research in Education* (SRE). By establishing experimental research and, preferably, randomized controlled trials as the gold standard for high-quality research, those two documents—one a federal law that mandated research methodology—exemplified the positivist and conservative restoration in the larger audit and accountability culture that privileges an instrumental, engineering model of social science that feeds on metrics to establish "what works." Notwithstanding claims of inclusiveness and in the fervor of a new scientism, qualitative research was rejected as not rigorous enough to count as high-quality science.

As time passed, it became clear that postmodernism had also become a whipping boy, a *codeword* for critiques of positivist tendencies offered by all those "turns" listed above and for critiques, more specifically, by feminist, race, Marxist, queer, postcolonial, and other theories. One of the first examples of how postmodernism was used to stand in for what was non-experimental and non-positivist was the following statement in the 2002 NRC report:

> We assume that it is possible to describe the physical and social world scientifically so that, for example, multiple observers can agree on what they see. Consequently, we reject the postmodernist school of thought when it posits that social science research can never generate objective or trustworthy knowledge. (p. 25)

A footnote to that statement is even more perplexing:

> This description applies to an extreme epistemological perspective that questions the rationality of the scientific enterprise altogether, and instead believes that all knowledge is based on sociological factors like power, influence, and economic factors. (p. 25)

Both statements assume views of reality and reason about which all the "turns," not just postmodernism, are skeptical. But even law enforcement officials experience social constructionism when eyewitnesses differently describe/construct what they "saw"; and many social *and* natural scientists acknowledge that power, politics, and economic factors influence knowledge production in the sciences.

The NRC report cited as its authority for those two statements rejecting postmodernism a book by Phillips (a member of the NRC committee) and Burbules (2000). But my careful reading of that book found almost no discussion of postmodernism or citations to postmodern scholars except Lyotard, so it cannot serve as a warrant for the committee's claims about postmodernism. Nonetheless, Phillips (2006) continued to critique postmodernism without citing postmodern scholars, calling postmodernism "extreme" and "at the left-hand end or pole" of some "continuum," claiming for himself a moderate, temperate position. Later, Phillips (2009) seemed surprised that researchers would object to the rampant orthodox positivism in the scientifically based research (SBR) debates and admonished resisters to SBR—those in a "diseased condition" (p. 164)—for being unruly, recalcitrant, querulous, vituperative, and filled with "postmodernist contumely" (p. 193).

Other examples of unsubstantiated, under-sourced critiques of postmodernism followed, especially from Grover Whitehurst, the former Director of the U.S. Institute of Education Sciences (IES). In his 2003 Presidential Invited Session at the American Educational Research Association, he proclaimed that we need less theory, naming postmodernism in particular, and more of "what works." Whitehurst (IES, 2008) continued to attack postmodernism in his final report to Congress in 2008, reporting that during his tenure at IES he had had to distinguish the institute's work "from what had become the dominant forms of education research in the latter half of the 20th century: qualitative research grounded in postmodern philosophy and methodologically weak quantitative research" (p. 5). In the report, he referred to "the ascendance of postmodern approaches to education research" (p. 6). Who knew? I, for one, was unaware that postmodern qualitative research had ever been dominant in any field. True to form, Whitehurst did not cite postmodern scholars or texts in either case, but the link between postmodernism and qualitative research was, nonetheless, established in their rejection.

Whitehurst's counterpart in England, Anne Oakley, Director of the Social Science Research Unit at the Institute of Education at the University of London, had been rejecting postmodernism for some time. In an odd twist, she called critiques of scientifically based research "resistance texts" and "conservative responses to real or imagined threats, including that of 'new' technology [the randomized controlled trial and the systematic review (SR); see MacLure, 2005, for a postmodern critique of SRs], and its ability to reveal *previously concealed features of academic work*" (Oakley, 2006, p. 64, emphasis added). Oakley laid the blame for poor social science research on postmodernism, chiding it for "fashionable nonsense and word games" (p. 78) though, like Whitehurst, she cited none of the key postmodern scholars.

Perhaps Henig's (2008) comment summed up the positivist concern about research that is not positivist. He wrote that educational research had become a fragmented field that was "overly abstract (e.g., neo-Marxist, post-structuralism, gender identity, or critical race studies) and seen as insufficiently rigorous—leaning toward qualitative over quantitative research and less concerned with causal mechanisms than telling convincing stories" (p. 51). Of course, it is only positivism that claims to be non-abstract, objective, and both theory- and value-free. Qualitative inquiry has always carried on its strong, supple back theory-, value-, power-, and politically-laden investigations of the lived experiences of people in the midst of living—hardly a neutral arena. It has never claimed science can be nowhere, disentangled from the humans who produce it.

The examples above illustrate how, in the SBR debates, postmodernism—without citational authority or warrant—became a code word for any philosophical approach that is not positivist. Linked to qualitative methodology, which could never be rigorous because it is not experimental, postmodernism was doubly damned. In writing about the resistance to Derrida's work, which has profoundly informed postmodern theories, Lamont (1987) suggested that

> this large opposition was related to Derrida's attack on the basic tenets of the humanist tradition and interpretive activity. The very violence of these attacks contributed to the institutionalization of deconstruction; it indicated that Derrida had become a force to be contended with. (p. 612)

Hodkinson (2004) pointed out that postmodernism's critique of foundationalism in educational research has been significant though both ignored and rejected in the new audit culture with its "increasing dominance of procedures of target setting, outcomes measurement, and the focus on effectiveness and efficiency, rather than purpose or values (p. 17). But a conservative, positivist restoration in social science research methodology has not been secured; postmodern and other approaches in the social sciences are entrenched and proliferate.

THE RESURGENCE OF POSTMODERNISM

This chapter is my contribution to the *resurgence of postmodernism,* a body of critique especially useful in times like these as positivism once again falters across the social sciences as evidenced in education, for example, by the failure of the "what works" mentality of the IES in too many "no effect" research results (Viadero, 2009) and, in economics, the hardest of the soft social sciences, by the recent failure of supposed rational free markets and consumers (see Cullenberg, Amariglio, & Ruccio, 2001). Postmodern critiques, along with those of the other "turns," emerged half a century ago in response to the excesses of the positivisms;

produced a sea change in the social sciences and humanities; and are needed once again to open up structures being disciplined, regulated, and normalized.

I wish to make it clear here at the beginning that the "posts" (e.g., post-colonialism, post-critical, post-humanist, post-Fordist, post-positivist, post-feminist, post-foundational, post-emancipatory, post-memory, post-subjective, post-everything—henceforth, I will abbreviate using "posts") have never offered alternative structures and that *I do not and cannot offer an alternative methodology*—a recipe, an outline, a structure, for post qualitative research—another handy "research design" in which one can safely secure oneself and one's work. The "posts" do not offer a corrective or a fix.

Instead, I use the occasion of writing this chapter to summarize and extend my continuing concerns with what I refer to as conventional humanist qualitative inquiry and to call for a renewed commitment to a *reimagination of social science inquiry* enabled by postmodernism in spite of the current positivist orthodoxy. My critique is not that qualitative research is unscientific; it is My critique is that, to a great extent, it has been so disciplined, so normalized, so centered—especially because of recent assaults by SBR—that *it has become conventional,* reductionist, hegemonic, and sometimes oppressive and has lost its radical possibilities "to produce different knowledge and produce knowledge differently" (St. Pierre, 1997, p. 175). I am well aware that work accomplished under the umbrella of "qualitative research" is also radical, unconventional, and exciting. I do not believe, however, that that is the qualitative inquiry described in most textbooks or taught in most university courses. I think it's time, therefore, to move away from a centering, defensive mode and get on with the invention of science.

I argue that the concepts/categories that structure conventional, humanist qualitative inquiry have increasingly tightened since 1985, for example, when Lincoln and Guba wrote one of the first qualitative research texts, *Naturalistic Inquiry.* We now have thousands of textbooks, handbooks, and journal articles that have secured *qualitative methodology* by repeating that structure in book after book with the same chapter headings so that we now believe it is true and real. *We've forgotten we made it up.*

The "post" in the title of this chapter can be thought of both chronologically—what comes after conventional humanist qualitative research—and, more importantly, deconstructively. I will discuss deconstruction in detail later in the chapter, but here I explain that I envision at least two deconstructive approaches. The first follows Derrida in putting a structure *sous rature,* or under erasure. In this approach, we retain the structure of qualitative research methodology—its structuring concepts and categories—because it appears necessary and, at the same time, cross it out because it is inaccurate. Thus, we could write qualitative research methodology to signal the opening up—not the rejection—of the structure. "Persistently to critique a structure that one cannot not (wish to) inhabit is the deconstructive stance" (Spivak, 1993, p. 284). Working within the enclosure of conventional humanist qualitative inquiry while troubling it is what I have done for almost 20 years, but I seem no longer content with that approach.

During the last decades, we've deconstructed many of qualitative methodology's concepts/categories: e.g., *interview* (Scheurich, 1995), *validity* (Lather, 1993), *data* (St.Pierre, 1997), *voice* (Jackson & Mazzei, 2009), *reflexivity* (Pillow, 2003). The deconstruction of even one concept/category disrupts other related structuring concepts/categories, as I illustrate later in this chapter, and initiates the cascading collapse of methodology's center, its failure in the wake of the "posts." The difficulty for the poststructural researcher lies in trying to function in the ruins of the structure after the theoretical move that authorizes its foundations has been interrogated and its limits breached so profoundly that its center no longer holds.

Of course, *the structure had always already been ruptured, ruined.* In self-defense, some wrote textbooks to convince us it was coherent and asked researchers to organize their work into inadequate existing concepts (e.g., *research design, data, data collection, data analysis, interview, observation, representation*) even though they could not contain it. Much, therefore, has been unintelligible, and science has, accordingly, been impoverished.

A second deconstructive approach helps here. Derrida also explained that deconstruction is more than working within and against a structure. It is also the overturning and displacement of a structure so that something(s) different can be thought/done. In this second approach, one is no longer "residing within the closed field [of the structure] thereby confirming it" (Derrida, 1972/1981, p. 41) but is "overturning and displacing a conceptual order, as well as the nonconceptual order with which the conceptual order is articulated" (Derrida, 1971/1982, p. 329). After that displacement, we are in play as we radically de-naturalize what we've taken for granted. Here, we refuse alternatives and pursue the *supplement,* what always already escapes the structure.

This is the science that beckons—this is the lure. And this is deconstruction at its finest—the rigorous reimagining of a capacious science that cannot be defined in advance and is never the same. This science is *différance,* not repetition. Borrowing from Deleuze and Guattari (1980/1987), it is not *is;* it is *becoming.* We move away from Plato's poisoned gift of ontological determination, a logic of identity and prediction—*Science is this; science is not that*—toward a logic of the "and"—*This and this and this and this.* . . . Thinking and doing that science is the invitation we risk accepting.

READING THEORY

Before one can put postmodernism or any theoretical approach to work, one must read and study it. Given the impossibility of "talking across differences" that I, and others, experienced in the SBR debates, I am convinced that the study of philosophy should precede the study of research methodology so that, for example, the typical social science researcher would understand the epistemological and ontological assumptions that structure positivist, interpretive, critical, postmodern, and other methodologies in the social sciences. Attempts to disentangle science and philosophy are always dangerous.

If such study were the norm, most readers of the 2002 National Research Council report, *Scientific Research in Education,* would recognize the following sample statements from that report as positivist (there are many others): "cumulative knowledge" (p. 1), "at its core, scientific inquiry is the same in all fields" (p. 2), "replicate and generalize across studies" (p. 4), and "multiple observers can agree on what they see" (p. 25). That many readers of the 2002 NRC report could not do so is the result of a failure to read, not necessarily a failure to teach. Students do not have to take doctoral courses in theory in order to read and study positivism or social constructionism or critical race theory or postmodernism, though such courses would surely help researchers understand that *science* is not one thing but a highly contested concept whose meaning and practices shift across philosophical approaches and historical and political moments.

Unfortunately, we hesitate to read outside our comfort areas and too casually reject texts that seem too hard to read. It's doubtful we would expect to quickly understand an advanced physics text, yet we expect a philosophy text to be welcoming and accessible. Why should we expect to understand Derrida or Foucault or Deleuze and Guattari on first reading? Perhaps it's arrogant to think we should quickly understand concepts that have age-old and contentious histories such as *knowledge, truth, reason, reality, power,* and *language* and new concepts such as *différance,* the *rhizome,* and Foucaultian *archaeology.*

But the idea that language should be clear is not only deeply embedded in our anti-intellectual culture but also in positivism. For example, Ayer (1936), a logical positivist, wrote in his mid-20s,

> For we shall maintain that no statement which refers to a "reality" transcending the limits of all possible sense-experience can possibly have any literal significance; from which it must follow that the labours of those who have striven to describe such a reality have all been devoted to the production of nonsense. (p. 17)

This view of language is commensurate with the positivist determination to eschew metaphysics, which is speculative, deals with concepts that can't be verified with empirical evidence, and are thus senseless according to Ayer. It also represents positivism's "search for certainty" (Reichenbach, 1951) echoed in the call for clear language. Following Ayer, Maxwell (2010), for example, could dismiss Deleuze and Guattari, who introduced new language that might enable new realities, and claim they are "simply 'running their mouths'" (p. 6), which, of course, one could say about Ayer, Carnap, Reichenbach, Husserl, Marx, Einstein, Neils Bohr, Grigori Perelman, and many other scholars, including Maxwell, if one were so inclined.

I advise students to take seriously Lacan's (as cited in Ulmer, 1985) advice, "to read does not obligate one to understand. First it is necessary to read . . . avoid understanding too quickly" (p. 196). I have little sympathy with excuses not to read difficult texts, and I advise students to read harder when the text seems too hard to read, to just keep reading, letting the new language wash over them until it becomes familiar. I encourage them to develop "reading management strategies," for example, dictionaries of concepts they don't understand. The dictionary I began as a doctoral student is now over 700 pages long. The entry on *subjectivity,* the focus of my work, is over 30 pages. Still, I don't know what subjectivity *means.*

If we don't read the theoretical and philosophical literature, we have nothing much to think with during analysis except normalized discourses that seldom explain the way things are. However, when we study a variety of complex and conflicting theories, which I believe is the purpose of doctoral education, we begin to realize, as Fay (1987) suggested, that *we have been theorized,* that we and the world are products of theory as much as practice, and that putting different theories to work can change the world. History, of course, tells us that.

I don't care whether students make the postmodern or any other turn. I do expect them to read hard. By the time they write their dissertation proposals, I expect them to have studied several bodies of high-level theory (e.g., feminist theories, race theories, phenomenology, postmodernism, social construction-ism), the theories of their disciplines that have taken up those high-level theories (e.g., in English education, reader response theory that is thinkable because of social constructionism), and the methodological literature.

In all this, I am increasingly interested in *readiness,* and find Butler's (1995) question apropos: "how is it that we become available to a transformation of who we are, a contestation which compels us to rethink ourselves, a reconfigura-tion of our 'place' and our 'ground'?" (p. 132). I expect we're inclined toward certain interests but, no doubt, that's as much a matter of experience and educa-tion as disposition.

Clearly, what I describe here is not the "training model" of the natural sciences. My desire is for students to go into a study immersed in a field of complex and contradictory theory rich enough to address the complex and contradictory nature of whatever they encounter in fieldwork and analysis. They desperately need theories, interpretive frameworks, for analyzing data rather than more and/or better methods for collecting it, else they produce poorly conceived and theorized work. Hurworth (2008), in her study of the teaching of qualitative inquiry, concurred and wrote that theory and practice should be taught together. And Neumann, Pallas, and Peterson (2008) wrote that we should focus research preparation on the challenge of the "management and use of epistemological diversity in research" (p. 1478). The following three sections of this chapter describe poststructural theories I have found particularly helpful, which, once read, studied, and taken up, will change the way one reads the world.

POSTMODERNISM AND POSTSTRUCTURALISM (THE "POSTS")

Postmodern and poststructural analyses include diverse and contradictory critiques that resist, subvert, and refuse any structural formation. Rajchman (1987) wrote that postmodernism "does not comprise a School of Thought" but refers to a "motley and elastic range of things" (p. 49). While taking account of the "turns" mentioned in this chapter, the "posts" announce a radical break with the humanist, modernist, imperialist, representationalist, objectivist, rationalist, epistemological, ontological, and methodological assumptions of Western Enlightenment thought and practice.

In the "posts," the "epistemological point of departure in philosophy is inadequate" (Butler, 1992, p. 8) and, some might argue, incommensurable. *Epistemology*—the branch of philosophy concerned with what counts as knowledge and how knowledge claims are justified as true—assumes a certain kind of subject, the sovereign, knowing subject secured in advance of knowing and always separate from it—the originating subject of knowledge and history. The "posts" deconstruct that subject as I will discuss later in the chapter. *Ontology* is the branch of metaphysics concerned with what exists (what "is"), with being and reality and how entities are organized. In the "posts," the ontological point of departure is also inadequate. In conventional philosophy, it is important to keep epistemological and ontological issues separate, and, if they are confused, we say a "category mistake" has been made. But postmodern theories disrupt the distinction between epistemology and ontology, as does physics, for example, "where the rise of quantum theory with its interpretational problems was one of the first major challenges to the ontic/epistemic distinction" (Atmanspacher, 2002, p 50).

The terms *postmodernism* and *poststructuralism* are often used interchangeably; however, there are acknowledged differences in their meaning. Thus far, I have used the term *postmodern* in this chapter, though I would describe my own work as *poststructural*. Lather (1993) differentiated these two terms as follows: postmodernism "raises issues of chronology, economics (e.g., post-Fordism) and aesthetics whereas poststructural[ism] is used more often in relation to academic theorizing 'after structuralism'" (p. 688).

Postmodernism has been used to refer to "the new stage of multinational, multiconglomerate consumer capitalism, and to all the technologies it has spawned" (Kaplan, 1988, p. 4) as well as to the avant garde in the arts, "the erosion of the older distinction between high culture and so-called mass or popular culture" (Jameson, 1988, p. 14). Flax (1990) wrote that

> postmodern discourses are all deconstructive in that they seek to distance us from and make us skeptical about beliefs concerning truth, knowledge, power, the self, and language that are often taken for granted within and serve as legitimation for contemporary Western culture. (p. 41)

Poststructuralism is a French term that represents the European, particularly French, avant garde in critical theory. Peters (1999) explained that poststructuralism, inspired by Nietzsche, is a "specifically philosophical response to the alleged scientific status of structuralism" (p. 1) in all its guises. "In philosophy," Harvey (1989) wrote,

> the intermingling of a revived American pragmatism with the post-Marxist and poststructuralist wave that struck Paris after 1968 produced what Bernstein calls "a rage against humanism and the Enlightenment legacy." This spilled over into a vigorous denunciation of abstract reason and a deep aversion to any project that sought universal human emancipation through mobilization of the powers of technology, science, and reason. (p. 41)

Poststructuralism offers critiques of the scientific pretensions of structural tendencies in all disciplines—linguistics, anthropology, psychology, economics, and so forth.

Interestingly, the word *postmodernism* first appeared in architecture to reflect a new way of thinking about space: Harvey (1989) credited Jameson for calling it "contrived depthlessness" (p. 58). This is consistent with the general postmodern critique of foundationalism, the idea that there are absolute truths propping up everyday human activity. Classical foundationalism encourages empiricism, the idea that all knowledge is derived from sensory experience. In his general introduction to postmodernism, Harvey (1989) cited the postmodern position of the editors of the architectural journal *PRECIS*, who in 1987 summarized postmodernism quite elegantly as follows:

> postmodernism as a legitimate reaction to the "monotony" of universal modernism's vision of the world. "Generally perceived as positivistic, technocentric, and rationalistic, universal modernism has been identified with the belief in linear progress, absolute truths, the rational planning of ideal social orders, and the standardization of knowledge and production." Postmodernism, by way of contrast, privileges "heterogeneity and difference as liberative forces in the redefinition of cultural discourse." Fragmentation, indeterminacy, and intense distrust of all universal or "totalizing" discourses (to use the favoured phrase) are the hallmark of postmodernism thought. The rediscovery of pragmatism in philosophy (e.g., Rorty, 1979), the shift of ideas about the philosophy of science wrought by Kuhn (1962) and Feyerabend (1975), Foucault's emphasis upon discontinuity and difference in history and his privileging of "polymorphous correlations in place of simple or complex causality," new developments in mathematics emphasizing indeterminacy (catastrophe and chaos theory, fractal geometry), the re-emergence of concern in ethics, politics, and anthropology for the validity and dignity of "the other," all indicate a widespread and profound shift. (p. 9)

As Eagleton (1987) announced, "we are now in the process of wakening from the nightmare of modernity, with its manipulative reason and fetish of the totality" (p. 9), a modernity that elevated science to a religion, appealed to a "surface rationality of proof, logic, axiom, explicitness" (McCloskey, 2001, p. 103).

Postmodernism argues against the values, practices, and goals of Enlightenment humanism as they play out in Modernism: "History, Progress, Freedom, Reason, Transcendence and Man" (Finn, 1993, p. 134). Such totalizing discourses are meta-theories "through which all things can be connected or represented" (Harvey, 1989, p. 45), including the idea of a unified theory of science (the positivist's claim), or a grand unified theory (GUT) of physics, or one all-embracing, deterministic principle such as social class found in Marxism. In his report on scientific knowledge, Lyotard (1979/1984) described postmodernism as a "condition," wrote that he found it in America, and defined it simply as an "incredulity toward metanarratives"(p. xxiv), grand, totalizing theories like Harvey's listed above.

The catastrophic events of World War II interrupted centuries-old Western traditions. Spivak (1993) explained the French response as follows:

> The critique of humanism in France was related to the perceived failure of the European ethical subject after the War. The second wave in the midsixties, coming in the wake of the Algerian revolution, sharpened this in terms of disciplinary practice in the humanities and social sciences because, as historians, philosophers, sociologists, and psychologists, the participants felt that their practice was not merely a disinterested pursuit of knowledge, but productive in the making of human beings. It was because of this that they did not accept unexamined human experience as the source of meaning and the making of meaning as an unproblematic thing. And each one of them offered a method that would challenge the outlines of a discipline: archaeology [Foucault], genealogy [Foucault], power/knowledge reading [Foucault], schizo-analysis [Deleuze & Guattari], rhizo-analysis [Deleuze & Guattari], nonsubjective psychoanalysis [Lacan], affirmative deconstruction [Derrida], paralogic legitimation [Lyotard]. (p. 274)

There is much to read about each of these and other "methods" used in the "posts," but here I provide a brief description only of Derrida's affirmative deconstruction, which I mentioned earlier. It is deconstruction that made me aware early on that any concept/category is a structure attempting to contain and close off meaning and, at the same time, that that concept/category is available to rupture and rethinking.

DERRIDA'S DECONSTRUCTION

Derrida (1988) made it clear that "deconstruction is not a method" and cannot "be reduced to some methodological instrumentality or to a set of rules and transposable procedures" (p. 4). Further, "in spite of appearances, deconstruction is neither an *analysis* nor a *critique*" (p. 4). He cautioned that "all sentences of the type 'deconstruction is X' or 'deconstruction is not X' a priori miss the point, which is to say that they are at least false" (p. 4). He continued,

> Deconstruction is neither a theory nor a philosophy. It is neither a school nor a method. It is not even a discourse, nor an act, nor a practice. *It is what*

happens [emphasis added], what is happening today in what they call society, politics, diplomacy, economics, historical reality, and so on and so forth. (Derrida, 1990, p. 85)

To acknowledge the ethical nature of deconstruction, Derrida (as cited in Caputo, 1993) wrote simply, "deconstruction is justice" (p. 86). Spivak (1989) added to Derrida's list of what deconstruction is not, commenting that "Deconstruction is not an essence. It's not a school of thought; it is a way of reading" (p. 135). But Derrida (1989/2002) wrote that deconstruction is not something done to a text: "This deconstruction does not apply itself to such a text. It never applies itself to anything from the outside. It is in some way the operation or rather the very experience that this text, it seems to me, first does itself, by itself, on itself" (p. 264). Again, deconstruction is not something done to a text or any other structure; *the text, the concept, the structure undoes itself.* More generally, Spivak (1993) claimed that "deconstruction has always been about the limits of epistemology" (p. 123) and, in particular, an argument against the Western metaphysics of *presence.*

If it now seems impossible to understand what deconstruction *is,* what it *means,* that is precisely Derrida's point, that the meaning of any signifier—*deconstruction, reason, truth, science*—cannot be secured, cannot be *present,* but is constantly deferred, absent. Given this, we can no longer ask, "What is science? What exactly does it mean, once and for all?" because the sign (e.g., *science*) has no center, no constant, essential meaning that holds across time and all instances of its use. Science is always already different from itself.

Deconstructive discourses critique *essentialism,* then, an ontological concept that characterizes the work of thinkers such as Plato, Aristotle, Descartes, Spinoza, Leibniz, Kant, and Husserl. According to Fuss (1989), "essentialism is classically defined as a belief in true essences—that which is most irreducible, unchanging, and therefore constitutive of a given person or thing" (p. 2). In humanist thought, without that essence—the *center*—that unique and unchanging core that guarantees the thing its meaning, the thing would cease to exist. Essentialism pervades Western thought. For example, Derrida (1972/1981) questioned the idea in phenomenology of an *a priori* "layer of pure meaning, or a pure signified . . . a layer of prelinguistic or presemiotic (preexpressive, Husserl calls it) meaning " (p. 31), some preexisting meaning that language brings to light, to presence, and expresses.

A companion example is the phrase, "the thing in itself," as opposed to its appearance, which much concerned Plato and, later, Kant. Nietzsche (1887/1967) argued that "Kant no longer has a right to his distinction between 'appearance' and 'thing-in-itself' (p. 300) because there are no things-in-themselves. "If we were to remove all the relationships and actions of a thing, the thing does not remain" (p. 302). Things—and some will say people as well—exist not by themselves but only in relations. In deconstruction, "the thing itself always escapes" (Derrida, as cited in Spivak, 1974, p. lxix). Meaning appears only fleetingly and then begins to decay as it misfires and re-forms within the play of language. The sign, then, is not a structure of identity, of presence, but a radical structure of difference, absence. Derrida used the concept *différance* (meaning both "to differ" and "to defer") to account for the endless differences in and the deferral of the meaning of a sign. As Spivak explained, "word and thing or thought never in fact become one" (p. xvi). Because of this, the linguistic system cannot be totalized, and language, then, is always "being born" and exists between the "already" and the "not yet" (Derrida, 1967/1974, p. 244); meaning is always "to come" [*avenir*].

In an early lecture about deconstruction, Derrida (1966/1970), in his careful way, explained the problem of essence, the presumed centered structure:

> Thus it has always been thought that the center, which is by definition unique, constituted that very thing within a structure which while governing the structure, escapes structurality. This is why classical thought concerning structure could say that the center is paradoxically, *within* the structure and *outside it*. The center is at the center of the totality, and yet, since the center does not belong to the totality (is not part of the totality), the totality *has its center elsewhere*. The center is not the center. The concept of centered structure—although it represents coherence itself, the condition of the *episteme* as philosophy of science—is contradictorily coherent. And as always, coherence in contradiction expresses the force of a desire. The concept of centered structure is in fact the concept of a freeplay based on a fundamental immobility and a reassuring certitude, which is itself beyond the reach of the freeplay. With this certitude anxiety can be mastered. (p. 248)

The notion of a centered structure (presence, essence, core), then, is the illusion, the ruse, the cheat, the grounding mistake of Western metaphysics and positivist philosophy of science. Because there is no pure center, *presence*, "the structure of the sign is determined by the trace or track of that other which is forever absent" (Spivak, 1974, p. xvii). The authority for the coherence of the structure lies not in its center, in the interior of the structure (presence), but elsewhere—in exteriority (absence). The structure cannot (it never could) authorize itself and comes undone (has always already been undone).

Yet deconstruction demonstrates that that idea—presence, essence—is but a *description* of the world that, one might argue, releases us from responsibility, from the difficult intellectual, political, and ethical struggles of dealing with the ambiguity and contingency of human existence. As Keenan (1997) wrote, responsibility comes not with certainty but with "the removal of grounds, the withdrawal of the rules or the knowledge on which we might rely to make our decisions for us. No grounds means no alibis, no elsewhere to which we might refer the instance of our decision" (p. 1). Once we give up appeals to transcendental/foundational truth, essence, and originary meaning (the universal, the eternal), responsibility and justice assume their full weight. As Mouffe (1996) explained, "the absence of foundation 'leaves everything as it is,' as Wittgenstein would say, and obliges us to ask the same questions in a new way" (p. 38). Along those lines, Scott (1988) suggested we stop asking essentializing questions like "What does it mean?" and ask instead, "How do meanings change? How have some meanings emerged as normative and others been eclipsed or disappeared? What do these processes reveal about how power is constituted and operates?" (p. 35).

Deconstruction not only decenters structures that presume foundational/transcendent meaning, it also deconstructs the structure of binary oppositions (e.g., Self/Other, identity/*différance*) also organized by *presence*. The first term of the binary represents "presence and the logos; the inferior serves to define its status and mark a fall" (Spivak, 1974, p. lxix). The privileged term in the binary can only be thought in opposition to the other term; that is, the unmarked term depends on the marked term for its meaning. For example, Said (1978) illustrated that the Occident had to create the Orient in order to define itself, and to define itself as superior.

Derrida wrote that the binary oppositions of metaphysics are violent hierarchies because those on the wrong side of the binary can be brutalized for their difference. For that reason, the binary can't simply be neutralized. It must first be reversed—"fight violence with violence" (Spivak, 1974, p. lxxvii). The first step in deconstruction, then, is to reverse the binary. So in the binary, heterosexual/homosexual, for example, homosexual should hold the privileged position so that heterosexuals can feel the violence of being called abnormal, deviant, sinful, evil, and so on. In the next step, the winning term is displaced to make room for a new concept that can't be understood in terms of the old structure, a concept that not only undoes the binary but also encourages entirely different thinking about sexuality. This is the affirmative move of deconstruction, the overturning and opening up of a violent structure so that something different might happen.

Some call deconstruction, and other poststructural "methods," nihilistic, relativist, anarchist, antipolitical, deliberately obfuscatory, and on and on, but for many they are ethical practices of freedom, as Culler (1982) described below:

> If "sawing off the branch on which one is sitting" seems foolhardy to men of common sense, it is not so for Nietzsche, Freud, Heidegger, and Derrida; for they suspect that if they fall there is no "ground" to hit and that the most clear-sighted act may be a certain reckless sawing, a calculated dismemberment or deconstruction of the great cathedral-like trees in which Man has taken shelter for millennia. (p. 149)

If one has been on the wrong side of binaries and trapped in essentialist structures that control and shut down meaning and lives, the persistent critique of deconstruction against their founding violence can, indeed, be liberating. In conclusion, deconstruction is not just attention to language but to the very material structures we create through language and social practice, including that very material structure we call the *human being*.

ENTANGLEMENT/HAECCEITY/ASSEMBLAGE

In my own work, I have used Deleuze and Guattari's concepts *haecceity* and *assemblage* and the notion of *entanglement* from quantum physics to deconstruct one of the most powerful legacies of Enlightenment humanism—the *human being,* the *individual,* the *self,* the *person.* Once that master concept ruptures, every single related structure fails because we humans are at the center of them all—or, at least, we've been led to believe we are. In this section, I briefly describe the following: the humanist description of the human being, *entanglement* from quantum physics, and a Deluzoguattarian reconception of the human being. The failure of the humanist subject produces the failure of humanist methodology as I illustrate later.

Enlightenment humanism produced a particular description of the human being—an epistemological subject. Descartes' (1637/1993) foundationalism provided one description of that human being, a knowing subject who knows chiefly through rational deduction—"I think, therefore I am" (p. 18). Locke (1690/1924) would later dispute Descartes—Locke argued that the mind is a blank slate with no innate ideas—and describe a "self," an "individual," with a personal identity based on consciousness. Locke, the first of the British empiricists, believed that knowledge is determined only by experience derived from the senses, the chief tenet of empiricism. The human beings these two Enlightenment thinkers, in particular, described (invented) have had remarkable staying power in modernism and in conventional social science.

Elsewhere (St.Pierre, 2000) I have discussed and will not repeat here a postmodern critique of the liberal individual of Enlightenment humanism—a sovereign, lucid, transparent, free, agentive, self-sufficient, rational, knowing, meaning-giving, conscious, stable, coherent, unified, self-identical, reflective, autonomous, intentional, and ahistoric individual who is "endowed with a will, a freedom, an intentionality, which is then subsequently "expressed" in language, in action, in the public domain" (Butler, 1995, p. 136). But both Descartes' and Locke's beliefs, their descriptions of the human, prevail in the human sciences, and we believe the human is, indeed, separate from everything else and, usually, master of the universe. Many binary oppositions follow from that assumption: Self/Other, subject/object, knower/known, man/nature, and so forth.

It is the *principle of individuation,* the criterion of identity, that enables us to organize the undifferentiated into identity, to determine when/where one thing ends and another begins, to divide and separate. Typically, we individuate by establishing an essence and then claim that everything that has that essence is identical, the same. At some point, it became possible to think that one human being could be individuated/divided from other human beings—that each human has a center, an identity (an "inner self," "inner voice"). We also individuated the human from everything else, from all that is not human. Clearly, individuation (the creation of categories such as *man* and *nature*) is an act of power.

In postmodernism, however, the aim is to de-individualize, to disrupt individuations we believe are real, and, in that work, Deleuze and Guattari are most helpful. They borrowed from Duns Scotus an old concept, *haecceity,* that he borrowed from Aristotle to describe a non-subjective assemblage of humans, time, space, physical objects, and everything else: "It should not be thought that a haecceity consists simply of a décor or a backdrop that situates subjects. . . . It is the entire assemblage in its individual aggregate that is haecceity . . . that is what you are, and . . . you are nothing but that" (Deleuze & Guattari, 1980/1987, p. 262). Rajchman's (2000) examples of this impersonal assemblage follow: "An hour of a day, a river, a climate, a strange moment during a concert can be like this—not one of a kind, but the individuation of something that belongs to no kind" (Deleuze & Guattari, 1980/1987, p. 85). Deleuze (1990/1995) rethought the idea of the human being as *assemblage:* "Felix [Guattari] and I, and many others like us, don't feel we're persons exactly. Our individuality is rather that of *events* [emphasis added] . . . a philosophical concept, the only one capable of ousting the verb 'to be' and its attributes" (p. 141). Haecceity is not stable but is always becoming. It is not *is* but *and*. "A haecceity has neither beginning nor end, origin nor destination; it is always in the middle. It is not made of points, only of lines. It is a *rhizome*" (Deleuze & Guattari, 1980/1987, p. 263).

I think, then, of *haecceity* as mingling, assemblage, as relation, as becoming, perhaps as Benjamin's (1999) *constellation* or *entanglement*. In quantum physics, when "two entities interact, they entangle. . . . No matter how far they move apart, if one is tweaked, measured, observed, the other seems to instantly respond. . . . And no one knows how" (Gilder, 2008, p. 3). Barad (2007) explained entanglement in quantum theory as follows:

> To be entangled is not simply to be intertwined with another, as in the joining of separate entities, but to lack an independent, self-contained existence. Existence is not an individual affair. Individuals do not preexist their interactions; rather, individuals emerge through and as part of their entangled intra-relating. Which is not to say that emergence happens once and for all, as an event or as a process that takes place according to some external measure of space and of time, but rather that time and space, like matter and meaning, come into existence, are iteratively reconfigured through each intra-action, thereby making it impossible to differentiate in any absolute sense between creation and renewal, beginning and returning, continuity and discontinuity, here and there, past and future. (p. ix)

Quantum physics seems quite Nietzschean and Deleuzean, and here we see that Science and Philosophy do not have to be at odds.

Experimental physics also disrupted our conventional understanding of space and time in which we believe objects and people exist in a stable space that moves through time so that, for example, one can supposedly observe the same phenomena as they pass through time and change, progress, or "develop"—linearity. With entanglement in mind, Massey (1994) argued, "it is not that the interrelations between objects occur in space and time; it is these relationships which create/define space and time" such that "the spatial is social relations 'stretched out'" (p. 263). It is only manmade history that brings time into being and establishes clear connections. The shift from the vertical (history, depth) to the horizontal (simultaneity, surface) characterizes the shift from modernism to postmodernism.

Space-time from physics is dynamic, fractured, porous, paradoxical, and non-individual with sets of space-time relations existing simultaneously, rhizomatically and overlapping, interfering with each other. "There is no choice between flow (time) and a flat surface of instantaneous relations (space)" (Massey, 1994, p. 265) because time is not linear and space is not flat. The human desire to measure and control everything extended to time itself (we invented clocks), but time is out of joint and always has been. "In the theory of relativity," Hawking (1988) wrote, "there is no absolute time. Each observer has his own measure of time" (p. 87), so we all live different times.

Even so, some descriptions have great purchase in the social sciences, especially positivist approaches that mimic ideas no longer supported in the natural sciences. Ideas of absolute time, linearity, and sequenced progression enable positivist ideas such as cause and effect, the accumulation of knowledge, and so on. But such linearity is unintelligible in space-time because "people are everywhere conceptualizing and acting on different spatialities" (Massey, 1994, p. 4). Thus, there cannot be a fixed point from which a fixed individuation can observe another fixed individuation at another fixed point. And the positivist statement in the 2002 NRC report that the world can be described so that "multiple observers can agree on what they see" (p. 25) is not thinkable in space-time because everything is entangled and always already overlapping, dynamic, contested, multiple, antagonistic, becoming, in process.

So the positivist social science ideas of replication and generalizability are unthinkable in space–time, along with the subjectivity/objectivity distinction and related concepts such as *bias* and *brute fact/data*. In a similar fashion, the interpretive and critical social science idea of, for example, *culture*—a coherent set of people traveling together in space and time—is also unthinkable. In all those examples, we attempt to "stabilize the meaning of particular envelopes of space-time" (Massey, 1994, p. 5) and study them.

Quantum physics' entanglement and space—time require a different description of the human being. On the one hand, it might be difficult to give up the "I" one is familiar with; on the other, why should we rank Descartes' "I" and Locke's "self" (both inventions) above Deleuze and Guattari's "assemblage" or "haecceity" (another invention) or, indeed, some other description of the "human" we may have forgotten and/or not yet thought?

Clearly, language strains and stutters here. I have not yet learned to write easily without saying "I," "me," "myself," "one," "oneself," though I do not need them so much anymore for living. But as Deleuze and Guattari (1980/1987) explained, the goal is not to reach the "point where one no longer says I, but the point where it is no longer of any importance whether one says I" (p. 3). They did advise that to resist subjectification, "You have to keep enough of the organism for it to reform each dawn and you have to keep small supplies of significance and subjectification, if only to turn them against their own systems when the circumstances demand it" (p. 160). That is the work of politics, "to refuse what we are" (Foucault, 1982, p. 216).

The implications of entanglement are staggering. If one no longer thinks of oneself as "I" but as entangled with everyone, everything else—as haecceity, as assemblage—what happens to concepts in social science research based on that "I"—the *researcher,* the *participant, identity, presence, voice, lens, experience, positionality, subjectivity, objectivity, bias, rationality, consciousness, experience, alienation, reflexivity, freedom, transformation, dialogue?* In space–time, how does one think of *research design, research process, timeline, narrative, cause and effect, accumulation of knowledge, generalizability, replicability, predictability, scaling up?* In entanglement, how does one think about "face-to-face" methods like *interviewing* and *observation,* methods that privilege *presence,* Derrida's bane?

It is indeed difficult to escape the "I." Even those who've studied the "posts," and, in particular, poststructural theories of subjectivity, seem unable *not* to write the humanist human being. For example, they may include a "subjectivity statement" to describe themselves even though *subjectivity* in the "posts" is incommensurable with that practice. They may write lengthy, rich, thick descriptions of individual participants to whom they've assigned pseudonyms, producing them as autonomous, coherent, intentional, knowing, speaking subjects. But in the posts, participants are not an "epistemological dead-end" (Sommer, 1994, p. 532)—an object of knowledge—but rather a line of flight that takes us elsewhere—participants as provocateurs. It should be clear that if we no longer believe in a disentangled humanist self, individual, person, we have to rethink qualitative methods (interviewing and observation) grounded in that human being as well as humanist representation.

DECONSTRUCTION HAPPENS

Putting deconstruction and entanglement to work in conventional humanist qualitative methodology renders it not only incomprehensible but also without an alternative that can be described in advance of the study in a proposal or captured at the end in representation. Each researcher who puts the "posts" to work will create a different *articulation* (e.g., Hall, 1986/1996; Laclau & Mouffe, 1985), *remix, mash-up, assemblage,* a *becoming* of inquiry that is not *a priori,* inevitable, necessary, stable, or repeatable but is, rather, created spontaneously in the middle of the task at hand, which is always already *and, and, and. . . .* I argue that this has always been the case but that researchers have been trained to believe in and thus are constrained by the pre-given concepts/categories of the invented but normalized structure of "qualitative methodology," its "designs" and "methods," that are as positivist as they are interpretive, often more so.

In general, qualitative inquiry, especially after SBR, comes with so many instructions and limits that rigor seems impossible. By rigor, I mean the demanding work of freeing oneself from the constraints of existing structures, what Foucault (1966/1970) called the "order of things," so that one can think the unthought. Rigor is the work of différance, not repetition, work that bell hooks (1989) called "too deep" and the poet Rilke, "too large." I can barely think into that space though I do find myself there, most often when I write, because, for me, writing, that old technology (absence) Plato feared, "can free thought from what it silently thinks and enable it to think differently" (Foucault, 1984/1985, p. 9).

I don't believe the rigorous inquiry I desire can be taught in a sequence of research courses or described in textbooks, but I've thought a great deal about how one might become available to deconstructive work and the transformations it can enable. I cannot explain how deconstruction happens, but it does if one has read enough and puts it to work.

I have written elsewhere about how I came to theory (St.Pierre, 2001) in my own doctoral program. Briefly, I quickly exhausted the mid-level theories of my field, English education, which seemed mostly focused on preservice teacher education, did not situate itself within larger theoretical frameworks, and therefore seemed to come from nowhere. I had studied philosophy as an undergraduate when the "turns" were being thought and written but missed them entirely after I became a high school English teacher and, later, a librarian. Still, I knew there were larger conversations I was missing as a doctoral student.

I took as many qualitative research courses as I could find and studied methodology with feminist professors in education and sociology making the postmodern turn. Their casual references in class to Foucault, Butler, Trinh, Said, Derrida, Omi and Winant, Habermas, and other theorists were my only guidance to the "turns."

I never had a theory course in my doctoral program; instead, as scholars have done for centuries, I followed the citational trail from one text to another, finding and reading on my own, for example, feminism, Frankfurt School critical theory, interpretive anthropology, postcolonialism, critical race theory, social constructionism, poststructuralism, postmodernism, and theories of space–time and memory. I felt far behind some of my fellow students and read harder to catch up. Much of the work I read had been written during my own lifetime, and it spoke eloquently to me. Loving language, I reveled in Butler's and Derrida's rich, complex, perfectly formed sentences. Deleuze and Guattari's new concepts (e.g., *bodies without organs, becoming animal, smooth space*) spilled over me, immediately useful. I formed and then shed attachments to scholars and their theories as I read, and those shifts taught me there would always be another sentence in another book that might well shatter my life again. Reading guaranteed transformation, and I couldn't get enough.

I began to understand that *theory produces people.* Theory was no longer an abstract, sometimes impenetrable discourse but a powerful, personal tool I needed to study for my own good. I realized I and my culture had been theorized by Enlightenment humanism whose projects seldom served women well and that the "posts," in particular, combined with other theories, offered many analyses to resist humanism's oppressive structures, especially its foundational structure, the *human being.*

To study the construction of subjectivity (including my own), I dutifully designed and accomplished a qualitative study that was a combination of an interview study with older women who lived in my hometown and an ethnography of their community. Until I began to write my dissertation, the two bodies of literature I had diligently studied—theory and qualitative research methodology—mostly remained separate. But as I wrote the dissertation, qualitative methodology, so clearly grounded in the humanism (and positivism) I no longer believed, ruptured.

No doubt the nature of my study intensified that breakdown. I returned to my hometown in Essex County where my family still lived 20 years after I had left, to study women who had taught me how to be a woman. As I interviewed them, they were simultaneously old women happy to help a hometown girl get her doctorate *and* the lovely, formidable young women I remembered from childhood. I never knew who/when/where I was during fieldwork. Subjectivity, space–time, and "reality" exploded and overwhelmed me. It was not simply that I "had multiple subjectivities" or "moved among subject positions" but that I was always already a simultaneity of relations with humans and the nonhuman (I could no longer think/live that dichotomy)—the "women" and "me" in all times and places; my father, long dead, loving me; the streets and storefronts of the town; all us cousins catching lightning bugs on a summer evening; Essex County's red clay tobacco fields; my beloved aunt whose smile saved everyone who met her; all of us, everything, de-individualized, de-identified, *dis-individuated.* A rhizome, assemblage, haecceity, my life. *A life.* Theory produced me differently, and I am not the same. I never was.

But I could not have thought those thoughts by thinking alone. That work about subjectivity (an inadequate concept) required a simultaneity of living, reading, and writing. I needed living (*experiences* is inadequate) for which humanist individuations no longer worked (me with the women in space–time simultaneously); theories that provided language to think living differently (the "posts" and theories of space–time and memory), and the setting-to-work of writing that forced the rupture and demanded I move on. When writing the next word and the next sentence and then the next is more than one can manage; when one must bring to bear on writing, in writing, what one has read and lived, that is thinking that cannot be taught. *That is analysis.*

So writing became a field of play in which the study took place, a space (never just textual) as important as Essex County. *In the thinking that writing produced,* the humanist subject was the first humanist concept/category to fail, but many others did as well.

Here, I briefly discuss the failure of one other key concept, *data* (and data collection and data analysis and others). I have written in detail elsewhere (St.Pierre, 1997) about my troubles with data. Until I began analysis—the thinking that writing enables—I believed the textbook definition of qualitative data: that which is textualized, fixed, and made visible in words in interview transcripts and fieldnotes. That is a foundationalist description that enables us to treat words as brute data—transparent, neutral, independent of theory, *waiting to be analyzed.* However, words are always thinkable, sayable, and writable (in interviews and fieldnotes) only within particular grids of intelligibility, usually dominant, normalized discursive formations. What this means is that words we collect in interviews and observations—data—are always already products of theory.

The researcher's first task is to recognize the theory(ies) that enabled others' words in interviews, and she can do that only if she's studied theory. Her next task is to theorize those already theorized words that reflect "experiences," living. Of course, the theory(ies) she uses determines whether those words even count as data because words (or anything else) become data only when theory acknowledges them as data. In this way, theory is deeply imbricated in the concept *data* and in every related concept, e.g., "methods" of collecting data, data analysis. I believe the understanding of data in conventional humanist qualitative methodology, strongly influenced now by SBR and scientism in general, is increasingly positivist because, first, it must be fixed and visible in words, and, second, because we increasingly treat words as brute, uninterpreted data rather than as already interpreted data we must explain. It should not be surprising, then, that one who thinks with poststructural theories of language would have trouble with humanist qualitative methodology's description of data.

Here's a brief description of how deconstruction happened for me. As I wrote about subjectivity, I realized I was thinking/writing not only with textualized data in interview transcripts and fieldnotes, but also with data that were not textualized, fixed, and visible. I therefore decided to claim and name some of those other data so they might be accounted for. For one thing, I believed that if participants' words about subjectivity in interview transcripts counted as data, so did theorists' words about subjectivity in books I had read—why discount their expertise? I thought with everyone's words as I wrote—Foucault's and my former Latin teacher's—and it no longer made sense to separate those data into chapters called "literature review" and "interpretation." It has since occurred to me that that artificial separation actually encourages researchers *not* to theorize data from interviews and observations.

I also identified what I called "transgressive data" clearly at work in my study—*emotional data, dream data, sensual data, memory data,* and *response data*—data that were not visible and that disrupted linearity, consciousness, and the mind/body dichotomy. (Recently, several of my students have, unaware of each other's work, identified *spectral data.*) Much data—*what we think with when we think about a topic*—were identified *during* analysis and not before. Until one begins to think, one cannot know what one will think with. In that sense, data are collected during thinking and, for me, especially during writing.

I wrote earlier in this chapter and elsewhere (Richardson & St.Pierre, 2005) that, for me, writing is analysis. Twenty years ago, I did not believe that coding data was analysis, and I haven't changed my mind. It's certainly something one can do with data—label and sort (and count)—but I'm not sure one would do it if one had never heard of it. There are many ways to "stay close to the data" (conventional data, that is), for example, reading transcripts and fieldnotes and listening to tapes repeatedly. But if those data are only a portion of the data we use in thinking, in analysis, coding makes even less sense, e.g., how/why would one code sensual data?

I strongly advise my own doctoral students not to code data because I have seen too many students, even those who've done their hard theoretical reading, become exhausted after months of tedious coding and never do the theoretical analysis they could. Their findings are pedestrian, and they produce low-level, insignificant themes; untheorized stories; or extended descriptions that do not get to the intellectual problem of explaining why things are as they are. I do, however, ask them to explain what they did when they thought they were "doing analysis," and they describe a multitude of activities—washing the car and weeding the garden (*the physicality of theorizing*), making charts and webs, talking with friends, writing, listening to music, reading transcripts, reading more theory, dozing on the couch, and so forth. The positivism imbedded in qualitative research quickly fails—audit trails can't capture that work, it can't be triangulated, and it is never saturated.

If we agree with Derrida and many others that language cannot contain and close off meaning and cannot transport meaning from one person to another, it's difficult to understand why we believe that isolating and labeling a word or group of words (a chunk) with another word (a code) is scientific or rigorous or "analysis"—even if we do that work with computer software, which makes the process seem detached, objective, systematic, and even more scientific. If a word is data, isn't a code (a word) data as well? Do we code codes? I expect some do because I have read entire books on coding and discovered that there are, for example, supercodes. Some even count the occurrence of codes, giving weight to codes that appear most frequently even though we know that the most significant data in a study might occur only once. I argue that coding is a positivist practice, a relic from the positivist social science of the 1920s and 1930s when qualitative data were handled in a quasi-statistical fashion, when words were considered *brute data,* when it seemed best to treat words as numbers and even to turn them into numbers for the sake of clarity and simplicity, for the sake of scientific analysis—the pathology of quantification.

I expect we teach coding because we don't know how to teach thinking. But I will always believe that if one has read and read and read, it's nigh onto impossible *not* to think with what others have thought and written. (If one has not read much, perhaps one needs to code.) I imagine a cacophony of ideas swirling as we think about our topics with all we can muster—with words from theorists, participants, conference audiences, friends and lovers, ghosts who haunt our studies, characters in fiction and film and dreams—and with our bodies and all the other bodies and the earth and all the things and objects in our lives—the entire assemblage that is *a life* thinking *and, and, and.* . . . All those data are set to work in our thinking, and we think, and we work our way somewhere in thinking. My advice is to read, and analysis, whatever it is, will follow. *(Do tell me what you think you are thinking with when you think—what are your data? And do tell me what you think you do when you think—when you do analysis? Do that.)* In the end, it is impossible to disentangle *data, data collection,* and *data analysis.* Those individuations no longer make sense. We could just give them up.

Any concept/category can be deconstructed as I've deconstructed data here. This work is not only playful in the Derridaean sense but also necessary if we're to move out of the structures that prevent us from thinking differently. Here we do not repeat the same—this work is *différance,* not repetition.

A RETURN TO PHILOSOPHY

What can be said here at the end of this chapter? I have reviewed some post-structural theories, stressed the importance of studying those theories if one wants to use them, and then used them to deconstruct several concepts/categories that ground conventional humanist qualitative inquiry: language, the human being, data, and related structuring concepts. I suspect that some familiar, naturalized concept becomes troublesome in every study, but deconstruction requires that instead of suppressing or ignoring that trouble, we "take it with the utmost seriousness, with literal seriousness, so that it transforms itself" (Spivak, 1989, p. 129) and overturns the structure it helps to organize. What happens next is not predictable, and, for that reason, the "posts" do not and cannot offer an alternative methodology.

It is critical at this deconstructive moment that is always already a political moment that we do not, in fear or confusion, submit to the positivist resurgence or any other foundationalist legitimating authority that promises to secure science and save us. The urge to create new structures of comfort is almost insurmountable, but we must work against the current conservative restoration in favor of a time to come, a future that is "no more historical than it is eternal: it must be untimely, always untimely" (Deleuze, 1995/2001, p. 72).

The "posts" and interpretive and critical theories were described half a century ago in a time much like this one in response to crippling foundationalist, especially positivist, dogma. The conventional humanist qualitative inquiry described in textbooks—the structure we call a "methodology" with "research designs" and "methods" that still mimics a simulacrum of the natural sciences—emerged as one project of the interpretive turn, the critique of positivist social science, which itself began in earnest in the 1920s with the logical positivism and logical empiricism of the Vienna Circle and continued well into post–World War II social science. But it is difficult to escape what one critiques, and qualitative inquiry has always been organized as much by positivism as by interpretivism. Its latent positivism was clearly evident when it almost immediately hardened in response to the scientific- and evidence-based movements and accommodated, for example, epistemologically and ontologically incommensurable "mixed methods." In any case, it is entirely humanist.

Conventional humanist qualitative inquiry organized and established itself mainly through a proliferation of publications that convinced us it was real. The scattered post critiques, never well-organized into rival publications, nonetheless gnawed away at it throughout the social sciences, even economics, and ruptured and ruined it beyond recognition. Those working those ruins deconstructively (working within/against the structure) who paused—for too long, I suspect—to defend qualitative inquiry from the resurgence of positivism are now countering with a *resurgence of postmodernism,* calling it out to continue work it began in the 1960s.

I believe qualitative inquiry is more vulnerable than ever now that its positivist tendencies have been outed. More importantly, I suggest that we've worked within/against the ruined structure long enough. We could now, if we wish, give up conventional humanist qualitative inquiry and its structuring concepts and categories—just let it go.

We can now do something different from the beginning. Am I saying "anything goes"? Well, anything always goes until someone who has some power draws a line. But many of us are weary of all the lines drawn around social science inquiry these days. I believe inquiry should be provocative, risky, stunning, astounding. It should take our breath away with its daring. It should challenge our foundational assumptions and transform the world. We must, even so, be vigilant in analyzing the consequences of human invention and the structures it endlessly creates. Humanism's projects created spectacular failures that the "turns" identified half a century ago. Why not try something different?

But what happens next, is happening now, and has always happened, cannot be predicted or controlled. People everywhere always re-think, deconstruct, invent, and we theorists and researchers are always catching up, trying to make sense of their work. We individuate, we order, we name, we try to control, we draw lines. Nonetheless, they resist structural boundaries as they create entanglements that may initially seem incongruous. I propose we worry less—so much angst—about what might happen if we give up exhausted structures and attend to what *is* happening. *Deconstruction has already happened; it is happening at this moment, everywhere.*

My desire is for post inquiry to remain *unstable* as we create different articulations, assemblages, becomings, mash-ups of inquiry given the entanglement that emerges in our different projects. Whether it will be called "science" depends, as always, on who has the power to make such decisions. Some will work to keep science capacious, others won't, and still others won't care much at all.

I am reminded of Foucault's (1984) questions about subjectivity here at the end because whether we, each of us, is available to a transformation of inquiry, much less of ourselves (the "I") and our world, is always already personal *and* philosophical: "How are we constituted as subjects of our own knowledge? How are we constituted as subjects who exercise or submit to power relations? How are we constituted as moral subjects of our own actions" (p. 49). Foucault's projects focused on how power relations constitute human beings within discursive formations that are only *descriptions,* albeit sometimes powerful descriptions with very real material effects. Rorty (1986) explained that those descriptions are not necessarily rational, intentional, ethical, or progressive:

> The urge to tell stories of progress, maturation and synthesis might be overcome if we once took seriously the notion that we only know the world and ourselves *under a description.* For doing so would mean taking

seriously the possibility that we just *happened* on that description—that it was not the description which nature evolved us to apply, or that which best unified the manifold of previous descriptions, but just the one which we have now *chanced* to latch onto. (p. 48)

At this very moment, we are latched onto descriptions that are producing us and the world, descriptions that, over time, have become so transparent, natural, and real that we've forgotten they're fictions. We accept them as truth.

What philosophy can do, what the "posts" can do, is reach "for the speculative possibilities that exceed our present grasp, but may nevertheless be our future" (Rorty, 1986, p. 48). The resurgence of positivism evidenced in SBR once again attempted to detach science from philosophy as positivism always does; to reduce knowledge to that produced by science; and to reduce science to systematic procedures and protocols, mechanistic technique, statistical manipulation, and causal structures. The call for the resurgence of postmodernism in this chapter has, of course, all along, been a call for philosophically informed inquiry accomplished by inquirers who have read and studied philosophy. It seems we have to keep on learning that philosophy and science are not individuated but always already entangled. The most important task of post qualitative inquiry is to attend to that false and grievous distinction.

References

Atmanspacher, H. (2002). Determinism is ontic, determinability is epistemic. In H. Atmanspacher & R. Bishop (Eds.), *Between chance and choice: Interdisciplinary perspectives on determinism* (pp. 49–74). Thoveton, UK: Imprint Academic.

Ayer, A. J. (1936). *Language, truth, and logic.* London: Victor Gollancz.

Barad, K. (2007). *Meeting the universe halfway: Quantum physics and the entanglement of matter and meaning.* Durham, NC: Duke University Press.

Benjamin, W. (1999). *The arcades project* (H. Eiland & K. McLaughlin, Trans.). Cambridge, MA: Harvard University Press.

Butler, J. (1992). Contingent foundations: Feminism and the question of "postmodernism." In J. Butler & J. W. Scott (Eds.), *Feminists theorize the political* (pp. 3–21). New York: Routledge.

Butler, J. (1995). For a careful reading. In S. Benhabib, J. Butler, D. Cornell, & N. Fraser (Eds.), *Feminist contentions: A philosophical exchange* (pp. 127–143). New York: Routledge.

Caputo, J. D. (1993). *Against ethics: Contributions to a poetics of obligation with constant reference to deconstruction.* Bloomington: Indiana University Press.

Cullenberg, S., Amariglio, J., & Ruccio, D. F. (Eds.). (2001). *Postmodernism, economics and knowledge.* London: Routledge.

Culler, J. (1982). *On deconstruction: Theory and criticism after structuralism.* Ithaca, NY: Cornell University Press.

Deleuze, G. (1995). *Negotiations: 1972–1990* (M. Joughin, Trans.). New York: Columbia University Press. (Original work published 1990)

Deleuze, G. (2001). *Pure immanence: Essays on a life* (A. Boyman, Trans.). New York: Zone Books. (Original work published 1995)

Deleuze, G., & Guattari, F. (1987). *A thousand plateaus: Capitalism and schizophrenia* (B. Massumi, Trans.). Minneapolis: University of Minnesota Press. (Original work published 1980)

Derrida, J. (1970). Structure, sign, and play in the discourse of the human sciences. In R. Macksey & E. Donato (Eds. & Trans.), *The structuralist controversy: The languages of criticism and the sciences of man* (pp. 247–272). Baltimore: Johns Hopkins University Press. (Lecture delivered 1966)

Derrida, J. (1974). *Of grammatology* (G. C. Spivak, Trans.). Baltimore: Johns Hopkins University Press. (Original work published 1967)

Derrida, J. (1981). *Positions* (A. Bass, Trans.). Chicago: University of Chicago Press. (Original work published 1972)

Derrida, J. (1982). Signature, event, context. In J. Derrida, *Margins of philosophy* (A. Bass, Trans.) (pp. 307–330). Chicago: University of Chicago Press. (Original work published 1971)

Derrida, J. (1988). Letter to a Japanese friend. In D. Wood & R. Bernasconi (Eds.), *Derrida and différance* (pp. 1–5). Evanston, IL: Northwestern University Press.

Derrida, J. (1990). Some statements and truisms about neologisms, newisms, positisms, parasitisms, and other small seismisms. (A. Tomiche, Trans.). In D. Caroll (Ed.), *The states of "theory": History, art, and critical discourse.* New York: Columbia University Press.

Derrida, J. (2002). Force of law: The "mystical foundation of authority." In J. Derrida, *Acts of religion* (G. Anidjar, Ed.) (pp. 230–298). New York: Routledge. (Original work circulated 1989)

Descartes, R. (1993). *Discourse on method and Meditations on first philosophy* (4th ed., D. A. Cress, Trans.). Indianapolis, IN: Hackett Publishing Company. (*Discourse on Method* first published 1637 and *Meditations on First Philosophy* first published 1641)

Eagleton, T. (1987, February). Awakening from modernity. *Times Literary Supplement, 20*, 6–9.

Fay, B. (1987). *Critical social science: Liberation and its limits.* Ithaca, NY: Cornell University Press.

Feyerabend, P. K. (1975). *Against method* (3rd ed.). London: Verso.

Finn, G. (1993). Why are there no great women postmodernists? In I. Taylor (Ed.), *Relocating cultural studies: Developments in theory and research* (pp. 123–152). New York: Routledge.

Flax, J. (1990). Postmodernism and gender relations in feminist theory. In L. J. Nicholson (Ed.), *Feminism/Postmodernism* (pp. 39–62). New York: Routledge.

Foucault, M. (1970). *The order of things: An archaeology of the human sciences* (A. M. S. Smith, Trans.). New York: Vintage Books. (Original work published 1966)

Foucault, M. (1982). The subject and power. *Critical Inquiry, 8*(4), 777–795.

Foucault, M. (1984). What is enlightenment? (C. Porter, Trans.). In P. Rabinow (Ed.), *The Foucault reader* (pp. 32–50). New York: Pantheon Books.

Foucault, M. (1985). *The history of sexuality. Volume 2. The use of pleasure* (R. Hurley, Trans.). New York: Vintage Books. (Original work published 1984)

Fuss, D. (1989). *Essentially speaking: Feminism, nature & difference.* New York: Routledge.

Gilder, L. (2008). *The age of entanglement.* New York: Knopf.

Hall, S. (1996). On postmodernism and articulation: An interview with Stuart Hall. In D. Morley & K.-H. Chen (Eds.), *Stuart Hall: Critical dialogues in cultural studies* (pp. 131–150). London: Routledge. (Reprinted from *Journal of Communication Inquiry, 10*(2), pp. 45–60, 1986)

Harvey, D. (1989). *The condition of postmodernity: An enquiry into the origins of cultural change.* Cambridge, MA: Blackwell.

Hawking, S. (1988). *A brief history of time: From the big bang to black holes.* New York: Bantam Books.

Henig, J. R. (2008). The evolving relationship between researchers and public policy. In F. M. Hess (Ed.), *When research matters: How scholarship influences education policy* (pp. 41–62). Cambridge, MA: Harvard Education Press.

Hodkinson, P. (2004). Research as a form of work: Expertise, community and methodological objectivity. *British Educational Research Journal, 30*(1), 9–26.

hooks, b. (1989). *Talking back: Thinking feminist, thinking black.* Boston: South End Press.

Hurworth, R. E. (2008). *Teaching qualitative research: Cases and issues.* Rotterdam, The Netherlands: Sense Publishers.

Institute of Education Sciences. U.S. Department of Education. (2008). *Rigor and relevance redux: Director's biennial report to Congress* (IES 2009–6010). Washington, DC.

Jackson, A. Y., & Mazzei, L. A. (2009). *Voice in qualitative inquiry: Challenging conventional, interpretive, and critical conceptions in qualitative research.* New York: Routledge.

Jameson, F. (1988). Postmodernism and consumer society. In E. A. Kaplan (Ed.), *Postmodernism and its discontents: Theories, practices* (pp. 13–29). New York: Verso.

Kaplan, E. A. (1988). Introduction. In E. A. Kaplan (Ed.), *Postmodernism and its discontents: Theories, practices* (pp. 1–9). New York: Verso.

Keenan, T. (1997). *Fables of responsibility: Aberrations and predicaments in ethics and politics.* Stanford, CA: Stanford University Press.

Kuhn, T. S. (1970). *The structure of scientific revolutions* (2nd ed.). Chicago: University of Chicago Press. (Original work published 1962)

Laclau, E., & Mouffe, C. (1985). *Hegemony and socialist strategy: Towards a radical democratic politics.* London: Verso.

Lamont, M. (1987). How to become a dominant French philosopher: The case of Jacques Derrida. *American Journal of Sociology, 93*(3), 584–622.

Lather, P. (1993). Fertile obsession: Validity after poststructuralism. *Sociological Quarterly, 34*(4), 673–693.

Lincoln, Y. S., & Guba, E. G. (1985). *Naturalistic inquiry.* Newbury Park, CA: Sage.

Locke, J. (1924). *An essay concerning human understanding.* Oxford, UK: Clarendon Press. (Original work published 1690)

Lyotard, J-F. (1984). *The postmodern condition: A report on knowledge* (G. Bennington & B. Massumi, Trans.). Minneapolis: University of Minnesota Press. (Original work published 1979)

MacLure, M. (2005). "Clarity bordering on stupidity": Where's the quality in systematic review? *Journal of Education Policy, 20*(4) 393–416.

Massey, D. (1994). *Space, place, and gender.* Minneapolis: University of Minnesota Press.

Maxwell, J. A. (2010, January 19). Review of the book, *Theory and Educational Research: Toward Critical Social Explanation,* by J. Anyon. Available at http://edrev.asu.edu/reviews/rev882.pdf

McCloskey, D. (2001). The genealogy of postmodernism: An economist's guide. In S. Cullenberg, J. Amariglio, & D. F. Ruccio (Eds.), *Postmodernism, economics, and knowledge* (pp. 102–128). London: Routledge.

Moss, P. A., Phillips, D. C., Erickson, F. D., Floden, R. E., Lather, P. A., & Schneider, B. L. (2009). Learning from our differences: A dialogue across perspectives on quality in educational research. *Educational Researcher, 38*(7), 501–517.

Mouffe, C. (1996). Radical democracy or liberal democracy? In D. Trend (Ed.), *Radical democracy: Identity, citizenship, and the state* (pp. 19–26). New York: Routledge.

National Research Council. (2002). *Scientific research in education* (R. J. Shavelson & L. Towne, Eds.). Committee on Scientific Principles for Education Research. Washington, DC: National Academies Press.

Neumann, A., Pallas, A. M., & Peterson, P. L. (2008). Exploring the investment: Four universities' experiences with the Spencer Foundation's research training grant program: A retrospective. *Teachers' College Record, 110*(7), 1477–1503.

Nietzsche, F. (1967). *The will to power* (W. Kaufman, Ed.; W. Kaufman & R. J. Hollingdale, Trans.). New York: Vintage Books. (Original work published 1887)

Oakley, A. (2006). Resistances to "new" technologies of evaluation: Education research in the UK as a case study. *Evidence and policy: A journal of research, debate and practice, 2*(1), 63–87.

Patton, C. (2008). Finding "fields" in the field: Normalcy, risk, and ethnographic inquiry. *International Review of Qualitative Research, 1*(2), 255–74.

Peters, M. (1999). (Posts-) modernism and structuralism: Affinities and theoretical innovations. *Sociological Research Online, 4*(3). Available at http://www.socreson line.org.uk

Phillips, D. C. (2006). A guide for the perplexed: Scientific educational research, methodolatry, and the gold versus platinum standards. *Educational Research Review, 1,* 15–26.

Phillips, D. C. (2009). A quixotic quest? Philosophical issues in assessing the quality of education research. In P. B. Walters, A. Lareau, & S. H. Ranis (Eds.), *Education research on trial: Policy reform and the call for scientific rigor* (pp. 163–195). New York: Routledge.

Phillips, D. C., & Burbules, N. C. (2000). *Postpositivism and educational research.* Lanham: Rowman & Littlefield.

Pillow, W. S. (2003). Confession, catharsis, or cure? Rethinking the uses of reflexivity as methodological power in qualitative research. *International Journal of Qualitative Studies in Education, 16*(2), 175–196.

Rajchman, J. (1987, November/December). Postmodernism in a nominalist frame: The emergence and diffusion of a cultural category. *Flash Art, 137,* 49–51.

Rajchman, J. (2000). *The Deleuze connections.* Cambridge: MIT Press.

Reichenbach, H. (1951). *The rise of scientific philosophy.* Berkeley: University of California Press.

Richardson, L., & St.Pierre, E. A. (2005). Writing: A method of inquiry. In N. K. Denzin & Y. S. Lincoln (Eds.), *The SAGE handbook of qualitative research* (3rd ed., pp. 959–978). Thousand Oaks, CA: Sage.

Rorty, R. (1979). *Philosophy and the mirror of nature.* Princeton, NJ: Princeton University Press.

Rorty, R. (1986). Foucault and epistemology. In D. C. Hoy (Ed.), *Foucault: A critical reader* (pp. 41–49). Cambridge, MA: Basil Blackwell.

Said, E. W. (1978). *Orientalism.* New York: Vintage Books.

Scheurich, J. J. (1995). A postmodernist critique of research interviewing. *International Journal of Qualitative Studies in Education, 8*(3), 239–252.

Scott, J. (1988). Deconstructing equality-versus-difference: Or, the uses of poststructuralist theory for feminism. *Feminist Studies, 14*(1), 33–50.

Sommer, D. (1994). Resistant texts and incompetent readers. *Poetics Today, 15*(4), 523–551.

Spivak, G. C. (1974). Translator's preface. In J. Derrida *Of Grammatology* (G. C. Spivak, Trans.) (pp. ix–xc). Baltimore: Johns Hopkins University Press.

Spivak, G. C. (1989). In a word: Interview (E. Rooney, Interviewer). *Differences, 1*(2), 124–156.

Spivak, G. C. (1993). *Outside in the teaching machine.* New York: Routledge.

St.Pierre, E. A. (1995). *Arts of existence: The construction of subjectivity in older, white southern women.* Unpublished doctoral dissertation, The Ohio State University, Columbus.

St.Pierre, E. A. (1997). Methodology in the fold and the irruption of transgressive data. *International Journal of Qualitative Studies in Education, 10*(2), 175–189.

St.Pierre, E. A. (2000). Poststructural feminism in education: An overview. *International Journal of Qualitative Studies in Education, 13*(5), 477–515.

St.Pierre, E. A. (2001). Coming to theory: Finding Foucault and Deleuze. In K. Weiler (Ed.), *Feminist engagements: Reading, resisting, and revisioning male theorists in education and cultural studies* (pp. 141–163). New York: Routledge.

Ulmer, G. L. (1985). *Applied grammatology: Post(e)-Pedagogy from Jacques Derrida to Joseph Beuys.* Baltimore: Johns Hopkins University Press.

Viadero, D. (2009). "No effect" studies raising eyebrows. *Education Week, 28*(27), 1 & 14.

Whitehurst, G. J. (2003). *The Institute of Education Sciences: New wine and new bottles.* Paper presented at the annual meeting of the American Educational Research Association, Chicago.

15

Qualitative Research and Technology

In the Midst of a Revolution

Judith Davidson and Silvana di Gregorio

In the early 1980s, as qualitative researchers began to grapple with the promise and challenges of computers, a handful of innovative researchers brought forth the first generation of what would come to be known as CAQDAS (Computer Assisted Qualitative Data Analysis Software), or QDAS (Qualitative Data Analysis Software) as we will refer to it here. These stand-alone software packages were developed, initially, to bring the power of computing to the often labor-intensive work of qualitative research. While limited in scope at the beginning to text-retrieval tasks, for instance, these tools quickly expanded to become comprehensive all-in-one packages that offered qualitative researchers the following:

(1) A convenient digital location in which to organize all materials related to one study;

(2) A suite of linked digital tools that could be applied to those materials, including the ability to store and organize data as well as fragment, juxtapose, interpret, and recompose that same material;

(3) Easy portability; and

(4) A remarkable new form of transparency that allowed the researcher, and others, the opportunity to view and reflect upon the materials (di Gregorio & Davidson, 2008).

QDAS packages were flexible enough that they could be used by qualitative researchers from diverse disciplinary and methodological perspectives (although many early developers and users were from sociology). Over time, as the technological context advanced, these tools came to incorporate possibilities for working with multimodal data, as well as to provide new ways for multiple researchers to work together on the same project. A small but robust literature on the use, applications, and implications of QDAS also burgeoned.

Close to 30 years later, QDAS packages are comprehensive, feature-laden tools of immense value to many in the qualitative research world. However, with the advent of the Internet and the emergence of web-based tools known as Web 2.0, QDAS is now challenged on many fronts as researchers seek out easier-to-learn, more widely available and less expensive, increasingly multimodal, visually attractive, and more socially connected technologies to support their qualitative research endeavors (Anderson, 2007).

Truly, qualitative research and technology is in the midst of a revolution. The purpose of this chapter is to set a historical context for understanding the development of QDAS and to bring that discussion into alignment with the broad stream of methodological discussions in qualitative research, examine the challenges that face qualitative researchers at this pivotal moment, and attempt to predict how the current technological dilemma of our field will be resolved.

Definitions and Delimitations

Our primary aim is to examine those tools that support qualitative researchers in the organization and analysis of qualitative research projects. Silver's (2009) adaptation of Lewins and Silver's (2007) model presents a particularly robust view of these functions.

As illustrated above, qualitative analysis is a process that requires the exploration, organization, interpretation, and integration of research materials (data). These four components require that researchers retrieve, rethink, compare subsets, and identify patterns and relationships. Various QDAS program features support analysis tasks including linking and grouping, annotating and searching, writing and making connections, and incorporating references and combining or converting findings.

These are the same tasks researchers using traditional methods perform except that without the power of the computer, it is difficult to retrieve data, so you are limited in comparing subsets and identifying patterns, which then have a limiting effect on your ability to rethink data.

Figure 15.1 The Basic Idea of QDAS Packages

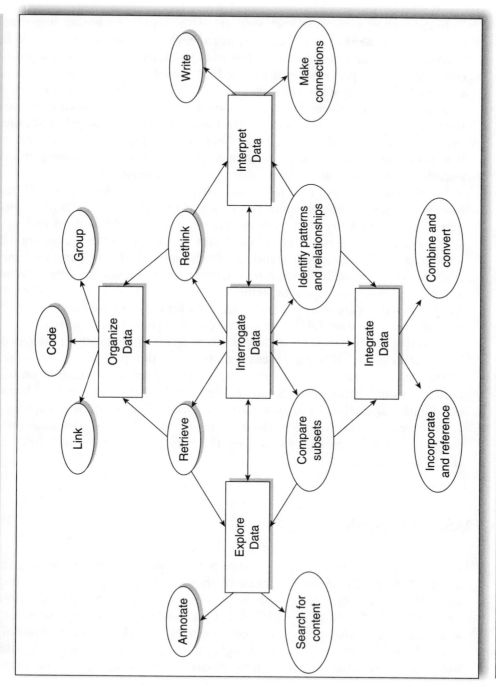

Adapted from Lewins, A., & Silver, C. (2007), *Using Software in Qualitative Research: A Step-by-Step Guide.* London: Sage.

In the earliest versions of such software, data preparation was an important concern. Materials had to be prepared in particular ways so that they could be entered into the program. As computers and QDAS have become more sophisticated, less special preparation is required. MS word formats, jpegs, and video formats can be imported with ease. However, to take advantage of certain affordances of the software (such as automatic coding), you still need to prepare the materials in specified ways (although the preparations are simple and minimal in nature). It could be argued that these affordances may have an impact on how researchers—particularly novice researchers—would design their projects, attending to the affordances rather than the research questions.

In this piece, our goal is to focus on tools providing specific support for the functions described above in the Lewins and Silver (2007) model. QDAS programs are comprehensive stand-alone packages providing a kind of one-stop shop for the technologically savvy qualitative researcher. In this article, we will use the term QDAS to refer to stand-alone software tools that perform the functions described above. It is true, however, that with the explosion of the Internet and Web 2.0, tools with these capacities come in a variety of forms (stand-alone and net-based), opening up uncharted territory for the qualitative researcher. We will introduce the term *QDAS 2.0* to describe this hybrid state of affairs.

In setting parameters for this piece, we have decided not to include the area of "Internet Research," where the focus is on the collection of Internet data or the Internet as a virtual site of study (Hine, 2008). For more information on this topic, we would direct you to Sarah Gatson's article in this volume "The Methods, Politics, and Ethics of Representation in Online Ethnography" (Chapter 8).

We have also shied away from those discussions of technologies for qualitative research that are primarily focused on the presentation of research findings (Dicks & Mason, 2008).

QDAS: An Overview

Discussions of QDAS rely upon a range of frameworks for understanding the development of QDAS or the nature of the tools (see, for instance, Fielding, 2008; Hesse-Biber & Crofts, 2008; Kelle, 1995; T. Richards & Richards, 1994; Tesch, 1990; Weitzman & Miles, 1995). For the most part, these discussions have focused on the developments of the technology itself and less on the relationship of the changing technology to the changing methodological currents of qualitative research. For that reason, we have chosen to anchor our discussion of the development of QDAS around Denzin and Lincoln's (2003, 2008) eight critical moments in the chronology of qualitative research. In using the Denzin and Lincoln chronology, we are aware of its possible ethnocentric limitations (Cisneros, 2008a, 2008b, 2009), but we feel that this is a broadly recognized stage structure among qualitative researchers.

Taking a historical approach to qualitative research and QDAS should help the reader to see how technology has always been a part of qualitative research (di Gregorio & Davidson, 2008; see Table 15.1).

Table 15.1   Lincoln and Denzin's Stages of Qualitative Research Tweaked and Integrated With Davidson and di Gregorio's Stages of QDAS Development

Moments in Qualitative Research	Stages in the Development of QDAS
1. Traditional Period—Early 1900s to WWII	Stage I: Pre–Qualitative Data Analysis Software notebooks; typewriter and carbon paper
2. Modernist—Post WWII to 1970	Stage I continues . . . McBee Keysort Cards; InDecks Information Retrieval cards; manual to electric portable typewriters; photocopying
3. Blurred Genres—1970 to 1986	Stage II: QDAS begins
4. Crisis of Representation—Mid-1980s to early 1990s	Stage III: The Typology Era: Matching program to project
5. Postmodernism—Early to mid-1990s	Stage IV: Focus on developing similar and competing features: Experimentation with generic tools for qualitative research (QR) functions
6. Post-Experimental Inquiry—1995–2000	Stage IV continues . . .
7. Methodologically Contested Present—2000–2008	Stage V: Development of meta-perspectives on the use of QDAS
8. A Fractured Future	Stage VI: Development of Web 2.0/3.0. Networked technologies move to the fore. QDAS 2.0 comes into being.

STAGE I: PRE-QDAS

Traditional Period—early 1900s to WWII	Stage I: Pre-QDAS: Notebooks; typewriters and carbon paper
Modernist—post WWII to 1970	Stage I: Pre-QDAS continues: McBee Keysort cards, InDecks Information Retrieval cards, manual to electric portable typewriters, photocopying

In Stage I, a period that spans more than half the 20th century, the classical set of qualitative research technologies was established. The lionized anthropologist of the "traditional moment" in qualitative research was pictured with a pad and pen in hand, or perhaps in a tent slaving away on his or her manual typewriter, eyes on a notebook full of notes, or a pile of note cards. A significant technological development of this era was the advent of carbon paper. This enabled the researcher to type multiple copies of an interview transcript or observation notes. The copies could be cut up and sections of text could be filed according to themes. The development of QDAS-like tools—notched index cards such as McBee Keysort Cards and InDecks Information Retrieval Cards (Kelly, 2008) and tabs (Tenner, 2005)—represented important technological steps forward in the field. Each index card contained notes from an interview. A mastercard would have descriptors associated with the holes around its periphery. Each card was "coded" by punching out the relevant hole(s) in a card. Retrieval was done by inserting a needle in the stack of cards in the hole for a particular descriptor—those cards that were not lifted out by the needle were the ones relevant for the query. Using two needles simultaneously would achieve a Boolean AND.

Toward the end of the modernist period of qualitative research, important changes were taking place in the computer arena that would make QDAS possible. The early mainframe computers were developed (1965) with a focus on the conduct of quantitative content analysis. In 1968, the University of Chicago released the quantitative analysis program—SPSS—and McGraw-Hill published the first user's manual for this program in 1970 (http://www.spss.com/corpinfo/history.htm).

While quantitative researchers were quick to integrate the use of software in their practice, qualitative researchers were not. It may be that statistical software packages mapped more readily onto already existing practices. Computers were associated with counting and mathematical calculations that were consistent with statistical analysis. Qualitative researchers, on the other hand, could only see computers contributing to a quantitative reduction of their analysis.

Toward the end of this period, Glaser and Strauss published *The Discovery of Grounded Theory* (1967). It would have a deep and reverberating effect on the future of QDAS and its place within the field of qualitative research (Fielding, 2008). In this work, Glaser and Strauss challenged the dominant sociological perspectives of the time as exemplified in the works of Talcott Parsons, Robert Merton, and Peter Blau. Glaser and Strauss provided the rationale for the use of qualitative data in capturing "the unfolding nature of the meanings, interpretations and processes that the sociologist is studying" (Layder, 1993). Their book inspired an upsurge of interest in the use of qualitative data in sociology.

Our discussion of noncomputer qualitative research technologies may seem unrelated to the birth of QDAS, but in truth they have great significance for the emergence of QDAS. The concept of *skeuomorphs* is critical in explaining the connection between earlier technologies and QDAS: "A skeuomorph is a design feature that is no longer functional in itself, but that refers back to a feature that was functional at an earlier time. . . . Skeuomorphs visibly testify to the social or psychological necessity for innovation to be tempered by replication" (Hayles, 1999, p. 17).

In Stage I, qualitative researchers struggled to find effective means of organizing and analyzing research materials. In that process, they developed techniques from card sorts and indexing to annotations and searching that informed the structure and form of QDAS in Stage II. These earlier forms lived on as skeuomorphs embedded in the design and structure of QDAS.

STAGE II: QDAS BEGINS

Blurred genres—1970 to 1986	Stage II: QDAS begins

QDAS was born as qualitative researchers struggled with the issue of blurred genres and as the boundaries between academic areas become fuzzy, allowing for new kinds of intersection and overlap between the social sciences and humanities (Denzin & Lincoln, 2003). As qualitative research struggled with this internal argument, it also struggled with an external context within universities and funding agencies that emphasized science-like approaches to research, which was to have implications for qualitative research and QDAS.

The 1980s are described by Fielding and Lee (1998) as a period of experimentation in computer use in general—databases, quantitative content analysis, word processors, and QDAS. NUD*IST (Non-numerical Unstructured Data Indexing, Searching, and Theorizing) was released in 1981; the Ethnograph was released in 1984. Both are forms of QDAS.

Seidel (1998), developer of the Ethnograph, describes how he identified the analysis processes of pre-QDAS qualitative researchers, as he developed the components of his QDAS tool. Noticing and collecting, which he identified as key analysis processes, were then translated into the computer method. A criticism of the Ethnograph and similar tools was that noticing and collecting could be mistakenly seen as the sum total of the researcher's work (Seidel, 1998).

In research computing in general, the trend was toward programs that were operated from individual computers, as opposed to the large, immoveable mainframe machines.

What also characterizes the beginnings of QDAS is the relative isolation of the various developers. Programs were developed with little knowledge of what other software developers were doing to develop related solutions. The early QDAS programs were developed in noncommercial environments either by social scientists themselves or by social scientists working with programmers (Fielding, 2008).

STAGE III: THE TYPOLOGY ERA— MATCHING PROGRAM TO PROJECT

Crisis of Representation—Mid-1980s to early 1990s	Stage III: The Typology Era: Matching program to project

The "crisis of representation" raised its head in the mid-1980s as qualitative researchers "made research and writing more reflexive and called into question the issues of gender, class, and race" (Denzin & Lincoln, 2003, p. 26).

The corresponding development in QDAS we have dubbed "The Typology Era," which represents the period in which users were concerned with methodological alignment of tool and project. As a consequence, much thought was given to the paradigmatic or methodological perspectives of the developer, as it was believed that these were embedded in the software design and would shape the work of users in specific directions congruent with the developer's methodological bias, regardless of the user's intent.

QDAS came to the fore at the same moment that Strauss and Corbin's (1990) step-by-step guide for doing grounded theory was published. While Glaser and

Strauss (1967) provided the justification for qualitative analysis and developing theory from analysis grounded in empirical data, their book did not elaborate on how to conduct such an analysis. Strauss and Corbin produced a text that represented grounded theory as a highly structured set of procedures. Indeed, their text overpowered many voices within the field, and it is only recently that the full breadth of grounded theory possibilities are being discussed (Bryant & Charmaz, 2010). The result was that newcomers from traditionally quantitative disciplines were attracted to the method, as it provided a "cookbook" for conducting qualitative analysis. At the same time, their book also created great antipathy within the field from researchers who felt that alternative perspectives on grounded theory were not represented.

QDAS emerged at this moment and was quickly drawn into the fray. QDAS had been developed as generic tools to support researchers working with unstructured data through providing computerized assistance to the common tasks required when working with this kind of data. QDAS developers were quick to state that their tools were certainly compatible with grounded theory approaches. This apparent association between grounded theory and QDAS led to concerns about the epistemologies of the software developers and the influence their methodological perspectives might have had on the shape of the tool (Coffey, Holbrook, & Atkinson, 1996; for a response to this critique, see Kelle, 1997, and Lee & Fielding, 1996). As a result, QDAS came to be seen as more prescriptive in nature than traditional (noncomputerized) methods of qualitative research. This was the state of affairs in QDAS as qualitative research entered the crisis of representation.

In 1989, the Department of Sociology at the University of Surrey, United Kingdom, organized the first international conference on qualitative computing where, for the first time, a dialogue was established among developers and early adopters (Fielding & Lee, 2007). While this group of QDAS enthusiasts was attentive to the developments in the wider world of qualitative analysis, the same cannot be said for the wider world of qualitative research, which paid little attention to the developments in QDAS. QDAS users were a kind of subcultural movement, and their concerns were not incorporated in the contemporary debates around qualitative analysis.

Another important landmark occurred in 1990 when Renata Tesch published the first book to provide an overview of types of qualitative analysis and software tools. While Tesch identifies 46 "brands" of qualitative research, she argues that there are not 46 approaches to analysis. Instead, she describes 10 principles that are common across most types of qualitative research. She makes a distinction between *structural* analysis (event structure analysis, discourse analysis, ethnoscience, ethnography of communication, and structural ethnography) and *interpretational* analysis (which includes the bulk of types of qualitative analysis; they can be subdivided into theory-building and interpretive/descriptive analysis). The structural analysis approaches differ in that their goal is to create a model—the organizing system common to all approaches is not a means to an end but the end itself. For this approach to analysis, she recommends text retrievers and database managers, which are general tools that can be adapted. However, at the time there were two tools that specifically supported structural analysis—ETHNO and TAP. Interpretational analysis was best supported by the qualitative analysis programs that were evolving at the time—QUALPRO, the Ethnograph, TEXTBASE ALPHA, and HyperQual. AQUAD, NUD*IST, and HyperResearch are briefly mentioned as supporting theory building.

It is important to note two things from Tesch's (1990) seminal work: (1) Grounded theory is featured as only 1 of the 46 types of qualitative analysis, and (2) apart from a couple of Mac-based programs, the rest were for the DOS operating system. The software developed at the time was restricted by the possibilities offered by a DOS system. And the DOS system was soon to be replaced by the Windows operating system. Those software programs that did not make the transition to Windows quickly were left behind. In the next period, software that became dominant had made that transition quickly. NUD*IST (later NVivo), the Ethnograph and HyperResearch, and a few software packages that did not feature in Tesch's review—namely, ATLAS.ti and WinMax (later MAXQDA), became prominent in the field.

Tesch's (1990) book was a key text for the new group of qualitative software users. However, unlike Strauss and Corbin (1990), it did not have the same impact on the wider qualitative research community. The common principles of analysis across most approaches to qualitative analysis that software supported were lost in the discussion and justification of the epistemological bases of these different approaches.

Tesch's (1990) points are amplified by Fielding and Lee in a 2007 presentation overviewing the history of QDAS:

> There was also an assumption that we were seeking to establish some kind of orthodoxy around the analytic process, particularly in relation to grounded theory. This is an assumption we have always strongly resisted. For us, identification of the coding features found in many qualitative data analysis programs with grounded theory has tended to elide program features, analytic procedures and methodological approaches (p. 10)

STAGE IV: SIMILAR AND DIFFERENT—AN ERA OF COMPETITION

Postmodernism—Early to mid-1990s	Stage IV: Focus on developing similar and competing features: Experimentation with generic tools for qualitative research (QR) functions
Post-Experimental Inquiry—1995–2000	Stage IV continues

The postmodern turn in qualitative research refers to the "triple crisis of representation, legitimation, and praxis . . . in the human disciplines" (Denzin & Lincoln, 2003, p. 28). New forms of representation emerged in the field at the same time that social justice concerns were ardently pushed forward.

Following on the heels of the University of Surrey's conference on qualitative computing, Stage IV represents a radical shift away from methodological alignment of software and project to a broader perspective on the common qualities expected from a basic QDAS package. This stage is illustrative of the increasing sophistication of experienced QDAS users, with the skills and knowledge to look critically across packages, compare features, and explain similarities and differences. A mark of this era is the emergence of key texts on the topic of QDAS; of particular note are the volumes by Fielding and Lee (1991, 1998), Miles and Weitzman (1994; Weitzman & Miles, 1995), and Kelle (1995).

In discussing the publication of their 1991 volume, Fielding and Lee (2007) commented, "It took three proposals before our publisher agreed but the book based on the 1989 conference became their best seller" (p. 5). Fielding and Lee's 1998 book is one of the few studies based on empirical work that looks at how researchers use software to support qualitative data analysis.

Miles and Weitzman (1994; Weitzman 2002; Weitzman & Miles, 1995) built on the work of Tesch (1990) but hardened the distinction between different types of software—text retrievers, textbase managers, code-and-retrieve programs, code-based theory builders, and conceptual network builders. Their focus on comparing technical features of each package had the unfortunate consequence of reinforcing the procedural, scientific image of these programs. While this image attracted users from disciplines without a qualitative analysis tradition, it pushed away many experienced qualitative analysts. In addition, many of the DOS programs they covered transitioned into Windows packages or ceased to exist, as did many of the Apple Macintosh programs—following a downturn in Apple's fortunes during the 1990s.

Kelle's (1995) edited volume, which is dedicated to Tesch, contains a rich collection of articles by the small but hardy group that was creating the software and trying to figure out how to apply it to practical research questions. The contributors included developers and other academics in a relatively egalitarian mix, far different from the more commercial and distanced relationships that were to prevail in a later period. This volume makes a significant contribution to pushing the theoretical perspectives necessary to bring QDAS into the qualitative research field.

In this era, there were many notable and significant developments that supported and exploited this growing knowledge of QDAS. In 1994, the Economic and Social Research Council (ESRC) in Great Britain funded the CAQDAS Networking Project (which emerged out of the awareness raised by the 1989 conference). Based in the Sociology Department at the University of Surrey, it provided (and still provides) advice and training in multiple QDAS packages (http://caq das.soc.surrey.ac.uk/). Freelance trainers with specialization in QDAS begin to emerge at this time, including one of the authors of this article (di Gregorio). Many of these trainers have specialized in one specific tool, and a smaller number have offered support in multiple tools.

Sage Publications played a key role in disseminating information about and marketing these packages. In 1995, they agreed to market the QSR's newly formed software package—NUD*IST. This was followed subsequently by marketing a number of other qualitative packages, such as ATLAS.ti, Hyper Research, and WinMAX (later MAXQDA). Sage's involvement as a market center for QDAS was short-lived, but their brief involvement did provide important visibility for many of the packages. QSR's NVivo was released in 1999 and marks the close of this era of QDAS development and comparison. NVivo is unusual in the annals of QDAS in that it has been the focus of several book-length texts by the developer and independent writers (Bazeley, 2007; Bazeley & Richards, 2000; Gibbs, 2002; L. Richards, 1999).

As QDAS users compared packages, other qualitative researchers used on-the-shelf software such as Word or Excel to support their analysis. Hahn (2008) has illustrated how Word can be used to support qualitative analysis, while Ritchie and Lewis (2003) have documented how Excel can be used to support their approach to qualitative analysis. It is interesting to note that the National Centre for Social Research (where Ritchie and Lewis were based) have since developed their own QDAS—FrameWork (http://www.framework-natcen.co.uk/).

By the end of this period, three major QDAS packages had come to dominate the scene: ATLAS.ti (www.atlasti.com), MAXQDA (www.MAXQDA.com), and NVivo (www.qsrinternational.com). While the dominant packages of this era were generic tools, other packages emerged with enhanced features that supported particular types of analysis, e.g., Transana (http://www.transana.org/) for video analysis and QDAMiner (http://www.provalisresearch.com/QDAMiner/QDAMinerDesc.html) for mixed methods.

While QDAS made remarkable growth during this period, seeds of contention had been sown. Qualitative researchers debated postmodernism and theories of representation, and QDAS developers and friends, who were also qualitative researchers, listened and examined the tools in light of these arguments. However, the reverse could not be said to be true. Qualitative researchers who had not been introduced in a positive way to QDAS did not gravitate toward using these tools. Some believed the rumors they had heard about the epistemological problems, others did not have access to the tools and were not motivated to find access, and still others did not know that such tools existed. Fear of technology itself was, undoubtedly, an important factor in the failure of senior researchers, in particular, to integrate these new tools into their practices.

On this point, Fielding and Lee (2007) have pointed out, "Since qualitative researchers traditionally learn their craft in apprenticeship mode, the approach we were suggesting [QDAS] seemed to take some mystique out of the analytic process, potentially challenging in consequence the charismatic authority of the teacher" (p. 10).

STAGE V: DEVELOPMENT OF META-PERSPECTIVES

Methodologically Contested Present—2000–2008	Stage V: Development of meta-perspectives on the use of QDAS, 2000–2008

The methodologically contested seventh period of qualitative research continues to explore the issues of form and justice, legitimation and representation.

Moment seven corresponds to our Stage V, the development of meta-perspectives on the use of QDAS. In Stage V, QDAS adherents sought to develop strategies for research analysis grounded in a cohesive theoretical perspective on QDAS. The Strategies Conferences in the UK (1999–2006), international conferences focused on strategies for using the two QDAS packages developed by QSR International—NUD*IST and NVivo—were important in this process (Fielding & Lee, 2007). These conferences enabled a small and dedicated group of users to discuss ways of working with these packages, including using them for literature review (di Gregorio, 2000), teamworking (di Gregorio, 2001; Gilbert & di Gregorio, 2004;

L. Richards, 2006), ways of managing analysis—in general (di Gregorio, 2003a, L. Richards, 2004; T. Richards, 2004) and for specific types of research—including narrative analysis (Gibbs, 2004), and evaluation research (Kaczynski & Miller, 2004; Richter & Clary, 2004), and grounded theory (di Gregorio, 2003b). While the focus was on using NUD*IST and NVivo, it became clear to some participants that many of the principles of use under discussion were relevant regardless of which QDAS package was used. Some of the papers from these conferences are still accessible from www.qual-strategies.org.

The software package MAXQDA has also been the focus of a series of annual conferences beginning in 2005 (Computergestut zen Analyse Qualitatirer Daten, or CAQD; see http://www.caqd.de/).

The development of a meta-perspective was crystalized by Lewins and Silver (2007). Their book not only incorporates a step-by-step guide for working with the three major packages of the time (ATLAS.ti, NVivo, and MAXQDA), but it is also organized around the processes and tasks involved in qualitative analysis (rather than the features and functions of each software package).

Our work (di Gregorio & Davidson, 2008) looked across software packages to offer a common framework for representing a qualitative research design when setting up a project in QDAS regardless of the software package adopted. In this work, the term *E-Project* is introduced, meaning the electronic container that is used for storing and organizing all materials related to one project. The E-Project is described for the first time in the QDAS literature as a research genre, and theories of the literary or social science genre are applied to discussion of standards and procedures that cut across individual software packages (see also Davidson 2005a, 2005b, 2005c, 2005d; Davidson & di Gregorio, 2007; di Gregorio, 2005, 2006a, 2006b, 2007; di Gregorio & Davidson, 2007).

This new foundation (the e-project as a generic term for qualitative research projects in any QDAS package, and the notion of the e-project as a genre) serves as the basis for a new approach to research design. The approach described in *Qualitative Research Design for Software Users* (di Gregorio & Davidson, 2008) presents the notion of (1) a software shell representing the research design of a study, (2) the development of an interpretive system through disaggregation and re-contextualization of the data, and (3) thorough reliance on an interactive practice that sustains dialogue between technology and methodology. Whereas earlier QDAS writers had given greater weight to the methodological fit of the tool to the methodological perspective of the researcher, the E-Project approach assumes all tools have limitations and that tools for research are in constant flux and development. Therefore, researchers must engage in an active dialogue between methodology and technology in order to craft the appropriate fit for their work.

Other developments that characterize this period include the expanding use of QDAS in diverse disciplines and various kinds of institutions—academia, business, and other sectors. Sectors that are starting to look at the use of QDAS include market research (di Gregorio, 2008b; Rettie, Robinson, Radke, & Ye, 2007; Vince & Sweetman, 2006), law firms (Coia, 2006), research institutes, and the public sector (di Gregorio & Davidson, 2008). This expansion of QDAS use brought increasing demand for information on best methods for research design with these tools (di Gregorio, 2005; di Gregorio, 2006b; di Gregorio & Davidson, 2008). However, expansion in the market research and commercial sectors has been slow and piece-meal with suspicion of QDAS being associated with quantitative methods (Ereaut, 2002) or not understanding the benefits of its use (di Gregorio, 2008b) despite efforts to demonstrate its value (Ereaut & di Gregorio, 2002, 2003).

The increased awareness and use of QDAS during this time led inevitably to discussions about the teaching of qualitative research using QDAS (Bringer, Johnston, & Brackenridge, 2004; Davidson, 2004, 2005c; Davidson & Jacobs, 2008; Davidson, Siccama, Donohoe, Hardy-Gallagher, & Robertson, 2008; di Gregorio & Davidson, 2008; Gilbert, 1999; Jackson, 2003; Kuhn & Davidson, 2007). In 2003 and 2005, the University of Wisconsin campus was the venue for two conferences on teaching qualitative research with QSR products (Davidson, 2005b; di Gregorio 2003b). The 2003 conference resulted in a special issue of the *Qualitative Research Journal* devoted to the topic of teaching qualitative research with QSR software (*Teaching Qualitative Research With QSR Software,* 2003). Concern about the instruction of QDAS has led software developers to increas-ing training activities and developing licensing incentives for university settings as well as to developing materials specifically for trainers and teachers.

The majority of discussion about teaching with QDAS has focused on doc-toral-level work in higher education. Di Gregorio and Davidson (2008) spend considerable time discussing how QDAS can change pedagogical practices related to qualitative research instruction and advisement for the dissertation. For instance, the new transparency and portability afforded by QDAS allow advi-sors and doctoral students to engage in interpretive work in ways that were not possible before. Texts, coding systems, and the very coding itself are easily shared through projects sent as file attachments or the joint viewing of the e-project in class or supervision sessions. This has led to the need for new standards for the writing and reading of the e-project as a genre, and the need for faculty to gain fluency in this new literary form.

Issues related to scaling up QDAS use within and across institutions also began to be discussed more widely in Stage V, including issues related to the role of professional organizations in setting standards for qualitative research conducted in QDAS and the ethical issues that QDAS raises for researchers in this era of institutional review boards (Davidson & Jacobs, 2007; Davidson et al., 2008; di Gregorio & Davidson, 2008, 2009; ESRC, 2005; Office of Public Sector Information, 1998; Strike et al., 2002). See the subsequent section on ethics for a fuller discussion of this issue.

In Europe, the high point of Stage V was the CAQDAS 2007 Conference organized by the CAQDAS Networking Project to celebrate 13 years of their work in this area. This international conference drew developers and users together to discuss their use of and experiments with different forms of media and software tools. Innovative papers pointing to future developments included Dario Da Re's (2007) study on the use of video, multimedia, and the web as a new form of qualitative representation (see www.raccontiditerra.it); Parmegianni (2007) on visual sociology; and Tutt and Shaukat's (2007) presentation on MiMeG—a tool for remote collaborative video analysis (see conference materials at http://caqdas.soc.surrey.ac.uk/Resources/Caqdas07conference/caqdas-07conferenceintro.html).

In the United States, the conclusion of Stage V might well be the May 2008 "A Day in Technology in Qualitative Research," a preconference day of the Fourth International Congress of Qualitative Inquiry, where an international group of scholars came together to share perspectives on the use of technology in qualitative research. Presentations offered opportunities to explore many of the new frontiers of the field, from the integration of QDAS and geospatial concerns (Cisneros, 2008a; Kwan, 2008) and discussions of e-portfolios as a form of qualitative research (Arndt, 2008), to issues related to teaching QDAS (Davidson et al., 2008), deeper integration of QDAS across disciplines (Gilbert et al., 2008), and the application of QDAS in new liberatory ways (Lapadat, 2008), as well as discussions of directions beyond QDAS, including the use of wikis (Bhattacharya & McCullough, 2008).

As this stage of work began to come to a close, the divisions between the mainstream of qualitative research and the world of QDAS had become increasingly apparent to those in the QDAS world. Although humanistic and arts-based forms of qualitative research were proliferating in this period, it was next to impossible to find examples of qualitative research of this nature employing QDAS (Davidson, 2009; Davidson et al., 2009). New possibilities for QDAS were arising in the world of the Internet, but it was unclear how this would affect the stand-alone packages (di Gregorio, 2009, 2010).

STAGE VI: NETWORKED TOOLS TO THE FORE

A Fractured Future	Stage VI: Development of Web 2.0–networked tools to the fore: QDAS 2.0

As we enter Stage VI, a period characterized by powerful new movements within qualitative research, from autoethnography and performance ethnography to indigenous methodologies and the rise of discussion about mixed methods, QDAS use stands at an uncomfortable juncture. The concerns come from within and without—from QDAS developers and qualitative researchers; to institutions of higher education, nonprofits, and commerce; to the world of rapid Internet development.

Among many qualitative researchers, there continues to be a sense of unease with QDAS, and a lingering problem is the close association of grounded theory and QDAS (Fielding, 2008; Hesse-Biber & Crofts, 2008). For some, QDAS seems to embody the divide between scientific and humanistic or artistic approaches that qualitative researchers have struggled so hard to sort out, and QDAS is allied with the scientific side in their minds. For those who seek to conduct qualitative research in more humanistic ways, there appears to be a resistance to the transparency afforded by QDAS, and an unspoken belief that their interpretive strategies should not be put on the public chopping block in this manner (Jackson, 2009). Here, too, the fear of failing with the use of technology may be an important factor.

Some of the difficulty with adopting QDAS seems to be related to the complexity of the comprehensive software packages. Early QDAS packages were limited in functionality and had a fairly simple format with only a few menus and drop-down selections. As the programs became more powerful, they also became richer with features, and menus and drop-downs have become more deeply buried and complicated to the average user. Beginning users can easily feel overwhelmed by the choices available (Mangabeira, Lee, & Fielding, 2004).

Not surprisingly, we find that many of those using the packages do so in a very limited way and are often not aware of the features that could assist them. Some researchers have tried these packages, and lacking adequate support, failed in their attempts. Lack of technical support for these tools has been an ongoing problem since their inception. As a result, they warn off other potential users as they share experiences of their QDAS disasters. Newcomers can also be put off by the lack of an intuitive interface and, with some packages, a visually uninteresting interface.

QDAS has not become the practice of most senior researchers in the field of qualitative research, and many rising researchers still lack exposure to QDAS use in their graduate training. Technologically savvy graduate students have forged ahead using QDAS for their research, but in some cases must proceed without adequate technical support, and with advisors who cannot make sufficient sense of QDAS use. For those graduate students working with advisors with knowledge of QDAS, other faculty with whom they work may not be equally skilled. To date, there have been few exemplars of integrated QDAS use at the institutional level from which to learn (Davidson & Jacobs, 2007; Davidson et al., 2008; di Gregorio & Davidson, 2008b). Some developers are taking innovative steps to change these circumstances, such as QSR's recent Teaching Grant Award program (QSR International, 2009).

The lack of institutional support for QDAS in higher education has been a significant issue. While there are signs that QDAS support is increasing within selected institutions, overall support remains uneven within and across institutions. Support also varies depending upon the national context. The problems with building institutional capacity in QDAS are multifaceted. Until recently, universities had been slow to provide researchers with licenses for these products, technical support for their use, and acknowledgment for researchers and teachers who explore these tools. On many campuses, support for QDAS lags far behind support for basic quantitative technologies. Moreover, requests from qualitative researchers for these basic technological tools may be greeted with greater skepticism from administrators, requiring greater justifications than what quantitative researchers face making similar requests (Davidson & Jacobs, 2007; Davidson et al., 2008). As di Gregorio and Davidson (2008) report, "lacking a critical mass of users and adequate paths of knowledge distribution, users are often isolated within organizations or fields" (p. 2).

The lack of institutional support could be attributed to several issues. First, senior faculty are not advocating for it because they are less likely to be users. Newer faculty and graduate students, who are users, may lack the institutional clout to acquire and implement QDAS use. Second, information technology departments have a significant say in technology purchases despite the fact that they may have limited knowledge about higher education curricular needs. Given their technical backgrounds, it may be that quantitative tools have more sway with them than qualitative research tools. Third, the entry point for QDAS into an institution is usually an individual faculty member, so there may be many hives of QDAS activity within an institution that are not aware of each other's activities. In other words, QDAS implementation does not fall under any unified policy direction of the institution.

Institutional support for QDAS differs significantly based upon the national context. The UK has been at the forefront in providing national leadership for the development of digital capacity for qualitative researchers. The ESRC National Centre for Research Methods and the Joint Information Systems Committee (JISC) have provided leadership and resources for the development of qualitative research methodology in many ways, including the provision of training and the development of e-resources.

At the same time that many universities have proven resistant to QDAS, there is significant expansion of the use of QDAS in governmental, commercial, and other nonprofit settings (di Gregorio, 2006b; di Gregorio & Davidson, 2008). These include such diverse fields as health, criminal justice, law, and social policy. Virtually every field in which unstructured data are present, and there is the need for fine-grained studies of small pockets of such data, is discovering that QDAS could help ease the burden. Many of these studies fall into the arena of evaluation or evaluation-like research, with little use being made of the capacity of QDAS to support less scientific and more humanistic forms of qualitative research. In some cases, new converts to QDAS are coming without training or experience in qualitative research and, lacking other reference points, develop their QDAS use with only quantitative research training as background. Such studies only exacerbate some qualitative researchers' beliefs that QDAS is really quantitative research in disguise. And, indeed, discussions regarding the possibilities of using computer capacities to integrate qualitative and quantitative data have also been on the rise (Fielding, 2008; Nasukawa, 2006).

QDAS developers are closely attuned to the market possibilities for their wares. In addition to expanding disciplinary markets, they are also looking to expand language markets as they make their tools available in different language formats. Developers have also expanded their training and educational forces, and developed new and attractive licensing strategies. Each new version of the software packages demonstrates attentiveness to user demands, from better tools for visualization, geospatial work, and multiple media modalities to the capacity for greater collaboration and teamwork and integration of quantitative data.

To date, there has been little discussion among academic and nonacademic users of these tools. Thus, we know little about the ways these different audiences are using these tools, the unique challenges they have encountered, or the standards for use that are developing in these different arenas. However, the Merlien Institute, an independent organization founded in 2006, offers a unique platform for connecting various communities interested in qualitative research and the use of QDAS through its mini-conferences on these topics (http://merlien .org/).

THE CHALLENGE OF THE INTERNET

At the same moment that QDAS has come to this pass, qualitative researchers have encountered another challenge. With the rapid growth of the Internet, we are faced with an avalanche of unstructured data—words, images, video, and even sensory data. The rise of Web 2.0 applications, such as YouTube, Flickr, Twitter, and Facebook, allows anyone with access to the Internet to upload their own data—be it photos, video, or chat—to share with others, to comment, and to organize.

These opportunities come paired with their own set of challenges for qualitative researchers: How can we make best use of this information? What are the tools of the future for qualitative researchers? What are the ethical guidelines for qualitative research in QDAS 2.0? How can we ensure the security of data in online environments?

Software developers with no relationship to the world of qualitative research and its rich traditions in the arena of interpretation of unstructured data have created tools that will help users to organize and analyze unstructured information in this virtual world. In so doing, they must ask and answer the same kinds of questions that have long been discussed among qualitative researchers: How do we deal with unstructured data of many formats? How does one best organize, search, sort, pattern, and manipulate this kind of data? An example of the most recent innovations at the time of this writing is the development of Web 3.0—moving from a web of documents to a web of data (Berners-Lee, 2009).

A feature of this amazing amount of unstructured data is that it is available everywhere to just about anyone. Not only is the data readily available in the forms of texts, images, and video, but also the tools and services with which one can work with the data. There has been a huge growth in technologies to decipher and search among these forms of unstructured data. Digital text searches are essential in today's world, and one can also search sound and visual images (di Gregorio, 2010).

It is becoming increasingly apparent that many kinds of people want to research and work with various kinds of unstructured texts (Greif, 2009). The things they do to the texts they examine (search, tag, index, annotate, memo, interpret, represent) bear close resemblance to the things qualitative researchers have long done to unstructured data. These ordinary people are actively engaged as indigenous qualitative researchers in the virtual world. Examples of these indigenous researchers include teenagers who tag and organize YouTube videos and crafters of all sorts engaging in their community of practice (di Gregorio, 2009, 2010). They use a range of tools, pulled off the web, to achieve their personal research goals. The analysis of this phenomenon of tagging items on the

Internet and the development of *folksonomies,* a user-created, bottom-up categorical structure development with an emergent thesaurus (Vander Wal, 2007), has been dominated by those in library science, information architecture, and new media (di Gregorio, 2008a).

Unlike the restricted world of QDAS, the developers of these new QDAS-like Web 2.0 tools represent a broad cross-section of the information community. There are the major computer companies that survived the shift into the Internet age, such as Microsoft, IBM, Xerox, and Apple, all of which are conducting important research leading to new tool possibilities. There are also web-based companies that emerged from the Web 2.0 revolution, including such well-known names as Google, Amazon, and Apple iTunes, who have also made important contributions to the possibilities of QDAS-like tools. The new forms of the telephone/Internet provider companies are also serious contenders. AT&T, Verizon, Apple—creator of the iPhone—and Telenor are a few of the names in this marketplace. Governmental agencies have also played a role in the development of new QDAS-like tools. In the UK, the Joint Information Systems Committee and the Economic and Social Research Council have been particularly active in this area with the funding of projects that will develop new digital tools and training available to qualitative researchers. Finally, there are thousands of independent Web 2.0 developers scattered across the globe that are working on their own to create new products that can do the kinds of things that QDAS has done. They are so prolific that even the most tuned-in leaders in the field complain that it is hard to keep abreast of these developments (Greif, 2009). An example of this work can be found in the emergence of an application for iPhone use designed specifically for qualitative market researchers—EverydayLives (www.everydaylives.com)—which allows the researcher to document activities in the field, tagging or coding the text, audio, or visual records and sharing them with researchers in other locations from a mobile (cell) phone.

For qualitative researchers, an important portal to the world of these new tools has been DiRT (the Digital Research Tools wiki), which provides a comprehensive list of QDAS and Web 2.0 research tools (http://digitalresearchtools .pbworks.com). There are a few promising net-based tools emerging that appear to have capabilities very close to QDAS. A good example of this development is A.nnotate, a tool created by developers in the UK, with financial support from the Scottish government, that allows researchers to annotate or tag text and visual data, and index and organize these tags. The annotations can be viewed and worked upon by collaborative groups (A.nnotate.com).

Qualitative researchers have also begun to experiment with new net-based tools that have special affinity with the ways qualitative researchers work. Wikis are very important in this category. Dicks and Mason (2008) experimented with qualitative hyperlinking in their Ethnographic Hypermedia Environment project. They used StorySpace to do this but see wikis as a way to turn this kind of an analysis into an interactive endeavor, "which allows informants and participants, other academics and indeed the general public to make contributions, allowing the work to grow and develop organically over time" (p. 584). Melanie Hundley (2009a) of Vanderbilt University has used wikis in qualitative research courses as a collective e-project site to house multimodal data collected by students and has explored the ways the hypertext capacities of a wiki support the notion of "data as event." Hundley (2009b) has also used a website for her autoethnography—*The Bard on the Digital Porch*—which invites the reader to decide how to traverse the hyperlinks she constructed so that the reader can participate in the co-construction of the interpretation of meaning. Kakali Bhattacharya (2009) has also explored the possibilities of wikis for qualitative research teaching; while more oriented toward the use of wikis for theoretical study, her work offers possibilities for thinking about wiki's as a collaborative tool for qualitative research in general. Di Gregorio has developed an online course on qualitative analysis based in a Wetpaint wiki, which incorporates videos, collaborative work on analysis, a discussion board, and a chat area (http://qdas01.wetpaint.com). Again, while focused on teaching, it illustrates how researchers can reflect and share insights on each other's work. Bennett (2008) has produced a YouTube video on how to use wikis for qualitative analysis (www.youtube.com/watch?v=JwfceBwNmuk&feature=related). We (Davidson and di Gregorio) wrote this chapter in a PBWorks wiki—where we constructed collaboratively the initial outline of the chapter, created a resource section where we uploaded documents and links to references, and used the comments feature to communicate and keep a record of our developing thinking. We saw strong parallels between the ways we use QDAS e-projects and the process of collaborative writing in the wiki, and for this reason we believe wikis are very worthy of closer study by qualitative researchers concerned with the development of digital tools for qualitative research analysis.

Di Gregorio (2010) has related QDAS tools to existing Web 2.0 tools, as exemplified in Table 15.2. As can be seen in the table, there are equivalent Web 2.0 tools for the core QDAS tools. Unsurprisingly, Web 2.0 tools are stronger with hyperlinking, visualizing, and collaborating, while QDAS tools are stronger in fine coding and sophisticated searching. However, as there are considerable investments in Web 2.0 tools from large companies such as Google, IBM, and Microsoft, the capabilities of Web 2.0 tools in fine coding and searching could soon surpass the QDAS tools.

Table 15.2   Comparison of Web 2.0 and QDAS tools

	Web 2.0	**QDAS**
Organizing	Tagging	Coding
	Grouping	Sets, families
	Hyperlinking	Hyperlinking
Reflective tools	Blogging	Memoing
	Annotating	Annotating
	Mapping	Mapping
Exploring tools	Visualizing	Model, map, network
	Searching	Text search, coding search
Integrating tools	Blogging with hyperlinks	Memoing with hyperlinks
	Collaborating through wikis	Merging projects

In the United Kingdom, as mentioned earlier, a strong push for development of research tools has come from JISC, the ESRC and their associated National Centre for E-Social Science (NCeSS), as well as the National Centre for Research Methods (NCRM). Grants from the NCRM have funded Qualitative Innovations in CAQDAS (QUIC), the University of Surrey's work on expanding qualitative research computing into the areas of mixed methods, visualization and geospatialization, and large-scale collaboration (http://caqdas.soc.surrey.ac.uk/QUIC/quicheader.html). In addition, through QUIC, Surrey will expand their training program to encompass online training including on interactive protocols and software exemplars. NCeSS funded the development of MiMeg, a collaborative video analysis tool (www.ncess.ac.uk/tools/mimeg/) and DRS, a tool to integrate multimodal data (audio and visual records) with GPS and sensory probe data, which is billed as the "next-generation CAQDAS" (http://caqdas.soc .surrey.ac.uk/PDF/DRSdistinguishingfeatures.pdf). NCeSS was closed in 2009, and its key work is being carried forward by the Manchester eResearch Centre (MeRC) (www.merc.ac.uk/)

These new developments emerging at the intersection between QDAS and the Internet raise important issues for qualitative researchers as they seek out digital tools that will be beneficial to their work.

MOVING FROM QDAS TO QDAS 2.0

The next movement in the evolution of technology in qualitative research will include both QDAS and QDAS-like tools available on the Internet. For this reason, we would like to offer the term *QDAS 2.0* to refer to this hybrid state of affairs that will probably persist for some time. If this new movement is to successfully integrate QDAS 2.0 with the work of qualitative researchers, we need to develop tools that meet basic user requirements, create a shared vision of the qualitative analysis process that will allow us to make the best use of QDAS 2.0, and to engage in conversation with the new field of developers.

Basic Requirements

Both older tools (QDAS) and newer tools (QDAS 2.0) will have to meet evolving user standards. In addition to meeting the standards for one or more components of QDAS in the realm of data organization and analysis, it will be essential that these new tools

- Possess an intuitive and visually attractive interface;
- Are easily accessible;
- Have powerful, intuitive, and contextualized search tools;
- Are easily combined to create new user-specialized tools;
- Provide opportunities for visualization and spatialization;
- Offer ease of integration with quantification tools; and
- Offer strong functionality for collaborative work.

Other issues that QDAS 2.0 must grapple with as it moves forward are the new challenges to privacy and ethics that web-based tools raise—for instance, housing data on a third-party server controlled by a commercial interest (see discussion below).

CREATING A SHARED VISION OF THE QUALITATIVE ANALYSIS PROCESS

In order to mend the rift between qualitative research and QDAS 2.0, we feel it is necessary to re-present the critical discussion that those engaged in QDAS

2.0 have been making about the nature of QDAS 2.0 in relationship to the nature of the qualitative analysis process. In her landmark book on QDAS, Tesch (1990) concluded that while there are many brands of software programs, they provide a similar range of features for the conduct of qualitative research analysis. In other words, qualitative analysis processes, regardless of the methodological approach of the researcher, must basically do a range of similar things. While they may vary in particulars, the overall range of things one does in analysis is similar across methodological approaches. Thus, QDAS is a generic tool tailored to do these basic tasks that must occur in qualitative research analysis.

T. Richards and Richards (1994) support this conclusion when they point to the importance of the researcher's skills, perspectives, and ability to work with the tools. Morse and Richards (2002) add to this discussion, emphasizing the importance of the researcher's epistemological stance in shaping a research project. They demonstrate how different questions dictate different approaches, but also how analysis processes are composed of a similar range of possibilities. Lewins and Silver (2007) are essentially making the same point; that is, the research process is composed of a range of common tasks, and QDAS are generic tools designed to support the researcher to do these tasks. Hesse-Biber and Crofts (2008), in a similar vein, discuss the commonalities of the qualitative research process as the backdrop to understanding the generic nature of QDAS packages. Fielding (2008) also makes the point that these software packages provide generic support that works with the range of qualitative research methodologies, emphasizing that users have to make the decisions about what the computer will be asked to do. Di Gregorio and Davidson (2008) stipulate the importance of ongoing dialogue between technology and methodology. There is always, we believe, a dialectic between researcher and technology, regardless of whether the technology is a software program or a note card. It is the researcher, not the technology, that decides the question that will guide the research and how it will be approached, as well as deciding critical methodological stances toward gender, power, and voice. This point is similar to the stand taken by L. Richards (2005).

Many of the arguments we have heard made against the use of technology (it imposes unnecessary hierarchy, it is variable dependent, it leads to artificial understanding, it presumes an objective observer, etc.) are arguments about issues that are in the realm or control of the researcher and are not a function of the technology itself. These are arguments that could be applied to many technologies employed by qualitative researchers, not just those of the digital sort.

Following Tesch's (1990) lead, we would describe qualitative analysis as distinct because of the nature of the process (iterative, flexible, and reflexive), the characteristic tasks (disaggregation and reaggregation driven by the search for patterns and comparison of categories), and the role of the researcher (responsible for integrating methodology and substance).

EXPANDING THE CONVERSATION: ADDRESSING ETHICAL CONCERNS

QDAS has, until recently, flown under the radar of ethical discussions in qualitative research. QDAS was considered simply a place in the computer where the data was stored, and, for that reason was no more or less problematic than any kind of electronic data stored on a stand-alone computer. Similar restrictions were applied to QDAS as to documents in a word processing software, that is, ethical bodies sought to make sure that adequate safeguards of privacy and security were in place so that information would not be inadvertently released or inappropriately available to prying eyes.

Because of software restrictions, e-projects have not been stored on the Internet. However, this restriction is on the verge of change as increasing numbers of users need to be able to work with data in an Internet environment, as opposed to a stand-alone computer environment. IRBs are also increasingly sophisticated about the technological issues that can infringe on the privacy of research participants, and they will need to be assured that the new cycle of digital tools can be used in a way that will protect the safety of human subjects. While these discussions will be challenging, we have no doubt that these issues are solvable.

A greater ethical dilemma, however, looms on the horizon for qualitative researchers working with QDAS 2.0. In regard to Internet research ethics, Bassett and O'Riordan (2002) argue that

> the use of spatial metaphors in descriptions of the Internet has shaped the adoption of the human subjects research model. Whilst this model is appropriate in some areas of Internet research such as email communication, we feel that researchers, when navigating the complex terrain of Internet research ethics, need also to consider the Internet as cultural production of texts. (p. 233)

In this volume, Gatson (Chapter 8) discusses the ethical complexities facing Internet researchers and points to the guidelines of the Association of Internet Researchers as a starting point for designing policies (http://aoir.org).

Buchanan, Delap, and Mason (2010) identify seven issues that fuel concern regarding ethics with research and new digital technologies. These are "malleability of technology; black box nature of systems; increasing complexity of systems; potential scope and magnitude of impact; difficulty of anticipating consequences; potential irreversibility; [and] rapid pace of technical development . . . lack of precedents" (n.p.).

These challenges have led, in some cases, to creative responses. As an example, researchers working on the VIBE (Virtual Information Behavior Environments) project at the University of Washington Information School have developed a "consent bot, named Harvey, to allow them to gain consent from participants in Second Life where they are conducting research" (Lin, Eisenberg, & Marino, 2010, n.p.).

The ethical dilemmas facing researchers working with QDAS 2.0 cannot be underestimated. This issue will require strong attention from qualitative researchers and other information technology specialists.

Conclusion

QDAS 2.0 offers spectacular possibilities to qualitative researchers. From their inception as simple text-retrieval programs to their current state as comprehensive stand-alone packages and what is emerging—Web 2.0 tools with various capacities—they have been a controversial subject among qualitative researchers. As we move more deeply into the digital age, their use, which was once a private choice, will become a necessity.

We recognize that there is strong resistance to the notion that elements of analysis are common among diverse methodological approaches to qualitative research. This resistance is a residue, we believe, of the tough battles of legitimacy qualitative researchers fought to gain a position in academic and other circles. It is time, however, to put this one to rest. As the pressure for participation in the digital world increases, it is critical that qualitative researchers get beyond these artificial and self-imposed barriers they have erected and get on with more important tasks.

The possibilities and development of QDAS 2.0 will depend in large part upon the capacity of qualitative researchers to enter discussions about QDAS and Web 2.0. It will require our field to initiate or join conversations taking place, not only among academic colleagues and QDAS developers, but also with the wider world of Internet entrepreneurs, from the IBMs and Amazons of the world to the range of small, savvy developers creating exciting new tools for use with fine-grained analysis of unstructured data in all its forms.

References

Anderson, P. (2007, February). What is Web 2.0? Ideas, technologies and implications for education. *JISC Technology and Standards Watch.* Available at: http://www.jisc.ac.uk/publications/reports/2007/twweb2.aspx

Arndt, A. (2008, May). *Artifacts and assemblages: Electronic portfolios in educational research.* Paper presented at "A Day in Technology in Qualitative Research," a preconference day of the Fourth International Congress on Qualitative Inquiry, University of Illinois, Urbana-Champaign.

Bassett, E., & O'Riordan, K. (2002). Ethics of Internet research: Contesting the human subjects research model. *Ethics and Information Technology, 4*(3), 233–247.

Bazeley, P. (2007). *Qualitative data analysis with NVivo.* Thousand Oaks, CA: Sage.

Bazeley, P., & Richards, L. (2000). *The NVivo qualitative project book.* Thousand Oaks, CA: Sage.

Bennett, N. (2008, April 5). *Using wikis to conduct qualitative research* [YouTube video], Available at http://www.youtube.com/watch?v=JwfceBwNmuk

Berners-Lee, T. (2009, March 13). The next web of open, linked data [YouTube video]. Available at http://www.youtube.com/watch?v=OM6XIICm_qo

Bhattacharya, K. (2009). *Portal to three wiki spaces developed by K. Battacharya's qualitative research classes.* Available at http://kakali.org/memphiswebsite/kakaliorg1/community.html

Bhattacharya, K., & McCullough, A. (2008, May). *De/colonizing democratic digital learning environments: Carving a space for wiki-ology in qualitative inquiry.* Paper presented at "A Day in Technology in Qualitative Research," a preconference day of the Fourth International Congress on Qualitative Inquiry, University of Illinois, Urbana-Champaign.

Bringer, J., Johnston, L., & Brackenridge, C. (2004). Maximizing transparency in a doctoral thesis: The complexities of writing about the use of QSR*NVIVO within a grounded theory study. *Qualitative Research, 4*(2), 247–265.

Bryant, A., & Charmaz, K. (2010). *The SAGE handbook of grounded theory.* Thousand Oaks, CA: Sage.

Buchanan, E., Delap, A., & Mason, R. (2010, January). *Ethical research and design in cyberspace.* Paper presented at the 43rd Hawaii International Conference on Systems Science, Koloa.

Cisneros, C. (2008a, May). *Emergent approaches on linking qualitative software to qualitative geography.* Paper presented at "A Day in Technology in Qualitative Research," a preconference day of the Fourth International Congress on Qualitative Inquiry, University of Illinois, Urbana-Champaign.

Cisneros, C. (2008b). On the roots of qualitative research. In J. Zelger, M. Raich, & P. Schober (Eds.), *Gabek III: Organisationen und ihre Wissensnetze* (pp. 53–75). Innsbruck, Austria: StudienVerlag.

Cisneros, C. (2009, May). *Qualitative data analysis software: Challenges from the periphery.* Paper presented as part of a panel titled Humanistic Issues Regarding Qualitative Data Analysis Software (QDAS): Teaching, Learning, and the Representation of Data in a Digital Age, at the Fifth International Congress on Qualitative Inquiry, University of Illinois, Urbana-Champaign.

Coffey, A., Holbrook, B., & Atkinson, P. (1996). Qualitative data analysis: Technologies and representations. *Sociological Research Online, 1*(1). Available at http://www.socresonline.org.uk/1/1/4.html

Coia, P. (2006, June). How a global law firm works with NVivo 7. *Nsight, 29.*

Da Re, D. (2007, April 18–20). *Research results showed by a video and by a website.* Paper presented at the CAQDAS 2007 Conference: Advances in Qualitative Computing, Royal Holloway, University of London, Egham, UK. (website for the project discussed in this paper is http://www.raccontiditerra.it/)

Davidson, J. (2004, September 1–3). *Grading NVivo: Making the shift from training to teaching with software for qualitative data analysis.* Paper presented at the Fifth International Conference on Strategies in Qualitative Research: Using QSR Nivo and NUD*IST, University of Durham, UK.

Davidson, J. (2005a, April). *Genre and qualitative research software: The role of "the project" in the post-electronic world of qualitative research.* Paper presented at the American Educational Research Association Annual Meeting, Montreal, Quebec, Canada.

Davidson, J. (2005b, April). *Learning to "read" NVivo projects: Implications for teaching qualitative research.* Paper presented at the Second Teaching Qualitative Research Using QSR Products Conference, University of Wisconsin, Madison.

Davidson, J. (2005c, Spring). Learning to think as a teacher within the NVivo container. *QSR Newsletter.*

Davidson, J. (2005d, April). *Reading "the project": Qualitative research software and the issue of genre in qualitative research.* Paper presented at the First International Congress of Qualitative Inquiry, University of Illinois, Urbana-Champaign.

Davidson, J. (2009, May). *Autoethnography/self-study/arts-based research/qualitative data analysis software: Mixing, shaking, and recombining qualitative research tools in the act of recreating oneself as qualitative researcher, instructor, and learner.* Paper presented at the Fifth International Congress on Qualitative Inquiry, University of Illinois, Urbana-Champaign.

Davidson, J., & di Gregorio S. (2007, May). *Research design in qualitative research software.* Paper presented at the Third International Congress on Qualitative Inquiry, University of Illinois, Urbana-Champaign.

Davidson, J., Donohoe, K., Tello, S. Christensen, L., Steingisser, G., & Varoudakis, C. (2009, May). *Initiating qualitative inquiry: Report on an experiment with a cluster of powerful tools—autoethnography, arts-based research, and qualitative data analysis software.* Poster session presented at the Fifth International Congress on Qualitative Inquiry, University of Illinois, Urbana-Champaign.

Davidson, J., & Jacobs, C. (2007, May). *The qualitative research network: Working cross-campus to support qualitative researchers at the University of Massachusetts-Lowell.* Paper presented as part of a panel titled Institutionalizing Qualitative Research: Emerging Models, at the Third International Congress on Qualitative Inquiry, University of Illinois, Urbana-Champaign.

Davidson, J., & Jacobs, C. (2008). The implications of qualitative research software for doctoral work: Considering the individual and institutional context. *Qualitative Research Journal, 8*(2), 72–80.

Davidson, J., Siccama, C., Donohoe, K., Hardy-Gallagher, S., & Robertson, S. (2008, May). *Teaching qualitative data analysis software (QDAS) in a virtual environment: Team curriculum development of an NVivo training workshop.* Paper presented at the Fourth International Congress on Qualitative Inquiry, University of Illinois, Urbana-Champaign.

A Day in Technology in Qualitative Research. (2008, May 17–21). Preconference day at the Fourth International Congress on Qualitative Inquiry, University of Illinois, Urbana-Champaign.

Denzin, N. K., & Lincoln, Y. S. (2003). Introduction: The discipline and practice of qualitative research. In N. K. Denzin & Y. S. Lincoln (Eds.), *The landscape of qualitative research* (2nd ed., pp. 1–46). Thousand Oaks, CA: Sage.

Denzin, N. K., & Lincoln, Y. S. (2008). Introduction: The discipline and practice of qualitative research. In N. K. Denzin & Y. S. Lincoln (Eds.), *The landscape of qualitative research* (3rd ed., pp. 1–44). Thousand Oaks, CA: Sage.

Dicks, B., & Mason, B. (2008). Hypermedia methods for qualitative research. In S. Hesse-Biber & P. Leavy (Eds.), *Handbook of emergent methods* (pp. 601–612). New York: Guilford Press.

di Gregorio, S. (2000, September 29–30). *Using NVivo for your literature review.* Paper presented at the Strategies in Qualitative Research: Issues and Results From Analysis Using QSR NVivo and NUD*IST conference, Institute of Education, London.

di Gregorio, S. (2001, November). Teamwork using QSR N5 software: An example from a large-scale national evaluation project. *NSight Newsletter.*

di Gregorio, S. (2003a, May 8–9). *Analysis as cycling: Shifting between coding and memoing in using qualitative software.* Paper presented at the Strategies in Qualitative Research: Methodological Issues and Practices Using QSR NVivo and NUD*IST conference, Institute of Education, London.

di Gregorio, S. (2003b). Teaching grounded theory with QSR NVivo [Special issue]. *Qualitative Research Journal,* 79–95. Available at http://www.latrobe.edu.au/aqr

di Gregorio, S. (2005, May 11–13). *Software tools to support qualitative analysis and reporting.* Paper presented at the Business Intelligence Group Conference, The New B2B: A Widening Horizon, Chepstow, UK.

di Gregorio, S. (2006a, June). The CMS Cameron McKenna Project—How it looks in NVivo 7. *Nsight, 29.*

di Gregorio, S. (2006b, September 13–15). *Research design issues for software users.* Paper presented at the Seventh International Strategies in Qualitative Research Conference, University of Durham, UK.

di Gregorio, S. (2007). Qualitative Analysesoftware. In R. Buber & H. Holzmuller (Eds.), *Qualitative Marktforschung: Konzpete, Methoden, Analysen.* Wiesbaden, Germany: Gabler.

di Gregorio, S. (2008a). *Folksonomies: A tool to learn from others?* [Online wiki]. Available at http://folksonomiesanddelicious.pbworks.com/

di Gregorio, S. (2008b, Fall). Is technophobia holding back advances in the analysis of qualitative data? *QRCA Views, 7,* 1.

di Gregorio, S. (2009, June 4–5). *Qualitative analysis and Web 2.0.* Paper presented at the Second International Workshop on Computer-Aided Qualitative Research, Utrecht, The Netherlands.

di Gregorio, S. (2010, January 5–8). *Using Web 2.0 tools for qualitative analysis: An exploration. Proceedings of the 43rd Annual Hawaii International Conference on System Sciences (CD-ROM).* Washington, DC: IEEE Computer Society Press.

di Gregorio, S., & Davidson, J. (2007, February 13). *Research design, units of analysis and software supporting qualitative analysis.* Paper presented at the CAQDAS 2007 Conference: Advances in Qualitative Computing, Royal Holloway, University of London, Egham, UK.

di Gregorio, S., & Davidson, J. (2008). *Qualitative research design for software users.* London: Open University Press/McGraw-Hill.

di Gregorio, S., & Davidson, J. (2009, May 20–23). *Research design and ethical issues when working within an e-project.* Paper presented at the Fifth International Congress of Qualitative Inquiry at the University of Illinois, Urbana-Champaign.

Economic and Social Research Council. (2005). *Research ethics framework.* Available at http://www.esrcsocietytoday.ac.uk/ESRCInfoCentre/opportunities/research_ethics_framework

Economic and Social Research Council. (n.d.). *Our research.* Available at http://www.esrcsocietytoday.ac.uk/ESRCInfoCentre/research

Ereaut, G. (2002). *Analysis and interpretation in qualitative market research.* London: Sage.

Ereaut, G., & di Gregorio, S. (2002, June). *Qualitative data mining.* Presentation at Association for Qualitative Research Conference, London.

Ereaut, G., & di Gregorio, S. (2003, June 6). *Can computers help analyse qualitative data?* Presentation at Association for Qualitative Research Conference, London.

Fielding, N. (2008). The role of computer-assisted qualitative data analysis: Impact on emergent methods in qualitative research. In S. Hesse-Biber & P. Leavy (Eds.), *Handbook of emergent methods* (pp. 675–695). New York: Guilford Press.

Fielding, N., & Lee, R. (1991). *Using computers in qualitative research.* London: Sage.

Fielding, N., & Lee, R. (1998). *Computer analysis and qualitative research.* Thousand Oaks, CA: Sage.

Fielding, N., & Lee, R. (2007, April 18–20). *Honouring the past, scoping the future.* Plenary paper presented at CAQDAS 07: Advances in Qualitative Computing Conference, Royal Holloway, University of London, Egham, UK.

Gibbs, G. (2002). *Qualitative data analysis: Explorations with NVivo.* Buckingham, UK: Open University Press.

Gibbs, G. (2004, September 1–3). *Narrative analysis and NVivo.* Paper presented at the Fifth International Strategies in Qualitative Research Conference, University of Durham, UK.

Gilbert, L. (1999). *Reflections of qualitative researchers on the uses of qualitative data analysis software: An activity theory perspective.* Doctoral dissertation, University of Georgia: Athens, GA.

Gilbert, L., Boudreau, M., Coverdill, J., Freeman, M., Harklau, S. L., Joseph, C., et al. (2008, May). *Faculty learning community: Experiences with qualitative data analysis software.* Paper presented at "A Day in Technology in Qualitative Research," a pre-conference day of the Fourth International Congress on Qualitative Inquiry, University of Illinois, Urbana-Champaign.

Gilbert, L., & di Gregorio, S. (2004, September 1–3). *Team research with QDA software: Promises and pitfalls.* Paper presented at the Fifth International Strategies in Qualitative Research Conference, University of Durham, UK.

Glaser, B., & Strauss, A. (1967). *The discovery of grounded theory.* Chicago: Aldine.

Greif, I. (2009). *Web 2.0 Expo NY: Irene Greif (IBM), what ManyEyes knows* [YouTube video]. Available at http://www.youtube.com/watch?v=nXSOM7WUNaU

Hahn, C. (2008). *Doing qualitative research using your computer: A practical guide.* Thousand Oaks, CA: Sage.

Hayles, N. K. (1999). *How we became posthuman: Virtual bodies in cybernetics, literature, and informatics.* Chicago: University of Chicago Press.

Hesse-Biber, S., & Crofts, C. (2008). User-centered perspectives on qualitative data analysis software: Emergent technologies and future trends. In S. Hesse-Biber & P. Leavy (Eds.), *Handbook of emergent methods* (pp. 655–674). New York: Guilford Press.

Hesse-Biber, S. N., & Leavy, P. (2007). *The practice of qualitative research.* Thousand Oaks, CA: Sage.

Hine, C. (2008). Internet research as emergent practice. In S. Hesse-Biber & P. Leavy (Eds.), *Handbook of emergent methods* (pp. 525–541). New York: Guilford Press.

Hundley, M. (2009a, May). *Data as event.* Paper presented at the Fifth International Congress on Qualitative Inquiry, University of Illinois, Urbana-Champaign.

Hundley, M. (2009b, May). *Gilding the lily: Creating the Bard on the digital porch.* Paper presented at the Fifth International Congress on Qualitative Inquiry, University of Illinois, Urbana-Champaign.

Jackson, K. (2003). Blending technology and methodology: A shift toward creative instruction of qualitative methods with NVivo [Special issue]. *Qualitative Research Journal, 15.*

Jackson, K. (2009, May 20–23). *Troubling transparency: Qualitative data analysis software and the problems of representation.* Paper presented at the Fifth International Congress of Qualitative Inquiry, University of Illinois, Urbana-Champaign.

Kaczynski, D., & Miller, E. (2004, September 1–3). *Evaluation team design considerations using NVivo.* Paper presented at the Fifth International Strategies in Qualitative Research Conference, University of Durham, UK.

Kelle, U. (1995). Introduction: An overview of computer-aided methods in qualitative research. In U. Kelle (Ed.), *Computer-aided qualitative data analysis: Theory, methods and practice* (pp. 1–17). London: Sage.

Kelle, U. (1997). Theory building in qualitative research and computer programs for the management of textual data. *Sociological Research Online, 2*(2).

Kelly, K. (2008). One dead media. *The Technium Blog.* Available at http://www.kk.org/thetechnium/archives/2008/06/one_dead_media.php

Kuhn, S., & Davidson, J. (2007). Thinking with things, teaching with things: Enhancing student learning in qualitative research through reflective use of things. *Qualitative Research Journal. 7*(2), 63–75.

Kwan, M. (2008, May 17–21). *Geo-narrative: Extending Geographic Information Systems for narrative analysis in qualitative research.* Keynote presentation at "A Day in Technology in Qualitative Research," a preconference day of the Fourth International Congress on Qualitative Inquiry, University of Illinois, Urbana-Champaign.

Lapadat, J. (2008, May). *Liberatory technologies: Using multimodal literacies to connect, reframe, and build communities from the bottom up.* Paper presented at "A Day in Technology in Qualitative Research," a preconference day of the Fourth International Congress on Qualitative Inquiry, University of Illinois, Urbana-Champaign.

Layder, D. (1993). *New strategies in social research.* Cambridge, UK: Polity Press.

Lee, R., & Fielding, N. (1996). Qualitative data analysis: Representations of a technology: A comment on Coffey, Holbrook, and Atkinson. *Sociological Research Online, 1*(4).

Lewins, A., & Silver, C. (2007). *Using software in qualitative research: A step-by-step guide.* Thousand Oaks, CA: Sage.

Lin, P., Eisenberg, M., & Marino, J. (2010). *"Hi! I'm Harvey, a consent bot": How automating the consent process in SL addresses challenges of research online.* Poster session at the February 2010 iConference, University of Illinois, Urbana-Champaign.

Mangabeira, W., Lee, R. M., & Fielding, N. G. (2004). Computers and qualitative research: Adoption, use, and representation. *Social Science Computer Review, 22,* 167.

Miles, M., & Weitzman, E. (1994). Appendix: Choosing computer programs for qualitative data analysis. In M. B. Miles & M. A. Huberman (Eds.), *Qualitative data analysis* (2nd ed., pp. 311–317). Thousand Oaks, CA: Sage.

Morse, J. M., & Richards, L. (2002). *Readme first for a user's guide to qualitative methods.* Thousand Oaks, CA: Sage.

Nasukawa, T. (2006). *TAKMI (text analysis and knowledge mining) and sentiment analysis, IBM research, Tokyo Research Laboratory.* Paper presented at agenda-setting workshop, Bridging Quantitative and Qualitative Methods for Social Science Using Text Mining Techniques, at National Centre for e-Social Science, Manchester, UK.

Office of Public Sector Information. (1998). *Data Protections Act of 1998.* London: Her Majesty's Stationery Office.

Parmeggiani, P. (2007, April 18–20). *Using computer-assisted qualitative data analysis software for visual sociology.* Paper presented at the CAQDAS 2007 Conference: Advances in Qualitative Computing, Royal Holloway, University of London, Egham, UK.

QSR International. (2009, August 12). *What's new? Recipients of NVivo teaching grants announced.* Available at http://www.qsrinternational.com/news_whats-new_detail .aspx?view=168

Rettie, R., Robinson, H., Radke, A., & Ye, X. (2007, April 18–20). *The use of CAQDAS in the UK market research industry.* Paper presented at the CAQDAS 2007 Conference—Advances in Qualitative Computing, Royal Holloway, University of London, Egham, UK.

Richards, L. (1999). *Using NVivo in qualitative research.* Victoria, Australia: Qualitative Solutions and Research.

Richards, L. (2004, September 1–3). *Validity and reliability? Yes! Doing it in software.* Paper presented at the Fifth International Conference on Strategies in Qualitative Research: Using QSR NVivo and NUD*IST, University of Durham, UK.

Richards, L. (2005). *Handling qualitative data.* Thousand Oaks, CA: Sage.

Richards, L. (2006, September 13–15). *Farewell to the Lone Ranger? What happened to qualitative=small?* Paper presented at the Sixth International Strategies in Qualitative Research Conference, University of Durham, UK.

Richards, T. (2004, September 1–3). *Not just a pretty node system: What node hierarchies are really all about.* Paper presented at the Fifth International Conference on Strategies in Qualitative Research: Using QSR NVivo and NUD*IST, University of Durham, UK.

Richards, T., & Richards, L. (1994). Using computers in qualitative research. In N. K. Denzin & Y. S. Lincoln (Eds.), *Handbook of qualitative research* (pp. 445–462). Thousand Oaks, CA: Sage.

Richter, D., & Clary, L. (2004, September 1–3). *Using NVivo in the analysis of data from a site visit program.* Paper presented at the Fifth International Strategies in Qualitative Research Conference, University of Durham, UK.

Ritchie, J., & Lewis, J. (2003). *Qualitative research practice: A guide for social science students and researchers.* London: Sage.

Seidel, J. (1998). *Qualitative data analysis.* Available at http://www.qualisresearch.com (originally published as Qualitative data analysis, in *The Ethnograph v5.0: A Users Guide,* Appendix E, 1998, Colorado Springs, CO: Qualis Research)

Silver, C. (2009). *Choosing the right software for your research study: An overview of leading CAQDAS packages.* Paper presented at the 2009 Computer Assisted Qualitative Research Conference, Utrecht, The Netherlands.

Strauss, A., & Corbin, J. (1990). *Basics of qualitative research: Grounded theory procedures and techniques.* Newbury Park, CA: Sage.

Strike, K., Anderson, M., Curren, R., van Geel, T., Pritchard, I., & Robertson, E. (2002). *Ethical standards of the American Educational Research Association: Cases and commentary.* Washington DC: American Educational Research Association.

Teaching qualitative research with QSR software. (2003). *The Journal of the Association for Qualitative Research* [Special issue].

Tenner, E. (2005, February). Keeping tabs: The history of an information age metaphor. *Technological Review.*

Tesch, R. (1990). *Qualitative research: Analysis types and software tools.* Basingstoke, UK: Falmer.

Tutt, D., & Shaukat, M. (2007, April 18–20). *Evaluation of MiMeG in use: Technical and social issues in remote collaborative video analysis.* Paper presented at the CAQDAS 2007 Conference: Advances in Qualitative Computing, Royal Holloway, University of London, Egham, UK.

Vander Wal, T. (2007, February 2). *Folksonomy coinage and definition.* Available at: http://www.vanderwal.net/folksonomy.html

Vince, J., & Sweetman, R. (2006, September 29). *Managing large scale qualitative research: Two case studies.* Paper presented at Words Instead of Numbers: The Status of Software in the Qualitative Research World, the Association for Survey Computing, Imperial College London.

Weitzman, E. (2000). Software and qualitative research. In N. K. Denzin & Y. S. Lincoln (Eds.), *Handbook of qualitative research* (2nd ed., pp. 803–820). Thousand Oaks, CA: Sage.

Weitzman, E., & Miles, M. (1995). *Computer programs for qualitative data analysis.* Thousand Oaks, CA: Sage.

QUALITATIVE DATA ANALYSIS SOFTWARE

ATLAS.ti. *ATLAS.ti home page,* http://www.atlasti.com/
MAXQDA. http://www.MAXQDA.com/
NVIVO. A product of QSR International, http://www.qsrinternational.com/
QDAMiner. http://www.provalisresearch.com/QDAMiner/QDAMinerDesc.html
QSR. *QSR International home page,* http://www.qsrinternational.com/
Transana. http://www.transana.org/index.htm

TECHNOLOGIES, TECHNOLOGY COMPANIES, AND RESEARCH RESOURCES

Amazon. *About Amazon,* http://www.amazon.com/Careers-Homepage/
A.nnotate. *About A.nnotate,* http://a.nnotate.com/about.html

Apple. *Apple science,* http://www.apple.com/science/

AT&T Labs, Inc. *Research,* http://www.research.att.com

CAQDAS. *CAQDAS Networking Project,* http://caqdas.soc.surrey.ac.uk/

DiRT. *Digital Research Tools wiki,* http://digitalresearchtools.pbworks.com

DReSS. http://www.esrcsocietytoday.ac.uk/esrcinfocentre/viewawardpage.aspx?award number=RES-149–25–0035

EverydayLives. http:// www.everydaylives.com

Google. *Google Labs,* http://www.googlelabs.com

IBM. *IBM Center for Social Research,* http://www.research.ibm.com/social/index.html

Microsoft. *Microsoft Live Labs,* http://livelabs.com

MiMeg. http://www.esrcsocietytoday.ac.uk/esrcinfocentre/viewawardpage.aspx?award number=RES-149–25–0033

PARC (Palo Alto Research Center). http://www.parc.com

Telenor. *Telenor Research and Innovation,* http://www.telenor.com

16

The Elephant in the Living Room, or Extending the Conversation About the Politics of Evidence[1]

Norman K. Denzin

There is a current dispute between qualitative and quantitative research. It is international, acrimonious, and there are elements of state-sponsored support "in the West" for a return to a kind of neopositivist quantitative inquiry.

—I. Stronach (2006, p. 758)

To serve evidence-based policymaking we probably need to invent a . . . myth for qualitative work, that is we too have clear-cut guidelines and criteria, maybe not randomized control trials, but we have our criteria.

—M. Hammersley (2005a, p. 4)

Qualitative researchers are caught in the middle of a global conversation concerning emerging standards and guidelines for conducting and evaluating qualitative inquiry (St.Pierre, 2006). This conversation turns on issues surrounding the politics and ethics of evidence, and the value of qualitative work in addressing matters of equity and social justice (Lather, 2006). In some senses, this is like old wine in new bottles, 1980s battles in a new century.

Like an elephant in the living room, the evidence-based model is an intruder whose presence can no longer be ignored. Within the global audit culture,[2] proposals concerning the use of Cochrane and Campbell criteria,[3] experimental methodologies, randomized controlled trials, quantitative metrics, citation analyses, shared data bases, journal impact factors, rigid notions of accountability, data transparency, warrantablity, rigorous peer-review evaluation scales, and fixed formats for scientific articles now compete, fighting to gain ascendancy in the evidence-quality-standards discourse (Feuer, Towne, & Shavelson, 2002; Lather, 2004; NRC, 2002; Thomas, 2004).

The interpretive community must mount an articulate critique of these external threats to our "collective research endeavor" (Atkinson & Delamont, 2006, p. 751; Freeman, deMarrais, Preissle, Roulston, & St.Pierre, 2007). We must create our own standards of quality, our own criteria.

I want to read the controversies surrounding this discourse within a critical pedagogical framework, showing their contradictions, their overlaps, the gaps that stand between them (Denzin, 2003). Standards for assessing quality research are pedagogies of practice, moral, ethical and political institutional apparatuses that regulate and produce a particular form of science, a form that may be no longer workable in a trans-disciplinary, global, and postcolonial world. Indeed, within the evidence-based community, there is the understanding that qualitative research does not count as research unless it is embedded in a randomized controlled trial (RCT)! Further, within this community, there are no agreed-upon procedures, methods, or criteria for extracting information from qualitative studies. These interpretations must be resisted.

In reviewing these multiple discourses, I hope to chart a path of resistance. Because the qualitative research community is not a single entity, guidelines and criteria of quality need to be fitted to specific paradigmatic and genre-driven concerns, e.g., grounded theory studies versus performance ethnographies. I favor flexible guidelines that are not driven by quantitative criteria. I seek a performative model of qualitative inquiry, a model that enacts a performance ethic based on feminist, communitarian assumptions.

I align these assumptions with the call by first and fourth world scholars for an indigenous research ethic (Bishop, 1998; Rains, Archibald, & Deyhle, 2000; L. T. Smith, 1999). This call opens the space for a discussion of ethics, science, causality, and trust and a reiteration of moral and ethical criteria for judging qualitative research (Denzin, 2003, 2007; Denzin, Lincoln, & Giardina, 2006). I will conclude with a set of recommendations concerning review panels, scholarly associations, journals, and criteria for evaluating qualitative research.

The Elephant in the Living Room

I agree with Atkinson and Delamont (2006) who state, "We are appalled by the absurd proposal that interpretive research should be made to conform to inappropriate definitions of scientific research. . . . Equally disturbing is the argument that qualitative research should not be funded if it fails to conform to these criteria" (p. 751; see also Erickson & Gutierrez, 2002, p. 221). Hammersley (2005a), in turn, observes that "[q]ualitative research tends to suffer by comparison with quantitative work because there is a myth that quantitative researchers have clear-cut guidelines which are available for use by policymakers (Was it a randomized controlled trial? Was there a control group?)" (p. 3).

Morse (2006a) extends the argument: " Indeed, qualitative inquiry falls off the positivist grid. Why it barely earns a Grade of C- on the Cochrane scale! It gets worse! It receives the 'does not meet evidence standard' on the 'What Works Clearinghouse' (WWC) Scale" (p. 396; Cheek, 2005, 2006).

Feuer et al. (2002) offer the counterargument:

> Although we strongly oppose blunt federal mandates that reduce scientific inquiry to one method . . . we also believe that the field should use this tool in studies in education more often than is current practice. . . . Now is the time for the field to move beyond particularized views and focus on building a shared core of norms and practices that emphasize scientific principles. (p. 8)

A report by the National Center for Dissemination of Disability Research (2007) states, "We need criteria for comparing research methods and research evidence, we need terms like credibility (internal validity), transferability (external validity), dependability (reliability), confirmability (objectivity)" (n.p.).

A skeptic must ask, "Whose science? Whose scientific principles?"

Two Other Elephants

The elephant wears two other garments, the cloak of meta-analysis and the disguise of mix methods research. The meta-analysis disguise invites the production of systematic reviews that incorporate qualitative research into meta-analyses (Dixon-Woods et al., 2006). The mixed methods disguise revisits the concept of triangulation, asking how qualitative and quantitative methods can be made to work together (Moran-Ellis et al., 2006).

There are problems with both disguises. Meta-analyses of published articles hardly count as qualitative research in any sense of the term. The return to mixed methods inquiry fails to address the incommensurability issue—the fact that the two paradigms are in contradiction (Smith & Hodkinson, 2005). Any effort to circumvent this collision, through complementary strengths, single-paradigm, dialectical, or multiple-paradigm, mixed methods approaches seems doomed to failure (see Teddlie & Tashakkori, 2003, pp. 19–24).[4]

Whose Criteria? Whose Standards?

Extending J. K. Smith and Deemer (2000), within the qualitative inquiry community there are three basic positions on the issue of evaluative criteria: foundational, quasi-foundational, and non-foundational (see also Creswell, 2007; Guba & Lincoln, 1989, 2005; Lincoln & Guba, 1985; Spencer, Ritchie, Lewis, & Dillon, 2003). *Foundationalists,* including those that apply the Cochrane and Campbell Collaborations, are in this space, contending that *research is research,* quantitative or qualitative. All research should conform to a set of shared criteria (e.g., internal, external validity, credibility, transferability, confirmability, transparency, and warrantability (see Dixon-Woods, Shaw, Agarwal, & Smith, 2004; Dixon-Woods et al., 2006; Teddlie & Tashakkori, 2003).

Quasi-foundationalists contend that a set of criteria, or a guiding framework unique to qualitative research, needs to be developed. These criteria may include terms like reflexivity, theoretical grounding, iconic, paralogic, rhizomatic, and voluptuous validity (Eisner, 1991; Lather, 1993; Lincoln & Guba, 1985). In contrast, *non-foundationalists* stress the importance of understanding, versus prediction (Denzin, 1997; Wolcott, 1999). They conceptualize inquiry within a moral frame, implementing an ethic rooted in the concepts of care, love, and kindness (see also Christians, 2005).

Policy and Praxis

Evaluative criteria, as pedagogical practices, are shaped by what is regarded as the proper relationship between qualitative inquiry and social policy. Within the critical qualitative inquiry community, at least four pedagogical stances, or identities, can be distinguished, each with its own history: (1) discipline-based qualitative research focused on accumulating fundamental knowledge about social processes and institutions; (2) qualitative policy research aimed at having an impact on current programs and practices; (3) critical qualitative approaches that disrupt and destabilize current public policy or social discourse; and (4) public intellectuals, public social scientists, and cultural critics who use qualitative inquiry and interpretive work to address current issues and crises in the public arena (Hammersley, 2005a, p. 3).

Hammersley (2005a,) cautions that, "We should not allow the close encounters promised by the notion of evidence-based policymaking, or even 'public social science,' to seduce us into illusions about ourselves and our work" (p. 5). Torrance (2006) is quite assertive:

> This new orthodoxy seems perversely and willfully ignorant of many decades of debate over whether, and if so in what ways we can conduct enquiry and build knowledge in the social sciences, pausing only to castigate educational research for not being more like . . . medical research. (p. 127)

The Politics of Evidence

The term *politics* (and ethics) *of evidence* is, as Morse (2006a) observes, an oxymoron in more than one way. Evidence "is something that is concrete and indisputable, whereas politics refers to 'activities concerned with the . . . exercise of authority [and power]'" (p. 395). Evidence in a countable or measurable sense is not something that all qualitative researchers attend to. Few critical ethnographers (Madison, 2005) think in a language of evidence; they think instead about experience, emotions, events, processes, performances, narratives, poetics, and the politics of possibility.

Moreover, evidence is never morally or ethically neutral. But, paraphrasing Morse (2006a), who quotes Larner (2004, p. 20), the politics and political economy of evidence is not a question of evidence or no evidence. It is rather a question of who has the power to control the definition of evidence, who defines the kinds of materials that count as evidence, who determines what methods best produce the best forms of evidence, whose criteria and standards are used to evaluate quality evidence. On this, Morse is quite clear: "Our evidence is considered soft . . . it is considered not valid, not replicable, not acceptable! We have failed to communicate the nature of qualitative evidence to the larger scientific community . . . we have failed to truly understand it ourselves" (pp. 415–416). The politics of evidence cannot be separated from the ethics of evidence.

State- and Discipline-Sponsored Epistemologies

This ethical, epistemological, and political discourse is historically and politically situated. It plays out differently in each national context (see Atkinson & Delamont, 2006; Cheek, 2006; Gilgun, 2006; Morse, 2006a, 2006b; Preissle, 2006). In the United States, the United Kingdom, Continental Europe, New Zealand, and Australia, the conversation criss-crosses audit cultures, indigenous cultures, disciplines, paradigms, and epistemologies, as well as decolonizing initiatives. Depending on the nation-state, the discourse goes by various acronyms. In the United States, it is called SBR (scientifically based research), or SIE (scientific inquiry in education). In the United Kingdom, the model goes by the letters RAE (the British research assessment exercise), and in Australia, it goes by RQF for the research quality framework. All of these models are based, more or less, on the assumption that since medical research is successful, and randomized experimental designs are used and appreciated in medical science, this should be the blueprint for all good research (but see Timmermans & Berg, 2003).

There is not a single discourse. In the postpositivist, foundational, and quasi-foundational U.S. communities, there are multiple institutions (and conversations) competing for attention, including (1) the Institute of Education Science (IES) within the U.S. Department of Education; (2) the What Works Clearinghouse (WWC), funded by the IES; (3) the Cochrane-Campbell Collaboration (CCC), which contracts with the WWC; (4) the National Research Council-SBR framework (2002), which implements versions of CCC and WWC; (5) the recently IES-funded ($850,000) Society for Research on Educational Effectiveness (SREE); and (6) the 2006 standards for reporting adopted by the American Education Research Association (AERA), which explicitly addresses standards for qualitative research, some of which are contained in documents prepared by members of the Cochrane Qualitative Methods Group (Briggs, 2006).[5]

National Research Council

The federally funded National Research Council (NRC) scientifically based research (SBR), or evidence-based movement, argues that educational, health care, and other social problems can be better addressed if we borrow from medical science, and upgrade our methods and create new gold standards for evaluating evidence (National Research Council, 2002; NRC, 2005).

For this group, quality research is scientific, empirical, and linked to theory; it uses methods for direct investigation and produces coherent chains of causal reasoning based on experimental or quasi-experimental findings, offering generalizations that can be replicated and used to test and refine theory. If research has these features, it has high quality, and it is scientific (NRC, 2005).

In the United States, such research must also conform to the Office of Human Subject Research definition of scientific inquiry—namely, that scientific research is

> any activity designed to test an hypothesis, permit conclusions to be drawn, and thereby to develop or contribute to generalizable knowledge expressed in theories, principles, and statements of relationships. Research is described in a formal protocol that sets forth an objective and a set of procedures designed to reach that objective. (U.S. Code of Federal Regulations, Title 45, Part 46, as quoted in American Association of University Professors [AAUP], 2001, p. 55; see also AAUP, 1981, 2002, 2006)

Hand in glove, ethics and models of science now flow into one another. IRB panels can simultaneously rule on research that is ethically sound and of high quality. If these assumptions are allowed, we have lost the argument even before it starts.

Cannella and Lincoln (2004) are clear on this point:

> The NRC report is a U.S. government–requested project designed to clearly define the nature of research that is to be labeled as representing quality. . . . Accurately referred to as methodological fundamentalism . . . contemporary conservative research discourses . . . have ignored critical theory, race/ethic studies, and feminist theories and silenced the voices and life conditions of the traditionally marginalized. (p. 165; see also Feuer, 2006; Freeman et al., 2007; Hammersley, 2005a; St.Pierre, 2006; St.Pierre & Roulston, 2006)

Implementing the NRC Model

Thirteen recommendations for implementing the NRC model are directed to federal funding agencies, professional associations and journals, and schools of education. These recommendations state that

RESEARCH AGENCIES SHOULD

- Define and enforce better-quality criteria for peer reviewers;
- Ensure peer reviewer expertise and diversity;
- Create infrastructures for data sharing.

PUBLISHERS AND PROFESSIONAL ASSOCIATIONS SHOULD

- Develop explicit standards for data sharing;
- Require authors to make data available to other researchers;
- Create infrastructures for data sharing;
- Develop standards for structured abstracts;
- Develop a manuscript review system that supports professional development.

SCHOOLS OF EDUCATION AND UNIVERSITIES SHOULD

- Enable research competencies;
- Ensure that students develop deep methodological knowledge;
- Provide students with meaningful research experiences.

There are several problems with these NRC formulations and recommendations. I start with Maxwell (2004a, 2004b). He unravels and criticizes the centrally linked assumptions in the model. His six points constitute powerful criticisms of SBR. He argues that the model assumes a narrow, regularity view of causation; privileges a variable-oriented, as opposed to a process-oriented, view of research; denies the possibility of observing causality in a single case; neglects the importance of context, meaning, and process as essential components of causal and interpretive analysis; erroneously asserts that qualitative and quantitative research share the same logic of inference; and presents a hierarchical ordering of methods for investigating causality, giving priority to experimental and other quantitative methods (2004b, p. 3).

Feuer et al. (2002) attempt to finesse this criticism, creating a special place for qualitative research, suggesting it can be used to capture the complexities involved in teaching, learning, and schooling, that is, when a problem is poorly understood, and plausible hypotheses are scant—qualitative methods such as ethnographies . . . are necessary to describe complex phenomena, generate theoretical models and reframe questions. . . . We want to be explicit . . . [that] we do not view our strong support for randomized field trials and our equally strong argument for close attention to context . . . as incompatible. Quite the contrary: When properly applied, quantitative and qualitative research tools can both be employed rigorously and together. (p. 8)

Finessing aside, the NRC is clear on this point, that "a randomized experiment is the best method for estimating [causal] effects" (Feuer et al., 2002, p. 8).

Flashback to 1926. Déjà vu all over again. Lundberg (1926), sociology's arch-positivist, is arguing against the use of the case method:

The case method is not in itself a scientific method at all, but merely the first step in the scientific method . . . . [T]he statistical method is the best, if not the only scientific method . . . . [T]he only possible question . . . is whether classification of, and generalizations from the data should be carried out by random, qualitative, and subjective method . . . or through the systematic, quantitative, and objective procedures of the statistical method. (p. 61)

Fast forward to 1966, to Howard S. Becker:

The life history method has not been much used by contemporary sociologists, a neglect which reflects a shift in the methodological stance of the researcher. Rigorous, quantitative, and (frequently) experimental designs have become the accepted modes of investigation. This situation is unfortunate because the life history, when properly conceived and employed, can become one of the sociologist's most powerful observational and analytic tools. (p. xviii)

The presumption that only quantitative data can be used to identify causal relationships is problematic. Maxwell (2004b) shows how the SBR model neglects meaning, context, and process. He demonstrates that causality can be identified (after Hume) in the single case; that is, multi-case, variable-based causal arguments are just one form of causal interpretation. Other causal, or quasi-causal, models of course are based on multi-variant, process, contextual, and interactionist-based assumptions. Further, causality as a type of narrative is only one form of interpretation. Autoethnographic, performative, arts-based, ethnodramatic, poetic, action-based, and other forms of narrative representation are equally powerful methods and strategies of analysis and interpretation.

In addition to Maxwell's six basic criticisms, I add the following. First, amazingly, there is little attention given to the process by which evidence is turned into data. This is not a simple process, and is not accomplished by waving a wand over a body of observations. Second, there is also no detailed discussion of how data are to be used to produce generalizations, test and refine theory, and permit causal reasoning. It is clear, though, that data become a commodity that does several things. That is, third, evidence as data carries the weight of the scientific process. This process works through a self-fulfilling, self-validating process. You know you have quality data that are scientific when you have tested and refined your theory. How you have addressed problems in the real world remains a mystery.

Fourth, the focus on data sharing is critical, and of central concern. It is assumed that quality data can be easily shared. But complex interpretive processes shape how evidence is turned into data, and how data, in turn, are coded, categorized, labeled, and assembled into data banks (Charmaz, 2005). Data are not silent. Data are commodities, produced by researchers, perhaps owned by the government or by funding agencies. What would it mean to share my data with you? Why would I want to do this? If I own my data, I want to have ownership over how it is used, including what is published from it. The injunction to engage in data sharing requires amplification. Data sharing involves complex moral considerations that go beyond sending a body of coded data to another colleague.

Fifth, money and concerns for auditing from the audit culture seem to drive the process. This is evidenced in the emphasis placed on funding and quality peer reviews. If quality data can be produced and then shared, then granting agencies get more science for less money. However, in order for greater data sharing to occur, more quality projects need to be funded. For this to happen, granting agencies need a better peer review system with better-trained reviewers, who are using more clearly defined rating scale levels. Reviewers will be helped if researchers write proposals that use rigorous methodologies and the very best research designs. Such projects will surely have high standards of evidence. Thus does the self-fulfilling process reproduce itself. We know we are getting quality science of the highest order because we are using methods of the highest order. Reviewers can easily identify such work. The blind peer review, based on presumptions of objectivity, is the key to this system.[6]

The peer review system is not immune to political influence. Kaplan (2004) has demonstrated that the George W. Bush administration systematically stacked federal advisory and peer review committees with researchers whose views matched the president's on issues ranging from stem-cell research to ergonomics, faith-based science, AIDS, sex education, family values, global warming, and environmental issues in public parks (see also Monastersky, 2002).

Sree

The Society for Research on Educational Effectiveness (SREE) extends the federally sponsored NRC agenda. It appears to oppose recent efforts within AERA to soften NRC guidelines (see below). The code words for SREE, which plans its own journal (*Journal of Research on Educational Effectiveness*—JREE), handbook (*Handbook of Research on Educational Effectiveness*), and electronic journal (*Research Notes on Educational Effectiveness*), are rigorous research design and randomized control experiment. The mission of SREE is

> to advance and disseminate research on the causal effects of education interventions, practices, programs, and policies. As support for researchers who are focused on questions related to educational effectiveness, the Society aims to: 1) increase the capacity to design and conduct investigations that have a strong base for causal inference, 2) bring together people investigating cause-and-effect relations in education, and 3) promote the understanding and use of scientific evidence to improve education decisions and outcomes. (www.sree-net.org; see also Viadero, 2006)[7]

There is no place in SREE here for qualitative research. This is hardcore SBR: evidence-based inquiry. Scientific research becomes a commodity to be sold in a new journal, a commodity that serves and embodies the interests of educational science as narrowly defined.

The Cochrane, Campbell, What Works Clearinghouse Collaborations

The Cochrane, Campbell, and What Works Clearinghouse Collaborations are inserting themselves into the qualitative research conversation. All three represent state-sponsored projects. All three are dedicated to producing so-called scientific peer reviews of quality (evidence-based) research that can be used by policy makers. The Cochrane Qualitative Methods Group focuses on methodological matters arising from the inclusion of findings from qualitative studies into systematic reviews of evidence-based inquires. The Campbell Methods Group focuses on methodological issues associated with process evaluations, which use mixed methods, while including evidence gathered via qualitative methods. It is understood that qualitative research can help in understanding how an intervention is experienced, while providing insight into factors that might hinder successful implementation.

Randomized controlled trials are central to all three collaborations. Hence, qualitative evidence is of primary interest only when it is included as a data gathering technique in an experimental, or quasi-experimental, study (Briggs, 2006). There is some debate on this point, that is, whether "only qualitative research embedded within relevant RCTs should be included" (Briggs, 2006). The Campbell Collaboration only includes qualitative materials if they are part of controlled observations (Davies, 2004). However, there is no consensus on how to include qualitative evidence in such work—namely, how to identify, record, appraise, and extract data from qualitative studies.

Appraisal Tools

Enter CASP—the Critical Appraisal Skills Program (Briggs, 2006), which was developed in conjunction with the Cochrane Qualitative Research Methods Group (CQRMG). The Cochrane Group (Briggs, 2006) has a broad, but conventional definition of qualitative research, encompassing specific methods (interviews, participant and nonparticipant observation, focus groups, ethnographic fieldwork), data types (narrative), and forms of analysis (ethnography, grounded theory, thematic categories).

CASP, like any number of other checklists (Dixon-Woods, et al., 2004; Jackson & Waters, 2005; Popay, Rogers, & Williams, 1998; Spencer et al., 2003), is an assessment tool developed for those unfamiliar with qualitative research. The tool presents a series of questions focused around three broad issues: rigor, credibility, and relevance. Ten questions concerning aims, methodology, design, subject recruitment, data collection, researcher–participant relationship, ethics (IRBs), data analysis, statement of findings, and value of research are asked. The reviewer of a study writes comments on each of these issues.

CASP implements a narrow model of qualitative inquiry. Methods are not connected to interpretive paradigms (e.g., feminism, critical theory). Multiple strategies of inquiry and analysis (case or performance studies, narrative inquiry, critical ethnography) go unidentified. Nor is the complex literature from within the interpretive tradition on evaluating qualitative research addressed (see Christians, 2005). Thus, CASP offers the reviewer a small, ahistorical tool kit for reading and evaluating qualitative studies.

CHECKLISTS

Here, Hammersley (2005a) is again relevant. This is the myth of the checklist, the myth of the guideline. Consider the guidelines prepared for the British Cabinet Office (Spencer et al., 2003). This is another checklist with 16 categories (scope, timetable, design, sample, data collection, analysis, ethics, confirmability, generalizability, credibility, etc.), 80 specific criteria (clearly stated hypotheses, outcomes, justification of analysis methods, triangulation, etc.), and 35 broad criteria (explicit aims, appropriate use of methods, assessment of reliability and validity, etc.).

This is old-fashioned postpositivism, applying a soft quantitative grid (confirmability, hypotheses, credibility) to qualitative research. But there is more going on. Like CASP, the Spencer et al. (2003) tool kit introduces the notion of credibility, that is, whether the findings can be trusted. If they can be trusted, they must be confirmable, valid, and reliable, which means they can be generalized. If they are not credible, the whole house of cards falls down.

Torrance (2006) exposes the underlying theory at work here, noting that "it is a traditional, positivist model, that is the truth is out there to be discovered" (p. 128). Yet, as he observes, "these scholars still cannot solve the problem of epistemological incommensuration . . . but . . . this is little more than experts 'rating' qualitative evidence on an agreed scale so it can be included in meta-analyses of effect sizes" (p. 140).

Aera

The American Education Research Association (AERA, 2006, 2008) has recently added its collective voice to the conversation, supplementing and departing from the NRC recommendations. Two sets of guidelines, one for empirical research, the other for humanities-based work, have been offered. Both sets are intended to help authors and journal editors and reviewers who may not be familiar with expectations guiding such work. They are also intended to foster excellence in the production of high-quality research.

STANDARDS FOR EMPIRICAL SOCIAL SCIENCE RESEARCH

Two global standards are offered for reporting empirical research: warrantability and transparency (AERA, 2006).[8,9] Reports of research should be warranted, that is, adequate evidence, which would be credible (internal validity), should be provided to justify conclusions. Reports should be transparent, making explicit the logic of inquiry used in the project. This method should produce data that have external validity; reliability; and confirmability, or objectivity. Like the NRC guidelines, these standards are to be used by peer reviewers, research scholars, and journal publishers, and in graduate education programs where researchers are trained.

There is extensive discussion of quantitative procedures (AERA, 2006, pp. 6–10), but trust is not an issue.

Trust

Trust *is* an issue for qualitative researchers. The AERA (2006) report is explicit, asserting that

It is the researcher's responsibility to show the reader that the report can be trusted. This begins with the description of the evidence, the data, and the analysis supporting each interpretive claim. The warrant for the claims can be established through a variety of procedures including triangulation, asking participants to evaluate pattern descriptions, having different analysts examine the same data (independently and collaboratively), searches for disconfirming evidence and counter-interpretations. (p. 11)

This is all clear enough, but these validating procedures and standards are not held up for quantitative researchers. When qualitative evidence does not converge, the report recommends that

critical examination of the preexisting perspective, point of view, or standpoint of the researcher(s), of how these might have influenced the collection and analysis of evidence, and of how they were challenged during the course of data collection and analysis, is an important element in enhancing the warrant of each claim. (AERA, 2006, p. 11)

Here is the heart of the matter. The perspective of the qualitative researcher can influence the collection of evidence in such a way as to introduce a lack of trust into the research process. That presence potentially undermines the credibility and warrantability of the report. But why would the qualitative researcher's effects on the research process be greater or less than the effects of the quantitative researcher? Doesn't the quantitative researcher have an effect on the collection, analysis, and interpretation of evidence, including deciding what is evidence?

The 2006 AERA recommendations call for the responsible use of quasi-foundational tools; that is, threats to trust can be overcome. Transparency—that is, trust—is increased by clearly discussing the process of interpretation, highlighting the evidence and alternative interpretations that serve as a warrant for each claim, providing contextual commentary on each claim. When generalizations extend beyond a specific case, researchers must clearly indicate the sampling frame, population, individuals, contexts, activities, and domains to which the generalizations are intended to apply (external validity). The logic supporting such generalizations must be made clear.

A sleight of hand is at work in the AERA recommendations. The intent of the report is now clear. Two things are going on at once—a familiar pattern. Qualitative research is downgraded to the status of a marginal science, second-class citizenship. Since it lacks trustworthiness, it can be used for discovery purposes, but not for the real work of science, which is verification. Only under the most rigorous of circumstances can qualitative research exhibit the qualities that would make it scientific, and even then, trust will be an issue. Trust becomes a proxy for quality; transparency and warranted evidence function as proxies for objectivity.

Clearly, AERA wants a space for qualitative research that is not governed by the narrow NRC experimental and quasi-experimental guidelines. We all want this. To its credit, AERA wants a broad-based, multimethod concept of quality. But they falter in asserting that empirical research reports should be warranted and transparent. These are criteria for doing business as usual. No wonder SREE was created. AERA's educational science does not require randomized controlled experiments. SREE's does.

Rereading Trust and Ethics

Trust in this discourse resurfaces as a proxy for more than quality. It spills over to the researcher who does research that lacks trust. Untrustworthy persons lie, misrepresent, cheat, engage in fraud, or alter documents. They are not governed by measurement and statistical procedures that are objective and free of bias.

They may not be shady characters; they may be well-intended, gifted actors, poets, fiction writers, or performers, but they are not scientists! Qualitative researchers are not to be trusted because their standpoints can influence what they study and report. Somehow quantitative researchers are freed from these influences. This of course is a sham!

By implication, qualitative scientists are being charged with fraud, with misrepresenting their data. This may be because many qualitative researchers do not have data and findings, tables and charts, statistics and numbers. We have stories, narratives, excerpts from interviews. We perform our interpretations and invite audiences to experience these performances, to live their way into the scenes, moments, and lives we are writing and talking about. Our empirical materials can't be fudged, misrepresented, altered, or distorted because they are life experiences. They are ethnodramas.

Apples Turned Into Oranges: Turning Interpretations Into Data

Like the NRC, AERA's ethical guidelines focus on issues relevant to reporting results. Authors have an obligation to address the ethical decisions that shaped their research, including how the inquiry was designed, executed, and organized. Incentives for participating, consent waivers and confidentiality agreements, and conflicts of interest should be presented and discussed. Reporting should be accurate, free of plagiarism, fully accessible to others, and without falsification or fabrication of data or results. Data should be presented in such a way that any qualified researcher with a copy of the relevant data could reproduce the results.

Thus are interpretive materials turned into data. The interpretive process becomes an exercise in seeking patterns of evidence, presenting evidence in a way that will engender trust on the part of the reader, while avoiding charges of misrepresentation or fabrication (more on ethics below). But this is not how qualitative researchers work.

STANDARDS FOR REPORTING ON HUMANITIES-ORIENTED RESEARCH IN AERA PUBLICATIONS[10]

The 2008 Draft of Standards for Humanities-Oriented Research extends the place of qualitative inquiry in educational research.[11] The document recognizes that traditional social science standards for empirical research cannot be automatically applied to humanities-oriented research. The document focuses on five genres of humanities-linked inquiry: philosophy, history, arts-based educational research (ABER), literary studies, and studies of the politics of knowledge.[12] Space prohibits a discussion of all five genres. I will focus on ABER because of its overlap with experimental forms of qualitative inquiry (see Barone, 2001; Cahnmann-Taylor & Siegesmund, 2008; Eisner, 1991; Finley, 2008; Leavy, 2009; Richardson, 2000a, 2000b).

Two strands of arts-based inquiry, the humanistic or traditional, and the activist, critical pedagogical, can be identified. The traditional strand, the one emphasized in the AERA (2008) report, contrasts empirical and artistic approaches to qualitative research. Dance, film, poetry, drama, and the plastic arts are used to explore various facets of the human condition: the relationship between reason and emotion, the ethical life, self, identity, and meaning (p. 3; see also Finley, 2008). Activist, radical, performative, ethical, and revolutionary forms of arts-based work, projects which disrupt, interrupt and challenge structures of oppression, are not taken up (see Finley, 2008).

The report defers to those forms and methods of humanities-oriented research that are empirical and use interpretive methods in the analysis of texts, text analogues, and textual artifacts (AERA, 2008, p. 4). It is asserted that such work is inextricably empirical, which means it can be counted, assessed, and evaluated in terms of a politics of evidence. This means there is overlap between empirical and humanities-oriented research (p. 4).

Accordingly, the standards for evaluating humanistic work overlap with those applied to empirical work. Seven standards, each with a series of substandards[13] that elaborate the major standard, are offered: (1) significance, (2) conceptualization, (3) methods, (4) substantiation, (5) coherence, (6) quality of communication, and (7) ethics.[14] (These could have been included in the 2006 empirical standards document.)

Substantiation and coherence are key standards, and they are intertwined. Together they establish the warrant for the arguments in a text, the adequacy or credibility of its interpretations, the quality and use of evidence, its transparency, and critical self-awareness. A warrantable humanities-based text, like its empirical counterpart, uses evidence that justifies its conclusions. Such a text demonstrates internal and external coherence, offering compelling confirming and disconfirming evidence, and an awareness of competing, external perspectives.

What if a work is deliberately not empirical? What if it disrupts the concept of the empirical. What if it disallows the concept of the text, and turns the text into a performance, into a site where meaning is multiple, plural, and unclear? In such a case, an empirical-textual model no longer applies, and the standards of coherence and substantiation no longer apply.

Reading the New Standards

As with the discussion of qualitative research, it is clear that AERA wants a space for humanities-based inquiry that is not governed by narrow SBR guidelines. But the window it creates for this form of inquiry is quite narrow. AERA wants to hold humanistic inquiry to a modified set of evidence-based standards. Underneath its claim for inclusiveness, it brings the same criteria—transparency, coherence, evidence, trust—to the humanities that it applied to qualitative inquiry.

Its discussion of arts-based educational research (ABER) ignores, as it did in the discussion of qualitative inquiry, a large methodological and interpretive literature concerning empowerment discourses, critical performance ethnography, art-for-social-action purposes, dialogic spaces, public art, censorship, and neoliberal forms of governmental regulation (see Finley, 2003, 2005). It seems that this document was produced outside the discourse it was intended to regulate.

The effect, however, is disarming. There is the impression that we are one big happy family, with different people doing different things. That is not the case. In fact, we are better described as a "house divided."[15] Accordingly, we should resist the "new orthodoxy." By asserting that everything we do is inextricably empirical, the AERA seeks to diminish, if not erase, hard-fought distinction, and all in the name of science!

✶ ✶ ✶

It is as if the NRC, SREE, and AERA guidelines were written in a time warp. Over the last three decades, the field of qualitative research has become a interdisciplinary field in its own right. The interpretive and critical paradigms, in their multiple forms, are central to this movement. Complex literatures are now attached to research methodologies, strategies of inquiry, interpretive paradigms, and criteria for reading and evaluating inquiry itself. Sadly, little of this literature is evident in any of the recent national documents. It seems that the qualitative community is hemmed in from all sides. But before this judgment is accepted, the "for whom" question must be asked—that is, high-quality science, or evidence, for whom? (Cheek, 2006). NRC, AERA, and SREE's umbrellas are too small. We need a larger tent.

The Qualitative Inquiry Community

There are tensions over the politics of evidence within the interpretive community: (1) Interpretivists dismiss postpositivists, (2) poststructuralists dismiss interpretivists, and now (3) the postinterpretivists dismiss the interpretivists (Preissle, 2006, p. 692; see also Hammersley, 2005b; Hodkinson, 2004; MacLure, 2006). Some postpositivists are drawn to the SBR standards movement, seeking to develop mixed or multiple methodological strategies that will conform to the new demands for improving research quality. Others reject the gold standard movement, and argue for a set of understandings unique to the interpretive, or postinterpretive, tradition (St.Pierre & Roulston, 2006). Atkinson and Delamont (2006) call for a return to the classics in the Chicago School tradition. The American Education Research Association (2006) aims to strike a middle ground, neither too postpositivist nor too interpretivist.

The immediate effects of this conversation start at home, in departments and in graduate education programs where PhD's are produced and tenure for qualitative research scholars is granted. Many fear that the call for SBR will drown out instruction, scholarship, and the granting of tenure in the qualitative tradition, or confine them to a narrow brand of interpretive work (Eisenhart, 2006). Worse yet, it could lead to a narrow concept of orthodoxy.[16]

Resistance

We must resist the pressures for a single gold standard, even as we endorse conversations about evidence, inquiry, and empirically warranted conclusions (Lincoln & Cannella, 2004). We cannot let one group define the key terms in the conversation. To do otherwise is to allow the SBR group to define the moral and epistemological terrain that we stand on. Neither they nor the government own the word *science.* Habermas (1972) anticipated this nearly 40 years ago:

> The link between empiricism, positivism and the global audit culture is not accidental and it is more than just technical. Such technical approaches deflect attention away from the deeper issues of value and purpose. They make radical critiques much more difficult to mount . . . and they render largely invisible partisan approaches to research under the politically useful pretense that judgments are about objective quality only. In the process human needs and human rights are trampled upon and democracy as we need it is destroyed. (p. 122)

Bourdieu (1998) elaborates:

> The dominants, technocrats, and empiricists of the right and the left are hand in glove with reason and the universal. . . . More and more rational,

scientific technical justifications, always in the name of objectivity, are relied upon. In this way the audit culture perpetuates itself. (p. 90)

There is more than one version of disciplined, rigorous inquiry—counter-science, little science, unruly science, practical science—and such inquiry need not go by the name of science. We must have a model of disciplined, rigorous, thoughtful, reflective inquiry, a "postinterpretivism that seeks meaning but less innocently, that seeks liberation but less naively, and that . . . reaches toward understanding, transformation and justice" (Preissle, 2006, p. 692). It does not need to be called a science, contested or otherwise, as some have proposed (Eisenhart, 2006; Preissle, 2006; St.Pierre & Roulston, 2006).

Lather (2006) extends the argument:

The commitment to disciplined inquiry opens the space for the pursuit of 'inexact knowledges' (p. 787), a disciplined inquiry that matters, applied qualitative research . . . that can engage strategically with the limits and the possibilities of the uses of research for social policy (p. 789). The goal is a critical "counter-science." . . . that troubles what we take for granted as the good in fostering understanding, reflection and action (p. 787). We need a broader framework where such key terms as science, data, evidence, field, method, analysis, knowledge, truth, are no longer defined from within a narrow policy-oriented, positivistic framework. (pp. 787 & 789)

A New Terrain: Trouble With the Elephant

Let's return to the elephant in the living room. Consider the parable of the blind men and the elephant. Lillian Quigley's children's book, *The Blind Men and the Elephant,* is a retelling of an ancient fable about six blind men who visit the palace of the Rajah. There, the men have their first encounter with an elephant. As each man touches the animal in turn, he reports to the others what he feels:

The first blind person touches the side of the elephant and reports that it feels like a wall. The second touches the trunk and says an elephant is like a snake. The third man touches the tusk and says an elephant is like a spear. The fourth person touches a leg and says it feels like a tree. The fifth man touches an ear and says it must be a fan, while the sixth man touches the tail and says how thin, an elephant is like a rope.

There are multiple versions of the elephant in this parable, multiple lessons. We can never know the true nature of things. We are each blinded by our own perspective. Truth is always partial.

To summarize,

Truth One: The elephant is not one thing. If we call SBR the elephant, then according to the parable, we can each know only our version of SBR. For SBR advocates, the elephant is two things: an all-knowing being who speaks to us, and a way of knowing that produces truths about life. How can a thing be two things at the same time?

Truth Two: For skeptics, we are like the blind persons in the parable. We only see partial truths. There is no God's view of the totality, no uniform way of knowing.

Truth Three: Our methodological and moral biases have so seriously blinded us that we can never understand another blind person's position. Even if the elephant called SBR speaks, our biases may prohibit us from hearing what she says. In turn, her biases prevent her from hearing what we say.

Truth Four: If we are all blind, if there is no God, and if there are multiple versions of the elephant, then we are all fumbling around in the world just doing the best we can.

Two Other Versions of the Elephant

The version above is the blind person's version of the elephant. There are at least two other versions, 2.1 and 2.2. Both versions follow from the version above, but now the elephant refers to a painfully problematic situation, thing, or person in one's life space. Rather than confront the thing, and make changes, people find that it is easier to engage in denial, to act like the elephant isn't in the room. This can be unhealthy because the thing may be destructive. It can produce code-pendency. We need the negative presence of the elephant in order to feel good about ourselves.

This cuts two ways at once, hence versions 2.1 and 2. 2. In **Fable 2.1,** SBR advocates treat qualitative research as if it were an elephant in their living room. They have ignored our traditions, our values, our methodologies; they have not read our journals, or our handbooks, or our monographs. They have not even engaged our discourses about SBR. Like the six blind men, they have acted as if they could create us in their own eye. They say we produce findings that cannot be trusted, we are radical relativists, we think anything goes. They dismiss us when we tell them they only know one version of who we are. When we tell them their biases prevent them from understanding what we do, they assert that we are wrong and they are right.

In **Fable 2.2,** the elephant is located in our living room. With notable exceptions, we have tried to ignore this presence. Denial has fed codependency. We need the negative presence of SBR to define who we are. For example, we have not taken up the challenge of better educating policy makers, showing them how qualitative research and our views of practical science, interpretation, and performance ethics can positively contribute to projects embodying restorative justice, equity, and better schooling (Preissle, 2006; Stanfield, 2006). We have not engaged policy makers in a dialogue about alternative ways of judging and evaluating quality research, nor have we engaged SBR advocates in a dialogue about these same issues (but see St.Pierre, 2006). And, they have often declined the invitation to join us in a conversation. As a consequence, we have allowed the SBR elephant to set the terms of the conversation.

If we are to move forward positively, we have to get beyond Fable 2.2, beyond elephants, blind persons, and structures of denial. We must create a new narrative, a narrative of passion and commitment, a narrative that teaches others that ways of knowing are always already partial, moral, and political. This narrative will allow us to put the elephant in proper perspective. Here are some of the certain things we can build our new fable around:

1. We have an ample supply of methodological rules and interpretive guidelines.

2. They are open to change and to differing interpretation, and this is how it should be.

3. There is no longer a single gold standard for qualitative work.

4. We value open peer reviews in our journals.

5. Our empirical materials are performative. They are not commodities to be bought, sold, and consumed.

6. Our feminist, communitarian ethics are not governed by IRBs.

7. Our science is open-ended, unruly, and disruptive (MacLure, 2006; Stronach, Garratt, Pearce, & Piper, 2007).

8. Inquiry is always political and moral.

9. Objectivity and evidence are political and ethical terms.

We live in a depressing historical moment of violent spaces, unending wars against persons of color, repression, the falsification of evidence, the collapse of critical, democratic discourse, and repressive neoliberalism disguised as dispassionate objectivity prevails. Global efforts to impose a new orthodoxy on critical social science inquiry must be resisted; a hegemonic politics of evidence cannot be allowed. Too much is at stake.

Notes

1. This chapter revises and extends arguments in Denzin (2009).

2. Audit culture refers to a technology and a system of accounting that measures outcomes and assesses quality in terms of so-called objective criteria such as test scores. Some argue that the global audit culture implements conservative, neoliberal conceptions of governmentality (Bourdieu, 1998; Habermas, 1972, 2006).

3. Lather (2004) offers a history and critical reading of this alphabet soup of acronyms: CC (Cochrane Collaboration), C2 (Campbell Collaboration), AIR (American Institutes for Research), WWC (What Works Clearinghouse), IES (Institute of Education Science). There has been a recent move within CC and C2 to create protocols for evaluating qualitative research studies (see Briggs, 2006; National CASP Collaboration, 2006; see also Bell, 2006, and below).

4. Over the past four decades, the discourse on triangulation, multiple operationalism, and mixed methods models has become quite complex and nuanced (see Saukko, 2003, and Teddlie & Tashakkori, 2003, for reviews). Each decade has taken up triangulation and redefined it to meet perceived needs.

5. The common thread that exists between WWC and C2 is the No Child Left Behind (NCLB) and Reading First Acts. These acts required a focus on identifying and using scientifically based research in designing and implementing educational programs (What Works Clearinghouse).

6. Ironically, the blind peer review recommendation flies in the face of a recent CC study, which argues that there is little hard evidence to show that blind peer reviews improve the quality of research (Jefferson, Rudin, Brodney Folse, & Davidoff, 2003; White, 2003; see also Judson, 2004, pp. 244–286). Indeed, the Cochrane Collaboration researchers found few studies examining this presumed effect.

7. Their first annual conference (March 2–4, 2008) was outcomes based, calling for rigorous studies of reading, writing, and language skills; mathematics and science achievement; social and behavioral competencies; and dropout prevention and school completion.

8. Warrantability and transparency are key terms in the new managerialism, which is evidence based, and audit driven; that is, policy decisions should be based on evidence

that warrants policy recommendations, and research procedures should be transparently accountable (Hammersley, 2004). Transparency is also a criterion advanced by the Cochrane Qualitative Methods Group (Briggs, 2006).

9. The reporting standards are then divided into eight general areas: problem formation, design, evidence (sources), measurement, analysis and interpretation, generalization, ethics, title and abstract.

10. I thank Kenneth Howe for his comments on this section. He was a member of this AERA committee.

11. The revised and finalized version of these standards is published in *Education Researcher, 38*(6), August/September 2009, 481–486.

12. The report reduces interpretive work to three generic categories, or kinds of objects: texts, text analogues (reports, narratives, performances, rituals), and artifacts (works of art).

13. For example, the significance standard has four levels, involving topic and scholarly contribution. The methods standards have three levels, conceptualization has five levels, and so forth.

14. Ethically, humanities research, as with empirical research, should be carried out in accordance with IRB approval. Scholars should announce their values and discuss any conflicts of interest that could influence their analysis.

15. I thank Ken Howe for this phrase.

16. In the last two decades, qualitative researchers have gone from having fewer than 3 journals dedicated to their work to now having 20 or more (Chenail, 2007).

References

American Association of University Professors. (1981). Regulations governing research on human subjects: Academic freedom and the institutional review board. *Academe, 67,* 358–370.

American Association of University Professors. (2001). Protecting human beings: Institutional review boards and social science research. *Academe, 87*(3), 55–67.

American Association of University Professors. (2002). Should all disciplines be subject to the common rule? Human subjects of social science research. *Academe, 88*(1), 1–15.

American Association of University Professors, Committee A. (2006). *Report on human subjects: Academic freedom and the institutional review boards.* Available at http://www.aaup.org/AAUP/About/committees/committee+repts/CommA/

American Education Research Association. (2006). *Standards for reporting on empirical social science research in AERA publications.* Available at http://www.aera.net/opportunities/?id =1480

American Education Research Association. (2008, August/September). Standards for reporting on humanities-oriented research in AERA publications. *Educational Researcher, 38*(6), 481–486.

Atkinson, P., & Delamont, S. (2006, November/December). In the roiling smoke: Qualitative inquiry and contested fields. *International Journal of Qualitative Studies in Education, (19)*6, 747–755.

Barone, T. (2001). *Touching eternity: The enduring outcomes of teaching.* New York: Teachers College Press.

Becker, H. S. (1966). Introduction. In C. Shaw, *The jack-roller* (pp. v–xviii). Chicago: University of Chicago Press.

Bell, V. (2006). *The Cochrane Qualitative Methods Group.* Available at http://www.lancs .ac.uk/fass/ihr/research/public/cochrane.htm

Bishop, R. (1998). Freeing ourselves from neo-colonial domination in research: A Maori approach to creating knowledge. *International Journal of Qualitative Studies in Education, 11,* 199–219.

Bourdieu, P. (1998). *Practical reason.* Cambridge, UK: Polity.

Briggs, J. (2006). *Cochrane Qualitative Research Methods Group.* Available at http://www .joannabriggs.eduau/cqrmg/role.html

Cahnmann-Taylor, M., & Siegesmund, R. (Eds.). (2008). *Arts-based research in education: Foundations for practice.* New York: Routledge.

Cannella, G. S., & Lincoln, Y. S. (2004, April). Dangerous discourses II: Comprehending and countering the redeployment of discourses (and resources) in the generation of liberatory inquiry. *Qualitative Inquiry, 10*(2), 165–174.

Charmaz, K. (2005). Grounded theory in the 21st century: A qualitative method for advancing social justice research. In N. K. Denzin & Y. S. Lincoln (Eds.), *The SAGE handbook of qualitative research* (3rd ed., pp. 507–535). Thousand Oaks, CA: Sage.

Cheek, J. (2005). The practice and politics of funded qualitative research. In N. K. Denzin & Y. S. Lincoln (Eds.), *The SAGE handbook of qualitative research* (3rd ed., pp. 387–410). Thousand Oaks, CA: Sage.

Cheek, J. (2006, March). What's in a number? Issues in providing evidence of impact and quality of research(ers). *Qualitative Health Research, 16*(3), 423–435.

Chenail, R. J. (2007). Qualitative research sites. *The Qualitative Report: An Online Journal.* Available at http://www.nova.edu/sss/QR/web.html

Christians, C. (2005). Ethics and politics in qualitative research. In N. K. Denzin & Y. S. Lincoln (Eds.), *The SAGE handbook of qualitative research* (3rd ed., pp. 139–164). Thousand Oaks, CA: Sage.

Creswell, J. W. (2007). *Qualitative inquiry and research design: Choosing among five approaches* (2nd ed.). Thousand Oaks, CA: Sage.

Davies, P. (2004). Systematic reviews and the Campbell Collaboration. In G. Thomas & R. Pring (Eds.), *Evidence-based practice in education* (pp. 21–33). New York: Open University Press.

Denzin, N. K. (1997). *Interpretive ethnography.* Thousand Oaks, CA: Sage.

Denzin, N. K. (2003). *Performance ethnography: Critical pedagogy and the politics of culture.* Thousand Oaks, CA: Sage.

Denzin, N. K. (2007). The secret Downing Street memo, the one percent doctrine, and the politics of truth: A performance text. *Symbolic Interaction, 30*(4) 447–461.

Denzin, N. K. (2009). The elephant in the living room: Notes on the politics of inquiry. *Qualitative Research, 9*(1), 139–160.

Denzin, N. K., & Giardina, M. D. (2006). Qualitative inquiry and the conservative challenge. In N. K. Denzin & M. D. Giardina (Eds.), *Qualitative inquiry and the conservative challenge* (pp. ix–xxxi). Walnut Creek, CA: Left Coast Press.

Denzin, N. K., & Lincoln, Y. S. (2005). The discipline and practice of qualitative research. In N. K. Denzin & Y. S. Lincoln (Eds.), *The SAGE handbook of qualitative research* (3rd ed., pp. 1–32). Thousand Oaks, CA: Sage.

Denzin, N. K., Lincoln, Y. S., & Giardina, M. D. (2006, November/December). Disciplining qualitative research. *International Journal of Qualitative Studies in Education, 19*(6), 769–782.

Dixon-Woods, M., Bonas, S., Booth, A., Jones, D. R., Miller, T., Sutton, A. J., et al. (2006, February). How can systematic reviews incorporate qualitative research? A critical perspective. *Qualitative Research, 6*(1), 27–44.

Dixon-Woods, M., Shaw, R. L., Agarwal, S., & Smith, J. A. (2004). The problem of appraising qualitative research. *Quality & Safety in Health Care, 13*, 223–225.

Eisenhart, M. (2006, November/December). Qualitative science in experimental time. *International Journal of Qualitative Studies in Education, 19*(6), 697–708.

Eisner, E. W. (1991). *The enlightened eye.* New York: Macmillan.

Erickson, F., & Gutierrez, K. (2002, November). Culture, rigor, and science in educational research. *Educational Researcher, 31*(8), 21–24.

Feuer, M. J. (2006). Response to Bettie St.Pierre's "Scientifically Based Research in Education: Epistemology and Ethics." *Adult Education Quarterly, 56*(3), 267–272.

Feuer, M. J., Towne, L., & Shavelson, R. J. (2002, November). Science, culture, and educational research. *Educational Researcher, 31*(8), 4–14.

Finley, S. (2008). Arts-based research. In J. G. Knowles & A. L. Cole (Eds.), *Handbook of the arts in qualitative research* (pp. 71–81). Thousand Oaks, CA: Sage.

Freeman, M., deMarrais, K., Preissle, J., Roulston, K., & St.Pierre, E. A. (2007). Standards of evidence in qualitative research: An incitement to discourse. *Educational Researcher, 36*(1), 1–8.

Gilgun, J. F. (2006, March). The four cornerstones of qualitative research. *Qualitative Health Research, 16*(3), 436–443.

Guba, E., & Lincoln, Y. S. (1989). *Fourth-generation evaluation.* Newbury Park, CA: Sage.

Guba, E., & Lincoln, Y. S. (2005). Paradigmatic controversies, contradictions, and emerging confluences. In N. K. Denzin & Y. S. Lincoln (Eds.), *The SAGE handbook of qualitative research* (3rd ed., pp. 191–216). Thousand Oaks, CA: Sage.

Habermas, J. (1972). *Knowledge and human interests* (2nd ed.). London: Heinemann.

Habermas, J. (2006). *The divided West.* Cambridge, UK: Polity.

Hammersley, M. (2004). Some questions about evidence-based practice in education. In G. Thomas & R. Pring (Eds.), *Evidence-based practice in education* (pp. 133–149). New York: Open University Press.

Hammersley, M. (2005a, December). Close encounters of a political kind: The threat from the evidence-based policy-making and practice movement. *Qualitative Researcher, 1,* 2–4.

Hammersley, M. (2005b, April). Countering the "New Orthodoxy" in educational research: A response to Phil Hodkinson. *British Educational Research Journal, 31*(2), 139–156.

Hodkinson, P. (2004, February). Research as a form of work: Expertise, community and methodological objectivity. *British Educational Research Journal, 30*(1), 9–26.

Jackson, N., & Waters, E. (2005). Criteria for the systematic review of health promotion and public health interventions. *Health Promotion International, 20*(4), 367–374.

Jefferson, T., Rudin, M., Brodney Folse, S., & Davidoff, F. (2006). Editorial peer review for improving the quality of reports of biomedical studies. *Cochrane Database of Methodology Reviews, 1.*

Judson, H. F. (2004). *The great betrayal: Fraud in science.* New York: Harcourt Brace.

Kaplan, E. (2004). *With God on their side: How the Christian fundamentalists trampled science, policy, and democracy in George W. Bush's White House.* New York: New Press.

Larner, G. (2004). Family therapy and the politics of evidence. *Journal of Family Therapy, 26,* 17–39.

Lather, P. (1993). *Getting smart: Feminist research and pedagogy with/in the postmodern.* New York: Routledge.

Lather, P. (2004). This is your father's paradigm: Government intrusion and the case of qualitative research in education. *Qualitative Inquiry, 10*(1), 15–34.

Lather, P. (2006, November/December). Foucauldian scientificity: Rethinking the nexus of qualitative research and educational policy analysis. *International Journal of Qualitative Studies in Education, 19*(6), 783–792.

Lather, P. (2007). *Getting lost: Feminist efforts toward a double(d) science.* Albany: SUNY Press.

Lincoln, Y. S., & Cannella, G. S. (2004, February). Dangerous discourses: Methodological conservatism and governmental regimes of truth. *Qualitative Inquiry, 10*(1), 5–10.

Lincoln, Y. S., & Guba, E. (1985). *Naturalistic inquiry.* Beverly Hills, CA: Sage.

Lundberg, G. (1926, October). Quantitative methods in sociology. *Social Forces, 39,* 19–24.

MacLure, M. (2006, November/December). The bone in the throat: Some uncertain thoughts on baroque method. *International Journal of Qualitative Studies in Education, 19*(6), 7239–7746.

Madison, D. S. (2005). *Critical ethnography: Methods, ethics, and performance.* Thousand Oaks, CA: Sage.

Maxwell, J. A. (2004a). Causal explanation, qualitative research, and scientific inquiry in education. *Educational Researcher, 23*(2), 3–11.

Maxwell, J. A. (2004b, August). Using qualitative methods for causal explanation. *Field Methods, 16*(3), 243–264.

Monastersky, R. (2002, November 25). Research groups accuse education department of using ideology in decisions about data. *Chronicle of Higher Education, 2.*

Moran-Ellis, J., Alexander, V. D., Cronin, A., Dickenson, M., Fielding, J., Sleney, J., et al. (2006, February). Triangulation and integration: Processes, claims, and implications. *Qualitative Research, 6*(1), 45–60.

Morse, J. M. (2006a, March). The politics of evidence. *Qualitative Health Research, 16*(3), 395–404.

Morse, J. M. (2006b, March). Reconceptualizing qualitative inquiry. *Qualitative Health Research, 16*(3), 415–422.

National CASP Collaboration. (2006). *10 questions to help you make sense of qualitative research, Critical Appraisal Skills Program (CASP).* Milton Keynes Primary Care Trust. Available at http://www.pdptoolkit.co.uk/Files/Critical%20Appraisal/casp .htm

National Center for Dissemination of Disability Research. (2007). Available at http://www .ncddr.org/kt/products.focus.focus9/

National Research Council. (2002). *Scientific research in education.* Committee on Scientific Principles for Education Research (R. J. Shavelson & L. Towne, Eds.). Washington, DC, National Academies Press.

National Research Council. (2005). *Advancing scientific research in education.* Committee on Scientific Principles for Education Research (L. Towne, L. Wise, & T. M. Winters, Eds.). Washington, DC, National Academies Press.

Popay, J., Rogers, A., & Williams, G. (1998). Rationale and standards for the systematic review of qualitative literature in health services research. *Qualitative Health Research, 8,* 341–351.

Preissle, J. (2006, November/December). Envisioning qualitative inquiry: A view across four decades. *International Journal of Qualitative Studies in Education, 19*(6), 685–696.

Quigley, L. (1996). *The blind men and the elephant.* New York: Scribner.

Rains, F. V., Archibald, J., & Deyhle, D. (2000). Introduction: Through our eyes and in our own words—The voices of indigenous scholars. *International Journal of Qualitative Studies in Education, 13*(4), 337–342.

Richardson, L. (2000a). Evaluating ethnography. *Qualitative Inquiry, 6*(2), 253–255.

Richardson, L. (2000b). Writing: A method of inquiry. In N. K. Denzin & Y. S. Lincoln (Eds.), *Handbook of qualitative research* (2nd ed., pp. 923–948). Thousand Oaks, CA: Sage.

Saukko, P. (2003). *Doing research in cultural studies: An introduction to classical and new methodological approaches.* London: Sage.

Smith, J. K., & Deemer, D. K. (2000). The problem of criteria in the age of relativism. In N. K. Denzin & Y. S. Lincoln (Eds.), *Handbook of qualitative research* (2nd ed., pp. 877–896). Thousand Oaks, CA: Sage.

Smith, J. K., & Hodkinson, P. (2005). Relativism, criteria and politics. In N. K. Denzin & Y. S. Lincoln (Eds.), *The SAGE handbook of qualitative research* (3rd ed., pp. 915–932). Thousand Oaks, CA: Sage.

Smith, L. T. (1999). *Decolonizing methodologies: Research and indigenous peoples.* Dunedin, NZ: University of Otago Press.

Spencer, L., Ritchie, J., Lewis, L., & Dillon, L. (2003). *Quality in qualitative evaluation: A framework for assessing research evidence.* London: Government Chief Social Researcher's Office, Crown Copyright.

Stanfield, J. H. (2006, November/December). The possible restorative justice functions of qualitative research. *International Journal of Qualitative Studies in Education, 19*(6), 723–728.

St.Pierre, E. A. (2006). Scientifically based research in education: Epistemology and ethics. *Adult Education Quarterly, 56*(3), 239–266.

St.Pierre, E. A., & Roulston, K. (2006, November/December). The state of qualitative inquiry: A contested science. *International Journal of Qualitative Studies in Education, 19*(6), 673–684.

Stronach, I. (2006, November/December). Enlightenment and the "Heart of Darkness": (Neo) imperialism in the Congo, and elsewhere. *International Journal of Qualitative Studies in Education, 19*(6), 757–768.

Stronach, I., Garratt, D., Pearce, C., & Piper, H. (2007, March). Reflexivity, the picturing of selves, the forging of method. *Qualitative Inquiry, 13*(2), 179–203.

Teddlie, C., & Tashakkori, A. (2003). Major issues and controversies in the use of mixed methods in the social and behavioral sciences. In A Tashakkori & C. Teddlie (Eds.), *Handbook of mixed methods in social and behavioral research* (pp. 3–50). Thousand Oaks, CA: Sage.

Thomas, G. (2004). Introduction: Evidence: Practice. In G. Thomas & R. Pring (Eds.), *Evidence-based practice in education* (pp. 1–20). New York: Open University Press.

Timmermans, S., & Berg, M. (2003). *The gold standard: The challenge of evidence-based medicine and standardization in health care.* Philadelphia: Temple University Press.

Torrance, H. (2006). Research quality and research governance in the United Kingdom. In N. K. Denzin & M. Giardina (Eds.), *Qualitative inquiry and the conservative challenge* (pp. 127–148). Walnut Creek, CA: Left Coast Press.

Viadero, D. (2006). New group of researchers focuses on scientific study. *Education Week, 25*(21), 1 & 16.

White, C. (2003, February 1). Little evidence for effectiveness of scientific peer review. *British Medical Journal, 326*(7383), 241.

Wolcott, H. F. (1999). *Ethnography: A way of seeing.* Walnut Creek, CA: AltaMira Press.

17

Writing Into Position

Strategies for Composition and Evaluation

Ronald J. Pelias

When I write it feels like I'm carving bone. It feels like I'm creating my own face, my own heart.

—G. Anzaldúa (1999, p. 95)

I'm sitting at my desk considering how the self is positioned in scholarly writing, how the self commands attention even when the self is not seemingly central to the discussion. As this argument gathers in my head, I remember Joan Didion's initial claim in her essay, "Why I Write" (2000):

> In many ways writing is the act of saying I, of imposing oneself upon other people, of saying *listen to me, see it my way, change your mind.* It's an aggressive, even hostile act. You can disguise its aggressiveness all you want with veils of subordinate clauses and qualifiers and tentative subjunctives, with ellipses and evasions—with the whole manner of intimating rather than claiming, of alluding rather than stating—but there's no getting around the fact that setting words on paper is the tactic of a secret bully, an invasion, an imposition of the writer's sensibility on the reader's most private space. (pp. 17–18, emphasis original)

I am drawn to Didion's insight, seduced by its logic. It seems, in part, to write my experience of writing, positioning me in a productive place, a place where I might see myself writing. Being pulled in by Didion, I transcribe her comment in my journal and jot the following note:

> When I write, I am asserting a self, insisting that I matter. In general, I would argue, research is a way of claiming space. It takes an extended turn with the implication that one's writing merits attention. Such a commitment is a call to arrogance and to significance. Research cannot exist without a belief in its seriousness; it cannot prosper in the belief in its singular truth. Research lives in possibility and in promise.

In that moment of composition, I come to see what I believe, what I did not know before I started writing. I arrive at a place of resonant articulation. I move toward clarity, toward, as Robert Frost (1963) would suggest his poems are, "a momentary stay against confusion" (p. 2). I perform myself into being and I emerge within and through the consequences of my always political and material assertions. I am engaging in a process that Laurel Richardson (2000; see also Richardson & St.Pierre, 2005) would call "writing as a method of inquiry" (p. 923).

Following Richardson, in this chapter I build on the idea that writing is a "method of inquiry." I write myself into a position that identifies what I have come to understand by that claim as well as what I presently believe about qualitative writing. Part I argues that writing functions as both a realization and a record. As a realization, it locates itself on a continuum of possibility to certainty, of the subjunctive to declarative, as well as situates itself on a continuum of personal discovery to public argument. As a record, realizations find their form as poetic, narrative, and dramatic utterances and emerge as descriptive, deconstructive, and critical claims. Part II argues that the evocative, reflexive, embodied, partial and partisan, and material characteristics often associated with qualitative research encourage certain compositional strategies. Part III, using the device of juxtaposition, outlines how the more and less effective essay establishes itself.

Part I: Positioning Self, Positioning Writing

I am sitting at my desk trying to remember some of the creative writers I have read that suggest in some way that writing is a method of inquiry. I open my journal and quickly find Stephen Dunn's (1993) claim that an essayist might best be seen as "a person who believes there's value in being overheard clarifying things for himself" (p. ix). On another page, I discover Lee Smith (2007) echoing Dunn's suggestion:

> Whether we are writing fiction or nonfiction, journaling or writing for publication, writing itself is an inherently therapeutic activity. Simply to line up words one after another upon a page is to create some order where it did not exist, to give recognizable shape to the sadness and chaos of our lives. (p. 41)

This clarifying function of writing I see on another page of my journal when Theodore Roethke (2001) notes that a poem is "one more triumph over chaos" (p. 77). My search continues with Natalie Goldberg (1986): "Writing is the act of burning through the fog in your mind" (p. 86). What these and other creative writers have come to understand is that writing is a strategy of circling, of making present what might have slipped away, of calling into focus through an attentiveness to and negotiation with language. It is a process, as Marvin Bell (2002) would have it, where the writer "listens" to the writing "as it goes" (p. 13). In that way, writing is, as M. L. Rosenthal (1987) explains, "the unfolding of a realization, the satisfying of a need to bring to the surface the inner realities of the psyche" (p. 5). As Don Geiger (1967) says of the lyric poem, writing "records the process of the speaker's realization" (p. 152). With such surrounding discourse, it is not surprising that Richardson would up the stakes by arguing for writing's methodological status and that her argument would be embraced by many scholars who engage in qualitative research.

Joining those who align themselves with Richardson, I want to outline how writing might function as a realization and as a record. These terms—*realization* and *record*—point toward the writer's process and completed text. Writers come to realize what they believe in the process of writing, in the act of finding the language that crystallizes their thoughts and sentiments. It is a process of "writing into" rather than "writing up" a subject. When writing *up* a subject, writers know what they wish to say before the composition process begins. When writing *into* a subject, writers discover what they know through writing. It is a process of using language to look at, lean into, and lend oneself to an experience under consideration. This "languaging" unearths the writer's articulate presence. It positions, marks a place, a material stance in the world. In short, languaging matters.

As writers proceed, their realizations come forward on a continuum between the declarative and the subjunctive. These realizations might be called "is-ness" or "perhaps-ness" utterances. "Is-ness" claims assert, "This is . . ."; "perhaps-ness" statements reside in "may be." For writers, then, a realization may carry considerable authority, materialize without doubt, feel certain, or may exist tentatively, appearing as a possibility among many, contingent upon circumstances. Realizations settle into writers in different ways, often guiding the stance they take toward their subjects. Moving with assurance or caution, believing they possess overwhelming evidence or only perhaps a small piece of a larger puzzle, writers stand behind their ideas, sometimes pushing them forward as points that seem obvious and worthy of attention and sometimes holding them close by, keeping them from making too much noise. On the "is-ness" side of the continuum, arguments come forward as definitive and, at times, sufficient for public advocacy. On the "perhaps-ness" side, claims invite further dialogue, call for further research, live in their questions.

Realizations, whether emerging as "is-ness" or "perhaps-ness" claims, also unfold on a continuum from the personal to the public. Personal realizations inform writers about themselves as individuals. They place them in touch with their own attitudes, beliefs, and feelings; with their own relational attachments and political investments; with their own sense of the world. Such writing might be located in personal identity (e.g., Alexander, 2006; Myers, 2008; Trujillo, 2004; Warren, 2001; Young, 2007); in trauma, illness, and loss (e.g., Defenbaugh, 2011; Ellis, 1995; Rambo Ronai, 1996; Richardson, 2007; Watt, 2005, 2008); or in relational dynamics (e.g., Adams, 2006; Poulos, 2009; Tillmann-Healy, 2001). In short, personal realizations tell writers how they might see themselves, how they might make sense of their experiences. When sharing their insights, they invite readers to acknowledge their perspectives and perhaps to identify with them. Their writing becomes a location for readers' consideration.

Public realizations place writers in contact with the social or cultural sphere. They come to understand how the social world unfolds, highlighting how structural schemes guide human behavior, how institutional practices control human desires and dictate entitlements, how cultural understandings privilege some but not others. Such writings might focus on colonial and postcolonial logics (e.g., Anzaldúa, 1999; Bhabha, 1994), corporate and governmental behaviors (e.g., Goodall, 1989, 2006; Tracy, 2003), or social and political injustices (e.g., Denzin, 2008; Lockford, 2008). They often carry an implicit or explicit call to action. They may come forward as a utopian dream, as a location of hope, or as an ethical imperative. They may call for a reordering in the name of social justice. They may appear radical, even anarchist, when change from within seems insufficient or impossible. They may excite; they may incite.

The familiar feminist insight that the personal is political is a quick reminder of the dangers of separating the personal and the public. Personal utterances are revelatory in the public sphere, particularly when previously silenced or minimized, and public pronouncement and legislation find their most profound articulation as they impact individual bodies. By contemplating the personal, public realizations emerge; by considering the public, personal insights become apparent. The personal/public distinction is useful, however, for noting what seems rhetorically foregrounded in a given work.

Realizations find their form by becoming a record of what a writer has come to discover. They take shape as a poetic, narrative, or dramatic record. While these forms share much in common, scholars tend to gravitate to one form or another in their work and, in so doing, their scholarly efforts unfold differently. The poetic record comes forward as poem, an inquiry that depends upon the power of poetic devices (e.g., figurative language, prosody, lining) to structure its insights. Whether turning to their own or others' experiences as data, as a source for their evidentiary claims, researchers (e.g., Brady, 2003; Hartnett, 2003; Prendergast, Leggo, & Sameshima, 2009) working with poetic form use the condensed emotional intensity of poetry as well as careful research to render their subjects. As Hartnett explains, turning to the poetic merges "the evidence-gathering force of scholarship with the emotion-producing force of poetry" (p. 1). In this sense, such efforts stand as what some have called "investigative poetry" (e.g., Hartnett, 2003; Hartnett & Engels, 2005; Sanders, 1976).

The narrative record is the form most frequently found in scholarly circles. It is a formed tale, told by a narrator, relying upon point of view, plot, and character. In most cases, the narrators in scholarly research are reliable; that is, they share the same values as their authors. As readers engage these tales, they expect authors to operate under a contract of truth-telling. They assume that authors will try to render their stories as honestly as they can, recognizing, of course, that no account is the final word. "Storying" is a self-making process. It helps authors construct their perceptions of the world, see new terrain, and live with alternative views. It is also a culture-making process. Stories often carry a sense of social responsibility, a need to tell to further social justice. Such stories come forward as acts of witnessing, as testimony on behalf of others. Ellis (2009a) offers a telling description of the power of story for scholars:

> Stories are what we have, the barometers by which we fashion our identities, organize and live our lives, connect and compare our lives to others, and make decisions about how to live. These tales open our hearts and eyes to ourselves and the world around us, helping us change our lives and our world for the better. (p. 16)

The dramatic record taps into theatrical practice, highlighting conflict and dialogue. It may emerge as a script on the page (e.g., Ellis & Bochner, 1992) or on the stage (e.g., Gray & Sinding, 2002; Pineau, 2000; Saldana, 2005). Relying upon the artistic techniques of performance, scholars working with dramatic forms write their research findings as scripts designed to display multiple speakers engaged in interaction with one another or multiple voices reflecting varying perspectives. The labels most commonly associated with the dramatic record are ethnodrama (e.g., Mienczakowski, 2001; Saldana, 2005) and performance ethnography (e.g., Alexander, 2005; Denzin, 2003; Madison, 2005) The aim of such renderings is to offer embodied representations, portrayals that bring to life research findings, often with the desire to participate in "a cultural politics of hope" (Denzin, 2003, p. 24).

Whether realizations take shape as poetic, narrative, or dramatic utterances, they also take form as interpretive, deconstructive, or critical utterances. Realizations, in an interpretive form, rely most heavily on description; in deconstructive form, they open possibilities; in critical form, their investigative pulse pushes toward social action. To think of writing as a realization recorded in a given form is to suggest that writing is a performative act. It is a speech act that participates in the world, a material utterance that matters. It may function to simply reinforce current construction or it may provide alternative ways of seeing the world. It is always political. The speaker is always, for better or worse, positioned. To say that writing is a method of inquiry best understood as realization recorded in a given form, however, does not offer the specific strategies that qualitative scholars often employ. The next section turns to some of these compositional strategies.

Part II: Compositional Strategies

I am sitting at my desk trying to identify how qualitative researchers make their cases, how they shape words on the page, how they bring readers into their essays. I remember some of the key descriptions of qualitative work, descriptions that point in similar directions across numerous arguments on behalf of qualitative work (e.g., Colyar, 2009; Denzin & Lincoln, 2005; Ellis, 2004; Goodall, 2000, 2008; Pollock, 1998). I begin by noting how qualitative scholars often indicate that their work is evocative, reflexive, embodied, partial and partisan, and material, and that each of these dimensions pushes these scholars toward certain compositional strategies. Although separated here for explanatory purposes,

I should note that readers are likely to discover writers using multiple strategies within their essays. All essays are necessarily partial and partisan as well as material. Writing, for better or worse, matters. Essays vary in their degree of evocativeness, reflexivity, and embodiment. Readers, however, often have a feel for what strategy or strategies are being privileged in a given essay.

EVOCATIVE

Qualitative researchers who employ the evocative do so to enrich or disrupt normative understanding. Their work relies on the *literary* and *possibilizing*. In calling upon the literary, they use literary devices (e.g., figurative language, dialogue, rhythm) to create an experience for the reader. They see their work as aesthetic, borrowing from various literary traditions and believing that the affective has a place in scholarly writing. Tillmann-Healy (2003), for example, offers a compelling rendering of her family relationships during a time of loss through the use of metonymy. She describes her own and other family members' hands to establish the situation's relational and emotional force. In a particularly poignant moment, she tells the reader her thoughts as she looks at her grandfather's hands:

> I stare at the eighty years ingrained in my grandfather's hands. Culinary hands that kept enlisted men fed in the Second World War. Supple hands that stroked my grandmother's raven hair. Strong hands that repaired the dam restraining the eager Mississippi. Calloused hands that constructed my father's childhood home on Elm Street. Proud hands that cradled three boys, and later, eight grandchildren. Paternal hands that carved holiday turkeys. Nurturing hands that cultivated the garden soil that burst open in spring in symphonies of crimson and marigold. Tired hands soothed by sweating glasses of lime Kool-Aid. Forgetful hands that rattled the cup of Yahtzee dice for one too many turns. Aging hands stained with the burgundy of exploded blood vessels. Incorrigible Parkinson's hands that played invisible pianos as he sat in his napping chair, watching "wrastling." (p. 176)

This passage finds its power in the rhythmic repetition, in the carefully selected details, and in the chronological structure that delays the telling hands of her grandfather's illness. Through the literary, the reader, guided by Tillmann-Healy, learns about loss.

Possibilizing works by putting on display multiple readings and alternative actions that the reader can consider. It strives for an escape from the crisis of representation, fully aware that it cannot fully satisfy its own desire. It values writing, to use Derrida's term, in excess in order to create a space for dialogue and different ways of being. As Pollock (1998) suggests, "Performative, evocative writing confounds normative distinctions between critical and creative (hard and soft, true and false, masculine and feminine), allying itself with logics of possibility rather than of validity or causality" (p. 81). Madison (2005) further explains,

> In a performance of possibilities, the possible suggests a movement culminating in creation and change. It is active, creative work that weaves the life of the mind with being mindful of life, of merging the text with the world, of critically traversing the margin and the center, and of opening more and different paths for enlivening relations and spaces. (p. 172)

Writers who rely on possibilizing might present conflicting narratives of the same event, generate a proliferation of readings of a given episode, identify various actions that could be taken, call attention to the inadequacy of their rendering, and so on. They write cautious of language's hegemony, cautious that their advocacy does not become another gesture of power. They write for the possible.

Often, both literary and possibilizing strategies take form by deploying multiple speakers. Some calling upon these strategies aspire to the aesthetic standards of dramatic scripts and find their complete articulation in full theatrical staging. Such is typically the case with ethnodrama, performance texts, and performance ethnography. Spry's "From Goldilocks to Dreadlocks: Hair-Raising Tales of Racializing Bodies" (2001a), Smith's *Fires in the Mirror* (1993) and *Twilight: Los Angeles, 1992* (2000), and Kaufman's *The Laramie Project* (Kaufman & Members of the Tectonic Theater Project, 2001) are clear examples of this type of work. Others using these strategies are content to have their drama on the page, using multiple speakers to establish various perspectives, juxtapositions, and collaborations. Ellis's "Telling Tales on Neighbors: Ethics in Two Voices," (2009b), Denzin's *Searching for Yellowstone* (2008), and Gale and Wyatt's "Two Men Talking: A Nomadic Inquiry Into Collaborative Writing" (2008) serve as instructive examples.

REFLEXIVE

Reflexive writing strategies allow researchers to turn back on themselves, to examine how their presence or stance functions in relationship to their subject. Reflexive writers, ethically and politically self-aware, make themselves part of their own inquiry. Reflexive writing strategies include indicating how the researcher emerged as a *contaminant,* how the researcher's *insider* status was revelatory or blinding, and how the researcher is *implicated* in the problem being addressed. Researchers who see themselves as a contaminant might argue that their own positionality or procedures negatively influenced the study. In such cases, researchers offer a cautionary note suggesting that their claims be read in full awareness of the researcher's influence. Rhetorically, this strategy often proves effective because the reader trusts that the researcher is sensitive to the issue and is likely to temper his or her arguments accordingly.

Researchers who claim insider status indicate that they share cultural membership with the group under investigation. Often, insider status comes unquestioned (e.g., "as a Japanese immigrant living in the United States," "as a single mother of three children," "as a person with cancer"). Other times, insider status may become a point of discussion. In such cases, researchers describe their relationship to the group they are studying to argue that they have spent sufficient time or been accepted by others warranting their claim of insider membership. Once insider status is established, researchers may assert that their insider position allowed them to have insights that outsiders could not or, conversely, that their insider status may have kept them from seeing operative cultural logics.

Chawla (2003) offers an instructive example. She presents a deeply reflexive essay about her research on East Indian arranged marriage. As a woman of Indian background, Chawla first notes that she wrote her own story before collecting tales from other Indian women. Then she questions her procedure: "I began to ask myself why I wrote my story before I listened to my participants. I wondered if I had imposed my story on them by writing first" (p. 276). Later, she troubles her own insider status:

> While I do have incomplete stories from my memories of the different arranged marriages that surround me, these are stories about other people in these marriages, and not stories about *myself.* In these memories, I remain an observer, albeit an observer to myself. My lack of a direct involvement in the reality of an arranged marriage makes me question my legitimacy to do this research. I am still worried that I am too much on the *outside* in this existential and intellectual displacement. (p. 277, emphasis original)

Such arguments are particularly useful writing strategies because they acknowledge that researchers cannot be separated from their research, that the researchers' relationship to those they study as well as their procedures influence their findings, and that researchers who reflect about their stance offer more trustworthy and honest accounts.

Researchers who see themselves as implicated write about their complicity in the problem they are trying to address. In short, they position themselves as contributing to the predicament. For example, one might argue that he or she, as a meat eater, has some responsibility for deforestation; that he or she, although arguing for racial equality, has participated in racist speech; or that he or she served in a war he or she did not support. Structurally, this strategy often first acknowledges one's mistakes and ends with a pledge to alternative conduct. It has the advantage of pointing one's finger at oneself instead of at others. In doing so, it invites others who may have committed similar "sins" to join with the researcher in enlightened behaviors. Denzin (2008) offers a powerful example. He implicates himself as he tracks his own family history with Native Americans. Following an introductory chapter, he begins his discussion, "In the 1950s my brother, Mark, and I spent our summers, until we were young teenagers, with our grandparents on their farm south of Iowa City, Iowa. Saturday nights were special. Grandpa loved those 'cowboy and Indian' movies, and so did I" (p. 25). In the next paragraph, he writes, "In fourth grade I was Squanto in the Thanksgiving play about the pilgrims" (p. 25). Throughout, Denzin places his previous behavior under suspicion as he writes "our way into a militant democratic utopian space, a space where the color line disappears, and justice for all is more than a dream" (p. 23). In a similar fashion, Myers (2008) uses the trope of dentistry to uncover his straight and White privilege. His line, "When I was about 12 years old, it was obvious to my parents and my peers (and myself whenever I looked in the mirror) that I was simply not straight enough" (p. 161), offers a flavor of how he implicates himself throughout his essay.

EMBODIED

Qualitative researchers who value embodiment write from a location of corporeal presence. They see the body as a site of knowledge demanding scholarly attention (Conquergood, 1991; Madison, 1999, 2005; Spry, 2001b, 2009). As Spry (2001a) explains, "Coaxing the body from the shadows of academe and consciously integrating it into the process and production of knowledge requires that we view knowledge in the context of the body from which it is generated" (p. 725). To do so, researchers write into the *mind/body split* as a corrective to cognitive renderings, call upon the *sensuous* body, and tap into *bodily experiences*.

Writing into the mind/body split, researchers make the body present. Instead of privileging mind over the body, they insist that the body provides flesh to sterile, distant, cognitive accounts. They proceed by writing from affective space, often with the desire to provide a more complete picture of human experience. For them, purely cognitive descriptions of human behavior fail to give rich and nuanced portrayals, erase the individual in the name of generalizability, and lack resonant validity. Closely associated is sensuous writing. As a writing strategy, it asks researchers to speak from the senses, to recognize how the body takes in the world around it, to allow the body to be alive in research. Stoller (1997) explains that sensuous scholarship "is an attempt to reawaken profoundly the scholar's body by demonstrating how the fusion of the intelligible and the sensible can be applied to scholarly practices and representations" (p. xv). Another related strategy is writing from bodily experience. In this case, researchers speak about some incident where the body was the site of the incident's happening. Scholars have used this strategy to write about such topics as illness, trauma, violence, grief, race, sexuality, gender, ethnicity, and so on. Common to such studies is that the body becomes a location of knowledge, a place where the researcher speaks from felt experience, from an awareness of what the body endured, from a sense of self. In doing so, the vulnerable body gains agency by asserting its history and living presence. It turns victim into survivor and the voiceless into a cultural worker. It carries the potential for identification and for social change.

Spry (2001b) presents a telling example of how her body becomes deployed on behalf of scholarly inquiry. Writing about her decision as a White woman to grow dreadlocks, she says,

> Their time had come.
>
> And as they emerged, they evoked many comments from many people.
>
> A most interesting theme of comments emerged from White women:
>
> "Tami, aren't you afraid of offending Black people
>
> by wearing dreads?" "I mean, what will they think?"
>
> "Aren't you 'taking something away' from Black people
>
> by growing dreads?"
>
> As if I could
>
> As if I were in   racial drag
>
> As if I were   drag racing   to the finish line
>
> of an essentialized,   homogenized   *Blackness.*

But what began to emerge for me

were essentialized, homogenized images of

Whiteness.

And I began to see the ways

that I had been living much of my life

In White   racial   drag.   (p. 724)

Spry, in this brief excerpt from a longer work, writes about and from her body, allowing the reader to consider how White privilege and, more generally, race functions in U.S. culture. Readers sense her resistance to those who through their questions would essentialize race, feel her struggle to make sense of her own racialized body, and question their own racial positioning and understanding. Spry gives readers a performative encounter with race, fully embodied, felt, and emotionally honest.

PARTIAL AND PARTISAN

Researchers proceed with the knowledge that their work is always partial and partisan. That is, they understand that they can never say everything about anything (partial) and that everything they say carries ideological weight (partisan). Given such awareness, researchers may elect to write into the heart of the matter by calling attention to *linguistic limitations,* by highlighting how a given argument is *ideologically laden,* or by *uncovering* the hidden. Using the strategy of noting linguistic limitations permits researchers to acknowledge how language is slippery, never in perfect correspondence to the subject it attempts to capture. Noting linguistic limitations draws attention to the elusive and inexpressible that haunts all qualitative inquiry. It reminds readers what is at stake in any rendering. Researchers might put this strategy into play by discussing the implications of a given word choice, by calling into question their own representations (e.g., specifying what is missing, suggesting why their writing is inadequate), by offering multiple narratives of the same event, or by continuously adding to a previous account. Such maneuvers remind the reader to stay alert, to accept any claim with caution, to be suspicious of language's ability to represent human experience.

Holman Jones (2002) offers a poignantly expressed example:

Some days I wonder if, after all the hours I've spent in seminar rooms and alone in front of my computer writing, I have been reduced to making lists of words, to scripting fragments. Unable to express in finely wrought sentences the injustices of oppression or the beauty of a solution, I make lists that signify worlds. Words that set off explosions of thought and feeling. (p. 187)

In this moment, Holman Jones offers the reader a glimpse into her struggle to write in a way that satisfies her. She hints that her academic position and her isolation as a writer may be contributing factors. She does not have the words to capture what she desires. She has only fragments, lists, that point to her subject, but she is unable to write what troubles her most. As her essay progresses, the reader sees that she does, in part through the use of fragments and lists, write her desire. This turn is not uncommon in qualitative inquiry. Readers often encounter researchers who lament language's limitations while demonstrating its power.

Researchers, recognizing that all utterances are ideologically laden, point to language itself as well as their own language practices. When discussing language itself, they might demonstrate how language privileges some at the expense of others, how a word's etymology points to its unproductive connotations, or how language conceals as much as it reveals. Such writing shows how language as a discursive system is never innocent, without bias. When turning on their own language practices, researchers might make explicit their ideological commitments and their operative hidden assumptions. They often do so by revealing their personal beliefs, noting their private agendas, or specifying their ethical stance. Closely associated to the strategy of making ideology explicit is the tactic of *uncovery*. Uncovery is a deconstruction, an act of revealing the absent in a given assertion. Its primary approach is proliferation, excess, with the aim, at times, of reconstruction.

Russel y Rodriguez (2002) argues that her own discipline, anthropology, requires "static and uncomplicated single identities of its subjects and theoreticians" (p. 347) that are at odds with her own positionality:

The Chicana among feminists, the feminist among Chicanos. The Chicano nationalist among Euro-Americans, the bridge builder among Chicano nationalists. Half Anglo, half Chicana. The newcomer in academe, the over-educated at home. The minority among the majority, the mainstream among raza. (pp. 347–348)

Russel y Rodriguez recognizes how each of these descriptors places her in differing ideological currents. Uncovering these currents and marking their force, she writes to free herself and others from a space where "both normative and oppositional stances contribute to a silencing praxis in anthropology" (p. 348).

MATERIAL

As I hope I made clear earlier in this essay, writing as a realization and record is a performative act, a material manifestation of a writer's labor and ideology, an enunciation that carries weight in the social world. Material texts often demonstrate what matters through personal, scholarly, and social articulations. Among the strategies available to researchers foregrounding the material are the *curative,* the *citational corrective,* and the *socially consequential.* Writing curatively, researchers work therapeutically in the desire to heal their own and others' wounds. They may be struggling, for instance, to come to terms with illness, relational tensions, oppression, or physical violence. Poulos (2009) gives a seductive explanation of why researchers call upon the curative:

> As I inquire into the depth and contours and possibilities of the secret world of families, I necessarily encounter some of the "darker" moments of the human spirit. But, along the way, I discover—in the eruption of a story, in the soft reminiscent light of accidental talk, in a burst of memory overstepping memory—a world of hope. (p. 15)

The hope functions not only for the authors of curative texts but also for those who might see themselves in the account and for those whose understanding of a given problem is enlarged.

Kiesinger (2003), writing of her sexual abuse and of her resulting binge eating and purging in her powerful poem, "He Touched, He Took," stands as a useful example. The reader is first given a description of the assault. Here is a small sample:

> She will put language to the images and sensations as they come to her.
>
> His breath, hot on her neck.
>
> His scent—an odd mixture of dirt and Lysol.
>
> The feel of his hands, rough and calloused, as he places candy in hers—
>
> soft and small. (p. 177)

The poem next moves to her descriptions of binging and purging—binging to fill the void he left, purging to rid herself of him. The poem ends with the following: "She writes from and through her memories with the hope of recovering what he took when he touched—with the hope of rediscovering what was fundamentally her own" (p. 184). Kiesinger's text becomes another purging. She writes of her own horrific experience, an experience that, unfortunately, others have lived. She writes with hope for her own healing and marks a space where others might find comfort in seeing their own story told. She writes to teach us all.

Researchers who use citational corrective as a writing strategy start from dissatisfaction with a given scholarly claim. They proceed by writing against what stands as an adequate account. They challenge ongoing logics by such tactics as juxtaposing their own personal experience against disciplinary claims, speaking from the margins, and adding the affective to cognitive accounts. My desire, for example, to write "Confessions of an Apprehensive Performer" (Pelias, 1999) initiated with the belief that despite the considerable amount of research on communication apprehension, none captured the felt experience of the apprehensive speaker. I placed myself in dialogue with research findings to demonstrate how as an apprehensive I seldom saw myself in these cognitive claims, or when I did, the claims rang empty. In one section, I quote several scholars on the topic and offer flippant responses to their points. Here is one instance:

Watson, Monroe, and Atterstrom:

Communication apprehension (CA), the fear of oral communication with another person or persons, is found to affect many individuals negatively by inhibiting amounts of communication and interfering with effectiveness in life experiences. (*Communication Quarterly, 37*, 1989, p. 67)
   No shit. (p. 83)

My aim was not to denigrate other scholars but to put on display my emotional response as an apprehensive when reading such points and to suggest that research on apprehension might benefit by attending to apprehensives' personal accounts.

The writing strategy that foregrounds the socially consequential puts on display alternative social constructions and practices. Scholars who are committed to the idea that research should matter to everyday lives take as their charge to articulate new ways of being. Their work comes forward as an emancipatory pedagogy, ethically charged, calling for action. They strive to move beyond description, to become critically engaged, to create utopian spaces. They are cultural workers, laboring on behalf of social justice. Denzin and Giardina (2009) offer an eloquent statement of how socially consequential writing would ideally unfold:

> Inquiry grounded in critical indigenous pedagogy should meet multiple criteria. It must be ethical, performative, healing, transformative, decolonizing, and participatory. It must be committed to dialog, community, self-determination, and cultural autonomy. It must meet peoples' perceived needs. . . . It seeks to be unruly, disruptive, critical, and dedicated to the goals of justice and equity. (p. 29)

I am sitting at my desk knowing that any listing of writing strategies is incomplete. Language, despite its limitations, is too rich and generative to be nailed down into simple categories. There are no limits to the productive procedures a researcher might employ. There is no simple formula for writing success. Likewise, writing strategies are not stable; they overlap, slip away, change. They may prove effective for one study but not for another. There are no magic techniques that, abracadabra, turn an essay into a "must read." Yet, if employed with rhetorical skill; with sensitivity to the task at hand and with an eye toward writing evocatively, reflexively, and in an embodied fashion; deploying language's partial and partisan nature for the material, for social justice, then certain writing strategies may prove to be a helpful way in.

Part III: An Evaluative Position

I am sitting at my desk trying to contemplate what qualitative work I want to applaud and what efforts seem lacking. I'm curious why I am seduced by some work but not others, why the best work seems to engage and the weaker work seems to fall flat and leaves me cold. I wish to articulate what I like and what I don't without imposing my evaluative stance but acknowledging that I have one that guides my practice as a reviewer, teacher, and writer. I leave open the possibility of other evaluative and more productive schemes, but I believe that the following assessments live in the company of other scholars' values (e.g., Bochner, 2000; Ellis, 2004; Goodall, 2000, 2008; Richardson, 2000). I am sitting at my desk ready to consider other readings, but I continue, putting an evaluative self forward.

The flat piece, a cold dinner, is forced down, taken in with little pleasure. It lacks the heat of the chef's passions, the chef's sensuous self who knows, without spice, all is bland. The engaging piece makes each mouthful worthy of comment, encourages lingering, savoring, remembering. In its presence, I want to invite my colleagues and students to enjoy its flavors.

The flat piece does not know its place. It carries on as if no one has ever spoken before. It once again invents the wheel. The engaging piece knows it place, bows in the direction of the previous as it takes its conversational turn. It does so, not with the perfunctory review, but with the respectful incorporation of others' ideas. At times, it works as a process of sense making, of letting others carry it along, but it is always as interesting as those it quotes. It proceeds without creating a killing field.

The flat piece clothes itself in fancy garb, often hiding its essential simplicity. The engaging piece knows just how to dress for the occasion, perhaps adorning itself in the unfamiliar but always with an eye toward making any flourish an expressive part of the whole. Instead of an ostentatious display, its design encourages further conversation.

The flat piece lives in the abstract, speaks across and above the individual. The engaging essay resides in the precise. It puts leaves on bare limbs, but never bowling balls or toasters. It realizes what leaves are needed to create its tree. And as the leaves accumulate, become thick, each one counts.

The flat piece structures its ideas with familiar models. It learned too well the lessons from first-year English composition and scientific reasoning. It forgets the vibrant relationship of form and content; instead, it unfolds in a predetermined manner. The engaging work allows structure to emerge, guided by the necessity of its subject. When its form is fulfilled, it satisfies. It knows the imperatives of its content.

The flat piece has easy and ready answers. It says what it knows, finding its way to where it began. It works to prove itself right. The engaging essay exists in struggle, searching for what it may come to realize. It becomes a small, nervous solution, offered with humility. Its ideas slide into cautious claims, noting its limitations.

The flat piece thinks its author can be invisible, above it all, bodiless. It is a megaphone speaking from on high, producing pronouncements. The engaging essay has its author own his or her bodily presence. Knowing that all bodies are historically, culturally, and individually saturated, it brings forward its own situatedness to suggest a context for reading and to demonstrate how its account is tainted. It understands how it is fettered. It speaks from the body to those who wish to listen.

The flat piece thinks its head can be separated from its heart. Its passion is buried; its politics is denied. It is a doctor with a scalpel. The engaging essay joins the head and the heart. It resists Descartes' logic, but if trapped by his binary, it turns "think" into "feel." It works best when it speaks from the heart through the power and passion of its heady constructions to render human experience, albeit never completely, in its lived complexity. It is the nurse with your chart by her side telling a comforting and clear tale.

The flat piece accepts the given, trusts in the already forged. It ornaments the already built, decorates the status quo. The engaging piece plays, opens closed doors, discovers hidden passageways, creates new spaces. It is mischievous, utopian, saying the unsayable, the forbidden, the dangerous. It knows the master's house can be rebuilt. It believes there should be no master.

The flat piece errs by thinking it has the truth. It believes it has covered all the bases, exhausted all the angles, handled all the counterarguments. Its smugness sticks to the page. The engaging essay situates itself in the conditional, aware of language's slippery slide, aware that today's certainty is tomorrow's joke, aware that it is always located in its author.

The flat piece turns politics into sloganeering, easy platitudes. It rails against known enemies, pointing its finger in a familiar direction. It is full of fury, often signifying a liberal education, but nothing more. Too often, it is merely correct. The engaging piece locates politics in the body, shows how politics matters to individual lives, speaks of and to the heart. It positions readers in another's life, brings forward their empathic selves, even while at times implicating them, so that they want to work on behalf of social justice.

The flat piece proceeds unaware of its moral consequences. It rushes in, claims space, forgetting others may be present. Its emissions pollute the social environment. The engaging essay looks both left and right. It finds its ethical stance with its hand in another's hand.

A Summary Positioning

I am sitting at my desk, positioned, having taken an extended turn, asking perhaps more of my reader than I am entitled to request or that my prose might bear. My narrative is, of course, only one story that might be told about writing qualitative research. I invite the reader to decide if it is flat or engaging. In either case, it is a record of what I've come to realize, a statement that lobbies for space, a material gesture on behalf of qualitative inquiry designed to enhance our efforts at writing the social world, of making the social world a more habitable and just place. I offer it in the hope of dialogue and of new possibilities. I am sitting at my desk, trying.

References

Adams, T. (2006). Seeking father: Relationally reframing a troubled love story. *Qualitative Inquiry, 14*(4), 704–723.

Alexander, B. K. (2005). Performance ethnography: The reenacting and inciting of culture. In N. K. Denzin & Y. S. Lincoln (Eds.), *The SAGE handbook of qualitative research* (3rd ed., pp. 411–442). Thousand Oaks, CA: Sage.

Alexander, B. K. (2006). *Performing Black masculinity: Race, culture, and queer identity.* Walnut Creek, CA: AltaMira Press.

Anzaldúa, G. (1999). *Borderlands/la frontera: The new mestiza* (2nd ed.). San Francisco: Aunt Lute Books.

Bell, M. (2002). Thirty-two statements about writing poetry (work-in-progress). *The Writer's Chronicle, 13.* Available at http://www.coppercanyonpress.org/400_opportunities/430_gettingpub/bell.cfm

Bhabha, H. K. (1994). *The location of culture.* New York: Routledge.

Bochner, A. P. (2000). Criteria against ourselves. *Qualitative Inquiry, 6,* 266–272.

Brady, I. (2003). *The time at Darwin's reef. Poetic explorations in anthropology and history.* Walnut Creek, CA: AltaMira Press.

Chawla, D. (2003). Rhythms of dis-location: Family history, ethnographic spaces, and reflexivity. In R. P. Clair (Ed.), *Expressions of ethnography: Novel approaches to qualitative methods* (pp. 271–279). Albany: State University of New York Press.

Colyar, J. (2009). Becoming writing, becoming writers. *Qualitative Inquiry, 15*(2), 421–436.

Conquergood, D. (1991). Rethinking ethnography: Towards a critical cultural poetics. *Communication Monographs, 58,* 179–194.

Defenbaugh, N. (2011). *Dirty tale: The chronically ill journey.* Creskill, NJ: Hampton Press.

Denzin, N. K. (2003). *Performance ethnography: Critical pedagogy and the politics of culture.* Thousand Oaks, CA: Sage.

Denzin, N. K. (2008). *Searching for Yellowstone: Race, gender, family and memory in the postmodern West.* Walnut Creek, CA: Left Coast Press.

Denzin, N. K., & Giardina, M. D. (2009). Qualitative inquiry and social justice: Toward a politics of hope. In N. K. Denzin & M. D. Giardina (Eds.), *Qualitative inquiry and social justice* (pp. 11–50). Walnut Creek, CA: Left Coast Press.

Denzin, N. K., & Lincoln, Y. S. (Eds.). (2005). *The SAGE Handbook of qualitative research* (3rd ed.). Thousand Oaks, CA: Sage.

Didion, J. (2000). Why I write. In J. Sternburg (Ed.), *The writer on her work* (pp. 17–25). New York: W. W. Norton.

Dunn, S. (1993). *Walking light: Essays and memoirs.* New York: W. W. Norton.

Ellis, C. (1995). *Final negotiations: A story of love, loss, and chronic illness.* Philadelphia: Temple University Press.

Ellis, C. (2004). *The ethnographic I: A methodological novel about autoethnography.* Walnut Creek, CA: AltaMira Press.

Ellis, C. (2009a). *Revision: Autoethnographic reflections on life and work.* Walnut Creek, CA: Left Coast Press.

Ellis, C. (2009b). Telling tales on neighbors: Ethics in two voices. *International Review of Qualitative Research, 2*(1), 3–28.

Ellis, C., & Bochner, A. P. (1992). Telling and performing personal stories. The constraints of choice in abortion. In C. Ellis & M. Flaherty (Eds.), *Investigating subjectivity: Research on lived experience* (pp. 79–101). Newbury Park, CA: Sage.

Frost, R. (1963). The figure a poem makes. In *Selected poems of Robert Frost* (pp. 1–4). New York: Holt, Rinehart & Winston.

Gale, K., & Wyatt, J. (2008). Two men talking: A nomadic inquiry into collaborative writing. *International Review of Qualitative Research, 1*(3), 361–380.

Geiger, D. (1967). *The dramatic impulse in modern poetics.* Baton Rouge: Louisiana State University Press.

Goldberg, N. (1986). *Writing down the bones: Freeing the writer within.* Boston: Shambhala.

Goodall, H. L. (1989). *Casing the promised land: The autobiography of an organizational detective.* Carbondale: Southern Illinois University Press.

Goodall, H. L. (2000). *Writing the new ethnography.* Walnut Creek, CA: AltaMira Press.

Goodall, H. L. (2006). *A need to know: The clandestine history of a CIA family.* Walnut Creek, CA: Left Coast Press.

Goodall, H. L. (2008). *Writing qualitative inquiry: Self, stories, and academic life.* Walnut Creek, CA: Left Coast Press.

Gray, R., & Sinding, C. (2002). *Standing ovation: Performing social science research about cancer.* Walnut Creek, CA: AltaMira Press.

Hartnett, S. J. (2003). *Incarceration nation: Investigative prison poems of hope and terror.* Walnut Creek, CA: AltaMira Press.

Hartnett, S. J., & Engels, J. D. (2005). "Aria in time of war": Investigative poetry and the politics of witnessing. In N. K. Denzin & Y. S. Lincoln (Eds.), *The SAGE handbook of qualitative research* (3rd ed., pp. 1043–1068). Thousand Oaks, CA: Sage.

Holman Jones, S. (2002). Torch. In N. K. Denzin & Y. S. Lincoln (Eds.), *The qualitative inquiry reader* (pp. 185–215). Thousand Oaks, CA: Sage.

Kaufman, M., & Members of the Tectonic Theater Project. (2001). *The Laramie Project.* New York: Vintage Books.

Kiesinger, C. E. (2003). He touched, he took. In R. P. Clair (Ed.), *Expressions of ethnography: Novel approaches to qualitative methods* (pp. 177–184). Albany: State University of New York Press.

Lockford, L. (2008). Investing in the political beyond. *Qualitative Inquiry, 14,* 3–12.

Madison, D. S. (1999). Performing theory/embodied writing. *Text and Performance Quarterly, 19,* 107–124.

Madison, D. S. (2005). *Critical ethnography: Method, ethics, and performance.* Thousand Oaks, CA: Sage.

Mienczakowski, J. (2001). Ethnodrama: Performed research—limitations and potential. In P. Atkinson, A. Coffey, S. Delamont, J. Lofland, & L. Lofland (Eds.), *Handbook of ethnography* (pp. 468–476). Thousand Oaks, CA: Sage.

Myers, B. (2008). Straight and White: Talking with my mouth full. *Qualitative Inquiry, 14,* 160–171.

Pelias, R. J. (1999). *Writing performance: Poeticizing the researcher's body.* Carbondale: Southern Illinois University Press.

Pelias, R. J. (1999). Confessions of an apprehensive performer. In R. J. Pelias, *Writing performance: Poeticizing the researcher's body* (pp. 79–87). Carbondale: Southern Illinois University Press.

Pineau, E. (2000). Nursing mother and articulating absence. *Text and Performance Quarterly, 20,* 1–19.

Pollock, D. (1998). Performative writing. In P. Phelan & J. Lane (Eds.), *The ends of performance* (pp. 73–103). New York: New York University Press.

Poulos, C. (2009). *Accidental ethnography: An inquiry into family secrets.* Walnut Creek, CA: Left Coast Press.

Prendergast, M., Leggo, C., & Sameshima, P. (Eds.). (2009). *Poetic inquiry: Vibrant voices in the social sciences.* Rotterdam, The Netherlands: Sense Publishers.

Rambo Ronai, C. R. (1996). My mother is mentally retarded. In C. Ellis & A. Bochner (Eds.), *Composing ethnography: Alternative forms of qualitative writing* (pp. 109–310). Walnut Creek, CA: AltaMira Press.

Richardson, L. (2000). Writing: A method of inquiry. In N. K. Denzin & Y. S. Lincoln (Eds.), *Handbook of qualitative research* (2nd ed., pp. 923–948). Thousand Oaks, CA: Sage.

Richardson, L. (2007). *Last writes: A daybook for a dying friend.* Walnut Creek, CA: Left Coast Press.

Richardson, L., & St.Pierre, E. A. (2005). Writing: A method of inquiry. In N. K. Denzin & Y. S. Lincoln (Eds.), *The SAGE handbook of qualitative research* (3rd ed., pp. 959–978). Thousand Oaks, CA: Sage.

Roethke, T. (2001). *On poetry and craft.* Port Townsend, WA: Copper Canyon Press.

Rosenthal, M. L. (1987). *The poet's art.* New York: W. W. Norton.

Russel y Rodriguez, M. (2002). Confronting anthropology's silencing praxis: Speaking of/from Chicana consciousness. In N. K. Denzin & Y. S. Lincoln (Eds.), *The qualitative inquiry reader* (pp. 347–376). Thousand Oaks, CA: Sage.

Saldana, J. (2005). *Ethnodrama: An anthology of reality theatre.* Walnut Creek, CA: AltaMira Press.

Sanders, E. (1976). *Investigative poetry.* San Francisco: City Lights Books.

Smith, A. D. (1993). *Fires in the mirror.* New York: Doubleday.

Smith, A. D. (2000). *Twilight: Los Angeles, 1992.* New York: Random House.

Smith, L. (2007). A life in books. *The Writer's Chronicle, 40*(2), 37–41.

Spry, T. (2001a). From Goldilocks to dreadlocks: Hair-raising tales of racializing bodies. In L. C. Miller & R. J. Pelias (Eds.), *The green window: Proceedings of the Giant City*

Conference on Performative Writing (pp. 52–65). Carbondale: Southern Illinois University.

Spry, T. (2001b). Performing autoethnography: An embodied methodological practice. *Qualitative Inquiry, 7*, 706–732.

Spry, T. (2009). Bodies of/as evidence in autoethnography. *International Review of Qualitative Research, 1*, 603–610.

Stoller, P. (1997). *Sensuous scholarship.* Philadelphia: University of Pennsylvania Press.

Tillmann-Healy, L. M. (2001). *Between gay and straight: Understanding friendship across sexual orientation.* Walnut Creek, CA: AltaMira Press.

Tillmann-Healy, L. M. (2003). Hands. In R. P. Clair (Ed.), *Expressions of ethnography: Novel approaches to qualitative methods* (pp. 175–176). Albany: State University of New York Press.

Tracy, S. J. (2003). Watching the watchers: Making sense of emotional constructions behind bars. In R. P. Clair (Ed.), *Expressions of ethnography: Novel approaches to qualitative methods* (pp. 159–172). Albany: State University of New York Press.

Trujillo, N. (2004). *In search of Naunny's grave: Age, class, gender, and ethnicity in an American family.* Walnut Creek, CA: AltaMira Press.

Warren, J. T. (2001). Absence for whom? An autoethnography of White subjectivity. *Cultural Studies <=> Critical Methodologies, 1*, 36–49.

Watt, J. (2005). A gentle going? An autoethnographic short story. *Qualitative Inquiry, 11*, 724–732.

Watt, J. (2008). No longer loss: Autoethnographic stammering. *Qualitative Inquiry, 14*, 955–967.

Young, V. A. (2007). *Your average Nigga: Performing race, literacy, and masculinity.* Detroit, MI: Wayne State University Press.

18

Evaluation as a Relationally Responsible Practice

Tineke A. Abma and Guy A. M. Widdershoven

E valuation is an applied science, and evaluators do their work amidst the sociopolitical dynamics of the practice evaluated. Although evaluation requires methodological steps, in this chapter we emphasize that evaluation is first of all a relationally responsible endeavor. In their work, evaluators enact a shared understanding of what it means to be an evaluator and do evaluative work. We argue that evaluators should engage with the world around them, taking fully into account their relationship with those in the practice being evaluated. This engagement includes a responsibility for the relationships developed as well as a shared responsibility for the development of socially just practices. A case example is presented from the field of psychiatry to illustrate the ideas in the chapter.

Evaluation as a Practice Involving Implementation and Education

Evaluation is first of all a practice, meaning that evaluators are workers, acting and conducting all kinds of activities like negotiating contracts, talking to people, typing out transcriptions, and writing reports. Much of their actions are based on a shared understanding of what it means to be an evaluator. "Shared" refers here to a way of doing things that is common in the evaluation field. Defining evaluation as a practice stresses that evaluation is much more complex than just the application of textbook knowledge; evaluators also have to deal with the sociopolitical complexity of their practice (impatient clients, bureaucratic managers, invisible users, etc).

The practice of evaluation is not inwardly focused, but very much grounded in the problems arising in the real world. Evaluation should be useful for practice. Therefore, implementation has always been an issue of concern in the field. From their beginnings, it was clear that evaluation studies have to inform and be useful for decision making and practice, whether these findings influence ways of thinking gradually, and as part of other information sources in an incremental policy-making process, or are directly used to adjust less complicated decision-making processes at the micro level (Patton, 1988; Weiss, 1988). Evaluation work is thus part of a sociopolitical process (Abma & Schwandt, 2005; Greene, 1994, 2000; House, 1981; Palumbo, 1987). This sociopolitical context creates a complicated dynamic; evaluative work often needs to be done within a short time frame, there may be a sponsor who may claim a special say, or the evaluator may encounter resistance or interest groups trying to influence the outcomes. The responsibilities of the evaluator are therefore demanding; there are many actors with conflicting interests and perspectives. In addition, programs or policies can be stopped as a result of the evaluation and people can be sanctioned. Implementation thus requires a political awareness and sensitivity on the part of the evaluator.

An important dimension of implementation is the pedagogical one. Evaluation fosters learning processes and can do so in various ways. A didactic approach to learning will strive for the application of findings after the evaluation has been conducted. It follows a linear conception of knowledge production: dissemination—translation—application. This transmissional view of information processing understands learning as a cognitive act, something that occurs in the mind of an individual and separate from the rest of one's activities. Acquiring knowledge and applying it are considered as distinct steps. A pedagogical approach to learning will place more emphasis on the learning that occurs in the action and interaction between practitioners. Learning is then understood as a social and collective process, and directly related to the working context of participants. This means that the evaluation process itself will foster learning experiences when it challenges participants to reflect on their practice and to ask themselves critical questions regarding the goodness of their practice. Qualitative evaluations foster such processes through face-to-face interactions. Deliberately engaging participants in a learning process concerning their practice will create co-ownership for practice improvements, and facilitates the implementation right from the start of the evaluation. Reasoning from a pedagogical stance, one should not consider the evaluation as an add-on after the intervention or program has been developed, but rather as a reflective learning process that is part of the development of practice. Action, reflection, and evaluation will then become intensively intermingled. Such a process is not the sole responsibility of the evaluator, we will argue, but a shared responsibility of all involved. The evaluator will engage all and foster interactions and relationships of trust in the interest of a more inclusive society.

The purpose of this chapter is to argue for an approach that takes the relational responsibility of evaluation seriously, both in term of relations as well as in terms of the normative horizon of social justice. Let us first go back into history, without pretending to cover all, to gain an insight into the intellectual history of the field, and qualitative evaluation in particular.

History of the Field

Evaluation is a young, typically modernist discipline and profession. It was just after the Second World War that evaluation as a formal way of thinking and discipline came to life in the United States, closely related to developments in the field of education. Its birth is marked by the U.S. frontier ethos and federal attempts to improve the situation of poor people, concurrent with the launch of Sputnik by the Russians and a movement toward developing and enhancing the knowledge of children (Guba, personal communication, summer 1994). Massive educational programs were federally sponsored, with the obligation to evaluate their effectiveness. Evaluation was connected to social engineering; evaluators had to find out which programs worked best, what causal relations explained the program's effectiveness in order to generalize, predict, and control the performance of these programs elsewhere, as a basis for social betterment. Since evaluating programs had not been done before, social scientists and other professionals had to develop ways to measure, monitor, describe, control, and judge practices. Initially, scholars and practitioners in the field focused on the development of appropriate methodologies, which were initially predominantly quasi-experimental in design. In such a design, hypotheses—the articulated policy goals and assumptions—are a priori formulated (program theory) and then tested with the use of quantitative methods and techniques.

Qualitative evaluation can be defined as inquiry that establishes the value and goodness of a practice based on insiders' and contextual knowledge. The rise of qualitative evaluation dates back to the 1970s when Cronbach (Cronbach et al., 1980) proposed that the evaluation field needed good social anthropologists, a call that inspired many evaluators to become naturalistic or field researchers with a special focus on social relations (Stake, 1991; personal communication, summer 1994). In the UK, Parlett and Hamilton (1972) further elaborated the metaphor of the evaluator as social anthropologist. The authors proposed an approach to evaluation that is adaptive to situations. Central features were that the evaluator familiarizes him- or herself "thoroughly with the day-to-day reality" in order to "unravel the complexity." Being present and recording observations were the predominant activities. The evaluator was to record discussions with and between participants, and keep track of the language, jargon, and metaphors in order to gain insight into implicit pre-assumptions and interpersonal relations. In the USA, Stake also proposed a broader conceptualization of evaluation that included social interactions (Abma & Stake, 2001; Stake, 1967). Evaluators should not only gather data about program input and outcomes, but also describe its context and judge the quality of intermediary processes. Guba and Lincoln (1981) refer explicitly to Stake's work in the development of their "naturalistic" approach to evaluation.

These qualitative approaches have in common that they aim to holistically understand the evaluated program from the insider perspectives of the program participants and other stakeholders. This holistic understanding implies that the evaluator pays attention to many mutually influencing "factors" that shape the program and its context, such as the history of the program, the organization and culture in which it is embedded, the persons and personalities that take the lead, the political dynamics, and the social interactions and relations among stakeholders. All these factors are important in evaluation, because they are integral to and partly constitutive of the quality and effectiveness of the program being evaluated. Stake (1991) and others mention "personalities to be determining factors" (p. 12), but other aspects of social relations also count: leadership and charisma, caring and respect, reciprocity and collaboration, safety and structure, opportunities to learn and grow, but also hierarchy, conflict, envy, suspicion and mistrust, and many more. These are all aspects of stakeholders' relationships with one another that become interwoven in the fabric of the program being evaluated and thereby are integral to program quality and effectiveness. A program or policy should therefore be understood as a social practice; it is never just an intervention, but always a socially, historically, and culturally determined pattern of relations, interactions, and values. An example can be found in the work of Mabry (1991) who evaluated the arts education in an inner-city school. Here is a vignette based on her work:

> Alexandre Dumas is an elementary school located in the south side of Chicago. The evaluator aims to see how they teach the arts at Dumas. The evaluation is part of a larger study of arts education in elementary schools. A single step in the foyer and the evaluator realizes Dumas doesn't fit the generalized descriptions of a school in a poor neighborhood. It doesn't fit the expectations she has not tried to preconceive. Ushering in a sea of attentive black faces the evaluator suddenly realizes she is white. Having talked to many teachers and attended several classroom lessons, she concludes that at Dumas the arts are seen as a way out, a way to acknowledge and celebrate being African American as well as an entrée into mainstream culture, an opportunity to experience the good things in life. With no exception everyone attributes Dumas' success to the charisma and dedication of the principal, Ms. Silvia Peters. Her leadership makes Dumas a dream amidst the nightmare of many of Chicago's all–African American public schools. The evaluator presents a rich portrayal in order to show us who Sylvia Peters is and how she did it: She made the arts fun; she made them accessible; and she made them important.

Within qualitative approaches, like the one presented above, there is an awareness that evaluators should attend to the plurality of values and interests of those participating in the program and those of other stakeholders. Stake (1975) was among the first to draw attention to the one-sidedness and shortcomings of an approach that just took the program goals as the criterion for evaluation. This would lead to a management bias, and Stake therefore enlarged the scope of evaluation to include the issues of all possible stakeholders. This was based on the idea that a phenomenon has various, sometimes conflicting meanings for different stakeholders (Abma & Stake, 2001; Stake & Abma, 2005). Being responsive to the issues of stakeholders assumes an appreciation of their experiential knowledge. Methodologically, the acknowledgment of plurality implies that the "design" gradually emerges in conversation with the stakeholders. Metaphorically one may compare the designing process in such an evaluation with improvisational dance (Janesick, 2000). Whereas the minuet prescribes the definite steps, definite turns, and foot and arm movements, improvisation is spontaneous and reflexive of the social condition. The evaluator charts the progress and examines the route of the study as it proceeds by keeping track of his or her role in the research process. Since the design is not preordained, important methodological decisions have to be made along the way, like determining a point of saturation and selecting issues that require further exploration.

Also, the users of these approaches are well aware of the interpretive character of the evaluative work. Issues of stakeholders are not there to be discovered or revealed, they are not ready-made, but have to be elicited by the evaluator as a midwife. The birth of meaning is never just a matter of demonstration. Human beings, evaluators included, are interpreters. In order to make sense of our world and endow our experiences or those of others with meaning, we bring in our own background, training, prior experiences, desires, and standpoints. Every description is laden with interpretation. Yet, qualitative evaluation studies try to stay as close to the stakeholders' accounts and narratives as possible and are skeptical about the use of conceptual frameworks to prevent foreclosure or reduction of the data. In order to illuminate the quality of the practice, the evaluator has to use his or her judgment. This should not be understood as judgment in terms of calculation against preordained criteria. The qualitative evaluator does not predefine a set of evaluation criteria, but uses the stakeholder issues and their experiences as well as his or her observations as a source to come to an assessment of the program's quality. Stake explains that this is partly an intuitive process; one develops an understanding of the quality and later rationalizes what makes the practice good (personal communication, summer 1994; Stake & Schwandt, 2006). Schwandt (2005) refers to the Aristotelian virtue of *phronesis,* or wise judgment, to indicate what it means to evaluate the quality of a practice.

Wise judgment is a kind of ordinary, empirical, quasi-aesthetic, contextual knowing. Berlin (as quoted in Schwandt, 2005) aptly describes it as follows:

> Capacity for integrating a vast amalgam of constantly changing, multi-colored, evanescent, perceptually overlapping data, too many, too swift, too intermingled to be caught and pinned down and labeled like so many individual butterflies. . . . To seize a situation in this sense one needs to see, to be given a kind of direct, almost sensuous contact with the relevant data, and not merely to recognize their general characteristics, to classify them or reason about them, or analyze them, or reach conclusions and formulate theories about them. (p. 325)

Wise judgment requires a power to attend to the particulars of a situation, to discriminate, and to see relevant details. Part of the evaluator's wisdom is also that he or she finds a balanced, middle-ground position in between antipathy and sympathy, between emotional and rational, and does justice to all stakeholders.

The Aristotelian middle-ground position is also crucial in describing the practice. Stake (1982) notes, "The wisdom of the evaluator's findings will be little appreciated if couched in words that hurt too little or too much" (p. 80). Developing such wisdom is a process that never ends in the scholarly life of an evaluator; it is fostered among novices by a process of *Bildung,* which entails more than learning about qualitative methods and techniques. It requires a safe and friendly context where exploration and reflection on the self-as-evaluator (and of his or her authority, responsibility, obligation, and so forth) are stimulated.

New Interpretative Paradigms

The qualitative evaluation approaches described above emphasize the contextual understanding of programs by the evaluator as a wise judge. Wise judgment is detached. The evaluator as a wise judge wants to understand the world of the practitioners without taking into account the relevance for him- or herself and the input of the evaluator. This is quite different from interactive and dialogical evaluation approaches; here the relations between the evaluator and practitioners are central.

The difference between old and new interpretative approaches can be clarified by the work of the hermeneutic philosopher Hans Georg Gadamer (1960). According to Gadamer, there are three ways of understanding the world. The first stance is objectivist: The knower is detached from the outside world, stands above or outside that world (at least claims such a stance), and tries to explain the world with the use of universal laws. The perspectives of others in that world can be wrong, and their incorrect vision can be explained by underlying causalities or motives. We recognize this stance in the objectivist judgment approaches following a quantitative design. The second stance is subjectivist. Now the knower tries to understand the world by placing him- or herself in the footsteps of practitioners living in that world. The perspectives of other people are not wrong, but different. This empathic understanding of the uniqueness of the other from within can be recognized in the qualitative approaches described above. It can lead to relativism. Both the objectivist and subjectivist stance are problematic according to Gadamer. In both these stances, the knower does not relate to world; he does not take into account what the world means for himself nor what his input means for the world. The third position goes beyond objectivism and relativism (Bernstein, 1983) and is dialogical: Now the knower engages with the world around, taking fully into account what the world means for him, and vice versa. The knower listens to the other from a readiness to accept the other's input as being relevant for himself. Knower and known engage in a joint learning process in which both change in identity and new horizons emerge. The knower no longer just looks at the world, but interacts and takes responsibility for the process of development in the world. This intersubjective position can be found in interactive, dialogical approaches to evaluation. In these approaches, the evaluator and the participants in practice learn from each other and are jointly responsible for the outcome of this learning process.

Relevant evaluative traditions that embody the idea that the evaluator has a relationship with and thus a responsibility for the evaluated practice include those that promote transformation and change in the interest of human flourishing, such as feminist and transformative approaches to evaluation (Mertens, 2002, 2009; Whitmore et al., 2006), empowerment evaluation (Fetterman, 1994), democratic evaluation (MacDonald, 1977; Murray, 2002), participatory evaluation (Greene, 1997, 2006; Suarez-Herrera, Springett, & Kagan, 2009; Themessl-Huber & Grutsch, 2003), critical evaluation (Segerholm, 2001), social justice promoting traditions in evaluation (House, 1981, 1993), and fourth- and fifth-generation evaluation (Guba & Lincoln, 1989; Lincoln, 1993). The evaluator establishes particular relationships in his or her evaluation as a way of challenging such relationships—especially of power—in the context outside the evaluation. The evaluative purpose is the establishment of equal and just relations in society and the empowerment of marginalized groups in society, and therefore engagement and ownership is valued. In order to help effect the kinds of transformations desired, the evaluator purposefully uses the relational dimensions of evaluation. He or she purposefully establishes certain kinds of relationships—those that are accepting, respectful, and reciprocal—in order to help promote the overall social changes desired.

There is thus more emphasis on the evaluator's responsibility to foster the interactions among practitioners as a way to jointly develop socially responsible practices. Active partnership and participation are central values. In traditional qualitative approaches, the evaluator does all the interpretive and judgmental work alone; in an interactive approach, this is a joint responsibility of the evaluator and all the practitioners (including clients, patients, citizens, etc.). In interactive evaluation, the social relations between the evaluator and various practitioners and among practitioners are therefore central. Interactions and relationships always matter because these shape the evaluative knowledge that is generated in an evaluation and because these relationships convey what particular norms and values are being advanced in the evaluation. It matters, for example, that evaluators kneel in the mud alongside psychiatric patients because relationships thus formed are respectful, equitable, and accepting. With this action, they communicate the values of respect, attentiveness, and engagement (as opposed to the more distanced and hierarchic relation in objectivist evaluation approaches). In interactive evaluation, the social relations in the setting are not just an object of study, but there is an active engagement with the people in the setting. This broader responsibility stems from the critical consciousness and awareness that social practices are often marked by inequalities and social injustice, and the desire to create more responsible practices through evaluative work.

The underlying ontological notion is that human beings are fundamentally relational. Our social world is a product of social interactions and relations. Understanding of our socially constructed world can only be generated by developing a relation and dialogue with and between the inhabitants of this world. Epistemologically these traditions are grounded in the notion that object and subject mutually influence each other. There is a dialogical relationship: Instead of two independent entities standing in front of each other, knower and known are now engaged in a conversation. In this conversation, participants may change. Mertens (2002) describes the relationship between object and subject, knower and known as follows: "interactive, sensitive to those with the least power, and empowering to those involved in the process" (p. 106). Others point out that relations between evaluator and program participants become more democratic: The locus of control shifts from the evaluator as an expert to program people and other stakeholders who also have a say in the process (Greene, 1997; MacDonald, 1977; Murray, 2002; Themessl-Huber & Grutsch, 2003). Instead of being objective and impartial, evaluators working in these traditions show a "multiple partiality"; they identify with all people involved, which enables them to act as teachers who can explain the various experiences to the groups. At the same time, they are open to learning from each of the participants.

Evaluators working in these traditions understand evaluation as a political practice; it has unequal consequences for various stakeholders in the evaluation. They ask themselves *whose* interests they want to serve (Schwandt, 1997; Segerholm, 2001). Social relations and societal structures are not taken for granted, but critically examined and transformed. The evaluator criticizes power imbalances and the status quo, often on the grounds of critical theories. He or she acts as a social critic, arguing against domination, oppression, exploitation, cruelty, and violence (Segerholm, 2001; Mertens, 2002), and as an advocate of a particular silenced and marginalized group (Lincoln, 1993), not just to promote the interests of this group, but to allow the group to participate equally in the overall learning process. The intention to pay attention to social relations is driven by emancipatory and democratic ideals and a human rights agenda

(Mertens, 2009). There is an engagement to empower people; to enlarge people's abilities to govern their own lives. On an individual level, empowerment refers to the development of voice, to more creative ways of interacting with one's social environment and the ability to take action in a more self-conscious way. On the collective level, empowerment refers to obtaining more influence and power in organizations and, eventually, in the processes of decision making in organizations and institutions.

FOSTERING ACTION, INTERACTION, AND DIALOGUE

Qualitative evaluation aims to develop a rich and holistic understanding of the complexity of social practices from the insider's perspective of various stakeholder groups. This is taken a step further in interactive evaluation where the aim is to enhance the mutual understanding between practitioners. The interactive evaluator helps the practitioners to develop new and richer ways of dealing with actual problems in their practice. They are engaged in dialogues about real problems. This distinguishes a dialogue from a theoretical debate. A dialogical approach implies a crucial role for action, experience, and learning. A dialogue presupposes that the participants already have some interest in and insight into the matter at hand. It also presupposes that the participants can elaborate their interest and knowledge through an exchange of perspectives.

In qualitative evaluation, practitioners are approached as meaning-making persons. They are invited to share their experiences with the evaluator. Interactive evaluation turns the process of sharing information into a two-sided relationship in which both the evaluator and the practitioner are active. The role of the practitioners goes beyond that of providing information. In interactive approaches, practitioners are actively involved in the evaluation process from beginning to end. Ways to engage practitioners may range from being an advisor to the process or a full member of the evaluation team to being participant in a learning community. Each time anew the evaluator will search for the best ways to engage people in the process. This means that data are gathered, not about participants in practice, but together with practitioners (professionals, clients, and other stakeholders). Likewise, the interpretation of the data in light of their consequences requires a dialogue with participants in practice. Methodological decisions made along the way will also be part of the negotiation with practitioners. The idea of emergence—not planning everything ahead—is an important prerequisite for the development of voice and inclusion. Generally, the emerging character of the process fosters the feeling of co-ownership.

PHASES IN THE PROCESS

Step 1: Ideally, the interactive evaluation process starts with the group least heard to ensure a balanced and fair process (Abma, Nierse, & Widdershoven, 2009; Baur, Abma, & Widdershoven, 2010). Their voice is unknown and needs to be articulated and elaborated. Also along the way, deliberate attention should be paid to the identification of "victims" or "silenced voices," those whose interests are at stake but remain unheard (Lincoln, 1993). Such voices may be hard to find, for example, because people want to remain anonymous or because they fear sanctions. To fully articulate the voice of those least heard often involves an intensive process. The evaluator needs to establish contact and develop a trusting relationship. Patience is an important virtue, and sometimes one needs to work with "cultural brokers" to be acceptable as an evaluator and to develop sensitivity for the specific cultural values and norms of the marginalized group.

Step 2: To prepare these groups for a dialogue with other groups often entails a process of empowerment where individuals first need to develop their own intimate voice, and then are brought into contact with each other to develop a shared agenda. Enclave deliberation among those with the same interests helps to turn an intimate voice into a political voice. Methods such as surveys and experiments are often not very appropriate to reach those who are marginalized (Mertens, 2002). Evaluators should therefore consider other methods to gain access to experiences, for example, in-depth interviews, focus groups, or story-telling workshops. Via interviews, people gain personal acknowledgment for their experiences (Koch, 2000). Sometimes other methods are more appropriate, such as focus groups. This depends on the population, so flexibility is needed with an attentive eye for the material conditions (timing, location, restitution for traveling costs, etc.) that create a comfortable space to speak up. The issues of established groups are often easier to determine. Their issues and agenda are often already documented, and persons from these groups are more articulate and able to provide focused information. Hence, this takes less time and energy.

Step 3: Having identified the issues for each stakeholder group, the next step is to create conditions and to organize dialogues and interactions between groups of stakeholders whose interests may diverge. Interaction between stakeholder groups is a deliberative process. *Deliberation* refers to the interaction and dialogue between participants. They will not just accept each other's beliefs and persuasions, but will explore these. Listening, probing, and questioning characterize this process, rather than confronting, attacking, and defending. Central features of dialogue are openness, respect, inclusion, and engagement (Abma et al., 2001; Greene, 2001). Dialogue may lead to consensus. Absence of consensus is, however, not problematic; on the contrary, differences stimulate a learning process (Widdershoven, 2001). Conditions for dialogue involve the willingness of stakeholders to participate, to share power, and to change in the process (Abma et al., 2001; Widdershoven & Abma, 2007).

Dialogue requires respect and openness, and that the evaluator should create a social infrastructure to facilitate participation and stakeholder communication. Deliberate attention should be paid to the power relations (Koch, 2000; Mertens, 2009). If a face-to-face encounter is impossible given asymmetries between stakeholder groups, one may organize a virtual meeting to stimulate a learning process between participants (Widdershoven, 2001). Experiences that have been exchanged in the safe environment of homogeneous groups are then introduced as issues in other stakeholder groups. By presenting such issues through stories, a climate of open discussion and dialogue may be fostered (Abma & Widdershoven, 2005). Active engagement of as many stakeholders as possible and deliberation minimize the chance of bias and domination of one party. Of course, bringing people together does not imply that everyone is heard. The moderator of the dialogues should therefore be alert for subtle mechanisms of exclusion. Afterward, evaluators should assess whether the dialogical process was really open. A careful reading of the transcript and an evaluation of the deliberative process with participants can give insight into this. During the process, the evaluator should also be prepared for the fact that those who are established and who feel superior may not be willing to participate in the process (They may think, what is there to learn?), or may join the process but find it hard to listen to the voices of other groups. Those who are not established might feel uncertain and need extra support to bring in their voice.

Dialogue and deliberative forums can be explicitly used to give voice to program participants who don't usually have a voice (House & Howe, 1999). This experience hopefully can affect participants' political power outside the evaluation context. Segerholm (2001) notes, however, that inclusion of stakeholders does not guarantee that values like equity and social justice will be prominent. There is always the risk of pseudo-participation. Evaluators should therefore ask who will profit from an inclusive deliberation.

ROLES OF THE EVALUATOR

The roles of the interactively working evaluator include those of facilitator, teacher, and Socratic guide, and indicate an equal, friendly, and cordial relationship.

The evaluator should engage with the people in the setting (Kushner, 2000). The evaluator has a "relational responsibility" and should pay deliberate attention to the "social relations of inquiry" (Greene, 2002). This means that the evaluator will try to create a "safe space" for participants and stakeholders "to learn how to relate and communicate equally and justly, a space that is unfettered by outside status and role differentials and animated by norms of reciprocity, parity, and respect" (Greene, 1997, p. 176; Greene, 2001). The evaluator must be sensitive to subtle mechanisms of exclusion. This is in line with what Aristotle (1997) said about wise judgment. The Aristotelian view of wise judgment goes beyond the detached view described above; it recognizes a hermeneutic and dialogical relationship between judge and world (Gadamer, 1960). The wise evaluator not only has a good perception of the practice and an adequate moral relation with the practice (unbiased, respectful), but he also strives toward just relations in the practice and is sensitive to power relations and helps practitioners to solve moral problems, not by placing him- or herself outside or above the practice, but by engaging in that practice.

Case Example: Reduction of Coercion in Psychiatry

In this part, we present a story from the field to illustrate our idea of evaluation as socially responsible practice. It concerns an evaluation as part of a movement to reduce coercion and restraint in psychiatry in The Netherlands. The purpose of the evaluation was to engender a dialogue about the application of coercive interventions and to develop normative guidelines for professionals in practice. In the first phase (1999–2001), six psychiatric hospitals participated in the process. The emphasis was on developing guidelines. The second phase also took 3 years (2002–2005). At this point, 12 psychiatric hospitals were involved. In this phase, the focus was on implementation of the guidelines. A learning community was set up among the project coordinators to foster active learning and connect experiments.

INCLUSION, VOICE, LEARNING COMMUNITY, AND OWNERSHIP

The evaluation processes were set up in a responsive way. In line with the notion that one needs to start with the group having least influence, a lot of time and energy was invested to contact patients, and to gain an insight into their experiences with coercion. It proved, however, to be difficult to include patients for in-depth interviews. They did not feel comfortable enough to tell their story to a professional who was an outsider, and the issue touched on a sensitive period in their lives. Therefore, we started working along with a research partner from an advocacy group who helped us to set up a series of communal meetings with client representatives. In the safe environment of this group, participants began to tell what had happened to them. The testimony of Jenny (pseudonym), a woman with a bipolar disorder, was recognized as expressing well the patients' perspective on coercion. The responses and recognition turned her personal testimony into a collective story witnessing the experiences inside the institutions. The story aptly revealed the interactional character of crises, how professionals were part of the problem situation without seeing it. Sharing and recognizing each other's stories helped the patients to transform personal issues into collective ones, and to build support among themselves as a group to place their issues on the agenda.

Jenny's Testimony, or Developing a Political Voice

Jenny was taken into care in a psychiatric hospital where she felt ill at ease and was hot-tempered. She says, *I could be very angry, because I felt powerless. I would be warned, and this would make me feel rebellious. If a nurse would say, "Do not extinguish your cigarette in that plant," I would not see this as reasonable, and I would become more and more obstruse.*

As a result, Jenny was often put in an isolation cell. The cell makes her feel miserable: *It is not humane to be in a cell without a toilet. These cardboard chamber pots are very awkward.*

After a while the medication starts to work. Yet, she is anxious about the risk of becoming numbed by it. Luckily, this does not occur: *I was really worried, that I would not have any feelings any more. Well, it did not turn out that way.*

She is hesitant about leaving the hospital and returning home. In the end, she is forced to go. At home she often feels down and lonely: *I stayed in the hospital for three years, and then I had to go home. I went home one day, and never returned to the hospital. I experienced a lot of anxiety and loneliness. I felt left alone by the hospital. I often called the emergency phone.*

Subsequently, in order to foster the interaction between stakeholder groups, heterogeneous dialogue groups (managers, nurses, psychiatrists, patients, and family) were organized to discuss the issues derived earlier in the process. In these mixed groups, the focus was on ethical problems regarding coercion. We were not so much interested in the question of when coercion is legitimate (a legal question), but how coercion can be prevented and, if needed, be carried out in a careful and responsible manner (an ethical question). Analyzing the material, we (the research team) were able to establish ethical problems about coercion and restraint, and to develop guidelines for action, which we called quality criteria. These criteria were again discussed within dialogue groups to validate them and to facilitate stakeholder interaction and mutual learning. The criteria changed in this iterative process (see Table 18.1 for an overview of the most important criteria). To make the quality criteria assessable for those working in practice, a short brochure was composed and widely disseminated. In addition, a longer document was crafted that grounded the quality criteria in concrete experiences and theoretical insights (Berghmans, Elfahmi, Goldsteen, & Widdershoven, 2001).

After the drafting of the document, the second phase of the project started. In 12 institutions, implementation activities were set up. These were different for each institution, based upon local context and expertise. Staff from the institutions coordinated the activities, while the evaluators focused on giving feedback and organizing meetings among the local organizers to exchange experiences and learn from one another. Also, a learning community was set up among the project coordinators in each institution. The learning community aimed to foster "situated learning" (versus learning from material abstracted from context) in relationships between people. It was based on the assumption of an intimate connection between knowledge, relationships, and action. The learning process of the project coordinators was intimately connected with and embedded in their practice. The knowledge produced was context-specific, practice- and experience-based, and interactively derived. Below, an example is given of the

Table 18.1   Quality Criteria for Coercion and Compulsion

- Be aware of contradictory obligations in handling situations of coercion.
- Create room for emotions, reflect upon them, and discuss them.
- Pay attention to the process character of coercion: Anticipate and evaluate incidents.
- Pay attention to communication: Be attentive and open toward the patient; reflect upon goals and means.

knowledge generated among the project leaders in response to a problematic situation presented and discussed in one of the collegial meetings. It concerns the question of whether or not the institution should build extra seclusion rooms concentrated in a specialized unit. The problem was brought in by a project coordinator, called Larry (pseudonym), who was also the head of the closed units in one of the participating hospitals.

Larry's Problem, or Generating Support

Larry, project coordinator of the implementation of the quality criteria, has been asked to give his Board of Directors advice about the number of rooms required in the new seclusion unit. There appears to be a growing group of youngsters with aggressive behavior. Seclusion is considered to be the only option for them. A specialized seclusion unit is proposed as the solution for the problems at hand.

The participants in the meeting ask questions about Larry's power. He responds that he has at least some influence on the formation of the seclusion unit and the number of seclusion rooms. In response to a question concerning the vision of care underlying the plans, Larry explains, *The management reasons, How should these bricks be piled and what is the most logical and cheap way to do that? There is not much talk about our vision of quality of care.*

Participants recognize the case and bring several negative experiences with specialized seclusion units to the fore, such as that patients may experience it as a punishment to go to another unit; the seclusion unit easily becomes a sort of internal police service within the organization and the availability of seclusion rooms will create a demand. One of the participants calls it a "logistics story" and misses the underlying ideas about what quality of care means. Participants also question the necessity of the reorganization: *For whom is this? It is certainly not in the interest of the staff and patients!* The group gives the advice to pay more attention to the means to prevent seclusion, such as creating "healing environments" and enhancing communication and interaction with patients.

Larry's story shows how work experiences were shared within the learning community. Participants shared stories about failures, hard-earned knowledge that if not narrated might not be known. These stories were used by Larry, who presented the perceived problems and alternative solutions in discussions with his Board of Directors. In the end, the Board decided to build four instead of the planned six seclusion rooms.

Evaluators and local staff wrote down their experiences in a book, describing both the tensions in the project and the positive outcomes (Abma, Widdershoven, & Lendemeijer, 2005). During the implementation, the formulation of the guidelines did not change. Yet the meaning of the guidelines for practice was further specified through experiments and the development of so-called "good practices." (It was agreed between organizing staff and ethicists that we should not use the notion of "best practices." At that time, the hospitals had just started to experiment with new approaches, and we did not expect to gain a shared understanding of a "best" practice.)

PERSPECTIVE, EXPERIENTIAL KNOWLEDGE, DIALOGUE, SHARED UNDERSTANDING

One of the key assumptions of interactive evaluation regards the notions of perspective and exchange of perspective, or, in terms of Gadamer (1960), fusion of horizons. Qualitative evaluation aims to articulate and explore the various, sometimes conflicting perspectives on a situation under consideration and to foster communication and dialogue among these perspectives.

In the project, we deliberately explored the perspectives of all stakeholder groups on coercion; managers, psychiatrists, nurses, patients, and family were consulted so we could understand their experiences and point of view. It soon became clear that their perspectives varied. Patients like Jenny focused on the negative side of coercion, and expressed their feelings of dehumanization, powerlessness, anger, loss of control, and fear. They brought to the fore that seclusion, the preferred method of coercion in The Netherlands, was often experienced as a punishment. They also complained about the fact that such incidents were never discussed afterward.

The nurses took another perspective, focusing on the constraining organizational conditions (lack of staff, shortage of time, too many administrative tasks, large caseload) that complicated their work. They also reported about the difficulties involved in assessing the risk of danger, and mentioned problems in the decision-making process. Dialogue about coercion assisted the nurses to articulate their identity; instead of being a "guardian," they began to redefine their identity in terms of being a "coworker" of the patient, developing a new, more cordial relationship (Landeweer, Abma, & Widdershoven, 2010). Psychiatrists focused on the means of coercion and lacking the legal conditions to substitute seclusion by (enforced) medical treatment. Family members felt that the communication with professionals was not always optimal: Why were they not informed about the situation of patients and consulted about proper courses of action? Finally, the project coordinators and managers like Larry reported about the culture of control (versus negotiation) in their institutions and resistance to change. Each of these perspectives was articulated, explored, and placed in the context of the background, training, experiences, and position of each of the groups. In other words, meanings and (moral) judgments were associated with the concrete context and the positions of stakeholders.

Interactive evaluation conceives dialogue as a learning process. Stakeholders were engaged in genuine dialogues. This was unique, since in public debates on coercion these parties tended not to talk, but to discuss and debate with each other and act strategically toward each other. In public, parties would bring their standpoints to the fore, taking different positions without engaging in dialogue. In the project, however, parties gained a name and face and became persons who were starting to talk with each other, exchanging perspectives.

An example concerns the conversation about the role of the patient's history in decisions about coercion. Professionals stressed that one should place a patient's behavior in the larger context of former ways of behaving. In order to judge whether a certain action is dangerous, one should take into account previous experiences with the patient. This obligation was stressed by psychiatric nurses. On the other hand, patients brought to the fore that the patient should get a chance to show different behavior. If the staff intervenes because they predict problems, based on prior events, they do not trust the patient to be able to handle the situation better this time. As a consequence, the patient is "locked up" in his or her history. Nurses and patients agreed that there is no simple solution to this dilemma. The best thing to do is to recognize that it is unfair not to take the history into account (since that would take away possibilities of prevention) and to see the patient's history as a causal determinant for the current situation. This example shows that nurses and patients learned from each other and developed new and enriched insights. They not only learned about the concrete perspectives of the others, but they also became aware of the more general fact that concrete situations are multi-interpretable and that certain methods or communication strategies (like dialogue) bring out these various interpretations.

The example also shows the relevance of practical rationality and wise judgment that guides interactive qualitative evaluation, as a characteristic not just of the evaluator, but of all the participants in the process. Our conversations always started from practice, with practical case examples, appreciating and using the experiences of participants as a valid source of moral wisdom. The practical knowledge of the participants was articulated and further developed by dialogical exchanges. By these means, participants gained more general knowledge of the situation and developed rules to deal with it in the form of quality criteria. They were able to develop wise judgment, not as an individual quality, but as a group capacity.

The shared understanding between parties—all supported the quality criteria—was largely due to the fact that people listened to each other's experiences around coercion and restraint, and came to understand uncertainties and worries. The inclusion of many voices and (disciplinary) perspectives enhanced the insight into the moral problems encountered in the care for psychiatric patients and led to a fuller understanding of what is required to improve the quality of coercion and care in general. For example, the input of the patients helped to further unravel the complexities in communication between patients and professionals. We also noted that people with various disciplinary backgrounds learned from each other. For example, nurses and psychiatrists came to appreciate each other's view of the situation. The dialogues enhanced the mutual understanding among participants and gave a voice to those who often have no say in policy processes. Moreover, the continuous dialogue on and reworking of the documents enabled the participants to influence the process and secured their commitment.

An important characteristic of the process was the commitment to and responsibility for creating change and improving practice, shared by the evaluators and the participants. Everybody was convinced that the existing way of dealing with coercion was unsatisfactory, and that reduction and quality improvement were urgent. Thus, the project had a political nature. By seeing this as a shared responsibility, strategic action by individuals was prevented. All parties recognized that they were unable to develop solutions individually, and needed each other to create a better practice. Both the evaluators and the participants showed their vulnerability: Since they would not be satisfied with simple but inadequate solutions, they would sometimes show emotions like frustration and even anger. By being open and sincere about this, the participants created an atmosphere of trust and mutual support, which was experienced as unique and helped to overcome problems along the way.

Discussion and Conclusion

In this chapter, we presented the basic notions of an interactive approach to evaluation. Interactive evaluation is relational and socially responsible. It goes beyond objective approaches to evaluation in that it takes into account the meanings of participants in practice. In this sense, interactive evaluation is part of the qualitative tradition in evaluation. It differs from classical qualitative approaches in that it does not regard the interpretation of meanings in practice as an activity of the evaluator, listening to the participants as a wise judge, but as a dialogical process; both the evaluator and the participants in practice are active in the process of meaning making and interpretation; wise judgement is an activity shared by all. Interactive evaluation is relationally responsible in that the evaluator engages in the practice and stimulates the participants to be active and responsible themselves for the quality of their interactions, communication, and relations. In addition, the evaluator tries to develop a shared responsibility with the participants to jointly work toward the normative ideal of a more inclusive society. We described how this worked in the case of reduction of coercion in psychiatry. The evaluation was based on the political idea that the practice of coercion should be improved. This presupposition was shared among all the participants. The role of the evaluator was to foster a dialogue on experiences around coercion and to stimulate the parties involved to take and share responsibility for improvement.

One may question whether the evaluator, in giving voice to the group least heard, does not take sides, and thus strategically influences the evaluation process. In order to create conditions for dialogue, the evaluator does have to support weaker parties and thus empower them. This process of empowerment is, however, not dictated by the evaluator. The participants in the weaker group themselves become confident by listening to each other and sharing emotions and knowledge. In the case of Jenny, the story was developed in interaction with and through the responses of the other patients. They shared her indignation, and as a group became *self*-conscious. The group helped Jenny to articulate her intimate voice, and in the chorus with other voices the group developed a political voice and agenda. This prepared them for the dialogue with other, more established parties. Likewise, Larry was empowered, not by the evaluators, but by the group of colleague project leaders. In the political science literature, developing a voice within a group of participants with the same interests is known as "enclave deliberation" (Karpowitz, Raphael, & Hammond, 2009). Enclave deliberation helps to deal with power differences between groups and prevents domination of established groups. It serves as an alternative to proportional deliberation, a process with equal amounts of participants with diverging interests. Creating preconditions for dialogue is not a strategic activity. It requires trust in the participants and respect for their ability to express their experiences. The evaluator can only succeed if the members of the group take responsibility for helping each other in making explicit issues and concerns.

By emphasizing that interactive evaluation is relationally responsible, we do not deny that other approaches to evaluation can and should be responsible. Objective approaches to evaluation have to be fair and measure outcomes in a valid way. This is an example of being responsible. Interpretive approaches presuppose wise judgment of the evaluator. Interactive evaluation underlines the importance of validity and wisdom, but defines and realizes these notions in a new and radical way. In interactive evaluation, validity and wisdom are regarded as social and relational products. What counts as valid measurements should be agreed upon by all parties involved. Practical wisdom should be shared between participants and developed in a joint learning process. The responsibilities as interactive evaluators define them also to have consequences for the quality criteria that guide their work. Many years ago, Guba and Lincoln (1989) provided a set of trustworthiness, authenticity, and fairness criteria. We find these still to be very helpful. Interactive evaluation is not only good when it results in better understandings, it should also lead to an enhanced insight among all participants, so that they are better equipped to interact creatively with their surroundings. The process toward such shared understanding and responsibility should be fair and just. Striving for one codified set of quality criteria does not acknowledge that various approaches have diverse sets of responsibilities and goals.

What are the challenges for interactive evaluation as a socially responsible practice? One challenge is to develop ways of making cultural change enduring. Through dialogue, participants in a practice can be stimulated to become more open toward each other, to understand various perspectives and give up traditional oppositional views. This openness is a precondition for practice change. Yet, developing shared understandings is not enough to make change enduring. In the case of reduction of coercion in psychiatry, we saw a large change in views. Whereas coercion used to be regarded as a normal element of psychiatric practice, it is now seen as problematic and unwanted. In many institutions, initiatives to reduce coercion have been set up, resulting in a decrease in the number and the length of seclusions. These successes are, however, fragile. It may become difficult to develop new ideas because so much has already been achieved. Thus, new input is constantly needed. When project leaders move to new jobs, the project is vulnerable. This shows that the project is still too dependent on individual people, and structural implementation is weak.

A further challenge and new territory is the trend toward intercultural diversity. Over the years, it has become more common for nurses, patients, and families to have a voice in health care policy; these groups have become more empowered and accepted as equal participants. Yet, professionals, patients, and families from a non-Western cultural background are less involved in processes of policy making. The participants in the project of reduction of coercion in psychiatry were mainly White. Over the years, the population of institutions of mental health care in The Netherlands has become more diverse, with a larger proportion of patients coming from other cultures. A challenge for the future will be to ensure their participation, giving them voice and stimulating them to be responsible partners in interactive evaluation. Evaluators may seize the opportunity to develop and evaluate diversity-sensitive practices with the communities concerned (Burlew, 2003). Working in a globalized context may then actually result in an enrichment of our practice, as it will confront us with new values and norms and place our own ideas in perspective.

References

Abma, T. A., Greene, J., Karlsson, O., Ryan, K., Schwandt, T. S., & Widdershoven, G. (2001). Dialogue on dialogue. *Evaluation, 7*(2), 164–180.

Abma, T. A., Nierse, C., & Widdershoven, G. A. M. (2009). Patients as research partners in responsive research. Methodological notions for collaborations in research agenda setting. *Qualitative Health Research, 19*(3), 401–415.

Abma, T. A., & Schwandt, T. S. (2005). The practice and politics of sponsored evaluations. In B. Somekh & C. Lewis (Eds.), *Research methods in the social sciences* (pp. 105–112). London: Sage.

Abma, T. A., & Stake, R. (2001). Stake's responsive evaluation: Core ideas and evolution. *New Directions for Evaluation, 92*, 7–22.

Abma, T. A., & Widdershoven, G. A. M. (2005). Sharing stories: Narrative and dialogue in responsive nursing evaluation. *Evaluation and the Health Professions, 28*(1), 90–109.

Abma, T. A., Widdershoven, G. A. M., & Lendemeijer, B. (Eds.). (2005). *Dwang en drang in de psychiatrie, De kwaliteit van vrijheidsbeperkende maatregelen.* Utrecht, The Netherlands, Lemma.

Aristotle. (1997). *Ethica Nicomachea* (Book IV). Amsterdam: Kallias.

Baur, V., Abma, T. A., & Widdershoven, G. A. M. (2010). Participation of older people in evaluation: Mission impossible? *Evaluation and Program Planning, 33*(3), 238–245.

Berghmans, R., Elfahmi, D., Goldsteen, M., & Widdershoven, G. A. M. (2001). *Kwaliteit van dwang en drang in de psychiatrie.* Utrecht/Maastricht: GGZ Netherlands/ Universiteit Maastricht.

Bernstein, R. J. (1983). *Beyond objectivism and relativism.* Oxford, UK: Oxford University Press.

Burlew, A. K. (2003). Research with ethnic minorities: Conceptual, methodological, analysis issues. In G. Bernal, J. E., Trimble, A. K. Burlew, & F. T. L. Leong (Eds.), *Handbook of racial and ethnic minority psychology.* Thousand Oaks, CA: Sage.

Cronbach, L. J., et al. (1980). *Toward reform of program evaluation.* San Francisco: Jossey-Bass.

Fetterman, D. (1994). Empowerment evaluation. *Evaluation Practice, 15,* 1–6.

Gadamer, H. G. (1960). *Wahrheit und Methode.* Tübingen, Germany: J. C. B. Mohr.

Greene, J. C. (1994). Qualitative program evaluation: Practice and promise. In N. K. Denzin & Y. S. Lincoln (Eds.), *Handbook of qualitative research* (pp. 530–544). Thousand Oaks, CA: Sage.

Greene, J. C. (1997). Participatory evaluation. In L. Mabry (Ed.), *Evaluation and the postmodern dilemma. Advances in program evaluation* (Vol. 3, pp. 171–189). Greenwich, CT: JAI Press.

Greene, J. C. (2000). Understanding social programs through evaluation. In N. K. Denzin & Y. S. Lincoln (Eds.), *Handbook of qualitative research* (2nd ed., pp. 981–1000). Thousand Oaks: Sage.

Greene, J. C. (2001). Dialogue in evaluation: A relational perspective. *Evaluation, 7*(2), 181–203.

Greene, J. C. (2002, October). *Evaluation as education.* Paper presented at the European Evaluation Society, Seville, Spain.

Greene, J. C. (2006). Evaluation, democracy, and social change. In I. F. Shaw, J. C. Greene, & M. M. Mark (Eds.), *The SAGE handbook of evaluation* (pp. 141–160). London: Sage.

Greene, J. C., & Abma, T. A. (Eds.). (2001). Responsive evaluation. *New Directions for Evaluation, 92.*

Guba, E. G., & Lincoln, Y. S. (1981). *Effective evaluation.* San Francisco: Jossey-Bass.

Guba, E. G., & Lincoln, Y. S. (1989). *Fourth-generation evaluation.* Newbury Park, CA: Sage.

House, E. R. (1981). *Evaluating with validity.* Beverly Hills, CA: Sage.

House, E. R. (1993). *Professional evaluation.* Newbury Park, CA: Sage.

House, E. R., & Howe, K. R. (1999). *Values in evaluation and social research.* Thousand Oaks, CA: Sage.

Janesick, V. J. (2000). The choreography of qualitative research design: Minuets, improvisations, and crystallization. In N. K. Denzin & Y. S. Lincoln (Eds.), *Handbook of qualitative research* (2nd ed., pp. 379–400). Thousand Oaks, CA: Sage.

Karpowitz, C. F., Raphael, C., & Hammond, A. S. (2009). Deliberative democracy and inequality: Two cheers for enclave deliberation among the disempowered. *Politics & Society, 37,* 576–615.

Koch, T. (2000). Having a say: Negotiation in fourth-generation evaluation. *Journal of Advanced Nursing, 31,* 117–125.

Kushner, S. (2000). *Personalizing evaluation.* London: Sage.

Landeweer, E. G. M., Abma, T.A., & Widdershoven, G. A. M. (2010). The essence of psychiatric nursing: Redefining nurses' identity through moral dialogue about reducing the use of coercion and restraint. *Advances of Nursing Science, 33*(4), E1–E12.

Lincoln, Y. S. (1993). I and thou: Method, voice, and roles in research with the silenced. In D. McLaughlin & W. Tierney (Eds.), *Naming silenced lives* (pp. 29–47). London: Routledge.

Mabry, L. (1991). Alexandre Dumas Elementary School, Chicago, Illinois. In R. Stake, L. Bresler, & L. Mabry (Eds.), *Custom & cherishing: The arts in elementary schools* (pp. 137–176). Chicago: University of Illinois, National Arts Education Research Center.

MacDonald, B. (1977). A political classification of evaluation studies. In D. Hamilton, D. Jenkins, C. King, B. MacDonald, & M. Parlett (Eds.), *Beyond the numbers game* (pp. 224–227). London: Macmillan.

Mertens, D. (2002). The evaluator's role in the transformative context. In K. E. Ryan & T. S. Schwandt (Eds.), *Exploring evaluator role and identity* (pp. 103–118). Greenwich, CT: IAP.

Mertens, D. M. (2009). *Transformative research and evaluation.* New York: Guilford Press.

Murray, R. (2002). Citizens' control of evaluations: Formulating and assessing alternatives. *Evaluation, 8*(1), 81–100.

Palumbo, D. J. (Ed.). (1987). *The politics of program evaluation.* Newbury Park, CA: Sage.

Parlett, M., & Hamilton, D. (1972). Evaluation as illumination: A new approach to the study of innovatory programs. In G. Glass (Ed.), *Evaluation review studies annual* (Vol. 1, pp. 140–157). Beverly Hills, CA: Sage.

Patton, M. Q. (1988). The evaluator's responsibility for utilization. *Evaluation Practice, 9,* 5–24.

Schwandt, T. S. (1997). Whose interests are being served? Program evaluation as conceptual practice of power. In L. Mabry (Ed.), *Evaluation and the post-modern dilemma: Advances in program evaluation* (Vol. 3, pp. 89–104). Greenwich, CT: JAI Press.

Schwandt, T. S. (2005). On modeling our understanding of the practice fields. *Pedagogy, Culture and Society, 13*(3), 313–332.

Segerholm, C. (2001). Evaluation as responsibility, conscience, and conviction. In K. E. Ryan & T. S. Schwandt (Eds.), *Exploring evaluator role and identity* (pp. 87–102). Greenwich, CT: IAP.

Stake, R. E. (1967). The countenance of evaluation. *Teachers College Record, 68,* 523–540.

Stake, R. E. (1975). To evaluate an arts program. In R. E. Stake (Ed.), *Evaluating the arts in education: A responsive approach* (pp. 13–31). Columbus, OH: Merrill.

Stake, R. E. (1982, August). How sharp should the evaluator's teeth be? *Evaluation News,* pp. 79–80.

Stake, R. E. (1991). Retrospective on "The Countenance of Educational Evaluation." In M. W. McLaughlin & D. C. Phillips (Eds.), *Evaluation and education: At quarter century, ninetieth yearbook of the National Society for the Study of Education (NSSE)* (pp. 67–88). Chicago: University of Chicago Press.

Stake, R. E., & Abma, T. A. (2005). Responsive evaluation. In S. Mathison (Ed.), *Encyclopedia of evaluation* (pp. 376–379). Thousand Oaks, CA: Sage.

Stake, R. E., & Schwandt, T. S. (2006). On discerning quality in evaluation. In I. F. Shaw, J. C. Greene, & M. M. Mark (Eds.), *The SAGE handbook of evaluation* (pp. 404–418). London: Sage.

Suarez-Herrera, J. C., Springett, J., & Kagan, C. (2009). Critical connections between participatory evaluation, organizational learning and intentional change in pluralistic organizations. *Evaluation, 15*(3), 321–342.

Themessl-Huber, M. T., & Grutsch, M. A. (2003). The shifting locus of control in participatory evaluations. *Evaluation, 9*(1), 92–111.

Weiss, C. (1988). If program decisions hinged only on information: A response to Patton. *Evaluation Practice, 9,* 15–28.

Whitmore, E., Gruijt, I., Mertens, D. M., Imm, P. S., Chinnan, M., & Wandersman, A. (2006). In I. F. Shaw, J. C. Greene, & M. M. Mark (Eds.), *The SAGE handbook of evaluation* (pp. 340–359). London: Sage.

Widdershoven, G. A. M. (2001). Dialogue in evaluation: A hermeneutic perspective. *Evaluation, 7*(2), 253–263.

Widdershoven, G. A. M., & Abma, T. A. (2007). Hermeneutic ethics between practice and theory. In R. E. Ashcroft, A. Dawson, H. Draper, & J. R. McMillan (Eds.), *Principles of health care ethics* (pp. 215–222). West Sussex, UK: Wiley.

Author Index

Subject Index

⑨SAGE research**methods**

The essential online tool for researchers from the world's leading methods publisher

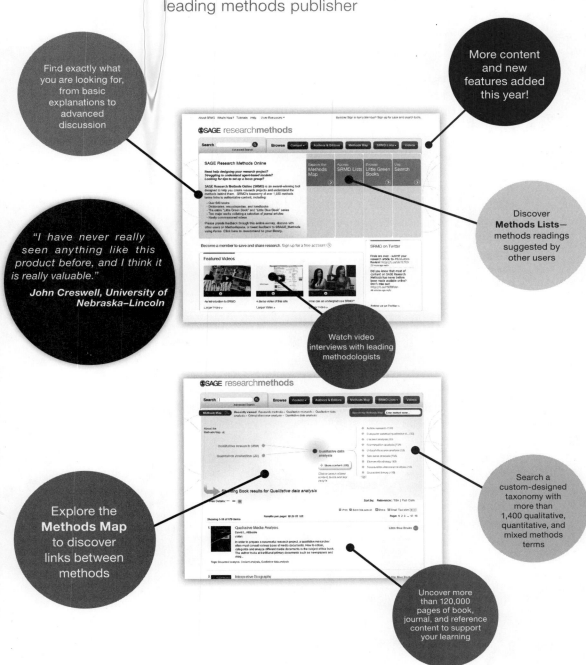

Find exactly what you are looking for, from basic explanations to advanced discussion

More content and new features added this year!

"I have never really seen anything like this product before, and I think it is really valuable."

John Creswell, University of Nebraska–Lincoln

Discover **Methods Lists**— methods readings suggested by other users

Watch video interviews with leading methodologists

Explore the **Methods Map** to discover links between methods

Search a custom-designed taxonomy with more than 1,400 qualitative, quantitative, and mixed methods terms

Uncover more than 120,000 pages of book, journal, and reference content to support your learning

Find out more at
www.sageresearchmethods.com